D1376670

SALUTE TO HISTORIC BLACK ACHIEVERS

SALUTE TO HISTORIC BLACK ACHIEVERS

Introductory Essay by
CORETTA SCOTT KING

THE VARSITY COMPANY
P.O. Box 141000
Nashville, TN 37214

Copyright © 1992 by Chelsea House Publishers,
a division of Main Line Book Company.
All rights reserved.
Published by Thomas Nelson, Inc., Nashville, TN 37214
Printed and bound in the United States of America.

ISBN 0-8407-3436-0

1 2 3 4 5 — 94 93 92

CONTENTS

———— ❧ ————

INTRODUCTION

Coretta Scott King

BEFORE YOU BEGIN this book, I hope you will ask yourself what the word excellence means to you. I think that it's a question we should all ask, and keep asking as we grow older and change. Because the truest answer to it should never change. When you think of excellence, perhaps you think of success at work; or of becoming wealthy; or meeting the right person, getting married, and having a good family life.

Those important goals are worth striving for, but there is a better way to look at excellence. As Martin Luther King, Jr., said in one of his last sermons, "I want you to be first in love. I want you to be first in moral excellence. I want you to be first in generosity. If you want to be important, wonderful. If you want to be great, wonderful. But recognize that he who is greatest among you shall be your servant."

My husband, Martin Luther King, Jr., knew that the true meaning of achievement is service. When I met him, in 1952, he was already ordained as a Baptist preacher and was working towards a doctoral degree at Boston University. I was studying at the New England Conservatory and dreamed of accomplishments in music. We married a year later, and after I graduated the following year we moved to Montgomery, Alabama. We didn't know it then, but our notions of achievement were about to undergo a dramatic change.

You may have read or heard about what happened next. What began with the boycott of a local bus line grew into a national movement, and by the time he was assassinated in 1968 my husband had fashioned a black movement powerful enough to shatter forever the practice of racial segregation. What you may not have read about is where he got his method for resisting injustice without compromising his religious beliefs.

He adopted the strategy of nonviolence from a man of a different race, who lived in a distant country, and even practiced a different religion. The man was Mahatma Gandhi, the great leader of India, who devoted his life to serving humanity in the spirit of love and nonviolence. It was in these principles that Martin discovered his method for social reform. More than anything else, those two principles were the key to his achievements.

The book you are holding tells my husband's story. It describes his childhood in Atlanta, Georgia, his interests as a young adult, his study of theology as a college student, and his work as a minister before he got so deeply involved in the civil rights movement. But this is also the story of that movement itself, for it was Martin who brought to it his unique—and ultimately successful—approach.

I was there when it began, in the winter of 1955. During one of his very first speeches Martin said this: "If you will protest courageously, and yet with dignity and Christian love, when the history books are written in future generations, the historians will have to pause and say, 'There lived a great people—a black people—who injected new meaning and dignity into the veins of civilization.' This is our challenge and our overwhelming responsibility." That was the message he never forgot, even during the darkest of times, and it is one we cannot afford to forget today.

Of course, the history of black men and women in America contains many important messages. Not all of the people in this history had the same ideals, but I think you will find something that all of them have in common. Like Martin Luther King, Jr., they all decided to become "drum majors" and serve humanity. In that principle—whether it was expressed in books, inventions, or song—they found something outside themselves to use as a goal and a guide. Something that showed them a way to serve others, instead of living only for themselves.

Reading the stories of these courageous men and women not only helps us discover the principles that we will use to guide our own lives but also teaches us about our black heritage and about America itself. It is crucial for us to know the heroes and heroines of our history and to realize that the price we paid in our struggle for equality in America was dear. But we must also understand that we have gotten as far as we have partly because America's democratic system and ideals made it possible.

We are still struggling with racism and prejudice. But the great men and women in this series are a tribute to the spirit of our democratic ideals and the system in which they have flourished. And that makes their stories special and worth knowing. ◆

THE
AFRICAN
AMERICANS

The Peoples of North America

THE AFRICAN AMERICANS

Howard Smead

SENIOR CONSULTING EDITOR

SENATOR DANIEL PATRICK MOYNIHAN

Sharecroppers face eviction in Missouri in about 1935.

A HEROIC HERITAGE

O f all the peoples who have journeyed to America from foreign lands, Afro-Americans have the saddest yet most inspiring story. Unlike immigrants of every other nationality and race, the Africans arrived on our shores naked and in chains. They came as captives, sold into involuntary servitude by European slave traders and their reluctant partners, local African rulers. European slave merchants—who first arrived in Africa in the 16th century—eventually brought a total of approximately 15 million slaves to New World colonies in Central and South America, to the "sugar islands" of the West Indies, and, finally, to North America.

In 1619, British colonists located in Jamestown, Virginia, purchased America's first African workers, 20 in all. These arrivals were not slaves but indentured servants. The African population in America remained tiny until the turn of the 18th century, when Virginians began importing slaves from West Africa at a rate of about 1,000 per year. By that time slavery had spread throughout the colonies. Africans worked as field hands in the South and as domestic servants in the North. From 1776 to 1783, slaves bolstered the ranks of George Washington's army, as Americans waged their War of Independence against the British. In fact, a 47-year-old slave, Crispus Attucks, earned a place in revolutionary history by leading colonial forces during the Boston Massacre in 1770.

5

The revolutionary era was a promising time for slaves. In 1783, for example, a Massachusetts court granted liberty to Quork Walker—a slave who claimed the right to freedom on the grounds that the preamble to the state constitution declared all men "free and equal." That year, Massachusetts prohibited slavery. In 1784, Connecticut, New Jersey, and Rhode Island followed suit.

At the very same time, however, blacks in the American South were about to suffer a major setback. In 1793, Eli Whitney invented the cotton gin, a machine that revolutionized the nation's cotton industry, which became the backbone of the economy in the South. During the first decade of the 1800s, cotton exports nearly tripled—from 30 to 80 million pounds—and the demand for slave labor escalated quickly on the large farms, or plantations, of the South.

At the same time, an antislavery movement—called "abolitionism"—gained momentum in the North. Abolitionists launched a crusade, and many lost their lives in sectional conflicts that divided the nation from about 1820 until the start of the Civil War in 1861. The abolitionist movement not only catalyzed the Civil War, but also spawned a new generation of black leaders.

The most influential of these leaders was Frederick Douglass, a freed slave who became an eloquent voice for the Afro-American community. His autobiographical work *Narrative of the Life of Frederick Douglass*, published in 1845, remains an important document of slave conditions and one of the classics of American literature. As the racial climate changed, Douglass served as a barometer of Afro-American feelings. He joyfully welcomed the emancipation of slaves and later expressed horror at the racist backlash that denied to blacks the hard-won gains of the Civil War. Shortly before his death, in 1895, he told a group of whites, "The rich inheritance of justice, liberty, prosperity and independence, bequeathed by your fathers is shared by you, not by me. The sunlight that brought light and healing to you, has brought stripes and death to me. The Fourth of July is yours, not mine. You may rejoice, I must mourn."

By 1890 the promise of freedom won during the Civil War had soured, as yet another form of oppression took root in the South, where a block of racist legislation known collectively as "Jim Crow" laws forced Afro-Americans into second-class citizenship. Worse than these unjust laws was the covert sanction southern states gave to violence unleashed against blacks. Throughout the 1890s, whites shot, burned, and lynched blacks at an alarming rate; an average of one black was killed every two and a half days. Like the fugitive slaves of an earlier generation, Afro-Americans fled north to safety, but in far greater numbers. In only 10 years, from 1910 to 1920, nearly 1.5 million blacks escaped the South.

In the North, most Afro-Americans settled in urban enclaves and together forged a new identity as city dwellers. In the 1920s, New York City boasted the largest and grandest black neighborhood in the nation: Harlem. Here more than 200,000 blacks lived and worked together, creating a vibrant culture—the Harlem Renaissance—alive with gifted poets, novelists, painters, and performers. Another metropolis, Chicago, emerged as the mecca of black music. There, ragtime, blues, and Dixieland merged to form one of the century's great art forms, jazz.

Hard times hit in 1929, when the Jazz Age crashed into the Great Depression, which lasted through the 1930s. This economic crisis put millions of Americans on breadlines, but Afro-Americans suffered the most. Yet the very bleakness of the decade spurred blacks in a new direction—toward social reform. In 1937, for instance, black train porters banded together to form their own union. Buoyed by this success, black labor leaders galvanized the community to change its second-class status.

Afro-Americans were thus ready to defend their rights in the 1940s, when the nation's fortunes changed again, this time as a result of World War II. The war effort opened up lucrative job opportunities in the booming factories that supplied weaponry to the U.S. Army. But blacks, though desperate for work, were ignored by employers. Instead of mutely accepting this

A studio portrait of Frederick Douglass, taken in 1856.

injustice, black union organizer A. (Asa) Philip Randolph pried open the doors of the all-white defense industry in 1941 by threatening to stage a mass protest in Washington, D.C. Randolph's bold move paid off. The U.S. Congress passed legislation that outlawed job discrimination.

This triumph set the stage for one of the most stirring chapters in American history, the civil rights movement of the 1950s and 1960s. Protests in strongholds of Jim Crow such as Birmingham, Alabama, and Albany, Georgia, drew widespread attention to the plight of Afro-Americans. Their struggle for justice aroused the sympathy of the nation and thrust into international prominence a young black preacher, Martin Luther King, Jr., who in 1964 was awarded a Nobel Peace Prize.

But as blacks made gains, dissension arose within the civil rights community. Some leaders found King's method of nonviolent protest too tame; others thought the movement should shift its focus from the South and its institutional (or *de jure*) segregation, to the North, where blacks had legal rights but were locked into ghettos and locked out of decent housing and jobs. Malcolm X, Stokely Carmichael, and others argued that white Americans would never give blacks a fair shake and that the minority community must strengthen its own economic and political base independent of the larger society.

The civil rights movement became splintered and nearly collapsed in the mid-1960s, when a rash of rioting broke out in American cities such as Los Angeles, California, Detroit, Michigan, and Newark, New Jersey. Blacks and whites squared off in mobs that left peaceful cities in ruins. The crisis culminated in 1968, when King was assassinated in Memphis, Tennessee, at the age of 39.

For the next two decades black leaders struggled to fill the vacuum left by King's death. Yet Afro-Americans continued their drive for equality and made some gains, especially on the political front. By the early

1980s, many large cities had black mayors. Blacks also made an impact on national politics. Two congressmen, for example—Charles Rangel of New York and William Gray of Pennsylvania—ranked among the leaders in that legislative body.

The late 1980s saw the emergence of the most remarkable political figure of all, the Reverend Jesse Jackson, who in 1988 ran a highly successful campaign for the Democratic presidential nomination. For the first time, Americans of all descriptions—including whites long mired in racism—voiced their belief that an Afro-American deserved to occupy the highest office in the land. Jackson ultimately lost the nomination—to Massachusetts governor Michael Dukakis—but his campaign caused an entire nation to reassess its prejudices.

Afro-Americans continue to excel, too, on another front—culture. Black dance troupes, such as the Dance Theatre of Harlem and the Alvin Ailey American Dance Theater, delight audiences around the world because they encapsulate America itself, its energy, passion, and humor, its willingness to improvise new forms. The same is true, to an even greater degree, of Afro-American music. Americans have blacks to thank for jazz, blues, rhythm and blues, rock 'n' roll, and rap. These forms have added sparkle to our own culture and have helped create the international myth of American glamor.

Today, most Americans acknowledge the tremendous contributions of the black community, but many obstacles still bar the way to true equality. An alarming percentage of blacks remain trapped in the ghetto, with its shabby housing, dismal schools, broken homes, teenage pregnancies, and rampant drug culture. Many Afro-Americans hurdle these obstacles only to face the subtle racism of employers, landlords, and—most disappointing of all—the framers of public policy. Blacks can draw strength, however, from the legacy of their forebears, whose capacity for hope finally overcame the cruelty of their oppressors. ❧

In 1979 Andrew Young, then U.S. ambassador to the United Nations, defends his meeting with the Palestinian Liberation Organization, a terrorist group not officially recognized by the United States.

A limestone relief dating from about 1370 B.C. shows the head of an African taken prisoner.

FROM FREEDOM TO SLAVERY

The story of the Afro-Americans begins not on this continent but on another approximately 4,800 miles away: Africa, a vast land mass of nearly 12 million square miles. Most ancestors of today's Afro-Americans lived in West Africa. This region, located on the northwestern coast of Africa, had a highly diverse population. More than 250 languages were spoken there, all subgroups of the three major West African tongues: Sudanic, Bantu, and Hamitic. The region's culture was equally varied. Different communities practiced distinct customs and developed unique civilizations. In fact, hundreds of years before the discovery of America, three great empires—in the countries of Ghana, Mali, and Songhai—flourished on the grasslands south of Africa's Sahara Desert.

It was in this region that slave trade began at the end of the 15th century. It was initiated by European countries, which had recently entered an age of exploration that led them to colonize foreign lands in North and South America—the New World. The competition to annex new territories became especially fierce between two seafaring powers, Spain and Portugal, which raced to establish settlements across the Atlantic. By 1494, relations between the two nations had grown so strained that Pope Alexander VI issued the Treaty of Tordesillas. It provided for Spain's control of all of

11

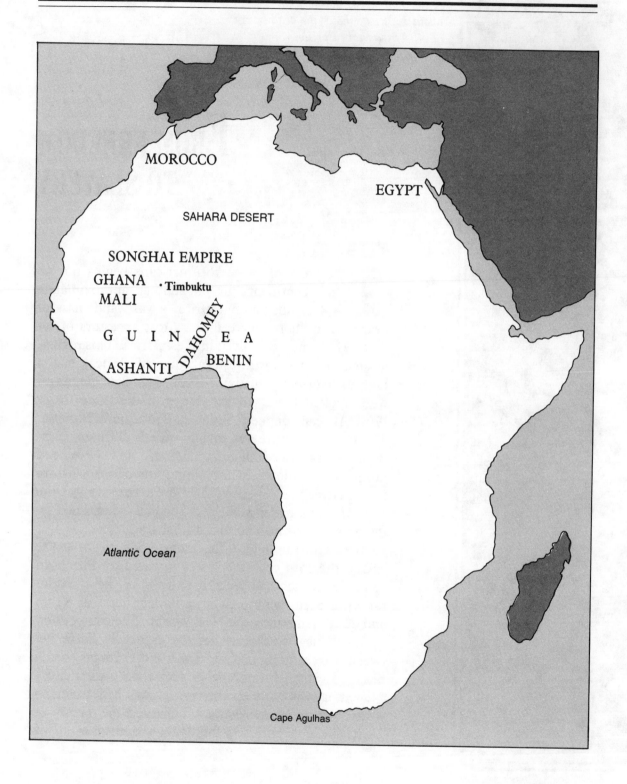

MOROCCO

EGYPT

SAHARA DESERT

SONGHAI EMPIRE

GHANA · Timbuktu

MALI

G U I N DAHOMEY E A

ASHANTI DAHOMEY BENIN

Atlantic Ocean

Cape Agulhas

South America save for Brazil, which fell under the sovereignty of Portugal. So did Africa. In this era, Portugal started trading with African tribal chiefs. At first the Portuguese coveted gold and ivory. But over the next 50 years, their interest shifted toward another precious natural resource, human beings, to fill a growing need for free labor in the burgeoning colonies of the New World. African traders willingly obliged the Portuguese because slave trade enabled them to dispense with people whom they viewed as undesirable, particularly warriors taken captive during battles with enemy tribes and nations.

As time wore on, the demand for human beings escalated. It could not be satisfied by the small supply of wartime prisoners African chiefs had been offering. The Europeans threatened to take their business to rival tribes, and Africans began hunting slaves with the sole intention of selling them to whites for a profit. Soon African traders grew dependent upon the slave trade and were easily manipulated by the Europeans, who

Spanish explorer Fernando de Soto terrorizes a tribe native to Florida in this 16th-century engraving. The cruelty of the Spanish toward indigenous peoples of the Americas led to the outlawing of Indian slavery by the Spanish Crown and the importation of African slaves to take their place.

This bronze figurine of a Portuguese slaver was made in the West African kingdom of Benin during the 16th or 17th century.

used every available means of increasing the slave supply.

One ruse was to exploit the hostilities that often put tribes at odds with each other. For example, Europeans armed the Dahomeans—a people from the Guinea coastal territory first called the Kingdom of Benin, later known as the country of Nigeria and now called Benin—with enough weaponry to conquer and capture neighboring adversaries. The Dahomeans balked at the plan, but when the Europeans threatened to transfer their loyalties to the enemy tribe, the Dahomeans became hopelessly ensnared in the slave trade, delivering other Africans to whites in order to save themselves from enslavement.

African slave traders, known as *caboceers*, captured their victims singly, in small groups, or in large numbers, but in every case they sought those best suited for the rigors of the New World—healthy males and females between the ages of 18 and 35, although some children also were captured. Sometimes slavers were outnumbered by their prey, but they generally had superior weaponry and could overpower their victims, whom they chained together at the ankle or wrist or linked at the neck by a wooden yoke. Thus bound, the captives then embarked upon a grueling march—sometimes as long as 600 miles—to the coast, where European ships awaited them. Not all the prisoners made it. Some resisted their captors and were killed. Others died from the rigors of the trip. A lucky few managed to overpower their captors or simply slipped away.

Once they reached the coast, the tired and bewildered Africans were stripped naked and penned into *barracoons*, or stockades. But the worst of their ordeal lay ahead of them—the harrowing voyage to the New World aboard slave ships. These ships lay at anchor until their holds had a full cargo of slaves. Then the "middle passage" got under way. This term referred to the second leg of a three-part trading system. The first part began when European ships—first Portuguese, but mostly British after the 18th century—sailed to Africa bearing manufactured wares. Cotton textiles, pewter, gunpowder and guns, whiskey, and boxes of beads went to Africans who, in return, handed over slaves. Next came the second step—the middle passage—whereby Europeans shipped the captive Africans across the Atlantic to the West Indies. There the slavers traded their human cargo for sugar, which they took back to Europe, completing the final part of the journey.

The Atlantic Crossing

For the captives, only the middle passage mattered, and it was a nightmare. The Atlantic crossing took four to eight weeks, and for its duration women, men, and children were crammed into tightly packed quarters in the "between decks" of a vessel, located below the main deck and above the cargo hold. The ceiling of this area usually reached no higher than five feet and ran the length of the boat. From the side of the ship, rough wooden planking extended six to nine feet toward the center. This planking formed the slaves' quarters for the entire journey. There were no mattresses, no sheets, no blankets, no pillow—just hard wood. During storms

Captured Africans—shown in a European engraving— begin the long trek toward slavery.

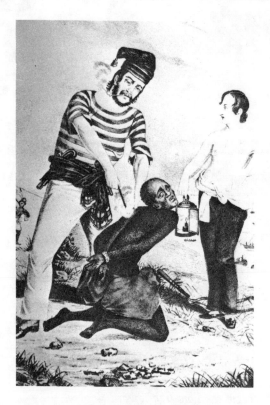

A joint work by American lithographers Nathaniel Currier and James Merritt Ives depicts the branding of slaves on the coast of Africa.

or rough seas the slaves sustained numerous cuts and scrapes.

A typical slave ship had two or three such shelves, which held a total of up to 700 people. The space between them never exceeded three feet. Only the smallest children had room to sit up. Bound in pairs by the wrists and ankles, the male slaves occupied the longest shelves, filling the center of the vessel. Each shelf had two or three buckets for the slaves to use as toilets. If a slave was too cramped or too weak to maneuver the bucket under himself, he relieved himself where he lay and had to lie in his own excrement. The buckets often spilled or were knocked over during the night, further befouling the already stifling conditions. The sick generally languished in their own corner. But those who suffered from ill health rarely made it to the New World. An English clergyman named John Newton, writing in 1750 about the slave trade, commented, "Every morning, perhaps, more instances than one are found of the living and the dead fastened together."

The wretchedness of the slaves' existence was worsened by the monotony of their days. If weather permitted, the crew brought the slaves on deck at about 8:00 A.M. They fastened down the men, either by attaching their leg irons to ringbolts set into the deck or by chaining them to the gunwales, the upper edges of the boat's side. Women and children could roam freely. At 9:00 A.M. the slaves ate their first meal, usually boiled rice, millet, or cornmeal, sometimes flavored with a few lumps of salted beef. The fare might also include starchy vegetables such as plantains, yams, or manioc, an edible root. The slaves washed down their meals with half a pint of water, drunk out of a pannikin, a small, hollowed-out pan rather like a large deep spoon.

The ordeal was so demoralizing that slaves often sank into a condition known as suicidal melancholy or fixed melancholy. A slave so afflicted lost the will to live, slipped into a deep depression, and died. According to one eyewitness, "Notwithstanding their apparent

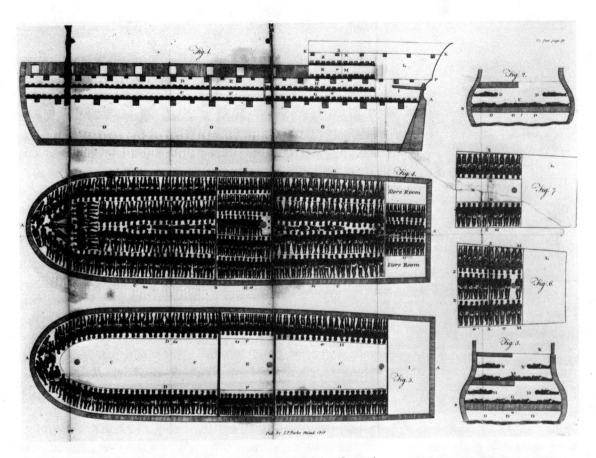

good health each morning three or four would be found [dead]. One of the duties of the slave-captains was when they found a slave sitting with knees up and head drooping, to start them up, run them about the deck, give them a small ration of rum, and divert them until in a normal condition." Some slavers hired a musician to play a drum, banjo, or even a bagpipe in order to boost the spirits of the slaves. Others merely directed a sailor to beat out a crude rhythm on an upturned kettle.

Another practice was "dancing" the slaves. After breakfast, chained men were dragged on deck where they stood in their fetters and exercised either by hopping in place or by jangling their arms and bodies. The crew walked among them with cat-o'-nine-tails making sure they complied with this forcible recreation, a process meant to keep the slaves "healthy" in body and mind.

An engraving published in Philadelphia in 1808 diagrams the packed interior of a 19th-century slave ship.

While the slaves "jumped in their irons," crew members went below to carry out the sickening task of cleaning out the slave quarters, a job performed no more than three times a week. They scrubbed the fouled planking with stiff brushes and hot water, scraped and swabbed the deck, then dropped red-hot iron pellets into bowls of vinegar to freshen the sour air. The captain had to maintain strict discipline to make sure his crew performed this onerous job. If he relaxed his rule or if the seas were rough or the slaves rebellious, the task went undone.

After dancing the slaves and cleaning out "'tween decks," the sailors served the second and final meal of the day at about 3:00 or 4:00 P.M., a healthful but unappetizing mixture of boiled horsebeans—the cheapest food available in Europe—mixed with flour, palm oil, water, and malagueta pepper, a spice obtained on the African coast. The sailors themselves found the mixture disgusting and derisively referred to it as "slabber sauce." Their revulsion was shared by the slaves, who often refused to eat their food, instead throwing it at the crew or at each other. When the meal ended, the slaves returned below to their planked shelves.

An illustration from the book Revelation of a Slave Smuggler (1856) *dramatizes a scene in the hold of the ship* Gloria.

Slaves could escape this grim routine only by taking their own lives, an option they sometimes chose over enslavement. But slavers, seeking to protect their investment, did all they could to prevent suicides. If vigilant crew members restrained the captives from jumping overboard, the slaves often fell into such despair they tried to starve themselves to death. Many received severe beatings for refusing to eat, a form of passive resistance that became so widespread that European slavers invented an instrument—called a *speculum orris*—used to force-feed those who fasted. This device operated like pliers in reverse and enabled slavers to pry and hold open a slave's mouth so the slavers could pour food into it through a funnel. Slavers frequently discouraged self-starvation by shoving hot coals down a slave's throat; the victim died but served as a warning to others.

Often slaves who retained their will to live and who ate died anyway, either from the diseases that ravaged the slave ships or from suffocation due to lack of oxygen in the air between decks. The filthy living conditions on board bred pestilence; in fact, the crewmen fell ill and died more often than the slaves themselves. Dysentery—caused by slaves' wallowing in their own filth below deck or by eating with soiled fingers—claimed lives on nearly every voyage and often led to bloody flux, a dreaded condition in which slaves excreted blood and mucus.

Flux was widely feared, but it inspired less terror than another ailment, smallpox, an incurable virus that afflicted crew and slaves alike. Smallpox doomed whomever contracted it. If the illness itself did not claim the victim's life, he would perish as a result of the practice—common on board slave ships—of throwing overboard anyone bearing its symptoms, a drastic method of avoiding contagion.

Slaves were tossed into the sea not only to halt epidemics but also to decrease the weight of a ship. For example, if winds were not blowing, the crew sometimes jettisoned part of its cargo in order to gain speed

European sailors jettison slaves in this woodcut created in about 1750.

on the waves. This practice originated during the first transatlantic voyages of the Spanish, who pitched their horses overboard when they reached the doldrums—an area of the mid-Atlantic known for its listless winds and currents. Slave ships followed suit by sacrificing not horses but human beings.

This practice was so widespread that slave merchants took out insurance—from Lloyds of London and other companies—that covered the eventuality of jettisoning some or all of their human cargo. The British were still jettisoning slaves as late as 1781. That year the *Zong*, after completing an arduous middle passage lasting 3 months and 16 days, jettisoned 132 slaves within sight of Jamaica, their destination. The ship's insurance company agreed to pay the merchants £30 for each dead slave, but an English court found the payment illegal and stated "that a higher law applies to this very shocking case." After this decision, the practice of jettisoning slaves, by British slavers at least, came to an end.

In any case, it benefited the slavers to deliver their cargo not only intact but, if possible, in good health. Often they promoted a false appearance of robustness in the slaves in order to fetch a higher price at the market. They fattened their captives by feeding them all the remaining food left on board and by keeping them on deck, where there was fresh air, as long as possible. Slavers also tried to disguise any sign of disease. Someone suffering from the bloody flux had his anus plugged with candle wax. Other afflictions, such as yaws (a tropical disease marked by ulcerating lesions), running sores, or scrapes, were concealed with a mixture of gunpowder and iron rust. Slavers also oiled the bodies of the slaves to highlight their muscles.

Once in port, a ship's captain might arrange for the sale of slaves himself, but usually that chore fell to factors, slave traders who received a commission on each sale of 15 percent per slave plus a smaller percentage of the total proceeds. Factors sold slaves either individ-

A copper engraving details the auctioning of slaves on the coast of Africa.

ually or by lot. The most profitable deals were made when the owner of a large sugar plantation—or a group of wealthy planters—bought an entire cargo of newly arrived slaves. The most barbaric of all sales venues was the auction block, though only the choicest slaves—those who were already "seasoned" by years of servitude or those born in the Americas—underwent this indignity.

In general, planters bought inexperienced slaves in large lots. Sometimes they bid "by inch of the candle," a process whereby factors lit a candle and took offers on the slaves until the wick had burned down an inch. But most Africans were sold in "the scramble," so called because at the sound of a cannon shot, the planters or their agents scrambled about the stockade attaching a handkerchief or colored ribbon to the slaves they wanted to purchase. In some cases the scramble took place aboard the ship.

These rites of sale officially marked the end of the abominable middle passage, but not of the slaves' sufferings. Ahead lay a life of bondage to the slave master and his subordinates. ∾

Four generations of a slave family pose for a photographer in Beaufort, South Carolina, in 1862.

SLAVERY

During the more than 350 years of the slave trade, most of the 15 million Africans arriving in the Western Hemisphere were put to work in South and Central America and in the sugar islands of the West Indies: Cuba, Hispaniola (an island now shared by the countries of Haiti and the Dominican Republic), Jamaica, and Puerto Rico.

In 1619, a Dutch merchant ship unloaded 20 Africans in the English colony of Jamestown, Virginia—the first to set foot in North America. These early arrivals were not really slaves, however; they eventually earned enough laboring in the tobacco fields to purchase their freedom, in the manner of indentured servants. After several decades the demand for workers exceeded the supply, and Virginians turned to the slave trade. They did not buy slaves fresh from Africa. They preferred slaves who had already logged some time in the West Indies, where previous owners had already broken them into the rigors of slavery. North American colonists also favored "Creole" slaves, American-born children of African parents. Not until the 18th century did British colonists begin large-scale importation of slaves directly from Africa.

Although slaves became commonplace in the South, they played a far more limited role in the northern colonies, where they generally lived in cities. Things changed after the American Revolution, when merchants from the cities of Boston, Massachusetts, Newport, Rhode Island, and Philadelphia, Pennsylvania, began importing Africans to the New World. Northern slaves usually performed household duties or were rented out by their owners to work in urban shops and factories.

King Cotton

Slaves never became an integral part of the North's industrial economy; the region produced no cash crop that required a large permanent labor force. In the South, however, slavery grew into a major institution. In the 1600s and 1700s, slaves had raised tobacco in Maryland, Delaware, and Virginia, and along the Carolina coast they cultivated rice and indigo, a plant used to make dye. In the 19th century, the need arose for thousands more slaves in a new industry, the cotton trade, which revolutionized the economy of the South.

First domesticated in Africa, cotton cultivation spread to the Middle East and India before the Christian Era and had long been a significant force in the world economy. Two types of cotton grew in the American South. Long-staple or long-fiber cotton—used in the production of fine lace—flourished in the islands off the Georgia coast, but nowhere else. A heartier plant, short-staple cotton—also known as green-seed, piedmont, or upland cotton—grew easily throughout the Deep South, from Georgia to east Texas.

At first short-staple cotton seemed unsuitable for mass production because its short fibers made the removal of seeds by hand an extremely difficult task. This problem was solved—and the slaves' hopes of freedom ended—in 1793, when northerner Eli Whitney invented the cotton gin, a machine designed to separate cotton fiber from seeds, hulls, and foreign matter. Whitney's simple machine, which he patented in 1794, used teeth to comb the cotton through a grating, thereby leaving the troublesome seeds behind. It allowed cotton to be cultivated on a grand scale—an endeavor requiring widespread labor.

As cotton agriculture spread, slavery spread with it, from the Tidewater states of Maryland and Virginia to the Georgia and North Carolina Piedmont into south-

Slaves in South Carolina prepare cotton for the gin.

western Virginia. Soon Tennessee and new U.S. territories acquired under the Louisiana Purchase of 1803—including Mississippi, Alabama, Louisiana, and Arkansas—began importing slaves to cultivate cotton. Plantation owners, aided greatly by the cotton gin, grew rich from the fibers of this plant.

The cotton gin was not the only invention that spurred the American cotton industry. The textile industry in England—the largest importer of U.S. cotton—had already benefited from the automation of weaving, made possible by such innovations as the water-powered loom and the spinning jenny, a machine that could spin 8 to 11 strands of cotton simultaneously. This invention and others elevated cloth making from a cottage industry to a factory enterprise.

These developments boosted English imports of cotton from the American South. In 1790 merchants in Richmond, Virginia, exported 30 small bags of cotton. But after the cotton gin was invented, exports rose sharply to 30 million pounds in 1800 and rose again to 80 million pounds by 1810. Cotton had become king in the South.

This growth depended entirely on the labor of slaves. Their population in the South more than quadrupled from 700,000 in 1790 to 3.2 million in 1850 and rose still higher to 4 million in 1860. By the eve of the Civil War, three-fourths of all the slaves in the United States produced cotton.

This enormous population of slaves was owned by only 385,000 whites. They represented some of the wealthiest and most powerful people in American society, including 12 of the nation's first 16 presidents. Most slave owners held fewer than five slaves. But the planters—who by definition possessed 20 slaves or more—owned most of the slaves in the South. By 1860, 25,000 planters owned 2 million slaves between them, an average of 80 each.

The Slave Codes

Slavery was an institution, and as such a complex set of rules developed to regulate it. In the colonial era, "slave codes" severely restricted the legal rights of slaves. Codes prohibited enslaved blacks from participating in lawsuits, from testifying in court against whites, from owning property or firearms, or from possessing alcohol. Most slave states did not recognize slave marriages, and many prohibited slaves from learning to read and write in order to make them even more dependent upon their owners and thus forestall rebellion.

Laws also limited religious practices. Whites generally had to approve the choice of preachers, and the preachers themselves could not freely address their congregations. Again, the fear among whites was that churches might become cradles of revolt. Slave codes set up a system of armed patrols that guarded against insurrection and apprehended runaway slaves. Under these laws any white person could stop any black person he encountered and demand to see either proof of freedom or the pass that all slaves had to carry when they left the plantation. These regulations reduced even the 250,000 free blacks living in the South to second-class citizenship.

Plantation Life

The basic unit of cotton production was the plantation. The largest of these sprawling farms were located in Louisiana, the Mississippi Delta, the Alabama Black Belt (so-called because of its rich black soil), and coastal

South Carolina. Plantations also sprang up around Natchez Trace, a 449-mile commercial route linking the cities of Natchez, Mississippi, and Nashville, Tennessee. In some plantation counties, slaves outnumbered whites by more than two to one. Other counties had no slaves at all. Many white Southerners went through their entire lives without ever laying eyes on a slave. Yet slavery was the foundation of southern society.

On plantations, slaves performed various jobs and held different ranks. For example, slaves who became skilled carpenters, blacksmiths, and coopers enjoyed greater privileges than the majority, who worked in the fields. Field slaves were usually divided into gangs of 5 to 10, supervised by a slave driver, usually a slave himself, who was held accountable for the performance of his gang.

In addition to field slaves, drivers, and artisans were those who belonged to another class altogether—the house servants. A large plantation might include a domestic staff composed of two entire families, who held the posts of maid, cook, butler, and gardener. The "mammy" served as governess, taking charge of the owner's children. She teamed up with the butler, generally her husband, to oversee the other servants.

Black country churches, such as this one in Louisiana, were a mainstay of many slave communities.

Afro-Americans sit outside the remains of slave quarters in Florida, in the late 19th century.

With the exception of the domestic slaves, who worked directly for the planter and his family, all others answered to an overseer, in almost every case a white man hired by the planter to keep the slaves in line. The master allowed the overseer to handle discipline and punishment, which could be severe. Overseers became hated figures among slaves.

Field slaves lived on a subsistence level, surviving on a minimum of food, clothing, and shelter. Most slave cabins had a dirt floor, one window covered with a burlap flap, and an opening rather than a doorway in the front. These shabby quarters were aligned in rows. At the end of the rows stood a larger dwelling, which housed the overseer. The cabins were situated near to the manor house but hidden from the line of vision of the planter and his family.

The cabins were crudely furnished with a table, perhaps one or two chairs, and a single bed where parents and the smallest children slept. The rest of the family slept on the ground on mattresses filled with hay, grass, or straw. The cabins let in rain and wind and provided little warmth during the winter, which in the cotton regions was mercifully short.

Slave codes required planters to issue each male slave two shirts, two pairs of trousers, and a pair of shoes each year. Women received one or two dresses. The children wore hand-me-downs and went barefoot. Food rations were even stingier. Most codes stipulated that slaves receive a weekly ration of a peck (about eight quarts) of cornmeal and three to four pounds of salt pork per family. Slaves supplemented their diet by growing their own vegetables, trapping game, and, when they were permitted to do so, fishing.

The treatment slaves received from their masters varied tremendously. Some owners were brutal sadists who worked their slaves mercilessly and threatened them with corporal discipline so painful it amounted to torture. The whip was the most common means of punishment on plantations. Most slaves—men and women alike—felt its stinging heat or the imminent possibility of it at least once in their life. Masters instructed their overseers to use the whip whenever necessary to quell restlessness among the slaves or to enforce discipline. Instead of whipping slaves en masse, the overseer usually singled out one unfortunate victim as an example to the others. One whipping of a rebellious slave effectively instilled terror in the rest. A slave had no protection from this mistreatment because the law considered him another man's property, not a human being. When a slave suffered a whipping, he could not take his master to court nor could he fight back with his fists.

Overseers on large plantations used the whip more frequently than did small farmers who owned five slaves or less. But the whip was not the only means of enforcing discipline. For example, a master might extend work hours beyond the normal limit (slaves usually worked dawn to dusk during much of the growing season, but did not have to labor for half of Saturday and all of Sunday). The master sometimes bribed his slaves into good behavior by rewarding them with gifts of extra clothing or food or by offering them a special holiday or an extra day off per month if the slaves raised their individual quotas.

Masters also manipulated the slaves' private lives. They knew they valued their bonds with one another above anything else. Because many slaves had loved ones on neighboring plantations, a master often denied weekend visitation passes as a punitive measure. Even more to the slaves' disliking, he might refuse to sanction their marriages as a means of enforcing discipline. Most slave codes outlawed slave marriages, but it was not at all uncommon for a master to ignore this law and permit his slaves to wed. Some masters encouraged matrimony in the belief that it promoted stability and happiness. But even if a master allowed his slaves to marry, he often threatened to break up these unions by selling one of the spouses and separating the couple for life.

The master also retained his authority by restricting the slaves' right to practice religion, one of the chief comforts of their life. Yet, even the most merciless masters realized that religion played a central role in the slave community and could not be stamped out altogether. In essence, Afro-American religion blended Christianity with the faiths indigenous to West Africa. This hybrid creed taught that the law of God was superior to the law of man and thus gave slaves spiritual independence from the whites who controlled their daily lives.

Masters usually reserved the right to choose who preached to their slaves and the contents of their sermons, often prescribing pious sermons about such topics as brotherly love and the rewards of the afterlife. But slave communities greatly preferred black preachers who drew on the great oral traditions of their African forebears to develop a powerfully rhythmic style of oration. These preachers delivered a gospel of liberation. They interpreted the tenets of Christianity to emphasize the importance of freedom, dignity, and self-respect. The churches they organized—the earliest of which predated the Civil War—encouraged the black quest for independence from white control.

Slave Culture

Christianity represented just one aspect of the culture slaves developed in their plantation communities. Only recently have historians come to recognize the sophistication of slave culture, which they long believed had been thoroughly inhibited by the hardships of servitude. Nothing could have been further from the truth. Within their quarters, slaves developed an independent culture unknown to their masters. The slave community, for instance, included its own—benevolent—figures of authority whom the others looked up to, men and women of great integrity who offered hope in the face of the overseer's bullwhip. Enclosed slave societies gave their members a group identity that enabled them, in the words of black historian Nathan Huggins, "[to] hold together through deep trauma and adversity. . . . slaves laid claim to their humanity and refused to compromise it, creating families where there would have been none, weaving a cosmology and a moral order in a world of duplicity, shaping an art and a world of imagination in a cultural desert."

One testament to the richness of slave culture survives in its folktales. Forbidden by law to read and write, blacks spun fantastic spoken narratives that passed from one generation to the next. These fables expressed the slaves' own aspirations for a better life by describing how small, seemingly weak animals (who represented the slaves) defeat larger beasts (the slaves' hated owners). The most popular stories centered around either the adventures of the small but sly Brer Rabbit or the triumphs of a slave named John or Jack, who ingeniously outwitted his oafish white master.

Slave Families

At the core of slave society was the family, and slaves struggled valiantly to maintain this vital institution. If the master prohibited slave marriages, blacks conducted their own ceremonies in secret, often drawing on the traditions of West Africa. For example, instead of taking their vows in a church, slaves jumped over a broom, a ritual that can be traced back to their homeland. Couples usually created two-parent households, although circumstances often tore them apart: About one-third of all slave families unraveled when one member was sold to another plantation. Owners usually kept women and children together, selling off the father or the sons. On the well-established plantations, black families had a better chance of remaining intact—some endured for three or four generations.

The emphasis slaves placed on the family lent dignity to relations between the sexes. But sometimes wedlock proved impossible, as, for example, when lovers lived on separate plantations. In these cases, the slave community usually tolerated intimate relations between the couple. This tolerance was not extended to adultery.

The community also objected fiercely to the sexual favors planters and overseers often demanded of slave women. This form of abuse was outlawed under slave codes, but whites often disregarded the law and took

Toussaint L'Ouverture, known as the George Washington of Haiti, stands in military dress in a 19th-century engraving.

young female slaves as their mistresses. The offspring of these liaisons lived as slaves and were usually accepted into the slave community.

Slave Rebellions

Although family life, religion, and folk tales softened the horrors of slavery, they did not lessen the humiliating fact of servitude, and slaves sought more direct means of resisting their bondage, either through violent rebellion or through subtle and covert acts of resistance. Wherever there were slaves in the Western Hemisphere, there were slave revolts. The success of these uprisings varied greatly from region to region, depending on several factors.

Slaves stood a better chance of freedom if their region had places to escape to, such as dense jungles or rugged mountains. They also fared better if the region's slave population exceeded that of owners; if the slaves rebelling were African-born and shared a common ethnicity; if plantations were large and produced only a single crop; and if the owner resided far from his plantation and visited infrequently. In addition, slaves were more likely to stage a revolt if the slave-holding society lacked cohesiveness. This combination of circumstances occurred most frequently in the Caribbean, a region whose blacks developed a proud history of armed resistance.

Fugitive West Indian slaves, known as maroons, established independent societies in several Caribbean islands, including Jamaica and Haiti. Throughout the 1700s, Jamaican slaves fought full-fledged wars against planters and eventually united under Cudjo, a maroon leader. From 1733 to 1738 Cudjo masterminded a guerrilla war against the vastly superior British army, winning 1,500 acres of land for his people. In 1791 Cudjo's counterpart in Haiti—Toussaint L'Ouverture—helped rid the island of European domination by organizing other maroons into a standing army of several thousand troops. His decisive victory against the French army stunned European and American slaveholders alike and made him a national hero among Haitian blacks.

Perhaps the most successful maroon society was the Republic of Palmares, founded deep in the Amazon jungle of Brazil in 1605. According to historian John Hope Franklin, "Palmares was a remarkable political and economic achievement for the fugitive slaves of Brazil . . . it grew into a complex political organism of many settlements of which Cerca Real do Macaco was the capital." At its height, Palmares boasted 20,000 inhabitants who traded with nearby towns and lived peaceably within a system of law. Although Palmares fell to a European invasion in 1695, stories of its success reached slaves in many other communities, including those in the American South. Centuries after Palmares disappeared, slaves told tales of the great maroon kingdom that had thrived for nearly 100 years.

The First Stirrings of Rebellion

Slaves did not enjoy similar success in the United States, where the total number of organized revolts equaled only a fraction of those staged in Central or South America or the Caribbean. Despite repeated defeats, American slaves never became resigned to their lot. Since the time of the American Revolution, slaves in the United States fought on plantations and also in courts of law in order to end their bondage.

In fact, slaves made great headway during the revolutionary era. Their first triumph came in 1783 when Quork Walker sued his master for his freedom on the grounds that the preamble to the state constitution declared all men "free and equal." The court ruled in his favor and in its decision ended slavery not only for Walker, but for all blacks in Massachusetts. The Walker case set a legal precedent and several New England slaves successfully won their freedom in the courtroom, victories that ultimately led to the abolition of slavery in the North. But the trend of freeing slaves traveled no farther south than Virginia. In 1831 the Virginia legislature came within one vote of abolishing the institution of slavery.

The liberation of northern blacks can be traced to the important role they played during the revolutionary war. In 1770, for example, an escaped slave named Crispus Attucks led the attack on British troops in what became known as the Boston Massacre, shouting, "The way to get rid of these soldiers is to attack the main guard!" Some historians consider Attucks the first man to die in the American Revolution.

During the War of Independence, many slaves volunteered to fight against England and received their freedom in exchange for military service. This arrangement aided the revolution by supplying rebel troops with auxiliary soldiers and by countering a similar offer from the British, who also needed an infusion of men into their forces. Thus, at the end of the war many former slaves lived as free men. The Revolutionary era offered blacks the best conditions they would know until the Civil War brought about the abolition of slavery.

American Slave Revolts

Once the booming cotton industry reinforced slavery in the South, blacks staged just four revolts, only two of which gained any momentum. The first occurred in 1800 in Richmond, Virginia, under the leadership of a slave name Gabriel Prosser. Gabriel's Revolt was secretly planned for months. It involved 1,000 slaves, all of whom had organized into a small fighting force, armed with guns, pikes, scythes, and bayonets. The rebel slaves met six miles outside of Richmond, intending to capture the city and to occupy it until the state legislature guaranteed that slavery would be outlawed. The plan was foiled when a slave betrayed the plot to authorities. Virginia governor James Monroe led the local militia out to meet the slaves and to turn them back. No battle ensued, but the leaders of the uprising, including Gabriel Prosser, were arrested and executed.

In 1811 the least-known but largest slave revolt in American history took place in St. John-the-Baptist Parish, Louisiana, just outside New Orleans. The revolt included some 500 slaves who had been brought to Louisiana by their French colonial masters, who were themselves refugees from the Haitian slave revolt. After arriving in North America, these slaves escaped, armed themselves, and marched on New Orleans with drums beating and flags flying. The militia, much better armed, rode out to meet them and attacked. Although the slaves fought bravely, they had no chance of winning and the militia triumphed.

Eleven years later in Charleston, South Carolina, Denmark Vesey, a slave who had purchased his own freedom, organized a plot among slaves to seize the city and ransom it in exchange for an end to slavery. Vesey devised a complex scheme to kidnap government leaders. On the eve of the revolt, however, a slave disclosed the plot to whites, and Vesey and his coconspirators were arrested. South Carolina authorities apprehended 131 slaves in all and hanged 37, including Vesey.

The best-known slave revolt in U.S. history occurred in 1831 in Southampton, Virginia. It was led by a plantation headman named Nat Turner, who rose up

An illustration from A Popular History of the United States—*published in about 1880—portrays the arrest of slave insurrectionist Nat Turner.*

in revolt with other slaves and killed his master and the master's family. These slayings initiated a wholesale slave insurrection that progressed from one plantation to another as slaves murdered their owners and liberated each other. Turner's uprising led to the deaths of about 60 whites and included among its participants approximately 70 slaves. The rampage was halted when federal and state troops crushed the rebellion and captured and executed Turner.

Slave revolts were just one means by which slaves in the South offered resistance to their bondage. Because outright rebellion posed great dangers for them, slaves employed more subtle means of protest. For example, slaves would covertly and purposely break plantation machinery or would set fire to a barn—acts that disrupted the daily life of the plantation and thereby lightened their own burden.

The slaves' prime target was the overseer. When this hated figure drove slaves especially hard or otherwise mistreated them, they sometimes resorted to outright murder. More often, slaves tried to sabotage the overseer, either by getting him drunk on corn liquor, a staple in the slave quarters, or by informing the master, through one of the house servants, that the overseer had committed an indiscretion.

When all else failed, slaves ran away. Between 200 and 300 slaves escaped every year, most of them from the upper South and the border states. In all, some 60,000 slaves escaped to free territory. They usually journeyed north via one of two routes: through eastern Maryland into Delaware and Pennsylvania or through western Maryland and across the Mason-Dixon Line—the border between Pennsylvania, a free state, and Maryland, a slaveholding state—into central Pennsylvania. Sometimes slaves followed trails farther west, such as those along the Mississippi or Ohio rivers, that led them north.

The vast majority of slaves ended their flight in Canada, where slavery had been outlawed by the mother country, England. Canada was much more enlightened about slavery than the United States. Canadian law not only admitted runaways into the country; it also denied entry to professional slave catchers—poor whites known as "patty rollers"—sent to track the blacks down.

The United States, in contrast, granted federal assistance to slave owners trying to recover their slaves. In 1793 Congress passed the Fugitive Slave Law, which made it a criminal offense for a citizen to harbor a fugitive slave or to prevent his or her arrest. A second piece of legislation—the Fugitive Slave Act of 1850—increased sanctions against aiding runaway slaves. Nowhere in the United Sates, not even in the antislavery North, could runaway slave be completely safe from capture and re-enslavement.

Slave-state legislatures feared political pressure from antislavery groups would seriously damage the "peculiar institution," a euphemism used by some apologists for slavery. By 1860 the slave codes had become so tyrannical that it was nearly impossible even for willing masters to *manumit*, or free from bondage, their own slaves. The only recourse the master had was to obtain passage of a special act by the state legislature, a process that cost time and money.

In any case, few slaves relied on the kindness of masters. Instead they plotted their own journey to freedom. Many who succeeded did so by escaping along a series of trails and paths collectively known as the Underground Railroad. This secret route from the South to the North was led by "conductors," brave men and women who sneaked into slave territory to guide runaway slaves out of bondage. The most famous conductor was Harriet Tubman. She had escaped from a Maryland plantation in 1849 and at great risk to her own safety—a bounty had been put on her head—returned to the South as many as 19 times to lead slaves on the Underground Railroad. She alone escorted 600 slaves to freedom, including her sister, both her children, and her mother and father.

Tubman plotted these escapes down to the smallest detail. She preferred to start her journeys on a Saturday night because owners could not print newspaper announcements of runaways until Monday morning, and the time in between gave her a headstart. Tubman had great sympathy for enslaved blacks, but none for cowards. If one of her party lost his nerve, Tubman pulled out the pistol she always carried and then threatened to kill him with the words "live free or die." She also brought along a small vial of tincture of opium, a sedative for crying babies, when slave catchers lurked nearby.

Harriet Tubman was just one of many men and women known as abolitionists because they worked to abolish slavery. They viewed the peculiar institution as immoral and unchristian and could not comprehend how Americans, who were steeped in the tenets of their Declaration of Independence, could sanction the enslavement of human beings in their midst. The abolitionist movement attracted members of both races, including the prominent journalist William Lloyd Garrison, who published the *Liberator*, the leading antislavery newspaper of the day.

Underground Railroad conductor Harriet Tubman (far left) poses with some slaves she led to freedom.

THE LIBERATOR.

VOL. I.]   WILLIAM LLOYD GARRISON AND ISAAC KNAPP, PUBLISHERS.   [NO. 33

BOSTON, MASSACHUSETTS.]   OUR COUNTRY IS THE WORLD—OUR COUNTRYMEN ARE MANKIND.   [SATURDAY, AUGUST 13, 1831.

The vast majority of abolitionists, however, were blacks. Many made their home in the North and worked as clergymen. Others, like Frederick Douglass, an escaped slave who held several government-appointed posts after the Civil War, published abolitionist newspapers such as the *North Star*, named after the star that guided conductors on the Underground Railroad. Douglass used this journal to publicize the antislavery cause and to promote the works of black writers such as Phillis Wheatley, a poet who lived at the time of the American Revolution.

Some abolitionists grew so disillusioned with the United States that they simply left the country. Reverend Alexander Crummell and Edward Wilmot Blyden founded a colony of freed American blacks in Liberia, a country on the coast of West Africa. Martin R. Delany, a black physician, led an effort to establish a colony in Africa at the bend of the Niger River. He returned to the United States in 1865 and led black troops who fought in the Union army. Like other abolitionists, he threw himself wholeheartedly into the violent struggle over slavery between Northern and Southern states, a bloody conflict that would claim the lives of more than 500,000 soldiers and countless civilians, known to history as the Civil War. ⧯

The masthead of the August 3, 1831, edition of The Liberator.

The Shores family poses in front of their house in Custer County, Nebraska, in 1887.

THE CIVIL WAR AND RECONSTRUCTION

The Civil War claimed more lives than any other armed conflict in American history. This four-year contest between the Northern Union and the Southern Confederacy—lasting from 1861 to 1865—was sparked by bitter controversy about the future of slavery in the United States. Much of the strife centered around the South's desire to extend slavery into newly acquired U.S. territories and the North's determination to confine it to the Southern states.

The Missouri Compromise

In 1803 the United States had completed the Louisiana Purchase, a transaction that doubled the nation's land mass. Under this agreement, the United States acquired from France territory in what are today the states of Arkansas, Kansas, Louisiana, Nebraska, Oklahoma, South Dakota, Iowa, Minnesota, North Dakota, Colorado, Missouri, Montana, and Wyoming.

In 1820 a crisis arose concerning the expansion of slavery into the land gained through the Louisiana Purchase. The new territory of Missouri stood to the north of the Mason-Dixon Line, the traditional boundary between free and slaveholding states, but many of the Southern whites who claimed settlements in Missouri had brought their slaves with them.

Then Missouri applied for statehood. The House of Representatives approved a bill admitting it to the Union but with an amendment that prohibited the entrance of additional slaves into the state. Northerners in the Senate, however, prevented the bill's passage, claiming that the admission to the Union of a new slaveholding state would upset the balance of power between the 11 free states of the North and the 11 slaveholding states of the South.

Debates raged in the Senate. Each side advanced its cause with such fervor that it seemed enmity about the expansion of slavery might hopelessly poison relations between the two regions. "This momentous question, like a fire bell in the night, awakened and filled me with terror," wrote Thomas Jefferson. John Quincy Adams echoed this sentiment in his diary: "I take it for granted that the present question is a mere preamble—a title-page to a great, tragic volume."

In January 1820, Congress averted a schism by passing a series of measures known collectively as the Missouri Compromise. The Senate voted to admit Missouri as a slave state and to counterbalance this act by speeding the admission of Maine into the Union as a free state. The compromise also extended the boundary between slave and free states to territory west of the Mississippi River, using the southern border of Missouri, near the 36th parallel, as the northernmost point where slavery could be practiced. Henceforth, Missouri was to be the only slave state above this line.

From 1820 until the outbreak of the Civil War in 1861 violent debates about the future of slavery factionalized Congress.

THE AFRICAN AMERICANS

This agreement stemmed the conflict until the 1840s, when the cultivation of cotton spread into what is now Texas, an area that at the time belonged to Mexico. In 1845, Congress annexed Texas, and war broke out with Mexico. The United States won in 1848, and the expansion-minded country controlled not only Texas, but also the territory that would become Arizona, California, New Mexico, and Utah.

Bloodshed in Kansas

Texas's admittance to the Union in 1845 and the acquisition of new land in the West renewed debates about slavery and ushered in an era of furious sectional strife. The slave states threatened to secede from the Union if the Senate prohibited slavery in the newly gained territories, and America came perilously close to civil war. Armed battle was postponed by the resulting Compromise of 1850. Under its provisions, California joined the Union as a free state, offsetting the earlier admittance of Texas. Most of the remaining territory was given the right to decide the slavery issue for itself. To placate the abolitionist forces in the country, the Senate abolished the slave trade in Washington, D.C.; to appease the South, it strengthened the Fugitive Slave Law of 1793.

The fragile peace effected by the compromise lasted only until 1854 when a senior senator from Illinois, Stephen A. Douglas, reawakened the bitter enmity between North and South. A seasoned politician, Douglas favored a "continuous line of settlements [from the Atlantic] to the Pacific Ocean" and thus introduced into the Senate a bill proposing that the Great Plains be reorganized as the Territory of Nebraska. This vast acreage lay north of the 36th parallel, the boundary of slave states as set forth in the Missouri Compromise. Its designation as a territory—the first step to achieving statehood—would eventually tip the balance of power toward the free states of the North.

Douglas knew he faced opposition from his Southern colleagues in the Senate. He won their support by

The Swan Swamp Massacre in 1858, one of many vicious confrontations between abolitionists and pro-slavery forces that earned Kansas the sobriquet "Bleeding Kansas."

incorporating a proposal for an outright repeal of the Missouri Compromise into his Nebraska bill: Each U.S. territory and state—even those north of the 36th parallel—would adopt the policy of popular sovereignty, deciding for itself by vote whether to nullify or legalize slavery. Douglas's proposal outraged Northern politicians. For three months they tried unsuccessfully to defeat this measure, which nonetheless was passed by Congress in 1854. The Great Plains gained official status as not one, but two territories: Kansas and Nebraska.

In 1855, Kansas became the battleground of abolitionist and pro-slavery forces when slaveholding residents of neighboring Missouri tried to influence the elections that would ultimately legalize or outlaw slavery in Kansas. Partisans on both sides engaged in armed warfare. So many people lost their lives that the observers dubbed the territory "Bleeding Kansas." The abolitionists won the struggle after much loss of life, and a slave-free Kansas finally achieved statehood in 1861.

Dred Scott and John Brown

In 1857 the growing abolitionist movement suffered a setback when the United States Supreme Court handed down a controversial decision in the case of *Dred Scott V. Sandford*. Dred Scott, a black slave, had been taken by his Missouri master to the free-soil state of Illinois, from which both later returned to Missouri. Back home again, he brought suit against his owner on the grounds that he had legally become emancipated by living within a free-soil state.

The Supreme Court ruled against Scott, declaring that as a black man he was not a United States citizen and thus had no right to bring a suit in a federal court. More important, the Court ruled that a slave did not automatically gain his liberty by entering a free state. Under this logic, a man who resided in free territory could nevertheless own slaves. He had only to travel into a slave state, buy as many slaves as he desired, and take them home, where they would remain slaves ever after. After the *Dred Scott* ruling no former slave could find a safe haven within the United States. This decision made it increasingly obvious to abolitionists that slavery would never be ended without a full-scale war.

Two years after the *Dred Scott* case, an abolitionist named John Brown—a veteran of Bloody Kansas—organized a plot to free Southern slaves through armed intervention. In order to secure sufficient weaponry, he led a raiding party of 13 whites and 5 blacks into the federal arsenal at Harpers Ferry, Virginia. Brown wrested control of the armory, killed the town's mayor, and seized several hostages before he was captured by federal authorities and hanged two months later on December 2, 1859.

An oil portrait of Dred Scott painted by 19th-century artist Louis Schultze.

The Republican Party

In 1854, a new political party, known as the Republican party, was formed. It was a coalition that included not a single member from a Southern state. In 1860, an election year, the Republican party adopted a plank in its presidential platform opposing further expansion of slavery. The nominee of the party that year was Abraham Lincoln, a former congressman from Illinois and a Republican since 1856.

Lincoln considered slavery a moral evil, but he himself was not an abolitionist. He favored not an abrupt ending to slavery, but a gradual liberation of blacks

Abraham Lincoln sat for this studio portrait on August 13, 1860, when he was the Republican nominee for the presidency.

from bondage, to be completed by the year 1900. Lincoln also believed that slave owners should be compensated for the loss of their property and that freed blacks should establish colonies somewhere outside the United States, perhaps in Africa or the Caribbean. Lincoln won support throughout the North for his stand against the expansion of slavery. In 1860 he was elected 16th president of the United States.

Lincoln's victory threw the South into revolt. By the day of his inauguration in March 1861, seven states—Alabama, Florida, Georgia, Louisiana, Mississippi, South Carolina, and Texas—had seceded from the Union to form a coalition they called the Confederacy. One month later, on April 12, Confederate gunfire sounded over Fort Sumter, a federal stronghold located off the coast of South Carolina. Lincoln responded to this attack by issuing a call for 75,000 volunteers to man the Union army. His rallying of military troops forced states in the upper South to proclaim their loyalty for one of the two sides, and Arkansas, North Carolina, Virginia, and Tennessee joined the Confederacy. Lincoln later summed up his reasons for embarking on war in a single sentence: "My paramount object in this struggle is to save the Union, and is not either to save or to destroy slavery."

Once the war began, abolitionists presented the president with two ultimatums: They called for the emancipation of the slaves and for the right of freed blacks to fight with the Union against slavery. Eventually, Lincoln acceded to both demands. Nearly 185,000 blacks fought valiantly during the Civil War and about 38,000 of them gave their lives to the Union cause. Sixteen blacks received Congressional Medals of Honor for bravery in action. Despite countless acts of heroism on the part of black soldiers, fewer than 100 were promoted to officer. Black troops, which were segregated from white Union forces, usually fought under white officers and received lower pay than white soldiers. Until 1864, every black enlisted received only $7 a month, whereas their white counterparts earned $13 or more. Black soldiers faced other forms of discrimination as well. Several white officers, such as Union general William Tecumseh Sherman, refused to command them at all. To their credit, black enlisted men fought with a tenacity that impressed their white officers.

On September 23, 1862, Lincoln satisfied the first of the abolitionists' demands when he issued the Emancipation Proclamation, a document that freed the slaves in all states still in rebellion as of January 1, 1863. Lincoln explained the logic behind his proclamation in an interview with the New York *Tribune* in 1862: "If I could save the Union without freeing any slave, I would do it; and if I could save it by freeing all the slaves I would do it; and if I could save it by freeing some and leaving others alone, I would also do that."

Ultimately, Lincoln chose this last course of action. The Emancipation Proclamation bolstered the Union's efforts, but it produced no instant victory for the North. The War Between the States—as it was called by the Confederacy—dragged on until April 1865, the historic day that Confederate general Robert E. Lee surrendered to Union general Ulysses Grant in Appomattox, Virginia.

The end of the Civil War brought freedom to nearly 4 million slaves and a great sense of optimism to blacks throughout the United States. During the days immediately after the North proclaimed victory, liberated slaves were filled with jubilation. Freedmen, as both males and females were called, celebrated on plantations or at crossroads between them. In December 1865, Congress passed the 13th Amendment to the Constitution of the United States, guaranteeing the hard-won freedom of black slaves: "Neither slavery nor involuntary servitude . . . shall exist within the United States."

The 107th U.S. Colored Infantry Guard of the Union army stand in front of their guardhouse.

After Appomattox

The end of the Civil War destroyed the institution of slavery in the South, but it did not vanquish the racism of white Southerners, who wanted their former slaves to retain their inferior status. Confederates showed little remorse for having enslaved the blacks. In fact, they insisted the South be readmitted to the Union without further delay or punishment from the North. Southerners argued that the Union had already exacted a terrible retribution in their territory: Nearly 250,000 men had been lost (and thousands more incapacitated), and the region's economy was shattered from the wreckage of Southern cities, small farms, and plantations.

But the Northerners were not satisfied with just the military defeat of the South. They wanted to effect permanent political and social change there and to ensure that slavery would never rear its ugly head again. In particular, a core of Republican politicians insisted that the Southern states recognize the civil rights of blacks and that legislatures below the old Mason-Dixon line redistribute privately held land. Thus, they hoped, political control in the South would be wrested from an elite group of planters, who might well mount another drive to secede.

Presidential Reconstruction

Activities in the South during the era of Presidential Reconstruction—as the years 1865–67 were later known—aroused considerable apprehension on the part of Northerners. Southern legislatures contained many former Confederate army officers and politicians. They voted to renounce secession and to ratify the 13th Amendment, but in truth they wanted to keep blacks in a position of subservience.

Claiming they, better than Northerners, truly understood "their" blacks, whites passed a series of laws, known as *Black Codes*, meant to curtail the activities of freedmen. The codes varied from state to state, but all of them forbade freedmen from carrying firearms; set restrictions on jobs freedmen could hold; and limited the amount of property they could acquire.

The worst aspect of the Black Codes was the vagrancy laws, which provided that any unemployed or idle freedman could be arrested and arbitrarily placed in a job. Although the war left thousands unemployed among both whites and blacks, the former were allowed to go free, but the latter now found themselves "assigned" to work on the plantations where they had once been slaves. The vagrancy laws enabled courts of law to order freed blacks back onto plantations. They also provided for the forced apprenticeship of black children to the former white masters of their parents. It was a strange kind of freedom for blacks.

The Republican-controlled legislature was appalled by the Black Codes and refused to seat new Southern congressmen and senators when Congress convened in late 1865. Aroused by Southern intransigence, the Republican legislators passed a series of laws (many of them over presidential vetoes) that overturned the first phase of Reconstruction and instituted a new program of change, called *Radical Reconstruction*, within the South. As a part of this revolutionary program, Congress extended the right to vote to all freedmen, thus granting formerly unheard of power to blacks while also enabling Republicans to win a constituency in the South for the first time.

In 1867 Congress divided the South into five military districts, each operating under the authority of a presidentially appointed army general, and also disenfranchised most Confederate army officers and politicians. The acts encouraged a new political order by providing for state constitutional conventions to meet with delegates elected by members of both races. For the first time, blacks were to have the right to participate in the governing process.

The South complied with the dictates of the Reconstruction Acts only because the military now occupied their territory, enforcing the new laws. By 1868 each state had held a constitutional convention, attended by black delegates, in which universal manhood suffrage was adopted, the black codes abolished, and a public school system set up for children of all races. The 14th Amendment and the civil rights acts of 1866 and 1875 gave freedmen additional liberty by granting them access to public places on an unrestricted basis.

In this 1872 cartoon General Ulysses S. Grant sits atop a carpetbag, symbol of the "carpetbaggers" who dominated Southern politics during Reconstruction.

Afro-Americans

Emancipation throughout the South was followed by a period of intense confusion in which blacks made the dramatic transition from slavery to citizenship. Afro-Americans tested their unfamiliar freedom by leaving the plantations and migrating to new areas, refusing to work for overseers, and voting and holding office. They were aided in their efforts by the Freedmen's Bureau, an organization created and funded by the Congress. The bureau performed acts of public service such as enrolling black children in schools, representing blacks in courts of law, and supervising their labor agreements with white companies. Most important, the Freedmen's Bureau provided a refuge for blacks, a place where they could usually find sympathy, help, and protection.

The bureau encouraged blacks to remain on the plantation and to work in agriculture. This would give blacks a means of economic support and also help counter the chaos disrupting Southern society. Most blacks followed this advice and remained on the plantation as sharecroppers, farmers who rented their land not with money but with a portion of their yearly crop. The arrangement was agreed upon with a bank or a private landowner. Sharecropping proved instrumental to restoring the Southern economy. By 1866 most freedmen were living and working on farms and plantations, for themselves or for wages. Very few blacks possessed the means to purchase their own land outright.

Major changes had altered the lives of the freedmen. Slavery was only a few years dead and most blacks were still poor, uneducated, and ruled by white society, yet their lives were vastly improved compared to the degradation of slavery. They could no longer be bought and sold or forcibly separated from their families. They could no longer be physically punished without a trial. They received wages for their labor. A new black community was growing out of the ashes of slavery. Blacks developed new independence and sought to separate themselves from their former oppressors as much as was possible.

The central institution in the black community became the church. Blacks in the South broke away from white Christian sects, such as the Baptists and Methodists, and set up their own churches as soon as possible. And black ministers—along with politicians, educators, and other professionals—stood at the top of black society.

Blacks in Southern Politics

During Reconstruction, the most important government positions were held by scalawags, white southern Republicans, and carpetbaggers, northerners who came south during this era. Contrary to popular perceptions, black officials did not form a majority in the South. With the exception of the lower house of the South Carolina legislature, where for a time blacks held a majority of the seats, the proportion of black officeholders fell below their percentage of the population. Fourteen black men served in the House of Representatives between 1869 and 1877. And two black Mississippians— Blanche K. Bruce, a former slave, and Hiram Revels— served in the Senate between 1870 and 1881. No black ever achieved the rank of governor, although the black lieutenant governor of Louisiana, P. B. S. Pinchback, served as acting governor for more than a month.

Black politicians contributed greatly to the Reconstruction effort: They led the way in establishing the South's first public school system and they expanded and modernized the public transportation system. But these improvements created new dilemmas for the South. In order to pay for schools, bridges, roads, and railroads, many Reconstruction legislatures levied a new set of duties and those who did not incurred a considerable debt for their state.

Blanche K. Bruce was elected U.S. senator from Mississippi in 1874.

Ku Klux Klansmen, recognizable by their white hoods, were largely responsible for the racial violence that for much of the 20th century kept Southern blacks in a state of terror.

States suffered from not only increased taxes but also widespread corruption within their governments. Republican politicians—the vast majority of them white—participated in graft, jobbery, and bribe taking. They padded expense accounts and skimmed funds from public appropriations. The 1860s and 1870s were a time of widespread corruption throughout the nation, not just in the South. Indeed, the moral laxness of southerners occurred on a small scale, and blacks acted much less fraudulently than their white counterparts. But white opponents of Radical Reconstruction accused blacks of being at the forefront of the corruption and turned public opinion against the Republican governments. When their enemies combined the corruption issue with appeals to white solidarity, blacks found themselves winning fewer and fewer elections.

Whites seized upon the opportunity to rob blacks of their political gains. They first used fraudulent practices to reduce the number of black ballots. When that tactic failed, they began a campaign of terror designed to drive blacks from office and the polls. Organizations such as the Ku Klux Klan—a secret society established by ex-Confederates in 1866—lynched, murdered, beat, harassed, and threatened black voters. Although often outnumbered and unarmed, blacks fought back in pitched battles that raged through Memphis, Tennessee, in 1866; Meridian, Mississippi, in 1871; and Hamburg and Charleston, South Carolina, in 1876.

These events drove black and white politicians out of the Republican party. Conservative white southerners—all of them Democrats—gradually returned to power and "redeemed" their home territory from Republican and black rule. Some states, such as Tennessee and Virginia, were "redeemed" as early as 1869 and 1870, respectively. Democrats presented themselves as the white man's party and branded all those who refused to support or cooperate with them as traitors to their race and to the South.

By the mid-1870s, Republicans outside of the South were beginning to see blacks as a liability, and a majority of the party had begun to believe that their grand experiment of social transformation in the South had failed. Black Republicans became increasingly isolated, and the party factionalized into a black wing, called the *black and tans*, and a white wing, known as the *lily-whites*. In order to salvage their political careers many white politicians bolted for the Democratic party.

By 1877 the Radical Republicans had lost control of the South. They agreed to end Reconstruction, withdraw federal troops, and let the South solve its own racial problems. The great experiment had ended. Whites then embarked on a 20-year campaign of racial disenfranchisement and discrimination that forced blacks into second-class citizenship. White supremacy came to dominate every area of southern life. According to historian Carl Degler:

> The inability of the radicals to translate their egalitarian ideals into reality through the use of force brought an end to the first phase of the search for a place for the black man in America. During the years which followed, the South was left free to work out for itself what it considered the Negro's proper niche. Contrary to popular conceptions of Reconstruction and its aftermath, the South was neither united nor decided on what that position should be. The evolution of the region's place for the Negro would take another generation. ❧

Mr. and Mrs. Emmet J. Scott pose with their children in about 1900.

JIM CROW AND SEGREGATION

After Reconstruction and the withdrawal of federal troops from the South, blacks found themselves at the mercy of a hostile white population that subjected them to discrimination, mob violence, and, worst of all, political disenfranchisement. Blacks continued to vote and hold office until late in the 1890s, in some cases risking their personal safety to do so. But by the turn of the century they had lost virtually all their political power. The last black congressman from the South left Congress in 1901. Not until 1967 did another black man from the South, Andrew Young of Georgia, win election to the House of Representatives. Some conservative blacks even voted for the Democratic ticket in order to be allowed a small voice in party politics.

As the number of successful Democratic candidates increased, the whites who supported them grew bolder in their tactics, often resorting to illegal measures to ensure Democratic victories: They stuffed ballot boxes, threw out black votes during the counting process, and issued false election returns. Finally, whites passed a series of discriminatory voting laws that effectively silenced blacks. In time, prejudicial laws would extend into other realms, namely schools and public transportation. As a body, this legislation was known as Jim Crow laws, named after the buffoonish central character of a racist 19th-century song-and-dance act that mocked blacks.

Because the Constitution prohibited racially based discrimination, Jim Crow laws avoided specific mention of race and did not openly prohibit blacks from voting. The only Jim Crow voting law that specifically mentioned race was the white primary ban, which forbade blacks from voting in Democratic primaries. Otherwise, the laws consisted of requirements that seemed to have no racial purpose, though they strategically worked against blacks. For example, under Jim Crow laws all voters had to pay a two-dollar poll tax when they registered to vote. Most black voters, and many whites as well, were simply too poor to afford the tax and thus were deemed ineligible to cast their ballot.

(continued on page 65)

An etching from Frank Leslie's Illustrated Newspaper *depicts South Carolina blacks traveling to the polls. After "redemption" Southern legislatures disenfranchised the majority of black citizens.*

A PANORAMA OF
THE PERFORMING ARTS

(Overleaf) *The Alvin Ailey American Dance Theater performs* Revelations, *a ballet choreographed to a selection of spirituals.*

Black dance ranges from the glamour of Broadway, epitomized by tap and jazz veteran Maurice Hines (left), to the classical elegance of the Dance Theater of Harlem's Swan Lake, to the urban vitality of break dancing (above).

60

Black excellence in two musical forms, opera and blues, is personified in baritone Simon Estes and singer B. B. King: (clockwise from left) King accompanies himself on his guitar, "Lucille"; Estes takes center stage in Porgy and Bess; *he plays opposite diva Leontyne Price in Verdi's masterpiece* Aida.

Rock 'n' roller Chuck Berry jams at his 60th-birthday concert, backed up by Rolling Stone member Keith Richards (opposite); Louis Armstrong improvises a horn solo (above); and bandleader Cab Calloway rehearses for a Washington gala.

The Fat Boys have helped popularize rap songs, in which performers rhythmically speak lyrics that often carry a social or political message.

(continued from page 56)

In addition to the tax, legislators instituted "literacy and understanding" tests in which the voter had to prove his ability to read and understand a specific document, usually the state or federal constitution or the Declaration of Independence, in order to register. Later many states added the requirement that voters hold a certain value of land or property. Generally, known as the Mississippi Plan (for the state that first implemented them), these laws kept tens of thousands of black adults off the voting lists.

One problem created by the Jim Crow laws was that they also disenfranchised thousands of poor white voters. Thus many states adopted a "Grandfather Clause," which enabled a voter to forgo the poll tax if his ancestor had voted in 1860—when blacks were still slaves. The Supreme Court declared the grandfather clauses unconstitutional in *Guinn v. U.S.* in 1915.

In cities, where better educated, middle-class blacks could circumvent the discriminatory laws, whites resorted to race riots to drive black politicians from office and in some cases from the city as well. In 1898, whites in Wilmington, North Carolina, staged an effective coup d'état that drove both black members of the city council and the black sheriff from office amid much bloodshed. In Atlanta, Georgia, a white-instigated race riot in 1906 culminated in pitched street battles that discouraged blacks from political participation.

White supremacy became so nearly complete that even well-to-do blacks finally gave up hope and acceded to the inevitable. In 1877, the South Carolina legislature had 39 black members in its lower house. By 1890 the number had shrunk to 6, and by 1900 there were none. Mississippi followed a similar course, as did other Southern states. The Democratic party, the bastion of an elite planter class and of former Confederate officers, was winning 96 percent of all elections. The South's 9 million blacks, numbering just more than 11 percent of the nation's entire population, had disappeared from the public arena.

Fusion Politics

In order to resist annihilation, black politicians of the 1880s resorted to an old trick and allied—or fused—themselves and their constituents with political parties willing to be of some service to the black community. In return, black leaders instructed their followers to vote for the candidates of that party.

The most successful fusion was born of an alliance between poor black and white farmers, who composed the membership of three agrarian parties: the Northern Farmers Alliance, the Southern Farmers Alliance, and the Colored Farmers Alliance. In the 1880s, these groups formed a National Farmers Alliance, a forerunner of the Populist movement of the 1890s. The marriage between Republicans and Populists worked well for a time, but the conservative Democrats, who were losing seats to fusion candidates, responded with a massive wave of disenfranchising legislation that hurt Populists as well as blacks. Gradually, the Populist party turned against blacks, unleashing the racist tirades of Tom Watson and other former supporters of the black community. In the late 1890s, whites solidified behind color lines and thereafter race became a primary consideration in regional and national politics.

Segregation in Education

Throughout the South, the races became polarized not just in the realm of politics but in all areas. States passed laws that legalized the preexisting custom of keeping blacks and whites apart, or segregated. This system advocated a policy of maintaining "separate but equal" schools, transportation, and housing for the races; in truth, whites alone benefited from the system. It increased their domination of the South politically, economically, and socially.

The first segregation laws affected public schools. Since they were founded—after the Civil War—these

A black delegate speaks at the 10th annual convention of the Knights of Labor. During the late 19th century blacks maintained some of their political power by forming alliances with white organizations and political parties.

had never mixed black and white students. During Reconstruction, the Freedmen's Bureau actually supported such schools, on the assumption that special institutions for blacks would include a curriculum developed expressly to suit them. But over the years black schools got the short end from state legislatures, which skimped on equipment, building maintenance, and teachers' salaries. After 1900, schools for white pupils received twice as many funds as those for blacks.

Similar injustices also occurred at the university level. Black colleges, which depended on financial contributions from Northern white philanthropists, had trouble obtaining support unless their curriculums emphasized manual and vocational training. The issue of higher education split the black community. Liberals maintained that students deserved a chance to develop their intellect and creativity. Conservatives argued that training students as skilled craftsmen was better than not training them at all—an argument also advanced by many racist whites. In the end, black education proved "separate" but not "equal."

Students gather in front of a "Negro school" in about 1900.

The Spread of Jim Crow

In time, Jim Crow laws applied to public transportation. Many Southern cities started separating whites from blacks in streetcars, and states quickly followed by keeping them apart in railroad cars. In 1881, the Tennessee legislature became the first in the country to require "colored" travelers to sit in Jim Crow cars, which were nothing more than the smoking cars. Throughout the South, wealthy black travelers who for years had purchased a first-class ticket and sat in the first-class coach found themselves forced to tolerate uncomfortable bench seats.

In 1887, W. H. Council, the president of an all-black college in Alabama, suffered just such an indignity when, in spite of his first-class ticket, the conductor forced him to move to the Jim Crow car. He filed a complaint with the Interstate Commerce Commission, which responded with a ruling that permitted separate facilities on public transportation so long as they were equivalent to white ones. Black Americans were outraged at this decision. They well knew that the separate

A black passenger is expelled from a Philadelphia railway car in this etching from the Illustrated London News *in 1856.*

facilities were not equal and were not intended to be.

In 1896, Jim Crow was again challenged in the historic case *Plessy v. Ferguson*. Homer Plessy, a black man from New Orleans, was arrested for refusing to move from the whites-only coach on the East Louisiana Railroad line. He challenged his conviction on the grounds that it violated his rights under the 14th Amendment. The case eventually found its way to the Supreme Court, which in its ruling deemed separate facilities for blacks constitutionally valid if they were equal to those reserved for white people. Justice John Marshall Harlan, the lone dissenter in the case, declared the decision as harmful to the country as that in the *Dred Scott* case. He further added that, "Our Constitution is color-blind and neither knows nor tolerates classes among citizens. In respect of civil rights, all citizens are equal before the law."

The landmark decision in *Plessy v. Ferguson* opened the door to a new wave of segregation laws. Southern states segregated waiting rooms, lavatories, water fountains, lunch counters, prisons, poorhouses, public parks, restaurants, even cemeteries and factories. Southern cities adopted segregated housing ordinances and went so far as to use a Jim Crow Bible in courtrooms. Piece by piece the bricks were cemented into the wall of segregation, and blacks were forced to tolerate second-class citizenship.

As historian C. Vann Woodward has pointed out, segregation was by no means uniform throughout the South. In some areas the black middle class grew and prospered free from daily harassment and humiliation. In other areas, whites ignored Jim Crow laws and allowed or even encouraged black voting. Blacks continued to hold local offices, such as sheriff and justice of the peace, and sat on city councils until 1900. And in many southern cities, blacks challenged Jim Crow by boycotting segregated streetcar lines and stores. Still, the rule of the day was segregation. And to black people living in the South it seemed that the occasional victory was followed by more setbacks. Afro-Americans in the North, too, suffered racial prejudice, but the North never approached the South in the viciousness and pervasiveness of its discrimination.

Mob Rule

Worse even than segregation was the racial violence that terrorized blacks during the 1890s. During this period, a wave of lynchings, unprecedented in their frequency, swept through the rural South. Some occurred in cities, but most took place in isolated rural areas where blacks composed between 40 and 50 percent of the population and thus were perceived by hostile whites as a potential threat to white domination.

During a lynching, mob members openly flaunted their identity before hundreds or even thousands of onlookers. People from all levels of society attended lynch-

An Indiana mob attends a lynching in 1930. The practice of lynching was not limited to the South and was responsible for thousands of deaths.

ing bees, as they were called. Men, women, and children dressed in their Sunday best for this special event and looked on in fascination as the victim, often a young black man falsely accused of murder or arson, was hanged. During the 1890s, this scene was repeated more than 1,400 times. Sometimes the victim was a black politician who had refused to resign in favor of a white man. Southern whites claimed the chief cause of lynching was interracial rape, but the statistics did not support their contention. In fact, less than 20 percent of all lynchings involved a charge of rape or sexual assault against a white woman. The lynch mob acted with virtual impunity; less than one percent of their participants were ever arrested and indicted, let alone tried and convicted.

The lynch mob became the most feared symbol of white supremacy in the South, upholding the sentiment of Jim Crow. In the few areas where segregation laws did not extend, a single lynching might discourage black voting for years. How could the South so freely discriminate against and terrorize Afro-Americans? For a combination of reasons: Republicans had all but deserted the cause of racial equality, and northerners withdrew their support of southern blacks by ignoring their plight, even denying civil rights to blacks who had moved northward. Thus, blacks found themselves isolated, and oppressed. The white South had achieved what it once had under slavery—the creation of a work force it could control.

Booker T. Washington at the Tuskegee Institute in 1906.

The Black Response to White Supremacy

During this bleak era in their history, black Americans had little to comfort them: neither relief from daily toil nor certainty that their lot would someday improve. But they did find hope in a succession of black leaders who devoted their own lives to bettering those of American blacks. The first to rise to prominence was Booker T. Washington, an Afro-American born into slavery in 1856. Washington headed the Tuskegee Institute—an

Black women students learn millinery at the Tuskegee Institute in 1906.

industrial school located in Tuskegee, Alabama—and advocated vocational education for blacks, saying that they must learn a trade in order to earn economic independence and self-respect. During his tenure at Tuskegee, Washington made the acquaintance of George Washington Carver, who served as the school's director of agricultural research and achieved his own fame for scientific work. He discovered hundreds of uses for the sweet potato, the peanut, and the soybean—crops he believed would revolutionize southern agriculture.

Through his "Tuskegee machine" Booker T. Washington became a leader as well as an educator. In 1895 he stirred controversy within the black community and attracted international attention by telling a predominantly white crowd at the Cotton States Exposition in Atlanta, Georgia, that blacks would temporarily accept disenfranchisement and the loss of political power and accept segregation. "In all things that are purely social," he said, "we can be as separate as the fingers, yet one as the hand in all things essential to mutual progress."

Washington faced fierce opposition from other blacks, including a Harvard-educated intellectual named William Edward Burghardt (W. E. B.) Du Bois.

Du Bois was born in Great Barrington, Massachusetts, in 1868, and in 1895 he became Harvard's first black Ph.D. In 1903 Du Bois published a scathing essay entitled "Of Mr. Booker T. Washington and Others" in his book *Souls of Black Folk*, denouncing Washington's willingness to accept a "temporary" second-class citizenship for Afro-Americans. Du Bois demanded immediate restoration of political rights for blacks and advocated a "Talented Tenth" to act as racial leaders. He also encouraged blacks to embrace their African heritage. In 1909, Du Bois joined with leading white reformers to create the National Association for the Advancement of Colored People (NAACP), an organization pledged to the elimination of segregation and other forms of discrimination.

Du Bois's views proved as controversial as Washington's, and before long they, too, caused spirited debate within the black community. His chief adversary was William Monroe Trotter, born in 1872 in Hyde Park, New York. Trotter earned an undergraduate degree from Harvard, then made his reputation as editor

W. E. B. Du Bois sits in his office at the Crisis, *a magazine published by the NAACP.*

William Monroe Trotter helped found the Niagara movement— a forerunner of the NAACP— along with W. E. B. Du Bois.

of the *Guardian*, a newspaper he founded in Boston, Massachusetts, in 1901. From its pages Trotter argued that if blacks tolerated adversity (as Washington had advised) or overemphasized their African heritage (as Du Bois thought they should), they would only impede the process of their integration and assimilation into American society. His advocacy of immediate integration foreshadowed the civil rights movement of the 1960s.

The Emigration Movement

While Washington, Du Bois, and Trotter fought against the late 19th-century oppression of blacks, another black leader, Bishop Henry McNeal Turner, became the spokesman for Afro-Americans who decided their best hope for a decent life lay in a return to Africa. Born to freedmen in South Carolina in 1834, Turner grew to adulthood with a keen awareness of his family's low social status. Of America, Turner said, "We were born here, raised here, fought, bled and died here, and have a thousand times more right here than hundreds of thousands of those who help to snub, proscribe and persecute us, and that is one of the reasons I almost despise the land of my birth." His message held a special appeal for poor southern blacks, who had despaired of hoping that life in the United States held any promise for them.

In the early 1890s, Turner joined forces with the American Colonization Society (ACS). This group had already sponsored the migration of approximately 100 black Americans to Liberia annually. Turner and the ACS helped smooth the way for additional emigrants. In 1891 Turner himself visited his ancestral homeland and wrote glowingly of its opportunities, all but ignoring the widespread poverty and disease in western Africa. His accounts of life across the ocean captured the imagination of blacks back home, and by 1892 thousands had begun to apply for passage aboard the small ships leaving New York for Liberia. Strapped by a lack of funds, the ACS was forced to turn all of them away and as a consequence collapsed entirely.

Migration North

For the great majority of black people living in the South, a less distant journey seemed a sure means of obtaining relief from their daily oppression. At the beginning of the 20th century, they turned their gaze not toward Africa but toward the industrial cities of the North, whose factories offered better wages than the fields of the South.

Some blacks—and whites—had moved as early as the 1860s, but the exodus did not gather force until the 1900s. In 1910, three-fourths of the nearly 10 million Afro-Americans lived in rural areas and nine-tenths lived in the South. By 1950, three-fourths of the black population—which totaled more than 15 million—dwelled in cities and slightly more than half lived outside the South. This exodus—called the "Great Migration"—was the most significant population shift in American history and brought about a profound change in the texture of black life. ✎

In 1863 President Lincoln appointed Bishop Henry McNeal Turner chaplain to the Union army's First Regiment of Colored Troops.

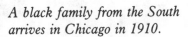
A black family from the South arrives in Chicago in 1910.

LIFE IN THE GHETTO

The Great Migration was a major turning point in the Afro-American experience. A huge portion of the black population no longer resided in the rural South but in urban centers in the North. Most black migrants took on unskilled jobs in industry—laborious and often dangerous work—that offered them higher wages than they had ever before received.

Soon reports detailing the wonderful opportunities available in Chicago, Detroit, New York City, Philadelphia, and St. Louis filtered into the South, stimulating further waves of migration. But at the close of World War I, the Northern wellspring suddenly went dry. European nations reduced their demand for U.S. goods, decreasing the production rates of American factories. The nation's economy sagged, and the number of available jobs declined. Blacks found themselves vying for employment against white veterans of the Great War—a competition that kindled resentment within both groups.

The Urban Ghetto

New arrivals from the South faced a similar struggle in their quest for decent housing. In New York City, for example, blacks who arrived at the outset of the Great Migration had lived along the northern edge of Manhattan in a neighborhood called Harlem. Once a wealthy white quarter, Harlem began accepting black

Blacks and whites work together in this New York cigar factory in about 1915.

residents in 1903, and by 1910 was home to about 5,000 black families, all squeezed into a 6-block section of the neighborhood.

In an effort to prevent the influx of more blacks, worried white residents organized the Harlem Property Owners Association. It failed to keep out blacks, and "white flight" began in earnest. Unscrupulous real estate agents capitalized on whites' fears through a practice called blockbusting. The realtors sneaked a black family onto a previously white block, thereby panicking the whites, who sold their property cheaply to the real estate company. Once the block had been busted, real estate developers renovated the housing, dividing space meant for a single family into rooms for five times as many, usually with a common kitchen. This opened up more apartments for a while, but there was not enough room for the steady stream of blacks. By the 1930s, 233 black people crowded into every square block of Harlem, whereas white Manhattanites lived with the more comfortable ratio of 133 people per square block.

Black neighborhoods across the country suffered a similar fate and rapidly deteriorated into dangerous and dirty ghettos. To make matters worse, these districts' longtime black residents often blamed their ruin on the newcomers and developed a revulsion against their brethren from the rural South. Northern blacks disdained new migrants as "country bumpkins" and often refused to admit them to fraternal organizations, churches, social clubs, and other community groups that could have eased their transition into city life. Instead, the new arrivals had to fend for themselves in an alien and often hostile environment.

Disillusioned Anew

Eventually, the antagonism between established blacks and newcomers relaxed into a mutual understanding and the two groups banded together to form a unified community of urban blacks. The turning point was World War I. By war's end nearly 367,000 Afro-Americans were called into service, 50,000 of whom actually fought overseas. Veterans returned home from the fox-

Interior of a Harlem apartment in about 1910.

holes of France with a new outlook. Europeans often treated them equitably—as Americans rather than blacks—and the soldiers learned that it was possible to live in a society free from discrimination. Veterans passed this discovery on to family and friends, and—perhaps unintentionally—fortified fellow blacks for their long struggle for equality.

America was less ready than Europe to acknowledge the accomplishments of Afro-American soldiers. Historian John Hope Franklin has pointed out that black troops were the first Allied troops to push into German-controlled territory and reach the Rhine river. The Germans called them Hell Fighters. But when the Hell Fighters returned home they were hardly honored and once again they found themselves mired in racism.

The postwar era was a time of dashed hopes not only for black veterans, but for all Afro-Americans. Their dreams of a prosperous city life curdled as they

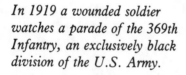

In 1919 a wounded soldier watches a parade of the 369th Infantry, an exclusively black division of the U.S. Army.

confronted the harsh realities of workplace discrimination and the urban ghetto. They found, too, that they had failed to escape the racist violence of the South, as the Ku Klux Klan took root in Northern metropolises.

In the ill-fated summer of 1919, later called the Red Summer, Afro-Americans publicly vented their anger and frustration. Twenty race riots erupted in cities across the country, spilling blood in larger urban centers, such as Chicago, and smaller towns, such as Elaine, Arkansas. Generally, police in the various cities where the riots occurred did nothing to quell them, and in some cases they actually aided white rioters or took part in the frays themselves.

These melees signaled a new militancy among blacks, who—concentrated for the first time in small, urban neighborhoods—actively engaged whites in violent confrontation, something that had been unthinkable in the rural South. Fighting in Houston, Texas, for example, marked the first time in history that a race riot took more white than black lives. The black community had finally dared to retaliate, and Afro-Americans interpreted this new boldness as a sign that they could win victories not only in the streets but also in the arenas of politics and economics.

The Reign of Garvey

During this volatile period, one man arose to capture the attention of the masses crowded into America's ghettos—Marcus Moziah Garvey. Born on the island of Jamaica in 1887, Garvey was a self-taught orator with a magnetic personality. As a young man, he read widely, especially in the works of Booker T. Washington, and found inspiration in Washington's theories about the importance of self-help and racial solidarity for blacks.

Garvey developed his own philosophy about race and adopted a more radical stance than Washington's. He believed whites would always be prejudiced against people of African descent. He rejected integration and assimilation, arguing instead that the African in the United States and the Caribbean should develop "a distinct racial type of civilization of his own and . . . work out his salvation in his motherland."

In 1914, Garvey founded an organization that later served as the base for his back to Africa movement, the Universal Negro Improvement Association (UNIA). In its earliest days, the UNIA aimed not to relocate blacks but to heighten black pride and to introduce a program of educational and economic opportunity. Garvey also established the African Orthodox church, in which he preached that God was black and the devil white. When the UNIA failed to find a responsive audience in Jamaica, Garvey traveled to New York in 1916 and established the headquarters of his international organization in the rapidly growing black community of Harlem.

At first the UNIA attracted scant support in Harlem but, after the Red Summer politicized New York blacks, its membership grew. Garvey spread his views through his newspaper, the *Negro World*, and he soon stood at the head of a black nationalist movement that first blossomed through Afro-American communities in the 1840s and later in the 1890s, under the leadership of Du Bois and Turner. The UNIA's message of political liberation and African nationalism struck a chord deep within the oppressed masses in big-city ghettos. By August 1920, when the movement reached its peak, total membership in the UNIA—according to Garvey— numbered approximately 2 million in 30 chapters around the world. Also in 1920, Garvey presided over the First International Convention of the Negro Peoples of the World, attended by thousands of his supporters. In honor of the event, the UNIA staged an elaborate parade through the streets of Harlem.

Much of the district closed down as thousands lined the streets to watch the procession. Garvey rode in an open car, wearing an elegant uniform topped with a plumed hat. In his wake followed an army of UNIA groups. The African Legions and the Black Cross

Nurses marched with military precision and waved the UNIA's red, black, and green flag ("red for the blood that was shed in slavery, black for the noblest of all races, and green for the land of Africa"). As they paraded, the UNIA members sang their anthem, "Ethiopia, Thou Land of Our Fathers."

Later, the charismatic Garvey gave a speech, in which he told the crowd that he wanted to "retake every square inch of the 12,000,000 square miles of African territory belonging to us [all persons of African heritage] by right divine." His slogan, "Africa for the Africans at Home and Abroad," became a symbol of united opposition to the racism blacks in the Western Hemisphere endured and to the oppression that Africans faced from the European colonial powers dominating their homeland.

At the very moment of Garvey's triumph, his reign was about to end. In 1919, he had founded the Black Star Line of steamships to conduct trade between blacks in America and the Caribbean. When word of this endeavor reached UNIA members, they believed that he had established the steamship line to transport the faithful back to Africa. Indeed, in the 1920s, Garvey sent delegations to the black nation of Liberia in order to open the way for UNIA settlers. The Liberians were initially receptive to Garvey's emigration plan, but by 1924 Liberian president Charles D. B. King viewed the UNIA with extreme suspicion. He suspected Garvey of secretly scheming to take over the Liberian government. Faced also with the financial collapse of the Black Star Line, Garvey soon abandoned his plans for emigration.

At home, Garvey faced mounting opposition from the black elite, especially W. E. B. Du Bois, who labeled Garvey the worst enemy of the black race and called him an uneducated foreigner and a demagogue. Another influential man, labor and protest leader A. Philip Randolph, joined in the chorus of criticism and warned the black community that any government led by Garvey would be a reactionary dictatorship, not

In August 1924, Marcus Garvey rides in a parade to celebrate a meeting of the International Convention of the Negro Peoples of the World, which first convened in 1920.

Fashionable Harlemites stroll down Lenox Avenue, a main thoroughfare of the neighborhood during the 1930s.

a democracy. Black church leaders also aligned against Garvey. His African Orthodox church threatened to woo away the masses of black poor who composed their congregations.

In 1922, Robert Abbott, the editor of the Chicago newspaper the *Defender* and an adversary of Garvey's made it known that Garvey was about to sell stock in the UNIA without a license. A federal investigation began and uncovered irregularities in the UNIA's financial affairs. Garvey was indicted and convicted of mail fraud. Historians still debate the question of Garvey's guilt. Some have defended him as an honest man who too easily trusted unreliable "lieutenants" to run his complex and far-flung organizations. Others believe he knowingly defrauded his followers.

Garvey appealed his conviction but in 1925 was sent to the Atlanta Penitentiary. Two years later the U.S. government commuted his sentence and deported him to his native land, Jamaica, where Garvey carried on his work until his death in 1940.

The Harlem Renaissance

The decade dominated politically by Garvey also witnessed a flowering of black culture now known as the Harlem Renaissance. By 1920 Harlem had become the capital of the black world, a city within a city, in which 200,000 Afro-Americans lived within an area of 2 square miles. There some of the most talented artists in the United States gathered together and forever changed the face of American music, theater, and literature.

The Advent of Jazz

The 1920s was a period when, in the words of poet Langston Hughes, "Harlem was in Vogue." New Yorkers from every walk of life flocked uptown to Harlem to spend long evenings—they often stretched until dawn—in an array of night spots. Forty years before races generally mingled, white millionaires casually brushed shoulders with black factory hands. The main attraction for whites were fashionable clubs such as The Bamboo Inn, Mexico's, and Connie's Inn, where patrons could hear the sounds of jazz.

Jazz traced its roots to the American spirituals of the late 19th century and even further back, to the rhythms, melodies, and harmonies of West Africa. The earliest jazz musicians hailed from New Orleans, where in the early 1900s they played "Dixieland," an ensemble style that featured several instruments playing together at breakneck tempos. In the mid-1920s, Dixieland evolved into the "Western" or "Chicago" style. Its greatest figure was Louis Armstrong, a New Orleans native, whose trumpet solos introduced the spontaneous invention—or improvisation—that distinguished jazz from every other variety of music. Armstrong and other jazz masters, such as clarinetist Sidney Bechet and pianist Earl "Fatha" Hines, elevated jazz solos into musical statements of great sophistication and beauty.

The best jazz playing often occurred in jam sessions or in cutting contests. In these, young musicians competed with each other in order to win an opportunity to play with jazz giants. Milton "Mezz" Mezzrow, a white reedman from Chicago, often played in Harlem and described an after-hours cutting contest held at Mexico's:

> The contests generally happened in the early morning, after the musicians came uptown from their various jobs. There was always a small private club or a speakeasy that had a piano in it, and when some new musician came to town he was obliged to come up with his instrument and get off for the older musicians. . . . before the night was over all the cats were in some smoky room, really blowing up a breeze. If it was a close call . . . and people couldn't come to much decision about who was best—then somebody would sneak out and get [saxophonist] Coleman Hawkins, and when he unwrapped his horn it settled all arguments and sent the boys back to practice some more.

Blues queen Bessie Smith smiles for a publicity photo in 1925.

Instrumental music was the domain of male players, but women prevailed in the field of jazz singing, often performing blues numbers characterized by the themes of love, sex, poverty, and death. Harlem clubs were never more packed than when Bessie Smith, Empress of the Blues, belted out "Gulf Coast Blues" or "Baby Won't You Please Come Home" to a crowd that hung on her every note.

Born in about 1898 in Chattanooga, Tennessee, Smith was herself the protégée of Gertrude (Ma) Rainey, a vocalist who raised the singing of blues to an art form. Smith moved to New York in the early 1920s—after several years on the road—and enjoyed stardom both onstage and through best-selling sound recordings. One fan recalled her in performance:

Bessie Smith was a fabulous deal to watch. She was a pretty large woman and she could sing the blues. . . . She dominated a stage. You didn't turn your head when she went on. You just watched Bessie. You didn't read any newspapers in a night club when she went on. She just upset you. When you say Bessie— that was it. She was unconscious of her surroundings. . . . If you had any church background, like people who came from the South as I did, you would recognize a similarity between what she was doing and what those preachers and evangelists from there did, and how they moved people. Bessie did the same thing on stage. She could bring about a mass hypnotism. When she was performing, you could hear a pin drop.

The Dean of Harlem Poets

As Armstrong enchanted listeners with his trumpet, and Bessie Smith captivated them with her song, poet contemporary Langston Hughes moved readers with his lyrical verse. Born in Joplin, Missouri, in 1902, Hughes spent his early youth working at a variety of odd jobs, including busboy, and traveling widely. In 1925 his work was introduced to white audiences by the American poet Vachel Lindsay, and one year later Hughes's first book of poems, *The Weary Blues*, was published to great acclaim. Hughes's poetry incorporated the rhythms of jazz and blues with the cadences of black speech. He drew upon all sides of black experience in his work—particularly the struggles of urban blacks.

Another major black author was novelist and folklorist Zora Neale Hurston. Like Hughes, she made music out of the rhythms of ordinary black speech. In the words of one critic, "In the speech of her characters, black voices . . . come alive. Her fidelity to diction, metaphor and syntax rings with an aching familiarity that is a testament to Hurston's skill and to the durability of black speech."

Born in 1901 in Eatonville, Florida, Hurston struggled all her life to celebrate and promote the rich heritage of American blacks, particularly rural blacks. Her most famous novel, *Their Eyes Were Watching God* (1938) describes the life of Janie, a headstrong woman who gives up a loveless but financially secure marriage in order to embark on a love affair and a subsequent journey of self-discovery. Hurston published five more novels as well as a folktale collection, an autobiography, and many short stories. Then she hit hard times. She suffered from a stroke and heart disease before dying in a welfare home in her home state in 1960. Hurston lay in an unmarked grave for more than a decade. Then another important black writer, Alice Walker, discovered Hurston's burial site and had a tombstone erected there. Walker also rescued Hurston's work from obscurity, using her own influence (much of it gained from her own success as a writer) to persuade publishers to reissue several of Hurston's novels. Thanks to Walker's efforts, Hurston's work has once again found a wide following, and she has emerged as one of the great American authors of her time.

According to novelist Sherley Anne Williams, the Harlem Renaissance amounts to "the first concerted outpourings of formal artistic expression among Afro-Americans." Even after the glory days of Harlem had ended, black artists continued to reap the rich tradition established by an earlier generation. Black authors, for

Langston Hughes visits New York's Public School 113 in 1943.

A native of Florida, Zora Neale Hurston journeyed north to study at Barnard College and—along with her contemporary Langston Hughes— introduced a uniquely black idiom into American literature.

example, produced important work in the 1930s and 1940s, especially the fiction of Richard Wright, author of *Black Boy* and *Native Son*. The 1950s saw the publication of *The Invisible Man*, by Wright's protégé Ralph Ellison. In 1965, a poll of critics and writers named this masterpiece the single best novel written by any American since World War II. Another major black writer, James Baldwin, excelled as a novelist, playwright, and essayist. His searing account of black experience—*The Fire Next Time*—caused a sensation when it appeared in The *New Yorker* magazine in 1963. Today, leading black writers include Walker, Toni Morrison, and John Edgar Wideman.

The New Deal

During the Harlem Renaissance, Afro-Americans forged a new identity, based on a decade of artistic and cultural achievement among blacks. This era saw the birth of what Howard University professor Alain Locke has called "The New Negro," whose confidence and energy seemed to overcome a sorrowful past. But at the close of the 1920s, the Jazz Age euphoria that had galvanized Harlem abruptly stopped.

In October 1929, stocks in the United States declined in value by an average of 40 percent. The crash of the stock market, in the words of one historian, "confronted the United States with its greatest crisis since the Civil War. Factories slashed production; construction practically ceased; millions of investors lost their savings; over 5,000 banks closed their doors in the first three years of the [economic] depression." A worldwide depression ensued that took its toll on Americans across the country. No group suffered more than the blacks.

The administration of President Herbert Hoover— whom the executive director of the NAACP, Walter White, referred to as "the man in the lily white house"—did so little to aid Afro-Americans that by 1933 between 25 and 40 percent of urban blacks depended on federal relief to avoid starvation. Many private charities sustained whites during this difficult

period but discriminated against blacks in the distribution of food; some organizations bluntly refused to sponsor integrated soup kitchens.

Hope came with the election of Franklin D. Roosevelt to the presidency in 1933. He promised that "no citizen shall be permitted to starve" and that "in addition to providing emergency relief, the Federal Government should and must provide temporary work whenever that is possible." Shortly after taking office, Roosevelt inaugurated the New Deal, a program aimed at helping those hurt by the Great Depression. Many Americans, blacks among them, found employment through the New Deal's temporary work programs, such as the Public Works Administration, the Civilian Conservation Corps, and the Works Progress Administration. Roosevelt did not openly advocate equal rights for blacks, but he ensured that they reaped the benefits of his policies. Indeed, the New Deal marked the beginning of 20th-century federal involvement in civil rights. To that extent, apart from the short-term aid it gave during the depression, it set the stage for the next dramatic chapter of Afro-American history, the civil rights movement. ∾

Eleanor Roosevelt (fourth from left) championed black rights throughout her lifetime.

THE CIVIL RIGHTS REVOLUTION

During World War II approximately 1 million black men and women served their country with distinction. Although they still faced discrimination, they gained entry into more branches of the armed forces than ever before, bolstering the ranks of fighting and tranportation units, the engineer corps, the signal corps, and many other divisions of Selective Service. In January 1945, the army initiated a bold plan to intermingle platoons of white and black troops to fight within Germany. The experiment met with great success, and blacks' accomplishments equaled those of the Hell Fighters feared by Germans during World War I.

At home, industrial plants joined the war effort by producing the weaponry needed to supply the troops. In the process, they won lucrative government supply contracts that enabled them to hire millions of workers and pay them more than ever before. The boom in the defense industry, along with Roosevelt's New Deal employment programs, lifted the American workforce out of its depression slump. But black workers did not share in this new abundance and stood no chance of employment in defense plants, which were controlled, by and large, by white-dominated unions.

The First March on Washington

In all of the United States, one man commanded the organizational expertise blacks desperately needed to gain access to the defense plants. He was A. Philip Randolph, the organizer and president of the Brotherhood of Sleeping Car Porters (an all-black union since 1937, the year it was founded). Randolph was a seasoned labor negotiator. He clearly perceived the racism that shut blacks out of defense plants and denied them many other opportunities enjoyed by white Americans.

In 1941, Randolph decided to combat the racist policies of defense plants in order to advance the cause of winning equality and justice for blacks. To that end, he spread news of a planned march on the nation's capital throughout the black community, calling for 50,000 to 100,000 blacks from across the country to travel to Washington, D.C., and protest the policies that withheld employment from them.

The mere threat of the march on Washington pressured President Franklin D. Roosevelt into negotiating with Randolph. Roosevelt feared social unrest among blacks and also knew that a mass demonstration against racism in Washington would tarnish the United States's image abroad as a champion of democracy. The president met several times with Randolph, who agreed to cancel the march if Roosevelt guaranteed the end of discrimination against blacks in the defense industry. On June 25, 1941, Roosevelt complied by issuing Executive Order 8802—a landmark document in black American history. It declared that "there shall be no discrimination in the employment of workers in defense industries or Government because of race, creed, color, or national origin." This was the first presidential directive on race relations since Reconstruction and once again aligned the federal government with the well-being of the country's black citizens.

As a result of the executive order, defense plants hired about 2 million blacks, admitting many of them into unionized jobs. The number of blacks enrolled in labor unions rose to 1.23 million, an increase of nearly

100 percent. In addition, 200,000 blacks found employment with the federal government, which began hiring Afro-Americans in greater numbers than ever before. From 1941 until the war's end in 1945, black Americans achieved significant economic gains—the first step in preparing them for the struggle to come.

As the nation entered the peaceful and prosperous 1950s, Afro-Americans grew even more determined to end racial injustice. In 1947, they saw two of their own break into America's favorite pastime, when second baseman Jackie Robinson donned the uniform of the Brooklyn Dodgers and infielder (later outfielder) Larry Doby joined the Cleveland Indians. Blacks knew, however, that such advancements, though significant, would never substitute for full integration into the American mainstream.

In 1948, Afro-Americans (only one quarter of whom qualified to vote; Jim Crow still shut them out of southern polls) supported Democratic incumbent Harry S. Truman in his victorious presidential campaign. Today, historians credit Truman's narrow margin of success to the black urban vote he received. Blacks anticipated his return to office with great happiness and hoped that his administration would help advance the cause of civil rights. Truman made some important moves (such as ending segregation in the armed forces) but he did not actively press for civil rights legislation. Black Americans realized that, in the words of A. Philip Randolph, they would have to begin exacting the justice owed them by the federal government.

In 1936 A. Philip Randolph delivers an address to the National Negro Congress, for which he served as president.

Separate but Not Equal

In the early 1950s, black leaders decided the time had come to challenge the principle of segregation. They focused their attack on the public schools of the South, which cheated black children of an opportunity to receive an education comparable to that of white students.

In 1951, Thurgood Marshall, the head of the NAACP's Legal Defense Fund, began to develop a case challenging the legality of school segregation. Local

NAACP lawyers (from left to right) George Hayes, Thurgood Marshall, and James N. Nabrit stand outside the Supreme Court on the day of their victory in Brown v. Board of Education. *Marshall won appointment to the Supreme Court in 1967.*

branches of the NAACP had already brought into federal court antisegregation suits against school systems in five different states. Marshall combined the arguments underlying all five suits into one case: *Oliver Brown et al v. the Board of Education of Topeka, Kansas.* As Marshall designed the case, it would ask the Supreme Court to overturn the 1896 *Plessy v. Ferguson* decision that had sanctioned segregation on the grounds that public facilities that were "separate" for the races were constitutional as long as they were "equal."

From the outset, a majority of the Court favored overturning the notorious *Plessy,* but Chief Justice Earl Warren wanted a unanimous decision, so that opponents of integration would find no reason to continue their opposition. Finally, after months of deft persuasion, Warren prevailed on his colleagues. On May 17, 1954, the Supreme Court handed down its momentous ruling in *Brown v. Board of Education.* Warren read the court's decision:

> Does segregation of children in public schools solely on the basis of race, even though the physical facilities and other "tangible" factors may be equal, deprive children of the minority group of equal educational opportunities? We believe that it does. . . . We conclude that in the field of public education the doctrine of "separate but equal" has no place. Separate educational facilities are inherently unequal.

With its ruling, the Supreme Court invalidated segregation, paving the way for equal rights for all Americans.

The Struggle Continues

Now all eyes in the nation turned to the South. Would its leaders comply and desegregate their educational systems? Several border states did so immediately: Delaware, Kentucky, Maryland, Missouri, Oklahoma, and West Virginia. But throughout the following year, discouraging rumblings emanated from the Deep South, which refused to comply with the *Brown* ruling.

One year after the *Brown* decision, the Supreme Court ruled on another NAACP suit, one designed to force southern schools to obey the order to desegregate. Much to the disappointment of the black community, the Supreme Court did not demand obedience from southern states but instead declared that school systems need only show a "prompt and reasonable start towards full compliance" and that desegregation proceed "with all deliberate speed." The words were so vague as to be undefinable. Earl Warren later revealed he had been forced to compromise on the enforcement of the *Brown* case in order to obtain the unanimous vote he had originally wanted. Furthermore, Warren realized he was working at odds with the executive branch of the government. President Eisenhower regretted his appointment of Warren to the Supreme Court, later calling it "the biggest damn fool mistake I ever made." In addition, he offered no support to the principle of desegregation, privately saying that "the fellow who tries to tell me you can do these things by force is just plain nuts."

But in September 1957, the federal government finally intervened in the South on behalf of school desegregation in Little Rock, Arkansas, a racially moderate town that planned to integrate its Central High School by admitting nine black students when school resumed after the summer recess that year. This design probably would have suceeded had it not been implemented on the eve of a state gubernatorial election. The incumbent candidate, Governor Orval Faubus, saw the desegregation of Central High as an opportunity to butter up his most conservative constituents.

Faubus appeared on television the night before school opened and declared he could not guarantee the safety of the nine black students. Racists heard his announcement as an invitation to stir up trouble. Indeed, they staged violent protests outside Central High for weeks. Faubus did nothing to protect the nine black teenagers and, in fact, called out the National Guard to help block their entrance into the school building. A

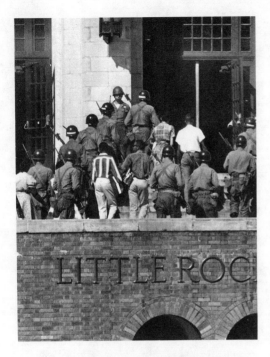

In September 1957, black students enter Little Rock Central High School flanked by federal troops.

federal district judge ordered these troops to disband, but a white mob quickly replaced them. This act of defiance finally galvanized President Eisenhower into action and on September 24, he ordered the 101st Airborne Division of the United States Army into Little Rock to protect the black students.

The Minister of Montgomery

The desegregation movement spread out from the schools and soon encompassed other public facilities, namely transportation. In December 1955, Rosa Parks, a black seamstress living in Montgomery, Alabama, refused to yield her seat on a bus to a white man. Unable to make her move, the bus driver summoned a police officer and had Rosa Parks arrested.

E. D. Nixon, head of the local branch of the NAACP—in which Parks was an active member—saw her arrest as a golden opportunity to challenge the city's Jim Crow bus laws. A former Pullman porter, Nixon had once been a member of the union led by A. Philip Randolph. In Demember 1955, Nixon summoned the leaders of the black community to a meeting to plot a citywide boycott of the bus lines as a means of protesting Jim Crow laws. They demanded the city integrate its buses and hire more black drivers.

Nixon searched for the ideal leader of the boycott and selected a young minister who had recently moved into the city, Martin Luther King, Jr. At first, King was uncertain he wanted to take part in the campaign, but Nixon insisted. He argued that because King was new to the community he could act more freely than others who had been forced to make compromises. Besides, Nixon told him, "I've already told everyone to meet at your church tonight."

The boycott began—and lasted more than a year, as black citizens walked rather than ride the buses. The economic drain on the city was so great that city leaders finally caved in and agreed to a compromise. Then the federal courts intervened and struck down the city's Jim Crow transportation laws. The boycott ended in complete victory and its leader, Martin Luther King, Jr., was elevated to national prominence at the age of 26.

King was born in 1929, the son of a Baptist minister, and was raised in a middle-class black community in Atlanta, Georgia. A scholarly, introverted youth, he entered Morehouse College in Atlanta at age 15. He graduated with honors four years later, then headed north to study first at Crozer Theological Seminary in Pennsylvania and later at Boston University, where he received a Ph.D. in theology in 1955. During his tenure at Boston University he met and married a woman who would herself become a leader in the movement for civil rights, Coretta Scott King.

King's studies in Boston had introduced him to the teachings of Mohandas Gandhi, a politician and spiritual leader in India. Gandhi had led fellow Indians in their struggle for independence against the colonial British throughout the 1930s and 1940s. King saw many parallels between the battle being waged by blacks in the United States and that fought by Indians several decades earlier. He admired Gandhi's doctrine of nonviolent resistance to oppression and emulated Gandhi's belief in *Satyagraha* (soul force) as a means of opposing social injustice.

King eventually would write that blacks must reach a point where they could tell whites: "We will not hate you, but will not obey your evil laws. We will soon wear you down by pure capacity to suffer." While still a student, King had also read the works of Henry David Thoreau, a giant of 19th-century American literature and thought, and found himself intrigued by Thoreau's ideas about civil disobedience as a means of protest. In 1960, King began to put his principles into action. He left Montgomery for a pulpit in Atlanta, Georgia, and during that year founded the Southern Christian Leadership Conference (SCLC), an organization dedicated to nonviolent protest against segregation.

In March 1956, Martin Luther King, Jr., and his wife Coretta Scott King stand amid a cheering crowd during the Montgomery bus boycott.

The Sit-In Movement and Freedom Rides

Soon the black community began staging peaceful acts of civil disobedience, both in conjunction with King and independently of him. On February 1, 1960, four black freshmen from the Negro Agricultural and Technical College in Greensboro, North Carolina, decided to challenge segregation near their campus.

After a night's planning in their college dorm rooms, the students took seats at the whites-only lunch counter at Woolworth's Department Store. They sat there all day until the store closed. The next day they came back with more people. In a matter of days dozens of students, including some whites, joined the sit-in. They encountered violence and insult and attracted national attention. They refused to move until, finally, Greensboro officials agreed to begin desegregating public facilities.

The sit-in movement spread rapidly across the South as blacks continued their challenge to segregation. In April 1960, black college students—inspired by the success of their Greensboro comrades—met in Raleigh, North Carolina, to form the Student Nonviolent Coordinating Committee (SNCC). SNCC members embarked upon a two-front campaign of nonviolent direct action: sit-ins, picketing, and boycotts; and voter registration drives. The organization, which capitalized on the youthful energy and optimism of its members, became a powerful force within the civil rights movement of the 1960s and rejected guidance offered by either Martin Luther King and his SCLC or the NAACP.

In 1961, the SNCC, SCLC, and the NAACP were joined in their desegregation efforts by the Congress of Racial Equality (CORE), an integrated civil rights organization created in 1942. The Congress sponsored a series of "Freedom Rides" on Trailways and Greyhound buses from Washington, D.C., to Jackson, Mississippi, and New Orleans, Louisiana. The Freedom Riders' goal was to challenge segregated bus seating, bus station facilities, waiting rooms, lavatories, lunch counters, and drinking fountains.

CORE had first attempted Freedom Rides in 1947,

but without success. Now the time was ripe. In May 1961, black and white Freedom Riders led by CORE's James Farmer and the SNCC's John Lewis left Washington on two buses. They encountered no trouble until they neared Anniston, Alabama, where hostile whites stood on a highway just outside of town, awaiting the first bus. One among the group threw a fire bomb into a bus window, and as the Freedom Riders came out amid billowing black smoke, the mob beat them mercilessly. One of the white Freedom Riders sustained brain damage. The outrages against the Freedom Riders continued in other cities and prompted angry intervention from the Kennedy administration, which sought first to stop the rides and ended up providing police protection for them.

In 1961 freedom riders escape from their bus after it was set afire by a group of hostile whites in Anniston, Alabama.

Albany and Birmingham

In November 1961, the SNCC pushed on in the brave spirit of the Freedom Rides and launched a desegregation and voter registration campaign in Albany, Georgia. Its enthusiastic but ill-conceived project nearly caused the civil rights movement to disband. Organizers rushed into Albany without advance planning and began their demonstrations and marches. Local ministers asked Martin Luther King to join in the protests there, and King was ultimately arrested and jailed. In order to prevent King's arrest from becoming a nationally celebrated cause, the local sheriff, Laurie Pritchett, raised money within the white community for King's bail.

When King returned from jail, he found that the Albany Movement had disintegrated into a competition between warring factions of black protest leaders: The young radicals of the SNCC, the older and more staid members of the NAACP, and the black churches all regarded each other with suspicion and vied for the control of the civil rights movement. Furthermore, the Albany Movement attracted no broad base of support, thanks to the shrewd strategies of Laurie Pritchett, who had studied King's work. Pritchett knew that although

King's movement was nonviolent, it nevertheless relied on confrontations with the police—and these he refused to provide. He ordered his entire force to treat the protesters gently, thus denying them any opportunity to gain media attention and national recognition for their efforts. Never again would King or other civil rights leaders act without careful advance planning.

The Albany debacle set the stage for dramatic confrontations in Birmingham, Alabama, during the spring of 1963. Birmingham's notorious commissioner of public safety, T. Eugene "Bull" Connor, was not inclined toward gentility with black protesters. He was determined to block their attempts at desegregation in every possible way. After the setback in Albany, King and the SCLC moved into Birmingham knowing they would have to score a victory or face the dissolution of the civil rights movement. King was determined to provoke a confrontation in Birmingham and capture the attention of the American public. Bull Connor was all too willing to oblige him in this effort.

On April 12, 1963, King led a march on the Birmingham city hall and was arrested. While in jail, he wrote "A Letter from a Birmingham Jail," his response to a letter that white clergymen had addressed to King and published in the local newspaper. These men of the cloth had urged King not to create a national crisis over the issue of civil rights for blacks.

King penned his eloquent response on scrap paper and had it smuggled out of the jail. He argued that Afro-Americans could no longer wait for rights that should have been theirs centuries ago. King justified civil disobedience by showing it was the only way blacks could overturn unjust laws because they were barred from full participation in the political process. He claimed they had a moral responsibility not to obey immoral laws. His eloquent words moved a nation of white moderates to embrace his position.

In May, King hit upon the idea of using high school students in his demonstrations. This decision met with widespread criticism from within the movement; nevertheless, it worked. The nation watched in stunned horror as Bull Connor turned fire hoses and unleashed police dogs on thousands of black teenage protest marchers. The news footage of the dogs tearing at the demonstrators and of people being swept away by the torrent of water shocked and moved white Americans. President Kennedy said the pictures made him sick— but still claimed he lacked a constitutional mandate to act on behalf of the demonstrators.

The violence in Birmingham stirred black Americans to further action. More arrests followed "The Children's Crusade." This time in addition to police dogs and fire hoses Bull Connor sent in tanks. Several days later negotiations with embarrassed white leaders brought a promise to desegregate public facilities and the Birmingham campaign ended in victory.

That summer, flushed with success, black leaders planned a massive protest rally in Washington over the lack of government action in civil rights. The more conservative organizations, such as the NAACP and National Urban League, had before shied away from such a protest march in the nation's capital fearing the violence it might provoke. But after witnessing the terrible police brutality in Birmingham, they joined in the planning. The Kennedy administration attempted to block the march, but failing to do so they instead sought to guide its course.

The March on Washington for Jobs and Freedom drew national attention. Approximately 250,000 people came to Washington on August 28, 1963. Protesters anxiously awaited the speech of SNCC representative John Lewis. He planned to criticize the federal government for its failure to enforce the *Brown* decision and the Kennedy administration for failing to fulfill its promises on civil rights. At the last minute, the administration was able to persuade Lewis to moderate his speech.

But the historic moment of the event arrived when Martin Luther King ascended the platform to say a few words of his own. His 15-minute speech, echoing the refrain "I have a dream," stirred both the crowd and the nation and gave him an indelible place in history.

Members of the Birmingham, Alabama, fire department turn their hoses on a crowd of civil rights protesters in 1963.

Toward Federal Legislation

The events in Birmingham, the stirring March on Washington, and the November assassination of John F. Kennedy, who had slowly begun to embrace civil rights, combined to impel Congress toward the passage of the Civil Rights Act of 1964, the most sweeping civil rights legislation since Reconstruction. It outlawed discrimination on the basis of race, religion, or sex in all places of public access and in those supported by federal tax dollars; authorized the attorney general to hasten the process of school desegregation by bringing suits to court; strengthened voting rights laws; established the Equal Opportunity Commission to abolish all job discrimination; and gave federal agencies the power to withhold funds from state-administered programs that discriminated against blacks.

The year 1964 proved a watershed, too, in the registration of black voters by the SNCC, which launched the Mississippi Freedom Summer that year. The SNCC targeted Mississippi because only 5 percent of the state's eligible black voters were registered, the fewest of any state in the nation. At first the SNCC intended to bar whites from participation in the campaign, so strong had antiwhite sentiment become within the organization.

It was finally decided, however, that the presence of thousands of white college students in the Deep South would publicize the drive and also protect it from local police who, it was certain, would not harm the children of the white middle class. SNCC leaders underestimated their enemies. On June 22, SNCC leaders received word that three young civil rights workers—two white, one black—were missing in rural Mississippi. The eventual disclosure of their death outraged the nation.

In 1965 the campaign for voter registration shifted its focus to Selma, Alabama, and its leadership to Martin Luther King, who had won the Nobel Peace Prize in 1964. Of the Selma campaign, King said on January 2, 1965, "We will dramatize the situation to arouse the federal government by marching by the thousands to the places of registration. . . . We are not asking, we are demanding the ballot."

The local sheriff in Selma, James Clark, was already infamous to those within the movement for the vicious and violent manner in which his men treated civil rights workers. Within a month of their arrival in Selma, 2,000 people had been arrested, and the news media began focusing on the brutality of Selma's police. Organizers decided to address their grievances about Clark and his men to George Wallace, Alabama's governor.

On Sunday, March 7, the protesters began the 50-mile walk from Selma to Montgomery. As they approached the Edmund Pettus Bridge, leading out of town, the marchers found their way blocked by both the Alabama state police and Clark's men. The officers attacked them viciously, some charging through the crowd on horseback and wielding electric cattle prods. Others swung their nightsticks, clubbing even the children in the crowd. The nation witnessed this sickening scene on broadcast news and responded as it never had. Thousands of people from all over the country flooded into Alabama to participate in the massive protest march from Selma to Montgomery. The nation was properly indignant over the blatant brutality of "Bloody Sunday."

On March 21, 3,000 people marched from Selma to Montgomery. President Lyndon Johnson called out the Alabama National Guard to protect them. On the outskirts of Montgomery they were joined by King and 30,000 others. The two groups made their way to the state capitol where speaker after speaker denounced violence and racism and called for a voting rights campaign and crusades against poverty and segregated schools. In the stunned aftermath of Selma, Congress passed the Voting Rights Act of 1965, which provided federally supervised voter registration in the South. Thousands of blacks registered and eventually voted and brought to fruition the seed work done by the SNCC during its voter registration drives. The civil rights movement had reached its zenith. ∽

On the second march from Selma, Alabama, to the state capitol in Montgomery, civil rights sympathizers turned out by the thousands and completed their route with the protection of the National Guard.

In July 1968, members of the Black Panther party march along 42nd Street in New York City in order to protest the murder trial of Panther "defense minister" Huey P. Newton.

BLACK NATIONALISM AND BEYOND

Unlike their counterparts in the South, northern blacks could not revel in the demise of Jim Crow, because they had never been subject to legislated discrimination. In the North, blacks enjoyed free access to public transportation, polling places, and other facilities. Yet they, too, suffered white racism and were shunted into inferior urban schools, denied access to higher-paying jobs, and trapped in urban slums. In northern cities, however, this form of segregation was insidious; it existed everywhere but was not written into law.

Many Afro-Americans in the North expressed skepticism about the goal of a racially integrated society. They knew firsthand that greater intermingling between whites and blacks did not necessarily end either racism or, more importantly, the poverty endemic to black communities. Many ghetto dwellers, especially the young, viewed with disdain Martin Luther King's pleas for reconciliation between the races. They adopted a stance far more radical than King's, arguing that blacks should remove themselves from the society of whites and demand an equal share of political power—meeting white violence with retaliatory violence of their own. Afro-Americans espousing this na-

105

On the 21st anniversary of the Brown *decision, supporters of school desegregation march in Boston.*

tionalist philosophy turned for leadership to a black man many regarded as the antithesis of Martin Luther King, Jr., Malcolm X.

Malcolm X

Born Malcolm Little in 1925, he was the son of a West Indian mother and Afro-American father, a preacher who died at the hands of a white mob in Lansing, Michigan. This death splintered the family, and Malcolm was placed in the foster care of a white couple. He later recalled them with bitterness, telling an interviewer, "My presence in that home was like a cat or a parrot or any type of pet they had." After finishing the eighth grade, Malcolm dropped out of school and ran away first to Boston and later to Harlem, where he supported himself working as both a bookie and a bootlegger. His seedy career ended abruptly in 1946, when he was arrested for burglary and sentenced to 10 years in jail.

During his prison term, Malcolm experienced a spiritual redemption through exposure to the teachings of Elijah Muhammad, founder of a religious sect called the Nation of Islam, or the Black Muslims. Muhammad advocated a rejection of the white culture imposed on blacks by the institution of slavery. He denounced the adoption of Christianity, white surnames, and the identity of "so-called American Negroes." His radical doctrine appealed to Malcolm Little, who accepted it as his own, replacing his last name (that conferred on his ancestors by white slave owners) with an X.

By the time of his release from prison in 1952, Malcolm X had joined Elijah Muhammad's ministry. For the next 13 years he preached to a growing following, championing black nationalism and the embracing of African culture and heritage. His militant sermons drew fire from whites, who accused him of "inflaming" ghetto resentments. He also met with disapproval from Elijah Muhammad in 1963 and was suspended from the Black Muslims. In response, Malcolm X founded the rival Muslim Mosque, Inc. and in February 1965 was assassinated by three men claiming to be Black Muslims. However, historians still debate the identity of these killers.

Malcolm X addresses a Harlem rally in 1963.

Malcolm X and Martin Luther King, Jr.—one a Black Muslim leader and a survivor of ghetto poverty, the other a Christian clergyman from a middle-class Atlanta family—represented two significant but differing views about American racial problems. King advocated integration, Malcolm X urged voluntary separation from whites. He said the only thing he liked integrated was coffee, which he took with milk. King advocated Christian love and nonviolence. Malcolm X dismissed this "passivity" as foolish and urged his followers to counter racist violence with violence of their own, telling a Harlem crowd: "I don't believe we're going to overcome by singing. If you're going to get yourself a .45 and start singing 'We Shall Overcome' [the hymn of the civil rights movement], I'm with you." After Malcolm X's death, his separatist philosophy was perpetuated by black nationalist organizations such as the Black Panther Party, founded in 1966 in Oakland,

California, by Huey Newton and Bobby Seale. The following year, at a conference in Newark, New Jersey, the Panthers called for "the partitioning of the United States into two separate independent nations, one to be a homeland for white and the other to be a homeland for black Americans."

The Cities Riot

Six months after Malcolm X's death, the violence characterizing the Long Hot Summers began. In August 1965 urban blacks—whose rage Malcolm X had so eloquently voiced—rioted for five days in the Los Angeles neighborhood of Watts. Some 50,000 Afro-Americans looted stores, attacked whites and police, and burned buildings, until they were brought under the control of 1,500 Los Angeles Police and 14,000 National Guardsmen. In all, the fury injured 900 people and took 34 lives. Police, who arrested a total of 4,000 people during the days that chaos reigned in Watts, termed the upheaval an insurrection. There were many more to come.

As Americans stared in disbelief at the televised news reports of the Watts conflagration, Chicago, too, erupted in riot. On August 12, a black woman was run over by a truck from an all-white fire station. The incident set off two days and nights of looting and arson. In the summer of 1965, urban blacks across the country turned to violence in their frustration with racism and

The Los Angeles neighborhood of Watts burns during the riots of 1965.

In July 1966, National Guardsmen with bayonets push rioting blacks away from a burning building in Detroit.

poverty. A year later, similar scenes of looting, burning, and arrest were repeated in Atlanta, Georgia; Chicago, Illinois; Omaha, Nebraska; the Michigan cities of Lansing and Benton Harbor; and the Ohio cities of Dayton and Cleveland.

The Long Hot Summers of 1965 and 1966 were a mere prelude to the summer of 1967, when the United States witnessed the most destructive wave of racial violence in its history. Riots swept through 100 cities, including Newark, New Jersey, a town plagued by the nation's highest crime rate, highest percentage of black unemployment, and greatest number of condemned residential buildings. In July 1967, the arrest of a black Newark cab driver incited violence so bloody that New Jersey's governor Richard Hughes called it a city "in open rebellion." In all, 25 people were killed, 1,200 wounded, 1,300 arrested; and the city sustained property damages amounting to more than $10 million.

As Newark burned, the worst race riot in American history besieged Detroit, Michigan—then one of the most racially progressive cities in the United States. Blacks constituted almost half the city's elected officials, who had recently won a federal grant in order to implement antipoverty and urban renewal programs. Michigan's booming auto industry provided well-paying jobs to many workers. Two-thirds of all black families owned cars and half lived in their own homes during an era when more than one-third of all black families lived below the poverty level. Yet this relative prosperity was marred by a strained relationship between Detroit blacks and the predominantly white local police force, often accused of racially motivated police brutality.

On the night of July 18, 1967, the Detroit police arrested 18 young blacks at a nightclub on the charge that they were selling liquor illegally. The incident ignited 6 days of vicious rioting, in which 4,000 separate fires gutted 1,300 buildings. About 5,000 blacks lost their homes as the fires spread throughout the city. In all, Detroit withstood $250 million in property loss. Poorly trained National Guardsmen panicked and fired into houses and commercial buildings in an effort to stop the looting and protect themselves from snipers. Their indiscriminate gunshots left 43 people dead. As in previous years, the violence spread from one locale to many across America, taking 90 lives before the Long Hot Summer of 1967 finally came to a close.

A Time of Reflection

In 1965, President Lyndon Johnson sought to understand the causes of the violence rocking the United States and appointed a National Advisory Commission on Civil Disorders, naming Otto Kerner, a former governor of Ohio, as chairman. The Kerner Commission issued a report in 1968 and startled the public by placing the blame for the rioting not on the participants, but on racism: "White society is deeply implicated in the ghetto. White institutions created it, white institutions maintained it, and white society condoned it." The report recommended sweeping social changes to alleviate the plight of the ghetto dweller and warned: "We are moving toward two societies, one black, one white—separate and unequal."

The riots jarred not only white Americans, but also moderate blacks such as Martin Luther King, Jr. By

1967, King had broadened the purpose of his integration movement—fighting, too, for political and economic equality for blacks. King's rhetoric now reflected the increased militancy of Afro-Americans across the country, and he publicly addressed not only American domestic policies, but also international affairs. In particular, King voiced his objection to the Vietnam War, stating as early as 1965, "The long night of war must be stopped."

King's stand against the war in Vietnam cost him support from within the remnants of the civil rights movement. To regain lost momentum, in 1968, he planned a nationwide campaign to dramatize the realities of economic injustice in the wealthiest nation in the world. But on April 3, King embarked on a fateful trip to Memphis, Tennessee, to address a crowd of striking

Hosea Williams, Jesse Jackson, and the Reverend Ralph Abernathy, (left to right) stand with Martin Luther King, Jr., on the balcony where King was slain a day later.

sanitation workers, hoping to quell the violence resulting from their walkout. That night he gave his last speech, telling his audience about recent threats on his own life:

> But it doesn't matter with me now. Because I've been to the mountaintop. I don't mind. Like anybody, I would like to live a long life. Longevity has its place. But I'm not concerned about that now. I just want to do God's will. And He's allowed me to go up to the mountain! And I've looked over and I've seen the promised land! I may not get there with you, but I want you to know tonight that we as a people will get to the promised land. And I am happy tonight! I'm not worried about anything! I'm not fearing any man! Mine eyes have seen the glory of the coming of the Lord!

The next evening, King fell to white assassin James Earl Ray as he was standing on the balcony of the Lorraine Motel in Memphis. Once again, when word of King's death reached black communities across the country, the ghettos erupted in flames. On April 9, more than 300,000 people of all races marched behind King's coffin as it was pulled through the streets of

In 1971 black soldiers in Long Binh, Vietnam, observe the birthday of Martin Luther King, Jr.

Atlanta on a farm wagon drawn by two Georgia mules. Afro-Americans mourned not only King himself, but also the fading civil rights movement, which lost its momentum in the aftermath of King's death.

A Changing Community

Those within the civil rights movement took various paths in the years following King's murder, many assuming public office. The ranks of black elected officials swelled in 1968, when a record number of black men and the first black woman representative—Shirley Chisholm—were elected to Congress. The 10 Afro-Americans in Congress that year topped a previous record of 8 who had sat in the 44th Congress of 1875–77.

Afro-Americans continued to win votes throughout the 1970s and 1980s and made a particularly strong showing in mayoral elections in the country's major cities: In 1973 Detroit elected Coleman Young mayor and Los Angeles first voted Tom Bradley into its executive office; in 1981 former U.S. representative to the United Nations Andrew Young assumed the office of mayor in Atlanta; and in 1983 Chicago boosted Mayor Harold Washington to power. Despite the number of black elected officials, however, no single individual approached the stature of Martin Luther King until Jesse Jackson, a former member of King's inner circle, won several Democratic presidential primaries in 1988.

Jesse Jackson

Born in Greenville, South Carolina, in 1941, Jesse Jackson began his work in civil rights in 1965. In that year, as a student at Chicago Theological Seminary, he traveled to Selma, Alabama, in order to learn firsthand about Martin Luther King and the Southern Christian Leadership Conference. The young seminarian soon earned an important role in the SCLC and during the next three years established the movement's base in Chicago. After King's death in 1968, Jackson went on

In October 1987, Jesse Jackson announces his candidacy for the presidency of the United States.

to establish his own Chicago-based organizations, first directing Operation Breadbasket—which offered marketing and management services to minority-owned businesses—and later, in 1971, founding People United to Save Humanity (PUSH). As the director of PUSH he won almost $5 million in grants from the federal government and channeled the money into innovative inner-city public school programs for young blacks. Jackson remembered all too keenly the racism he knew as a boy growing up in South Carolina and wanted to spare young Afro-Americans that hardship. He told an interviewer: "[On] Saturdays I'd sell peanuts and soft drinks at the stadium. Whites sat all around drinking liquor. They'd say all kinds of vulgar things, call me nigger, try to shortchange me. . . . I couldn't go to the front at the movies, I couldn't use the bathrooms. It was humiliating."

For the next decade, Jackson worked within PUSH and other grass roots organizations, but in 1984 he entered the mainstream of American politics by launching a candidacy for that year's presidential election. Jackson forged a diverse constituency he dubbed the Rainbow Coalition. Although he won only one primary, he established himself as the leading Afro-American politician of his day and laid the groundwork for his next presidential campaign. He later recalled: "In 1984 my basic challenge was to open up the [Democratic] party to be fair. And I put a lot of focus on the Voting Rights Act. In 1984 we were encountering so much hostility—from the party, from the media—we had to spend a lot more time fighting for honor, fighting for dignity." Despite opposition from within the party, Jackson remained a loyal Democrat and registered 2 million new voters, many of whom cast their ballots for Democratic candidates in later elections. "I sit on the stage now," Jackson proclaimed, "and no one can challenge my Democratic Party credentials."

During the 1988 Democratic primaries, Jackson emerged as a serious contender for the nomination, winning a majority of the delegates in Michigan, the District of Columbia, his home state of North Carolina, and in other states in the Deep South. White voters as well as blacks jumped on the Jackson bandwagon and boosted him to national prominence.

Jackson's Rainbow Coalition united disparate factions within the black community. He spoke for the black middle class that had burgeoned as a result of Martin Luther King's movement for integration. He offered hope to the inner-city blacks who had been left behind in the ghettos. But Jackson also voiced the wishes and fears of an even broader segment of American society. In 1988, a white voter expressed the views of many in *Time* magazine: "I'm drawn to a candidate I believe in, someone who could possibly carry out the goals and ideals I found in the '60s. [Jackson's] talking about . . . drugs and economic devastation, issues that transcend ethnic and religious problems." Thus, in 1988 Jesse Jackson seemed to realize the dreams of generations of Afro-Americans, who—in the words of Martin Luther King, Jr.—saw Jackson judged not by the color of his skin but by the content of his character.

FURTHER READING

Anderson, Jervis. *This Was Harlem: 1900–1950*. New York: Farrar, Straus & Giroux, 1981.

Baldwin, James. *The Fire Next Time*. New York: Dial Press, 1963.

Franklin, John Hope, and Alfred Moss, Jr. *From Slavery to Freedom*. 6th ed. New York: Knopf, 1980.

Franklin, John Hope, and August Meier. *Black Leaders of the Twentieth Century*. Urbana: University of Illinois Press, 1982.

Garrow, David J. *Bearing the Cross*. New York: Morrow, 1986.

Genovese, Eugene G. *Roll, Jordan, Roll*. New York: Pantheon, 1976.

Litwack, Leon F., and August Meier. *Black Leaders of the Nineteenth Century*. Urbana: University of Illinois, 1988.

Meier, August, and Elliot Rudwick. *From Plantation to Ghetto*. 3rd ed. New York: Hill and Wang, 1976.

Smead, Howard. *Blood Justice: The Lynching of Mack Charles Parker*. New York: Oxford University Press, 1986.

Williams, Juan. *Eyes on the Prize*. New York: Penguin, 1987.

Williamson, Joel. *Rage for Order*. New York: Oxford University Press, 1986.

Woodward, C. Vann. *The Strange Career of Jim Crow*. 3rd ed. New York: Oxford University Press, 1974.

Wright, Richard. *Native Son*. 1940. Reprint. New York: Harper & Row, 1969.

MARTIN LUTHER KING, JR.

MARTIN LUTHER KING, JR.

Robert Jakoubek

Senior Consulting Editor
Nathan Irvin Huggins
Director
W.E.B. Du Bois Institute for Afro-American Research
Harvard University

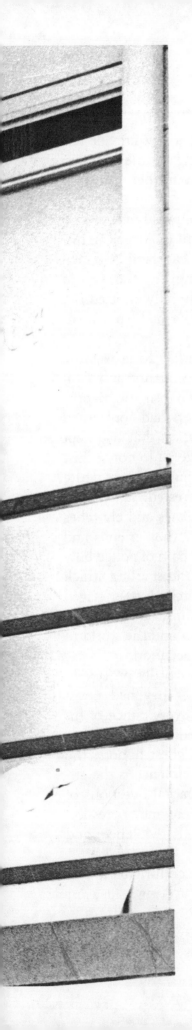

1

APRIL 3, 1968

❧

It WAS BEFORE dawn when the Reverend Ralph Abernathy brought his old Ford to a stop in front of the modest, pleasant home of Coretta and Martin Luther King, Jr., in Atlanta, Georgia. Abernathy half expected to see King waiting patiently on the stoop, a black valise at his side. But this morning King was running late. When Coretta answered the door, her husband was just getting up.

King mumbled an apology for oversleeping and hurried into the bathroom to shave. Abernathy, after declining Coretta's offer of breakfast, kept a close watch on the time. He and King had to catch an early flight for Memphis, Tennessee.

King was ready in nothing flat. As always, he wore a somber business suit, its well-tailored lines flattering his broad shoulders and subtly concealing his expanding waistline. He gave Coretta a quick good-bye kiss and said he would call her from Memphis. Once in the car, he reminded Abernathy that he wanted to stop by his office on the way to the airport.

When they reached the office on Auburn Avenue, King let himself in with his latchkey and swiftly gathered up some papers he would need in Memphis. In the early morning shadows, an outsider might have

King, flanked by his aides Jesse Jackson (left) and Ralph Abernathy, stands on the balcony of the Lorraine Motel shortly after arriving in Memphis, Tennessee, on April 3, 1968. Later in the day, King gave what turned out to be his last public address on civil rights.

121

taken the place for the office of a law firm or real estate business and King for a young attorney or salesman. Nothing could have been further from the truth.

The office on Auburn Avenue was home to one of the most significant organizations in American history—the Southern Christian Leadership Council (SCLC)—and Martin Luther King, Jr., the man in the dark suit, white shirt, and carefully knotted tie, was its founder and leader. And he had led a revolution.

The revolution of Martin Luther King was the struggle of black Americans for equality and civil rights. For a dozen years, this charismatic Baptist minister and his legion of followers had confronted the humiliating system of segregation that had kept black Americans second-class citizens. In doing this, he and his disciples had faced a raging storm of white abuse. They had been beaten, arrested, jailed, and spat upon. They had had their homes and churches burned, their families threatened, their friends and allies murdered. They had felt the pain of police billy clubs, high-pressure water hoses, and snarling attack dogs. Yet they kept on. They marched; they staged boycotts and sit-ins; they broke unjust laws; and, in the end, they awakened the nation and the world to the shame of American racial persecution.

Through it all, no matter how badly provoked, no matter how brutal their foes, they had never turned to violence, because with every ounce of his being Martin Luther King believed in nonviolence. In accepting one of the world's highest honors, the Nobel Peace Prize, he said, "Nonviolence is the answer to the crucial political and moral questions of our time—the need for man to overcome oppression and violence without resorting to violence and oppression."

During the heroic years of the civil rights movement, Ralph Abernathy had been at King's side, just as he was this morning as they dashed to the Atlanta airport. Others in the movement snickered at the way Abernathy fell asleep during meetings and elbowed his way next to King whenever photographers were around. One associate lamented, "What a burden Ralph was to Martin." Yet King trusted Abernathy absolutely, loved him as a brother, and, despite considerable opposition, had designated him as his eventual successor at the helm of the SCLC.

Abernathy was worried about his loyal friend. A few months before, he had returned from a trip to Europe and had found King dejected and melancholic. "He was just a different person," Abernathy said. "He was sad and depressed." Worst of all, King seemed obsessed by the subject of death and persisted in talking and speculating about his own end.

Those close to King knew he had every reason in the world to be preoccupied with death. As the man who symbolized black America's determination for justice and equality, he magnetically attracted the hatred of violent racists. Over the years, he had received nearly every kind of twisted, anonymous threat of death, and once in New York, a decade before, a deranged woman had stabbed him in the chest as he autographed books in a department store.

The latest reminder of the danger in which King lived took place at the Atlanta airport on this April morning. The scheduled time of departure for Memphis passed, and their plane did not budge. King and Abernathy shifted impatiently in their seats.

Finally, the pilot's voice crackled over the public address system: "Ladies and gentlemen, I want to apologize for the delay. But today we have on board Dr. Martin Luther King, Jr., and we have to be very careful—we had the plane guarded all night—and we have been checking people's luggage. Now that everything's clear, we are preparing for takeoff."

King laughed and shook his head. "In all my flights," he said, "I've never had a pilot say that. If

King returned to Memphis on April 3, 1968, to lead a peaceful march of striking workers that would help boost his Poor People's Campaign, a huge demonstration against poverty. Arriving with him were (from left to right) ministers Andrew Young and Ralph Abernathy and student activist Bernard Lee.

I'm going to be killed it looks like he's trying to make it only too plain to me."

At 10:30 a.m., they landed in Memphis. It was King's third trip to the city in less than three weeks, but it was not a place he particularly wanted to be. He had come to support the city's striking sanitation workers, but every moment in Memphis was one less he had for his principal order of business that spring of 1968: the Poor People's Campaign.

For months, King and the SCLC had been planning a massive demonstration to dramatize the plight of poverty-stricken Americans. It was an ambitious undertaking. King envisioned a great march in Washington, D.C., and the construction in the capital of a "poor people's city" of shacks and shanties that would remain standing until Congress approved sweeping antipoverty legislation. But all sorts of problems threatened to derail the campaign, and to keep it on track King wanted to give it all his time and effort.

Still, the 39-year-old minister could not say no to his friends in Memphis. Overwhelmingly black, the garbage collectors of Memphis were badly paid, overworked, and had no job security, no insurance, no pensions. When it rained, the black workers were sent home without pay, whereas their white supervisors were permitted to wait out the storm and draw their wages.

In February 1968, the garbage collectors went on strike, demanding higher pay and better working conditions and benefits. The local government refused them point-blank, and as the strike dragged on it became a paramount issue for the black community. In March, some black ministers appealed to King. Would he speak at a rally? Reluctantly, he rearranged his schedule, and on March 18 he spoke at Mason Temple. Fifteen thousand people packed the huge old building to hear him speak.

King loved addressing large crowds, and that day he was at the top of his oratorical form. Elated by the cheers, impressed by the sense of commitment in Memphis, he impulsively agreed to head a demonstration for the strikers. "I will lead you on a march through the center of Memphis," he told the crowd.

True to his word, on Thursday, March 28—a hot, uncomfortable day—King was back in town. The march began shortly after 11 o'clock in the morning, with King leading the way, Abernathy and the Memphis ministers at his side, their arms interlocked, their voices raised, singing "We Shall Overcome." Slowly, they moved through the streets toward City Hall, and thousands followed.

They had gotten only a few blocks when everything started to go wrong. Toward the rear of the march, some angry and undisciplined black youths started breaking store windows and looting merchandise. "We can't have that!" King shouted after he heard the sound of glass shattering.

But there was nothing he could do. The march disintegrated into chaos as the youths went on smashing windows and throwing stones and bottles. The Memphis police charged after them, and a full-scale riot was in the making.

On March 28, 1968, King joined forces with co-worker Ralph Jackson (second from left), the Reverend Ralph Abernathy (right), and hundreds of others in Memphis for a demonstration in support of striking laborers. Angry black youths disrupted the march by breaking shop windows and looting the stores, prompting King to set up a second march through the city's streets on April 8.

King himself appeared to be in danger. "You've got to get away from here!" someone yelled at him. Confused and frightened, the group around him pushed forward to Main Street, where King's bodyguard waved a white Pontiac to a stop. "Madam," he said to the black woman behind the wheel, "This is Martin Luther King—we need your car." She consented, and King and Abernathy piled into the backseat. The car then peeled off, racing for a hotel on the other side of town.

By nightfall, a 17-year-old black had been shot dead by the police, 60 of the marchers had been clubbed, and nearly 300 had been arrested. Memphis was declared in a state of emergency. Several thousand National Guardsmen were called in to patrol the streets.

At the Rivermont Holiday Inn, on the banks of the Mississippi, King lay on his bed, the covers pulled up to his chin. He was heartsick. His march had turned into a riot, and the marchers had started it. Had all the years of preaching nonviolence counted for nothing? Were people no longer listening to him? "Maybe we just have to admit that the day of violence is here," he said to Abernathy, "and maybe we have to just give up and let violence take its course. The nation won't listen to our voice—maybe it'll heed the voice of violence."

"It was the most restless night," Abernathy later said. "It was a terrible and horrible experience for him. I had never seen him in all my life so upset and so troubled." Throughout the night, King brooded over the damage done to his movement and to his reputation. His critics, he knew, would have a field day. White conservatives would point to the Memphis fiasco and say that King's nonviolence was a sham. Cautious, moderate blacks would urge him to slow down, to cancel the Poor People's Campaign in Washington. And the militant advocates of Black

Power would proclaim the days of nonviolence and "Martin Loser King" at an end.

Though agonized and in despair that night, King resolved not to give in to his critics or to give up on Memphis. He had to return and lead a peaceful march and demonstration. The Poor People's Campaign depended on it. "If we don't have a peaceful march in Memphis, no Washington," he said. "No Memphis, no Washington."

So, when King arrived in Memphis on April 3, a great deal was at stake. In five days—on Monday, April 8—there was to be another march. This time nothing could go wrong.

Some of the Memphis ministers greeted King at the airport and whisked him off to the Lorraine Motel, in the heart of a black neighborhood, where he checked into room 306, a $13-a-day room with double beds and a view of the parking lot and swimming pool. Almost immediately, he plunged into a long, exhausting series of meetings with the Memphis people and his SCLC associates.

They faced a problem. The city government had obtained an injunction from a federal court prohibiting the march on Monday as a danger to public safety. King decided that the march would proceed, injunction or no injunction. If need be, he would defy a court order. "I am going to lead that march," he said.

Taking a break from the staff meetings, King stepped from his room onto the porch and surveyed the sky. The weather was getting worse. All day there had been tornado warnings; now streaks of lightning flashed, and it started to rain hard.

The bad weather meant that there would not be much of a crowd for a rally that evening at Mason Temple. King had said he would speak there, but he had no desire to address a mostly empty auditorium. What was more, it had been a long day, he had a sore throat, and he was very, very tired. Back inside the room, he appealed to Abernathy, "Ralph, if this rain keeps up, will you go in my place?"

After some hesitation, Abernathy agreed, and around eight o'clock he left the Lorraine for the rally. King changed into his pajamas and settled in for a restful evening by himself.

At 8:30, the phone rang. It was Abernathy. "Martin," he said, "you've got to come over. There's not many people—less than two thousand—but they're so warm, so enthusiastic for you. . . ."

"Well, you don't have to talk that way to me. You know if you say come, I'll come."

King dressed in a hurry and was driven through the rain-swept streets to the temple. It was where he had spoken to a throng of 15,000 in March; this evening less than a seventh of that number awaited him. In soaked clothing, they sat up front. The relentless rain pounded on the building's high tin roof, and the wind seized the shutters at the windows, causing them to slam noisily back and forth. When King entered, the crowd raised a mighty cheer.

Great things were happening in Memphis, he said. Indeed, they were happening all around the world. If God were to give him the chance to live at any time in human history, "I would turn to the Almighty and say, 'If you allow me to live just a few years in the second half of the twentieth century, I will be happy.' " In Africa and Asia, in New York and Atlanta, and now in Memphis, the oppressed had arisen and they cried, "We want to be free." Nonviolence was the way for them. Today, he said, the issue was no longer a choice "between violence and nonviolence—it's nonviolence or nonexistence!"

King thanked God for allowing him to be in Memphis for the march on Monday. Then his voice became softer, more tender, as he recalled the time he had been stabbed in New York in 1958. The blade of the knife had come so close to his heart that a tiny movement, a sneeze even, would have killed him. A girl had written him to say how happy she was that he did not sneeze. "I too am happy I didn't sneeze."

If he had sneezed, he would not have been around for the sit-ins and freedom rides of 1960 and 1961, he said. He would not have seen the blacks of Albany, Georgia, "straighten their backs up" in 1962 as part of a campaign to desegregate the city. If he had sneezed, he would not have been part of the struggle in Birmingham and Selma, and he would never have spoken of his dream for a free and just America at the Lincoln Memorial in 1963. "If I had sneezed," he said, "I wouldn't have been in Memphis to see a great community rally around those brothers and sisters who are suffering.

"I'm so happy that I didn't sneeze."

Outside, bursts of thunder punctuated the hammering of the rain. But no one was paying the storm any mind. Everyone's attention was on the man in the pulpit, whose eyes were watering and whose brow was drenched with sweat, whose next words presaged what would take place on the following day.

King's voice wavered ever so slightly as he revealed the bomb threat on the plane that morning and the warnings against his life in Memphis:

> But it really doesn't matter with me now, because I've been to the mountaintop. And I don't mind. Like anybody, I would like to live a long life. Longevity has its place. But I'm not concerned about that now. I just want to do God's will. And He's allowed me to go up to the mountain, and I've looked over, and I've seen the promised land. I may not get there with you. But I want you to know tonight, that we, as a people will get to the promised land. And I'm so happy tonight. I'm not worried about anything. I'm not fearing any man. Mine eyes have seen the glory of the coming of the Lord. ✿

King addresses the congregation at Mason Temple in Memphis on April 3, 1968. Fellow civil rights activists Ralph Abernathy and Andrew Young later noted that King's speech, which marked his last public appearance, ended with a stirring—and ultimately prophetic—allusion to his own death.

2

"YOU ARE SOMEBODY"

❦

MARTIN LUTHER KING, Jr., was born on January 15, 1929, in Atlanta, Georgia, and learned about racial discrimination at an early age. When he was five years old, his most frequent playmate was a white boy whose father owned a neighborhood grocery store. One day, out of the blue, the boy's parents told Martin to go away and not play with their son any longer. Bewildered, Martin asked why. "Because we are white and you are colored," they said.

At home, Martin cried to his mother, "Why don't white people like us?" She dropped everything and for several hours explained the nature of race relations in America, the tragedy of slavery and of segregation. She told him to hold his head high and not let what whites said and did affect him. "You must never feel that you are less than anybody else," she said. "You must always feel that you are *somebody*."

King never really doubted that, but like every southern black, he lived in a segregated, unequal society. "On the one hand, my mother taught me that I should feel a sense of somebodiness," he later explained. "On the other hand, I had to go out and

King (bottom row, fourth from left) at the age of six, attending a birthday party with fellow first graders in his Atlanta neighborhood. "Love was central and . . . lovely relationships were ever present," he later said of his childhood years.

131

face the system, which stared me in the face every day, saying 'You are less than,' 'you are not equal to.' So this was a real tension within."

Throughout the South of King's youth, the system of segregation determined the patterns of life. Blacks attended separate schools from whites, were barred from pools and parks where whites swam and played, from cafés and hotels where whites ate and slept. Blacks never attended major southern universities, and only with the greatest difficulty could they vote in elections. On sidewalks, they were expected to step aside for whites, and if ever a black were to go inside the home of a white, he entered by the back door, never the front. When blacks traveled, they passed through bus and train stations with "colored" waiting rooms, water fountains, and toilets on their way to separate railway coaches or seats at the back of the bus.

It took a brave person to challenge the system. Yet in small ways blacks did their best to resist humiliation. When King was a child, his father took him to buy a pair of shoes at a white-owned store in Atlanta. Father and son took seats in front, near the window. A clerk approached and said, "I'll be happy to wait on you if you'll just move to those seats in the rear of the store."

"Nothing wrong with these seats," the elder King replied.

"Sorry, but you'll have to go back there."

Martin's father stayed put. "We'll buy shoes sitting here or we won't buy shoes at all," he insisted. The clerk shrugged and walked off. In a minute or two, King got up, took Martin by the hand, and strode from the store. On the sidewalk, he looked at his son and in a voice flushed with anger said, "I don't care how long I have to live with this system, I am never going to accept it. I'll oppose it till the day I die!"

Another time young Martin was riding with his father when a policeman pulled them over for a traffic violation. "Boy, show me your license," the officer drawled.

The elder King exploded. Pointing at Martin, he shouted, "Do you see this child here? That's a *boy* there. I'm a *man*. I'm Reverend King."

Indeed he was. The Reverend Martin Luther King, Sr., pastor of the Ebenezer Baptist Church, a leader of black Atlanta, demanded and claimed respect.

In his youth, he had been known as Mike, and he had come up the hard way. Born in 1899, he was from an unhappy family of poor sharecroppers in central Georgia. As a boy, Mike loved church, spent hours studying his Bible, and early on decided to become a minister. "I always felt extremely happy and completely at ease within the church setting," he recalled. "I never tired of going to the revivals, the baptisms, weddings, all the gatherings where people would be found bearing a particular witness."

When Mike reached the age of 15, the deacons of his church licensed him to minister, and he was soon traveling along back roads, preaching the gospel and singing hymns in black churches. Most of his days, however, were spent behind the plow, and he came to hate the tedium of farm work and rural life. After he turned 18, he left home for good, heading for Atlanta.

In the big city, Mike King took one job after another—vulcanizing tires, loading bales of cotton, driving a truck—and in a used Model T Ford that his mother had bought for him by selling a cow, he became something of a man about town. With such a fine car, he remembered, "Nothing I now felt, could stop me. Nothing."

The ministry was still his goal, but country preachers were a dime a dozen in Atlanta. To get

King's father, Martin, Sr., became a preacher at the age of 15 and pastor of Atlanta's well-attended Ebenezer Baptist Church in 1931. Thereafter, church activities played a central role in Martin, Jr.'s life.

ahead, to become the preacher of a leading church, he needed a degree in theology. For an uneducated young man from backcountry Georgia, that was a lot to ask. But Mike's ambition pulled him along. He worked during the day, and at night he studied for a high school diploma. Finally, in 1926, he was admitted to Morehouse College, a respected black school, where he began divinity studies.

Shortly after arriving in Atlanta, Mike King met Alberta Williams, the shy, genteel daughter of one of the city's prominent Baptist ministers. Mike was captivated. Before long, he was the most regular caller at the Williamses' large house on Auburn Avenue. On nice days, the properly chaperoned couple took long rides in Mike's Model T.

During Mike's courtship of Alberta, he won the respect of her father, the Reverend Adam Daniel Williams, pastor of the Ebenezer Baptist Church. The Reverend Williams had risen about as high as a black person could in Atlanta. He ministered to a large congregation, took part in black civic organizations, and was a leading light and charter member of the local chapter of the National Association for the Advancement of Colored People (NAACP), the nation's foremost antidiscrimination organization. Williams let his daughter know that Mike would make a fine husband, and, he added, a fine assistant minister at Ebenezer.

On Thanksgiving Day, 1926, Mike and Alberta were married. They moved in with Alberta's parents, there being plenty of space in the upstairs of the Williamses' 12-room house. Soon, King accepted his father-in-law's offer to become his assistant at Ebenezer, and when Williams died suddenly in 1931, Mike succeeded him in the pastorate.

When the Reverend King first settled in at Ebenezer, old friends still knew him as Mike. But as the years passed, more and more people were calling him

"Daddy," and for the rest of his life that was how he would be best known—as Daddy King. The name fit. Not only was he the fatherly head of a church, but he and Alberta had a family of three splendid children: a daughter, Willie Christine, born in 1927, and two sons, Martin Luther and Alfred Daniel.

Martin Luther King, Jr., arrived in the world at noon on January 15, 1929, in a bedroom of his grandparents' house at 501 Auburn Avenue. Daddy King was so overjoyed at the birth of his first son that he leaped into the air and touched the ceiling. The family quickly took to calling the pudgy, healthy baby "M. L.," and a year and a half later, when a second boy was born, they nicknamed Alfred Daniel "A. D."

Daddy constantly prayed, "God grant my children will not have to come up the way I did." His prayers were answered; the family was well-off. "Not really wealthy," his son Martin would recall, "but Negro-wealthy. We never lived in a rented house and we never rode too long in a car on which payment was due, and I never had to leave school to work."

Quite naturally, life revolved around the Ebenezer church. Among M. L.'s earliest memories were the Sunday mornings when his father preached emotional, heartfelt sermons and his mother, the church's musical director, played lovely Christian hymns on the great pipe organ. The King children spent all day Sunday at church, and they were there several afternoons during the week as well. By the time M. L. was five, he was performing gospel songs at church affairs. Accompanied on the piano by his mother, he never tired of singing "I Want to Be More and More Like Jesus."

At home, M. L. was no saint. Once, he clobbered his brother, A. D., over the head with a telephone, knocking him out, and his sister, Christine, could not help but notice how he always seemed to be in the bathroom when it was his turn to do the dishes.

King's mother, Alberta. Her father, the Reverend Adam Daniel Williams, preceded Martin Luther King, Sr., as head of the Ebenezer Baptist Church.

The three children could put aside their squabbling, though not always with a happy result. None of them cared for the piano lessons their mother insisted on, so they conspired against them. A. D. favored a direct approach and started assaulting the living-room piano with a hammer, but M. L. and Christine convinced him to try the more subtle tactic of loosening the legs of the piano stool. Their sabotage went like clockwork: The music teacher arrived, sat on the stool, and crashed to the floor. Had anything, the children

King was born and raised in this house at 501 Auburn Avenue. Located in the heart of black Atlanta, the house stood one block from the Ebenezer Baptist Church.

laughed, ever been so funny? Not in the least amused by the prank, their father gave each of them a thrashing.

It was not the first time M. L. had felt the sting of his father's switch. At home, Daddy meant to be obeyed absolutely. If something went wrong, somebody got a whipping. It was simple, quick, and persuasive, he explained.

"He was the most peculiar child whenever you whipped him," Daddy said of M. L. "He'd stand there, and the tears would run down and he'd never cry. His grandmother couldn't stand to see it." Grandmother Williams, who lived with the Kings, was closest to M. L., and after a spanking, Christine remembered, she always had for him "a hug, kiss, or kind word to help the hurt go away."

M. L. lovingly called her "Mama," and he could not bear the thought of living without her. One day when he was roughhousing with A. D., his brother slid down the banister of the front stairway, missed his mark, and slammed into Mama, knocking her down. When she did not get up, M. L. was sure he and A. D. had killed her. Tears pouring from his eyes, he rushed into a bedroom and threw himself out of a window, landing hard on the ground 12 feet below. When his family hurried to him, shouting that Mama was fine, just a little bruised, M. L. picked himself up and strolled away.

Not long afterward, on a Sunday, M. L. sneaked away to watch a parade—something Daddy had strictly forbidden. When the youngster returned home, the house was filled with sobbing relatives. His grandmother had suffered a heart attack and was dead. Shattered, sensing terrible guilt for having gone to the parade, he once more ran to a second-story window and jumped out. Unhurt beyond some bumps and scrapes, M. L. did not walk away this time. He cried and pounded the ground, a captive of grief.

M. L.'s leaps from upstairs windows naturally concerned his parents. What was he trying to do, they wondered—kill himself? But that seemed unlikely. He never again tried to do himself harm, and in every other way he was a normal, contented youngster. Like most boys, he did neighborhood jobs and delivered newspapers, once saving up $13 of his own. Although always a little small for his age, he enjoyed sports and competed fiercely, especially on the football field, where, said a friend, "he ran over anybody who got in his way." Sometimes, though, he left the playground, usually alone, usually with a book. "Even before he could read he kept books around him, he just liked the idea of having them," Daddy recalled. In school, he was a teacher's dream—smart, disciplined, and well mannered—and he breezed through with such good marks that he skipped grades in elementary school and high school.

By the time M. L. was in his early teens, people commented on how mature he seemed. They took special notice when he spoke. Almost overnight, his voice had changed from a child's chirp into a beautiful, vibrant baritone. Girls his age loved the deep voice and liked the careful way he dressed. In those days, he favored a brown tweed suit, with trousers tight at the ankles and baggy in the legs. Boys, not nearly as impressed, for years called him "Tweed."

At Booker T. Washington High School, M. L. saw his studies suffer a bit because of the time he devoted to romance and dancing. A. D. said of his brother, "I decided I couldn't keep up with him. Especially since he was crazy about dances, and just about the best jitterbug in town."

When M. L. put his mind to it, he could also be the best student in town. When he was 14 and in the 11th grade, he entered an oratorical contest sponsored by a fraternal group, the Negro Elks, and spoke on "The Negro and the Constitution." It was easily the best address, and M. L. won first prize.

The contest was held in Dublin, Georgia—quite a way from Atlanta—and M. L.'s teacher, Mrs. Bradley, accompanied him. On the trip home, the two sat together, talking happily, smiling about the prize-winning day. Then, everything turned to ashes. Twenty years later, King remembered the details vividly:

> Mrs. Bradley and I were on a bus returning to Atlanta, and at a small town along the way, some white passengers boarded the bus, and the white driver ordered us to give the whites our seats. We didn't move quickly enough to suit him, so he began cursing us, calling us "black sons of bitches." I intended to stay right in that seat, but Mrs. Bradley finally urged me up, saying we had to obey the law. And so we stood up in the aisle for the ninety miles to Atlanta. That night will never leave my memory. It was the angriest I have ever been in my life.

3

"I'M GOING TO BE
PASTOR
OF A CHURCH"

M. L. SAW THE world outside the South for the very first time after his final year in high school, when he took a summer job working in the fields of a Connecticut tobacco farm. Although the work was hard, living in the North gave him, he said, an "exhilarating sense of freedom." When he and his fellow black field hands went into Hartford, they were able to eat in any restaurant, relax in any park, and sit in any seat at a movie theater.

On the train back to Atlanta, M. L. reentered the bitter realm of segregation. He had his choice of seats for the first few hundred miles as the train raced across New York and New Jersey, but by dinnertime the train had reached Virginia. When he went to the dining car, a waiter escorted him to the rear table, and M. L. was asked to pull a curtain around him so whites would not have to see a black man eating. "I felt as though a curtain had dropped on my selfhood," he said.

But slowly, surely, times were changing. In December 1941, when M. L. was 12, the United States had entered World War II, and late in the summer of 1944, as he returned to Atlanta, the struggle was

King (front row, at far left) at the age of 19, attending a lecture at Morehouse College in Atlanta. In class, he was "quiet, introspective, and very much introverted," said one of his professors.

"We loyal Negro American citizens demand the right to work and fight for our country" became the slogan of civil rights activist A. Philip Randolph as he lobbied for black advancement during World War II. A tireless champion of the oppressed, he rose to national prominence after organizing America's first trade union for black workers in 1925.

approaching its climax. Moreover, the war was proving to be a turning point in American racial relations. Defense industries, desperate for labor, offered well-paying assembly-line jobs, and more than a million blacks flocked to factories. There they found themselves, often for the first time, working alongside whites.

The war also inspired a new militancy among black leaders. In 1941, labor organizer A. Philip Randolph prepared to lead a huge march on Washington to protest unfairness in the hiring practices of defense industries. Although many blacks were employed by defense plants, many more remained victims of discrimination and were denied jobs. At the last minute, President Franklin D. Roosevelt prevailed on Randolph to cancel the march. The president agreed to set up a Fair Employment Practices Commission to investigate discrimination against blacks in the war industry.

It was during these days of war and change that King entered college. Because so many 18 and 19 year olds were in the armed forces, Morehouse College in Atlanta offered special admission to high school students. King, only 15, passed the admission exam and in the fall of 1944 took his place in the freshman class.

It had been a foregone conclusion that King would attend Morehouse, an all-male, all-black college and the alma mater of his father and Grandfather Williams. Not so certain, however, was whether he would follow in their footsteps to the ministry. Daddy King envisioned M. L. as his eventual successor at Ebenezer, but M. L. was full of doubts about his father and about his religion. "I had doubts religion was intellectually respectable," he said years later. "I revolted against the emotionalism of Negro religion, the shouting, and the stomping. I didn't understand it and it embarrassed me."

King examined other professions. He considered becoming a doctor, but having little aptitude for science, he chose the law. "I was at that point where I was deeply interested in political matters and social ills," he said, looking back. "I could see the part I could play in breaking down the legal barriers to Negroes."

Sometimes King would stand in front of a mirror in his room at home, pretending to make courtroom speeches to imaginary juries. As it turned out, that was as close as he came to being a lawyer. His years at Morehouse directed him back to his roots, to his family's calling, and he decided to become a Baptist preacher after all. At Morehouse, he discovered a black minister did not have to be fiery and emotional like Daddy King. Instead, he could be like Dr. Benjamin Mays, the college president.

The tall, distinguished Mays was both a refined intellectual and an active champion of black rights. From the pulpit of the Morehouse chapel he called for the black church to put aside some of its religious fundamentalism and lead the protest for social change. When Mays spoke every Tuesday morning, King followed his every word, scribbling page after page of notes. In Mays he saw his vision of "a real minister"—eloquent, erudite, and committed to improving the lot of black Americans.

King's skepticism about the ministry and religion had nearly vanished by his junior year. Mays and the Morehouse faculty provided models of respectability, and King's classes in theology convinced him Christianity was intellectually defensible. During a course about the Bible, he recalled, "I came to see that behind the legends and myths of the Book were many profound truths one could not escape."

In the summer of 1947, when King was 18, he told his parents he meant to be a minister. Daddy masked his elation by gruffly demanding he prove it

At Morehouse College, King was deeply influenced by school president Benjamin Mays (shown here), who advocated social change during his weekly sermons. Mays's quietly dignified preaching style was quite unlike that of King's father, whose sermons were often thunderous and highly emotional.

by delivering a sermon at Ebenezer. Worshipers nearly filled the church's main sanctuary to hear his trial sermon, and the young man amazed them with his poise and power. "Anybody could see that he was going to make a great preacher right off to start," Daddy King remembered. That night, Daddy dropped to his knees and thanked God for having given him such a son. On February 25, 1948, Martin Luther King, Jr., was ordained a minister and made assistant pastor at Ebenezer.

Yet King's education in theology was just beginning. After graduating from Morehouse, the 19-year-old minister chose to attend the Crozer Seminary in Chester, Pennsylvania. "You're mighty young to go to Crozer," Daddy said, but he had no serious objections and wrote a glowing letter supporting his son's application. Crozer was a fine seminary, but more than scholarship recommended it. Far from Atlanta and his domineering father, Crozer offered King a chance to be his own man, to succeed or fail by himself.

For King, Crozer was a new world. Located a few miles south of Philadelphia along the Delaware River, the seminary enrolled fewer than a hundred students, only a handful of them black. Attending an integrated school for the first time, King was highly sensitive to what whites would think of him. Certain they viewed all blacks as lazy, laughing, sloppy, and tardy, he bent over backward to give the opposite impression. "If I were one minute late to class, I was almost morbidly conscious of it and sure that everyone noticed it," he said. "Rather than be thought of as always laughing, I'm afraid I was grimly serious for a time. I had a tendency to overdress, to keep my room spotless, my shoes perfectly shined and my clothes immaculately pressed." Gradually, he relaxed, discovering that most whites at Crozer accepted him as their equal. For a while, he dated a young white woman, a relationship unthinkable in Atlanta.

There was a limit to the tolerance at Crozer, however. On one occasion, a white student from the South burst into King's room, blamed him for a dormitory prank, and pointed a revolver in his direction. Others intervened and hauled the student away. King let the matter drop, neither pressing charges nor appealing to Crozer's administration, and his calm reaction to the incident won the respect of nearly everyone on campus. By the end of his first year, he was one of the most popular students around.

King was one of the brightest as well. His academic record at Morehouse had been mediocre, but at Crozer he started to shine, nearly always getting A's. As he studied works of theology, he gradually developed a personal philosophy that became the intellectual underpinning of his ministry.

One Sunday, King attended a lecture in Philadelphia by Dr. Mordecai W. Johnson, the president of Howard University. Johnson, who had recently returned from India, spoke about Mahatma Gandhi, the leader of the struggle of the Indian people for independence from Great Britain. Unique among political leaders, Gandhi believed in the power of love and insisted that any action or protest against the British imperialists be peaceful and nonviolent. In 1947, Gandhi, a tiny, simple man who did not eat meat and on occasion wore only a loincloth, saw the struggle won when the British admitted defeat and allowed India its freedom.

"I had heard of Gandhi," King recalled, but he had never given him much thought. Yet as Johnson described the man and his movement, King became intrigued. What he heard, he said, "was so profound and fascinating that I left the meeting and bought a half dozen books on Gandhi's life and works." In Gandhi's teachings, love and nonviolence were wedded to the force of a mass movement dedicated to ending oppression. He never talked of hating or destroying the British. He asked his followers to love

Indian leader Mahatma Gandhi's philosophy of nonviolent resistance ultimately served as the model for King's pacifist approach to social change. King later maintained that prior to reading extensively on Gandhi as part of his theological course work at Crozer Seminary, "I thought the only way we could solve our problem of segregation was an armed revolt."

the enemy as they loved themselves. Through love, he said, the oppressors would be redeemed, and they would see the error of their ways.

King was most attracted to Gandhi's concept of *satyagraha*, or the peaceful defiance of government. In response to continued British rule, Gandhi led boycotts, strikes, and marches, each nonviolent but each protesting the evils of imperialism, and each making it more difficult for the British to govern. King recognized in satyagraha a way for black Americans to break the back of segregation. Certainly there were vast differences between India and the United States, but the technique of active, nonviolent resistance to evil became for King the only moral and peaceful path to liberation.

In June 1951, King finished his studies at Crozer and received his bachelor's degree in divinity. He ranked at the top of his class, gave the valedictory address at the commencement, and won a $1,300 scholarship for further study at a graduate school. He decided to use the scholarship to pursue a Ph.D. and settled on the well-regarded School of Theology at Boston University. Daddy King, though impatient for him to return to Ebenezer, appreciated his son's scholarly ambition and rewarded his accomplishments at Crozer with a new bright green Chevrolet.

Early that fall, King loaded his books and clothes into the Chevy and drove from Atlanta to Boston. He found a pleasant apartment on St. Botolph Street and plunged into the demanding graduate curriculum at Boston University. As at Crozer, he excelled in his studies of philosophy and theology, making a powerful impression on the faculty. His academic adviser remembered him as one of the 5 or 6 best graduate students in his 31 years of teaching at the university.

King did not spend every evening in the library. "He just loved to party, he loved to enjoy life," a friend recalled. King had no trouble meeting attractive young women, although he complained to Mary

Powell, an old friend, that in Boston he missed the particular charm of southern women. Mrs. Powell said she knew just the girl for him and gave him the phone number of a young woman from Alabama: Coretta Scott. That night, he called her and asked for a date.

"He had quite a line," Coretta recalled. It was one he had used before. "You know every Napoleon has his Waterloo," he cooed into the phone. "I'm at my Waterloo, and I'm on my knees." Coretta laughed, and when he suggested having lunch together, she happily accepted.

The next day, stepping into his green Chevy, Coretta hastily sized up King as short and unimpressive. But over a long lunch in a cafeteria on Massachusetts Avenue, she changed her mind. "This young man became increasingly better looking as he talked so strongly and convincingly," she said.

On his side of the table, King was falling head over heels in love. "You have everything I have ever wanted in a wife. There are only four things, and you have them all," he said quietly, listing character, intelligence, personality, and beauty.

Those were the right words. Coming from a large family in Alabama, Coretta Scott had needed more than good luck to make it to Antioch College in

A future King: Coretta Scott (middle row, second from right) with classmates at Antioch College in Ohio, before she went on to study at the New England Conservatory of Music. She had planned to pursue a career as a singer before she met and married King and became an active figure in the civil rights movement.

Ohio and then to the New England Conservatory of Music in Boston, where she was studying voice. Determined to be independent, to have a career as a singer, she resisted the idea of marriage. But as King courted her in the spring, summer, and fall of 1952, she came to love him very much.

Daddy King did what he could to break up the couple. Wanting M. L. at Ebenezer, he insisted his son marry an Atlanta girl from a good solid family. At a tense gathering in Boston just before Christmas 1952, Daddy praised the fine, wonderful women M. L. knew and could marry back home. Coretta heard him out, then looked him straight in the eye. "I have something to offer too, Daddy King" she said.

M. L. kept quiet around Daddy but told his mother that nothing was going to prevent him from marrying Coretta. Daddy finally gave in and offered them his blessing, and on June 18, 1953, on the front lawn of Coretta's parents' house in Marion, Alabama, he conducted their marriage ceremony. The newlyweds went to Atlanta for the summer, and in the fall they returned to Boston, moving into a four-room apartment on Northampton Street.

Like his father, King held a traditional view of marriage. During their courtship, he told Coretta he expected his wife to be a mother and homemaker. He was glad for her to finish her musical studies in Boston, and he was delighted to help out around the house until she graduated, but a singing career for her was out. "I'm supposed to earn enough to take care of you and the family," he said.

Coretta accepted her role. "I always said," she recalled, "that if I had not married a strong man, I would have 'worn the pants.' Martin was such a very strong man, there was never any chance for that to happen."

By late 1953, King was hard at work on his doctoral dissertation, an analysis of the differing views of God advanced by two prominent theologians, Paul

Tillich and Henry Nelson Weiman. There was, however, no need to remain in Boston because his classes and research were nearly completed. He could write the dissertation elsewhere.

Several of King's professors encouraged him to take a teaching job. Staying in the academic world, living and working at a fine college—this was an attractive prospect. But for King it was never really tempting. He meant to preach. "I'm going to be pastor of a church," he told Coretta, "a large Baptist church in the South. . . . I'm going to live in the South because that's where I'm needed."

Coretta wished they could stay in the North, at least for a while longer. Growing up in rural Alabama, she had seen and felt a much harsher racial prejudice than her husband had. She lived with vivid, searing memories of bigoted and violent whites who got angry about her father's modest success in business and burned his sawmill to the ground. Martin understood her feelings, but his destiny, he repeated, was in the South.

Not in Atlanta, though. Daddy King begged M. L. to return to Ebenezer, but his son wanted the freedom of his own church.

In Montgomery, Alabama, the Dexter Avenue Baptist Church was looking for a new pastor. Around Christmas in 1953, King preached a sermon there and was impressed by the refined, respectful congregation. The worshipers liked what they saw and heard, and in April 1954 the church offered him the pastorate. He accepted.

By late August, Coretta had graduated from the conservatory, and King had completed his courses at Boston University. They stuffed their belongings into the Chevy and drove south. On September 1, they reached Montgomery, and in a few weeks they were in their new home: the church parsonage at 309 South Jackson Street, a white frame house in a quiet, tree-shaded neighborhood. ✿

In April 1954, King became pastor of the affluent Dexter Avenue Baptist Church in Montgomery, Alabama. He remained there until January 1960, when he left Dexter to devote himself more fully to the civil rights struggle. "History has thrust something upon me from which I cannot turn away," he said in resigning from his pastorship.

4

MONGOMERY

❧

MONTGOMERY, ALABAMA, IN 1954 was as segregated a city as there was in the South. White residents loved calling their home "the cradle of the Confederacy"—in 1861, Montgomery had been the Confederacy's first capital—and they did their best to preserve the ways of white supremacy. Of the city's 120,000 citizens, 48,000 were black, and, inevitably, they got the short end of everything. Most blacks lived in ramshackle houses, often without electricity and running water, located on dirty, unpaved streets. Whites owned nearly all the cars in town; blacks depended on city buses to get about. A municipal law even made it a crime for whites and blacks to play cards or checkers together.

To a newcomer like King, the blacks of Montgomery seemed apathetic, resigned to their fate. But the winds of change were beginning to blow more strongly, even in Alabama. In May 1954, the United States Supreme Court issued a monumental decision. In the case of *Brown v. Board of Education*, the court stated, by unanimous vote, "Separate educational facilities are inherently unequal . . . segregation is a denial of the equal protection of the laws." The court, in one stroke, had cut down a central tenet of southern life: segregating school children by race.

Anyone who hoped the system of separate schools for blacks and whites would disappear peacefully or quickly was to be sadly disappointed. The *Brown* decision infuriated the white South. All over Dixie, a cry arose among whites for "massive resistance" to

King with his wife, Coretta, and daughter Yolanda on the steps of the Dexter Avenue Baptist Church, just down the street from the state capitol, in 1956. His insistence that all church members support civil rights groups, register to vote, and regard their pastor as Dexter's chief authority and policymaker helped pave the way for him to become a leading spokesman for Montgomery's black community.

In May 1954, the U.S. Supreme Court ruled in the case of Brown v. Board of Education that racial segregation in America's schools is unconstitutional. Shown here, outside the U.S. Supreme Court building, are the National Association for the Advancement of Colored People (NAACP) lawyers who argued the case against segregation: (from left to right) Howard Jenkins, James Nabrit, Spottswood Robinson III, Frank Reeves, Jack Greenburg, Thurgood Marshall, Louis Redding, V. Simpson Tate, and George E. C. Hayes.

integration, and years would pass before blacks and whites would sit together in a classroom. Ominously, in the aftermath of the Brown decision, the ranks of the Ku Klux Klan, a white supremacist group, swelled with those who welcomed the organization's aim to thwart integration by terrorizing blacks.

In Montgomery, as in every other segregated southern city, a minority of blacks had done well for themselves. They were the lawyers and doctors, undertakers and store owners, teachers and accountants who served the black community. Quite a few members of this black middle class in Montgomery worshiped at the Dexter Avenue Baptist Church. It was, in Daddy King's words, "a big-shots church," its congregation generally prosperous, well dressed, and restrained. As a measure of their affluence, they paid their new minister $4,200 a year, the most offered by any black church in town.

The churchgoers received their money's worth. In his first year as pastor, King won the respect and affection of the congregation. Seeing him in the pulpit for the first time, some expressed amazement at his youth. But after hearing a sermon or two, they changed their mind. "Suave, oratorical and persuasive" were the words one worshiper used to describe him, and few disagreed.

In his sermons, King attempted to rouse the church into taking a more active part in resisting segregation. Praising the NAACP, he called for his congregation to join the nation's premier civil rights organization. He also wanted to see his flock at the polls. White officials made it extremely difficult for southern blacks to vote; but King told the congregation at Dexter Avenue that they had a duty to pass literacy tests, pay poll taxes, and overcome all the other obstacles to voting.

Across town, another Baptist preacher watched approvingly as King tried to light a fire under the Dexter Avenue parishioners. The Reverend Ralph David Abernathy of the First Baptist Church shared the newcomer's passion for social justice, and in no time the two were the best of friends. King liked Abernathy's direct, earthy manner, and King's sophistication and learning appealed to Abernathy. Often, the Kings got together with Abernathy and his wife, Juanita, for dinner, conversation, and laughter. The two men had a rich sense of humor and loved amusing one another, so dinner frequently dissolved into sidesplitting laughter as Abernathy, in his slow southern drawl, told joke after joke about country life in Alabama, and King provided hysterical imitations of other preachers. "I declare, you two could be on stage," said a friend.

King laughed easily in 1955. Life was treating him well. In the spring, he finished his doctoral dissertation, and not long afterward Boston University awarded him a Ph.D. Best of all, on November 17, 1955, Coretta gave birth to a girl, Yolanda Denise, whom they called Yoki. The new father could scarcely contain his joy.

Two weeks after Yoki's birth, on Thursday evening, December 1, 1955, a small, neatly dressed black woman in Montgomery left work at quitting time, walked across the street to do some shopping at a pharmacy, and then boarded a bus for the ride home. She took a seat toward the rear, in the row just behind the section marked Whites Only. Holding her packages, she was glad to sit down. After a long day, her feet hurt.

As the bus wound its way through Montgomery, it steadily filled with passengers, and soon every seat was taken. When two white men boarded and paid their fares, the bus driver called over his shoulder for the first row of blacks to move back. After some delay, three blacks rose and stood in the aisle. But Mrs. Rosa Parks, her feet aching, her lap covered with packages, did not budge. The driver shouted, "Look woman, I told you I wanted the seat. Are you going to stand up?"

Gently but firmly, Rosa Parks said, "No," and for that she was arrested and thrown in jail. She had

NAACP member Rosa Parks (second from right) and E. D. Nixon (second from left), a former head of the NAACP's Montgomery chapter, arrive at the Montgomery courthouse in March 1956 to appeal her conviction. Three and a half months earlier, she had refused to give her seat to a white man on a Montgomery bus and was promptly arrested for failing to comply with the city's segregation laws.

defied the law that established not only separate seating for blacks and whites but required blacks to surrender their places if buses were filled.

The next morning, King was working at the Dexter Avenue church when his telephone rang. It was
E. D. Nixon, a plainspoken Pullman sleeping-car porter and a leader in the Montgomery NAACP. "We
got it," he cried. "We got our case!" He explained
to King about Parks's arrest and said that this was
what he had been waiting for: an incident that could
be used to mount a legal challenge to Montgomery's
segregation laws. What was more, Nixon exclaimed,
the blacks in town should display their anger by
launching a boycott of the city buses.

At that moment, King did not completely share
Nixon's enthusiasm. To be sure, he knew how deeply
Montgomery blacks resented the buses and how they
particularly loathed the business of having to give up
their seats, something that was not required in many
other southern cities. He knew how bus drivers, all
of whom were white, insulted and abused black passengers. But he had doubts about a boycott. Nixon
assured him it was the only course of action.

A few minutes later, Abernathy called. He endorsed the planned boycott and asked for his friend's
backing. King agreed.

King later observed that the black women of
Montgomery lost their fear before the men did. The
day after the arrest of Rosa Parks, the Women's Political Council, an organization of black activists,
started handing out a leaflet calling for blacks to stay
off the buses the following Monday, the day Parks's
case would come to trial. "If we do not do something
to stop these arrests, they will continue," it read.
"The next time it may be you, or your daughter, or
your mother. . . . Don't ride the buses to work, to
town, to school, or anywhere on Monday."

Over the weekend, volunteers blanketed black
neighborhoods with leaflets, black cab firms promised

to carry riders for what it cost to ride a bus, and King, Abernathy, and others visited bars and nightclubs to speak in support of the boycott. On Sunday, black churchgoers heard their pastors urge them to stay off the buses. Still, it was anyone's guess what would happen on Monday. A Friday night meeting of black leaders at Dexter Avenue had revealed all sorts of disagreement and personal rivalry. As one dissatisfied participant got up to leave, he whispered to King, "This is going to fizzle out. I'm going."

"I would like to go too, but it's in my church," King said wanly. Given the short notice and all the argument, he thought that if 60 percent of the normal black ridership stayed home on Monday, the boycott would be a great success.

A bus stop was right in front of King's house on South Jackson Street, and very early on Monday morning the minister and his wife waited to see how many people were riding on the 6:00 A.M. bus, the first of the day. "Martin, Martin, come quickly!" Coretta cried. Her husband put down his coffee cup in the kitchen and raced to the front window. He could not believe his eyes. The South Jackson line served more blacks than any in the city, and the early bus was usually packed. "Darling, it's empty!" Coretta said. And so was the next bus. And the next.

His emotions surging, King jumped into his car and cruised about Montgomery. On every line, on every bus, black Montgomerians, nearly to a person, honored the boycott. Some took cabs, some drove with friends, one man rode a mule, and a great many walked. But as King crisscrossed the city, he counted only eight blacks riding on buses.

At nine o'clock that morning, hundreds of blacks crowded about the courthouse for the trial of Rosa Parks. In a matter of minutes, the judge found her guilty of violating a state segregation law and fined her $10 and court costs. She and her attorney appealed the verdict, setting in motion a legal challenge

On April 26, 1956, 5 months into the Montgomery bus boycott, King announces to a mass meeting of 3,000 supporters that the black protest against segregation on the city's buses would continue. Although the bus company had stated three days earlier that it would no longer enforce segregation, the city promised that segregation on the buses would continue.

to segregation. E. D. Nixon had been right; it was the case for which they had been looking.

In the afternoon, the local black leadership met to establish a new organization to direct the boycott. At Abernathy's suggestion, they decided to call the new group the Montgomery Improvement Association, or MIA. After agreeing on a name, they turned to electing a president. In a far corner of the room, Rufus Lincoln, a professor from Alabama State, the city's black university, called, "Mr. President, I would like to nominate Reverend M. L. King for president." No other names were placed in nomination, so King was asked if he accepted. "Well, if you think I can render some service, I will," he replied.

"The action had caught me unawares," King later said. It should have. Only 26 years old and not long in town, he assumed that an older, more established figure would be selected. But being a newcomer worked in his favor; he had not been around long enough to take sides in the feuds that divided the black community. Some in the MIA figured that whites would eventually crush the boycott and its leader. When the movement collapsed, they reasoned, why let it fall on us? Let it bury a youngster who could pick up and leave town. Not everyone, though, was cynical. They admired King's decency, eloquence, and the social activism he preached at Dexter Avenue.

A mass meeting that would determine the future of the boycott was scheduled for 7:00 P.M. at the Holt Street Baptist Church. As the MIA's new leader, King was to give the main address. He had not the slightest notion of what to say. He nearly panicked. All of his sermons were carefully written out, studied, memorized, rehearsed. Now he had but 15 minutes to collect his thoughts before heading out for the meeting. In his study at home, he dropped to his knees and prayed for God to be with him.

The church was filled far beyond its capacity. Outside, thousands clogged the streets, and loud-speakers were set up for them to hear the proceedings. After the others spoke, it was King's turn. He started with a calm description of the arrest of Mrs. Parks. Gradually, his voice grew louder and started to rise and fall in a singsong way. His words got stronger: "There comes a time when people get tired. We are here this evening to say to those who have mistreated us so long, that we are tired. Tired of being segregated and humiliated; tired of being kicked about by the brutal feet of oppression."

King asked that the protest adhere to "the deepest principles of our Christian faith. Love must be our regulating ideal." Above all, "we must not become bitter and end up hating our white brothers." The crowd, 1,000 in the church and 4,000 in the streets outside, cheered and shouted, "Amen," as he ended each phrase, but hushed when he spoke again: "If you will protest courageously, and yet with dignity and Christian love, when the history books are written in future generations, the historians will have to pause and say, 'There lived a great people—a black people—who injected new meaning and dignity into the veins of civilization.' This is our challenge and our overwhelming responsibility."

Then King sat down, emotionally drained. The throng exploded in a prolonged arm-waving, hand-clapping ovation. "It was the most stimulating thing I had ever heard," one person said. As King acknowledged the applause, he realized that his 16-minute address "had evoked more response than any speech or sermon I had ever delivered."

The crowd was so large and enthusiastic that there was no question the boycott would continue. That evening, the blacks of Montgomery endorsed the MIA's three demands of the bus company and municipal government: First, bus drivers must stop insulting black riders. Second, passengers should be seated on a first-come, first-served basis, blacks taking seats from the back of the bus and moving toward the front, whites from the front backward. And third, the bus company must consider hiring black drivers for the routes that had black patronage.

The demands did not in any way call for an end to segregation. If the MIA's plan were adopted, blacks would still sit apart from whites. All told, the MIA's proposals amounted to a request for a more polite system of segregation; and with such a modest agenda, King initially hoped for a speedy settlement. Even the most conservative white, he thought, could go along with them.

He was dead wrong. During the first week of the boycott, King and other blacks met with city officials and representatives of the bus company, who would not give an inch. It did not matter that the MIA's plan preserved segregation. "If we granted the Negroes these demands," said the attorney for the bus company, "they would go about boasting of a victory that they had won over the white people; and this we will not stand for."

King admonished himself for having been so optimistic. He should have known better. But it suddenly dawned on him that he and the MIA had taken on an enormous task. If the whites would not budge, neither could the blacks. That meant a boycott lasting not a few days or weeks, but one stretching into months, and such an undertaking called for coordination and planning.

The most pressing need was alternative transportation—some means to carry blacks from their homes on one side of town to their jobs on the other. On Tuesday, December 13, the MIA inaugurated a carefully organized, wonderfully effective car pool. Using 300 cars loaned by black motorists, volunteer drivers shuttled riders from 48 dispatch stations in the black neighborhoods to 42 drop-off stations in other parts of the city. Cars broke down, drivers sometimes got lost, but day after day the car pool efficiently shuttled riders back and forth.

The boycott and car pool united black Montgomery. Every morning at the crack of dawn, members

The Montgomery bus boycott owed a great measure of its success to an efficiently run car-pool system. Throughout the protest, privately owned vehicles, including this church-operated station wagon, delivered black passengers to their destination.

of the city's black elite—lawyers, doctors, professors—offered rides in their Cadillacs and Lincolns to the working poor. "The so-called 'big Negroes,'" King wrote, "who owned cars and had never ridden the buses came to know the maids and the laborers who rode the buses every day." Blacks—rich and poor—resented segregation, and the boycott enabled people to forget their different stations in life and join hands. They came together at the mass meetings of the MIA, held twice a week, on Mondays and Thursdays, in the black churches.

King was the star attraction. "Had he not been there, many people might have gone back to the buses," said one woman. Night after night, he explained the philosophy of nonviolent protest. At the first few meetings, he spoke in broad terms of Christian love and brotherhood, but after a while he came to talk of Gandhi and of the nonviolent resistance that had freed India. In the crowded, overheated churches of Montgomery, the young minister asked of his followers what Gandhi, years before, in a foreign land, had asked of his: "We must meet the forces of hate with the power of love; we must meet physical force with soul force. Our aim must never be to defeat or humiliate the white man, but to win his friendship and understanding."

The whites of Montgomery were in no mood to be loved. With each day of the boycott, blacks proved themselves resourceful, organized, and determined—precisely the opposite of what the whites had always said they were. And leading them was a preacher with a Ph.D. who talked of love, and of Gandhi, and of philosophers the whites had never heard of. They despised him and the disruption he was causing. As long as Montgomery's blacks stayed off the buses, King was a marked man.

Most upsetting were the anonymous threatening phone calls. One Saturday night, between 30 and 40 snarling whites called the Kings' number. "Listen, nigger," said one. "We've taken all we want from you. Before next week, you'll be sorry you ever came to Montgomery."

It was too much. Late one night, King answered the phone and heard another hate-filled voice call him "nigger" and order him out of town. Deathly afraid, he wandered to the stove and put on a pot of coffee. As he waited for the water to boil, he sat at the kitchen table. He bowed his head and said to the Lord that he could not continue. "I am at the end of my powers. I have nothing left. I can't face it alone." Suddenly, his cares vanished; his fears retreated. "At that moment," King said later, "I experienced the presence of the Divine as I had never experienced Him before." An inner voice said, "Stand up for righteousness, stand up for truth; and God will be at your side forever."

On January 30, 1956, King faced stark terror. It was a Monday, the day for an MIA rally, and that evening he spoke at Abernathy's First Baptist Church. Coretta stayed home with the baby. By 9:30, she had on her bathrobe and was in the living room, visiting with Mary Lucy Williams, a member of the Dexter Avenue congregation.

When a loud thump on the front porch interrupted their conversation, Mrs. Williams leaped to her feet. Coretta calmly said, "It sounds as if someone hit the house. We'd better move to the back." Just as they reached the next room, the floor trembled and a thunderous roar nearly deafened them. The living room was filled with broken glass and foul-smelling smoke.

At the MIA meeting, King noticed people scurrying around the church with worried, even tearful expressions. He looked for Abernathy. "Ralph, what's happened?" Abernathy shook his head. "Ralph, you must tell me."

"Your house has been bombed."

Some friends at the church drove King home, and there he embraced Coretta and Yoki. "Thank God you and the baby are all right," he said. The house was filled with people, even the mayor and commissioner of police offering their condolences.

Outside, South Jackson Street was swarming with people. Word of the bombing had flown through the black neighborhood, shocking and enraging all who heard the news. Some in the crowd, intent on revenge, had guns and knives. King stepped onto what was left of his front porch and told everyone that his wife and daughter were fine. Go home and put away your weapons, he said. More violence would not resolve a thing. "I want you to love our enemies," he urged his listeners. "Be good to them. Love them and let them know you love them." The crowd's anger subsided, and the people soon left.

King and his wife, Coretta, meet with reporters on the steps of the Montgomery County Courthouse before his trial in March 1956 for violating a state law forbidding boycotts. Immediately after his conviction, King told his supporters outside the courthouse, "We will continue to protest in the same spirit of nonviolence and passive resistance, using the weapon of love."

In the hours before daybreak, one more visitor arrived: Daddy King. Hearing of the bombing, he had left Atlanta at once, racing through the night in his big car to Montgomery. Come back home, he pleaded with his son, get out before they kill you. M. L. said he could not desert the MIA. "It's better to be a live dog than a dead lion," Daddy growled. But M. L. would not listen. He and Coretta and their baby were going to stay.

The violence kept on. Two nights later, some sticks of dynamite exploded in front of E. D. Nixon's house. The bombings, however, only intensified support for the MIA. Black Montgomery stayed off the buses.

In February, the city government attempted to break the boycott once and for all by obtaining an indictment against almost 100 MIA members for violating an obscure state law forbidding boycotts. To no one's surprise, King's name was at the top of the list. His was the first case to go before the court.

King's trial began on March 19, 1956, in the county courthouse. More than 500 black supporters tried to press into the small courtroom. Those who managed to find seats wore white crosses with hand-lettering that read "Father, forgive them." In King's defense, witnesses testified about the abusive bus system. They made no difference. Three days later, the judge routinely found King guilty and sentenced him to pay a $500 fine or serve 386 days of hard labor. His attorneys immediately appealed the decision.

Meanwhile, the case testing the constitutionality of Alabama's segregation statutes—the lawsuit that had begun with the arrest of Rosa Parks—was advancing through federal courts. In June, a panel of federal judges struck down the bus segregation laws, but the city of Montgomery appealed the decision to the U.S. Supreme Court. Accordingly, the boycott settled into a prolonged legal test of wills.

As long as the car-pool system ran smoothly, the boycott could continue indefinitely. This simple fact reached the whites in City Hall, and in the fall of 1956 they legally attacked the car pools. In November, the city went to court, seeking an injunction to halt the car pools, saying they were a public nuisance. If the car pools were declared illegal, the boycott was as good as dead.

At a Monday night rally, King did not try to minimize the peril. He asked for faith and hope: "This may well be the darkest hour before the dawn. . . . We must go on with the same faith. We must believe a way will be made out of no way."

The next day, November 13, 1956, King sat in the courtroom with the MIA's attorney as the judge considered the city's move to ban the car pools. "I was faltering in my faith and my courage," King recalled. Then a reporter handed him a slip of paper during a late-morning recess. "Here is the decision you've been waiting for," the man said with a smile. It was a wire service bulletin.

> Washington, D.C. (AP)—The United States Supreme Court today affirmed a decision of a special three-judge U.S. District Court in declaring Alabama's state and local laws requiring segregation on buses unconstitutional.

King read the words over and over. It was miraculous. At the very moment the movement in Montgomery looked to be in the deepest trouble, the nation's highest court declared that segregation on buses was illegal. The battle had been won.

A month later, one morning a little before six o'clock, a Montgomery city bus drew up in front of King's house on South Jackson Street. Several people were waiting at the bus stop, among them King, Abernathy, and Parks. King entered first and took a seat in one of the front rows. A white man occupied the spot next to him. ✺

King is cheered by his supporters following his conviction for helping to arrange the Montgomery bus boycott. The trial received national news coverage and gave renewed momentum to the city-wide protest.

5

"THE NUMBER ONE LEADER"

·❦·

IN LATE 1957, King and an associate were walking through the Atlanta airport on their way to a flight for Montgomery. Looking for a rest room, King saw two doors, one labeled Men, the other Colored. He went into the one marked Men. The whites inside paid him no attention, but the lavatory's black attendant was deeply upset. "Colored men don't come in here," he said.

When King did not depart, the attendant walked toward him, tapped him on the shoulder, and said, "You go in the colored room across the hall." King ignored him. Finally, he turned to the despairing attendant and asked, "Do you mean that every time you need to go to the bathroom you go out of here and all the way to that other room?"

"Yes, sir. That's the place for colored."

Back in the airport corridor, King told his friend what had happened in the rest room. Shaking his head, the 28-year-old minister said, "That's the way most of the Negroes of Montgomery acted before the boycott."

The boycott changed things, unleashing a powerful sense of pride and accomplishment within the black community. For the first time in anyone's memory, blacks, by themselves, had peacefully, successfully overcome segregation.

It was a landmark victory, but one that had flaws and limits. A ruling by the Supreme Court, after all,

"If anybody had asked me a year ago to head this movement, I tell you very honestly that I would have run a mile to get away from it," King said after the success of the Montgomery bus boycott. "As I became involved, and as people began to derive inspiration from their involvement, I realized that the choice leaves your own hands."

was what saved the day. Without the court's decision, the city probably would have put the car pool out of business and broken the boycott.

Furthermore, the movement that sought to love its enemies had not converted many whites. Instead, white Montgomery remained intolerant and prone to terrorism. Even though the boycott had ended, the violence persisted. Three days after Christmas 1956, white thugs opened fire on buses all over town, and in early January 1957, they firebombed four churches, including Abernathy's.

The violence and bigotry of whites, no matter how extreme, left King's commitment unshaken. Blacks in the South, he explained to a leading northern liberal in 1957, must say to whites, "We will match your capacity to inflict suffering with our capacity to endure suffering. We will meet your physical force with soul force. We will not hate you, but we will not obey your evil laws."

By 1957, King's message was reaching an audience that stretched far beyond Montgomery. The bus boycott had captured national attention and had transformed its leader into a celebrated spokesman for civil rights. Nearly every delivery of the mail to the Dexter Avenue Church contained for King speaking invitations, job offers from churches and universities, and publishers' proposals for books. In February 1957, he gained the ultimate stamp of celebrity: His picture appeared on the cover of *Time* magazine. On the inside pages, readers found a flattering profile of "this scholarly Negro Baptist minister."

Fame never went to King's head, and he declined nearly all of the offers. But one invitation he accepted eagerly. The leaders of the new African nation of Ghana requested he attend its independence day ceremonies. For King, the emergence of independent nations in Africa was immensely important. The struggle of American blacks against segregation, in

his view, was part of the worldwide quest of oppressed
colonial people for liberation. In Ghana, he met the
official American representative, Vice-president
Richard M. Nixon. "I'm very glad to meet you here,"
he told Nixon, "but I want you to come and visit us
down in Alabama where we are seeking the same
kind of freedom Ghana is celebrating."

Neither Nixon nor President Dwight D. Eisenhower came to Alabama to denounce segregation.
But in 1957, there came a glimmer of hope. Early in
the year, the Eisenhower administration sent to Congress a civil rights bill, the first of the 20th century.
In its original form, the measure provided for a civil
rights commission to investigate abuses against blacks
and permitted the Department of Justice to intervene
on behalf of those whose right to vote was denied by
southern officials.

Encouraged, King and other leading blacks decided the time was right for a major public demonstration to encourage congressional approval of the
civil rights bill. They organized a Prayer Pilgrimage
for Freedom, and on May 17, 1957, a crowd of 25,000
blacks and whites came together before the Lincoln
Memorial in Washington, D.C. On the monument's
steps, America's preeminent blacks, one after another, rose and spoke: Roy Wilkins, executive secretary of the NAACP; labor leader A. Philip
Randolph; New York congressman Adam Clayton
Powell, Jr.; former baseball great Jackie Robinson;
gospel singer Mahalia Jackson; singer Harry Bela-
fonte. Yet it was the 28-year-old preacher from Montgomery who outshone these luminaries and touched
the crowd in a way no one else could. "Give us the
ballot," King thundered, "and we will transform the
salient misdeeds of bloodthirsty mobs into the abiding
good deeds of orderly citizens."

Not long afterward, the *Amsterdam News*, the
largest black paper in the country, echoed the sen-

After arriving in Montgomery in February 1956, civil rights activist Bayard Rustin became one of King's chief aides and closest friends. Sharing King's commitment to nonviolence, he was instrumental in establishing the Southern Christian Leadership Conference (SCLC), a coordinating council to advise and stimulate black protest groups throughout the South.

timents of most who had heard and seen King in the nation's capital. Martin Luther King, Jr., the paper said, "emerged from the Prayer Pilgrimage to Washington as the number one leader of sixteen million Negroes in the United States."

Congress eventually approved the Civil Rights Act of 1957, but by the time it passed, southern senators and representatives had succeeded in gutting the sections protecting black voting rights. Though disappointed by the compromises, King supported the measure, telling Vice-president Nixon, "The present bill is far better than no bill at all."

King's rise to international fame upset older, more established blacks who envied his appeal. Roy Wilkins of the NAACP, in particular, disapproved of widespread nonviolent protest, and his relations with King were tense, often unfriendly. One prominent black, however, detected greatness in King and encouraged him to a large destiny: Bayard Rustin, who wrote to King at the time of the Prayer Pilgrimage, "The question of where you move next is more important than any other question Negroes face today."

A leading advocate of nonviolent protest, the tall, strikingly handsome Rustin had come on his own to Montgomery during the bus boycott. In a short time, he became King's friend and trusted adviser. Every time they talked, Rustin urged spreading the principles of the Montgomery boycott to the rest of the South.

King needed little convincing. In his view, organizations such as the NAACP had paid insufficient attention to the plight of the average southern black. He envisioned a new organization to coordinate civil rights activity throughout the South. Like the MIA, it would be dedicated to nonviolent mass protest, and, as in Montgomery, it would operate through local churches—the most stable, influential institutions in the black community.

At meetings in Atlanta and New Orleans in early 1957, King, with Rustin at his side, conferred with leading black clergymen and built a new organization. Several months later, in August, more than a hundred delegates convened at the Holt Street Church in Montgomery and officially named their group the Southern Christian Leadership Conference, or SCLC. From the outset, no one but King had been considered for its presidency. "King *was* the Southern Christian Leadership Conference," a supporter asserted.

Two years earlier, the young minister at Dexter Avenue had often sat hour upon hour in his study, meticulously preparing a single Sunday sermon. Now, with the SCLC, the MIA, speeches, fund-raising, and travel, he hardly had a moment for himself. Whenever he could, he worked on a personal account of the bus boycott that Harper and Brothers in New York had contracted to publish. Harper wanted to put the book out while the story of Montgomery was still fresh and had pestered him relentlessly for the manuscript. At last, in the spring of 1958, King completed the book. Carrying the title *Stride Toward Freedom*, it combined autobiography with a step-by-step story of the boycott.

King's growing reputation did nothing for him in Montgomery. On September 3, 1958, he accompanied Abernathy to the Montgomery courthouse for the preliminary hearing of a case that charged Edward Davis with chasing after Abernathy with a hatchet. Abernathy was slated to testify against Davis and had brought along a lawyer, Fred Gray, to counter Davis's anticipated testimony. When King asked if he could speak with Abernathy's lawyer, a guard exploded. "Boy," he yelled at King, "if you don't get the hell away from here, you will need a lawyer yourself." Two policemen rushed in. One grabbed King's arm and twisted it behind his back. In minutes, they had

King is arrested for loitering at the Montgomery courthouse, just before the Reverend Ralph Abernathy was to testify at a hearing. The police officers, unaware of the identity of their charge, treated King with obvious brutality.

dragged him from the courthouse to the police station, where a desk sergeant snarled, "Put him in the hole." The officers shoved, kicked, and twisted their captive into a cell.

Ten minutes passed. Some ranking officers hurried to King's cell and released him. They had discovered who their prisoner was, and, worse, that a news photographer had snapped pictures of the arm-twisting arrest. The police filed a charge against King for loitering, expecting that he would pay a fine and the matter would be dropped. At his trial a few days later, the judge found him guilty of disobeying the police and ordered him to pay $14 or serve 14 days in jail.

King startled the judge by refusing to pay the fine. "Your honor," he said, "I could not in all good conscience pay a fine for an act that I did not commit and above all for the brutal treatment I did not deserve." King decided that by staying behind bars he would dramatically illustrate the violence inflicted by police on other southern blacks. Officials in Montgomery realized they had blundered by arresting King—it had become national news—and a city commissioner quickly paid the $14 fine out of his own pocket. King was a free man, but from then on, he would not hesitate to go to jail for violating laws that protected segregation.

After King's arrest in Montgomery, a family friend warned him of the pitfalls of prominence. "You must be vigilant indeed," he cautioned the preacher. Danger seemed to be everywhere.

A few weeks later, King visited Harlem, Manhattan's sprawling black neighborhood, to promote *Stride Toward Freedom*. On a Saturday afternoon, he sat in Blumstein's department store on 125th Street, autographing copies of his book and surrounded by admirers. Suddenly, a middle-aged black woman burst through the crowd. "Is this Martin Luther King?" she inquired.

"Yes it is," King said, looking up. Hearing that, the woman reached into her handbag, pulled out a razor-sharp, seven-inch-long Japanese letter opener, and shoved it into King's chest. Amid the crowd's screams, guards and police handcuffed the woman and dragged her off. She was eventually confined to a mental institution. In shock but fully conscious, King did not move. With the blade still protruding from his chest, he was carried to an ambulance and taken to Harlem Hospital.

He was very fortunate. The letter opener had come to rest against his aorta. If the blade had entered his chest a fraction of an inch to the other side, or if he had made a sudden movement, sneezed even, he would have bled to death. A team of surgeons worked over him for hours, then assured his friends outside the operating room that he would live.

By late October, King was at home in Montgomery, taking it easy with Coretta, Yoki, and the newest family member, their son, one-year-old Martin Luther King III. Over the Christmas holidays, feeling

King waits for an ambulance moments after a deranged woman stabbed him with a letter opener at a New York store in September 1958. He later referred to this incident in his speeches whenever he was preoccupied with death.

much better, King decided to make a sentimental journey to India, the land of Gandhi.

In early February 1959, he and Coretta touched down in Bombay and started a month-long tour of the cities and villages of the vast country. In New Delhi, the capital, he said, "To other countries I may go as a tourist, but to India I come as a pilgrim. This is because India means to me Mahatma Gandhi." For four hours, he visited with Prime Minister Jawaharlal Nehru, Gandhi's ally in the struggle for Indian independence. King was impressed by Nehru and the Indian disciples of Gandhi, sensing in them a commitment to ending poverty and discrimination, something he doubted President Eisenhower and most American politicians possessed.

The most pressing business King faced as soon as he returned home was getting the SCLC voter registration campaign, its Crusade for Citizenship, off the ground. The SCLC had established headquarters in Atlanta, and it was nearly impossible for King to have a hand in day-to-day activities if he continued living in Montgomery. To give the SCLC his full attention, he and Coretta made the difficult decision to leave the Dexter Avenue Church, their home for five years. In late November 1959, he offered his resignation and told the congregation of his plans in Atlanta.

On Sunday, January 31, 1960, King concluded his farewell sermon at Dexter Avenue by asking for sustained protest "until every black boy and girl can walk the streets with dignity and honor." Monday, in Greensboro, North Carolina, four black freshmen from North Carolina Agricultural and Technical State University, seeking dignity and honor, sat down at a Woolworth's lunch counter. When no one waited on them, they stayed seated, opened their school books, and studied. Word that the four students had broken the whites-only law flashed across the campus.

The next day, more than two dozen students peacefully occupied the counter at Woolworth's. Within 10 days, the sit-ins had spread throughout North Carolina into Virginia and South Carolina. By the end of the year, some 50,000 people had joined the protest against segregation.

The sit-ins were remarkably effective. The well-mannered black students contrasted vividly with the whites who swarmed into the lunchrooms to denounce, abuse, and sometimes burn the protesters with lighted cigarettes. Bad for business, the sit-ins forced many places to give in; before 1960 was over, 126 southern towns had desegregated their lunch counters.

Sit-ins, organized protests against racial discrimination, became a powerful tactic in the battle against segregated lunch counters in 1960. Scenes such as this one, contrasting the abusive segregationists with the dignified protesters, sent a clear message to the nation and resulted in the desegregation of more than a hundred eating establishments in the South.

The first sit-ins were spontaneous and caught the leading civil rights organizations by surprise. But the young protesters, almost to a person, had in mind the example of Martin Luther King when they shunned violence and stoically withstood the taunts of whites. For his part, King admired their courage and tenacity and gave them his full support. Keep to nonviolence and coordinate your activities, he advised them.

In April 1960, King and the SCLC called a conference of the student leaders at Shaw University in Raleigh, North Carolina. His keynote address was enthusiastically received, as was his counsel to form a permanent student organization. His suggestion that they become a youth division within the SCLC, however, did not go over so well. The students liked their independence, so instead of joining the SCLC, they founded the Student Nonviolent Coordinating Committee, or SNCC. King's feelings might have been a little hurt, but he quickly joined SNCC's advisory board and offered its leaders a temporary office next to his own in Atlanta.

The SCLC was not King's sole responsibility. In returning to Atlanta, he had at last accepted his father's offer and become co-pastor at Ebenezer. Daddy King was delighted to have him back in Atlanta, telling the Ebenezer congregation, "He's not little M. L. anymore, now. He is 'Dr. King' now." He also assured friends that his son was "not coming to cause trouble."

Daddy and other prominent blacks in Atlanta had friendly relations with the city's white leadership and had no wish for an aggressive campaign of Atlanta sit-ins. This was, however, exactly what SNCC had in mind, and, reluctantly defying his father, King sided with the students.

At lunchtime on Wednesday, October 19, 1960, 75 blacks tried to be served in the whites-only restaurants of downtown Atlanta stores. At Rich's department store, King and 35 others were arrested for trespassing after the establishment's Magnolia Room refused to wait on them. The police packed them into paddy wagons, and by nightfall King and the others were in the cells of the Fulton County Jail. Refusing to pay a bond, he pledged to "stay in jail 10 years if necessary."

That was the last thing William Hartsfield, the mayor of Atlanta, wanted. Worried about unfavorable national publicity, Hartsfield worked out a compromise between black leaders and the store owners. At City Hall, he announced the release of all those arrested for trespassing with the promise that he would act as an intermediary in talks involving the students and the merchants.

King behind bars, though, was just what the officials of DeKalb County, Georgia, wanted. Months before, he had been arrested there for driving with an expired license, fined $25, and placed on a year's probation. He forgot about the matter, but county officials had not. Hearing of his trespassing arrest, the DeKalb sheriff contacted Atlanta officials, pointed out that King had violated the terms of his probation, and asked that they turn him over. The Atlanta officials agreed.

On Monday, October 24, after the others arrested at the sit-in had been released, the DeKalb sheriff's deputies picked up King and hustled him off to their jail. The following day, a judge found him guilty of breaking probation and cheerfully sentenced him to four months at hard labor in a state prison. King was awakened in his cell at three the next morning by a voice in the darkness: "Get up, King. Did you hear me, King? Get up and come out here. And bring all your things with you." The jailers slapped him into handcuffs, tightened chains around his ankles, and pushed him into the back of a squad car. They drove for hours, the officers silent about their destination.

At eight o'clock, they pulled into the state prison at Reidsville, where grinning guards outfitted their famous new charge in a white uniform with blue stripes and put him in a cell reserved for violent criminals. By himself, in a penitentiary infamous for its abuse of blacks, in a part of rural Georgia where the Ku Klux Klan thrived, King broke down and cried. Ashamed of his despair, he pulled himself together and decided to make the most of his four months in prison. He wrote to Coretta, asking her to send a long list of books.

Unbeknownst to King, his imprisonment had become a factor in national politics. In October 1960, the presidential race between the Republican nominee, Vice-president Richard M. Nixon, and the Democrat, Senator John F. Kennedy, was entering the homestretch, with the two candidates neck and neck.

Nixon kept quiet. Privately, he said King had gotten a "bum rap." The Republicans had been courting the votes of southern whites, however, and were worried that public support for a civil rights leader would cost them at the polls. Kennedy also did not want to disturb the traditionally Democratic whites in Dixie. Yet several members of his campaign staff had been trying to get King out of jail from the time of his arrest in Atlanta.

When King was sent to Reidsville, Kennedy himself acted. He called Coretta in Atlanta, expressed his concern, and said that she should call him if he could do anything else. More to the point, the candidate's brother and campaign manager, Robert F. Kennedy, telephoned the DeKalb County judge who sentenced King and in bold language expressed his outrage. The next day, the judge reopened King's case and allowed a bond to be posted and the prisoner released.

At a happy Atlanta homecoming, King said he was "deeply indebted to Senator Kennedy." The

Democratic presidential candidate John F. Kennedy (left) meets with the Republican candidate, Richard M. Nixon (right), before their first debate in the 1960 campaign. Although neither candidate was anxious to give King his public support and risk losing the votes of southern whites, Kennedy covertly engineered King's release from Georgia's Reidsville state prison in October 1960.

Democrat's intervention similarly impressed blacks throughout the nation. It was simply not the sort of thing white politicians normally did.

On election day, Kennedy defeated Nixon by a tiny margin. Some observers pointed to the Democrat's large number of votes among blacks as making the difference. Eisenhower went so far as to tell reporters that Kennedy had won because he had made "a couple of phone calls."

King, who never formally endorsed Kennedy's candidacy, was among those who celebrated the victory. Was it really possible, he wondered, that black America had a friend in the White House?

6

"I FEEL
THE NEED OF
BEING FREE NOW!"

I N OCTOBER 1961, eight months into his presidency, John F. Kennedy invited King to the White House. Their meeting had been a long time coming. King had wanted to talk about civil rights ever since the election, but the president kept putting him off. Finally, when they were together in the president's study, King pressed for legislation to safeguard black voting rights. He reminded the president that 100 years earlier Abraham Lincoln had worked in the very room where they were sitting. What better way to honor the great man's memory, King asked, than for Kennedy to issue a "second Emancipation Proclamation," declaring all forms of segregation illegal.

When King finished laying out his case, Kennedy replied with a lesson in practical politics. It was a bad time for civil rights legislation, he said. Elected narrowly, he faced strong opposition in Congress, and championing the cause of blacks would cost him the support of southern Democrats. Civil rights would have to wait.

King was disappointed but not surprised. By 1961, surely he realized that it was not in the cards for a president of either party willingly to join the civil

A common sight during the civil rights movement: King joining hands with other clergymen at the end of a meeting to sing "We Shall Overcome." The hymn quickly became the anthem of the movement.

181

rights movement. Kennedy and virtually every other American political leader would delay and temporize forever unless prodded and pushed. And blacks had but one way to pressure the federal government: Massive protest—the nonviolent direct action of demonstrations and sit-ins—got results. The Freedom Rides of 1961 had shown that.

In December 1960, the U.S. Supreme Court outlawed segregation in railroad stations and bus terminals as well as in the trains and buses that crossed state lines. But the South acted as if it had not heard of the decision and kept its facilities as segregated as ever. James Farmer, the head of a pioneer civil rights organization, the Congress of Racial Equality (CORE), decided to dramatize the South's defiance of the court.

In May 1961, two interracial groups, sponsored by CORE, boarded buses in Washington, D.C., and headed southward. Along the way, the Freedom Riders asserted their constitutional rights by ignoring Whites Only and Colored signs in southern bus stations. King gave them his support and had dinner with some of the riders when they passed through Atlanta. Although it was a CORE operation, the SCLC promised cooperation, even paying for the riders' bus tickets to Alabama.

Through Virginia, the Carolinas, and Georgia, the Freedom Ride proceeded uneventfully. This tranquillity bothered Farmer. "We planned the Freedom Ride with the specific intention of creating a crisis," he recalled. "We were counting on the bigots in the South to do our work for us. We figured that the government would have to respond if we created a situation that was headline news all over the world."

In Alabama, they finally got what they expected. At Anniston, a white mob burned one bus and attacked every Freedom Rider it could lay its hands on. The second bus raced to Birmingham, where the po-

lice told a gang of Ku Klux Klansmen they would not interfere with them for 15 minutes. The Klan, in that quarter hour, went after the riders in its preferred way: with lead pipes, baseball bats, and chains.

The outrageous brutality, as Farmer hoped, forced the federal government to act, and it fell to U.S. attorney general Robert F. Kennedy, the president's brother, to protect the Freedom Riders. He sent several assistants to Birmingham, and over the telephone he told an executive of the Greyhound line, "Somebody better get in that damn bus and get it going and get these people on their way." It got as far as Montgomery. There, howling whites surrounded the terminal, and when the Freedom Ride bus pulled in, they screamed, "Get 'em, get 'em, get 'em," and attacked. Clearly, local law enforcement was incap-

In the spring of 1961, an integrated group of Freedom Riders looked to draw national attention to the issue of discrimination on interstate buses by traveling through the South and inciting white segregationists. The passengers achieved their goal on May 14, after a white mob firebombed their bus outside Anniston, Alabama. Photographs of the incident soon circulated throughout the nation.

able of protecting the Freedom Ride, so Kennedy ordered 500 U.S. marshals to Montgomery to restore order.

King was in Chicago on SCLC business. Hearing of the violence, he flew at once to Montgomery. It was a Sunday evening, and at Abernathy's First Baptist Church a rally was quickly arranged. By early evening, more than a thousand blacks, angry about the violence at the bus station, had gathered to hear King. After being escorted from the airport to the church by 50 marshals, he stepped to the pulpit and called for a full-scale assault on segregation in Alabama. He demanded federal support: "Unless the federal government acts forthrightly in the South to assure every citizen his constitutional rights, we will be plunged into a dark abyss of chaos."

By the time King finished speaking, the "dark abyss of chaos" was right on the church's doorstep. A white mob, growing bigger by the minute, was in an early stage of riot. The federal marshals tried to drive them back by firing canisters of tear gas, but the hoodlums pressed in, hurled rocks through the windows, set fire to a car, and gave every sign they meant to burn down the church. Inside, the crowd prayed and bravely sang hymns.

A few minutes after 10:00 A.M., King went to a basement office and called the attorney general in Washington. He informed Kennedy that the mob was going to burn down the church. Kennedy assured him the marshals, who were reinforced by state troopers and the National Guard, could handle the crowd.

The marshals eventually managed to quell and disperse the mob. But it took them all night. Around five in the morning, the people in the church were escorted home by the marshals and guardsmen.

Later that day, the Freedom Riders decided to continue their journey to Mississippi. They expected King to accompany them, but he declined, pointing out that he was still on probation in Georgia for a traffic violation. His explanation satisfied few of the riders and enraged some. "I would rather have heard King say, 'I'm scared—that's why I'm not going,' " one complained, "I would have had greater respect for him if he said that." When King waved good-bye to the heavily guarded bus as it left Montgomery, the riders felt badly let down.

In Mississippi, the riders were arrested as soon as they arrived in Jackson, the state capital, for using the facilities at the main bus station. Attorney General Kennedy remembered, "My primary interest was that they weren't beaten up. So, I suppose I concurred with the fact that they were going to be arrested."

After the arrests, with the threat of white violence diminished, Kennedy tried to arrange their release. King called from Montgomery and informed the attorney general that "as a matter of conscience and morality" the Freedom Riders would stay in jail. Kennedy was nonplussed. What possible good could be done in a cell? "That is not going to have the slightest effect on what the government is going to do in this field or any other," he said to King.

"Perhaps," King replied, "it would help if students came down here by the hundreds—by the hundreds of thousands."

"The country belongs to you as much as to me," Kennedy said, his voice tense with anger. "You can determine what's best just as well as I can, but don't make statements that sound like a threat. That's not the way to deal with us."

Neither man spoke for a while. King broke the silence by trying to explain the philosophy of nonviolent resistance, of their need to dramatize the sufferings of blacks by remaining in jail. He could have saved his breath. Kennedy did not see his point. The riders already had the protection of the federal government, he said curtly.

Anxious to preserve the image of the federal government, U.S. attorney general Robert F. Kennedy was often forced to protect the Freedom Riders from violent white mobs. Accordingly, he kept close track of their journey in May 1961 from Montgomery, Alabama, to Jackson, Mississippi.

Ralph Abernathy (left), treasurer of the Southern Christian Leadership Conference (SCLC), and Wyatt T. Walker, the organization's executive director, examine the remains of a black church in Georgia that had been fire-bombed. Throughout the civil rights movement, white segregationists periodically attacked black institutions in an attempt to intimidate blacks.

Now it was King's turn to raise his voice. "I'm deeply appreciative of what the administration is doing," he said. "I see a ray of hope, but I am different than my father. I feel the need of being free now!"

If Kennedy could not see the utility of King's philosophy, he certainly knew political pressure when he saw it. The Freedom Riders gave the very clear lesson that unless segregated bus stations were eliminated, the disruptions would continue. On May 29, 1961, the attorney general requested that the Interstate Commerce Commission issue regulations ending segregation in bus terminals. Soon, the Whites Only signs started coming down all across the South.

Although King's choice not to join the Freedom Ride harmed his reputation with more militant blacks, the SCLC continued to grow impressively. Skillful fund-raising swelled the organization's treasury, and able, talented blacks, attracted to King and his cause, assumed key staff positions. There was, of course, Ralph Abernathy, King's closest friend, who moved to Atlanta to be closer to SCLC affairs. The organization lacked businesslike order until King made Wyatt T. Walker executive director. A minister who had led desegregation efforts in Virginia, Walker was a hard taskmaster, insisting on discipline in the Atlanta office.

If Walker was outspoken and always in motion, Andrew Young was tranquil and deliberate. In his late twenties, Young was an executive with the National Council of Churches in New York. But as he watched the sit-ins and Freedom Rides, he said, "It really disturbed me that things were happening in the South, and I wasn't there." In September 1961, he pulled up stakes and moved to Atlanta, almost at once becoming a central figure in the SCLC's voter education campaign and a trusted aide to King.

With the SCLC in good shape, King, in 1961, planned to accelerate the voter registration effort, and, as he told his friends, "We will have to carry the struggle more into South Carolina, Mississippi, and Alabama." His next and most severe challenge, however, would happen in none of those places, but somewhere the SCLC had not meant to become involved: Albany, Georgia, a city of 56,000 people, 270 miles from Atlanta.

In the summer of 1961, SNCC had initiated a voter registration campaign in Albany. It had been tough going at first, but the movement gradually picked up strength and the effort expanded into sit-ins against segregated public facilities. By mid-December, 471 blacks were in jail, and the town's black community had formed a loose coalition, the Albany Movement.

On the evening of December 15, 1961, King went to Albany with the intention of making a single, morale-boosting speech. When he entered the Shiloh Baptist Church, everyone arose spontaneously to shout and sing "Free-dom, Free-dom, Free-dom."

This marvelous spirit reminded King of Montgomery during the early days of the bus boycott.

In his speech, King talked about nonviolence and civil rights in words he had used hundreds of times to hundreds of audiences. Yet it did not matter to the people in the Shiloh Church, who responded with intense emotion. "Don't stop now," King cried. "Keep moving. Walk together, children. Don't get weary. There's a great camp meeting coming." When he concluded, the crowd sang verse after verse of the old spiritual that was becoming the anthem of the civil rights movement, "We Shall Overcome."

Elated by the response to his words and hearing that Albany's city government had refused to negotiate an end to local segregation, King decided to stay. Late on Saturday afternoon, December 16, he and Abernathy led 250 blacks on a march from the Shiloh Church to City Hall. When they reached the white section of town, Chief of Police Laurie Pritchett and 100 of his officers were waiting. The marchers refused to disband, so the police, using a minimum of force, arrested all of them for obstructing traffic.

From jail, King proclaimed, "I will not accept bond. If convicted I will refuse to pay the fine. I expect to spend Christmas in jail. I hope thousands will join me."

He was in jail only for the weekend. On Monday, he was told of a settlement between the city and local blacks. Accordingly, he allowed his bond to be posted.

Walking out of jail, King discovered he had been hoodwinked. The agreement, negotiated with just a few Albany blacks, was a sham, committing the city to nothing in the way of desegregation. "I'm sorry I was bailed out," he later admitted. "I didn't understand at the time what was happening. We thought that the victory had been won. When we got out, we discovered it was all a hoax."

The SNCC organizers who had started the whole campaign months before were embittered by King's blunder. Julian Bond, a SNCC leader, complained that King had been "losing for a long time. . . . More Negroes and more white Americans will become disillusioned with him, and find that he after all is only another preacher who can talk well."

Aware of this sort of criticism, King refused to give up on Albany. In February 1962, a court found him and Abernathy guilty of all charges stemming from the December march, and a few months later the judge sentenced them either to pay a $178 fine or spend 45 days in jail. Refusing the easy way out, both men chose imprisonment and the chance to draw attention to the injustice of their arrests.

Once more, they were not in jail for long. Albany's mayor, preferring not to have two martyrs in his jail, secretly ordered their release. King wanted to stay behind bars and protested the "subtle and conniving tactics" used to get him out. Abernathy joked, "I've been thrown out of lots of places in my day, but never before have I been thrown out of a jail."

Outmaneuvered again, King vowed to fight back. He summoned his SCLC staff to Albany and pledged a massive, nonviolent campaign to desegregate the city. He informed a cheering rally that they would "fill up the jails" and "turn Albany upside down." For the time being, he had the backing of thousands of the city's blacks, and waves of demonstrators picketed and sat in at segregated restaurants, stores, and public buildings.

Chief Pritchett took it all in stride. Unlike other southern police, he treated blacks respectfully. He bowed his head when the demonstrators prayed, then politely asked them to disperse. "He about stopped our movement," recalled Walter Fauntroy, a SCLC staffer, "because he was so kind."

King with his wife, Coretta, and their children (from left to right) Martin, Dexter, and Yolanda. A fourth child, Bernice, was born in 1963.

Nothing went right. A federal district judge issued an injunction against all forms of protest in Albany, and King obeyed the injunction and halted the demonstrations. This enraged the young SNCC members, who denounced King for timidity. Another court eventually lifted the injunction, but King's caution had cost him valuable support. Then, when he was out of town, a march broke up in disorder, with blacks hurling rocks and bottles at police. "You see them nonviolent rocks?" Pritchett called to reporters.

Still, King pressed on. In late July, he and Abernathy led another march to City Hall and deliberately got themselves arrested. Thrown into the same cell they had occupied before, King read, did some writing, and with Abernathy sang and listened to the radio. After a week, Coretta came for a visit. She brought along Yoki, three-year-old Marty, and Dexter, a baby born in January. (A fourth child, Bernice, was born in March of the following year.) Pritchett allowed their reunion to take place in a corridor so the children did not have to see their father in a cell.

Unfortunately, King's time in the city jail did nothing for the Albany Movement. When the city released him once more, the protest was in a shambles. Bitter disagreements among the city's blacks ruined the prospect of effective mass demonstrations. In late August, they were suspended, and King returned to Atlanta, with Pritchett boasting, "Albany is just as segregated as ever."

He was right. "Our protest was so vague that we got nothing, and the people were left very depressed and in despair," King lamented. The most he would ever claim for Albany was that "the Negro people there straightened up their bent backs; you can't ride a man's back unless it's bent."

King and the SCLC faced facts after their failure in Albany. Since Montgomery, he had been hoping

to convert his enemies. But in seven years, the strategy had not worked once. Southern whites were, by and large, as hostile to blacks as they had ever been.

If whites could not be converted, King decided, then whites would have to be displayed at their ugliest. That was what worked. The savage beatings handed out to the Freedom Riders had prompted the swift intervention of the federal government; but in Albany, where Pritchett had calmly maintained order, the Kennedy administration had kept its distance. Such a thing could not be allowed to happen again.

King with aide Ralph Abernathy (right) in July 1962, speaking to black youths about nonviolence and civil rights. "The old law of an eye for an eye leaves everybody blind," King was known to tell his listeners.

7

"I HAVE
A DREAM
TODAY!"

THERE WAS ONE place where civil rights would never be killed with kindness. Most every black knew that the meanest city in the South, with perhaps the meanest police in the country, was Birmingham, Alabama. Birmingham was Bull Connor's town. Commissioner of Public Safety T. Eugene "Bull" Connor had for years used fear and force to keep this city of 350,000 people (140,000 of whom were black) rigidly segregated. If the SCLC wished to confront a fortress of white supremacy, Birmingham was the ultimate test.

In late 1962 and early 1963, King and his colleagues decided they wanted such a confrontation. Wyatt T. Walker recalled selecting Birmingham "with the attitude we may not win it, we may lose everything. But we knew that as Birmingham went, so would go the South. And we felt that if we could crack that city, then we could crack any city."

The showdown began on April 3, 1963, when King issued a "Birmingham Manifesto" demanding that public facilities be desegregated and that blacks be hired by local merchants. That same day, 65 blacks

King addresses a crowd of nearly 250,000 civil rights marchers gathered at the Lincoln Memorial in the nation's capital on August 27, 1963. The huge, day-long demonstration concluded as the country's foremost civil rights leader told the audience, "I still have a dream. It is a dream deeply rooted in the American dream."

A member of the Student Nonviolent Coordinating Committee (SNCC), a student movement for nonviolent protest, teaches new recruits the art of civil disobedience. In these training sessions, SNCC members sought to show how to protect oneself during a demonstration in addition to controlling one's temper.

sat in at several downtown department stores. Connor's police arrested and jailed 20 of them.

Each evening, King spoke at a mass meeting in one of the city's black churches, recruiting volunteers to march, to sit in, and to be arrested the next day. "I got on my marching shoes!" he cried one night. "I woke up this morning with my mind stayed on freedom! I ain't going to let nobody turn me around! If the road to freedom leads through the jailhouse, then, turnkey, swing wide the gates!" And every night, scores of people would conquer their uncertainty, rise from their seats, and come forward, offering to enlist in the "nonviolent army."

They were divided into small groups, where SCLC staffers instructed them in the methods of nonviolent protest. Then they were told the target of the following day's protest, usually a store or lunchroom. When they were arrested, the SCLC would bail out the demonstrators and send them back into the streets for further protest. By the end of the first week, 300 blacks had gone to jail.

That was not enough. To his dismay, King discovered tremendous resistance to mass demonstrations from many influential Birmingham blacks, and, as a result, recruiting new demonstrators was difficult. Furthermore, Bull Connor had not lived up to his horrible reputation. During the first week of protest, the police had been restrained when making arrests. The city government had also obtained an injunction from a state court forbidding further demonstrations.

King was at a crossroads. If he obeyed an injunction, as he had in Albany, the movement might be stopped dead in its tracks. But if he led a march and went to jail, he would be unavailable to raise funds, and, at that moment, the SCLC had run out of bail money. In meetings at the Gaston Motel, his Birmingham headquarters, King listened to his colleagues argue back and forth. When he had heard enough, he went off to another room and prayed. Half an hour later, he returned to the group, in a change of clothes. Gone was the business suit. In its place was a pair of denim overalls. "The path is clear to me," he said, "I've got to march. I've got so many people depending on me. I've got to march."

In the early afternoon of April 12, 1963—Good Friday—King and Abernathy headed a column of 50 marchers to City Hall. The police intercepted them, made their arrests, and piled King and the others into paddy wagons. At the Birmingham jail, he faced "the longest, most frustrating and bewildering hours I have lived." The jailers—"unfriendly and unbelievably abusive in their language," he said—threw him into solitary confinement, in a cell without a mattress, pillow, or blanket. For a full day, he was held incommunicado—no visitors, no phone calls.

T. Eugene "Bull" Connor (second from right), the police commissioner of Birmingham, Alabama, leads his officers in a mass arrest of civil rights demonstrators in the spring of 1963. Connor's violent methods for keeping peace shocked the entire nation and prompted King to declare, "The eyes of the world are on Birmingham."

On Easter Sunday, at home in Atlanta, a very worried Coretta dialed the telephone number of the White House in Washington. She had been persuaded that a call to the president was the best way to draw attention to the deplorable condition of her husband's confinement. The president was away. But 45 minutes later, Robert Kennedy returned her call. "Bull Connor is very hard to deal with. . . . But I promise you I will look into the situation," the attorney general said. The next afternoon, the president himself called. Kennedy stressed that King was safe, and, he went on, "I have just talked to Birmingham, and your husband will be calling you shortly."

In Birmingham, suddenly polite guards entered King's cell and told him he could call home. On the telephone, he assured Coretta he was "pretty good"

King and the Reverend Ralph Abernathy lead a column of marchers through the streets of Birmingham, Alabama, on April 12, 1963, in a protest against racial segregation. Anticipating that they would be arrested by the police for heading the demonstration, both men had put on denims in preparation for being sent to jail.

and talked for a moment to Yoki and Marty. He then asked Coretta, "Who did you say called you?"

"Kennedy, the president," she replied.

"Did he call you direct?"

"Yes, and he told me you were going to call in a few minutes—"

"Is that known?"

The SCLC made sure it got known, and, before long, everyone was aware that the president had his eye on Birmingham, Alabama.

The president's display of concern caused the police to ease the conditions of King's confinement, and the 34-year-old civil rights leader put his time to good use. Earlier in the year, eight Birmingham clergymen, all of them white, had issued "An Appeal for Law and Order and Common Sense." It urged blacks to refrain from demonstrations. If you must, they advised blacks, seek change in the courts, not in the streets. In his lonely cell, writing first on the margins of a newspaper and then on yellow legal pads provided by his lawyers, King composed a reply to the ministers.

King's letter from the Birmingham jail chastised southern whites for not obeying the Supreme Court's decision of 1954 that declared segregated schools unconstitutional but defended blacks who broke the laws upholding segregation: "One may well ask, 'How can you advocate breaking some laws and obeying others?' The answer lies in the fact that there are two types of laws: just and unjust. I would be the first to advocate obeying just laws. One has not only a legal but a moral responsibility to obey just laws. Conversely, one has a moral responsibility to disobey unjust laws."

The days of segregation were numbered, King wrote. "Oppressed people cannot remain oppressed forever. The urge for freedom will eventually come. This is what happened to the American Negro.

Something within has reminded him of his birthright of freedom; something without has reminded him that he can gain it."

King's "Letter from Birmingham Jail," 6,400 words long, was published as a pamphlet and as a magazine article and soon had a circulation of nearly a million copies.

On April 20, after 8 days in jail, King and Abernathy posted $300 cash bonds and rejoined their SCLC associates at the Gaston Motel. There, pessimism hung in the air. The movement was falling to pieces. Too few people were volunteering to be arrested. Far from filling the jails, the demonstrations had nearly ceased. "We needed more troops," Wyatt T. Walker recalled. "We had run out of troops. We had scraped the bottom of the barrel of adults who would go. We needed something new."

Reluctantly, King decided to use children as demonstrators. All along, Birmingham's black high school and grade school students had been cheering on the protests and clamoring to become involved, but throughout April the SCLC had turned them down. But now, needing to keep the protest alive, King gave his approval to their participation, saying the children would gain "a sense of their own stake in freedom and justice."

On May 2, more than a thousand youngsters marched. They ranged in age from 6 to 16. The sight of what he called so many "little niggers" infuriated Bull Connor, and he ordered his police to arrest them. The next day, an even larger number marched, and this time Connor ordered his men not only to arrest but to repulse the demonstrators. When the marchers reached Kelly Ingram Park, they met a wall of Birmingham police, scores of firemen with high-pressure water hoses, and, on the leashes of handlers, barking, snarling German shepherd attack dogs. On the fringes of the park, a small crowd of black onlookers shouted abuse at the police and firemen.

Confined to an Alabama jail cell for eight days in April 1963, King composed one of his most passionate arguments for nonviolent resistance, "Letter from Birmingham Jail." "Any law that degrades human personality is unjust," he wrote in the essay. "All segregation statutes are unjust because segregation distorts the soul and damages the personality."

When rocks and bottles came flying from the crowd, Connor turned his forces loose. "I want to see the dogs work," he shouted. "Look at those niggers run!" The firemen switched on their hoses, and blasts of water slammed into the demonstrators, smashing them to the ground, ripping off their clothing, knocking them senseless. The dogs grabbed, clawed, and bit. Drenched and bleeding, the marchers broke ranks and fled.

Through it all, a large contingent of reporters and photographers did their jobs. On the evening television news broadcasts and in the next morning's newspapers, the American public saw and read how the police and fire departments of Birmingham, Alabama, had attacked children. The savage face of southern racism was being revealed.

In Washington, President Kennedy told some visitors that the pictures coming from Birmingham had made him "sick." Robert Kennedy was similarly affected and dispatched Burke Marshall, an assistant attorney general, to Birmingham. Marshall's charge was somehow to get negotiations going between blacks and whites. When he arrived, he found both sides suspicious. The whites refused to deal with King. "They wouldn't talk to anybody that *would* talk with him," Marshall remembered. King, too, wondered about Marshall's intentions. Did the Kennedys merely want the demonstrations stopped, or were they truly interested in a desegregated Birmingham?

Marshall convinced King that desegregation was the administration's goal, and the minister gave him his blessing. The city's white business establishment also came around. They preferred, even cherished, segregation, but violence in the streets was ruining their businesses and demolishing Birmingham's reputation. At Marshall's urging, they sat down with a handful of local black leaders and started bargaining seriously.

Meanwhile, the demonstrations continued with a seemingly inexhaustible supply of young marchers. Chanting "We want freedom! We want freedom!" day after day, they faced Connor's police, fire hoses, and dogs. By May 6, more than 3,000 blacks, most of them young, were in jail. "This is the first time in the history of our struggle that we have been literally able to fill the jails," King proclaimed.

On the afternoon of Tuesday, May 7, Birmingham approached utter chaos. Hundreds of demonstrators divided into small groups, tied up downtown traffic, and staged sit-ins at department stores. Once

more, Connor opened up with the fire hoses. The young marchers, schooled by the SCLC, stayed non-violent. But that afternoon, black bystanders threw rocks at the police, and it seemed, sooner or later, a riot was going to occur.

Fortunately, the white businessmen in town were fed up with Bull Connor and the relentless turmoil. On Friday, May 10, after several days of marathon bargaining sessions, they reached agreement with the black representatives. Their accord realized King's Birmingham Manifesto. Within months, lunch counters, rest rooms, fitting rooms, and drinking fountains in the downtown stores would be desegregated. Also, blacks would be hired for sales positions they had never before been allowed to hold.

King addresses a group of schoolchildren in Birmingham, Alabama. To increase the number of civil rights demonstrators and incite segregationist brutality, he asked the city's black youths to take part in the protest marches.

Schoolchildren in Birmingham, Alabama, are taken into custody by the police after participating in a civil rights demonstration. Southern Christian Leadership Conference (SCLC) officials James Bevel, Wyatt T. Walker, and Andrew Young directed the movements of the young troops.

The diehard segregationists did their best to sabotage the settlement. On Saturday evening, May 11, night-riding whites, most likely members of the Ku Klux Klan, firebombed the home of King's brother, A. D., a Birmingham preacher who had taken an active part in the demonstrations. Luckily, A. D. and his family escaped unhurt.

Minutes later, a second bomb exploded outside room 30 of the Gaston Motel, King's headquarters. King had returned to Atlanta for the weekend. Nevertheless, the bombings triggered a riot. Enraged blacks streamed into the streets yelling, "Let the whole city burn!" A car was overturned and set ablaze. Police were attacked. Bricks flew through store windows.

King raced back to Birmingham and did what he could to ease the wrath in the black neighborhoods. He toured bars and pool halls to plead for nonviolence, explaining to the denizens that "Bull Connor is happy when we use force." In his efforts to preserve the peace, King had the public support of the Kennedy administration.

The day after the riot, the president appeared on national television and praised the accord between the city's blacks and whites. The federal government, he warned, would "not permit it to be sabotaged by a few extremists on either side who think they can defy both the law and the wishes of responsible citizens by inciting or inviting violence." He backed up his words by dispatching federal troops to the Birmingham area. Facing such stern pressure from Washington, a new city government began implementing the planned desegregation.

Starting on May 2, 1963, police in Birmingham, Alabama, ordered their dogs to attack crowds of civil rights demonstrators. In addition, fire fighters employed high-pressure water hoses to repel the protesters.

King's brother, A. D., calls for calm following the bombing of his Birmingham, Alabama, home by white terrorists on the night of May 11, 1963. That same evening, a second bomb was detonated by Ku Klux Klan activists outside the motel room that served as King's Birmingham headquarters.

The message of black determination had reached the White House. On civil rights, recalled an assistant to the president, Kennedy always wanted to stay "one step ahead of the evolving pressures, never to be caught dead in the pressures, never to be caught dead in the water, always to have something new." After Birmingham, that "something new" meant requesting from Congress comprehensive civil rights legislation even though it was politically treacherous. The president had come to understand that black Americans would accept from him nothing less.

On June 11, 1963, the president delivered a nationally televised address that outlined his proposal for legislation barring segregation in public accommodations and schools. He asked whites to consider the plight of the American black: "Who among us would be content to have the color of his skin changed and stand in his place? Who among us would then be content with the counsels of patience and delay?" The time had come "for this nation to fulfill its promise" of freedom for all.

The president's strong, memorable words elated King. "He was really great," he enthused to a friend. But tragedy tarnished the day. Hours after Kennedy spoke, Medgar Evers, an NAACP leader, was shot dead in front of his house in Jackson, Mississippi. "This reveals that we still have a long, long way to go in this nation before we achieve the ideals of decency and brotherhood," King said sadly.

Birmingham, the rising tide of black activism, Kennedy's civil rights bill, and Evers's assassination gave a sense of urgency to a plan that had been in the works since early in the year—a plan for a march on Washington. It grew out of A. Philip Randolph's old vision of a massive, orderly, dignified parade in favor of civil rights through the streets of the national capital. Randolph's march, proposed for 1941, had never come off. There had been King's Prayer Pilgrimage in 1957, but for 1963 a much larger demonstration was envisioned, one that would bring the civil rights movement to the front and center of the public's attention.

Once more, Randolph, now 74, took a leading role. But it was King's friend Bayard Rustin who did the hard organizing. He enlarged the purpose of the march so that it embraced both economic opportunity and civil rights—Jobs and Freedom, the marchers' placards would read—and he cajoled virtually every civil rights leader and organization into participating.

On August 28, 1963, they marched. Nearly 250,000 people—black and white, farmers and machinists, northerners and southerners, a great cross section of the civil rights movement—proceeded from the Washington Monument to the Lincoln Memorial. In the symbolic shadow of Abraham Lincoln, speaker after speaker trooped to the rostrum. By three in the afternoon, the summer sun and the listless speeches had exacted a toll. The crowd was bored, restless. Then the magnificent gospel singer Mahalia Jackson sang the spiritual "I've Been 'Buked and I've Been Scorned," and the small talk and milling about stopped.

The white-haired, ramrod-straight Randolph introduced "the moral leader of the nation," and a quarter million voices hailed Martin Luther King, Jr., the last speaker of the day. "I started out reading the speech," he said later, when "just all of a sudden— the audience was wonderful that day—and all of a sudden this thing came to me that I have used—I'd used it many times before, that thing about 'I have a dream'—and I just felt I wanted to use it here."

To an assembly that stretched as far as he could see, and to a television audience that extended around the world, King said:

> I have a dream that one day on the red hills of Georgia, sons of former slaves and sons of former slave-owners will be able to sit down together at the table of brotherhood. . . .
> I have a dream my four little children will one day live in a nation where they will not be judged by the color of their skin but by the content of their character. I have a dream today!

He dreamed of an Alabama where "little black boys and black girls will be able to join hands with little white boys and white girls as sisters and brothers."

> I have a dream that one day every valley shall be exalted, every hill and mountain shall be made low, the rough places made plain, and the crooked places made straight and the glory of the Lord will be revealed and all flesh shall see it together.

He dreamed of freedom ringing from every mountaintop, even "from every hill and molehill of Mississippi."

And when we allow freedom to ring, when we let it ring from every village and hamlet, from every state and city, we will be able to speed up that day when all of God's children—black men and white men, Jews and Gentiles, Catholics and Protestants—will be able to join hands and to sing in the words of the old Negro spiritual, "Free at last, free at last; thank God Almighty, we are free at last."

The day of King's dream was a long way from being realized.

"Let the nation and the world know the meaning of our numbers," protest organizer A. Philip Randolph said in his opening speech at the March for Jobs and Freedom held in the nation's capital on August 28, 1963. Nearly a quarter million demonstrators participated in what King called an attempt "to arouse the conscience of the nation over the economic plight of the Negro."

Tragedy frequently followed triumph during the civil rights movement. Almost two weeks after the march on Washington, the Sixteenth Street Baptist Church in Birmingham, Alabama, was bombed (above) by white terrorists just as services were about to begin. Funeral services were held a few days later (opposite page) for the four young women who were killed in the blast.

SUNDAY, SEPTEMBER 15, 1963, was a hot, late-summer day in Birmingham, and the windows of the Sixteenth Street Baptist Church were open to catch what little breeze there was. Before 10 o'clock in the morning, a congregation of 400 black worshipers was moving down the aisles into the pews, chatting with the ushers and with one another. Toward the back of the church, four young girls talked and giggled as they slipped on their choir robes.

Just then, a package of dynamite was tossed through a window. One woman remembered hearing a sound like a great clap of thunder and then seeing an awful, blinding light. An explosion blasted a hole in the side of the church. Amid the rubble of broken furniture and shattered glass and in the stench of bluish smoke lay the lifeless bodies of Denise McNair, 11, and Cynthia Wesley, Carol Robertson, and Addie Mae Collins, all 14—the four girls who, a moment before, had been putting on their robes.

"My God, we're not even safe in church!" sobbed a woman fleeing the devastation. As word of the murderous assault spread, blacks poured into the streets, blindly striking back. The near riot only added to the tragedy; in the disturbances, two more young blacks were killed—one by police, the other by a gang of whites—and a half dozen were injured. King came to Birmingham that evening and walked through the ruined, bloodstained church, fighting to restrain his anger. "Not since the days of the Christians in the catacombs," he said, "has God's house, as a symbol, weathered such an attack as the Negro churches."

Nineteen sixty-three was a violent year. On November 22, King was spending the afternoon at home, half working, half watching television. Shortly before two, a program was interrupted by an appalling announcement. "Corrie," he shouted to his wife, "I just heard that Kennedy has been shot, maybe killed."

Coretta ran to him, and together they waited for a further bulletin. In a little while, there came the blunt news that President John F. Kennedy was dead, assassinated while riding in a motorcade through Dallas, Texas. After a long silence, King said, "I don't think I'm going to live to reach forty."

"Oh, don't say that, Martin," Coretta snapped.

"This is what is going to happen to me also. I keep telling you, this is a sick nation. And I don't think I can survive either." ✥

8

"WE ARE DEMANDING THE BALLOT"

P RESIDENT KENNEDY'S SUCCESSOR, Lyndon B. Johnson, entered the White House burdened with the reputation of being a masterful but devious political wheeler-dealer. For Johnson, someone once said, the shortest distance between two points was a tunnel. A southerner from the hill country of Texas, Johnson as a congressman and a senator had compiled a mixed record on civil rights. In the presidency, though, his doubts and equivocations vanished, and he used his considerable political skill to win congressional approval for Kennedy's civil rights bill. Less than two weeks after Kennedy's assassination, he invited King to Washington and convinced him that he was, King later said, "a man who is deeply committed to help us."

President Johnson was friendly, but across town there was a man who loathed King and everything for which he stood. He was J. Edgar Hoover, the director of the Federal Bureau of Investigation (FBI). Hoover was about the last person anyone would choose for an enemy. For 40 years, he had com-

President Lyndon B. Johnson (seated) signs the Civil Rights Act of 1964 on July 2 as King looks on. Later in the day, the president pointedly told King and other black leaders "that the rights Negroes possessed could now be secured by law, making demonstrations unnecessary and possibly even self-defeating."

211

manded the nation's premier law enforcement agency, and he wielded enormous power. During the long years of his leadership, the FBI had done great things by capturing killers, kidnappers, and spies. But, by the early 1960s, Hoover had outlived his usefulness. He had an increasingly paranoid obsession with communism and believed the Soviet Union's domestic agents were on the verge of overthrowing American freedom.

Hoover had no sympathy for civil rights and very little for blacks, so he and others at the FBI were almost automatically suspicious of King and his movement. FBI agents began keeping tabs on the minister in 1958. What bothered them most was his association with Stanley Levison, a New York lawyer who had helped launch the SCLC. For years, Levison had backed the activities of the American Communist party and, the FBI maintained, served on the party's secret national committee. King liked Levison and turned to him time after time for advice, particularly on matters of fund-raising.

King and fellow black leaders (from left to right) Roy Wilkins, executive director of the National Association for the Advancement of Colored People (NAACP), James Farmer, national director of the Congress for Racial Equality (CORE), and Whitney Young, executive director of the National Urban League, meet with President Lyndon B. Johnson at the White House on January 17, 1964, to discuss the new president's plans for a war on poverty. King supported Johnson's proposals, acknowledging the need "to bring the standards of the Negro up and bring him into the mainstream of life."

As far as is known, Levison never tried to push King into communism or communism into the SCLC. But Hoover refused to believe this. He preferred treating King as if he were a Communist.

In June 1963, President Kennedy told King how Hoover felt and advised him to avoid trouble by cutting his ties with Levison. King said he would think it over. When, ultimately, he did not abandon Levison, Hoover exploded and demanded that Attorney General Robert Kennedy approve the wiretapping of King's home and office. Kennedy, anxious to appease the director, gave him the go-ahead.

Hoover and the FBI got an earful by bugging not only King's Atlanta telephones but also his hotel rooms. The microphone surveillance did not uncover the slightest evidence of Communists infiltrating the civil rights movement, but it did provide the FBI with intimate knowledge of King's private affairs. The Bureau now had tape recordings of what it called "entertainment"—lively parties hosted by King.

During the spring and summer of 1964, as Hoover tried to spread dirt on King's reputation, Johnson worked to push the civil rights bill through Congress. On July 2, 1964, the president got the votes he needed, and Congress gave final approval to a measure that outlawed segregation in public accommodations, forbade unions and employers from practicing racial discrimination, and authorized withholding federal funds from institutions that continued to discriminate against blacks.

Three hours after the bill crossed its final congressional hurdle, Johnson signed it into law, using 72 pens to make a single inscription of his signature. He then passed out the pens as souvenirs. One of them went to King, who, along with other civil rights leaders and members of Congress, proudly watched the president sign the law that made segregation a federal crime.

J. Edgar Hoover, director of the Federal Bureau of Investigation (FBI), ordered constant surveillance of King's activities after the black leader complained that FBI agents had not fully investigated civil rights complaints in the South. In response to King's charge that no one had been arrested in 1963 for the murder of three civil rights workers in Philadelphia, Mississippi, or the bombing of the Sixteenth Street Baptist Church in Birmingham, Alabama, Hoover called King the nation's "most notorious liar."

That July day, in the East Room of the White House, King was the most famous black there, instantly recognized. At the end of 1963, *Time* magazine had acknowledged his stature, designating him its "Man of the Year." For a man who still lived in a rented house in Atlanta and drove a 1960 Ford with 70,000 miles on the odometer, awards and riches counted for little. He told Stanley Levison that the *Time* honor was nice, but with 200 other plaques and citations, "what's one more?"

There was, however, an award that meant a very great deal, and in October 1964, it was announced in Oslo, Norway, that King had won it: the Nobel Peace Prize. Bestowed by the Norwegian parliament on the individual who had done the most effective work in the interest of international peace, it is widely considered the highest honor in the world. At 35, King was the youngest Nobel recipient in history.

In December, he and Coretta led a large, lively entourage of family and friends to Norway for the award ceremony. Several days after his arrival, he traveled to Oslo University to accept the peace prize from King Olaf V of Norway. King delivered a brief, eloquent acceptance speech that called on the world to reject "revenge, aggression and retaliation."

"Only Martin's family and close staff members knew how depressed he was during the entire Nobel trip," Coretta recalled. J. Edgar Hoover and the FBI counted among his worries. Ironically, the award came at a time when the FBI was finally investigating and undermining the Ku Klux Klan's terrorist activities in the South.

Nevertheless, King's Nobel Peace Prize had sent Hoover into a fury. Privately, he raged that King should have gotten the "top alley cat" award, and to the press the FBI director branded him a "notorious liar . . . one of the lowest characters in the country." To prominent politicians, Hoover provided a collection of smears entitled "Martin Luther King, Jr.: His

Personal Conduct," while the Bureau fueled a whispering campaign that had King involved in financial, political, and sexual transgressions. By mid-1964, King knew the FBI had been eavesdropping on him, and he winced at the thought of what their tape recordings, if made public, might do to his reputation. Returning to Atlanta from Europe, he found out how low the FBI could sink.

In early January 1965, at the SCLC offices, Coretta opened a slim package containing a reel of tape and a letter. The tape, when played, revealed King's voice during a series of embarrassing private moments. The unsigned letter accused him of being a "dissolute, abnormal moral imbecile" and seemed to suggest he should commit suicide: "King, there is only one thing left for you to do. . . . You are done. There is but one way out for you. You better take it before your filthy, abnormal fraudulent self is bared to the nation."

King accepts the 1964 Nobel Peace Prize on December 10 in Oslo, Norway. He considered the award the "foremost of earthly honors" and accepted it on behalf of the entire civil rights movement.

King leaves the office of FBI di-rector J. Edgar Hoover in late 1964. One month later, the FBI threatened to discredit King by publicly releasing a tape recording that captured the black leader during a series of personal—and highly embarrassing—incidents.

When Coretta showed her husband the package, he immediately guessed it was the work of the FBI. "They are out to break me," he dejectedly told a friend. "They are out to get me, harass me, break my spirit." He was absolutely correct. The package was the work of William C. Sullivan, Hoover's right-hand man, and the tape was put together from the Bureau's surveillance of King's hotel rooms. Although distraught, King would not let himself be blackmailed. He bravely played the recording for Coretta and his SCLC associates, not denying that the voice on the tape was his.

The FBI had overplayed its hand with the crude blackmail attempt, but Hoover lost none of his interest in King. The surveillance, bugging, and wiretaps continued. Eventually, King and his SCLC friends were able to joke about how "all life is a recording studio for us," and they laughingly enrolled new members in "the FBI Golden Record Club." But humor provided small comfort from the calculated cruelty of J. Edgar Hoover.

Although the trouble with Hoover's FBI was unnerving, it did not dissuade King from proceeding with the SCLC's most ambitious campaign since Birmingham: a crusade for voting rights. The Civil Rights Act of 1964 dealt a swift, powerful blow to southern segregation, and the schools, theaters, restaurants, and hotels of Dixie finally opened their doors to blacks. But the measure did not effectively eliminate discrimination at the polling place. Across the Deep South, white officials used every trick in the book to intimidate blacks from exercising the franchise. In some places, the Klan and local police used force and terror against blacks who wanted to vote. In others, a literacy test that required blacks to do such things as recite the preamble to the Constitution word for word proved effective.

By the mid-1960s, only 6 percent of voting-age blacks were registered in Mississippi, 19 percent in

Alabama, and 32 percent in Louisiana. The situation was worst in rural sections. In 2 Alabama counties where blacks comprised 80 percent of the population, not a single black was on the voting rolls.

For King, the answer was the intervention of the national government. Send federal officials south to register blacks, he said. When he suggested that to Johnson in a meeting at the White House in late 1964, the president agreed: "Martin, you're right about that. I'm going to do it eventually, but I can't get a voting rights bill through in this session of Congress." It was too soon after the Civil Rights Act, Johnson explained.

King, of course, had heard that sort of thing from presidents before, and, once more, he turned to direct action. For the campaign for voting rights, King and the SCLC selected Selma, Alabama, the seat of Dallas County, where of 15,000 blacks eligible to vote, only 383 had succeeded in registering.

If Bull Connor had drawn the civil rights movement to Birmingham, then Dallas County sheriff Jim Clark was the attraction in Selma. A hefty, blustering six-footer, Sheriff Clark swaggered about town in a garish uniform set off by a gold-braided cap and a hand-tooled leather belt that carried his gun, billy club, and, for difficult criminals, his cattle prod. He commanded a volunteer posse of 200 devoted followers and said the only thing wrong with his job was "all this nigger fuss here of late." It was nothing to worry about, though: "We always get along. You just have to know how to handle them."

For more than a year, Clark had been "handling" a SNCC voter registration drive in Dallas County. "We found out SNCC had been driven out of Selma," recalled Hosea Williams, a senior SCLC organizer. "Jim Clark even sent deputies into churches where people would be having worship service, to see whether they were serving God or whether they were talking civil rights."

Although the SNCC effort had been a bust, many of its members did not want help from King and the SCLC. Young SNCC members had nicknamed King "de Lawd" and resented the way his fame overshadowed their movement. Nevertheless, SNCC chairman John Lewis, a soft-spoken former divinity student who greatly admired King, agreed to cooperate with the SCLC in Selma.

The day after New Year's 1965, King came to Selma and addressed 700 enthusiastic followers at Brown Chapel Methodist Church in the heart of the black community. "We are going to start a march on the ballot boxes by the thousands," he proclaimed. "We must be willing to go to jail by the thousands. We are not asking, we are demanding the ballot."

A little more than 2 weeks later, on January 18, 1965, the Selma campaign began when King and John Lewis conducted a march of 400 blacks to the courthouse, where they hoped to register to vote. Sheriff Clark was on the courthouse steps, but, surprisingly, he seemed restrained, not at all the mad dog everyone expected. He merely directed the marchers into an alley behind the courthouse, where he left them alone. The march soon broke up.

King and his associates worried about Clark's peacefulness. If the sheriff and his deputies did not abuse and arrest disenfranchised blacks, the Selma exercise was next to pointless. Clark had to show his true colors soon, King decided, or the SCLC would transfer the voter registration drive to another Alabama county.

That was music to the ears of the more moderate whites in Selma. Led by the director of public safety, Wilson Baker, they had prevailed on Clark not to rough up the demonstrators. With King on the verge of leaving town, their plan appeared to be working.

But Jim Clark could stand the sight of marching blacks only so long. On Tuesday morning, when a column of unregistered blacks paraded to the court-house, the sheriff blew up. He ordered 60 marchers arrested and personally grabbed a local black businesswoman by the back of her collar and shoved her around. On Wednesday, he gave another demonstration one minute to break up. When nothing happened, he had everyone arrested. By the end of the day, 226 blacks were in jail and the SCLC had what it wanted. "Jim Clark is another Bull Connor," an organizer said. "We should put him on the staff." The strategy of the moderate whites was in ruins.

Over the next few weeks, crowds of blacks kept on marching to the courthouse. On occasion, a few made it inside and actually filed their names with voting registrars, but their registration papers were usually thrown out on some technicality. And on more days than not they had to confront Jim Clark. During a march led by King, the sheriff scuffled with Annie Lee Cooper, a stout 53-year-old matron. "I wish you would hit me, you scum," she screamed at Clark. He promptly did, swinging his billy club across her head with a whack heard across the street. Press photographers captured the incident with their cameras, and hundreds of newspapers carried the picture of an Alabama sheriff clubbing a black woman for the crime of wanting to vote.

By February 1, the time had come for King to go to jail. In the morning, at Brown Chapel, the movement's headquarters, he addressed hundreds of supporters and then directed a march of 260 to the courthouse. After only a few blocks, Director of Public Safety Baker arrested the entire group for violating Selma's parade ordinance.

King's arrest and the daily marches were beginning to have an impact. Bailed out after five days in custody, he flew to Washington, where he met with administration officials and, after some maneuvering, with the president. This time Johnson did not say

King leads a group of 260 civil rights demonstrators in prayer following their arrest for violating a city parade ordinance in Selma, Alabama, on February 1, 1965. Once in jail, King and his aide Ralph Abernathy (center) turned down a meal of ham steak and turnip greens, explaining that they always fasted during their first two days behind bars.

that the political timing was bad. Instead, he assured King that he would be sending voting rights legislation to Congress "very soon."

Meanwhile, Alabama was doing its best to sicken the nation. The day following King's conference with Johnson, Sheriff Clark forced 165 black students who had been demonstrating at the courthouse to go at a fast trot to a lockup 6 miles outside of Selma, his posse of deputies poking and shocking them with electric cattle prods as they jogged. After three miles, with the students dropping from exhaustion and some vomiting on the roadside, Clark permitted them to "escape."

A week later, in neighboring Perry County, an evening march sponsored by the SCLC ended in tragedy. After a contingent of lawmen broke up the march, a state trooper chased 26-year-old Jimmie Lee Jackson and his mother into a small restaurant. As young Jackson tried to protect his mother from the trooper's billy club, the officer shot him in the stomach. Gravely wounded, Jackson was taken to Selma's black hospital, where Colonel Al Lingo, head of the Alabama State Police, came to his bedside and charged him with assault and battery with intent to kill a law officer. A few days later, Jackson was dead; on March 3, King preached at his funeral.

After Jackson's funeral, the SCLC announced that on March 7 King and his followers would begin marching from Selma to Montgomery—a distance of 54 miles—where they would present their grievances about voting rights and police brutality to the governor of Alabama, George C. Wallace. The governor had no intention of letting them come. A onetime Golden Gloves boxing champion, he brought to politics the same cocky combativeness he had shown in the ring. Upon becoming governor in 1963, he had sworn, "Segregation now! Segregation tomorrow! Segregation forever!" and in the two years since, he had emerged as the country's foremost opponent of civil rights.

On March 6, Wallace banned the scheduled march, saying it would disrupt traffic on the highway. Furthermore, he ordered Al Lingo of the state police to stop the marchers "with whatever means are available" if they tried leaving Selma.

Late in the morning on Sunday, March 7, 600 blacks assembled at Brown Chapel, ready to defy Governor Wallace and march to Montgomery. King was not among them. He assumed the state troopers would arrest all the marchers before they got out of Selma, and he saw no reason to return to jail. Therefore, he remained in Atlanta while Hosea Williams of the SCLC and John Lewis of SNCC led the march from the Brown Chapel through the streets of Selma to the Edmund Pettus Bridge, over which Highway 80 crossed the Alabama River on its way to Montgomery.

At one end of the bridge, a squadron of blue-uniformed state troopers waited, Sheriff Clark's mounted posse on their flanks. After the marchers came onto the bridge, the voice of a trooper blasted through a bullhorn: "You have two minutes to turn around and go back to your church!" The marchers held their ground, some by kneeling on the pavement.

John Lewis, chairman of the Student Nonviolent Coordinating Committee (SNCC), is felled by the nightstick of an Alabama state trooper during an abbreviated civil rights march from Selma to Montgomery on March 7, 1965. The troopers' violent intervention just past the Edmund Pettus Bridge became known throughout the nation as "Bloody Sunday."

"Troopers advance!" came the command. With that, the police surged forward, their billy clubs flailing. As the first few blacks were clubbed down, loud cheers and rebel yells went up from a group of approving white bystanders. Into the marchers, now in desperate retreat, rode Clark's posse, their horses spurred to a gallop.

Moments later, an acrid cloud of smoke spread over the chaotic scene. "Tear gas!" shouted a marcher. Protected by gas masks, the troopers pressed ahead into the coughing, blinded throng. "It was like a battle zone: all those people choking in the gas, being hit and beaten," remembered Lewis, himself clubbed by a trooper.

Heeding Clark's command, "Get those goddamn niggers!" the mounted posse chased the defenseless demonstrators all the way back to the Brown Chapel. Nearly 80 marchers were treated for fractured skulls, broken ribs, head gashes, and a dozen other injuries at the local hospital.

In Atlanta, King was horrified by the events of what came to be known as "Bloody Sunday." Experiencing what he called "an agony of conscience" for not having been in Selma, he at once announced his intention of personally leading a second march to Montgomery on Tuesday, March 9, just two days away. To his fellow ministers and to civil rights supporters around the nation, he issued a public appeal: Come to Selma; join us Tuesday in a ministers' march to Montgomery. In impressive numbers, his allies heeded the call, dropped what they were doing, and flew to Selma.

On Tuesday, once again at the Brown Chapel, 1,500 marchers, those from Selma now joined by activists from far parts of the country, heard King describe the path ahead: "There may be beatings, jailings, and tear gas. But I would rather die on the highways of Alabama than make a butchery of my conscience." Two abreast, they began walking to the Edmund Pettus Bridge. But King had no intention of leading them across it.

The day before, a federal district judge had issued an injunction against King's march to Montgomery. It presented a major problem. King had never before defied a federal court order, but ministers, expecting to march, were pouring in from all over, and the SNCC people were urging him to ignore the judge. United States attorney general Nicholas Katzenbach, by telephone from Washington, begged him not to. "Dr. King, you promised you would not," Katzenbach said repeatedly. Tugged one way by SNCC and the ministers, another by the administration, King at last

On March 9, 1965, King was among 2,000 civil rights demonstrators in Alabama who attempted for the second time in 3 days to march from Selma to Montgomery. But the protest failed once again to reach Montgomery. At the Edmund Pettus Bridge, a blockade of state troopers, backed by a court order, barred the marchers from advancing any farther.

decided to march. "Mr. Attorney General," he said, "you have not been a black man in America for three hundred years."

Alarmed by the prospect of another bloodbath, President Johnson dispatched Le Roy Collins, a former governor of Florida, to Selma as his personal emissary. He saw King and informed him the president did not want a march. Collins asked if he would consider leading the marchers to the Edmund Pettus Bridge, then return to town, provided the troopers did not interfere. Opening the door to compromise, King said he was not sure "what I can get my people to do, but if you will get Sheriff Clark and Lingo to accept something like that, I will try."

Sensing a deal, Collins located Clark and Lingo lounging about a local Pontiac dealership. They had gotten orders from Governor Wallace to avoid a repeat of Sunday's violence, and they accepted Collins's offer. "Both sides kept their word to the letter," Collins recalled. The troopers backed off, and King's people marched onto the bridge, knelt in prayer, sang "We Shall Overcome," then turned around and walked back to the Brown Chapel.

The turnaround may have preserved the peace, but it enraged SNCC. Kept in the dark about King's dealings with Collins, the SNCC workers had fully expected to battle through the troopers and attempt a march to Montgomery. The failure to do so ignited their anger. King was a coward, a traitor to the movement, some said. Back at the Brown Chapel, King only made matters worse by not leveling with the SNCC leaders about the compromise. There was no quelling their anger. With the exception of John Lewis, SNCC withdrew from the Selma campaign, thereby causing a serious rupture in the civil rights movement that would never be healed.

The night following the turnaround march, James J. Reeb, a white Unitarian minister from Boston, and two friends who had also heeded King's call to Selma ate dinner at a soul food restaurant. Afterward, walking back to the Brown Chapel, they heard someone call, "Hey, you niggers!" Before they could know what was happening, four young whites in windbreakers were on top of them, punching and clubbing. One smashed a two-by-four onto Reeb's head, crushing his skull. The minister fell into a coma, and two days later he died.

Reeb's death and "Bloody Sunday" speeded up the Johnson administration's plans for voting rights legislation. On the evening of March 15, 1965, President Johnson, on prime-time television, appeared before Congress to plead for a powerful voting rights law. Johnson, not normally a rousing speaker, delivered a spellbinding speech. "This time, on this issue, there must be no delay, no hesitation, and no compromise with our purpose," he said. Blacks were seeking their entitlement, "the full blessings of American life," and "their cause must be our cause, too." Every person, he concluded, must work to "overcome the crippling legacy of bigotry and injustice. And . . . we shall . . . overcome."

In Selma, King and his SCLC friends watched the president stand before Congress and the nation and join their ranks. In all their years of struggle, they had never seen King cry. But when Johnson said, "We shall overcome," tears flooded his eyes and rolled down his face.

It was left for King to complete what had twice been started: the march to Montgomery. President Johnson guaranteed the necessary security by taking control of the Alabama National Guard from Wallace and ordering the guard and U.S. marshals to protect the march along Highway 80. On March 21, a bright Sunday, King and 3,200 supporters left Selma by crossing the now placid Edmund Pettus Bridge. By arrangement, most of them peeled away outside town, leaving 300 freedom marchers to make the entire four-day trek to Montgomery.

Along the way, whites came to the roadside to wave Confederate flags and to shout, "Nigger King, go home!" but the National Guard prevented them from doing anything more. The band of 300 slogged through rain and mud, inspiring hope among the long-suffering blacks of central Alabama. "What do you want?" a marcher would shout. "Freedom!" the blacks along the highway would reply.

King was with the march most of the way, leaving it for a day, then rejoining it near the end. In Montgomery, nearly 25,000 people, many of whom had traveled thousands of miles to be there, followed King up Dexter Avenue and past his old church to the gleaming white state capitol building. "This is the day! This is the day!" cried a black woman as she marched.

The throng pressed in about the capitol, where 104 years earlier Jefferson Davis had assumed the presidency of the Confederacy and where George

"We are on the move now to the land of freedom," King said in leading a third protest march from Selma to Montgomery on March 21, 1965. An executive order by President Lyndon B. Johnson called for nearly 2,000 National Guardsmen to provide security for the demonstrators during the 4-day trek.

Wallace now preached segregation. But the day of white supremacy was nearly done. In a few months, Congress would approve Johnson's voting rights bill, and in a few years, black voters would change the face of southern politics. King acknowledged their great progress:

I know you are asking today, "How long will it take?" I come to say to you this afternoon, however difficult the moment, however frustrating the hour, it will not be long, because truth pressed to the earth will rise again.

How long? Not long, because no lie can live forever.

How long? Not long, because you will reap what you sow.

How long? Not long, because the arm of the moral universe is long but it bends toward justice.

How long? Not long, because mine eyes have seen the glory of the coming of the Lord. . . .

9

"WE DON'T WANT YOU HERE"

On AUGUST 6, 1965, in the President's Room of the Capitol, Lyndon B. Johnson signed into law the forceful, uncompromising Voting Rights Act. "Today is a triumph for freedom as huge as any victory that's ever been won on any battlefield," said the president. The Voting Rights Act was the deed that ratified the civil rights movement of Martin Luther King. The southern system of segregation and legal discrimination was a dead letter.

Less than a week later, Watts, the black ghetto of Los Angeles, erupted into one of the most frightening race riots in American history. Arsonists and snipers turned southeast Los Angeles into a combat zone. Mobs roamed the neighborhood, smashing windows, looting merchandise, screaming, "Burn, baby, burn," the slogan of a local disk jockey. Eventually, 14,000 National Guardsmen entered Watts, rumbling through the streets in tanks and armored cars, trying to restore order. When the sickening violence ended, death and ruin were everywhere. The riot took

After civil rights activist James Meredith was shot on June 6, 1966, during a one-man "walk against fear" to protest white violence in Mississippi, King (front row, center) and other black leaders took over the march. Despite the urging of some of his associates to respond with black militancy, King maintained: "I'm not going to use violence, no matter who says it."

229

34 lives, injured more than 1,000 people, resulted in 4,000 arrests, damaged or destroyed 977 buildings, and saw $35 million worth of property go up in smoke.

King got the news about Watts while on his way to Puerto Rico for a few days' rest. The more he heard about the riot, the less he felt like a vacation. Changing his plans, he flew to Los Angeles and toured the still-smoldering ghetto. The devastation of the area shocked him, and the attitude of many residents was profoundly depressing. Some pretended not to know who he was. Others heckled him when he spoke. The prophet of nonviolence, they were saying, had nothing to offer them. A group of youngsters told him, "We won."

"How can you say you won," King asked, "when 34 Negroes are dead, your community is destroyed, and whites are using the riots as an excuse for inaction?"

"We won because we made them pay attention to us," replied a young man.

In a way, the young man was right. The Watts riot, in its horror, forced attention on the northern ghettos and coincided with a shift in the civil rights movement from South to North. Half the blacks in the United States lived outside the South, and their problems were not with laws that kept them out of lunch counters or off the voting rolls. They had long had legal equality, but all too often their life was filled with unemployment, poverty, inferior housing, broken homes, crime, and disease.

When King looked north, he became outraged by "the Negro's repellent slum life," and he decided to employ the nonviolent direct action that had succeeded in the South to a northern city. In early 1966, King and the SCLC came to Chicago. It was the logical place. With a black population greater than 1 million, the nation's second-largest city practiced every typical northern form of racial discrimination.

King and his wife, Coretta, fix up their apartment in one of Chicago's poorest black ghettos during the 1966 campaign to win civil rights for urban blacks. "If we can break the system in Chicago, it can be broken anywhere in the country," King argued at the start of what became known as the Chicago Freedom Movement.

Chicago's political, financial, and real estate interests informally, but effectively, kept the black population segregated in the ghettos on the south and west sides of town. Segregated housing led to all-black schools where the quality of education was atrocious. Living in a ghetto, going to miserable schools, most blacks had two strikes against them when it came to finding a job—and poverty, unemployment, and welfare were the sad facts of life.

King's target was ghetto housing. "Our primary objective," he said, "will be to bring about the unconditional surrender of forces dedicated to the creation and maintenance of slums and ultimately to make slums a moral and financial liability upon the whole community."

"You can't really get close to the poor without living and being there with them," King said. So instead of staying in a comfortable hotel, in late January 1966 he rented an apartment for $90 a month in the part of the West Side known as Lawndale but more often called "Slumdale." For the next nine months, on and off, he commuted between Atlanta and this miserable Chicago apartment, with flaking plaster, broken-down appliances, and cramped rooms.

The Chicago movement began slowly. King toured the ghetto, met with community leaders, and denounced the tenement landlords. But, in truth, he had no idea how to eliminate slums, nor did the SCLC have a coherent plan for Chicago. Andrew Young conceded, "We haven't gotten things under control. The strategy hasn't emerged yet, but we know what we are dealing with and eventually we'll come up with answers."

What they were dealing with was the power of Richard J. Daley, mayor of Chicago, chairman of the Cook County Democratic Organization, and known far and wide as "the last of the big city bosses." A pudgy, narrow-shouldered man, given to purple-faced rages and slips of the tongue—"Racism doesn't have a Chinaman's chance in Chicago," he once said— Daley was nevertheless as shrewd a politician as there was in America. He bossed Chicago's fabled political machine, and, far from excluding blacks from its workings, he encouraged their participation. Chicago blacks loyally trooped to the polls every election day to give Daley and the Democratic ticket impossibly large majorities. In return, they received city jobs and city favors from the mayor, as did the Irish, Italians, Poles, Czechs, Jews, and every other ethnic group that backed the machine.

What Daley could not do for blacks was assist them out of their ghettos into the more pleasant, affordable homes in all-white neighborhoods. The bedrock of Daley's machine was white. If whites saw blacks moving in next door, they would surely blame it on the mayor, and, just as surely, his political goose would be cooked.

Through the spring of 1966, Daley kept one step ahead of King. He admitted things in the slums were bad but said Chicago had plans to improve conditions and the city did not need "outsiders telling us what to do." With charts, graphs, and position papers, the mayor outlined his commitment to slum clearance,

public housing, and antipoverty programs. To Lawndale, King's Chicago neighborhood, he sent an army
of building inspectors who wrote up violations of the
city code and forced landlords to make repairs. In
face-to-face meetings, Daley respectfully deferred to
King, saying he shared his goals and was doing all he
could to realize them.

As the Chicago movement fizzled, King was back
in the South. On June 6, 1966, James Meredith, the
first black admitted to the University of Mississippi,
was shot and wounded by a white assailant while on
a one-man voter registration march across Mississippi.
King at once decided to carry on for the fallen Meredith. For the next three weeks, the "James Meredith
March Against Fear" traveled 200 miles under the
scorching sun down U.S. Highway 51 from Memphis,
Tennessee, to Jackson, Mississippi.

It was neither a happy nor successful demonstration. Whites along the way bullied, taunted, and
abused the marchers. In Philadelphia, Mississippi—
strong Klan country—a white mob interrupted King's
speech by shouting and tossing cherry bombs. Afterward, the marchers' camp was strafed with rifle fire.
Miraculously, no one was hurt. Long years in the
South had prepared King to anticipate violence from
whites, but the great disappointment of the Meredith
march was division among blacks.

*Civil rights activist James Mere-
dith falls to the ground after being
shot during his one-man "walk
against fear." According to King,
the attack on Meredith clearly
demonstrated that "a reign of terror still exists in the South."*

King had hoped the march would recapture the black unity of earlier days, and in Memphis he planned the demonstration with Floyd McKissick, the national director of CORE, and Stokely Carmichael, the new chairman of SNCC. But they and their organizations were increasingly militant, and it did not take long on the highway to discover not everyone liked marching at King's pace. One day, he overheard some SNCC and CORE people talking. "I'm not for that nonviolence stuff anymore," said one. "If one of these damn Mississippi crackers touches me, I'm gonna knock the hell out of him." King appreciated the whites who joined the march, but Carmichael and the SNCC wanted an all-black affair. "We don't need any more white phonies and liberals invading our movement," he said.

As the march wound its way deeper into Mississippi, Carmichael got more militant. In Greenwood, after spending a brief time in jail, he told a crowd, "I ain't going to jail no more. Every courthouse in Mississippi ought to be burned down to get rid of the dirt." Then, over and over, he shouted, "We want black power," and each time the crowd cried back, "Black Power. Black Power."

King thought the phrase "unfortunate." It sounded too much like black supremacy or black separatism, both of which he totally opposed. It also drove a wedge into the march. At rallies, the SNCC and CORE people chanted, "Black Power," while the SCLC marchers called back, "Freedom now," their longtime cry. Finally, as the march neared Jackson, King had it out with Carmichael and SNCC. "I pleaded with the group to abandon the Black Power slogan," he said later. It refused, but after a long wrangle, it agreed to stop the shouting contest with the SLC.

The Black Power slogan quickly made Carmichael into a national figure. Before long, he was denouncing integration as "a subterfuge for the maintenance of white supremacy." In direct opposition to King, he said: "Black people should and must fight back."

King knew Black Power had strong appeal, particularly in the ghettos of the North. A day after the divided Meredith march reached its destination, he was on his way back to Chicago. There, the SCLC had to show that nonviolent direct action still worked. "We have got to deliver results—nonviolent results in a northern city—to protect the nonviolent movement," said Andrew Young.

On July 10, 1966, "Freedom Sunday," King launched his Chicago open housing drive. He declared to a crowd of 30,000 in sweltering 98-degree weather, "I do not see the answer to our problems in violence. . . . This day we must decide to fill up the jails of Chicago, if necessary, to end the slums." On Monday morning, Mayor Daley received him at City Hall, and, as before, he trotted out all of the housing and welfare programs Chicago had in the works.

Amid the blistering heat of the following day, some black youngsters near King's Lawndale apartment turned on the fire hydrants in the streets and cooled off in the gushing water. When the police

King speaks at a Mississippi voter registration drive in June 1966. At left is Stokely Carmichael, who replaced John Lewis as chairman of the Student Nonviolent Coordinating Committee (SNCC) and lobbied for blacks to take a more militant approach to gaining their rights.

arrived to close off the hydrants, it led to trouble. A few hours later, Martin and Coretta were returning from dinner, driving through the West Side. King noticed a group running along the avenue. "Those people—I wonder if there's a riot starting," he said. Indeed, there was, triggered by the hydrant episode. Over the next few days, violence gripped the West Side. Snipers appeared on the rooftops of tenements and housing projects, firing away blindly. Two blacks, one a 14-year-old girl, were killed, and incidents of arson and looting spread across several square miles.

On the worst night of the turmoil, King, Young, and the comedian Dick Gregory cruised the West Side, stopping at street corners, churches, bars, and barbecue joints. Everywhere, King pleaded for nonviolence, confronting members of the area's black gangs, notorious for their violent ways, to say they should put down their guns, knives, and Molotov cocktails. He invited some back to his Lawndale apartment.

When Assistant Attorney General Roger Wilkins, President Johnson's personal representative, called on King well after midnight, he found the place "jammed with people. . . . The apartment wasn't air conditioned. There was no fan. It was not a pleasant place to be." But there was King, "this Nobel Prize laureate, sitting on the floor, having a dialogue with semiarticulate gang kids. He was holding a seminar in nonviolence, trying to convince these kids that rioting was destructive; that the way to change society was to approach it with love of yourself and of mankind and dignity in your heart."

At the end of July, the ghetto was quiet again, but, of the SCLC campaign, Young said, "We haven't found the Achilles heel of the Daley machine yet." They soon did. King announced a series of demonstrations and marches—not on the lakefront, not in the riot-scarred West Side, but in the all-white, working-class neighborhoods that excluded blacks.

The plan jolted Daley. He had lived all his life in one of these neighborhoods, and if he knew anything, he knew that blacks marching in would cause terrible trouble. The mayor was in a tight spot. If the blacks marched without police protection, a race riot was virtually certain. But if the police protected the demonstrators, infuriated whites would blame City Hall for coddling blacks. Election day was only three months away.

King did not participate in the first few marches, leaving local leaders in control. A tall, outspoken 25-year-old Chicago minister named Jesse Jackson helped guide 500 demonstrators into the all-white Gage Park neighborhood. As they approached the office of real estate firms that refused to show homes to blacks, a white crowd showered them with rocks and bottles. Jackson was hit, as the police offered scant protection. The marches continued into other neighborhoods, and residents greeted the visitors by overturning cars and screaming, "Go back to Africa. We don't want you here."

A huge rally at Soldier Field in Chicago on July 10, 1966, launched an aggressive campaign to combat housing discrimination in the city. Immediately following the demonstration, King, backed by 5,000 supporters, marched into the heart of Chicago and taped a copy of the protesters' demands to the front door of City Hall.

King is stoned by white home-owners in a Chicago suburb during an August 1966 protest march for desegregated housing. He said afterward that he had "never seen anything so hostile and so hateful as I've seen here today."

On Friday, August 5, King himself led a pilgrimage of 600 marchers, including numerous white sympathizers, into Marquette Park. This time the Chicago police were out in force. Nearly a thousand blue-helmeted cops lined the streets to shield the marchers from the white homeowners.

When King drove up, the crowd was seething, but he seemed unconcerned. "Let's get out of the car. Nothing is going to happen. These people aren't going to do anything," he said to Al Raby, a Chicago organizer. As he left his car, the police closed in around him. They could not, however, protect him from a well-aimed rock that struck him on the right temple. The blow knocked King to one knee, and the crowd roared approval, bellowing, "Nigger, go home!" and, "We want Martin Luther Coon."

Escorted and sheltered by the police, the march proceeded through the neighborhood. The whites did not let up. When it was over, King, who thought he had seen it all, was shaking his head: "I think the people from Mississippi ought to come to Chicago to learn how to hate."

Over the next two weeks, the marches continued, sometimes several a day heading to different parts of the city. Then, on August 20, King raised the stakes by unveiling plans for a march into Cicero, a Chicago suburb with 70,000 residents, none of them black. "Jesus, they won't make it," said a Cicero politician. "If they get in, they won't get out." In 1951, a horrible riot had forced out a black who tried to buy a house there, and no one thought things would be any different in 1966.

The prospect of a march into Cicero was too much for Daley. Already, the white neighborhoods were up in arms about his police protecting blacks, and more marches, with more bloodshed, threatened the health of his political organization. He decided, for the moment, to let King have what he wanted. On August 26, the city agreed that all its agencies would uphold the principles of fair housing and would work to integrate all-white neighborhoods.

King hailed the agreement. Back in Atlanta, he explained to his congregation at Ebenezer that the Chicago accord was "the most significant and far-reaching victory that has ever come about in a northern community on the whole question of open housing."

It also was not worth the paper it was written on. For Daley, it made no difference what he agreed to as long as it got King out of town. With him back in Atlanta and the Chicago movement leaderless, the mayor simply forgot about the agreement and went back to business as usual.

But in March 1967, King was back in Chicago, once more leading a march, once more delivering an impassioned speech. This time, however, it was not a renewed drive for open housing. For the first time in his life, King was marching to protest a war—the American war in Vietnam.

On February 6, 1968, King and other clergymen joined forces with 2,500 supporters at the Tomb of the Unknown Soldier in Arlington National Cemetery for a demonstration against the Vietnam War. King said of his decision to take a public stand on the war, "I could no longer remain silent about an issue that was destroying the soul of our nation."

For several years, King had been watching with alarm the deepening American commitment to the anticommunist government of South Vietnam. In the spring and summer of 1965, as President Johnson ordered intense bombing raids of the enemy and deployed tens of thousands of American combat troops in Southeast Asia, King had spoken out. He declared, "The war in Vietnam must be stopped. There must be a negotiated settlement." Finding no encouragement for an antiwar position from other black leaders, King, for the best part of two years, kept his concerns about the war to himself.

By early 1967, he was quiet no longer. By then, a quarter million American soldiers were in Vietnam, and peace seemed nowhere in sight. Breaking his silence in Los Angeles, King referred to Vietnam as "one of history's most cruel and senseless wars." In Chicago, he said the nation's war policies left America "standing before the world gutted by our own barbarity." And on April 4, at the Riverside Church in New York City, he delivered his mightiest assault: "I knew that I could never again raise my voice against the oppressed in the ghettos without having first spoken clearly to the greatest purveyor of violence in the world today—my own government."

King's words placed him in the front rank of the peace movement. Yet in 1967, opposition to the war, while growing, was seen in some quarters as bordering on treason. After the Riverside Church address, a *Life* magazine editorial declared that by connecting "civil rights with a proposal that amounts to abject surrender in Vietnam . . . King comes close to betraying the cause for which he has worked so long." Within the civil rights movement itself, some felt the same way, and Roy Wilkins, A. Philip Randolph, and Bayard Rustin all distanced themselves from King's remarks.

Nineteen sixty-seven was a year during which nonviolence seemed to fail everywhere. In Vietnam, the war escalated and expanded. And at home, the ghettos exploded. During 5 days in July, 26 died in riots in Newark, New Jersey. Disturbances rocked Milwaukee, Rochester, Tampa, and Cincinnati. In Detroit, the worst race riot in half a century left 43 dead, 2,000 injured, and 4,000 fires burning. "There were dark days before," King muttered to Stanley Levison, "but this is the darkest." That summer, Coretta said, her husband's depression "was greater than I had ever seen it before." He would tell her, "People expect me to have answers and I don't have any answers. I don't feel like speaking to people. I don't have anything to tell them."

King would not surrender. Late in 1967, he developed the idea of an SCLC-sponsored Poor People's March on Washington. By bringing thousands of the impoverished to the nation's capital, the need for economic justice would be made plain. If they built a poor people's city of shacks and tents in sight of the Capitol, perhaps Congress would see the necessity of ending poverty. As he toured the nation, he talked not only of combating poverty and ending the war but of saving the American soul.

"We're going to build our shanties right in Washington and live right there," King would cry. "I'm not playing about this thing. I've agonized over it, and I'm trying to save America. And that's what you are trying to do if you will join this movement. We're trying to save this nation! We can't continue to live in a nation every summer going up in flames, every day killing our people in Vietnam like we're killing. We can't *continue* this way as a nation and survive."

The planning for the march did not go well. By spring 1968, things were far behind schedule. Then the striking garbage collectors of Memphis, Tennessee, asked for King's help, and he answered their plea.

10

APRIL 4, 1968

F EW THINGS IMPROVED King's mood like a good response to one of his speeches, and at Mason Temple in Memphis on April 3, 1968, the small rally cheered and cheered his address. As the SCLC people drove off to a late dinner, King seemed "happy and relaxed," according to Ralph Abernathy. Long after midnight, when the 39-year-old minister returned to the Lorraine Motel, there was a nice surprise. His brother, A. D., and several friends had driven in from Louisville. They all talked and joked for hours, not turning in until shortly before dawn.

Around noon on Thursday, April 4, Abernathy nudged his old friend. "Come on now, it's time to get up." Struggling to open his eyes, King nodded but stayed where he was. "You know, we can't win this nonviolent revolution in bed," Abernathy chided.

Soon, King was awake and dressed and meeting with various people, organizing down to the last detail Monday's march supporting the garbage collectors. As they worked, they considered all the things that could go wrong, and Abernathy thought King was "grim and businesslike." Another participant said he seemed "terribly depressed. He had a great deal of anxiety."

National Guardsmen were called into Memphis, Tennessee, to monitor a civil rights demonstration on March 29, 1968, the day after a protest march led by King had dissolved into turmoil. "Maybe we just have to admit that the day of violence is here," King said after the riot took place, "and maybe we have to just give up and let violence take its course."

But King lightened up. When Andrew Young came in, King scolded him for some mistake, and, Young remembered, "He picked up a pillow and threw it at me. And I threw it back, and we ended up with five or six of us in a pillow fight." Having his brother around also pleased King. In the afternoon, from A. D.'s room, they called their mother in Atlanta, at first disguising their voices, pretending to be each other. For almost an hour, they teased, joked, and chatted.

At five, King and Abernathy walked upstairs to their shared room and got ready for dinner. King shaved, as always using a foul-smelling product called Magic Shave to protect his sensitive skin, then splashing on generous amounts of Aramis cologne. Downstairs, in the motel's courtyard, a large chauffeured Cadillac pulled up. It was the car a Memphis funeral director had loaned King, and this evening it would be delivering everyone to a dinner at the home of Samuel B. Kyles, a local minister. Later, there would be another mass meeting, and King would speak.

Kyles entered room 306 and found King rummaging through his belongings. "Somebody on the staff took my tie," he said.

"Martin, why don't you just look down at that chair?" said Abernathy.

"Oh. I thought somebody took it on me." Knotting the black-and-gold striped tie, King turned to Kyles. "I think your wife is too young to cook soul food for us. She's only thirty-one, isn't she? How can she cook soul food at that age?"

"That's right," said Abernathy. "We don't want to come over to your house and get filet mignon. We want greens, soul food—does Gwen know how to cook soul food?"

"Don't you worry," Kyles assured them.

"This shirt is too tight," King complained.

April 4, 1968, 6:00 P.M.: A mortally wounded King lies on the balcony of the Lorraine Motel in Memphis, Tennessee, while his colleagues point to the rooming house from which James Earl Ray fired the fatal shot.

"You mean you're getting too fat," Abernathy laughed. "That's the shirt I washed for you."

"It's too tight." Making the best of it, King slipped on his jacket. "Okay, let's go eat. I sure hope you're not kidding us about Gwen."

The three men walked to the balcony, but Abernathy retreated to the room to put on some aftershave. Kyles and King waited. Downstairs in the parking lot, the other SCLC staffers stood around the big

Thousands of mourners follow the farm wagon that carried King's coffin through the streets of his hometown, Atlanta, on April 9, 1968. The wagon and mules were symbols of the Poor People's Campaign, the civil rights leader's attempt to call attention to the plight of the nation's poor.

white Cadillac. The car's driver called out that King should bring a topcoat; it was getting chilly. "Okay," King replied, and he asked Abernathy to fetch it.

It was six o'clock.

Kyles started downstairs. King glanced down and noticed Ben Branch, a Chicago musician, standing with Jesse Jackson. "Ben, make sure you play 'Precious Lord, Take My Hand' at the meeting tonight," he said. "Sing it *real* pretty."

Across the street, in the bathroom window of a cheap rooming house, James Earl Ray, a black-hating drifter, aimed his .30-06 rifle at the stocky black man on the balcony of the Lorraine Motel. He had a clean shot, and he fired.

It sounded like a firecracker or a car's backfire. From the door of their room, Abernathy saw King's body sprawled on the balcony. He rushed out, bent down, and saw a huge red wound on King's right jaw. He patted him on the cheek: "Martin, Martin, this is Ralph. Do you hear me? This is Ralph." King's lips seemed to move, but he did not speak.

An hour later, in a Memphis hospital, Martin Luther King, Jr., was pronounced dead at the age of 39.

His body was returned to Atlanta, and his funeral was held at the Ebenezer Baptist Church on April 9, 1968. An impressive number of prominent people—politicians and entertainers, public servants and civil rights activists—sat quietly in the congregation. Abernathy told the grief-stricken assembly, "We gather here this morning in one of the darkest hours in the history of the black people of this nation, in one of the darkest hours in the history of all mankind."

Outside, nearly 100,000 mourners surrounded the church. Mostly, they were humble and poor and black. Yet it was they—"the battered, the scarred, and the defeated," King called them—who possessed the courage and the love that had inspired him to greatness. ❧

Coretta Scott King comforts her youngest daughter, Bernice, during funeral services for the slain civil rights leader at the Ebenezer Baptist Church in Atlanta.

APPENDIX

THE WRITINGS OF
MARTIN LUTHER KING, JR.

Listed below are the books written by Martin Luther King, Jr. In addition to these works, he also wrote 60 articles that have appeared in such magazines and newspapers as *Ebony*, *The Nation*, and the *New York Times*. Many of these pieces have been reprinted in *A Testament of Hope: The Essential Writings of Martin Luther King, Jr.*, James M. Washington, ed. (New York: Harper & Row, 1986). Portions of King's writings have also been collected in *A Martin Luther King Treasury*, Alfred E. Cain, ed. (The Negro Heritage Library, Yonkers, New York: Educational Heritage, Inc., 1964).

The Measure of a Man. Philadelphia: Christian Education Press, 1959.

Strength to Love. New York: Harper & Row, 1963.

Stride Toward Freedom: The Montgomery Story. New York: Harper & Brothers, 1958.

The Trumpet of Conscience. New York: Harper & Row, 1968.

Where Do We Go from Here: Chaos or Community? New York: Harper & Row, 1967.

Why We Can't Wait. New York: New American Library, 1964.

CHRONOLOGY

1929   Born Martin Luther King, Jr., on January 15 in Atlanta, Georgia

1948   Graduates from Morehouse College; ordained as a Baptist minister

1951   Graduates from Crozer Theological Seminary

1953   Marries Coretta Scott

1954   Becomes pastor at Dexter Avenue Baptist Church in Montgomery, Alabama

1955   Receives Ph.D. degree in Systematic Theology from Boston University; joins the Montgomery bus boycott; becomes president of the Montgomery Improvement Association; first child, Yolanda, is born

1957   King founds the Southern Christian Leadership Conference (SCLC); organizes the Prayer Pilgrimage for Freedom; awarded the Spingarn Medal; second child, Martin Luther III, is born

1958   King stabbed in New York City

1959   Travels to India

1960   Becomes co-pastor at the Ebenezer Baptist Church in Atlanta; imprisoned at Reidsville state penitentiary in Georgia

1961   Launches desegregation campaign in Albany, Georgia; third child, Dexter, is born

1962   King joins racial protests in Birmingham, Alabama

1963   Arrested at a demonstration in Birmingham; writes "Letter from Birmingham Jail"; delivers "I Have a Dream" speech at the March on Washington; fourth child, Bernice, is born

1964   King awarded the Nobel Peace Prize

1965   Joins the SCLC in Selma, Alabama, for its march to Montgomery

1966   Launches the Chicago Freedom Movement; organizes the "James Meredith March Against Fear"

1967   Forms the Poor People's Campaign

1968   Assassinated on April 4 in Memphis, Tennessee

FURTHER READING

Bishop, Jim. *The Days of Martin Luther King, Jr.* New York: Putnam, 1971.

Branch, Taylor. *Parting the Waters: America in the King Years 1954–63.* New York: Simon & Schuster, 1988.

Garrow, David J. *Bearing the Cross: Martin Luther King, Jr., and the Southern Christian Leadership Conference.* New York: Morrow, 1986.

———. *The FBI and Martin Luther King, Jr.: From "Solo" to Memphis.* New York: Norton, 1981.

King, Coretta Scott. *My Life with Martin Luther King, Jr.* New York: Holt, Rinehart & Winston, 1969.

King, Martin Luther, Sr. *Daddy King: An Autobiography.* New York: Morrow, 1980.

Lewis, David L. *King: A Critical Biography.* New York: Praeger, 1970.

Lincoln, C. Eric, ed. *Martin Luther King, Jr.: A Profile.* Rev. ed. New York: Hill & Wang, 1984.

Oates, Stephen B. *Let the Trumpet Sound: The Life of Martin Luther King, Jr.* New York: Harper and Row, 1982.

Raines, Howell. *My Soul Is Rested: Movement Days in the Deep South Remembered.* New York: Putnam, 1977.

Williams, Juan. *Eyes on the Prize: America's Civil Rights Years 1954–1965.* New York: Viking Penguin, 1987.

Wofford, Harris. *Of Kennedys and Kings.* New York: Farrar, Straus & Giroux, 1980.

HARRIET TUBMAN

HARRIET TUBMAN

❦

M.W. Taylor

Senior Consulting Editor
Nathan Irvin Huggins
Director
W.E.B. Du Bois Institute for Afro-American Research
Harvard University

1

A WOMAN
CALLED MOSES

ON THE AFTERNOON of April 27, 1860, a tall black man named Charles Nalle stood defiantly before United States Commissioner Miles Beach in a courthouse in Troy, New York. A runaway slave, Nalle was being watched closely by an assortment of attorneys, court officers, and armed U.S. marshals, as well as Henry J. Wall, a plantation agent from Virginia. The marshals and Wall had just finished giving evidence against Nalle in their effort to send him back into slavery. Two years earlier, he had escaped from Virginia and made his way north to freedom.

But on this spring afternoon, 500 miles from the nearest slave state, Nalle faced the prospect of being told he was still a slave. According to the Fugitive Slave Act, federal legislation that was passed in 1850, he remained the property of his owner, even in a free state. The U.S. government was legally obliged to return a captured slave to bondage.

As the sounds of a crowd gathering outside the courthouse began to fill the second-floor room, Commissioner Beach disclosed his chilling decision to the court: Nalle must be turned over to Wall and returned to his southern master. Nalle edged toward the win-

Tubman escaped from slavery in 1849, then returned to the South at least 19 times during the next 10 years to lead more than 300 blacks to freedom in the North. According to one historian, "No fugitive was ever captured who had [her] for a leader."

dow. Below, on First and State streets, their eyes fixed on him, stood more than 1,000 people, black and white, women and men. Nalle knew that Troy, like most other northern cities, was home to many opponents of slavery. Some of these abolitionists favored ending slavery peacefully and lawfully. Others were ready and willing to help a slave escape any way they could.

Nalle lunged for the window. He almost made it through, but marshals seized his arms and dragged him back into the courtroom. At that moment, freedom must have seemed like a dream to Nalle. Even if the people outside the courthouse had wanted to come to his aid, how could they do it? He was now closely guarded by armed men, and he had no friends or allies nearby. The only black face in sight belonged to a spectator, a bent old woman wearing a shawl and bonnet and carrying a basket. The guards had probably let her in because they felt sorry for her. What could one old woman do, anyway?

A band of patrollers—white slave catchers—guns down a quartet of fleeing blacks in the mid-1800s. The passage of the Fugitive Slave Act in 1850 accelerated the South's relentless tracking of runaways.

Suddenly, a voice from the crowd below shouted a question that was heard in the courtroom: How much money would it take for the southern agent to free Nalle?

"Twelve hundred dollars," Wall replied.

Purses were opened and hats hastily passed. A few minutes later, the spectators announced that they had collected the price of Charles Nalle's freedom. Agent Wall responded by raising the figure to $1,500. A low, angry roar swept the crowd: The slave catcher was mocking them; he had no intention of releasing Nalle.

The abolitionists had tried to save Nalle and had failed. There was nothing else they could do. Now that the hearing was over, he would be put aboard a train and sent south, back into slavery.

Guards chained Nalle's hands and pushed him toward the stairs that led to the street. Near the landing, the guards brushed aside the old black woman, who was standing quietly, her head bowed. But as soon as they had passed her, she tore off her sunbonnet and raced to the window. "Here he comes," she shouted to the people below. "Take him!"

The crowd surged forward, meeting Nalle and his guards at the foot of the stairs. The marshals raised their clubs, yet the crowd continued to press in. Then down the stairs, like an avenging angel, charged the "old woman." Without her shawl, basket, and stooped pose, she revealed herself as a small, very dark-skinned woman of about 40. Her eyes were bright, even fierce; her arms were muscular, her fists clenched. The marshals ducked as she flew at them, punching furiously and shouting at the top of her lungs.

"Drag him to the river!" the woman cried. "Drown him! But don't let them have him!" Then, an eyewitness reported later, "like a wildcat" she

knocked down one of Nalle's guards and wrapped her arms around the manacled prisoner. Wrenching him away from a second guard, she pulled Nalle through the crowd toward the river. Marshals flailed at Nalle and his rescuer with fists and clubs, but the woman refused to let go. The crowd joined her.

The *Troy Whig* described the scene as "a regular battlefield." In the "surging mass" of people, said the newspaper, "the pulling, hauling, mauling, and shouting gave evidences of frantic efforts on the part of the rescuers, and a stern resistance from the conservators of the law." The street filled with screams, curses, and the smell of gunpowder.

"In the melee," a local attorney stated later, the small black woman "was repeatedly beaten over the

Slaves—men, women, and children—carry their harvest after a 16-hour day in the cotton fields. Escaping from such bondage in 1858, Virginian Charles Nalle was recaptured two years later in Troy, New York, but was eventually freed by Tubman and others.

head with policemen's clubs, but she never for a moment released her hold, but cheered Nalle and his friends with her voice, and struggled with the officers until they were literally worn out with their exertions, and Nalle was separated from them. True she had strong and earnest helpers in her struggle, some of whom had white faces as well as human hearts, and are now in Heaven. But she exposed herself to the fury of the sympathizers with slavery without fear, and suffered their blows without flinching."

Finally, the crowd managed to pull Nalle, chains and all, away from his captors. They rushed the bleeding, dazed fugitive to the riverbank and pushed him onto a waiting rowboat. As an oarsman pulled away from the shore, the black woman, along with some

400 allies, boarded a steam-powered ferryboat and followed the rowboat.

But more marshals, alerted by telegraph, awaited them across the river. They seized Nalle, locked him in a house, and placed armed guards at every window. Undeterred, the woman and her friends began to hurl rocks at the makeshift jail. The marshals responded with gunfire, and the crowd fell back. Then a man's voice shouted, "Who cares? They can only kill a dozen of us—come on!"

Eager to do his part, a huge black man emerged from the crowd, strode up to the house, and kicked down the door. Marshals swiftly felled him with an ax, but his body jammed the door open, and the abolitionists poured through. Strong hands picked up the battered Nalle, carried him outside, and put him into a wagon that rolled north, carrying the former slave toward Canada and freedom. Meanwhile, the crowd dispersed, and the black woman disappeared from view.

When the liberated slave revived, he asked about the woman who had engineered his rescue. Nalle's

A photographer in the mid-1800s created this powerful image of a slave on the run. In 1850 alone, more than 1,000 blacks fled their southern plantations for the free states of the North.

$100 REWARD.

Ran away from my farm, near Buena Vista P. O., Prince George's County, Maryland, on the first day of April, 1855, my servant MATHEW TURNER.

He is about five feet six or eight inches high; weighs from one hundred and sixty to one hundred and eighty pounds; he is very black, and has a remarkably thick upper lip and neck; looks as if his eyes are half closed; walks slow, and talks and laughs loud.

I will give One Hundred Dollars reward to whoever will secure him in jail, so that I get him again, no matter where taken.

MARCUS DU VAL.

BUENA VISTA P. O., MD.,
MAY 10, 1855.

Posted by a Maryland slave owner in 1855, a handbill offers $100 for the return of "servant" Mathew Turner. Notices about runaways, increasingly common in the decade before the Civil War, inspired widespread manhunts.

escorts told him she had gone into hiding because she carried a price on her head—she was wanted by authorities in both the North and the South for helping slaves escape from their masters. Her name was Harriet Tubman, they said, but she was better known as "Moses." A namesake of the biblical prophet who had brought his people out of bondage and into the Promised Land, Tubman had led more of her brethren out of Egypt—as she called the slaveholding South—than any other person, black or white, male or female, in American history.

2

THE SHORT
CHILDHOOD OF
A SLAVE

❧

H ARRIET TUBMAN WAS born into slavery
as Harriet Ross around 1820 on the Eastern Shore,
a peninsula shared by the state of Delaware and parts
of Maryland and Virginia. Bordered on the east by
the Atlantic Ocean and on the west by the shallow,
fish-filled waters of Chesapeake Bay, the area has a
moderate climate. The Eastern Shore's flat, rich farmland is also known as the Tidewater because its countless inlets, swamps, and small rivers rise and fall with
the tides of the nearby sea. Near the center of the
peninsula, where Delaware and Maryland meet, is
the nation's northernmost cypress swamp.

Although the Eastern Shore lies only a few miles
from the industrial cities of Baltimore and Philadelphia, its atmosphere resembles that of the Deep
South. Situated at the Confederacy's northernmost
edge, it was the birthplace of some of the most renowned and valiant warriors in the battle against
slavery, including Frederick Douglass and the woman
who would be known as Moses.

Harriet Ross's birthdate is approximate because
no one officially recorded it; few slaves could read or
write, and slave owners kept no more precise data on

*Facing a camera in the mid-
1800s, a young slave embraces
his little brother protectively. Tubman, like most children born into
slavery, started work early; she
was five years old when her master hired her out as a housemaid.*

A southern planter barks out a command to his field slaves. As an adult, Tubman said of her cruel masters: "They didn't know any better. . . . They were brought up with the whip in their hand."

the lives of their slaves than they did on the lives of their pigs and chickens. Harriet was one of 11 children born to Harriet Green and Benjamin Ross, slaves belonging to Maryland planter Edward Brodas. Harriet's mother, known as Old Rit, gave her daughter the "cradle name" of Araminta. The little girl's family usually called her Minty.

Both Green and Ross were full-blooded Africans; their parents had been brought to the United States in chains. According to legend, the family came from the Ashanti, a West African warrior people who successfully battled the British during much of the 19th century. Harriet Tubman believed in this version of her roots; as an adult, she sometimes remarked that she was "one of those Ashantis." In any case, she would prove to be a formidable warrior herself.

On his plantation, situated on the Big Buckwater River in the Tidewater's Dorchester County, Edward

Brodas raised apples, wheat, rye, and corn. His land also included vast stands of trees, including oak, cypress, and poplar, which he sold to the Baltimore shipyards across the Chesapeake Bay. Harriet's father, Benjamin ("Old Ben") Ross, spent most of his days cutting timber for his master. Harriet's mother worked for the Brodas family in their elegant home, called "the big house" by the slaves.

Like many slave owners in the Upper South, Edward Brodas bred and raised blacks as a cash crop, renting and selling them to others. Georgia slave traders made frequent appearances in the neighborhood; by the time she was 13, Harriet Ross had seen sisters, brothers, and friends sold "down the river" to work on the vast cotton and sugar plantations of the Deep South.

The childhood of a slave was short. When Harriet was five years old, her master rented her to a local couple named Cook. At their home, the little girl slept on the kitchen floor, poking her feet under the fireplace ashes when the nights grew cold. For meals, she shared table scraps with the Cooks' dogs.

Mrs. Cook put Harriet to work winding yarn, but when the young slave proved slow at the job, her mistress turned her over to her husband. He assigned Harriet to watch his muskrat traps. Now she spent her days, barefoot and wearing only a thin shirt, wading in the edge of the icy river, looking for animals on James Cook's traplines. Before long, she developed a cough and a high fever, which her masters accused her of faking to escape work. Calling her useless, lazy, and stupid, the Cooks finally sent her back to the Brodas plantation. There, under her mother's care, Harriet recovered from a six-week bout of measles and bronchitis. Then Brodas rented her again, this time to a woman who wanted a housekeeper and baby nurse.

Many years after the experience, Harriet Tubman described it to a friend who recorded her account:

I was only seven years old when I was sent away to take care of a baby. I was so little that I had to sit on the floor and have the baby put on my lap. And that baby was always on my lap except when it was asleep or its mother was feeding it.

One morning, after breakfast, she had the baby, and I stood by the table waiting until I was to take it; near me was a bowl of lumps of white sugar. My mistress got into a great quarrel with her husband; she had an awful temper, and she would scold and storm and call him all kinds of names.

Now, you know, I never had anything good, no sweet, no sugar; and that sugar, right by me, did look so nice, and my mistress's back was turned to me while she was fighting with her husband, so I just put my fingers in the sugar bowl to take one lump and maybe she heard me for she turned and saw me.

The next minute she had the rawhide down. I gave one jump out of the door and I saw that they came after me, but I just flew and they didn't catch me. I ran and I ran and I passed many a house, but I didn't dare to stop for they all knew my mistress and they would send me back.

By and by when I was almost tuckered out, I came to a great big pigpen. There was an old sow there, and perhaps eight or ten little pigs. I tumbled over [the fence] and fell in . . . so beaten out that I could not stir.

And I stayed there from Friday until the next Tuesday, fighting with those little pigs for the potato peelings and the other scraps that came down in the trough. The old sow would push me away when I tried to get her children's food, and I was awfully afraid of her. By Tuesday I was so starved I knew I had to go back to my mistress. I didn't have anywhere else to go, even though I knew what was coming. So I went back.

The terrified little girl returned to her mistress, who gave her a savage whipping, then brought her back to the Brodas plantation. Harriet, said the woman who had rented her, "wasn't worth a six-pence." Once again, Old Rit nursed her child, salving the fresh wounds that overlay the scars from earlier beatings. And once again, as soon as Harriet was able to work, Brodas hired her out. This time, she was put to work splitting fence rails and loading timber

on wagons. It was backbreaking labor, better suited
to a brawny adult male than a little girl. Nevertheless,
Harriet preferred it, she said later, to working in a
house under the harsh scrutiny of a "lady."

By the time she was in her early teens, Harriet
was known as a strong but surly laborer, unfit for
indoor work but useful as a field hand. She never
forgot her painful childhood, and she never had a
good word for any of her masters. If they had any
excuse for their cruelty, she asserted, it was igno-
rance. "They didn't know any better. It's the way
they were brought up . . . with the whip in their
hand," she said as an adult. "Now that wasn't the
way on all plantations," she added. "There were good
masters and mistresses, as I've heard tell. But I didn't
happen to come across any of them."

In 1831, when Harriet was about 11, exciting but
terrifying rumors swept the slave quarters of the Brodas estate. Nat Turner, a slave on a Virginia plantation—only 100 miles away, across the Chesapeake
Bay—had led an army of 60 rebel slaves against their
white masters. More than 50 whites, whispered the
Brodas slaves to one another, had been killed in the
uprising. True, Turner and his men had lost their
battle, but their daring revolt offered proof that Africans were men, not animals, and that they would
fight and die for their freedom.

Turner's was not the only black uprising in the
19th-century South. In 1800, a Virginia slave named
Gabriel Prosser had tried and failed to establish an
independent black state, and in 1822, Denmark
Vesey had organized hundreds of blacks in a spec-
tacular but futile bid for freedom in South Carolina.
These rebellions sparked hope and elation among the
South's blacks, terror among its whites.

Slaves found other ways, too, to establish some
degree of independence. Some pretended to be stupid, "accidentally" destroying their masters' tools and

*Nat Turner, the Virginia slave
who led a revolt in 1831, surren-
ders after evading pursuers for
two months. News of Turner's
rebellion, in which more than 50
whites were killed, sent waves of
fear—and pride—through the
Brodas plantation's slaves.*

Labeled like cattle, most slaves wore tags showing the name of their master. Free blacks carried medallions marked with the liberty cap (top), a token given to freed slaves in ancient Rome.

crops; others ran away when they saw their chance. Escape, however, was extremely difficult. When a planter reported a runaway slave, bands of mounted white men, known as patrollers ("patterollers" to the slave community), ranged through the countryside, tracking the fugitives with dogs. The standard punishment for runaways was whipping, branding with the letter *R*, and exile to the Deep South, where working conditions for slaves were more brutal than anywhere else. The slaves who trudged off in chains to Louisiana or Georgia never came back and rarely lived long.

During Harriet's childhood, even runaway slaves who managed to elude their pursuers had no place to go. Not until the mid-19th century, when the abolitionist movement began to develop in the North, was there any refuge for blacks fleeing their bonds.

It was an escaping slave who inadvertently brought disaster to 15-year-old Harriet. In the fall of 1835, she was shucking corn along with the rest of the plantation's workers when she noticed a tall black man sneaking away from the group. The overseer, carrying his snakeskin whip as usual, followed the black man. So did Harriet.

Catching up with the runaway at the crossroads store, the overseer prepared to whip him. He spotted Harriet and told her to hold the slave while he tied him up for the lashing. She refused. The black man bolted, and Harriet stationed herself in the doorway, blocking the overseer's way. Enraged, he grabbed a two-pound lead weight from the store counter and flung it after the running slave. The weight missed its mark and hit Harriet squarely in the head. She fell like a stone, blood pouring from a deep gash in her forehead.

When Harriet was carried home, her shocked mother dressed the wound, stopped the bleeding, and prayed. But the teenager remained in a coma for weeks, lying on a bed of rags in the corner of her family's windowless wooden cabin. Not until the following spring was she able to get up and walk unaided. Although her injury was never medically diagnosed (doctors were rarely wasted on slaves), Harriet had probably suffered a fractured skull and severe concussion.

She would carry a scar and a dent in her forehead for the rest of her life and, from that point on, would suffer periodic "sleeping fits." Without warning, wherever she might be, she would suddenly fall into a deep sleep. Such attacks took place as often as three or four times a day, even when Harriet was in the middle of a conversation. Until she regained consciousness by herself, nothing could rouse her.

While Harriet lay unconscious, the overseer who had struck her appeared at the cabin door—not to ask about her health but to see if she was fit enough to sell. He clearly wanted to be rid of this stubborn slave girl who had dared to defy him. Several times while Harriet was recuperating, the overseer pushed open the cabin door to give prospective buyers a look at her. But, as she later recalled, "They wouldn't give a sixpence for me."

Harriet had inherited her parents' strong religious faith, and as she slowly recovered from her head

A slave auctioneer takes bids for a black woman and her daughter. Slaves were considered easier to manage once they were separated from their relatives and friends.

wound, she prayed hard—for the soul of plantation owner Edward Brodas. Years later, she told her first biographer, Sarah Bradford, about these days. "As I lay so sick on my bed, from Christmas till March, I was always praying for old master," she said. "Oh, dear Lord," she begged, "change that man's heart and make him a Christian." Although Brodas kept sending possible purchasers to look at her, she kept praying for him. "All I could say," she recalled, "was, 'Oh, Lord, convert old master.' "

Then more grim news swept the slave quarters: Brodas had decided to sell Harriet and two of her brothers and send them south in chains. At this point, Harriet recalled later, "I changed my prayer, and I said, 'Lord, if you're never going to change that man's heart, *kill him*, Lord, and take him out of the way, so he won't do more mischief.' "

Not long afterward, Brodas suddenly fell ill and died. Harriet, who never questioned the power of prayer, was horrified. What had she done? "I would [have given] the world full of silver and gold, if I had it," she said years later, "to bring that poor soul back, I would give *myself*; I would give everything! But he was gone."

Brodas's death left Harriet with a sense of deep guilt, but it also slightly improved her prospects. In his will, the plantation owner had left his estate to a young relative, directing that it be managed by Anthony Thompson, a local clergyman, until the heir came of age. Brodas's will also stipulated that none of his slaves be sold outside the state of Maryland after his death.

Thompson, however, continued Brodas's practice of hiring out the plantation's slaves. By this time, Harriet's head wound had healed, and although she suffered from violent headaches and sudden blackouts, she was once again able to work. Harriet was hired out to John Stewart, a local builder. At the same time, the estate manager rented Harriet's father, Ben Ross, to Stewart as a woodcutter. Her father, Harriet recalled later, was pleased by the assignment; he knew and respected Stewart, at least as much as any slave could respect a white southerner in those times.

At first, Harriet was assigned to work as a maid in the Stewart home. She hated every minute of it, much preferring heavy outdoor labor. At the end of three months, she begged Stewart to let her work outdoors along with the men. Aware of her unusual strength, he agreed to let her try.

Stewart soon realized Harriet Ross was worth much more as a field hand than as a domestic. She could plow, chop wood, and drive a team of oxen more efficiently than most men. Ben Ross had been put in charge of a gang of rented slaves who cut timber for the Baltimore shipyards. Harriet began working with the timber crew, swinging an ax alongside her father.

Stewart was so impressed with Harriet's energy and will to work that he allowed her a privilege given only to the most trusted slaves: When times were slack on his farm, he let her hire herself out. In return, she paid him about $50 per year; any money she earned above that was hers to keep. For the next five years, she cut timber for Stewart and, in her spare time, chopped and hauled wood for the neighbors. Gradually, she accumulated a small amount of money of her own.

Harriet Ross liked her strenuous outdoor work, and she liked the feeling of money in her pocket, no matter how little. Still, she lacked what she considered the most important thing in life. It was something mentioned only in whispers by the slaves of the South, but it was talked about more and more openly in the free states only 90 miles to the north. It was freedom. ❧

Slave women wash their master's linens. Despising domestic work, Tubman much preferred outdoor labor—chopping trees or loading wagons along with her father and other male slaves of the Brodas plantation.

3

"A GLORY
OVER EVERYTHING"

IN THE MID-1840s, as millions of blacks toiled for their southern masters, a small but growing band of northerners worked toward ending more than two centuries of North American slavery.

The American colonies' first African slaves, a cargo of about 20 blacks, arrived at Jamestown, Virginia, in 1619. The number of slaves increased steadily; by 1763, the colonial population included about 230,000 blacks, most of them slaves. Of these, some 16,000 lived in New England, 29,000 in the Middle Colonies (New York, New Jersey, and Pennsylvania), and the remainder in the South.

Great Britain outlawed the slave trade in 1807, the United States a year later. But these moves only barred the importation of slaves; those already enslaved remained in bondage, as would their descendants. The British Empire, which included Canada, finally abolished slavery altogether in 1838. In the southern United States, however, the institution continued to flourish. Its strength rested largely on cotton.

In the late 18th century, the textile industry entered a period of rapid development in England and the northern United States. Its rise created a tre-

An Atlanta, Georgia, merchant advertises his wares: china, glass, and Negroes. Slave trading was big business in the prewar South; between 1850 and 1860 the average price of a slave increased by 70 percent.

273

Using inventor Eli Whitney's cotton gin, slaves rapidly remove the seeds from freshly picked cotton. Introduction of the machine vastly increased the South's cotton output; in 1860, the area produced 5 million bales.

mendous demand for southern cotton. But before it could be shipped to a textile mill, cotton had to be freed of its many sticky seeds. Seeding was a slow, labor-intensive process; even a skilled slave could clean only a few pounds of cotton per day. Then, in 1793, a Massachusetts-born inventor, Eli Whitney, developed a revolutionary new machine, the cotton engine. One slave using this engine, or "gin," as it came to be known, could clean as much cotton as four or five slaves working by hand.

Now the cultivation of cotton became hugely profitable; 10 years after Whitney invented his gin, southern cotton production had increased by 800 percent. Cotton became "king" not only in the Carolinas and Georgia but in the newly opened western lands of Alabama, Mississippi, and Louisiana. Needing more and more field hands, plantation owners turned to the long-established slave states of Virginia and Maryland. There, Edward Brodas and other slave owners began to breed and sell slaves as though they were livestock. The outlawed international slave trade was now replaced by an internal trade; thousands of blacks from the Upper South were sent to the Deep South to labor and die on the cotton plantations.

In 1860, 1 American family in 4 owned slaves; of a national population of almost 12 million, about 4 million were slaves, the vast majority of them in the South. Although a few voices were raised against slavery in the 18th century, most Americans seem to have taken the institution for granted. By the early 19th century, however, an increasing number of thoughtful people had come to see human bondage as a monstrous evil and its abolition as absolutely necessary.

In the South, slaves themselves were beginning to fight back, and in the North, free blacks took up the abolitionist cause with militant passion. Blacks and their white supporters had been deeply impressed by the actions of Toussaint L'Ouverture, a former slave who led a 1791 revolution in Haiti (then called St. Domingue). After freeing Haiti's black slaves, L'Ouverture had forced the departure of the British and the Spanish and then established the Western Hemisphere's first black republic. Another galvanic abolitionist was David Walker, a free black Bostonian. In 1829, he published *Appeal*, a fiery pamphlet that urged the slaves of the South to rise up and fight. Some historians credit Walker's powerful arguments with inspiring Nat Turner's revolt of 1831.

At the forefront of the abolitionist movement was William Lloyd Garrison, a white Massachusetts journalist and reformer. Garrison, who began publishing a journal called *The Liberator* in 1831, spoke a language that both blacks and whites could understand. "He that is with the slaveholder is against the slave," asserted Garrison. "He that is with the slave is against the slaveholder."

Former slave Toussaint L'Ouverture headed a revolt in 1791 that drove British and French forces from the Caribbean island of St. Domingue. Thirteen years later, the island became Haiti, the New World's first black republic.

Most abolitionists favored gradual emancipation and payments to slave owners for their property, but Garrison demanded immediate abolition with no compensation. In the first issue of *The Liberator*, he announced that he would never compromise on slavery. "I am in earnest—I will not equivocate—I will not excuse—I will not retreat a single inch—AND I WILL BE HEARD," he thundered.

Frederick Douglass, another towering figure in the antislavery movement, was born a Maryland slave in about 1817. Escaping to Massachusetts in 1838, he became an agent of the Massachusetts Anti-Slavery Society and a tireless lecturer on abolition. In 1847, Douglass founded an abolitionist newspaper, the *North Star*, later retitled *Frederick Douglass's Paper*. As dedicated as Garrison but less radical, Douglass recruited thousands of conservative Americans to the abolitionist cause.

By 1840, about 200,000 Americans belonged to some 2,000 antislavery organizations. As their movement gained strength in the North, these people

Publisher of the antislavery newspaper The Liberator, *William Lloyd Garrison was cofounder of the American Anti-Slavery Society and served as its president from 1843 to 1865. An uncompromising abolitionist, he urged the northern states to separate from the slaveholding South.*

began to look for practical ways to achieve their goal. Many otherwise law-abiding citizens proved willing to break the law in order to help runaway slaves escape. In the South, free blacks and other slaves were almost always willing to aid fugitive blacks. Thus was the Underground Railroad born.

According to one legend, this system of transport got its name during the 1831 pursuit of Tice Davids, a runaway Kentucky slave. When Davids reached the Ohio River, he plunged in and began a desperate swim for Ohio and freedom. His master followed closely in a boat, but when he reached the shore, his quarry had disappeared. Searching in vain, the frustrated slave owner reportedly cried, "He must have gone on an underground road!"

The Underground Railroad, of course, did not involve actual trains or tracks; it was a loose network of people willing to hide runaway slaves in their homes and "conduct" them to the next "station," or safe house. Slaves had always run away, but by the 1830s, they had allies willing to help them get out of the South and stay free. Word of these Good Samaritans began to spread through the slave quarters of the Upper South.

In 1839, news of a daring act at sea struck hope into the heart of all those who opposed slavery, black and white alike. A Spanish slave ship, the *Amistad,* was hijacked at sea by its captives, led by an African named Joseph Cinque. After killing most of the Spanish crew, the rebels sailed the ship to the coast of Long Island. There, they were arrested and jailed on charges of piracy and murder. Abolitionists across the country took up the cause of the mutineers, who eventually won their freedom in court and returned to Africa.

The *Amistad* case created a great furor. Harriet Ross and the other slaves at the Brodas plantation probably heard of it. Certainly, they were dreaming more and more of freedom.

Years afterward, Harriet Tubman told an interviewer about a recurring dream she had in those days: "I seemed to see a line, and on the other side of the line were green fields, and lovely flowers, and beautiful white ladies who stretched out their arms to me over the line, but I couldn't reach them. I always fell before I got to the line."

Such a line indeed existed. In 1767, a pair of English surveyors, Charles Mason and Jeremiah Dixon, had laid out the boundary between Pennsylvania and Maryland. That demarcation, later extended westward to mark the Pennsylvania-Virginia boundary as well, came to be known as the Mason-Dixon line. By the 1820s, the term was used to indicate the entire border between the free states of the North and the slave states of the South. Harriet Ross must have known that the line where freedom began was less than 100 miles from her home on the Eastern Shore.

In 1844, John Tubman, a free black man who lived in a cabin near the Brodas plantation, asked 24-year-old Harriet Ross to marry him. Already old for marriage by local standards, she agreed. Because his slave parents had been freed at their master's death, John Tubman had been born free. Marriage to a free man, however, did not change Harriet Tubman's slave status; it only meant that she was free to share her husband's cabin at night. Her children, if she had any, would belong to the Brodas estate.

Ironically, Harriet Tubman's husband used the slave system to control his own wife. She later said that he refused to listen to her talk about freedom and that he once told her he would betray her if she ever tried to run away. Nevertheless, she seems to have loved him; at any rate, she remained by his side for the next five years. But she never forgot her dream of freedom.

It was while she was married that Harriet Tubman learned she was being held in slavery illegally. Her

One of the nation's leading abolitionists, Frederick Douglass escaped from slavery in 1838 and published a best-selling account of his life 18 years later. A wartime adviser to President Abraham Lincoln, Douglass also served as a District of Columbia official and ambassador to Haiti.

mother, Old Rit, had often said she had been promised freedom years earlier but had been cheated out of it. Over the years, Harriet Tubman had managed to save five dollars, and in 1845, she took it to a local lawyer and asked him to look into her mother's records.

The lawyer discovered that Old Rit's original owner had willed her to one of his young relatives, specifying that the slave be freed when she reached the age of 45. But the relative had died soon afterward, and Rit had been sold despite the will's provisions. The lawyer told Tubman that her mother—and therefore she herself—was legally free. However, he said, because so much time had passed and because the women had always lived as slaves, no judge would even consider their case. With regard to black people, it seemed that justice was truly blind.

Harriet Tubman continued to suffer from blackouts, during which she often had strange and frightening dreams. She described them later as scenes from the "middle passage," the Atlantic crossing that cost the life of millions of captured Africans en route to America. She said she dreamed of ships where blacks

Slave-ship crew members in Africa, preparing for a voyage across the Atlantic Ocean, stow their human cargo below deck. Raised on firsthand reports of the dreaded "middle passage," Tubman had frequent nightmares about such journeys.

and whites fought on decks stained red with blood. She dreamed of a mother clutching a baby to her breast and leaping to her death in the sea.

Even after her marriage, Tubman lived in terror of being "sold South." During those years, she said later, "I never closed my eyes that I did not imagine that I saw the horsemen coming and heard the screams of women and children as they were being dragged away to a far worse slavery than they were enduring there." These dreams were not without foundation. Harsh as it was in the Upper South, slavery was much worse in the cotton states of Georgia, Mississippi, Alabama, and Louisiana.

In 1849, Tubman's worst fears came true. The young heir to the Brodas estate died, and word spread that his guardian planned to settle the plantation's bills by selling some of its slaves. One afternoon, Tubman learned that two of her sisters had just been sold and were already in chains, heading south. She knew it was time to go, and she persuaded three of her brothers to go with her. She told them what she had heard of the Underground Railroad and of the people in the North who would help them. Her father had showed her the North Star at night and told her how to use it as a compass; she assured her brothers she could guide them by watching it.

Tubman was reluctant to leave her husband, but she knew better than to ask him to come along—or even let him know she was going. He had already promised to betray her. She left late at night with her brothers, but they soon began to drag their feet. Even though she urged them on, they went slower and slower, worrying about what would happen when they were missed. Signs would be posted everywhere; alarm bells would be rung; the dogs would be set loose; and mounted patrollers with whips would track them down. They had no food, no money, no friends, and they were heading for unfamiliar country. Slavery,

Kidnapped by Spanish slavers in 1839, Joseph Cinque led his fellow prisoners in a revolt at sea. After killing most of their captors, the Africans sailed the slave ship to New York, where they were jailed, tried, and eventually freed.

A column of southbound slaves, chained to each other at wrist and ankle, makes its way through Washington, D.C. Tubman and her fellow slaves lived in constant fear of being "sold south"—led in chains to the Deep South's plantations, where living and working conditions were unbearable.

bad as it was, was at least familiar. The brothers feared the unknown. They turned back and made their sister turn back with them.

She crept back into her sleeping husband's bed, bitterly disappointed. But she had learned an important lesson, one she would never forget: Freedom is only for those bold enough to take it.

Two days after the botched escape, a slave from a nearby plantation gave Tubman bad news: She had been sold and was scheduled to start south the next day. This time she knew she would have to run alone. Years later, she described her thoughts at that moment: "There was one of two things I had a *right* to, liberty or death; if I could not have one, I would have the other; for no man should take me alive; I should fight for my liberty as long as my strength lasted, and when the time came for me to go, the Lord would let them take me."

Tubman wanted someone in her family to know she was leaving on her own, that she was not on her way south. After her last experience, she would not tell her brothers. How could she relay the news safely? Legend has it that she made her way toward "the big house," where one of her sisters was working in the kitchen. Walking back and forth near the window, Tubman sang an old spiritual:

> I'll meet you in the morning,
> When I reach the Promised Land,
> On the other side of Jordan.
> For I'm bound for the Promised Land.

That night, after her husband was asleep, Harriet Tubman wrapped up a little cornbread and salt herring, then tucked her favorite patchwork quilt under her arm. Did she kiss John Tubman good-bye as he slept? Did she regret leaving him? No one will ever know, for she never said. But perhaps she hinted at her feelings in her choice of a name: For the rest of her life, she identified herself as "Mrs. Tubman."

Tubman had heard of a local white woman who was said to help runaways, and she made her way through the woods to the woman's house. When she saw Tubman at her door, the woman seemed to know what her visitor wanted. She invited her in, then gave her two slips of paper, explaining that each contained the name of a family on the road north. When Tubman presented the slips, said the woman, these people would give her food and tell her how to get to the next house. The slips of paper were Tubman's first "tickets" on the Underground Railroad. In gratitude, Tubman gave the woman her precious quilt, then started on her way.

Reaching the first house just after dawn, Tubman presented her slip of paper. The woman of the house responded by giving her a broom and telling her to sweep the walk. Tubman was shocked. Was this a betrayal? Was she now this woman's slave? But she soon realized the move was for camouflage. A black woman with a broom would hardly be noticed, certainly not suspected as a runaway.

As soon as night fell, the woman's husband put Tubman in the back of his farm wagon, covered her with vegetables, and drove her north to the next "station." In this way, sometimes helped by others, sometimes left to her own devices, Harriet Tubman made her way north, walking up the Eastern Shore peninsula toward Pennsylvania. She began to learn the route she was to use so often and so effectively in the future.

Traveling by night, hiding in the daylight, Tubman trudged through 90 miles of swamp and woodland. At last, many days after she started, she found herself across the magic line, on free soil. Years later, she said of that morning: "I looked at my hands to see if I was the same person now that I was free. There was such a glory over everything; the sun came like gold through the trees, and over the fields, and I felt like I was in heaven."

4

"A FRIEND WITH FRIENDS"

I WAS FREE but there was no one to welcome me to freedom," recalled Harriet Tubman. "I was a stranger in a strange land."

Years later, Tubman talked to biographer Sarah Bradford about her arrival in Pennsylvania in 1849. "To this solemn resolution I came," she said. "I was free, and [my parents, brothers, and sisters] should be free also; I would make a home for them in the North, and the Lord helping me, I would bring them all there. Oh, how I prayed then, lying all alone on the cold, damp ground. 'Oh, dear Lord,' I said, 'I ain't got no friend but you. Come to my help, Lord, for I'm in trouble!' "

Tubman, however, was no woman to wait for help to come to her. Making her way to Philadelphia, she managed to get a job in a hotel kitchen. She spent the winter cooking, washing dishes, saving her money, and thinking about how she could rescue her family from Maryland. At that time, Philadelphia was second only to Boston as a center of abolitionist sentiment; the city was home not only to many whites working toward emancipation but also to a large number of blacks, some of them legally free, some of them escaped slaves like Tubman.

Horse-drawn traffic rumbles through the cobbled streets of mid-19th-century Philadelphia. Tubman, who arrived in the bustling Pennsylvania city in 1849, wasted no time in finding herself a job; she signed on as a hotel cook and dishwasher.

The Philadelphia Vigilance Committee greets Henry "Box" Brown, a slave who escaped from Virginia in a wooden crate. Clergyman James Miller McKim stands at the far left; next to him is William Still, who kept a written record of the fugitive slaves who passed through Philadelphia.

Both blacks and whites in Philadelphia (and the rest of the North) had been galvanized by the passage of the Fugitive Slave Act of 1850. Under this federal legislation, any Negro accused of being a runaway could be brought before a federal judge or a special commissioner. Denied a jury trial or even the right to testify on his or her own behalf, the alleged runaway could easily be returned to slavery. All the law required was a sworn statement from a white individual who claimed to be the black person's owner. The law also provided heavy penalties for anyone who helped a slave escape. Many northerners, even some who were not abolitionists, believed that the Fugitive Slave Act violated both the Constitution and basic human rights.

Soon after Congress passed the infamous law, Harriet Tubman paid a call on the Philadelphia Vigilance Committee. This organization, formed to assist fugitive slaves, was managed by two of the Underground Railroad's busiest "station masters": white clergyman James Miller McKim and William Still, a freeborn black Pennsylvanian. Still managed to meet just about every escaping slave who passed through Philadelphia. He fed them, listened to their stories, and helped them plan the next stage of their journey, no matter what the danger to himself.

One celebrated incident in McKim and Still's career involved Henry Brown, a slave from Richmond, Virginia. Brown persuaded a sympathetic white friend to nail him into a wooden packing box and ship it to the Vigilance Committee's office. After 25 hours in the small, suffocating crate, a beaming Brown emerged to greet the astonished Still and McKim. For the rest of his life, the ingenious escapee was known as "Box" Brown.

Unlike most of the fugitive slaves he helped, Still could read and write, and he used his talents well. He interviewed the runaways who passed through and recorded their names and stories in a ledger. It was Still's hope that one day all slaves would be free, and that when that day came, families might be able to trace their relatives through his records. He kept his ledger hidden in a graveyard, but in 1872, when it was at last safe to make it public, he published it under the title *The Underground Rail Road*. Still's book, one of the few written records of the legendary slave-escape system, has proved a gold mine to students of American history.

Tubman took to making frequent visits to Still's office, where she met and talked with many fugitive slaves. Meanwhile, she saved her pennies to help finance the trip she planned, back to the Eastern Shore to bring her family across the Mason-Dixon line. As it turned out, her first trip as a conductor was not to the Eastern Shore but to Baltimore, across the Chesapeake Bay.

Author Ann Petry described Tubman's first return to the South in her 1955 book, *Harriet Tubman: Conductor on the Underground Railway*. One night, according to Petry, Tubman was paying a call on Still and McKim when a stranger appeared, asking for help. He wanted the Vigilance Committee's assistance in rescuing a black woman and her two children from Cambridge, Maryland. The woman's husband was a free man, said the visitor, but his wife and children were about to be auctioned off to slave traders from the Deep South.

The visiting abolitionist said a local Quaker (a member of the Religious Society of Friends, a pacifist Christian sect) might be able to get the family out of Cambridge; but they would need someone to pilot them across the dangerous stretch from Baltimore to Philadelphia. As he outlined the escape plan, he mentioned the name of the free husband: John Bowley. Tubman must have looked startled; Bowley was her brother-in-law, husband of her sister Mary.

Baltimore, shown here in an
1849 photograph, was known as
a dangerous spot for fugitives.
The Philadelphia Vigilance Committee's William Still tried to talk
Tubman out of going to the
Maryland city in 1850, but she
knew she was needed there, and
she went.

At once, Tubman announced that she herself
would go to Baltimore and guide the Bowley family
to safety. Still objected. Tubman, he noted, was still
a fugitive herself, and Baltimore was a dangerous city
for runaways. Travel, too, was extremely hazardous.
Blacks who tried to board trains, even in the company
of their masters, were weighed and measured like
sacks of grain so they could be compared with the
ever-growing list of runaways.

But Tubman insisted. She knew the land, she
said; she had crossed it herself. And she could leave
at once. Time was growing short, and the mission
would have to be accomplished quickly. Reluctantly,
Still agreed to let Tubman try.

On the day of the Cambridge auction, a black
man claiming to belong to the auctioneer came to
the slave pen during the noontime break. He gave

the guard an official-looking letter, requesting him to turn the female captive and her children over to the bearer; the slaves, said the letter, were to be taken to the hotel where the auctioneer was having lunch.

The "auctioneer's slave" was John Bowley, and his official letter had been forged by his Quaker ally. Sensing nothing amiss, the guard unlocked the pen. Bowley marched his family through the streets of Cambridge to the home of his Quaker accomplice. The Quaker hid the fugitives in his attic until nightfall, then escorted them to the river. There, a small sailboat awaited them.

An experienced seaman, Bowley hustled his family aboard and set sail for the North. When he spotted the prearranged signal, one blue and one yellow lantern, he brought the boat ashore. A white woman met the fugitives, concealed them in a wagonload of potatoes, and took them to a brick house.

Bowley knocked on the door, and a voice from inside said, "Who's there?" He responded with the password: "A friend with friends." The door flew open, and Harriet Tubman rushed out to embrace her relatives. With her precious "shipment" in tow, Tubman made it back to Philadelphia safely, as indeed she was always to make it. "I never ran my train off the track," she proudly noted years later, "and I never lost a passenger."

Baltimore, as Still had pointed out, was a dangerous place for a fugitive slave, but the Eastern Shore was even more perilous. Nevertheless, it was there that Tubman's remaining family lived, and it was there she went. She made her first trip to Dorchester County in the spring of 1851. When she returned to Philadelphia, she brought one of her brothers and two other men, whom she entrusted to Still's care. She worked all that summer and fall, saving money for a trip she had dreamed of ever since the day she first left Maryland.

A slave pen, built to hold blacks designated for auction, stands ready to receive its human merchandise. It was from such an enclosure that Tubman's brother-in-law, John Bowley, spirited his wife and children out of Cambridge, Maryland, and into Tubman's arms.

Fugitive slave Thomas Sims (second row, center), after his 1851 arrest by Boston marshal Charles Devins, is escorted to the ship that will return him to Georgia. Boston's Vigilance Committee plastered the city with copies of a poster (opposite) warning all blacks to be wary of slave catchers after Sims was captured. (Despite a major attempt to rescue him, Sims was returned to Georgia. In 1863, he escaped again. In 1877, he showed up in Washington, D.C., where he was employed by the U.S. attorney general—Charles Devins, the man who had sent him back to slavery 26 years earlier.)

In December, Tubman made her way back down the peninsula to Dorchester County. She had to exercise extraordinary caution, because this was an area where she was well known. When she arrived at the Brodas plantation just after dark one evening, she went directly to her husband's cabin. Perhaps she hesitated before approaching his door. He had, after all, often ridiculed her dreams of freedom and had even threatened to betray her. What kind of welcome would she get? She knocked on the door. It swung open to reveal John Tubman—and a young, attractive black woman.

When Harriet Tubman told her husband she had come back for him, he laughed in her face. The young woman at his side, he said, was now his wife, and he had no interest in going anywhere. Late that night, Harriet Tubman left the plantation with several slaves and never looked back. She never laid eyes on John Tubman again and rarely spoke of him.

That was Tubman's third trip to the South. By now, she had developed the routes and techniques that would serve her so well as she conducted her people to freedom. Although every step was risky, Tubman's familiarity with the roads, the hiding places, and the "depots" allowed her to travel with increasing assurance.

On her rescue expeditions, Tubman usually traveled in Delaware as far as possible before crossing into Maryland. Delaware offered several advantages. First, it contained the headwaters of most of the rivers that drained the Eastern Shore, which meant she could use a small boat to reach almost any point. Even more important, Delaware was home to many more free black men and women than slaves. The state's black population in 1860 was 21,627, of whom only 1,798 were slaves. Delaware was, in fact, the only state in the South where a black person was assumed to be free unless proven to be a slave. Tubman could thus cross the state fairly openly, at least on the way down.

Tubman's return route took her past a number of Underground Railroad stations, or safe houses. When she approached one, she would hide her "passengers," then knock at the door. When someone responded from inside, she would answer with the magic words: "A friend with friends."

On most of Tubman's trips from the South, her last stop was Wilmington, Delaware, a city right on the Mason-Dixon line. Wilmington was the home of Quaker Thomas Garrett, a remarkable man who would become one of Tubman's closest friends. Garrett owned a large shoe store; when fleeing slaves arrived at his door, he hid them behind a false wall in his shop. He also provided each runaway with a pair of shoes, for many the first they had ever owned. According to William Still's records, Garrett helped some 2,700 slaves escape.

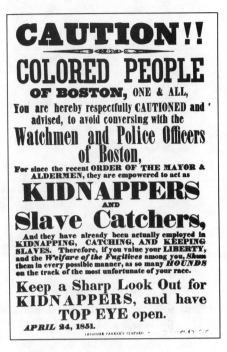

Several times arrested, found guilty, and heavily fined for assisting runaways, Garrett finally lost both his shoe business and his sizable personal fortune. Undeterred, he went back to work at the age of 60 and continued to help fugitives. He was arrested and fined again; this time, the presiding judge said he hoped the experience would teach Garrett to stop interfering "with the cause of justice by helping off runaway Negroes." Garrett, who spoke in the Quakers' biblical phrases, rose, looked hard at the judge, and said, "Friend, thee hasn't left me a dollar, but I wish to say to thee . . . that if anyone knows of a fugitive who wants a shelter, and a friend, *send him to Thomas Garrett!*"

In an 1868 letter to Sarah Bradford, Garrett referred with awe to "the remarkable labors" of Tubman. "In truth, I never met with any person, of any color, who had more confidence in the voice of God, as spoken direct to her soul," he said. "She has declared to me that she felt no more fear of being arrested by her former master . . . when in his immediate neighborhood, than she did in the State of New York, or Canada, for she said she ventured only where God sent her."

A runaway black family arrives at an Underground Railroad station. Operated by a loosely organized network of abolitionists, the Railroad consisted of a series of way stations where fugitives could rest, eat, and get directions to the next stop. Some historians believe that as many as 75,000 blacks escaped to freedom via the U.G.R.R., as the system was sometimes called.

By 1851, the Fugitive Slave Act was taking a heavy toll of runaways. Tubman heard ominous news of fugitive slaves arrested and returned to the South from such previously safe cities as Boston and Syracuse, New York. Abolitionists were outraged. "The only way to make the Fugitive Slave Act a dead letter," said former slave Frederick Douglass, "is to make a half dozen or more dead kidnappers."

Free blacks and their allies in the North began to fight back. In Boston, 300 armed men were needed to send 1 fugitive back to the South. The Fugitive Slave Act backfired in the long run because it increased northern opposition to slavery; yet it succeeded in making life difficult for Harriet Tubman. No longer able to work safely in Philadelphia, she moved to St. Catharines, Canada, a small town near Niagara Falls where many free blacks and former slaves had settled.

Between 1851 and 1857, Tubman made two trips to the Eastern Shore each year, one in the fall and one in the spring. Now instead of 90 miles, she had to conduct her passengers on a grueling journey of almost 500 miles. But the trips brought her people to genuine freedom, and they gave her the chance to meet the leaders of the abolitionist movement, many of whom lived in New York State and New England. It was on these pilgrimages that she met and befriended such giants of the movement as Frederick Douglass, Gerrit Smith, J. W. Loguen, and John Brown, the man who would most inspire her. ✺

John Brown (seen here in an early portrait) was to leave an indelible imprint on American history—and on Tubman. Along with the rest of the nation, Tubman probably first heard of the fiery abolitionist in 1856, when he staged a series of spectacular raids on proslavery settlements in Kansas Territory.

5

"MOVE OR DIE!"

❦

ALREADY, PEOPLE WERE calling her Moses. She traveled light and she traveled fast.

She knew the places where it was safe to hide: drainage ditches, hedges, and abandoned sheds or tobacco barns. Sometimes, she concealed her fugitives in potato holes, board-lined pits where farmers stored their winter vegetables. Once, she and her group hid in a manure pile and breathed through straws.

In addition to such hideouts, there were the more comfortable way stations, most of them operated by Quakers or free black people. Residents of the Cooper House in Camden, New Jersey, for example, regularly hid fugitives in a bunk-room over their kitchen. Another stopover for fleeing blacks was in Odessa, Delaware, where the Friends Meeting House (the Quaker version of a church) had a concealed loft over the sanctuary.

Harriet Tubman always carried a revolver on the Underground Railroad, and she was always ready to use it. "She could not read or write, but she had military genius," a contemporary said of her.

Tubman's standard procedure was to gather money and supplies in the North and then slip down the Eastern Shore, through Delaware and into Mary-

Tubman holds a musket in this engraving, but her choice of weapons was usually a pistol. Carrying her weapon—and willing to use it—the Underground Railroad conductor enforced iron discipline on the sometimes fainthearted fugitives she escorted to freedom.

This clergyman's residence in Ripley, Ohio, was among the Underground Railroad's busiest stations. High on a bluff overlooking the Ohio River, the house could easily be seen by escaping Kentucky slaves on the river's opposite bank.

land. There, she would make contact with the slaves who were ready to escape. She usually led them away on Saturday night, hoping they would not be missed and pursued until Monday. Before heading out, she paid someone to take down the wanted posters that would be sure to appear across the countryside.

In a 1907 article, the New York *Herald* described Tubman's methods:

> On some darkly propitious night there would be breathed about the Negro quarters of a plantation word that she had come to lead them forth. At midnight, she would stand waiting in the depths of woodland or timbered swamp, and stealthily, one by one, her fugitives would creep to the rendezvous. She entrusted her plans to but few of the party. . . . She knew her path well by this time, and they followed her unerring guidance without question. She assumed the authority and enforced the discipline of a military despot.

Once the slaves had left, there was no turning back. Tubman knew too well what happened to runaways who returned: They were beaten until they revealed their escape plans and the names of the people who had aided them. She would allow no one to betray her routes and secrets.

More than once, a slave grew fainthearted and wanted to go back, just as her brothers had the first time she tried to run away. Sometimes they were men twice her size. But now she was prepared. The hesitant slave would feel the cold steel of a revolver at his head and hear Tubman's voice harsh in his ear: "Move or die!" They moved. None of her passengers ever turned back, and she never lost one. To keep babies from crying, Tubman sometimes drugged them with opium, then readily available. When their mothers grew tired, she carried the babies in a basket on her arm.

To raise the flagging spirits of her followers, Tubman often sang to them as they plodded through woods and swamps. Hearing her strong, husky voice, the weary fugitives often joined in. The spiritual they most often sang referred to the biblical Moses' delivery of his people from Egyptian bondage:

> You may hinder me here, but you can't up there,
> Let my people go.
> He sits in the heavens and answers prayer,
> Let my people go!
>
> Oh go down, Moses,
> Way down in Egypt land,
> Tell old Pharaoh,
> Let my people go.

Tubman's blackouts still came upon her at unexpected times. She would simply collapse by the side of the road, and her passengers could only watch and wait until she awakened; then they would be off again. Sometimes, Tubman would steal a slave owner's buggy for the first stage of the journey. She knew the neighbors would assume the slaves were out on an errand for their master. When the horses grew winded, Tubman would abandon the buggy and continue the trip on foot, by boat, or in a cart heaped with vegetables.

Conductor Tubman became an expert at disguise and deception. Once, when she had to enter the village where her former master lived, she disguised herself as an old slave bringing chickens to market. The New York *Herald* told the story 50 years later: "As she turned a corner she saw coming toward her none other than her old master. Lest he might see through her impersonation, and to make an excuse for flight, she loosed the cord that held the fowls and amid the laughter of the bystanders, gave chase to them as they flew squawking over a nearby fence." In her 1869 biography of Tubman, Sarah Bradford added, "And [the master] went on his way, little thinking that he was brushing the very garments of the woman who had dared to steal herself, and others of his belongings."

On another occasion, Tubman disguised herself by pretending to read a book—hoping she was holding it right side up. Soon she heard one man whisper to another: "This can't be the woman. The one we want can't read or write."

By 1854, the woman called Moses was well known throughout the Eastern Shore, a legend among the slaves and a demon to the slaveholders. Try as they might, the plantation owners never got so much as a glimpse of this mysterious figure who came to the slave cabins at night and spirited away their valuable property.

In late 1854, Tubman got word that three of her brothers, Benjamin, John, and William Henry Ross, were going to be sold south the day after Christmas. It was time for a trip to Dorchester County. Tubman had a friend write to Jacob Jackson, a literate black man who lived near the estate where her brothers worked as hired slaves. "Read my letter to the old folks [Old Ben and Rit], and give my love to them," said the letter. "Tell my brothers to be always watching unto prayer, and when the good old ship of Zion comes along, to be ready to step on board."

On Christmas Eve, Tubman arrived on the East-ern Shore. Collecting her brothers, 2 other men, and a young woman, she headed for her parents' cabin, some 40 miles to the north. She would not take Ben and Rit this time; she knew that at their advanced age they were unlikely to be sold and shipped south. The group left in such a hurry that Tubman's brother William Henry had to leave his wife and newborn baby, promising to return for them soon. When it was time to go, Tubman waited for no one.

When the party arrived at Ben and Rit's cabin, they hid in an outbuilding where feed corn was stored. The parents knew nothing of the escape plan. Tub-man longed to see her mother, but she knew the old woman was unable to keep a secret and would tell the whole neighborhood. To make matters worse, Rit had been expecting her sons all day and had killed and cooked a pig for them. Tubman sent the two extra men to the cabin; they called Old Ben out into

Fugitives arrive at the Ohio farm of Levi Coffin, a dedicated sup-porter of the Underground Rail-road. Like his fellow Quaker Thomas Garrett of Wilmington, Coffin made no secret of the hos-pitality, financial assistance, and transportation he provided to fleeing slaves.

Louisiana runaways rest before heading north. Faced with immense distances through hostile country, fugitives from the cotton states were far more likely to be killed or captured than were those escaping from the Upper South.

the night and told him what was going on. He promised to keep the secret from Rit and said he would bring the hungry travelers some food.

Ben Ross, a slave for almost 50 years, had earned a widespread reputation for honesty. Indeed, he must have doubted his own ability to lie, for when he visited his children in the corncrib, he averted his eyes and never looked directly at them. And later, on Christmas Day, when he said good-bye to them, he tied a bandanna over his eyes.

Tubman and her passengers headed north toward freedom. A few days later, a team of slave chasers brought a report to the man who owned Ben and Rit. The men said they had questioned the fugitives' parents. They found the old woman heartbroken because she had been expecting her boys for Christmas. And the old man said he had not laid eyes on his children. The slaveholder accepted the story. He knew Ben Ross was no liar.

"Moses arrives with six passengers," noted the Vigilance Committee's William Still when Tubman brought her fugitives into Philadelphia. "Great fears were entertained for her safety, but she seemed wholly devoid of personal fear," wrote Still in his ledger. "The idea of being captured by slave-hunters or slaveholders, seemed never to enter her mind." Still added that he found it "obvious" that Tubman's "success in going into Maryland as she did was attributable to her adventurous spirit and utter disregard of consequences. Her like it is probable was never known before or since."

After escorting her brothers and their friends to Canada, Tubman prepared for her next mission. This one, undertaken in November 1856, involved a woman and three men. One of the men, Josiah Bailey, was the kind of slave every master wanted. Strong, healthy, and skilled as a farmer, he never talked back or gave any trouble. Bailey had been rented out by his master for six years to a planter named William Hughlett. In 1856, Hughlett decided to buy Bailey. He paid $2,000, a steep price but worth it to the purchaser, who planned to save money by making Bailey his overseer.

The day he bought him, Hughlett gave Bailey a savage whipping. The slave had done no wrong, said the master, but he needed to learn who owned him. Bailey submitted silently but, he later told Tubman, he said to himself, "This is the first and the last." That night he "borrowed" a rowboat and made his painful way down the river to Rit and Ben Ross's cabin. Speaking to Ross alone, he said, "The next time Moses comes, let me know."

Tubman arrived soon afterward. With Bailey and the other escapees, she headed north, closely followed by a small army of slave catchers. Because Bailey was so valuable, his master offered an unusually high reward for his capture. Hughlett posted signs all through the Eastern Shore. They showed the South's symbol of a runaway, a black figure with a knapsack and a walking stick. The signs read:

Heavy Reward
Two Thousand Six Hundred Dollars

After describing the runaways, the signs—which Bailey read to Tubman and the others—said that $1,500 was for Josiah Bailey alone; the rest was for the other slaves. Separate posters announced an even higher reward for a certain black woman. Harriet Tubman, "sometimes called Moses," was worth $12,000 to any person who delivered her to the authorities. The countryside swarmed with bounty hunters, but Tubman knew the Eastern Shore better than any of her pursuers. At one point, she led her shivering people across a deep creek, using a hidden ford that she said she had seen in a dream.

For the first time Tubman had a helper. Tough and courageous, Josiah Bailey pushed the group forward, singing in a low voice. Among his favorite verses was this one:

Who comes yonder all dressed in red?
I heard the angels singing—
It's all the children Moses led,
I heard the angels singing.

Keeping to the fields and hedges, the party made it as far as Wilmington, but they found the Delaware River bridge heavily guarded. Wanted posters were everywhere. Tubman scattered her group, placing them in the homes of sympathetic free blacks. She

believed her friend Thomas Garrett would find a way
to help, and she was right. Garrett sent a wagonload
of bricklayers across the bridge; when they returned
to Wilmington that night, seemingly drunk, they
carried five black fugitives hidden under the bricks.

From Wilmington, Tubman led the group to Philadelphia, then on to New York City. The trip had
gone as well it could have, but Bailey was growing
discouraged. He had thought they would be safe in
the North, but the wanted posters were on every wall
here, too. When the fugitives walked into the office
of the New York Anti-Slavery Society, its president,
Oliver Johnson, shook Bailey's hand and said jokingly, "Well, Joe, I'm glad to see the man whose head
is worth $1,500!"

Bailey did not laugh. "How did you know me?"
he asked. Johnson showed him a copy of the poster
and said that anyone who read it would recognize
Bailey easily. That meant that anywhere between
New York and Canada—a distance of more than 300
miles—someone might pounce on him and drag him
off for the reward. Disheartened, Bailey begged Tubman and the others to go on to Canada without him.
With him along, he said, they were all bound to be
caught. Tubman, of course, refused.

The rest of the trip north was easier. Much of the
Underground Railroad's route through New York
State involved real trains; Tubman and her charges
traveled in a baggage car, watched over by a sympathetic trainman. But Bailey, Tubman later told
Sarah Bradford, "was silent. He talked no more. He
sang no more. He sat with his head on his hand, and
nobody could rouse him, or make him take any interest in anything."

When the train approached Niagara Falls, the
conductor took the group into a coach so they could
see Canada on the other side of the bridge. Even
there, they were still in danger. Until the train

*The figure of a fleeing black often
appeared on the South's wanted
posters, most of which offered rewards. Few escapees, however,
were worth as much to bounty
hunters as Tubman; the price on
her head was $12,000.*

Nineteenth-century painter Thomas Mason caught the sense of terror felt by blacks who braved storms, swamps, and snarling dogs in their quest for freedom. Tubman must also have known fear on her many rescue missions, but by all accounts, she never showed it.

reached the center of the bridge, any slave catcher could legally arrest them and drag them all back into slavery. But the train moved steadily across the great iron bridge. When it reached the center, Tubman gave Bailey a shake and shouted, "Joe, you're in Queen Victoria's dominions! You're a free man!"

Bailey used his voice for the first time in days. With tears streaming down his face, he looked up and began to sing, "Glory to God and Jesus too, One more soul is safe!" He kept on singing, even after the train had stopped on the Canadian shore. A crowd of curious white people gathered around him on the platform, staring as he bellowed, "There's only one more journey for me now, and that's to heaven."

Tubman tugged at his sleeve, trying to quiet him. "Well, you old fool," she joked. "You might have looked at the Falls first and gone to heaven afterwards!"

AM I NOT A MAN AND A BROTHER?

6

"THE GREATEST HEROINE OF THE AGE"

⸎

T HE 1850s BEGAN with the passage of the infamous Fugitive Slave Act and ended with violence and bloodshed at Harpers Ferry, Virginia. In the years between, the storm clouds that had been gathering in the 1830s and 1840s grew darker. North and South eyed each other with increasing mistrust. The United States moved steadily toward division.

The abolitionist movement had been intensifying its crusade against slavery from the 1830s on. By the 1850s, a battalion of popular lecturers was sweeping through the North, driving home the message that slavery was a sin. Among the most effective speakers were such former slaves as Frederick Douglass and such white abolitionists as Wendell Phillips, an aristocratic Bostonian who later served as president of the Anti-Slavery Society. In Congress, Senator Charles Sumner of Massachusetts and other pro-abolition legislators made passionate speeches, which they transcribed and mailed to thousands of voters. Many northern newspapers, including the powerful New York *Tribune*, took an unreserved stand against slavery. Perhaps the most irresistible abolitionist message, however, was delivered by a remarkable book, *Uncle Tom's Cabin*.

Published by the American Anti-Slavery Society, an 1835 handbill shows an image widely used in abolitionist literature: a chained slave asking, "Am I not a man and a brother?" The Anti-Slavery Society, formed in 1833, flooded the North with such emotional appeals.

Abolitionist orator Wendell Phillips addresses an antislavery meeting on Boston Common. An admirer and good friend of Tubman's, Phillips served as president of the Anti-Slavery Society from 1865 to 1870.

Written by New Englander Harriet Beecher Stowe and published in 1852, *Uncle Tom's Cabin* struck America like a thunderbolt. Set in the plantation South, the novel tells the story of a devoutly Christian slave, Tom, and his friends and fellow slaves, George and Eliza Harris. George escapes from his cruel master, planning to buy his wife and son's freedom as soon as he can. Meanwhile, Eliza learns that circumstances have forced her kindhearted owner, Mr. Shelby, to sell both Tom and her son, Harry. Desperate, she flees with Harry.

Tom is shipped south, where he saves the life of Eva, a six-year-old white girl. Eva's grateful father, Augustine St. Clair, then buys Tom, but both St. Clair and his daughter soon die. Tom is bought by the sadistic Simon Legree, who viciously mistreats the patient old slave. Eliza and George Harris manage to escape with their boy to Canada, but Tom meets a grim fate. Just as George Shelby, the son of his former master, arrives to buy him back, Tom is beaten to death by Legree. Appalled, Shelby denounces slavery and becomes an abolitionist.

The first edition of *Uncle Tom's Cabin* sold out within a week of publication; little more than a year later, sales reached 1 million. The book, described by historian J. C. Furnas as "a verbal earthquake, an ink-and-paper tidal wave," sparked a wave of hatred against slavery, even among many previously neutral northerners. In the novel's wake came a flood of "Tom shows," popular dramatic portrayals of the horribly mistreated but always forgiving Uncle Tom.

According to Sarah Bradford, Tubman's friends once tried to persuade her to attend a Philadelphia performance of *Uncle Tom*. "I've heard *Uncle Tom's Cabin* read," she reportedly replied, "and I tell you, Mrs. Stowe's pen hasn't begun to paint what slavery is. . . . I've seen the *real thing*, and I don't want to see it on any stage."

The slavery issue continued to occupy the national stage as well, fanning ever-deeper anger between North and South. In 1857, the United States Supreme Court finally expressed its opinion on the issue, but instead of soothing the interregional quarrel, the Court's decision heightened it. The case involved Dred Scott, a Missouri slave whose master had taken him to the free territory of Minnesota and then back to the slave state of Missouri. Claiming that residence in free territory had made him a free man, Scott sued for freedom from his master. When the state supreme court decided against Scott, his abolitionist lawyers took his case to the U.S. Supreme Court.

After hearing lengthy arguments on both sides of the question, Chief Justice Roger B. Taney issued the Court's majority opinion. Scott, said Taney, was not a citizen and had no right to sue in a federal court. The Constitution had created a white man's government, and Negroes, "beings of an inferior order," had "no rights which a white man was bound to respect." Furthermore, stated the chief justice, Scott's resi-

Uncle Tom and Little Eva, characters in Harriet Beecher Stowe's Uncle Tom's Cabin, *appear on a 19th-century theatrical poster. "Tom shows"—stage versions of Stowe's best-selling novel about slavery—swept the nation in the 1860s, but Tubman refused to attend one. "I've seen the real thing," she said.*

dence in a free territory had not affected his status as a slave; he was property, and the Constitution forbade anyone to deprive a man of his property without "due process of law."

Meanwhile, a young Illinois politician named Abraham Lincoln was making a name for himself by engaging in public debates on the slavery issue. Like many Americans in the North and the Midwest, Lincoln—whose oratorical skills would help carry him to the White House—opposed slavery on moral, political, and ethical grounds. He did not, however, support social and political equality for blacks.

In Lincoln's view, slavery presented a threat to white Americans. If the United States accepted the idea that blacks were not created with equal rights, he said, it might next deny equal rights to other groups. "As a nation," Lincoln said in 1855, "we began by declaring that 'all men are created equal.' We now practically read it 'all men are created equal, except negroes.' " At that rate, continued the Illinois Republican, "it will [soon] read 'all men are created equal, except negroes and foreigners, and catholics.' "

Lincoln opposed the extension of slavery into the territories because, he said, white free labor would be unable to compete with black slave labor. Although his views would become less conservative over the years, in the 1850s Lincoln maintained that if slavery were confined to the South, it would eventually die of its own accord. Given enough time, he said, the "wrong" of human bondage would disappear from the United States.

As Lincoln addressed the citizens of Illinois about slavery, people were fighting and dying over the issue in the territory known as "bleeding Kansas." Soon after Kansas Territory was opened for settlement in 1854, large numbers of pioneers moved there. While most of the newcomers came to establish farms, many came to determine the status of slavery in the terri-

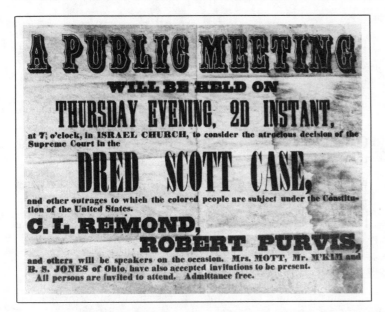

An 1857 poster advertises a meeting to protest "the atrocious decision of the Supreme Court in the Dred Scott case." The decision labeled blacks "an inferior order" and said they had "no rights which a white man was bound to respect."

tory. Both dedicated Free-Soilers and equally ardent supporters of slavery poured into Kansas, each side ready to fight for its beliefs.

In 1856, a band of proslavery adherents attacked the town of Lawrence, killing several antislavery residents. In revenge, John Brown, a fiercely dedicated white abolitionist who believed that God had appointed him to destroy slavery, attacked the proslavery settlement of Pottawatomie and killed five people. As a result of the 2 raids, civil conflict broke out in Kansas; more than 200 settlers died in the guerrilla warfare between the 2 factions.

In this climate of violence and turmoil, Harriet Tubman continued her work, traveling to the Eastern Shore, meeting with slaves who wanted to escape, and telling them about the North's abolition movement. During the mid-1850s, she began giving certain groups of runaways directions to Underground Railroad stations and sending them off on their own. In other cases, she escorted groups of escapees as far as Philadelphia or New York, left them in charge of friends there, then headed back south for more passengers. When Tubman felt unsure that a group of escaping slaves would be able to make the trip without her, she accompanied them all the way from Maryland to Canada. Tubman had now become a regular on the route that led north from New York City to Troy and Albany, then west across the Mohawk Valley to Niagara Falls and free Canada.

In 1855, journalist Benjamin Drew visited several Canadian towns where free blacks had settled. In the village of St. Catharines, Drew met and interviewed the celebrated woman known as Moses. He asked her to comment on slavery and recorded her response in his 1856 book, *The Refugee; or Narratives of Fugitive Slaves*:

> I grew up like a neglected weed—ignorant of liberty, having no experience of it. I was not happy or contented: Every time I saw a white man I was afraid of being carried away. . . . We were always uneasy. Now I've been free, I know what slavery is. . . . I think slavery is the next thing to hell. If a person would send another into bondage, he would, it appears to me, be bad enough to send him to hell if he could.

About a year after she talked to Drew, Tubman made her first visit to Boston, where she was invited to attend an antislavery meeting. Historian, playwright, and novelist William Wells Brown, a former slave who had become an ardent abolitionist and a popular speaker, noted her presence in one of his many books, *The Rising Son; or the Antecedents and Advancements of the Colored Race*:

> For eight or ten years previous to the breaking out of the Rebellion [the Civil War], all who frequented antislavery conventions, lectures, picnics, and fairs could not fail to have seen a black woman of medium size, upper front teeth gone, smiling countenance, attired in coarse, but neat apparel, with an old-fashioned reticule or bag suspended by her side, and who, on taking her seat, would at once drop off into a sound sleep.

Tubman, said Brown, became a frequent visitor at the homes of Boston's leading abolitionists. These highly educated, cultured men and women would listen spellbound as Tubman, who could neither read nor write, discussed slavery and abolition. Brown found himself awed by Tubman. "Men from Canada, who had made their escape years before, and whose families were still in the prison-house of slavery, would seek out Moses, and get her to go and bring their dear ones away," he wrote. "How strange! This woman—one of the most ordinary looking of her race; unlettered, no idea of geography, asleep half of the time. . . . No fugitive was ever captured who had Moses for a leader."

Tubman was resourceful, courageous, and dedicated to freedom. But like the rest of the human race, she was also capable of making human errors. Apparently very lonely in her midthirties, she committed one of the strangest acts of her life: She abducted a child. The episode began in 1855 or 1856, when she stopped at the Eastern Shore home of one of her brothers and became captivated by his daughter Margaret. More than 80 years later, Margaret's daughter, then Mrs. A. J. Brickler of Wilberforce, Ohio, recounted the story to an interviewer:

> My mother's life really began with Aunt Harriet kidnapping her from her home on Eastern Shore, Maryland, when she was a little girl eight or nine years old. Aunt Harriet fell in love with the little girl who was my mother. Maybe it was because in mother she saw the child she herself might have been if slavery had been less cruel. Maybe it was because she knew the joys of motherhood would never be hers and she longed for some little creature who would love her for her own self's sake. Certainly whatever her emotion, it was stronger than her better judgment, for when her visit was ended, she, secretly, and without so much as a by-your-leave, took the little girl with her to her Northern home.

Tubman, continued her grandniece, "must have regretted her act for she knew she had taken the child from a sheltered good home to a place where there was nobody to care for her." In any event, said Brick-

William Henry Seward was governor of New York (1839–43), U.S. senator (1849–61), and U.S. secretary of state (1861–69). He was also one of Tubman's staunchest admirers. "I have known her long," he once wrote, "and a nobler, higher spirit, or a truer, seldom dwells in the human form."

ler, not long after she had carried Margaret off, Tubman "thought of her white friends . . . and decided to place her dearest possession in their hands." She brought Margaret to her friend Frances Seward, wife of U.S. senator William H. Seward. (A former governor of New York and a dedicated abolitionist, Seward would serve as U.S. secretary of state from 1861 until 1869.)

"This kindly lady," said Brickler, "brought up mother, not as a servant but as a guest within her home. She taught mother to speak properly, to read, write, sew, do housework, and act as a lady. Whenever Aunt Harriet came back, mother was dressed and sent in the Seward carriage to visit her. Strange to say, mother looked very much like Aunt Harriet."

In 1857, soon after her short-lived experience as a mother, Tubman settled down in a home of her own. She had always been forthright about asking supporters to help finance her rescue missions, but she never asked for personal funds. Now, however, her friend William Seward took a firm stand. According to biographer Bradford, he said, "Harriet, you have worked for others long enough," and presented her with the deed to a little house in Auburn, New York. To avoid any appearance of charity, Seward "sold" Tubman the house; he required no cash but asked her to make a regular series of small payments. Situated in the central part of the state, Auburn served as a major station on the Underground Railroad. The small town was to be Tubman's home for the rest of her life.

Not long after she moved to Auburn, Tubman received troubling news. Her father had been arrested and was awaiting trial for helping a fellow slave escape. In the eyes of the South, Ben Ross's crime was enormous; Tubman knew that even though he was more than 70 years old, he would be punished severely if found guilty. She made plans to head south immediately. Needing money for her trip, she stopped off at the New York City office of the Anti-Slavery Society and asked for $20, a sizable amount in 1857.

Tubman later told Sarah Bradford what happened next. The abolitionist official said, "*Twenty dollars!* Who told you to come here for twenty dollars?" Tubman replied, "The Lord told me, sir." "Well," countered the official, "I guess the Lord's mistaken this time." Tubman lifted her chin. "No, sir," she said, "the Lord's never mistaken! Anyhow, I'm going to sit here until I get it."

As good as her word, Tubman sat down and immediately went to sleep, probably suffering one of her frequent blackouts. As she slept and woke, then slept again, she was aware of visitors coming and going through the office. Many must have been sympathetic to her plight; when she awoke late in the afternoon, she found a pile of bills—amounting to $60—in her lap. Tubman set off for the Eastern Shore. Her father's trial was imminent, and there was no time to spare.

Tubman's rescue of her parents was a model of simplicity—and extraordinary daring. Slipping into Ben and Rit's cabin late one night, she told the as-

After rescuing her elderly parents from Maryland, Tubman brought them to this house in Auburn, New York. The building, purchased on easy terms from William Seward in 1857 and still standing today, was Tubman's home for more than 50 years.

tonished old people to prepare for a trip north. Next, she walked over to the plantation stable, found a horse, and hitched it to a rickety farm wagon. Then, wrote Quaker Thomas Garrett later, "She got her parents . . . on this rude vehicle . . . and drove to town in a style that no human being ever did before or since." Three days later, Tubman and her parents arrived in Wilmington. "I furnished her with money to take them all to Canada," wrote Garrett. "I afterward sold their horse and sent them the balance of the proceeds."

Tubman brought her parents first to Canada, then to Auburn. "Harriet's abduction of her parents was an event in Underground annals," observed biographer Earl Conrad in his 1943 account of Tubman. "It was significant, not only because rarely did aged folks take to the Road, but because Harriet carried them off with an audaciousness and an aplomb that represented complete mastery of the Railroad and perfect scorn of the white patrol. Her performance was that, at once, of the accomplished artist and the daring revolutionary."

Not everyone, however, applauded Tubman's courage. John Bell Robinson, a Philadelphia supporter of slavery, characterized the rescue of Ben and Rit as "a diabolical act of wickedness and cruelty." In his 1860 book, *Pictures of Slavery and Freedom*, Robinson called "the bringing away from ease and comfortable homes two old slaves over seventy years of age . . . as cruel an act as ever was performed by a child towards parents." To help elderly people to freedom was "a thousand times worse than to sell young ones away," insisted Robinson. Even "confinement in the penitentiary for life," he said, "would be inadequate to [Tubman's] crime." There is no indication that Tubman ever heard of Robinson or his opinions. If she did, perhaps she just looked at her parents and smiled.

By now, as Conrad observed, the Eastern Shore was being "plucked of slaves like a chicken of its feathers before roasting." And Harriet Tubman was the primary culprit. She began arming the runaways she sent north: In 1857, for example, she equipped a departing group of 28 men, women, and children with revolvers, pistols, and butcher knives. All of them made it safely to the home of Thomas Garrett and then to Canada. Frantic plantation owners hired more slave hunters and raised the price on Tubman's head. "It now came to pass," noted a contemporary northern account, "that . . . rewards were offered for the apprehension of the Negro woman who was denuding the fields of their laborers and the cabins of their human livestock."

In the late 1850s, Tubman agreed to speak at a few New England antislavery meetings. She had little time for such activities; between her trips south, she

Their stolen wagon hitched to a pair of oxen, a band of fugitives crosses Virginia's Rappahannock River. As Tubman brought more and more slaves out of the South, slave owners became increasingly eager to catch the woman who was "denuding the fields of their laborers."

"Fighting Minister" Thomas Higginson feared for the life of his friend Tubman, whom he called "the greatest heroine of the age." She "will probably be burned alive whenever she is caught," said Higginson, "which she probably will be, first or last, as she is going again [to the South]."

had to work hard to support herself and her parents. (Strange as it seems, this daring commando earned her living as a domestic, usually in hotels.) When she did find time to address conventions, Tubman enthralled her audiences.

Clergyman Thomas Wentworth Higginson, president of the Massachusetts Anti-Slavery Society, often praised Tubman's abilities as a speaker. A celebrated orator himself, he said he had learned the art from "the slave women who had been stripped and whipped and handled with insolent hands and sold to the highest bidder . . . or women who, having once escaped, had, like Harriet Tubman, gone back again and again into the land of bondage to bring away their kindred and friends. . . . [I] learned to speak," he added, "because their presence made silence impossible."

Higginson, who was known as the Fighting Minister, wrote a letter to his mother about Tubman in 1859:

> We have had the greatest heroine of the age here, Harriet Tubman, a black woman and a fugitive slave. . . . Her tales of adventure are beyond anything in fiction and her ingenuity and generalship are extraordinary. . . . The slaves call her Moses. She has had a reward of twelve thousand dollars offered for her in Maryland and will probably be burned alive whenever she is caught, which she probably will be, first or last, as she is going again.

Despite her friend's grim predictions, Tubman was never caught. Before she changed her antislavery strategy, she would have made 19 excursions into the South, "stealing" more than 300 human beings from the land that had tried—and failed—to keep her in bondage. ◄♦►

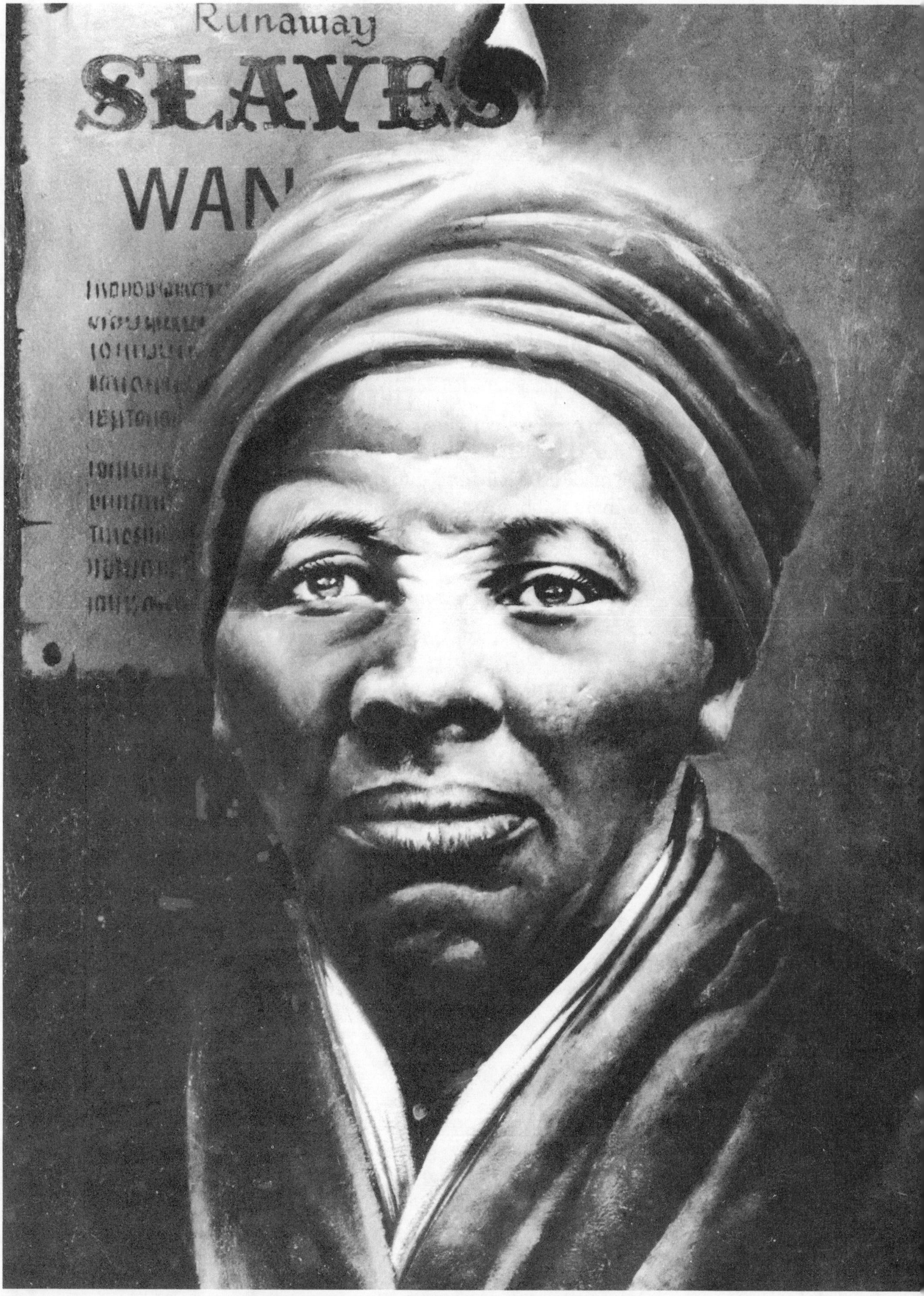
Runaway
SLAVES
WAN

7

GENERAL TUBMAN
GOES TO WAR

·❦·

ARRIET TUBMAN'S WORK had always involved stealth and secrecy; she chose, as Frederick Douglass once put it, "to labor in a private way," her activities observed only by "the midnight sky and the silent stars." She addressed occasional meetings only because her abolitionist friends insisted; a few words from her, they said, helped the cause more than dozens of speeches by its educated, well-to-do supporters. After she caught the attention of John Brown, however, Tubman lost any chance for obscurity.

Convinced he was God's instrument to destroy slavery, Brown had already battled proslavery forces in Kansas. By the late 1850s, he had decided it was time to take arms and end slavery everywhere. For his starting point, he settled on a little town at the northernmost corner of the South. He would assemble an army of abolitionists, both black and white, and strike at Harpers Ferry, Virginia, where the Potomac River passes through a gap in the Blue Ridge Mountains.

Brown planned to bring weapons to Harpers Ferry, seize more arms from the town's large arsenal, then retreat to the mountains, where he expected thousands of rebellious slaves to join him. With these

Tubman, probably about 40 years old in this portrait, still bears a scar on her temple from the ferocious blow she had received as a teenager. She also continued to suffer from the unpredictable "sleeping fits" induced by her near-fatal head wound.

319

John Brown, who believed he had a divine mission to end slavery by force, became a national figure during the Kansas Territory slavery battles of the mid-1850s. By the end of the decade, he was ready to start a full-scale war.

troops behind him, Brown expected to liberate all the slaves in the South, then establish a new national government. By late 1857, he had recruited a small band of free blacks and fugitive slaves. What he needed now was black leadership—charismatic figures who could inspire and lead these volunteers. He believed there were two such leaders in the United States: Harriet Tubman and Frederick Douglass. Brown would invite them both to join him in his great enterprise.

In the spring of 1858, Brown traveled through New England, rounding up support for his revolution among such leading abolitionists as Thomas Higginson and Franklin Sanborn of Massachusetts. From New England, Brown went on to New York State, meeting up with Frederick Douglass in Rochester. The celebrated orator, former slave, and abolitionist was apparently skeptical about Brown's plan, but he encouraged the fiery reformer to talk to Harriet Tubman, who had spent the winter working in St. Catharines. Accompanied by Tubman's friend, J. W. Loguen, the black clergyman and abolitionist, Brown accordingly headed for Canada. He arrived in April.

During the preceding winter, Tubman had had a recurring dream. Night after night, she recalled later, she dreamed of a "wilderness sort of place, all full of rocks and bushes." In the dream, a snake raised its head from among the rocks; as she watched, it turned into the head of an old man with a white beard and fierce, glittering eyes. He gazed at her, she said, "wishful like, just as if he was going to speak to me." Then, in the dream, two other heads, younger than the first, appeared. Finally, a crowd of men rushed in and struck down all three heads. Tubman told friends about the dream, which puzzled and disturbed her.

When she met John Brown, Tubman stared hard. His was the face—that of the old, bearded man with fire in his eyes—that she had seen in her dream. Still, the dream's meaning was unclear to her; maybe its message would reveal itself later. Meanwhile, Brown told Tubman of his planned revolution and asked her about the Underground Railroad, through which he hoped to channel slaves to join him at Harpers Ferry. He also asked her to recruit free blacks for the impending battle.

Clearly impressed with "General Tubman," as he called the militant black woman, Brown wrote a letter to his son about her. Curiously, he spoke of her as a man; perhaps he found it hard to believe that a woman could possess such strong qualities of leadership. "I came here direct with J. W. Loguen," said Brown's letter. "I am succeeding beyond my expectation. Harriet Tubman is the most of a man, naturally, that I ever met with. There is the most abundant material, and of the right quality, in this quarter, beyond all doubt."

During the following winter (1858–59), Tubman met with John Brown in Boston. There, the two conferred with Franklin Sanborn and other supporters of Brown's plan. Writing about that winter, Sanborn later noted that Brown "always spoke of [Tubman] with the greatest respect, and said that 'General Tubman,' as he styled her, was a better officer than most whom he had seen, and could command an army as successfully as she had led her small parties of fugitives."

Wendell Phillips, another great antislavery orator, met Tubman for the first time that winter. "The last time I ever saw John Brown," Phillips later recalled, "was under my own roof, as he brought Harriet Tubman to me, saying, 'Mr. Phillips, I bring you one of the best and bravest persons on this continent—General Tubman, as we call her.'"

Scheduled, delayed, and rescheduled several times, Brown's attack on Harpers Ferry would finally

Frederick Douglass shared John Brown's abolitionist goals, but he declined to join the old warrior's raid on Harpers Ferry, Virginia. "An attack on the federal government," Douglass warned Brown, "would array the whole country against us."

take place in October 1859. When the critical day arrived, however, Brown had neither of the black leaders he wanted at his side. Douglass, finally deciding that Brown's plan was doomed to failure, declined to join in the attack. Tubman, too, was absent.

Wholeheartedly admiring John Brown, Tubman had intended to join him for his historic battle. But in the summer of 1859, at the very moment she had planned to lend him her assistance, she fell ill. She had long suffered from the effects of the head wound she received as a young woman. Now almost 40, she found herself on the verge of exhaustion: The years of strenuous Underground Railroad journeys, combined with the heavy labor by which she supported herself and her parents, had caught up with her.

Tubman probably collapsed in Boston. In any case, friends took the sick woman to their home in New Bedford, Massachusetts, to recover. Meanwhile, Brown and his lieutenants had no idea where to find the "General," and she had no idea when the attack on Harpers Ferry would actually begin. In his biography of John Brown, the eminent black scholar W. E. B. Du Bois wrote, "Only sickness, brought on by her toil and exposure, prevented Harriet from being present at Harpers Ferry."

On the night of October 16, 1859, John Brown led his little band of abolitionist militants into the Virginia town and seized its federal arsenal. At his side were 5 blacks and 16 whites, 3 of them his sons. Almost immediately, Brown's fighters were attacked by citizens and local militia, who were soon joined by a company of United States Marines. With 10 of his men—including 2 of his sons—killed, Brown surrendered. Soon afterward, he was tried for treason, convicted, and hanged. Six of his remaining followers met the same fate.

When a horrified Tubman, still recovering from her illness, learned about the outcome of Brown's

raid, she must have recalled her dream of the previous winter; had those three stricken heads represented John Brown and his sons?

After Brown's trial, many abolitionists, including Tubman, kept as far away from the public eye as possible. They knew their names had been mentioned in the letters and papers that Brown had left scattered around the farmhouse from which he had staged his raid. Several prominent abolitionists, including Frederick Douglass, even left the country for a period. A Senate committee investigated the role played by the northern abolitionists, but in the end, none was accused of involvement in the Harpers Ferry raid. Tubman finally returned to her home in Auburn, still sick and now in mourning for the white man she had admired above all others of his race.

She must have been moved by Frederick Douglass's tribute to the slain visionary. "John Brown began the war that ended American slavery," said

Outnumbered and outgunned, John Brown's forces battle federal troops at the Harpers Ferry arsenal. Brown had hoped to enlist Tubman and Frederick Douglass in a mighty blow against slavery, but he went into action without either ally and with only 21 men behind him.

John Brown, a rope around his neck, heads for the gallows after his failed 1859 raid on Harpers Ferry. Devastated by the news of Brown's fate, Tubman said, "It was not John Brown that died. . . . It was Christ—it was the saviour of our people."

Douglass. "Until this blow was struck, the prospect for freedom was dim, shadowy, and uncertain. . . . When John Brown stretched forth his arm the sky was cleared—the armed hosts of freedom stood face to face over the chasm of a broken union, and the clash of arms was at hand."

By the following spring, Tubman was recovered and ready to renew her labors. In April, she staged her own raid, overwhelming scores of lawmen and rescuing fugitive slave Charles Nalle in Troy, New York. "Harriet Tubman's victory," commented biographer Earl Conrad, "was a high point of the fugitive slave history that racked the nation's breast for 10 years. If Brown's Virginia raid was a dress rehearsal for the Civil War, Harriet's action was a bugle call for the war to begin."

From Troy, Tubman went on to Boston. There, her friend and fellow Harpers Ferry conspirator, Frank Sanborn, escorted her from one gathering of social activists to another. She met many of the Bostonians passionately concerned with abolition, woman suffrage, economic theory, human rights, and civic reform. In a city preoccupied with the rights of women and blacks, Harriet Tubman became a highly sought-after speaker.

In drawing rooms all over Boston, men and women listened raptly as Tubman talked about her days as a slave, her travels on the Underground Railroad, and her association with the martyred John Brown. At one point, she said, "It was not John Brown that died at Charles Town [the Virginia town where he was hanged]. *It was Christ*—it was the saviour of our people."

Much of the talk in Boston revolved around the possibilities of ending slavery peacefully. Attired, as usual, in a well-worn gray cotton dress, its neck trimmed with lace and its full skirt reaching the floor, Tubman listened to such hopes silently but skeptically. At one point, Sanborn later recalled, she leaned toward him and whispered, "They may say, 'Peace, Peace!' as much as they like; I know there's going to be war!"

In Boston, Tubman spent most of her time with abolitionist groups, but she did make one speech at a women's rights convention, organized in 1860 by celebrated suffragists Susan B. Anthony and Elizabeth Cady Stanton. No record remains of Tubman's words, but a contemporary observer, author Robert W. Taylor, reported on their effects. "She made the weak strong, the strong determined, and the determined invincible," said Taylor. "After her words of untutored but fiery eloquence, her hearers stood like Martin Luther of old, body and soul and spirit devoted singly and untiringly to one end."

But for a woman of action, only so much time could be spent in drawing rooms and convention halls. As it happened, events in the fall of 1860 would plunge Tubman back into the tumultuous South. In November, Abraham Lincoln was elected president. Appalled by the victory of an abolitionist, South Carolina quickly seceded from the Union, virtually guaranteeing the flight of the rest of the cotton states. The specter of civil war loomed closer. Tubman, realizing that war would make it harder than ever to bring slaves out of the South, decided to make another foray into the Tidewater.

Supplied with traveling money by Boston abolitionists, Tubman headed for Maryland, where she picked up five slaves: Maria and Stephen Ennets and their three children, one of them a three-month-old baby. On her way north, Tubman collected two additional passengers, a man and a woman.

In December, Thomas Garrett of Wilmington sent a note to William Still of the Philadelphia Vigilance Committee. "I write to let thee know that Harriet Tubman is again in these parts. She arrived

By 1860, when he was elected president, Abraham Lincoln had made his position on slavery clear: "As I would not be a slave, so I would not be a master," he said in 1858. "This expresses my idea of democracy." Lincoln's election sparked South Carolina's secession from the Union and made civil war inevitable.

last evening from one of her trips of mercy to God's poor. . . . I gave Harriet ten dollars, to hire a man with a carriage to take them to [Philadelphia]. . . . I shall be very uneasy about them till I hear they are safe. There is now much more risk on the road . . . yet, as it is Harriet, who seems to have had a special angel to guard her on her journeys of mercy, I have hope."

The fugitives reached Philadelphia safely, and Still recorded their arrival in his book. Having learned from John Brown's mistakes, however, Still was now keeping less-detailed notes. The capture of Brown's letters and papers, he wrote, "with names and plans in full, admonished us that such papers and correspondence as had been preserved concerning the Underground Rail Road, might perchance be captured by a pro-slavery mob."

Tubman's 1860 Railroad trip was her last, although not by her own choice. As the North-South split widened, the South clamored ever more loudly for enforcement of the Fugitive Slave Act and for punishment of anyone who broke it. "Those anxious months, when darkness settled over our political prospects, were viewed by all classes with deep forebodings," Frank Sanborn recalled later. The times, said Sanborn, were especially dangerous "for those who, like Harriet, had rendered themselves obnoxious to the supporters of slavery by running off so many of their race from its dominions. Fear for her personal safety caused Harriet's friends to hurry her off to Canada, sorely against her will."

But Tubman was not to stay long in Canadian safety. In February 1861, the remaining six states of the Deep South (Alabama, Florida, Georgia, Louisiana, Mississippi, and Texas) withdrew from the Union to form the Confederate States of America. On April 12, Confederate troops opened fire on the federal garrison at Fort Sumter in Charleston, South

Confederate officers drive slaves away from approaching Union troops. Despite the rebels' efforts, thousands of blacks remained in South Carolina, flooding Union army bases in the Sea Islands and forcing overwhelmed commanders to call for civilian assistance. Heeding the call, Tubman headed south in 1862.

Carolina. The fort surrendered on April 13, and the nation went to war.

As Union troops advanced through Maryland in the spring and summer of 1861, large numbers of blacks left their plantations to join the northern soldiers. Officially called "contraband of war," these blacks were no longer slaves but were not yet legally free; Lincoln would not sign his Emancipation Proclamation, liberating the slaves of the South, until January 1, 1863.

In April 1861, when she learned that the federal armies needed help in caring for the "contrabands," Tubman headed south. Little is known of her activities during this period, but according to historian William Wells Brown, she remained on "the outskirts of the Union Army" until the fall, "doing good service for those of her people who sought protection in the Union lines."

Tubman was back in Auburn with her elderly parents when Union forces took Port Royal in South Carolina's Sea Islands. Plantation owners fled the islands for the mainland, leaving thousands of their slaves behind. These contrabands, many of them illiterate, malnourished and ill, flooded the Union army camps. Overwhelmed by this human tide, Union army commanders sent out a call for teachers

Newly released slaves line up outside a contraband school. Adding to their other problems, the contrabands around Beaufort spoke an African-flavored language that few outsiders—including Tubman—could understand.

and nurses. Hundreds of northerners responded; among them, not surprisingly, was Harriet Tubman.

Arriving at Beaufort, South Carolina, in March 1862, Tubman discovered that she could barely communicate with the local black people. Still linked closely to Africa—the last (illegal) slave ship had delivered its cargo to the area in 1849—these former slaves spoke a dialect called Gullah, which contained many African words. "Why, their language down there in the far South," Tubman later told Sarah Bradford, "is just as different from ours in Maryland as you can think. They laughed when they heard me talk, and I could not understand them."

Adding to the language problem was suspicion. These blacks of the Deep South had little trust for whites or those who worked for them. Isolated on their offshore islands, they had never heard of Moses or the Underground Railroad. Tubman, assigned to the contraband hospital, had to win her patients' confidence step by step. She was entitled to army rations and supplies, but when she learned that the contrabands were jealous of her privileges, she gave them up. To supply her personal needs, she sold pies and root beer, which she made at night, after working in the hospital all day.

While she was in Beaufort, Tubman dictated a letter to her friend Frank Sanborn. In it, she described her patients as "very destitute, almost naked." She said, "I am trying to find places for those able to work, and provide for them as best I can, so as to lighten the burden of the Government as much as possible, while at the same time they learn to respect themselves by earning their own living."

Tubman nursed both the blacks who poured into Beaufort and white soldiers injured in the field. It was sometimes discouraging work. Years later, she described it to Sarah Bradford:

As a Civil War nurse in South Carolina, Tubman worked in this Beaufort manor house, converted into a hospital for contrabands. Eager to teach these impoverished and homeless people "to respect themselves," Tubman not only cared for the sick but helped find jobs for the healthy.

> I'd go to the hospital early every morning. I'd get a big chunk of ice and put it in a basin, and fill it with water; then I'd take a sponge and begin. First man I'd come to, I'd thrash away the flies, and they'd rise, like bees around a hive. Then I'd begin to bathe their wounds, and by the time I'd bathed off three or four [soldiers], the fire and heat would have melted the ice and made the water warm, and it would be as red as clear blood. Then I'd go and get more ice, and by the time I got to the next one, the flies would be around the first ones black and thick as ever.

Although she could not read them, Tubman kept many of the notes and orders she received at Beaufort. One note, addressed by a hospital surgeon to the base commissary, reveals the lack of supplies available to Tubman and other medical workers. "Will Captain Warfield," read the note, "please let 'Moses' have a little Bourbon whiskey for medicinal purposes."

Tubman worked at several southern locations, reporting when she was needed, then moving on. " 'Moses' was in her glory," wrote historian William Wells Brown, "and travelled from camp to camp, being always treated in the most respectful manner. The black men would have died for this woman."

From Beaufort, Tubman went to a military hospital in Fernandina, Florida. There, she later re-

When Tubman ran into her old friend Thomas Higginson in 1862, he was commanding the all-black 1st South Carolina Volunteers. Deeply impressed by his men's fighting abilities, Higginson told the War Department that "the successful prosecution of the war lies in the unlimited employment of black troops."

ported, soldiers were "dying off like sheep" from dysentery. When she discovered no medicine to treat them, Tubman searched the woods for certain roots; these she used to treat the men, achieving remarkable results in many cases. She also nursed soldiers and contrabands stricken with smallpox and "malignant fevers," or malaria. Despite her willing exposure to these highly contagious diseases, Tubman never contracted one herself. "The Lord would take care of me," she told Bradford, "until my time came."

Back in Beaufort in December 1862, Tubman heard a bit of interesting news. Her old friend Thomas Higginson was at nearby Camp Saxton, where he was organizing a regiment of black soldiers. In a letter to his wife, dated December 10, Higginson wrote: "Who should drive out to see me today but Harriet Tubman who is living at Beaufort as a sort of nurse & general care taker; she sends her regards to you. All sorts of unexpected people turn up here."

Tubman's days as a "general care taker," however, were drawing to a close. Among the needs of the Union army in South Carolina was information: Where were the enemy encampments? How many men did they have? How well were they armed? Aware of her work on the Underground Railroad, Union officers assigned Tubman to a new job: spy. In the spring of 1863, she organized a scouting service, leading a small band of black men deep into enemy territory and returning with information on Confederate movements. She reported to Colonel James Montgomery, an expert in guerrilla warfare who had fought at the side of John Brown in Kansas.

Perhaps the most celebrated of Tubman's military exploits took place in the summer of 1863. Deciding the time was ripe for a raid up South Carolina's Combahee River, General David Hunter, commander of the Union's southern forces, called on Harriet Tubman. Her mission: to take "several gunboats up the

Combahee River, the object of the expedition being to take up the torpedoes [mines] placed by the rebels on the river, to destroy railroads and bridges, and to cut off supplies and troops." Hunter also wanted Tubman to lead out the hundreds of blacks known to be in the Confederate-held area. Tubman accepted the assignment.

On the night of June 2, 1863, she and Colonel Montgomery started up the river with a force of 150 black soldiers in 3 steam-powered gunboats. The expedition, as the Boston *Commonwealth* later reported, "dashed into the enemy's country, struck a bold and effective blow, destroying millions of dollars worth of commissary stores, cotton, and lordly dwellings, and striking terror into the heart of rebeldom, brought off near 800 slaves and thousands of dollars worth of property, without losing a man or receiving a scratch."

Aware that the spectacular raid had been led by a black woman, humiliated Confederate commanders chose to blame their defeat on one of their own officers. "On this occasion," said the official Confederate report, "[the officer's] pickets were neither watchful nor brave; they allowed . . . a parcel of negro wretches, calling themselves soldiers, with a

Confederate soldiers and their dogs attack a black South Carolina regiment. Black fighting men faced double jeopardy: they could be killed on the field, or they could be taken prisoner and murdered by rebel soldiers, who refused to treat them as legitimate prisoners of war.

few degraded whites, to march unmolested, with the incendiary torch, to rob, destroy and burn a large section of the country."

Tubman knew that Colonel Montgomery, the white officer technically in command of the Combahee raid, would get most of the credit for its success. Ordinarily self-effacing, she allowed herself a touch of defensive pride on this occasion. In a letter she dictated to Frank Sanborn, she said:

> You have without a doubt seen a full account of the expedition. Don't you think we colored people are entitled to some of the credit for that exploit, under the lead of the brave Colonel Montgomery? We weakened the rebels somewhat on the Combahee River, by taking and bringing away *seven hundred and fifty-six* head of their most valuable live stock, known up in your region as "contrabands," and this, too, without the loss of a single life on our part, though we had good reason to believe a number of rebels bit the dust. Of those seven hundred and fifty-six contrabands, nearly or quite all the able-bodied men have joined the colored regiments here.

In the same letter, Tubman said, "I have now been absent two years, almost. . . . My father and

A trio of "contrabands"—southern blacks no longer slaves but not yet legally free—reports to a Union officer and his staff. At first regarded with suspicion by the northern military, contraband volunteers proved able and willing recruits.

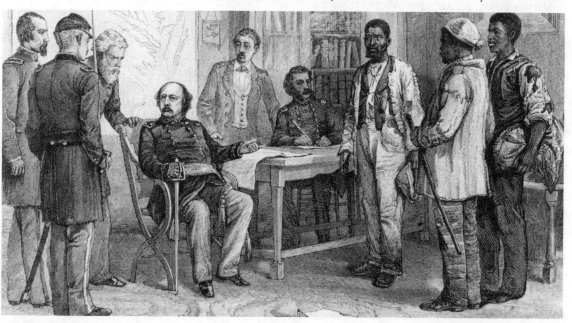

The 54th Massachusetts storms the parapet of Fort Wagner, in Charleston, South Carolina. Tubman probably saw the attack, which, observed the New York Tribune, "made Fort Wagner such a name to the colored race as Bunker Hill [Boston's revolutionary war battle site] had been for 90 years to the Yankees."

mother are old and in feeble health, and need my care and attention. I hope the good people [in Auburn] will not allow them to suffer, and I do not believe that they will. But I do not see how I am to leave at present the very important work to be done here."

Tubman would continue to perform that important work until the war ended, almost two years later. During that time, she would see some of the bloodiest battles of the Civil War. Among them was the celebrated Union assault on Fort Wagner, a Confederate bastion that guarded the harbor of Charleston, South Carolina. Leading the July 18, 1863, attack on Fort Wagner was the 54th Massachusetts, a black infantry regiment led by a 26-year-old white officer, Colonel Robert Gould Shaw. The battle marked the first important use of black troops, whose courage under fire was doubted by many whites, northerners as well as southerners.

Advancing through a murderous hail of shot and shell, the regiment captured Wagner's parapet, but

The men of Company E, 4th U.S. Colored Infantry Volunteers, prepare for inspection in 1865. President Lincoln vigorously supported the use of blacks in the army: "Abandon all the posts now possessed by black men," he said in 1864, "and we would be compelled to abandon the war in three weeks."

in the end, the entrenched Confederate position held. The 54th lost the battle, its young commander, and about half its men, but it demonstrated the extraordinary courage of its black soldiers. Their valor, however, failed to impress the South: When Colonel Shaw's father later asked for the return of his son's body, Confederate officers refused. "We have buried him," they said, "with his niggers."

But Fort Wagner transformed the North's view of the black fighting man. "Through the cannon smoke of that dark night," observed the *Atlantic Monthly*, "the manhood of the colored race shines before many eyes that would not see." After Fort Wagner, black soldiers fought on all fronts, with no one expressing doubts about their courage or ability.

Tubman probably witnessed the South Carolina battle. The night before, she served Shaw his dinner, and the next day, she helped bury the dead and nurse the wounded. Years later, she told historian Albert Bushnell Hart about a Civil War engagement that may have been Fort Wagner:

And then we saw the lightning, and that was the guns; and then we heard the thunder, and that was the big guns; and then we heard the rain falling, and that was the drops of blood falling; and when we came to get in the crops, it was dead men that we reaped.

For the next year, Tubman remained in the South. Taking part in numerous guerrilla operations, she earned respectful admiration from the military, foot soldiers and officers alike. As General Rufus Saxton, a Union officer responsible for organizing contraband regiments, later put it, "She made many a raid inside the enemy's lines, displaying remarkable courage, zeal, and fidelity." 🐾

Fernberger

8

"THIS HEROIC WOMAN"

❧

In MAY 1864, Harriet Tubman applied for leave from her duties at the Port Royal military hospital. Her boss, surgeon Henry Durrant, approved her request and gave her a note of reference. "I certify that I have been acquainted with Harriet Tubman for nearly two years," read the note, which Tubman saved. "My position as Medical Officer in charge of 'contrabands' in [Beaufort] has given me frequent and ample opportunities to observe her general deportment; particularly her kindness and attention to the sick and suffering of her own race. I take much pleasure in testifying to the esteem in which she is generally held." At the bottom of the note was a line signed by General Saxton: "I concur fully in the above."

Eager to see her aged parents, Tubman headed for Auburn, New York. Once there, her years of nonstop wartime service seemed to catch up with her; exhausted and ill, she suffered an intense bout of the sleeping seizures that had long plagued her. She spent almost a year in Auburn, resting and quietly visiting friends and neighbors. It was during this period that Tubman met and became friends with Sarah Bradford, the white woman from Geneva, New York, who was to become her first biographer.

Her face reflecting years of hardship and exhausting labor, Tubman sits for an Auburn photographer in the late 1860s. Despite her heroic war work as a nurse, spy, scout, and commando, Tubman never received a penny from the United States government.

A northern conductor orders a black passenger out of a postwar whites-only railroad car. Although the North had fought to free the South's slaves, Tubman and other blacks soon discovered that northern whites could be as bigoted as their southern counterparts.

By the early spring of 1865, Tubman felt well enough to return to the war. She set out for South Carolina, but by the time she reached Washington, D.C., a string of Union victories indicated that the war would soon be over. Tubman decided to remain in the Washington area, where she worked as a nurse for the U.S. Sanitary Commission, that era's equivalent of the Medical Corps.

On April 9, Confederate general Robert E. Lee surrendered to U.S. general Ulysses S. Grant at Appomattox, Virginia. A few months later, a weary Harriet Tubman once again turned her eyes toward Auburn and home. The Civil War was over. But for Tubman and millions of other free black Americans, another war had just begun.

Carrying a half-fare military pass, Tubman boarded a northbound train in Washington. The white conductor who looked at the pass refused to honor it. Tubman later told Bradford the story. "Come, hustle out of here!" shouted the conductor. "Niggers," he said, were not entitled to travel at reduced rates. When she protested, he grabbed her arm and said, "I'll make you tired of trying to stay here." With three other men, the conductor then dragged her out of the passenger car. The train's white passengers watched in silence. No one came to Tubman's aid as her four burly assailants wrestled her along to the baggage car and literally threw her in.

Tubman rode north alone, cradling a severely sprained arm. She rarely complained about anything, but she must have noted the incident's bitter irony. Harriet Tubman, the woman who had led troops in battle for the Union, the daring rescuer who had escaped bullets, bloodhounds, and angry slave owners, had suffered her first war injury from a civilian in the "free" North.

Although Tubman had been entitled to military pay for her services as a scout and nurse, she had never demanded it—and never received it. In 1864, the Boston *Commonwealth* had called attention to this injustice. "This heroic woman," said the newspaper, "[and] her services to her people and to the army seem to have been inadequately recompensed by the military authorities, and such money as she has received, she has expended for others as her custom is."

Tubman had carefully saved her receipts and records from the war years. Using these documents, Tubman's friends concluded that the United States government owed her $1,800 for her military services. When her own requests for payment went unheeded, Tubman's old friend William H. Seward, now secretary of state, along with such influential allies as Colonel Thomas Higginson and General Rufus Saxton, petitioned Congress in her behalf. "I can bear witness to the value of her services in South Carolina and Florida," wrote Saxton. "She was employed in the hospitals and as a spy . . . and is as deserving of a pension from the government for her services as any other of its faithful servants."

Tubman desperately needed the money to support herself and her parents and to continue helping others. Astonishingly, nothing happened; Tubman's special case, it seemed, came under no official law. In one session after another, an indifferent postwar Congress refused to recognize the rights of this black woman who had worked and fought for her country. The debt was never paid.

When Tubman returned to Auburn, she was about 45 years old, penniless, and responsible for 2 aged parents. She was also in steady pain from the arm the trainmen had savagely wrenched. Nevertheless, she went about her affairs with her customary verve. She planted apple trees and broke ground for a large vegetable garden to feed her family and those who came to her door. With the help of well-to-do

Former slaves work at a county poorhouse. Determined to keep as many blacks as she could from such a disheartening life, Tubman resolved to open a home where the sick and elderly could find health care, companionship, and peace.

neighbors, she established a kind of refuge for the many impoverished blacks who passed through the area in search of work and homes. She fed them, nursed their sick, and helped deliver their babies. Apparently with strength to spare, Tubman also began a fund-raising campaign to support schools for newly freed blacks in the South.

Tubman's good-humored energy may have flagged in October 1867, when a friend sent her a clipping from the *Baltimore American*. Asking a neighbor to read it to her, Tubman learned that her former husband was dead. John Tubman, the satisfied free black man who had once threatened to betray his wife for running away, had been shot down in broad daylight by a white man. Although John Tubman had been unarmed, and although witnesses testified to the cold-blooded killing, an all-white postwar Maryland jury had found the white man not guilty. Harriet Tubman's reaction to the news can only be guessed; she never said a word about it.

Meanwhile, she was finding it increasingly hard to make ends meet. Sarah Bradford illustrated the black woman's plight with an anecdote about the winter of 1867–68. A blizzard had all but buried Tubman's little house on the outskirts of Auburn, preventing her from working or going out for food. "At length," wrote Bradford, "stern necessity compelled her to plunge through the drifts to the city." Calling on "one of her firm and fast friends," Tubman "began to walk up and down, as she always [did] when in trouble." Her eyes filled with tears, Tubman seemed unable to speak. Finally, "with a great effort, she said, 'Miss Annie, could you lend me a quarter till Monday? I never asked it before.' Kind friends immediately supplied all the wants of the family, but on Monday Harriet appeared with the quarter she had borrowed."

At about this time, Bradford began writing her biography. First printed in 1869 under the title *Scenes in the Life of Harriet Tubman*, the book carried a slightly apologetic preface by Bradford. "There are those who will sneer, there are those who have already done so, at this quixotic [impractical] attempt to make a heroine of a black woman, and a slave," she observed. Nevertheless, with financial aid from Wendell Phillips and other friends, Bradford published the book, then turned its proceeds—some $1,200—over to its subject. A considerable sum for the time, the money allowed Tubman to pay her expenses, continue to support southern schools for blacks, and feed the hungry strangers at her door.

Appearing at her door in 1869 was another kind of visitor: a tall, handsome man named Nelson Davis. Some years earlier, in 1864, Tubman had met him at a South Carolina army base. Davis, then about 20 years old, was a private in Company G of the 8th U.S. Colored Infantry Volunteers. Whether Davis came to Auburn in search of Tubman or by chance is unknown; what is known is that the former soldier asked the former spy to marry him. Despite their age difference—Davis was at least 24 years younger than Tubman—she accepted.

Surrounded by friends, both black and white, the couple married on March 18, 1869. The next day, the Auburn newspaper reported on the ceremony. "Before a large and very select audience Harriet Tubman . . . took unto herself a husband and made one [Nelson Davis] a happy man," noted the paper. "Both born slaves . . . they stood there, last evening, *free*, and were joined as man and wife."

By all accounts, the good-looking Davis seemed unusually robust, but his appearance belied the truth. He had contracted tuberculosis in the army, and his health was fragile. Some people believed that Tubman, ever the care giver, married him so she could nurse him. In any case, Davis apparently never worked during the 19 years of his marriage.

Among the guests at Tubman and Davis's wedding had been William H. Seward. He and Tubman had not agreed on every issue (Seward had, for example, never supported Harriet's idol, John Brown), but the two remained staunch friends for decades. Seward was to die only a few years later, in 1872; at his funeral, hundreds of people passed his casket and the mountains of elaborate floral displays surrounding it. When the service ended, mourners saw a small black woman walk to the casket and lay a wreath of wildflowers at its foot.

The years were carrying away Tubman's most cherished possessions, the people she loved. She lost her parents, both nearing 100 years of age, in the 1870s. Quaker Thomas Garrett of Wilmington died in 1869, Colonel James Montgomery (Tubman's col-

Tubman's shawl hangs from the bed where she slept in her later years. Her Auburn house was small and sparsely furnished, but it was palatial compared to the ditches and "potato holes" in which she had stayed during her Underground Railroad days.

league on the Combahee raid) in 1871, Wendell Phillips in 1884, Frederick Douglass in 1895. By the 1890s, of all the thundering abolitionist band, only Thomas Higginson, Frank Sanborn, and Harriet Tubman lived on.

Tubman never changed: Needy people could always count on a meal or a place to stay when they came to her door. She dreamed of building a home for the poor and helpless, but the closing decades of the century were lean times, even for this gritty, resourceful woman.

In severe need of money, Tubman fell prey to a pair of black swindlers who came to Auburn in 1873. The men told her they had found a chest in the South containing $5,000 in gold. They said they did not want to exchange the gold for greenbacks (U.S. dollars) because the government would seize the gold and leave them penniless. If Tubman could raise

$2,000 in cash, the men said, they would turn the chest over to her. Tubman, who had seen such treasures hidden away by slaveholders, believed the story and persuaded friends to back her with $2,000. She agreed to meet the swindlers in the woods on a dark night: There, they knocked her unconscious, took the cash, and vanished. The episode became something of a scandal, but Auburn's citizens, even those who had lost their money, soon forgave Tubman. They knew she had been as much a victim as themselves.

In these years, Tubman earned her living as a peddler, traveling from house to house and selling vegetables from her garden. Neighbors welcomed her, eager to hear stories about her days on the Underground Railroad and her wartime activities. One of these friends later recalled: "Harriet when I knew her in her matriarchal phase was a magnificent looking woman, true African, with a broad nose, very black, and of medium height. I used to often sit and listen to her stories when I could get her to tell them. We always gave her something to eat. She preferred butter in her tea to anything else. That was a luxury."

In 1890, 2 years after her husband, Nelson Davis, died at the age of 44, Tubman finally got enough money to buy a few such "luxuries" herself: Congress approved pensions for the widows of Civil War veterans. Ironically, the government allotted Tubman $8 per month (increased to $20 in 1899) as the survivor of a soldier, but it steadfastly refused to reward her for her own gallant service.

Although her own government never recognized her, Great Britain's ruler did. After reading Bradford's biography of Tubman in 1897, a clearly impressed Queen Victoria had sent the American woman a silver medal and a letter inviting her to come to England. She never went, but her friends later reported that Tubman looked at the letter so many times, it "was worn to a shadow." The former slave had never forgotten her 1856 trip to Canada, when she had ushered the despairing Joe Bailey into "Queen Victoria's dominions" and freedom.

Another woman long admired by Tubman was Susan B. Anthony. Tubman had heard the great suffragist speak on a number of occasions, and she wholeheartedly endorsed Anthony's goals. Anthony, who returned Tubman's respect, referred to her fellow activist as "this most wonderful woman." Late in her life, Tubman received a visit from Elizabeth Miller, leader of a local suffragist group. Miller later described the occasion. "I remember seeing you years ago at a suffragist convention in Rochester," she told Tubman. "Yes," responded Tubman, "I belonged to Miss Susan B. Anthony's organization." Miller said she would like to enroll Tubman as a life member in her group. "You certainly have assisted in bearing the burdens," Miller continued. "Do you really believe that women should vote?" Tubman paused. Then she said softly, "I suffered enough to believe it."

As Tubman grew older, she became increasingly determined to establish a home for sick and needy black people. She had long had her eye on a 25-acre lot across the road from her house; the site, she thought, would be perfect for the poor people's shelter. In 1896, the property came up for public auction, and Tubman saw her chance. She had almost no money, but she had her usual supply of optimism and determination. She later told an interviewer about the auction:

> They were all white folks there but me, and I was there like a blackberry in a pail of milk, but I hid down in a corner, and no one knew who was bidding. The man began down pretty low, and I kept going up by fifties. At last I got up to fourteen hundred and fifty, and then others stopped bidding, and the man said, "All done. Who is the buyer?"
>
> "Harriet Tubman," I shouted.

Tubman left the astonished auction crowd and headed for the local bank, where she got the money

Women's rights activist Susan B. Anthony (left) confers with colleague Elizabeth Cady Stanton in 1900. Although Tubman focused most of her energies on abolition, she was also a strong supporter of Anthony and her suffragist movement. "Tell the women," she said a month before she died, "to stand together."

Tubman worshiped regularly at Auburn's African Methodist Episcopal Zion Church, where her strong, clear voice rang out in such favorite songs as "Swing Low, Sweet Chariot" and "Go Down, Moses." According to local reports, many parishioners attended the church as much to hear Tubman sing as for religious motives.

for her new land by mortgaging it (using it as security for a loan). Still, she lacked the funds to build the home. Seven years later, in 1903, she deeded the acreage to the African Methodist Episcopal Zion Church, an all-black congregation at which she had worshiped for years. The church built the home of Tubman's dreams in 1908. She was delighted to see the first residents move in, but she objected strenuously when the home's managers decided to charge an admission fee.

"When I gave the Home over to Zion Church," she told a local reporter, "what do you suppose they did? Why, they made a rule that nobody should come in without a hundred dollars. Now I wanted to make a rule that nobody could come in unless they had no money. What's the good of a Home if a person who wants to get in has to have money?" Tubman and the church finally reached a compromise, and in 1911, she moved into the home herself.

MOSES OF HER RACE ENDING HER LIFE IN HOME SHE FOUNDED read the headline of an article in the June 25, 1911, issue of the New York *World*. "She was the friend of great men," said the story, "but now, almost a centenarian, she awaits the last call. Now with the weight of almost a hundred years on her shoulders, she seeks rest during the few remaining days."

Tubman enjoyed more than a "few remaining days." Clear of mind, her always hearty appetite undiminished, she spent almost two years at the home, receiving visitors, telling stories, and, in late 1912, making out a will. (She left her house and its garden to a niece, a grandniece, and Frances Smith, the black woman who managed the home.) In February 1913, she chatted with an old friend, Mary B. Talbert, president of the New York State Federation of Colored Women's Clubs. Tubman, recalled Frances Smith, told Talbert "of the sweet spirit in that home, and of the happiness she felt was there." As Talbert prepared to leave, Tubman reached for her hand.

Holding it tightly, she expressed her hopes for the suffrage movement. "Tell the women," said Tubman, "to stand together."

A few weeks later, on March 10, 1913, Harriet Tubman died of pneumonia at the age of 93. Friends who had gathered at her bedside joined hands and sang her favorite spiritual, "Swing Low, Sweet Chariot."

Most of Auburn attended Tubman's last rites, a military service led by local Civil War veterans. As

In this photograph, probably the last ever taken of Tubman, the old fighter looks at the world with her usual unflinching gaze. As William Still had said so many years earlier, "Her like it is probable was never known before or since."

Erected in 1932, an Auburn plaque boasts of one of the town's distinguished residents. Eighteen years earlier, almost everyone in Auburn had attended a memorial service for Tubman, who died at the age of 93. Blacks and whites, free citizens all, stood side by side as educator Booker T. Washington praised Tubman for bringing "the two races nearer together."

she was laid to rest, the old soldiers stood at crisp attention, mourners bowed their heads, a bugler played taps, and the flag of the United States snapped in the breeze. A year later, the town's citizens, black and white, took part in a memorial service for "the Moses of her race." The crowd listened intently as celebrated black educator Booker T. Washington spoke about the woman who had "brought the two races nearer together" and "made it possible for the white race to place a higher estimate upon the black race."

Harriet Tubman's dramatic work on the Underground Railroad has sometimes overshadowed her other accomplishments. She conducted hundreds of people to freedom; she was also a skilled military leader, a compassionate nurse, a tireless abolitionist, and a lifelong humanitarian. Carrying the scars of slavery through her long life, Tubman was willing to break the law when she believed it wrong. She stood by her people from start to finish.

Tubman never sought power, and she never had any. Uninterested in wealth, she remained poor all her life. Although she acquired scores of famous friends, she preferred to work quietly, shunning attention whenever she could. Of all the testimonials to this remarkable woman, perhaps the most incisive was delivered by Frederick Douglass in an 1868 letter to Tubman:

> The difference between us is very marked. Most that I have done and suffered in the service of our cause has been in public, and I have received much encouragement at every step of the way. You, on the other hand, have labored in a private way. I have wrought in the day—you in the night. I have had the applause of the crowd and the satisfaction that comes from being approved by the multitude, while the most that you have done has been witnessed by a few trembling, scarred, and foot-sore bondmen and women, whom you have led out of the house of bondage, and whose heartfelt *"God bless you"* has been your only reward. The midnight sky and the silent stars have been the witnesses of your devotion to freedom and of your heroism. Excepting John Brown—of sacred memory—I know of no one who has willingly encountered more perils and hardships to serve our enslaved people than you have. ❧

CHRONOLOGY

———— •❦• ————

ca. 1820	Born Harriet Ross on the Brodas plantation in Dorchester County, Maryland
1827	Makes first attempt to escape from slavery
1835	Suffers a near-fatal blow to the head that leads to lifelong "sleeping fits"
1844	Marries John Tubman
1849	Escapes from slavery; befriends abolitionist leaders
1850	Makes first of 19 trips into the South as a conductor on the Underground Railroad
1852	Makes first trip to Canada
1857	Rescues parents from slavery; settles in Auburn, New York
1858	Meets abolitionist John Brown
1861	Travels to South Carolina to work with the Union army as a nurse
1863	Becomes a spy for the Union army; leads a raid on South Carolina's Combahee River; frees 750 slaves
1865	Works in Virginia hospital
1870	Marries Nelson Davis
1897	Receives a medal from Queen Victoria of England
1908	Builds a home for sick and elderly blacks
1911	Moves into home
1913	Dies of pneumonia

FURTHER READING

Aptheker, Herbert. *To Be Free: Studies in American Negro History.* New York: International Publishers, 1948.

Blockson, Charles L. *The Underground Railroad.* New York: Prentice-Hall, 1987.

Bradford, Sarah H. *Harriet Tubman: The Moses of Her People.* Secaucus, NJ: Citadel Press, 1974.

Campbell, Stanley W. *The Slave Catchers: Enforcement of the Fugitive Slave Law, 1850–1860.* Chapel Hill: University of North Carolina Press, 1968.

Conrad, Earl. *Harriet Tubman.* Washington, DC: Associated Publishers, 1942.

Duberman, Martin. *The Antislavery Vanguard: New Essays on the Abolitionists.* Princeton University Press, 1965.

Du Bois, W. E. B. *John Brown.* Philadelphia: Jacobs & Co., 1909.

Furnas, J. C. *Goodbye to Uncle Tom.* New York: William Sloane Associates, 1956.

Gara, Larry. *The Liberty Line: The Legend of the Underground Railroad.* Lexington: University of Kentucky Press, 1961.

McPherson, James M. *Battle Cry of Freedom.* New York: Oxford University Press, 1988.

Morris, Thomas D. *Free Men All: The Personal Liberty Laws of the North.* Baltimore: Johns Hopkins University Press, 1974.

Petry, Ann. *Harriet Tubman, Conductor on the Underground Railroad.* New York: Crowell, 1955.

Scott, John Anthony. *Hard Trials on My Way: Slavery and the Struggle Against It.* New York: Knopf, 1974.

THURGOOD
MARSHALL

THURGOOD MARSHALL

❦

Lisa Aldred

Senior Consulting Editor
Nathan Irvin Huggins
Director
*W.E.B. Du Bois Institute for Afro-American Research
Harvard University*

1

EQUAL JUSTICE UNDER LAW

❧

O N THE COLD morning of December 8, 1953, attorney Thurgood Marshall climbed a flight of white marble steps in Washington, D.C. Halfway up the stairs, the tall, dark-skinned lawyer glanced upward. He could see four familiar words carved across the front of the huge white building: Equal Justice Under Law. Marshall intended to make those words a reality.

Striding between the imposing columns, Marshall entered the vast sanctum of the United States Supreme Court. He laid his bulging briefcase on the table and drew a deep breath. Today, Marshall would offer his final arguments in the most important case of his distinguished career. If he won, the United States Supreme Court would rule that America's long-entrenched, segregated school systems were unconstitutional. If he lost, most of America's black children would continue to receive second-rate educations in substandard, ill-equipped schools.

Marshall's case, entitled *Brown v. Board of Education of Topeka*, was a consolidation of five separate lawsuits. Challenging the legality of their local school boards, black students and their parents had brought suits in Delaware, the District of Columbia, Kansas, South Carolina, and Virginia. The case of Virginia's 16-year-old Barbara Rose Johns was typical of the others. Dissatisfied with the only school open to her and other black students—a tar-paper shack lacking proper heat or other facilities—Johns had led 450 classmates in a strike that climaxed in legal action against the school board of Prince Edward County.

Marshall prepares to argue the most important case of his career: Brown v. Board of Education of Topeka. At stake in the 1952–54 U.S. Supreme Court case, which was a consolidation of five separate lawsuits challenging racial segregation in public schools, was the future of black education in the United States.

357

The South Carolina case involved gas station attendant Harry Briggs, a navy veteran from Clarendon County. Seeking improved school conditions for his 5 children, Briggs had joined 19 other black parents in a suit against the county's segregated school system. As a result, Briggs and his wife had lost their jobs and their credit at the local bank.

Defeated in each of the five locations, the black students and parents appealed to the Supreme Court. Because the Kansas case—in which Topeka parent Oliver Brown sued his city's school board—came first alphabetically, the five clustered cases came to be known as *Brown*. The case presented the court with a question of vital importance to millions of Americans: Is government-enforced school segregation unconstitutional?

When the segregation cases came before the Supreme Court, legal counsel, directed by attorney Thurgood Marshall, was supplied by the National Association for the Advancement of Colored People (NAACP). Founded in 1909, the NAACP—whose membership was biracial—had spent decades fighting racial discrimination and segregation. In its early years, the NAACP concentrated on obtaining black suffrage (the right to vote), eliminating lynching and other mob violence against blacks, and promoting integration in housing and public places.

By the early 1930s, NAACP officials realized that blacks could never achieve social and economic equality without educational equality, and the organization made improved schooling for blacks a top priority. Thurgood Marshall had joined the organization in 1934. Now, in 1953, the 45-year-old attorney hoped for a major victory in what had been a long, grueling struggle.

Marshall hoped to win the *Brown* case by demolishing the "separate but equal" doctrine established by *Plessy v. Ferguson*. A celebrated Supreme

Court case of 1896, *Plessy* began when a black man, Homer Adolph Plessy, refused to ride in the "Jim Crow" (segregated) car of a train passing through Louisiana. (The popular minstrel shows of the 19th century often featured white actors who wore blackface makeup and danced to the refrain, "Jump, Jim Crow!" The term Jim Crow, used as a patronizing name for black people, was also applied to post–Civil War segregation laws.)

Charged with violating a state law that required racial segregation in public facilities, Plessy was convicted by a Louisiana judge (Ferguson). When Plessy's lawyer appealed the conviction before the United States Supreme Court, he argued that enforced separation of the two races violated the Constitution's Fourteenth Amendment, which guarantees all citizens "the equal protection of the laws."

The Fourteenth Amendment was ratified in 1868, five years after President Abraham Lincoln's Emancipation Proclamation legally ended slavery in the South. The amendment was designed to guarantee newly freed blacks the same legal rights and privileges as whites. But the Supreme Court, in its 1896 *Plessy* decision, upheld the Louisiana segregation law, ruling that separate but "equal" facilities satisfied the amendment's "equal protection" guarantee.

Although the court's decision technically applied only to the Louisiana law, it established a *precedent* (a legal decision that serves as a rule or pattern for future, similar cases). When the Supreme Court establishes a precedent, the nation's lower courts are bound to follow it unless it is overturned by the Supreme Court itself. Because consistency is very important to a legal system, precedents are seldom overturned.

Plessy opened the gates for a flood of new Jim Crow laws—statutes that required racial separation in both private residential areas and public facilities.

Crowning the imposing Washington, D.C., building of the U.S. Supreme Court is the motto Equal Justice Under Law. *But until the 1950s, when Marshall successfully argued that segregation was unconstitutional, many Americans acted as though the motto read* Separate But Equal Justice Under Law.

Southern youngsters attend a one-room schoolhouse in the early 1950s. Until the U.S. Supreme Court outlawed segregation in 1954, most of the nation's black children had to enroll in racially separate, substandard schools.

By 1900, blacks in many states were restricted to Jim Crow drinking fountains, railroad cars, movie theater sections, hospitals, and schools. Despite the *Plessy* ruling, few state or local governments enforced the equality of the institutions and services available to blacks.

Guided by the separate-but-equal precedent, county and state courts routinely dismissed anti-segregation suits; black students could legally be compelled to attend segregated schools if these institutions were judged equal to the schools reserved for white students. The judgments, of course, were made by people committed to preserving the separation of the races. Segregation had become the law of the land.

To help him prepare his arguments in *Brown v. Board of Education of Topeka*, Marshall recruited dozens of experts: lawyers, constitutional scholars, sociologists, psychiatrists, anthropologists, and educators. Under Marshall's guidance, the team scrutinized all aspects of the Fourteenth Amendment, examined every available study of children's learning patterns, and pored over research on the history and psychological effects of segregation on youngsters of both races.

The Supreme Court agreed to hear the *Brown* case in its 1952 session. During the 1952 hearing, Marshall asserted that the whole weight of social science demonstrated that black and white children possessed equal learning potential. He pointed out that school segregation had no reasonable basis and that it had a devastating effect on black children, decreasing their motivation to learn, lowering their self-esteem, and blighting their futures.

The court's nine justices found Marshall's arguments impressive, but legal precedents were heavily stacked against the NAACP's position. Deciding that the issue bore further consideration, the justices scheduled a rehearing, which began on December 7, 1953. Now, on December 8, Thurgood Marshall would offer his final arguments in the case.

When Marshall entered the courtroom, spectators, both black and white, filled every seat. Eager to witness history, many had waited outside in the bitter cold since before daybreak. The crowd's excited murmurs ceased when the marshal of the court stepped forward and, in ringing tones, pronounced the ancient ritual words: "The honorable the Chief Justice, the Associate Justices of the Supreme Court of the United States. Oyez, oyez, oyez! All persons having business before the honorable the Supreme Court of the United States are advised to draw near and give their attention, for the Court is now sitting, and God save the United States and this honorable Court."

Everyone present stood and faced the long, highly polished bench at the front of the courtroom. Then the red velvet curtains behind the bench parted; nine black-robed men stepped forward and seated themselves in high-backed leather chairs.

Marshall eyed his opponent, John W. Davis. Tall, pale, and aristocratic in bearing, the 80-year-old Davis was known as the nation's leading constitutional lawyer. As a law student, Thurgood Marshall had sometimes skipped classes to hear Davis argue before the Supreme Court. By 1953, Davis had argued 140 cases before the high court. Marshall himself had participated in 15 Supreme Court cases, but *Brown* had brought him face-to-face with the formidable Davis for the first time.

Like Marshall, Davis argued *Brown* for moral rather than financial reasons. (His only payment for defending the South's segregated school systems, in fact, was a silver tea service, presented by the South Carolina legislature.) Davis believed segregation was not only fair but necessary. Marshall, of course, believed exactly the opposite, but he nevertheless respected the older attorney: John W. Davis was a force to be reckoned with, and Marshall knew it. Presenting his final points on the *Brown* case the day before, Davis had argued brilliantly. Although he referred to his notes more frequently than in the past, the elderly attorney had lost none of his eloquence. With his mane of snow-white hair and his formal, old-fashioned suit, he cut an impressive figure in the courtroom.

Davis regarded the separate-but-equal doctrine as a basic principle of American life. A time comes, he said, when such a principle "has been so often announced, so confidently relied upon, so long continued, that it passes the limits of judicial discretion and disturbance." Davis had no doubt that equality had been achieved in the segregated school system. "I am reminded," he said, "and I hope it won't be treated

as a reflection on anybody—of Aesop's fable of the dog and the meat: The dog, with a fine piece of meat in his mouth, crossed a bridge and saw [his] shadow in the stream and plunged in for it and lost both substance and shadow. Here is equal education, not promised, not prophesied, but present. Shall it be thrown away on some fancied question of racial prestige?"

Thurgood Marshall stepped up to the bar to make his final rebuttal. "I got the feeling on hearing the discussion yesterday that when you put a white child in a school with a whole lot of colored children, the child would fall apart or something," he said. "Everybody knows that is not true. These same kids in Virginia and South Carolina—and I have seen them

Marshall greets John W. Davis during the case of Brown v. Board of Education of Topeka. *America's foremost constitutional lawyer in the early 1950s, Davis argued 140 U.S. Supreme Court cases before Marshall defeated him in Brown.*

As the U.S. Supreme Court's pronouncement that "separate educational facilities are inherently unequal" makes headlines around the world, a mother and daughter celebrate the May 1954 overthrow of public-school segregation with a visit to the Supreme Court building.

do it—they play in the streets together, they play on their farms together, they go down the road together, they separate to go to school, they come out of school and play ball together. They have to be separated in school."

Marshall declared that school segregation laws were deliberately designed to oppress black people. The only way the Supreme Court could uphold them, he asserted, would be "to find that for some reason Negroes are inferior to all other human beings." Ending his argument, he said, "The only thing [segregation] can be is an inherent determination that the people who were formerly in slavery, regardless of anything else, shall be kept as near that stage as is possible. And now is the time, we submit, that this Court should make it clear that that is not what our Constitution stands for."

After the lawyers completed their arguments, the justices followed their standard procedure, conferring about the case in secret session. Five months later—on May 17, 1954—they reassembled at their great mahogany bench. As Chief Justice Earl Warren prepared to read the Court's opinion in *Brown v. Board of Education*, spectators leaned forward in silence. Wire-service reporters started filing their dispatches from the press table. At 12:57 P.M., the Associated Press wire carried a bulletin: "Chief Justice Warren today began reading the Supreme Court's decision in the public school desegregation cases. The court's ruling could not be determined immediately." The alarm went off in every newsroom in America. The nation waited.

But instead of delivering a crisp summary of the decision, Warren embarked on a long, discursive text. He referred to the evidence of psychologists, sociologists, and educators on the effects of segregation on black students. He discussed *Plessy v. Ferguson* and the Fourteenth Amendment's equal protection guarantee; thus far, he said, no precedent existed for the application of that guarantee to school segregation. After citing a number of earlier cases and outlining the history of black education in America, Warren called education "the most important function of state and local governments."

An hour after he started, the chief justice had yet to reveal the court's ruling. Warren, wired the AP correspondent at 1:12, "had not read far enough in the court's opinion for newsmen to say that segregation was being struck down as unconstitutional." Finally, at 1:20 P.M., Warren reached the crucial question: "Does segregation of children in public schools solely on the basis of race . . . deprive the children of the minority group of equal educational opportunities?"

Warren paused for a split second. Then he said, "We believe that it does." He continued: "To separate [black children] from others . . . solely because of their race generates a feeling of inferiority . . . that may affect their hearts and minds in a way unlikely ever to be undone."

Approaching the end of the decision, Warren read, "We conclude . . ." Then he paused, raised his eyes from the document, and added, "unanimously." A shock wave seemed to sweep the courtroom. The justice continued, ". . . that in the field of public education the doctrine of 'separate but equal' has no place. Separate educational facilities are inherently unequal."

Stop-press bulletins flashed across the land. Radio and TV stations interrupted their programming. The Voice of America network beamed the news across the world in 34 languages: The Supreme Court of the United States of America had declared school segregation unconstitutional. Word of the decision reached Thurgood Marshall and his colleague Roy Wilkins in the New York office of the NAACP. Decades of struggle had finally paid off in victory. Silently, the two campaign veterans embraced. 🕮

Marshall with NAACP colleagues George E. C. Hayes (left) and James Nabrit (right), smiling victoriously outside the U.S. Supreme Court after educational segregation was declared unconstitutional. "I was so happy I was numb," Marshall said of the historic 1954 Supreme Court decision.

2

"A PRETTY TOUGH GUY"

❦

THURGOOD MARSHALL WAS born on July 2, 1908, in West Baltimore, Maryland. His combative nature seems to mirror that of his ancestors, especially his maternal great-grandfather, a slave brought to America in the mid-1800s. "His polite descendants like to think he came from the cultured tribes in Sierra Leone," Thurgood Marshall said, "but we all know that he really came from the toughest part of the Congo." (Until 1971, the Republic of Zaire was known as the Congo.)

According to Marshall, his great-grandfather "grew up into one mean man. One day his owner came up to him and said: 'Look, I brought you here so I guess I can't very well shoot you—as you deserve. On the other hand, I can't with a clear conscience sell anyone as vicious as you to another slaveholder. So, I'm going to set you free—on one condition. Get to hell out of this county and never come back.' " That, Marshall added, was "the only time Massuh didn't get an argument from the old boy." Marshall's great-grandfather raised no arguments, but he had no intention of complying with the slaveholder's wishes. He settled down and raised his family just a few miles from his former owner's plantation. "He lived there until the day he died," added Marshall, "and nobody ever laid a hand on him."

Marshall told this story to a *Time* magazine reporter in his characteristically easygoing, humorous style. But beneath the casual manner lay a familiarity

A snapshot from Marshall's family album shows the future civil rights activist as a toddler. Family members later described young Thurgood as a beautiful baby with silky hair and large, expressive eyes.

with the brutal facts of black bondage. Although African slavery had been practiced for centuries, the New World's demands for cheap labor vastly increased the traffic in human beings. Most slaves were captured from their villages by black tribal chiefs and brought to coastal markets. Sold to white ship captains, they were crammed aboard reeking ships and brought to America. Historians estimate that as many as half the slaves shipped from Africa died at sea, victims of malnutrition, disease, and outright murder. Some even took their own lives, preferring death to slavery.

Those slaves who survived the appalling voyage to the New World were sold at auction. Most of them became the property of southern plantation owners. Separated from their families, the enslaved Africans—men, women, and children—were put to work in the fields, laboring for 16 hours a day under constant vigilance and frequent abuse.

Beginning in the 18th century, southern states passed "black codes"—laws that forbade slaves to defend themselves against their masters' mistreatment, to own property, or to testify against whites in court. Under these codes, a white who taught a black to read or write was a criminal; a white who killed a black while punishing him, however, was acting legally. Marshall's Congolese great-grandfather, who refused to let these conditions defeat him, clearly filled his descendant with a powerful sense of family pride.

In the mid-19th century, many blacks in the United States used only one name, often that of their former owners. Another Thurgood Marshall ancestor—his paternal grandfather—was a freedman (former slave) known only as "Marshall." When Grandfather Marshall enlisted in the Union army during the Civil War, he learned that soldiers needed both first and last names. He chose to be called "Tho-

roughgood" Marshall. "I was named after him," Thurgood Marshall told an interviewer, "but by the time I was in second grade, I got tired of spelling all that and shortened it."

After Union forces won the war, Thoroughgood Marshall spent several years in the United States merchant marine. Retiring from the sea, he married a woman named Annie and opened a grocery store in Baltimore. There, Annie Marshall fought and won her own small war. When Baltimore's electric company decided to install a light pole in front of the Marshalls' grocery store door, Annie Marshall objected. The sidewalk adjoining the store, she said, belonged to her and her husband, and they wanted no pole in the middle of it. After obtaining a court order, the company sent workmen to install the pole. When they got there, they found the site occupied by Annie Marshall, firmly seated in a kitchen chair. Day after day, the determined shopkeeper held her

A group of USCTs—United States Colored Troops—line up at a Civil War military base. Marshall's grandfather Thoroughgood was one of the 186,000 former slaves who served in the Union armies.

ground, finally forcing the company to find another site for its pole. Recounting the story with a smile, Thurgood Marshall said, "Grandma Annie emerged as the victor of what may have been the first successful sitdown strike in Maryland."

In a 1965 *Ebony* magazine interview, Marshall talked about his maternal grandfather, an opera-loving sailor named Isaiah Olive Branch Williams. As Thoroughgood Marshall had done, Williams served in the merchant marine, then married and settled down in Baltimore. But he never forgot a long-ago visit to Arica, a Chilean port where he had enjoyed a fine performance of Vincenzo Bellini's 1831 opera, *Norma*. When his wife gave birth to a daughter, Williams named the baby—Thurgood Marshall's mother—Norma Arica.

Now the head of a growing family, Williams bought a house in Baltimore. Unfortunately, his next-door neighbor turned out to be a bigoted white man who treated Williams with open contempt. When he needed Williams's help to mend the fence

Newly emancipated black families arrive in Baltimore in the 1860s. After the Civil War, both of Marshall's grandfathers opened grocery stores in the bustling Maryland city.

between the two properties, however, the neighbor changed his tune. "After all," he told Williams, "we belong to the same church and are going to the same heaven." Williams, the object of countless insults from his suddenly friendly neighbor, responded quickly. "I'd rather go to hell," he said.

Isaiah Williams also showed his assertiveness in the political sphere. In the 1870s, he organized a large public meeting to protest police brutality toward blacks. The rally produced no marked improvements, but it set a precedent, proving that Baltimore's usually passive black population could unite in a common cause. In the post–Civil War era, when white supremacist groups such as the Ku Klux Klan roamed the land, beating and sometimes murdering "uppity" blacks, any act of black defiance required extraordinary courage.

Isaiah Williams's daughter, Norma Arica, married William Canfield Marshall in 1904. The union produced two sons: William Aubrey, born in 1904, and Thurgood, who arrived four years later. The Marshalls lived on Druid Hill Avenue in West Baltimore, a middle-class neighborhood where black and white families coexisted in relative harmony. Druid Hill Avenue was a pleasant street lined with three-story brick row houses, each equipped with whitewashed front steps and an arched doorway.

When Thurgood was born, his father worked for the Baltimore & Ohio Railroad as a dining-car waiter. The job was a good one, especially for a black man at the turn of the century, but it kept Will Marshall away from his family for weeks at a time. Thus, when he got the chance to sign on as a waiter at the Gibson Island Club, he took it. Marshall eventually became chief steward at the club, a prestigious Chesapeake Bay sailing association whose members included powerful Washington politicians and social leaders.

Thurgood Marshall's mother, Norma Arica Marshall, taught in a segregated Baltimore elementary school. After graduating from an all-black Maryland college, she had earned graduate credits at Columbia University Teachers College in New York City. Like her father, Norma Marshall loved music. She was known as a talented pianist and singer and sometimes appeared in local opera and theater productions. Her sister-in-law, Elizabeth Marshall, recalled Norma as "a very strong person" and "a leader who went all out for her boys and had great influence on them."

According to his relatives, Thurgood was a beautiful baby with big, dark eyes. His aunt, Media Dodson, remembered him as a "timid" little boy. But, Dodson told a *Time* magazine reporter, "one day—he must have been around five—he stopped crying and became a pretty tough guy. Now, I don't know what caused the change. Maybe the boys slapped his head."

Whatever caused the change, Thurgood Marshall remained a "pretty tough guy." A *New York Times Magazine* story quotes him as saying, "We lived on a respectable street, but behind us there were back alleys where roughnecks and the tough kids hung out. When it was time for dinner, my mother used to go to the front door and call my older brother. Then she'd go to the *back* door and call me."

Reminiscing about young Thurgood, family friend Odell Payne told *Ebony* magazine that he "was a jolly boy who always had something to say." But, she added, Thurgood showed a serious side as well. "I can still see him coming down Division Street every Sunday afternoon about one o'clock," she said. "He'd be wearing knee pants with both hands dug way into his pockets and be kicking a stone in front of him as he crossed over to Dolphin Street to visit his grandparents at their big grocery store on the corner. He was in a deep study, that boy, and it was plain something was going on inside him."

But Thurgood's high-spirited side usually prevailed. His boisterous classroom behavior, in fact, often landed him in trouble. Thurgood's grade-school principal administered a standard punishment for rowdiness: banishment to the school basement with a copy of the United States Constitution. Not until he had memorized a passage from that document was the offender allowed to return to his class. "Before I left that school," Marshall later told a reporter, "I knew the whole thing by heart."

Parts of the Constitution, however, puzzled him. As an adult, Marshall remembered wondering about

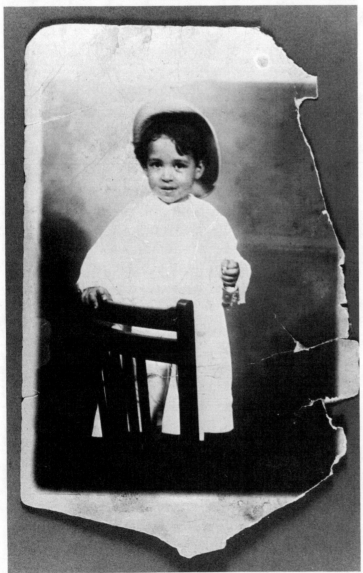

Two-year-old Thurgood's direct gaze gives a hint of the unflinching civil rights activist to come. One aunt, who described Marshall as a "timid" youngster, reported that by the age of five he had already become "a pretty tough guy."

Norma Arica Marshall, mother of Thurgood and William Aubrey Marshall, "went all out for her boys," according to one relative. A schoolteacher who demanded that her sons study hard, Norma Marshall lived to see the rewards of their labors: William became a prominent surgeon; Thurgood, a justice of the U.S. Supreme Court.

the Fourteenth Amendment's guarantee of "equal rights." Seeing inequality all around him, starting with his own segregated school, he asked his father what the guarantee meant. Will Marshall, recalled his son, simply said that the Constitution described things as they should be, not as they really were.

Thurgood Marshall's early acquaintance with the Constitution may have helped steer him toward the law, but his parents definitely influenced his future vocation. Will Marshall followed court cases as a hobby. He enjoyed reading newspaper accounts of impending trials, and he spent his occasional free afternoons in court, sometimes taking Thurgood with him.

In fact, William Marshall eventually became the first black to serve on a Baltimore grand jury. During his first two days on the jury, he observed that the jurors always asked whether the person under investigation was white or black. Blacks, he noted, were far more likely to be indicted (charged with a crime) than whites. On his third day as a juror, Marshall suggested that the jury drop the question of race when it was considering potential guilt or innocence. His words produced a tense silence in the jury room. Then, to Marshall's surprise, the white foreman agreed with him. That particular grand jury never again raised the question of race.

Although Will Marshall had received little formal education, he had an analytical mind and loved to debate. Thurgood Marshall later told a writer from *U.S. News & World Report* that it was his father who steered him toward a legal career. "He never told me to become a lawyer, but he turned me into one," said Marshall. "He did it by teaching me to argue, by challenging my logic on every point, by making me prove every statement I made."

Norma Marshall wanted her son to be a dentist, not a lawyer. Nevertheless, she helped him develop attitudes and skills that would prove useful in the career he chose. A bright student, Thurgood could have coasted through school, getting good grades with very little effort. But Norma Marshall put a high priority on education. She insisted that her son work hard and use his mind to its full capacity. According to Aubrey Marshall, Thurgood—like the boys' father—tended to be "very argumentive and aggressive." Norma Marshall's personality formed a sharp contrast. Conciliatory and diplomatic, she helped counteract Thurgood's sometimes tactless and impatient manner.

Norma and Will Marshall could provide their son with a secure and affectionate home, but they could not shelter him from prejudice against blacks. Marshall never forgot the day he discovered racism. Years later, he told a *Time* magazine reporter about the experience:

> I heard a kid call a Jewish boy I knew a "kike" to his face. I was about seven. I asked him why he didn't fight the kid. He asked me what would I do if somebody called me "nigger"—would I fight? That was a new one on me. I knew kike was a dirty word, but I hadn't known about nigger. I went home and wanted to know right that minute what all this meant. That's not easy for a parent to explain so it makes any sense to a kid, you know.

Although Will Marshall found it hard to define the word, he had no difficulty in telling his son how to react to it. "Anyone calls you nigger," he told Thurgood, "you not only got my permission to fight him— you got my orders to fight him."

A few years later, Thurgood Marshall followed those orders. By then a high school student, he led a busy life, managing to get excellent grades while participating in school clubs, going out for several sports, attending frequent dances, and, after school, delivering supplies for a hat company. One afternoon, he recalled later, he was carrying a stack of hatboxes

Thurgood Marshall's father, William, made his position on racism clear to his son. "Anyone calls you nigger," he told young Thurgood, "you not only got my permission to fight him—you got my orders to fight him."

so high he "couldn't see over them." Waiting for a trolley, he met and chatted with one of his father's friends, a man named Truesdale.

When the trolley arrived, Marshall arranged the bulky hatboxes as best he could and carefully stepped up to the platform. Suddenly, he felt himself seized by the arm and yanked backwards. "Nigguh, don't you push in front of no white lady again," snarled a male voice. "I hadn't seen any white lady," recalled Marshall, "so I tore into him. The hats scattered all over the street." The white man lunged back at Marshall, and the two were soon engaged in noisy battle.

Truesdale tried without success to break up the fight. At last, a policeman arrived and separated the combatants. The peacemaker turned out to be Army Matthews, a white neighborhood police officer known to be racially tolerant. Instead of automatically assuming that Marshall, because he was black, was at fault in the dispute, Matthews asked Truesdale for an eyewitness account. A deferential black man who preferred to avoid racial confrontations, Truesdale first apologized for Marshall's actions, then explained how the fight had started. After listening carefully, Matthews escorted both contestants to the police station. Charging neither with an offense, he dismissed them shortly afterward.

For a black man, striking—or even talking back to—a white man was dangerous business in the early 20th century, especially in a southern state. Truesdale's humble, apologetic manner exemplified what most whites expected—and got—from most blacks. Marshall's furious response to his white challenger might have earned him a savage beating, a jail sentence, or worse. Thanks to Army Matthews, the incident ended peacefully, but white policemen willing to listen to a black's version of an interracial squabble were rare. Marshall had been courageous. He had also been very lucky.

Despite Marshall's readiness to stand up for his rights, he sometimes had to compromise. Soon after his run-in at the trolley stop, he faced another challenge, this one less threatening but still uncomfortable. It started when his father helped him get a high school vacation job as a waiter on the Baltimore & Ohio Railroad. On the teenager's first day at work, the chief dining-car steward gave him a pair of waiter's pants. Finding them too short, the tall, lanky Marshall asked for another pair. "Boy," said the steward, "we can get a man to fit the pants a lot easier than we can get pants to fit the man. Why don't you scroonch down a little more?"

Marshall assessed the situation. Most work open to blacks, especially to male black teenagers, involved straight menial labor; a job on the B & O was a bonanza, not to be taken lightly, especially because he needed money for his education. Recalling the incident with a chuckle, he reported his next move: "I scroonched."

Although the adult Thurgood Marshall was able to joke about such incidents, growing up black—and ambitious—in early 20th-century America was no laughing matter. But even in that era of overt racism, Marshall grew up with a strong sense of dignity and self-respect. From his early years, he took pride in his family, starting with the tough-minded great-grandfather who fought his way out of slavery. Like his ancestors, Thurgood Marshall intended to claim his own position in American society.

3

THE EXTRA STEP

HURGOOD MARSHALL GRADUATED from high school in 1925, determined to continue his education. His parents, who had already managed to send their firstborn son to college, backed Thurgood's ambition enthusiastically. Aubrey Marshall, by this point a medical student, would become an eminent chest surgeon. Norma Marshall still hoped to make a dentist of her younger son.

In the 1920s, the United States offered its college-bound black students few choices. White colleges in the South were forbidden by law to accept blacks; white colleges in other parts of the country accepted very few. Thurgood Marshall decided to apply to one of the nation's all-black institutions. He chose Lincoln University, the nation's oldest black college.

Founded by a Presbyterian clergyman and his wife in 1854, Lincoln was chartered to provide "for the scientific, classical, and theological education of colored youth of the male sex." Although the distinguished Pennsylvania college is now open to students of all races and both sexes, its enrollment was all male and all black when Marshall entered. Specializing in liberal arts and teacher education, Lincoln sent about half of its alumni to graduate schools where they studied medicine, dentistry, education, and the law.

The college attracted a highly cosmopolitan group of young men, drawing its students from all sections of the United States and from such distant points as Africa and Asia. Among Thurgood Marshall's classmates were two future presidents of African nations:

Like other black high school graduates in the 1920s, 17-year-old Marshall faced limited educational options. Barred from the nation's exclusively white institutions, he selected Pennsylvania's distinguished Lincoln University, America's oldest black college.

379

Kwame Nkrumah of Ghana and Nnamdi Azikiwe of Nigeria. Another fellow student was Cabell Calloway, a young singer from Rochester, New York, who would later earn international fame as bandleader Cab Calloway.

Like countless college freshmen before him, Marshall played harder than he worked during his first semesters. The future lawyer became a charter member of the Weekend Club, a group of fun-loving students who swore they would never be found on campus over a weekend. True to his promise, Marshall used up his whole year's allowance of excused absences during his first semester. And when he was on campus, he later confessed, he spent most of his spare time playing cards. In his sophomore year, he and a group of friends were suspended for hazing new students, although they managed to shave several freshman heads before college officals caught them. "I got the horsin' around out of my system," Marshall said later.

Despite his antics, Marshall managed to maintain a B average and to read an impressive number of books. He was especially intrigued by the writings of W. E. B. Du Bois, the celebrated black scholar and activist who wrote *The Souls of Black Folk*, a searing collection of essays on black life, and edited the *Crisis*, the nation's largest black periodical. Published by the NAACP, the *Crisis* was renowned for Du Bois's powerful editorials.

Marshall was also exposed to the outpouring of black literature during the Harlem Renaissance. The 1920s, a time of general prosperity in America, produced a dazzling array of art from the New York City district of Harlem, the nation's unofficial black capital. Among the authors whose works appeared during Marshall's college years were poets Claude McKay, Countee Cullen, Jean Toomer, and Langston Hughes, perhaps the first major black poet whose writing specifically addressed members of his own

A founding member of the NAACP, William Edward Burghardt Du Bois spearheaded the fight for black equality in the first half of the 20th century. His long tenure at the NAACP's New York office briefly overlapped that of Marshall, who as a college student had been deeply impressed by The Souls of Black Folk *and other Du Bois works.*

race. Absorbed by the literature and social commentaries published by contemporary black authors, Marshall began to contemplate the role of the black individual in American society. It was a subject he would study for the rest of his life.

Marshall's college activities also included politics and protest. One evening, he and a group of friends decided to integrate the movie theater in nearby Oxford, Pennsylvania. When they bought their tickets, the seller sternly reminded them of the theater's rules: Black patrons were restricted to the balcony. Ignoring the reminder, the students marched into the theater and took seats in the "whites only" orchestra section.

An usher immediately ordered them to move to the balcony. When they stayed put, the usher loudly repeated his command, but the black students just gazed intently at the western on the screen. Then Marshall felt someone breathing on the back of his neck. "Nigger," said a harsh male voice, "why don't you just get out of here and sit where you belong?" Marshall quietly told the man that he had paid for his ticket and intended to stay where he was. Describing the episode in a letter to his family, he said, "You can't really tell what a person like that looks like because it's just an ugly feeling that's looking at you, not a real face."

Marshall's letter went on to report the incident's conclusion: "We found out that they only had one fat cop in the whole town and they wouldn't have the nerve or the room in the jail to arrest all of us. But the amazing thing was, when we were leaving, we just walked out with all those other people and they didn't do anything, didn't say anything, didn't even look at us—at least, not as far as I know. I'm not sure I like being invisible, but maybe it's better than being put to shame and not able to respect yourself."

During his college years, Marshall sometimes attended Philadelphia's Cherry Street Memorial

Until the 1950s, the South restricted its black residents to such separate facilities as this segregated movie theater in Leland, Mississippi. In the North, black moviegoers were usually obliged to sit in the balcony, called "nigger heaven" by patronizing whites.

Church with his friends. "We went in there because we learned that's where all the cute chicks went," he joked later. The "cute chick" he met was Vivian Burey, a University of Pennsylvania undergraduate. The two students fell in love almost immediately. "First we decided to get married five years after I graduated, then three, then one, and we finally did just before I started my last semester," Marshall recalled later.

Marshall and Burey, both 21 years old, were married on September 4, 1929. The Lincoln senior and his bride, who had already received her college degree, moved into a small apartment in Oxford. To help finance his education, both husband and wife worked: Thurgood Marshall as a bellhop and waiter and Vivian Marshall—whom everyone called "Buster"—as a secretary. According to friends, Buster Marshall exerted a stabilizing influence on her high-spirited young husband. "She helped 'turn him around' and inspired in him an academic zeal," said one observer.

Thurgood Marshall had enjoyed debates ever since his early discussions with his father. Known as "the Wrathful Marshall," he became the star of Lincoln's Forensic Society, leading the debating team to a string of impressive victories. In his senior year, dismayed by Lincoln's calamitous 1929 football season, Marshall reportedly jumped onto the stage during a pregame rally and delivered a fiery 20-minute pep talk. Ignited by his blazing rhetoric, the Lincoln football squad rushed onto the field and played its finest game of the year. The inspired performance produced only a scoreless tie, but Marshall cheerfully took credit for it. In any case, he had demonstrated the oratorical skill that would one day distinguish him in the courts.

In June 1930, Marshall received his A.B. degree, with honors in the humanities (literature, philosophy, and the arts). His interest in becoming a dentist,

Marshall (middle row, second from right) and his fellow Lincoln University freshmen sit for a class portrait in 1925. In spite of his mother's early guidance, Marshall earned a college reputation for being, as one friend later put it, "something of a playboy."

never strong, had steadily diminished during his college years. He was a gifted, persuasive speaker, and he enjoyed facing an audience. By the time he graduated, he had decided to enter the law. It was a decision he never regretted.

When Norma and Will Marshall invited their son and his wife to share their home in Baltimore, the young couple accepted quickly. They knew they needed to save every penny for law school. Norma Marshall, at last persuaded that law was a better choice for her son than dentistry, even sold her engagement ring to help pay his tuition expenses. Marshall applied to the University of Maryland's law school, a highly regarded Baltimore institution. The all-white university had never accepted a black student, and its administrators had no intention of changing its policy for Thurgood Marshall. They turned him down immediately.

Marshall next turned to Howard University's law school, which accepted his application. Founded in 1867 as a school for newly freed slaves, the Washington, D.C., institution had grown steadily in size and prestige. When Marshall entered law school in 1930, most of Howard's student body was black, although the college accepted students of all races and both sexes. Then as now, a large proportion of the nation's black doctors, dentists, engineers, architects, and lawyers held degrees from Howard.

Students stroll across the Washington, D.C., campus of Howard University, where Marshall attended the law school. Established in 1867 for young black males, Howard later opened its doors to men and women of all races.

Remembering his first week at law school, Marshall said he knew that "this was it. This was what I wanted to do for as long as I lived." Although he had been known, according to one old friend, as "something of a playboy" at Lincoln, Marshall changed his ways at Howard. He sped through his first year at a frantic pace. Up every day at 5:30 A.M., he caught a train to Washington, attended classes until 3 o'clock in the afternoon, boarded the return train to Baltimore, and then reported for his part-time job. After dinner with his wife and parents, he studied until midnight. "I heard law books were to dig in," he once recalled, "so I dug, way deep."

The long days took their toll on the young law student, whose weight fell from 170 to 130 pounds. But his hard work paid off. At the end of his first year, he was named top student in his class, an achievement that brought him the coveted job of assistant in Howard's law library. The position paid enough to keep him in law school, but it also kept him in Washington until 10 o'clock every night. In spite of his backbreaking schedule, however, Marshall acquired a large circle of friends and kept up an active social life. One law school classmate remembered him as "a dual personality. On the one hand, serious, and on the other hand, crazy." Marshall "was happy-go-lucky on the face of it," recalled another law school friend, "but he managed to get a lot of work done when nobody was looking."

When Marshall entered Howard, Mordecai Johnson, its first black president, was in the process of revolutionizing the school. Eager to promote what he called "higher individualism," Johnson rebuilt the college campus, expanded its curriculum, hired an impressive array of new instructors, and raised the university's academic standing to new heights. Johnson later credited a white friend, Supreme Court justice Louis Brandeis, with helping to inspire the transformation. "[Brandeis] told me that the one thing I should do was to build a law school and train men to get the constitutional rights of our people," Johnson recalled. "He said, 'Once you train lawyers to do this, the Supreme Court will have to hand your people their civil and constitutional rights.'"

Among the outstanding staff members recruited by Johnson was law professor William Henry Hastie, a Harvard graduate who later became the first black federal judge as well as a close friend and NAACP associate of Thurgood Marshall's. Another leading Howard figure was Charles Hamilton Houston, a brilliant attorney and pioneering civil rights activist. Appointed vice-dean of Howard's law school in 1929, Houston had remained active in the NAACP. He taught his students how to research and structure their cases, how to use existing laws to fight racial injustice, and how to act as "social engineers" as well as lawyers. Houston, who quickly spotted Marshall as a superior candidate for the law, paid special attention to the young student from Baltimore. And Marshall, recalled a law school contemporary, "idolized Charlie."

"Harvard was training people to join big law firms; Howard was teaching lawyers to go to court," Marshall told an interviewer years afterward. "Charlie's phrase was Social Engineer. He wanted us to be a part of the community. He wanted the lawyer to take over the leadership in the community." Part of Marshall's training under Houston and Hastie consisted of late-night sessions at which the lawyers plotted strategies for their current NAACP cases. Walter White, then chief executive of the NAACP, attended one such session. White was impressed by Marshall, whom he described as "a lanky, brash young senior law student who was always present," but he was also "amazed at [Marshall's] assertiveness in challenging positions [taken] by Charlie [Houston] and the other lawyers." However, added White, "I soon learned of his great value to the case in doing everything he was asked."

Charles Hamilton Houston taught Marshall in law school, worked with him on his first cases, and later hired him as NAACP counsel. "What Charlie beat into our heads," said Marshall later, "was excellence."

During their night sessions in the library, Marshall and his colleagues worked out legal research problems, some of them proposed by Houston, others by the students themselves. One evening, Marshall recalled later, "one guy started to work on something and we all joined in. And we found out that in codifying the Code of the District of Columbia, they had just left out the Civil Rights statute. Since it didn't apply to anyone but us, they left it out. We eventually got through the court and got that straightened out."

In 1932, Professor Hastie asked Marshall, then a second-year law student, to help prepare a *brief* (a written argument presented to a court by a lawyer) in a North Carolina desegregation case. The action involved a black college graduate who had been refused admission to the University of North Carolina law school because of his color. Claiming that his rejection violated the Constitution's equal protection guarantee, the applicant sued the university. He lost the case, then asked Hastie to handle an *appeal*: When a *litigant* (a person engaged in a lawsuit) loses in court, he or she may request the next higher court—the court of appeals—to review the case. The appeals court judge reads briefs from both sides before hearing the lawyers' oral arguments.

Despite Hastie and Marshall's carefully constructed brief, they lost their case in the North Carolina appeals court. The University of North Carolina was state supported, but its students paid tuition. Therefore, the court ruled, the university could be considered a private institution, under no obligation to extend equal rights to its applicants. This precedent has since been overturned.

Although Marshall met defeat in the North Carolina case, Howard and its professors taught him a great deal about the actual practice of law. Many law schools, even today, emphasize legal philosophy and history rather than hands-on experience. But at Howard, as Marshall later put it, "The emphasis was not on theory; the emphasis in this school was on practice, on how to get it done." Addressing Howard students many years after his own graduation, Marshall praised both the college and his mentor, Charles Houston. "[What] Charlie beat into our heads," said Marshall, "was excellence. He said, 'When a doctor makes a mistake, he buries his mistake. When a lawyer makes a mistake, he makes it in front of God and everybody else.' "

Thurgood Marshall had taken his training at Howard Law School to heart. In the same address, he endorsed the school's demand for hard work: "When you get in a courtroom, you can't just say, 'Please, Mr. Court, have mercy on me because I'm a Negro.' You are in competition with a well-trained white lawyer and you better be at least as good as he is; and if you expect to win, you better be better. If I give you five cases to read overnight, you better read eight. And when I say eight, you read ten. You go that step further; and you might make it."

As a law student, Marshall took that "step further": In 1933, he graduated first in his class. Harvard University immediately offered him a postgraduate scholarship, but he declined. It was a handsome tribute to his abilities, but Marshall had worked long and hard for the right to practice law. Now that he had his degree, that was exactly what he intended to do. He took the bar examination (a test required by each state before it allows a lawyer to practice) in Maryland, passed it with flying colors, and opened an office in Baltimore. Thurgood Marshall was on his way. ◖⦿◗

Judge William Henry Hastie (right) chats with members of a youth group in Louisville, Kentucky, in the 1940s. One of Marshall's professors and friends at Howard University, Hastie became the nation's first black federal judge in 1949.

4

FIGHTING
THE ODDS

THURGOOD MARSHALL MOVED into a small office in east Baltimore, hung out a sign, hired a secretary, and waited for business. In 1933, when Marshall began his practice, black lawyers were scarce; the ratio of black citizens to black attorneys in the United States stood at 200,000 to 1. Fewer than a dozen black lawyers practiced in Baltimore, a city with thousands of black residents. Despite their rarity, however, these lawyers faced formidable odds against success.

In the first decades of the 20th century, a black citizen who hoped to win a lawsuit, especially a suit against a white defendant, generally hired a white attorney. At a time when almost all judges and juries were white, and when many of those white people harbored racial prejudices, a white attorney clearly had a better chance of success than a black attorney. "Negroes weren't anxious to have Negro lawyers," recalled a colleague of Marshall's. "The feeling was that whites could get more for them . . . and the white lawyers, frankly, fed the feeling." Virtually the only black Americans who sought out attorneys of their own race were those without the funds to pay for legal services.

The state of America's economy added to the obstacles confronting Marshall and other black attorneys of the time. The Great Depression, triggered by the stock market crash of 1929, had reached its peak by the mid-1930s. Because few individuals of any race could afford to go to court, the entire legal

When Marshall opened his own law office in 1933, he got off to a slow start. In those days, recalled a black associate, "Negroes weren't anxious to have Negro lawyers. The feeling was that whites could get more for them."

profession suffered. Hardest hit, of course, were the already struggling black lawyers.

Marshall had not expected to become rich when he opened his office, but he had hoped for a few paying clients. During his first year as a lawyer, he had none. Rather than making money, in fact, he lost it: His books for his first 12 months of practice showed a net loss of $1,000, a sizable sum in 1933. Years later, Marshall told a reporter about his early days as a lawyer: "One day I'd bring two lunches and the next day, my secretary would bring two lunches and sometimes we'd be the only two people in that office for weeks at a time."

Clients finally began to appear: tenants evicted for nonpayment of rent, people who had received large penalties for small infractions of the law, or victims of police brutality. Very few could afford even modest legal fees, but Marshall turned no one away. He soon earned a reputation as "the little man's lawyer."

Years later, Marshall smiled as he told the story of an elderly black farm woman who had moved from South Carolina to Baltimore. Back home, the woman had received free legal advice from the county judge, but when she sought counsel from a Baltimore judge, he told her to get in touch with Thurgood Marshall. As she later confessed to Marshall, "He said you was a freebie lawyer."

Marshall, who prepared for each trial with painstaking care, won many of his early cases. The parade of needy clients passing through his door brought him no money, but it did help him polish his courtroom style. Poet Langston Hughes later described Marshall as a persuasive man who "has moved many a judge to search his conscience and come up with decisions he probably did not know he had in him." Another Marshall observer commented, "He is an effective lawyer because he has common sense and a good instinct for facts."

Marshall's *pro bono* (public service) work provided more than hands-on experience. As author Richard Kluger noted in his 1976 book, *Simple Justice*, "It was only a matter of time before word spread about [Marshall's] competence as well as his generosity of spirit. In effect, provision of his services *gratis* [free] or close to it was the best (and only) advertisement a struggling black attorney could have. . . . He began to pick up some solid clients."

Among Marshall's new, paying accounts were a large Baltimore laundry, several labor associations, and Carl Murphy, head of Baltimore's wealthiest and most influential black family. As publisher of a popular weekly newspaper, the *Afro-American*, Murphy had long backed the slowly expanding civil rights movement. Thus, when Lillie Jackson, a middle-aged Baltimore housewife, decided to reactivate the local chapter of the NAACP in 1934, she asked Murphy to bankroll the membership drive. Murphy promised his support, then chose Marshall to act as the chapter's lawyer. Like most of Marshall's jobs, the position of NAACP counsel paid nothing. For the young lawyer, however, the honor of working for the city's leading black-rights group was compensation enough.

Because the NAACP's Baltimore branch had dwindled to a mere handful of members, Marshall, Jackson, and Murphy began a vigorous campaign to revive local interest. Some potential recruits had been skeptical of the organization because of its reputation for admitting only the black elite. As Marshall put it, "When I was a kid, we used to say that NAACP stood for the National Association for the Advancement of *Certain* People." But now things would be different. Marshall visited every black neighborhood in town, talking to individuals, making speeches to crowds, and explaining how much a unified community could accomplish.

Richard Kluger discussed Marshall's early NAACP activities with the Reverend A. J. Payne,

Displaying a photograph of a lynching, an NAACP poster asks: "Can you look at this picture and refuse to help?" Marshall, who began working for the NAACP in 1934, devoted almost three decades to the black-rights organization.

then pastor of a large Baptist church in Baltimore. "The prevailing feeling here then among too many was that segregation was segregation, and it was going to be that way till kingdom come," Payne said. "Some very fine men in the community were just plain afraid. Young Marshall, though, was different. He showed his courage and his tenacity, and the people liked him, the common people and the professional people both. . . . He'd say that, Jim Crow or no Jim Crow, we were free citizens and as such we had rights but we were going to have to fight to get them. People in the community looked up to him. He was never arrogant and always accessible."

Briscoe Koger, a black Baltimore attorney, shared Payne's sentiments about Marshall: "Old-timers had

Following southern custom, North Carolinians quench their thirst at separate drinking fountains in 1945. Not until 1961 would Americans be able to travel without seeing "white" and "colored" signs in railroad stations and bus depots.

the feeling that here finally was a leader. Everybody was in his corner. Others had none of the assurance and power that whites were accustomed to, but Thurgood Marshall had that."

Marshall kicked off his NAACP career by leading a boycott of stores on Baltimore's Pennsylvania Avenue. Although they depended on black customers, the white owners of these shops flatly refused to hire any black workers. Marshall and his colleagues persuaded a group of unemployed black high-school graduates to form picket lines outside the stores, urging shoppers to stay away until the merchants changed their hiring policies. Sales plummeted, but instead of compromising, the shopkeepers sued the NAACP.

Marshall's Howard University mentor, Charles Houston, joined his protégé in defending the suit. The two lawyers worked as a team, Marshall researching the case and Houston presenting it in court. The spectators who packed Baltimore's federal courthouse during the trial gasped when the white judge announced his verdict: He not only ruled in favor of the NAACP but congratulated Marshall and Houston on their effective presentation.

Working with Lillie Jackson, Marshall next embarked on an NAACP campaign to organize Maryland's black schoolteachers. Like their counterparts throughout the South, the black teachers received much lower salaries than white teachers. The only way to correct the problem, asserted Marshall and Jackson, was through legal action. But most of the black teachers, afraid of being laid off, hesitated to sue their school boards. The NAACP team finally overcame the teachers' reluctance by raising money for an emergency fund to pay any teachers who lost their jobs. Although it took several years, the drive eventually succeeded. Its first beneficiary was a Maryland county school principal whose annual salary rose from $612 to $1,475 as the result of an NAACP-backed lawsuit.

In the 1930s, black Americans faced social injustice, segregation, and discrimination on numerous fronts, including education, criminal justice, voting, housing, recreational facilities, and public accommodations. With limited funds and personnel, the NAACP had to hit the most vulnerable targets first. Its executives, who regarded higher education as the "soft underbelly" of southern segregation, decided to concentrate their forces on graduate schools.

White resistance to integrated public schools formed a virtually unbreakable wall. Resistance to integration on the graduate and professional level, the NAACP believed, might be easier to overcome. Graduate students were far fewer in number than public school students, and systematic segregation at the graduate school level would be relatively simple to demonstrate. And Marshall and his colleagues believed that judges, who were lawyers themselves, might quickly grasp the argument that "separate" law schools could never be "equal." NAACP officials also believed that victory in a small number of cases would establish legal precedents that could eventually be applied to all black educational opportunities. By the mid-1930s, the NAACP had committed itself to an all-out attack on discrimination in law schools.

Joining Charles Houston in the first battle, Marshall scored his first major court victory in 1935. The case, *Murray v. Pearson*, pitted a 20-year-old black college graduate, Donald Gaines Murray, against the University of Maryland and its president, Raymond A. Pearson. When Murray applied to the university's law school, Pearson rejected him. Murray, he asserted, could obtain "separate but equal" training at the Princess Anne Academy, a segregated institution on Maryland's Eastern Shore.

Pointing out that the academy offered no legal degree, Murray renewed his application to the Maryland law school. "The university," responded Pearson, "does not accept Negro students." Murray then

Marshall (left) and Charles Houston (right) work with Donald Gaines Murray on their 1935 suit against the University of Maryland. Thanks to Marshall and Houston, Murray became the first black admitted to the law school at the previously all-white university.

took the university to court. Arguing his case, Marshall and Houston once again worked as a team, dividing up the research and the court presentation.

Murray came to trial in June 1935. Armed with Marshall's meticulously assembled precedents and arguments, Houston demolished the opposition. He forced Pearson to admit that Princess Anne Academy lacked the facilities, the faculty, and the educational resources of the University of Maryland; that Murray was fully qualified for admission to the university; and that the University of Maryland law school was the only institution at which Murray could receive training in Maryland law.

Presenting the final arguments of the case, Marshall demonstrated his mastery of constitutional law. The "separate" part of the separate-but-equal doctrine, he noted, had been upheld by the Supreme Court, but the "equal" part had never been tested. Now that the defendants had conceded that the separate facilities offered Murray were unequal, argued Marshall, the court had no choice but to order the university to admit him. "What's at stake here is more than the rights of my client," he said. "It's the moral commitment stated in our country's creed." Listening

An official at the NAACP's Manhattan headquarters points to the group's latest recruitment poster. When NAACP special counsel Charles Houston recruited Marshall as his assistant and told him that the job involved frustration and danger, Marshall took it without hesitation.

to his impassioned words were three especially attentive courtroom spectators: Norma, Will, and Buster Marshall.

Marshall and Houston's combined eloquence won the day. On June 25, the Baltimore City Court ordered Pearson to admit Donald Murray to the university law school at once. Marshall appeared calm and somber as he heard the verdict, but when he left the courtroom with his wife and parents, he expressed his real feelings: Seizing Buster Marshall in his arms, he swept her off her feet in a jubilant tango.

The university appealed the decision, but without success. "Whatever system is adopted for legal education now," ruled the Maryland Court of Appeals, "must furnish equality of treatment now." Donald Murray entered the University of Maryland law school without incident, earned his degree, and opened a practice in Baltimore. Throughout his career, he made his legal services available to the NAACP without charge.

Marshall continued to rally Maryland's teachers and to work toward improved public schools for black children. His personal financial picture, however, failed to improve. In a better economic climate, his nonpaying NAACP work might have been balanced by profitable private practice, but the depression still gripped the land, and Marshall still represented people who could not afford to pay him. Then, in 1936, he got a call from Charles Houston. The former Howard University dean, now first special counsel to the NAACP, invited Marshall to become his assistant at a salary of $2,400 per year. Houston told Marshall that the job would be sometimes discouraging, often frustrating, and usually dangerous. Marshall accepted immediately.

For the next two years, Marshall and Houston worked together closely, spending much of their time traveling from one southern courthouse to another as they filed lawsuits for black students and teachers. Talking to Richard Kluger about those days, Marshall recalled that "Charlie would sit in my car—I had a little old beat-up '29 Ford—and type out the briefs. And he could type up a storm—faster than any secretary—and not just with two fingers going. I mean he used 'em all." Because accommodations for black travelers in the South of the 1930s were either dismal or nonexistent, the two attorneys spent most of their nights with friends. Assisting Houston meant long days of nonstop labor for Marshall. "He used to work like hell and way into the night," recalled a former aide.

When he was not on the road with Houston, Marshall divided his time between New York City—headquarters of the NAACP—and Baltimore. Unwilling to abandon his many poor clients, he kept a small office in his family's home, attending to his townspeople's needs until, as he later put it, "they adjusted over to new lawyers." In 1936, he handled his first case as NAACP assistant special counsel. Another law school suit, this one involved black college graduate Lloyd Gaines, who had applied to the law school at the University of Missouri. Rejecting him on the basis of his race, the university offered to pay his tuition at an out-of-state law school. This policy, asserted the state of Missouri, complied with the separate-but-equal doctrine. Not so, said the NAACP, which called the policy unconstitutional, a violation of the Fourteenth Amendment.

Represented by Houston, who argued the case, and Marshall, who wrote the all-important brief, Gaines sued the state of Missouri. In November 1938, after a series of Missouri courts had ruled against Gaines, the Supreme Court agreed to hear the case. Marshall based his brief on the Fourteenth Amendment's "equal protection of the laws" section. Rather than challenging the separate-but-equal doctrine, the brief demanded equality: If Missouri refused to admit Gaines to its all-white law school, it must offer him— and other qualified black applicants—equal facilities within the state. By a vote of six to two, the Supreme Court agreed with the Marshall-Houston argument. State laws that called for segregation, ruled the court, were permissible only when they provided the separated races with equal privileges within the state. Because Missouri had failed to supply a separate-but-equal law school for blacks, the state was obliged to let Gaines enter the only law school available, the hitherto all-white University of Missouri.

The Gaines case had far-reaching implications. In effect, the Court said Missouri could maintain separate law schools for both races, but only if those schools were truly equal. Missouri—and other states—now faced two alternatives: integrating their law schools or building and staffing brand-new law schools for blacks, a crushingly expensive proposition. Elated NAACP officials realized that one day the Supreme Court's reinforcement of the separate-but-equal doctrine might extend to public schools at all levels, as well as to teachers' salaries and student facilities across the nation. Thurgood Marshall had helped breach a mighty wall.

In late 1938, Charles Houston resigned as NAACP special counsel because of ill health. Marshall, 30 years old, replaced him. With his wife, he moved into a walk-up apartment in Harlem and took over Houston's desk at the NAACP's lower Fifth Avenue headquarters. As chief counsel to the important civil rights organization, Marshall had become black America's most prominent attorney. But his personal style— relaxed, informal, and down-to-earth—remained unchanged.

Taking stock of the New York office, Marshall found it far too "tush-tush," as he put it, for his tastes. "It was Dr. Whoosis and Mr. Whatsis and all kind of nonsense like that, bowing and scraping like an embassy scene," he later told a *New York Times* reporter. "Well, I took a long look," he continued, "and I figured I'd have to bust that stuff up pretty quick. Believe me, I had them talking first names in nothing time and no more of that formality business." Describing his boss, an NAACP aide later said, "Thurgood was always one of the gang. He never put barriers between himself and the less exalted."

Soon after he took over as NAACP special counsel, Marshall traveled to Dallas, Texas, to investigate a recent incident of racial violence. It centered on a 65-year-old black man, the president of a local junior college, who had received a notice to report for jury duty. When he appeared at the Dallas courthouse, appalled officials discovered they had summoned a black man and told him to go home. The educator, however, insisted on exercising his rights as a citizen. Enraged, two white court workers grabbed the frail, elderly man, dragged him out of the jury room, and threw him down the courthouse steps.

The college president survived, but the episode sparked flames of hostility among both blacks and whites. By the time Marshall arrived in town, Dallas seethed with rage. Marshall appraised the situation, then called on Texas governor James Allred. Amazed that a black attorney from New York dared to come to Texas and explain the law to him, the governor gave Marshall a hearing. Apparently, the NAACP counsel spoke convincingly: The day after the meeting, Allred ordered the Texas Rangers to stand guard at the Dallas courthouse, requested an FBI investigation of the incident, and announced that he would tolerate no further harassment of potential black jurors. "No one," observed Richard Kluger, "could remember the last time a southern governor had demonstrated quite as much enthusiasm for enforcement of the law."

In October 1939, NAACP president Walter White created a new branch of the organization. Officially called the NAACP Legal Defense and Educational Fund, Inc., the body would provide free legal aid to blacks who suffered injustice because of their race. According to its charter, the Fund, as it came to be known, would also "seek and promote educational opportunities denied to Negroes because of their color" and publicize reports on "the status of the Negro in American life."

Appointed director-counsel of the Fund, Marshall was responsible for supervising all legal activities for the NAACP; he planned its overall courtroom strategy, oversaw individual lawsuits, prepared briefs, and often argued cases himself. During its early years, the Fund focused on two major targets: racial inequality in the nation's courtrooms and the exclusion of blacks from the voting process.

Marshall prepared his first Supreme Court brief in 1940, when the NAACP sought to overturn the convictions of three black men accused of murdering a white man in Florida. The three had confessed to the crime after a five-day, nonstop grilling by Florida police. During their interrogation, the defendants were not allowed to see lawyers, friends, or family members. The Supreme Court had already ruled that confessions extracted by force could not be used in court, but Florida courts had found that the men's confessions had not been obtained by force and were therefore admissible in court.

In his Supreme Court brief, Marshall maintained that such "sunrise confessions," wrung from terrified and isolated men, qualified as forced admissions. And such confessions, he argued, violated the Fourteenth Amendment's guarantee of "due process of law." Agreeing with Marshall, the Supreme Court reversed the convictions of the three Florida men. The decision in the case, known as *Chambers v. Florida*, by no means eliminated prejudice, violence, and injustice against blacks, but it was an important victory, encouraging to the black community and its defenders.

The next year, Marshall took on another case involving involuntary confessions, this one in Hugo, Oklahoma. After discovering the bodies of Elmer Rogers, his wife, and two children in the smoldering ruins of their home, the police arrested a young black handyman known as Lyons. Although they had no solid evidence against Lyons, police officers held him in a cell for 11 days, denying him food and sleep, beating him severely, and refusing him access to a

A sheriff and his deputies surround a black Oklahoman accused of murdering a white family in 1941. Despite evidence that the suspect, a handyman known as Lyons, had confessed to the crime only after savage beatings, Marshall was unable to prevent his conviction and sentence of life imprisonment.

lawyer. At last, after the officers placed the victims' bloody, charred bones in Lyons's lap, he confessed to the multiple murder. Twelve hours later, he signed a second confession at the state penitentiary.

Convinced that Lyons had been framed for the crime of another, Hugo's black community asked the NAACP to defend him. Marshall took the case himself. When he arrived in the small Oklahoma town, he found it boiling with racial hostility. Local blacks formed a network to protect the NAACP attorney, surrounding him with bodyguards and arranging for him to sleep in a different house each night of his stay.

Despite their precautions, Marshall received an unexpected nighttime visit from a white man. Quickly identifying himself as the murdered woman's father, the visitor said he had come with information. He told Marshall he did not know whether Lyons was guilty, but he did know that the accused man had been treated unfairly. A police official, he said, had showed him a "nigger beater" (a crowbar), boasting that it had been used to "beat a confession out of Lyons." The victim's father offered to testify at Lyons's trial.

Thanks in part to his testimony, the trial judge threw out Lyons's first confession, although he allowed the prosecution to refer to it throughout the trial. Under Marshall's relentless cross-examination, police witnesses admitted to their "bone tactic," and a hotel clerk testified that he heard policemen refer to a "nigger beater." But although Marshall introduced a telling exhibit—a photograph of a beaming police officer standing over the bruised and bleeding Lyons—no policeman would admit to the beatings. The officer pictured with Lyons claimed he could not identify the battered man; all blacks, he said under oath, looked alike to him.

The only evidence that could support a conviction was Lyons's second confession. And this, insisted

Marshall, had been obtained through a form of force: Lyons's terror of being subjected to further violent abuse. The Oklahoma court, however, disregarded Marshall's argument. Finding Lyons guilty of murder, it sentenced him to life imprisonment. Although he had failed to clear his client, Marshall's work was widely considered a victory because the court imposed a life sentence rather than the death penalty.

Believing that the *Chambers v. Florida* precedent applied to the Lyons case, Marshall appealed it to the Supreme Court. Again, he argued that Lyons's conviction had been based on inadmissible evidence—a nonvoluntary admission of guilt—and that he had thus been denied "due process of law." But by a vote of six to three, the justices of the Court decided against Marshall, ruling that Lyons's second confession was not "brought about by the earlier mistreatments." The decision marked Marshall's first defeat in a civil rights case. In the course of his career, he would argue 32 cases before the Supreme Court; 27 of these would be resounding triumphs.

Marshall next moved to the crucial area of voting rights. The Fifteenth Amendment, ratified in 1870, gave black men the right to vote. (Neither black nor white American women could vote until 1920.) But despite the amendment and several laws later enacted to strengthen it, the South's white population had no intention of allowing its black citizens to vote. No more than three percent of eligible blacks voted in the South during the 1930s.

The South employed a number of strategies to keep blacks away from the ballot box. Many states enacted poll taxes, or voting fees, that few blacks—the South's poorest residents—could pay. Other states required each would-be voter to pass a "literacy test"; whites were simply asked to spell their own names, but blacks received long, complicated examinations. Alabama, for example, obliged them to "understand and explain any article of the Consti-

Candidates address a segregated audience at a Marianna, Arkansas, election rally in the 1940s. Such events provided many southern blacks, routinely barred from the polls, with their only connection to the political process.

tution of the United States to the satisfaction of the registrars." The few black citizens who could both pass the literacy test and afford the poll tax still faced intimidation, threats, and violence if they tried to exercise their right to vote.

Still another means—perhaps the most effective—of preventing blacks from voting was the "white primary." In a primary election, usually held a few months before a general election, voters select their party's candidates for office. Because the states of the Deep South were solidly Democratic, the candidates who won the Democratic primary were virtually assured of winning the election that followed. Voters in a primary are required to belong to a political party. But the southern Democrats refused membership to blacks, effectively denying them any voice in the electoral process.

In 1944, Marshall decided to make a frontal assault on the white primary. His battlefield would be Texas; his weapon, a lawsuit brought by black Texan Lonnie E. Smith. When white election judge (supervisor) S. E. Allwright blocked Smith's attempt to vote in the 1940 Texas primary election, Smith sued the Democratic party. His suit was dismissed by the lower courts, which ruled that the Democratic party was a private institution with the right to include— or exclude—whomever it chose.

At this point, Marshall and his Legal Defense Fund team brought the case to the U.S. Supreme Court. They based their principal argument on the Fifteenth Amendment, which forbids the states to deprive citizens of their right to vote "on account of race, color, or previous condition of servitude." Marshall pointed out that the Texas primary "effectively controls the choice" of candidates in the Texas elections. Because the Texas election judge who prevented Smith from voting in the primary was a state official, he argued, the state of Texas had violated the Fifteenth Amendment. "The right to vote in Texas primary elections," he insisted, "is secured by the Constitution."

With only one dissenting vote, the Court upheld the Marshall team's argument, a decision that made racial discrimination in primary elections illegal. Southern states would continue to search for ways to get around the ruling, but in the long run, *Smith v. Allwright* sounded the death knell for the white primary.

Marshall saw the *Smith* decision as both a major triumph in the battle for social justice and as a stepping-stone to future victories. Speaking before an NAACP convention three months later, the exultant attorney asserted that the fight had just begun. "We must not be delayed by people who say, 'the time is not ripe,'" he told a cheering audience. "Persons who deny to us our civil rights should be brought to justice now. Many people believe the time is always 'ripe' to discriminate against Negroes. All right, then—the time is always 'ripe' to bring them to justice."

Not long afterward, Marshall experienced a frightening brush with people who believed the time was "always ripe to discriminate." It occurred near Columbia, Tennessee, on a dark November night in 1946. Earlier in the year, four Columbia policemen had been wounded during a raid on the town's black

A somber banner hangs from the window of the NAACP's New York office. Despite frequent reports of atrocities against blacks (according to police officials, 3,446 black Americans were lynched between 1882 and 1968), most legislators, afraid to incur the enmity of powerful southern politicians, looked the other way.

neighborhood. When 25 black men were subsequently charged with attempted murder, Marshall and 2 staff members sped to Columbia to defend them. After getting 24 of the defendants acquitted, the NAACP lawyers headed for their hotel in Nashville. Suddenly, three patrol cars, sirens wailing, signaled the black attorneys to pull over. Armed constables poured out of the squad cars.

After vainly searching the black lawyers' car for illegal liquor, the constables released Marshall and his friends. But a few miles farther on, they stopped them again. This time, they accused Marshall of drunk driving, ordered him into the squad car, and whisked him back to Columbia. There they told him to get out and walk across the street to the magistrate's office—alone. Aware that many blacks had been given similar orders, only to be shot in the back for allegedly "escaping custody," Marshall refused. The constables then escorted him into the office of the magistrate, a nondrinker famed for his tough approach to drinking drivers. He sniffed Marshall's breath, found him completely sober, and set him free. ("After that," Marshall joked later, "I really *needed* a drink!")

Hoping to avoid further harassment, Marshall's associates had meanwhile traded cars with a local friend. As the NAACP lawyers traveled to Nashville, a carload of deputies followed the friend, dragged him out of the car, and beat him severely. The next day, Marshall wired the U.S. attorney general, demanding a federal investigation of the episode. A week later, he returned to Columbia, strode into the courthouse, and obtained an acquittal for the last of the 25 black defendants.

Morgan v. Virginia, a second Marshall triumph in 1946, involved segregated transportation. Black traveler Irene Morgan, bound for Maryland, had boarded a bus in Virginia. Ordered to sit in the back of the bus as Virginia law dictated, Morgan refused; as an interstate vehicle, she said, the bus was not bound by local law. The driver called the police, who arrested Morgan and fined her $10. Marshall took her case to the Supreme Court, arguing that the Court had already banned state laws that placed "an undue burden" on interstate commerce and that Virginia's bus-passenger segregation law constituted just such a burden.

Concluding his argument, Marshall referred to World War II, which had ended the year before: "Today we are just emerging from a war in which all of the people of the United States were joined in a death struggle against the apostles of racism. How much clearer, therefore, must it be today . . . that the national business of interstate commerce is not to be disfigured by . . . racial notions alien to our national ideals." The Supreme Court agreed with the NAACP attorney, ruling segregation illegal on interstate buses. Although the decision covered only a narrow field, it was a breakthrough that would eventually lead to the end of Jim Crow transportation in America.

The year 1946 also brought Marshall the NAACP's highest award, the Spingarn Medal. Named for longtime NAACP chief Joel Spingarn, the coveted golden award is bestowed each year for the "highest or noblest achievement by an American Negro." A struggling Baltimore attorney only 13 years earlier, Marshall had beaten the odds facing any ambitious young black American in the 1930s. Now one of the nation's best-known lawyers, he had also become one of its most powerful crusaders for social justice. ❧

5

"MR. CIVIL RIGHTS"

B Y THE TIME Thurgood Marshall reached the age of 40, in 1948, he had earned a nickname from the press: "Mr. Civil Rights." Deeply respected by thousands of Americans of all races—and loathed by thousands of others—Marshall remained unchanged in his personal style. Like other associates, Marian Wynn Perry found him as informal and accessible as ever. Perry, a white labor lawyer who worked at the Fund from 1945 until 1949, later talked to Richard Kluger about her boss:

> He had a terribly deep and real affection for the little people—the people he called the Little Joes, and the affection was returned. . . . At a national convention, some little fellow might ask a not very penetrating question and . . . someone else on the rostrum might wave him off. But Thurgood would send me to find the fellow or go see him himself because he knew that question was terribly important to this Little Joe, even if not to anyone else. He had this enormous ability to relate. He was not only *of* them—he was *with* them.

In postwar America, the needs of the "Little Joes" were many. Perhaps most pressing, Marshall and his colleagues believed, was the need for decent housing, especially for the nation's black veterans. Marshall had long complained that the U.S. government itself practiced segregationist housing policies. In 1944, for example, the Federal Housing Administration had built several large public-housing units in Detroit. Addressing an NAACP meeting, Marshall noted that a year after the Detroit project was complete, "every single white family in the area eligible for public

NAACP branch-office director Gloucester Current points out trouble spots to Thurgood Marshall, counsel-director of the NAACP Legal Defense and Educational Fund. Constantly moving from one area of tension to another, Marshall logged thousands of miles of travel each year.

409

housing had been accommodated and there were still some 800 'white' units vacant with 'no takers.' At the same time there were some 5,000 Negroes inadequately housed and with no units open to them. This is the inevitable result of 'separate but equal' treatment."

Racially integrated American neighborhoods were virtually nonexistent in the 1940s. Blacks were largely confined to ghettos in the cities and to the least desirable sections in smaller towns. Even if a black family could afford a home in a middle- or upper-class neighborhood, no white owner would dream of selling or renting them any property.

Guarding the exclusivity of white neighborhoods were *restrictive covenants*, written agreements between white home buyers and sellers. In signing such an agreement, the buyer agreed never to sell or rent the property to anyone of a different race (or, sometimes, a different religion). In many cities and towns, entire neighborhoods signed restrictive covenants, making all the homes in the district unavailable to blacks. Although a number of prospective black home buyers had taken their cases to court, none had ever succeeded in overturning a restrictive covenant. Nothing in the Constitution, the Supreme Court had ruled in 1926, "prohibits private individuals from entering into contracts respecting . . . their own property."

In early 1947, Marshall and his Legal Defense Fund decided it was time to take action against racially restrictive covenants. Combining three separate anticovenant suits, each of which had lost in the lower courts, the NAACP asked the Supreme Court to consider the issue. Marshall handled *McGhee v. Sipes*, a case involving Orsel McGhee and his wife, blacks who had bought a house in a racially restricted Detroit subdivision. When the next-door neighbors, a white family named Sipes, learned of the purchase, they obtained a court order prohibiting the McGhees from moving into their new home. Michigan's highest court had upheld the ruling against the McGhees.

The Supreme Court took the combined covenant cases, known as *Shelley v. Kraemer*, in the fall of 1947. Lined up on the plaintiffs' side was a formidable array of NAACP legal muscle: Charles Houston, Thurgood Marshall, prominent West Coast attorney Loren Miller, and George Vaughn of St. Louis. Their force was strengthened by support from U.S. attorney general Tom Clark. Responding to Marshall's plea, Clark filed an *amicus curiae* (friend of the court: an individual who is not an actual party in a lawsuit but who has an interest in the matter) brief, urging the court to declare restrictive covenants illegal.

After presenting a long, painstakingly researched brief, Marshall summarized his position to the Court. "This case," he said, "is not a matter of enforcing an isolated private agreement. It is a test as to whether we will have a united nation or a nation divided into areas and ghettoes solely on racial and religious lines." Striking down restrictive covenants, he concluded, would "allow a flexible way of life to develop in which each individual will be able to live, work, and raise his family as a free American."

In May 1948, the Supreme Court handed down its verdict: Restrictive covenants could no longer be enforced by the courts of the land. Marshall and his associates had racked up another victory. Although blacks and other minorities would still face many difficulties in attempting to move into once-restricted neighborhoods, they now had the full weight of the Supreme Court behind them. As one measure of *Shelley*'s impact, 4 years after the decision 21,000 black Chicago families had moved into districts previously closed to them.

Meanwhile, under the leadership of President Harry S. Truman, the federal government was taking major civil rights action. In early 1947, before the

The dilapidated homes in a black Atlanta neighborhood and the Georgia State Capitol (in background) seem to belong to different worlds. In the years following World War II, Marshall and his associates waged a successful campaign against "restrictive covenants," agreements that had long prevented blacks from buying or renting homes in white neighborhoods.

U.S. attorney general entered the *Shelley* case as a "friend," Truman had appointed a prestigious, biracial group of citizens to study America's racial problems. In October 1947, the President's Committee on Civil Rights produced *To Secure These Rights*, a powerful document that called for swift action to end segregation and other abuses of blacks' civil rights. After receiving the committee's report, Truman asked Congress to make lynching a federal offense, to outlaw the poll tax, to eliminate segregated interstate transportation, and to establish a Fair Employment Practices Commission, which would stop racial discrimination in hiring. A year later, Truman ordered an end to all discrimination in federal employment and all segregation in the nation's armed services.

These were giant steps, greeted with jubilation by Marshall and other civil rights crusaders. The achievement of racial justice, however, would require many more steps. Education remained the biggest problem. For the moment, Marshall continued to aim his antisegregation attacks at the nation's graduate schools, reasoning that integration at this level would meet with far less impassioned resistance than integration at the public school level. Expanding on this idea to a friend, Marshall said, "Those racial supremacy boys somehow think that little kids of six or seven are going to get funny ideas about sex and marriage just from going to school together, but for some equally funny reason, youngsters in law school aren't supposed to feel that way. We didn't get it, but we decided if that was what the South believed, then the best thing for the movement was to go along."

Also directing the NAACP counsel's efforts toward graduate schools was the flood of black World War II veterans. Thousands of these former servicemen were not only eager to pursue their education but able to pay for it through the GI Bill, which provided government funds for the schooling of former soldiers. Ambitious black veterans, however, found few educational opportunities open to them, particularly in the South and Southwest. In all the southern states, there was 1 black medical school (but 29 for whites), 1 black law school (but 40 for whites), 1 black pharmacy college (but 20 for whites), and no black engineering school (but 36 for whites.) Clearly, only desegregation of the white institutions could provide the facilities required by black veterans and other black students.

Marshall's first major postwar desegregation battles began in Texas and Oklahoma. Their outcome, technically a victory, would also be a crushing disappointment to the NAACP and its chief counsel. The Texas case revolved around Heman Marion Sweatt, a black letter carrier who applied to the University of Texas Law School in 1946. Academically qualified, Sweatt was rejected because of his race. Texas, however, had no law schools open to blacks.

The U.S. Supreme Court ordered the Universities of Texas and Oklahoma to stop discriminating against Heman Marion Sweatt (right) and George McLaurin (left) after hearing Marshall's arguments. Marshall, who had hoped the McLaurin and Sweatt cases would finally demolish the Plessy v. Ferguson "separate but equal" doctrine, found the Court's narrow decision deeply disappointing.

When Sweatt sued the university, a Texas district judge ruled that the state must either open an "equal" law school within six months or admit Sweatt to its own law school.

Texas responded by slapping together a "colored" law school: two rented rooms for a campus and two black lawyers for faculty. Rejecting this feeble compromise, Sweatt sued again. Texas then opened a new black law school, this one boasting three rented rooms and three part-time instructors. Once again turning down the state's solution, Sweatt went back to court. At this point, Thurgood Marshall appeared on the scene.

Interviewed by a reporter when he arrived in Austin, Texas, Marshall made his intentions clear. "I think we've humored the South long enough," he said, "and it's only by lawsuits and legislation that we'll ever teach reactionaries [extreme conservatives] the meaning of the Fourteenth Amendment. . . . This is going to be a real showdown fight against Jim Crow in education."

Many of the university's students expressed solid support for Sweatt, even opening a temporary, all-white campus branch of the NAACP. The state of Texas, however, planned to defend Jim Crow with all the resources at its command. Marshall brought in a parade of expert witnesses, including the dean of a Pennsylvania law school and a celebrated anthropologist. He also produced an imposing array of statistics and examples to prove that Sweatt could not possibly obtain an equal legal education at the school Texas had opened. Countering Marshall's arguments was future Texas governor Price Daniel, a fervent segregationist and self-described white supremacist. Daniel cross-examined Marshall's witnesses, noted one observer, "as if they were cattle rustlers." The judge made no effort to restrain Daniel's racist remarks, but Marshall remained outwardly cool.

James Nabrit, Marshall's assistant at the Sweatt trial, later talked to Richard Kluger about his colleague. "[Marshall] had the rare ability to know when and where to draw the line in his fervor," said Nabrit. "He was fuming over the judge in Austin, and he said to me before court began one morning, 'I'm gonna tell that judge what I think of him today.' I told him to take it easy. He said nothing in court, but after the case was over and we were all heading for the cars, there was Thurgood standing over in the corner apparently muttering to himself. When he came back to join us, I asked him what that was all about, and he said, 'I told you I was gonna tell that judge what I thought of him—and I just did.' He could do that."

Nevertheless, Marshall lost the case. The Texas Court of Appeals ruled that the state had indeed provided equal opportunities for Sweatt. The NAACP counsel then appealed to the Supreme Court, which agreed to hear the case in due time. Meanwhile, Sweatt went back to delivering mail.

While *Sweatt v. Painter* (Painter was the president of the University of Texas) crept up the Supreme Court's crowded calendar, Marshall took on the Oklahoma graduate school case, which would come to be known as *McLaurin v. Oklahoma State Regents for Higher Education.* George W. McLaurin, a 68-year-old black college professor, had already earned a master's degree; in 1948, he decided to seek a doctorate in education from the University of Oklahoma. Rejected on the basis of his race, he sued. After Marshall convinced an Oklahoma district court that McLaurin could get the education he wanted only at the University of Oklahoma, the court ordered him admitted to the school.

University officials found their own way of coping with this unwelcome integration: They let McLaurin enroll, but "on a segregated basis." The black professor was required to sit outside classroom doors during lectures, given a screened-off desk in the library, and allowed to eat in the school cafeteria only when no white students were dining. Like their Texas counterparts, Oklahoma's white students warmly supported their black classmate, but university officials stood fast. Their treatment of McLaurin, they said, fully complied with Oklahoma's separate-but-equal laws.

Marshall then returned to the district court, arguing that McLaurin's "required isolation from all other students, solely because of the accident of birth, creates a mental discomfiture, which makes concentration and study difficult, if not impossible." The court ruled against him, whereupon he appealed directly to the Supreme Court.

The Supreme Court heard both *Sweatt* and *McLaurin* on the same day in April 1950. By this time, Marshall was determined to do more than try to force states to comply with the "equal" part of "separate but equal." He hoped to prove that, as he had put it in an earlier brief, "the terms 'separate' and 'equal' can not be used conjunctively. . . . *There can be no separate equality.*" Marshall, in short, was aiming at the destruction, once and for all, of the separate- but-equal doctrine, laid down in the *Plessy* decision more than half a century earlier.

Marshall presented his new attack on segregation in his standard tough-minded but nonagressive way, demonstrating respect for his adversaries along with his own unalterable convictions. Explaining his attitude about his opponents, Marshall once remarked to a reporter, "They believe what they believe just as hard as I believe what I believe."

As he waited for the Court's decision on *Sweatt* and *McLaurin*, Marshall must have been thinking of his old mentor and friend, Charles Houston. The battling black attorney, 54 years old, died of a heart attack just after Marshall completed his arguments in the 2 education cases. Marshall, who had learned his craft from the brilliant Houston, probably echoed the sentiments voiced by another old law school colleague, William Hastie, by then a judge of the United States Court of Appeals. "He guided us through the legal wilderness of second-class citizenship," said Hastie of Houston. "He lived to see us close to the promised land of full equality under the law . . . so much closer than would have been possible without his genius and his leadership."

The Supreme Court ruled in favor of both Heman Sweatt and George McLaurin, unanimously but narrowly: Decreeing that Texas had failed to offer Sweatt equal educational opportunity, the Court ordered him admitted to the University of Texas. And ruling that McLaurin's treatment at the University of Oklahoma had served to "impair and inhibit his ability to study," the Court ordered the school to remove its restrictions on the black professor-student. But in neither case did the Court suggest that the *Plessy* doctrine was in

As his mother and his friend Thurgood Marshall look on, young Charles Houston, Jr., accepts the 1950 Spingarn Medal on behalf of his late father, Charles Hamilton Houston. Presenting the coveted NAACP award is Dean Erwin Griswold of the Harvard Law School.

error. Marshall had won the battle, but not the war—at least not yet. Separate but equal remained the law of the land.

Determined to strike down *Plessy*, Marshall plotted his next move, a strategic attack on segregation at the college undergraduate level. One hot, humid night in July 1950, Associated Press reporter Warren Rogers, then stationed in Baton Rouge, Louisiana, received a news tip: Thurgood Marshall and his associates were going to try to enroll 12 black students at Louisiana State University the following day. Marshall, said the tipster, could be found in the back room of a fish-fry parlor in the black district known as Scotlandville.

Recounting the episode in a subsequent article, Rogers said he sped to the dilapidated restaurant. He heard muffled voices as he approached, but they stopped when he knocked on the door. At last, a man spoke from inside: "Who's that?" Rogers identified himself. "What do you want?" asked the man. The journalist said he wanted to talk to Marshall. "What about?" asked the interrogator, whom Rogers now recognized as local NAACP attorney A. P. Tureaud. "About those students you're going to register at LSU tomorrow," responded Rogers. "Another silence," he wrote later. "Somebody sighed. And then a voice, Thurgood Marshall's: 'Let him in.' Introductions all around. But the surliness held until Marshall finally broke it with a loud, thigh-slapping laugh. 'You caught us!' he said. 'Now, we'll talk if you promise not to write anything in advance. We need the surprise, OK?' "

Rogers agreed not to leak the story. The next morning, he watched Tureaud escort 12 nervous but resolute young black people into the admissions office of all-white Louisiana State University. As expected, LSU officials promptly rejected the applications. Just as promptly, Marshall and Tureaud filed suit on behalf of one of them, a prospective law student named Roy Wilson. After a district court decided for Wilson, Marshall asked for, and got, a confirmation from the Supreme Court of its *Sweatt* decision, a move that underscored the precedent. Another mile walked, another 10,000 to go.

In Marshall's case, mileage was more than a figure of speech. In each of the years since he had joined the NAACP, he had traveled thousands of miles, eating irregularly and sleeping when he had time— rarely more than four hours a night. The grueling pace had produced marked physical changes. In 1945, the *Afro-American* had run an illustrated article about the trim, 6-foot 2-inch, 35-year-old victor of *Smith v. Allwright*. Accompanying the newspaper's photograph of the movie-star-handsome lawyer was this comment: "Thurgood Marshall is the amazing type of man who is liked by other men and probably adored by women. He carries himself with an inoffensive self-confidence. . . . He wears and looks especially well in tweed suits."

The man who succeeded in enrolling a black law student at LSU in 1950 had lost some of his earlier sleekness. Marshall no longer had time to worry about his appearance. His tall frame now carried at least 25 more pounds, and his elegant tweed suits had given way to rumpled outfits often dusted with cigarette ashes. *Newsweek* magazine described him as "a disheveled bear of a man," *Time* as "a big, quick-footed man, with a voice that can be soft or raucous, manners that can be rude or gentle or courtly, and an emotional pattern that swings him like a pendulum from the serious to the absurd." To the *New Yorker*, Marshall was "a tall, vigorous man . . . with a long face, a long, hooked nose above a black mustache, and heavy-lidded but very watchful eyes."

Marshall may have stopped being a fashion plate, but he never slowed down. ("Isn't it nice," he once jokingly asked, "that no one cares which 23 hours of the day I work?") In 1951, he flew to South Korea for a six-week investigation of alleged mistreatment of black soldiers. American troops had been fighting in the Asian nation since Communist North Korea had invaded its non-Communist neighbor in 1950. An unusually high number of white southern officers commanded the American forces in South Korea, and an unusually high number of black soldiers were being convicted of crimes ranging from "disobedience" to "misbehavior" in battle. When the NAACP started receiving complaints from black soldiers, claiming they had been unjustly treated because of their race, Marshall had decided to take a firsthand look at the situation.

Reviewing military records, interviewing officers and enlisted men, even traveling to the front lines, Marshall examined the cases of 32 black soldiers who had been given heavy sentences. Very few, in his opinion, had received fair hearings. Four men, for example, had received life sentences after trials lasting less than one hour each. Marshall detailed his charges of racism to American commander Douglas MacArthur, but the general gave the attorney no

Black soldiers attack an enemy position at Heartbreak Ridge, site of some of the Korean War's toughest battles. In 1951, Marshall flew to South Korea to investigate charges that the American military was treating black troops unjustly.

assurance that he would take any action. When Marshall arrived back in the United States, therefore, he called a press conference to publicize his findings. Although the army made no official response to Marshall's charges, it soon proved it had heard them: Within weeks, military judges sharply reduced the sentences of 20 of the 32 convicted black soldiers.

Soon after he returned from South Korea, Marshall headed south. His next major case would be *Briggs v. Elliott*, the South Carolina lawsuit pitting Harry Briggs and 19 other black parents against Clarendon County school-board chairman Roderick Elliott. The plaintiffs aimed to force the county to provide their children with schools equal to those it provided white children. Thurgood Marshall and his associates, however, were after bigger game: *Briggs*, they hoped, would be the club with which they could finally kill Jim Crow.

Clarendon County's black citizens had sought at least minimal improvements in their schools for years, but to no avail. Although local white school officials claimed that they offered black students adequate educational facilities, no one could deny the enormous disparities between the county's black and white schools. Provided for the area's 276 white children were 2 brick schoolhouses; 1 teacher for each 28 children; special courses in biology, typing, and bookkeeping; flush toilets; cafeterias; and school buses. The county's 3 black schools, serving 808 pupils, offered a dismal contrast: rickety wooden buildings; 1 teacher for each 47 children; courses in agriculture and home economics; outhouses; no lunchrooms; and no school buses. To reach their assigned schools, black children as young as six had to walk five miles.

At stake in the Briggs case were tremendous issues. If Marshall won, proving not only that Clarendon County's black schools were unequal to its white schools but that they could never be equal

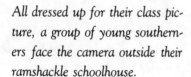

All dressed up for their class picture, a group of young southerners face the camera outside their ramshackle schoolhouse.

unless they were integrated, he could redefine civil rights in America. If he lost, or if he succeeded only in forcing the school board to upgrade the black schools, he would merely have reinforced the separate-but-equal doctrine. Marshall intended to prove that segregation was inherently unequal by proving that it created permanent psychological damage in black children. To strengthen his argument, he had enlisted several expert witnesses. Among them was Dr. Kenneth B. Clark, a 37-year-old assistant professor at City College of New York.

Clark, who would go on to become an eminent sociologist, educator, and author, had made a specialty of studying the effects of segregated schools on black children. With his psychologist wife, Mamie P. Clark, he had designed two tests to measure the attitudes of black children toward race. The tests, which the Clarks had administered to hundreds of young black children in segregated schools, looked simple. In the first test, children were shown four dolls, identical except for their color: Two were brown, two white. Asked which dolls they liked the best and which they considered the "nicest" or the "prettiest," the black children showed "an unmistak-

Most of the South's black schools—overcrowded, understaffed, and ill equipped—stood in sharp contrast to its white schools, where classes were smaller, teachers more numerous and highly trained, and buildings better supplied and maintained. The appalling condition of South Carolina's black schools prompted a group of Clarendon County parents to file Briggs v. Elliott, the 1951 lawsuit that eventually became part of Marshall's landmark Brown case.

able preference for the white doll and a rejection of the brown doll," reported the Clarks.

The second test involved crayons and outline drawings of girls and boys. The Clarks found that when black children in segregated schools were asked to color figures representing themselves, a surprising number chose white or pink crayons. To the Clarks and other sociologists, these results showed that black children who received segregated, inferior educations came to feel inferior themselves.

Black people from all over eastern South Carolina poured into Charleston for the *Briggs* trial. By the time the courthouse doors opened at 7:00 A.M. on May 28, 1951, more than 500 people had formed an orderly line from the street to the second-floor courtroom. Only 150 spectators could be seated inside the courtroom, but during the trial those inside whispered news of developments to the people outside; they in turn relayed it to their neighbors, until it finally reached the crowds in the street.

Briggs commanded the attention of South Carolina's white as well as its black population. The state's ruling white establishment realized that losing this case could mean losing the way of life it had carefully guarded ever since the Civil War. Attorney Robert Figg, representing the Clarendon County School Board, decided the best defense was an up-front admission that the county's black schools were indeed inferior to its white schools, followed by a promise to upgrade the black schools. In light of the county's position, said Figg, testimony on the inadequate facilities then available to blacks was irrelevant.

Marshall quickly asserted that this unexpected move had no bearing on the case. His aim, he told the court, was to prove the state's segregation laws unconstitutional. In order to do that, he insisted, his side "must be able to show the inequalities as they actually exist." Nevertheless, despite a parade of witnesses confirming the wretchedness of the county's black schools, despite the carefully delivered research of Kenneth Clark and other experts, despite Marshall's powerful arguments, he lost the case.

The court ruled that as long as all students received equal education, segregation could not be proven unconstitutional. Clarendon County's attorneys asserted that the school board would upgrade facilities for blacks within "a reasonable time." Leaving the Charleston courthouse after a subsequent hearing, Marshall was approached by a local attorney. "If you show your black ass in Clarendon County ever again," said the southern lawyer, "you're a dead man." Unimpressed—it was neither the first nor the last such threat he would hear—Marshall gathered his papers and strode from the courtroom.

As soon as the judge ruled on *Briggs*, Marshall made his next move: He appealed the decision to the United States Supreme Court. Meanwhile, he began to receive criticism from some sectors of the black community. In July 1951, the *Courier*, America's largest black newspaper, called *Briggs* "a serious legal setback in the civil rights fight." Marshall's frontal assault on segregation, said the newspaper, had "involved risk where none was necessary," producing a

Parents and children of Virginia's Prince Edward County, plaintiffs in one of the five lawsuits that comprised Brown v. Board of Education, assemble on the steps of Virginia's State Capitol building in Richmond. The Prince Edward case was a class action, a suit brought by one or more individuals on behalf of an entire group—in this case, all the black schoolchildren of the county.

decision that "infuses new vigor in the . . . doctrine of 'separate but equal.' "

"All our cases have involved risks," Marshall retorted. "It is completely unrealistic to believe the South will voluntarily . . . equalize school facilities," he replied in the *Courier*. "If we had not threatened to challenge the legality of the segregation system and if we do not continue the challenge to segregated schools, we will get the same thing we have been getting all these years—separate but never equal." Marshall's response drew the backing of black leaders across the nation. "We want our rights now, not a century hence," wrote one prominent black official.

After a series of delays and legal maneuvers, the Supreme Court finally agreed to hear *Briggs*, along with four NAACP segregation suits from Delaware, Kansas, Virginia, and the District of Columbia. Titled *Brown v. Board of Education of Topeka*, the consolidated appeals went before the court on December 9, 1952. After three days of intense oral arguments, both sides had used up the time allotted to them, and the Supreme Court justices retired to consider what they had heard. On his way out of the courtroom, Marshall's opponent, attorney John W. Davis, spoke to a colleague. "I think we've got it won," he said.

The following June, the Court announced that it wanted both Marshall and Davis to clarify certain constitutional points in their arguments. Their next appearance was scheduled for December 7, 1953. Marshall and his colleagues believed that the Court's questions justified optimism. But Marshall refused to be lulled into a sense of false security. The Court's request for clarification, he said, might even "turn out to be a booby trap with a bomb in it." He and his staff set to work with renewed vigor. To help him plan his strategy, Marshall convened a conference of 85 prominent sociologists, historians, political scientists, constitutional experts, and educators.

After grueling months of what one participant called "brain picking," Marshall wrote his brief for the Supreme Court showdown. Its main emphasis was on the Fourteenth Amendment and the intentions of those who had written it. "There can be no doubt," said Marshall, "that the framers were seeking to secure and to protect the Negro as a full and equal citizen." Earlier Supreme Court decisions, he continued, "compel the conclusion that school segregation . . . is at war with the Amendment's intent."

Listening intently to the measured rhetoric on that fateful morning were three of Marshall's closest associates: his old friend and early supporter, Carl Murphy of the *Afro-American*; his mother, Norma Marshall; and his wife and best friend, Vivian "Buster" Marshall.

John W. Davis countered Marshall's argument by asserting that the amendment's authors "did not contemplate and did not understand that it would abolish segregation in public schools." Marshall's case, he said, was nothing more than an effort to prove that black children would be happier or would become better students in integrated schools. And, he added, Marshall had not even proved *that*. The justices of the Supreme Court thought otherwise. Five months later, they unanimously declared school segregation unconstitutional.

For Thurgood Marshall, the decision crowned half a lifetime of dedicated labor. He later described his reaction to the news: "I was so happy I was numb." His happiness, however, was soon shadowed by sorrow. Shortly after the decision, Buster Marshall told her husband she was dying of cancer. Although she had known of her condition for months, she had kept it to herself, refusing to let it interfere with her husband's concentration on the most important case he would ever argue. When Marshall learned of his wife's fatal illness, he nearly collapsed. For 25 years, Buster Marshall had been not only his wife but his closest ally.

During the following fall and winter, Thurgood Marshall spent every available minute with his wife, and in the last six weeks of her life, he remained at her bedside constantly. Buster Marshall died in February 1955. "I thought the end of the world had come," Thurgood Marshall said afterward.

Most Americans believed the end of segregated schools had come with the 1954 *Brown* decision, but Jim Crow would not disappear so easily. Five weeks after Chief Justice Warren read the opinion, the governor of Virginia said, "I shall use every legal means at my command to continue segregated schools in Virginia." Similar responses echoed through much of the South. The governor of Georgia said the decision had turned the Constitution into "a mere scrap of paper." North Carolina's governor said he was "terribly disappointed." South Carolina's governor said he was "shocked."

Not all southerners, however, reacted negatively. Speaking for the region's many moderates, University of North Carolina scholar Howard Odum said, "The South is likely to surprise itself and the nation and do an excellent job of readjustment. We might want to delay a little so we can get ready, but in my opinion, the South for the most part will take it in stride."

Attending a racially mixed class for the first time in their lives, two Virginia schoolgirls exchange curious glances at a Fort Myer elementary school on September 8, 1954. The date, four months after the U.S. Supreme Court declared segregation unconstitutional, marked the beginning of integrated public schooling in Virginia.

Thurgood Marshall predicted that by 1963, the 100th anniversary of the Emancipation Proclamation, American school segregation would be history.

The *Brown* decision declared school segregation unconstitutional, but it did not say when it had to take effect. After its May 1954 decision, the Supreme Court heard months of testimony from southern spokesmen and from Marshall and his staff. The South, predictably, wanted as long a time period as it could get; the NAACP, predictably, wanted desegregation to begin at once. Finally, in May 1955, the Court delivered its decision on putting *Brown* into practice.

The states, said the Court, were required to admit to their public schools all eligible sudents "on a racially nondiscriminatory basis with all deliberate speed." Noting that "public interest" in some areas would make desegregation difficult, the Court allowed states to take whatever time was "necessary" to complete their desegregation plans, as long as they demonstrated "good faith." Thus, in spite of Marshall's passionate plea for a fixed date for the completion of desegregation, the segregationist states gained time to practice the strategy of delay. *Brown II*, as the 1955 decision came to be called, was a heavy blow to Marshall and his team. Full and immediate justice for America's black children, seemingly within reach a year earlier, had once more become a long-term goal.

Still, thanks to both *Brown* decisions, desegregation was on its way. Thurgood Marshall considered the situation, weighed his alternatives, and decided he had more than enough reason to hope. Soon after *Brown II* came down, he telephoned his friend Carl Murphy at the *Afro-American*. (Taped by Murphy's office, the dialogue was quoted by Richard Kluger in *Simple Justice*.) State laws mandating segregation, said Marshall, "have got to yield. They've got to yield to the Constitution. And yield means yield! Yield means give up!"

Murphy asked Marshall what he planned to do.

"We're going to do state by state, that's what we hope," responded the NAACP counsel. "For example, we're going to treat Georgia one way, we're going to treat Maryland another way. But now if Maryland doesn't act right, then we treat Maryland like we treat Georgia. . . . And we're going to give West Virginia a chance. Virginia we're going to bust wide open! . . . You can say all you want but those white crackers are going to get tired of having Negro lawyers beating 'em every day in court."

In a more solemn mode, Marshall addressed a Howard University forum. "The Negro who was once enslaved by law became emancipated by it, and is achieving equality through it. . . . I think *Brown v. Board of Education* demonstrates [that law] can also change social patterns. Provided it is adequately enforced, law can change things for the better; moreover, it can change the hearts of men, for law has an educational function also."

6

"A LONG, RESPECTFUL WHISTLE"

❧

THE *BROWN* DECISIONS provided Thurgood Marshall with both deep satisfaction and additional professional stress. New developments in his private life, however, helped ease the burden. In late 1955, the 47-year-old Marshall began courting Hawaiian-born Cecilia Suyat, an NAACP secretary known to her friends as Cissy. Colleagues saw the quiet, even-tempered Suyat and the boisterous, dynamic Marshall as perfect foils for each other. The couple apparently agreed: They married in December 1955.

A few months later, in February 1956, Marshall called a meeting of southern civil rights lawyers in Atlanta, Georgia. After hearing reports on local progress (or lack of it) in school integration, he called for ongoing pressure on a case-by-case basis. The lawsuits that followed inspired not only complex legal maneuvering but hostility, boycotts, and, sometimes, rioting that required armed intervention.

By far, the most violent resistance to integration took place in Little Rock, Arkansas. The Little Rock school board had prepared to admit black students to the city's Central High School in the fall of 1957 and to follow up with the desegregation of junior high and elementary schools. But Arkansas governor Orval Faubus had other ideas. A staunch segregationist, Faubus dispatched Arkansas National Guard units to Central High, ordering them to prevent the entrance

Trailed by photographers and reporters, Marshall and his wife, the former Cecilia (Cissy) Suyat, leave the U.S. Supreme Court after a hearing in the mid-1950s. The couple, who married in late 1955, met at the NAACP's New York office, where Suyat worked as a legal secretary.

431

of the nine black students who had registered there. The school board then petitioned the local district judge, who ordered the integration plan carried out immediately.

Faubus defied the court order, keeping the guardsmen at the school doors and blocking the black students' entry. For the next three weeks, the students arrived at the school every morning, greeted not only by armed soldiers but by a mob of white adults screaming racist epithets and threatening the teenagers with physical harm.

At this point, Thurgood Marshall stepped in. As counsel for the black students, he obtained another court order, this one forbidding Faubus or the national guard to interfere with the desegregation of Central High School. Not even that worked. No less an official than the president of the United States, Dwight D. Eisenhower, was required to maintain order in Little Rock. Eisenhower sent the 327th Battle Group of the 101st Airborne Division to Central High, and black students finally gained admittance. Racial tension in Little Rock remained sharp, how-

Marshall shares a laugh with colleagues at a 1955 meeting of civil rights lawyers in Atlanta, Georgia. Famed for his steely determination to obtain legal and social justice for blacks, Marshall has also gained renown for his hilarious—and occasionally mildly shocking—jokes and anecdotes.

Followed by a crowd of supportive Alabamans, Marshall strides through the streets of Birmingham in February 1956. The NAACP counsel was escorting Autherine Lucy (front row, left) to district court, where he later obtained an order forcing the University of Alabama to admit the 26-year-old black woman as a student.

ever, and in June the school board asked the district court to let it postpone desegregation for two and a half years.

Under Marshall's direction, the case eventually reached the Supreme Court. When Marshall addressed the Court in September 1958, he asserted that local resistance had no place in determining the law of the land. Even if desegregation produces unrest, he said, "this is preferable to the complete breakdown of education which will result from teaching that courts of law will bow to violence." The case, he added, gave the Court the chance to affirm "the supremacy of all constitutional rights over bigots—big and small."

The Court ruled in Marshall's favor. Still unwilling to give up, Faubus ordered the state's racially mixed public schools closed. Once again, Marshall appealed to the Supreme Court, which declared Faubus's action unconstitutional. Finally, by fall 1959, Little Rock's black and white children began their school year together and in peace.

During the next few years, Marshall engaged in seemingly unending legal combat, defending integration in Louisiana, Alabama, Virginia, South Carolina, and Texas. Alabama even tried to ban the NAACP from operating in the state, a move that brought Marshall back to the Supreme Court. "The right of freedom of association and free speech," he argued, belongs to "unpopular minorities" as well as to groups approved by "those in power." The safeguarding of these freedoms, he added, indicated "a belief in the fundamental good sense of the American people." The Alabama suit against the NAACP dragged on for five years, bouncing back and forth between the Supreme Court and the Alabama courts; but in the end, Marshall won: The NAACP continued to operate in Alabama.

In addition to waging a nonstop campaign against school segregation, Marshall and his Legal Defense Fund fought dozens of battles for individual rights. In 1961, for example, they took the case of Charles Clarence Hamilton, a black citizen of Alabama who had been convicted of raping a white woman and sentenced to death. Because Hamilton had not been advised of his rights or given legal counsel, Marshall argued, he had been deprived of "due process of law." Once again accepting a Marshall argument, the Supreme Court reversed Hamilton's conviction.

Marshall's attack points also included public housing, recreational facilities, interstate and local buses and trains, and professional sports arenas. He and his colleagues won blacks the right to use state-supported beaches in Maryland, to live in municipal housing in Missouri, to play on public golf courses in Georgia, to eat in railroad station restaurants in Virgina, to compete in boxing matches in Louisiana, and to sit at the front of buses in South Carolina.

The bus seat issue had become national news in 1955 when Rosa Parks, a 43-year-old black seamstress in Montgomery, Alabama, refused to give up her bus seat to a white passenger. Parks's arrest led to a black boycott of Montgomery's buses that lasted for more than a year. Organizing the boycott was Martin Luther King, Jr., a 26-year-old black Montgomery clergyman who soon became one of the 20th century's most influential black leaders.

King's struggle in Montgomery had the full support of Marshall and his Legal Defense Fund. In 1956, when King's advisers asked Marshall if he would back the Montgomery boycott—which eventually succeeded in desegregating the city's buses—the NAACP counsel guaranteed the legal protection of the Montgomery Improvement Association, the organization formed by King and other black leaders to direct the boycott. Marshall must have applauded King's words, spoken after his arrest during the bus boycott: "One thing the gradualists don't seem to understand: We are not trying to make people love us when we go to court; we are trying to keep them from killing us."

As the nation entered the 1960s, concerned Americans staged increasingly frequent, nonviolent protests against racial discrimination. Black southerners silently knelt on the steps of white churches, sat at "whites only" restaurant counters, and occupied train and bus seats traditionally reserved for whites. But even after the triumph in Montgomery, civil rights demonstrators faced harassment and arrest throughout the South. In 1960, Marshall publicly committed "the whole force of the NAACP" to defending civil rights demonstrators. "If a store is open to the public, anyone who enters is entitled to the same service anyone else gets," he said. "The right of protest is part of our tradition. It goes back to tea dumped in Boston Harbor. They have a right to say they want their rights. As long as they act lawfully, we will support them."

Marshall soon proved he meant what he said. The following year, police in Baton Rouge, Louisiana, arrested 16 black students for refusing to leave a segregated lunch counter. Although the neatly dressed

Marshall and NAACP attorney W. J. Durham lay plans to thwart the Dallas school board's 1959 request for a delay in integration. When one local segregationist said that the different educational levels of black and white children made integration a problem, Marshall replied, "Put the dumb colored children in with the dumb white children, and put the smart colored children with the smart white children—that is no problem."

students had remained silent during their sit-in, they had been booked for "disturbing the peace," a time-honored southern charge against unwelcome blacks. Found guilty in the Louisiana courts, each of the students received a $100 fine and a 30-day jail sentence. Thurgood Marshall took their case, known as *Garner v. Louisiana*, to the Supreme Court. He argued that the demonstrators' arrest, "based upon a vague statute which is enforced by the police according to their personal notions," violated their rights to both due process of law and freedom of expression. For the 29th time, the justices of the Supreme Court agreed with Marshall. They unanimously reversed the convictions of all 16 defendants, a victory that impressed even die-hard segregationists. The black attorney, grudgingly admitted Senator Richard B. Russell of Georgia, seemed to wield "an almost occult power" over the United States Supreme Court.

Garner v. Louisiana marked Marshall's last appearance as NAACP chief counsel. Although he remained passionately committed to the organization he had served for 27 years, he hoped it could disappear one day. In the early 1960s, a reporter asked him to define the NAACP's ultimate purpose. "To go out

Angry white youths, some of them carrying chains and hammers, accost black demonstrators after a Portsmouth, Virginia, lunch counter sit-in. Such confrontations became increasingly frequent during the 1960s, a decade of massive social change in the United States.

of business," replied Marshall, "with a realization that race is no longer a problem."

That realization, of course, lay far in the future. Meanwhile, Marshall had more work to do. In September 1961, 8 months after John F. Kennedy took office as the 35th president of the United States, he nominated Thurgood Marshall for a judgeship on the Court of Appeals for the Second Circuit.

The federal judicial system is made up of three tiers. At the lowest level are the district courts, where federal cases are tried and decisions rendered. If the losing party in a lawsuit is dissatisfied with the ruling of a district court, that party can appeal to the next highest tribunal, a circuit court of appeals. Appeals court decisions are final unless they are reviewed and overturned by the U.S. Supreme Court. A litigant dissatisfied with a circuit court decision may appeal to the Supreme Court, but most litigants' chances of being heard are slight. The Supreme Court receives about 5,000 requests for appeal every year—many more than it can handle—and it turns most of them down. The Court hears only about 200 cases, generally those that raise important constitutional issues, each year.

Each of the 11 circuits (geographic regions) within the federal court system has its own court of appeals. The Second Circuit Court of Appeals serves the states of New York, Vermont, and Connecticut. Because the Second Circuit decides an unusually high number of important cases, the legal world regards appointment to its bench as a high honor. Delighted by the president's recognition of their hero, civil rights advocates greeted Marshall's nomination with cheers. But there was no joy among white conservatives, none of whom wanted to see a liberal black lawyer on the federal bench.

Before they can be seated, nominees for federal judgeships must gain the approval of the Senate Ju-

Democratic senator James O. Eastland of Mississippi led the conservatives' 1961 fight against Marshall's confirmation as a federal judge. Deeply resentful of Marshall's success as a civil rights champion, Eastland first ignored the nominee, then hazed him, then said his background was inappropriate for a circuit judge, and finally suggested he was linked with "radical elements." Despite Eastland's attacks, the Senate confirmed Marshall's nomination.

diciary Committee. In 1961, the committee's members included its chairman, Mississippi's ultraconservative James O. Eastland, several other southern Democrats, and a few conservative Republicans. They subjected Marshall to a trial by fire, cross-examining him ferociously and dragging out his confirmation hearings for almost a year. Unflappable as always, Marshall sailed through the ordeal without impatience or apparent loss of temper.

Many senators, including Republican Kenneth B. Keating of New York, found the committee's tactics appalling. Marshall "has helped shape some of the most important legal advances of the decade in the field of civil rights," said Keating. "I propose that his selection be acted upon immediately, for our nation is not so rich in brilliance and talent that we can afford to pigeonhole it, as is being done in the case of Thurgood Marshall."

The Senate Judiciary Committee finally approved Marshall's nomination by a narrow margin. The full Senate then quickly confirmed him by a 54–16 vote. (The 16 nay votes were all cast by southern Democrats.) Senator Phillip A. Hart, a staunch Marshall supporter, probably spoke for many of his colleagues when he reacted to Marshall's victory. "Amen," he said, "and thank heaven."

Marshall took his seat on the federal bench in September 1962. He soon discovered that a judge and an attorney see a courtroom from very different perspectives. Accustomed to working with a battalion of noisy, impassioned lawyers in the always busy, sometimes frantic atmosphere of civil rights law, he now found himself in an isolated, somber environment.

Marshall's former secretary later told a *Life* magazine reporter that her boss "never complained about the court. In fact, he said he liked it." However, said the secretary, Marshall occasionally seemed lonely.

Chief Appeals Court judge J. Edward Lumbard swears Marshall in as a federal judge in 1961. To the surprise—and dismay—of those who had opposed his confirmation, Marshall chalked up an impressive record during his four years on the Second Circuit: Not one of his 98 majority opinions was ever reversed by the U.S. Supreme Court.

"Often his only visitor would be the bailiff," she said. "The other justices kept their chamber doors closed, but he insisted his be kept open."

During his 4-year tenure on the Second Circuit Court of Appeals, Marshall and his fellow justices decided some 400 cases each year. Marshall himself wrote 118 majority and dissenting opinions, many of them relating to cases totally unlike those he had spent his life practicing. He ruled on such issues as maritime law, patents and trademarks, and labor relations. One of his most admired opinions, however, dealt with familiar grounds: the First Amendment's guarantee of freedom of expression.

In 1965, the University of the State of New York ordered its faculty members to sign loyalty oaths, swearing that they had never been affiliated with the Communist party. The signing of loyalty oaths had become an important issue in the United States, stirring heated controversy between conservatives, who approved of the oaths, and liberals, who called them unconstitutional. Any faculty member who failed to sign the oath, said New York's university officials,

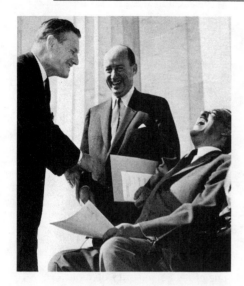

Marshall regales a group of dignitaries at a ceremony marking the Emancipation Proclamation's 100th anniversary. With the circuit court judge are Governor Nelson Rockefeller of New York (left), and UN ambassador Adlai Stevenson.

faced immediate dismissal. The university based its demand on the Feinberg Law, a state regulation that permitted the dismissal of public school teachers who refused to sign such oaths.

Believing that the law violated the Fourteenth Amendment's "due process" clause, faculty member Harry Keyishian and several colleagues sued the university in district court. The district court refused to hear the case, asserting that the educators had posed no substantial constitutional question. The faculty members then appealed to the Second Circuit Court.

Marshall, who delivered the court's opinion, ruled that the case, *Keyishian v. Board of Regents of the University of the State of New York*, did raise constitutional questions. He pointed out that the Supreme Court had specifically refused to pass on the constitutionality of laws that required school employees to swear they had never been Communists. In any case, said Marshall, the Feinberg Law applied to public school teachers, not to university faculty members. He also firmly noted that Feinberg had "significant similarity" to other laws that the Supreme Court had recently ruled unconstitutional.

Marshall sent *Keyishian* back to the district court, instructing it to hear the case. When the lower court accordingly reviewed *Keyishian*, it ruled the loyalty oaths constitutional. Two years later, however, the case went to the Supreme Court, which reversed the lower court's decision. Emphatically confirming Marshall's opinion, the Supreme Court held that the Feinberg Law indeed violated the Fourteenth Amendment.

Among circuit judge Marshall's most highly publicized opinions was one dealing with a man who had been tried three times on the same first-degree murder charge. Marshall insisted that states as well as the federal government were obliged to protect accused persons against "double jeopardy." (According to the

Fifth Amendment, "Nor shall any person be subject for the same offense to be twice put in jeopardy of life or limb.") Maintaining that this was exactly what New York State had done to the defendant, Marshall reversed the man's conviction.

"It was a difficult case," observed *New York Times* reporter Sidney Zion in 1965. "But few judges would have bothered to write a 42-page opinion, as he did. . . . It was advocacy at its purest and at the end, agree or not, one could only offer a long, respectful whistle. There wasn't a point that Marshall hadn't dealt with and then with great clarity in prose that could be understood by any intelligent layman. Judges do not usually do this. The general rule is to slide over the high, hard ones." Marshall, added Zion, "seems incapable of dodging the tough questions."

During his years as a federal judge, Marshall ruled on a wide variety of cases; their subjects ranged from the rights of defendants to the deportation of aliens to the use of illegally obtained evidence in criminal trials. In 4 years, not one of Marshall's 98 majority opinions was reversed by the Supreme Court, a remarkable record for a circuit court judge. That record did not go unnoticed in the corridors of power.

One day in July 1965, Marshall was having lunch with his colleagues in New York City when an aide arrived with a message. "The president is on the phone," said the aide. "The president of what?" asked Marshall. "Of the United States, sir," answered the aide. Marshall picked up the telephone and spoke to Lyndon B. Johnson. The president invited the judge to come to Washington, D.C., to talk about a new job: United States solicitor general, the third highest legal position—after attorney general and assistant attorney general—in the land. Marshall went to Washington.

7

SOLICITOR GENERAL

WHEN THURGOOD MARSHALL arrived at the White House in July 1965, President Lyndon Johnson formally asked him to accept the nomination to the post of U.S. solicitor general. "I want folks to walk down the hall at the Justice Department," Johnson reportedly told Marshall, "and see a [black man] sitting there." As solicitor general, Marshall—the first black citizen to hold the post—would be the nation's top-ranking courtroom advocate. On the other hand, taking the position would mean a cut in salary, from $33,000 per year to $28,500. It would also mean giving up a lifetime federal judgeship for an executive post held "at the pleasure of the president."

Marshall accepted the president's offer without skipping a beat. Reporters later asked him why he had made a "sacrifice," taking a position that provided less money and no security. "Because," he said, "the president asked me to." Then he added, "I believe that in this time, especially, we do what our government requests of us. Negroes have made great advances in government and I think it's time they started making some sacrifices."

Looking on as Marshall takes his oath of office as U.S. solicitor general are his wife, Cissy; President Lyndon Johnson; and (far right) U.S. attorney general Nicholas Katzenbach. After the ceremony, Johnson said it would be good for "schoolchildren to know that when the great United States government spoke in the highest court in the land, it did so through a Negro."

The U.S. solicitor general, probably the most publicly visible member of the Justice Department, represents the United States before the Supreme Court. This official directs all cases in which the United States government has an interest and argues the most important cases personally. The solicitor general also decides which cases the Justice Department will ask the Supreme Court to review and what position the department should take on cases being heard by the Court.

Because the president wanted Marshall confirmed as soon as possible, confirmation hearings were scheduled for July 29, only two weeks after the nomination was announced. Marshall took a small apartment in Washington, temporarily leaving his family in New York City. That family by now included not only his wife, Cissy, but two sons, nine-year-old Thurgood, Jr., and John William, seven. After his nomination, Marshall found himself besieged by reporters' questions about his professional and personal life.

One journalist, drawing on widespread rumors about Marshall, asked him how he found time to play poker and watch western movies. Marshall roared with laughter. "Now isn't that something else?" he said. "My newspaper friends keep saying all those things, and I wish to hell it was up to date. Once in a while I'll catch a western on television . . . and poker! Hah! I haven't pushed a chip in 10 years. You know what cards I'm down to now? I play 'War' with my two boys. Now that's hot action for you, isn't it?"

Reporters who interviewed Marshall's colleagues heard the same terms over and over: "natural advocate" and "warm human being." One NAACP lawyer told reporter Sidney Zion that "Thurgood is as comfortable at the Hogwash Junction function as he is at the home of a Supreme Court justice. He relates to everybody and anybody and it's this more than anything else that sets him apart from all the rest."

The hearings on Marshall's nomination as solicitor general contrasted sharply with those he had endured four years earlier. This time, the Senate Judiciary subcommittee approved Marshall's candidacy in exactly 29 minutes; the following day, the full Senate confirmed him with no debate. Thirteen days later, on August 11, Marshall was sworn in by Supreme Court associate justice Hugo Black. "He has good policy judgment and the power of self-control," Black commented afterward. "I know he will do a fine job."

For his swearing-in ceremony, Marshall wore the traditional outfit of the solicitor general: a cutaway morning coat, striped trousers, and a gray vest. "Now isn't this the silliest get-up in the world?" he asked with a broad smile. A reporter asked if he had considered skipping the formal attire. "No, no, I'm too old to worry about changing all that now," the 57-year-old Marshall replied, chuckling. "Besides, I've got a cutaway. . . . Now if I had to go out and buy a new one maybe I'd think about changing the tradition."

Marshall carried his informal manner into the solicitor general's office. During his first week on the job, for example, he burst into an aide's office. "How the hell do you work that noise box in my office?" he roared. "I can't get the World Series anywhere!" But Marshall confined his lighthearted moments to backstage. In the courtroom, he projected the measured dignity observers had come to expect. Between 1965 and 1967, he won 14 of the 19 cases he argued for the United States government. Most of them dealt with civil rights and privacy issues.

One of the major civil rights cases began in Philadelphia, Mississippi. It involved James Chaney, a 21-year-old black Mississippian, and 2 white New Yorkers: Andrew Goodman, 20, and Michael Schwerner, 24. In Mississippi to help register black

Following an official welcome from the U.S. Supreme Court, newly installed solicitor general Marshall leaves the Court with U.S. attorney general Nicholas Katzenbach. Speaking to a reporter after the formal ceremony, Marshall pointed to his attire and said, "Now isn't this the silliest get-up in the world?"

voters—an extremely unpopular and dangerous activity in the South of the early 1960s—the three civil rights workers disappeared in June 1964. After a massive search, FBI agents uncovered the young men's bodies beneath an earthen dam; all had been shot to death. The FBI arrested the local sheriff, his deputy, a patrolman, and 18 others, most of them members of the Ku Klux Klan.

Because murders are prosecuted on a state rather than on a federal level, the United States government may not bring murder charges, no matter how strong its case. In this instance, the Justice Department accused the Mississippi lawmen and Klan members of interfering with the civil rights of citizens—a federal crime. When the local district court dismissed the charges against all but three of the accused men, United States solicitor general Thurgood Marshall moved in. Marshall appealed the district court's ruling to the Supreme Court, requesting reinstatement of charges against all the accused men.

Unanimously agreeing with Marshall's arguments, the Court ordered the accused to stand trial. In the end, an all-white Mississippi jury found 7 of the defendants guilty; each received the maximum sentence of 3 to 10 years in jail. Although the rest were acquitted, Marshall and his staff celebrated the trial's historic outcome: It marked the first occasion that a white southern jury had convicted white defendants in a civil rights case. Civil rights history was on the march.

Marshall owed a number of his triumphs as solicitor general to the Civil Rights Act of 1964—which, in turn, owed its existence to the work of Martin Luther King, Jr., Marshall, and other crusaders for social justice. Among its several provisions, the Civil Rights Act outlawed discrimination in public accommodations—including hotels, theaters, restaurants, parks, and swimming pools—and empowered the Justice Department to bring suits against violators. In 1966, Marshall made use of the Civil Rights Act when he argued *Evans v. Newton*, a case that centered on a semipublic park in Macon, Georgia.

The Macon park had been left to the city by a wealthy resident who directed that it be used only by whites. After the enactment of the Civil Rights Act in 1964, Macon officials opened the park to blacks; as a public facility, they said, it could no longer be legally segregated. The landowner's heirs and other local whites challenged the city's action and won. The city then appealed to the Georgia State Supreme Court, which upheld the challengers.

When the United States Supreme Court agreed to hear the case, Marshall acted as amicus curiae. Although the park was technically private, he argued, it performed a "public function" and therefore came under the provisions of the Civil Rights Act. Writing for the majority of the Court, Associate Justice Wil-

The Reverend Martin Luther King, Jr., displays photographs of (left to right) Michael Schwerner, James Chaney, and Andrew Goodman, the civil rights workers murdered near Philadelphia, Mississippi, in 1964. After hearing Marshall's arguments, the U.S. Supreme Court ordered the young men's accused killers to stand trial in Mississippi, where they were eventually convicted of civil rights violations and sentenced to jail terms.

liam O. Douglas responded to Marshall's argument. "Under the circumstances of this case," he said, "we cannot but conclude that the public character of the park requires that it be treated as a public institution." After the decision, Macon's park once more served residents of all races.

Another important Marshall case centered on tenants' rights. In 1964, the California legislature repealed the state's fair housing statutes—laws that prohibited landlords from practicing racial discrimination. When a black couple, the Mulkeys, were refused an apartment by white landlords, the Reitmans, the Mulkeys sued and won in the California courts. Asserting that the California legislature had legalized discrimination, the Reitmans appealed to the United States Supreme Court, which heard the case in 1967.

Marshall argued that, in repealing fair housing laws, the California legislature had violated the Fourteenth Amendment's equal protection clause. According to the Constitution of the United States, he said, the Mulkeys were entitled to live in any apartment they could afford. After listening to Marshall, the Supreme Court ruled that California had illegally taken action "designed to make private discrimination legally possible." The state's constitutional amendment, said the Court, had made it a guilty partner in a discriminatory act and had, as Marshall asserted, violated the Fourteenth Amendment. Marshall had won his case. The Mulkeys—and thousands of other black families—had won the right to live wherever they wanted to live.

As solicitor general, Marshall was also concerned with voting rights. Representing the United States in a 1965 challenge brought by South Carolina, he successfully defended the federal government's right to oversee elections in areas where discrimination had been clearly practiced. In 1966, he secured the right

Solicitor General Marshall discusses a legal point with one of his longtime admirers, Senator Robert Kennedy of New York. As attorney general from 1961 to 1964, Kennedy had strongly supported the black struggle for civil rights, entering school-desegregation cases on the side of black petitioners, encouraging efforts to register black voters in the South, and filing dozens of cases against communities and individuals suspected of infringing on blacks' voting rights.

of non-English-speaking citizens to vote. That year, he also scored a major victory against the poll tax, the Deep South's favorite method of depriving impoverished blacks of their right to vote.

Although the Constitution's Twenty-fourth Amendment (ratified in 1964) prohibited the use of poll taxes in national elections, the issue of poll taxes in local and state elections remained unresolved. Five southern states, including Virginia, continued to require citizens to pay a fee before they cast their state ballots. In 1966, several black Virginians brought suit against the state and its poll taxes. The district court ruled against them, holding that the states, not the federal government, had the right to set voting requirements in state elections.

When the Supreme Court heard the Virginians' appeal, *Harper v. Virginia Board of Elections*, Marshall argued the case on behalf of the United States. The authority of the states to establish voters' qualifications, he maintained, did not extend to the "unbridled license to exclude any citizens from the electoral process that it may choose." By restricting the vote to those with money to pay for it, Marshall said, Virginia was violating the Fourteenth Amendment's guarantee of "equal protection of the laws." Once more, the solicitor general's arguments prevailed. In a 6–3 decision, the Supreme Court struck down the Virginia poll tax. "Wealth, like race, creed, or color," said Justice Hugo Black, "is not germane to one's ability to participate intelligently in the electoral process."

During Marshall's tenure as solicitor general, the Supreme Court heard a number of cases dealing with the right to privacy, another subject close to Marshall's heart. The Fourth Amendment protects Americans from "unreasonable searches and seizures." Years earlier, in 1928, the Supreme Court had ruled that the prohibition against unreasonable searches applied to speech as well as the "persons, houses, papers, and effects" listed in the amendment. Evidence obtained by wiretapping had been banned in all courtooms since 1934. But Marshall, who held an even broader view of unreasonable searches, considered all electronic eavesdropping illegal.

In 1966, when the Supreme Court scheduled *Black v. United States*, a government case against a man accused of evading federal taxes, Marshall dropped a bombshell. The government's case, he told the Court, had been based on FBI wiretaps of telephone conversations between the defendant and his attorney. To Marshall's way of thinking, this procedure had resulted in an unfair trial. Instead of arguing for the United States, then, he asked the Court to send the case back to the district court, where the evidence obtained by the wiretap could be reevaluated. To the surprise of many legal observers, the Supreme Court granted Marshall's request, reversing the defendant's conviction until the evidence was reexamined.

Despite a staggering load of legal work, the apparently tireless Marshall found time to make frequent speeches at colleges and public meetings across the country. In a National Law Day speech in 1966, he lit into lawyers and "intellectuals" who criticized the Supreme Court's constantly shifting interpretation of the Constitution. Such criticism, he said, "reflects a profound element of misunderstanding [and] a refusal to . . . view the law, not as a set of abstract and socially unrelated commands . . . but as an effective instrument of social policy."

The Marshalls relax at home with their sons, Thurgood, Jr. (left), and John William, in the 1960s. A once-legendary poker player, Marshall told a reporter that since the arrival of the boys, his card playing had been reduced to games of War.

In another speech, this one delivered to the White House Conference on Civil Rights, Marshall outlined the long history of American blacks' battle for their rights. The Supreme Court's rulings on school segregation, "white primaries," and restrictive covenants, he said, had produced impressive improvements, but the time to relax had not arrived. "I advocate more laws and stronger laws," Marshall stated emphatically. "And the passage of such laws requires untiring efforts."

Arguing before the Supreme Court, writing briefs, holding conferences with his staff at the Justice Department, and making speeches required what Marshall once estimated as 23 hours a day. Nevertheless, the solicitor general found time to enjoy his home life. On weekends, the boys played touch football with their father on the lawn; during the week, they attended the Georgetown Day School. Cissy Marshall's many activities included planning and presiding over the family's frequent dinner parties, whose guests comprised some of the capital's most glittering personalities.

At home, Marshall liked to relax in the kitchen. When he was a boy, his maternal grandmother, Mary Eliza Williams, had taught him to cook. "I'm all with your parents in wanting you to be a professional man," she told him, "but I want to be sure you can always earn a dollar. You can pick up all that other stuff later, but I bet you never saw a jobless Negro cook." Marshall managed to "earn a dollar" outside the kitchen, but he enjoyed cooking for friends. Fans of his cuisine especially praised his she-crab soup, a Baltimore specialty, and his horseradish-laden concoctions. One longtime friend, singer Lena Horne, insisted that Marshall "cooks the best pig feet in the world."

Other Marshall spare-time pursuits included horse racing and listening to jazz and symphonic music. "I don't know all the titles and composers," he once confessed, "I just like it." And, despite his denials, Marshall was a confirmed addict of movie westerns, sometimes watching TV reruns of his old favorites for hours. As he once explained, he was "still waiting to see one showing where the Indians win."

In 1967, Marshall was comfortably settled in both public and private life. But changes lay ahead. The president of the United States had new plans for his solicitor general. ✤

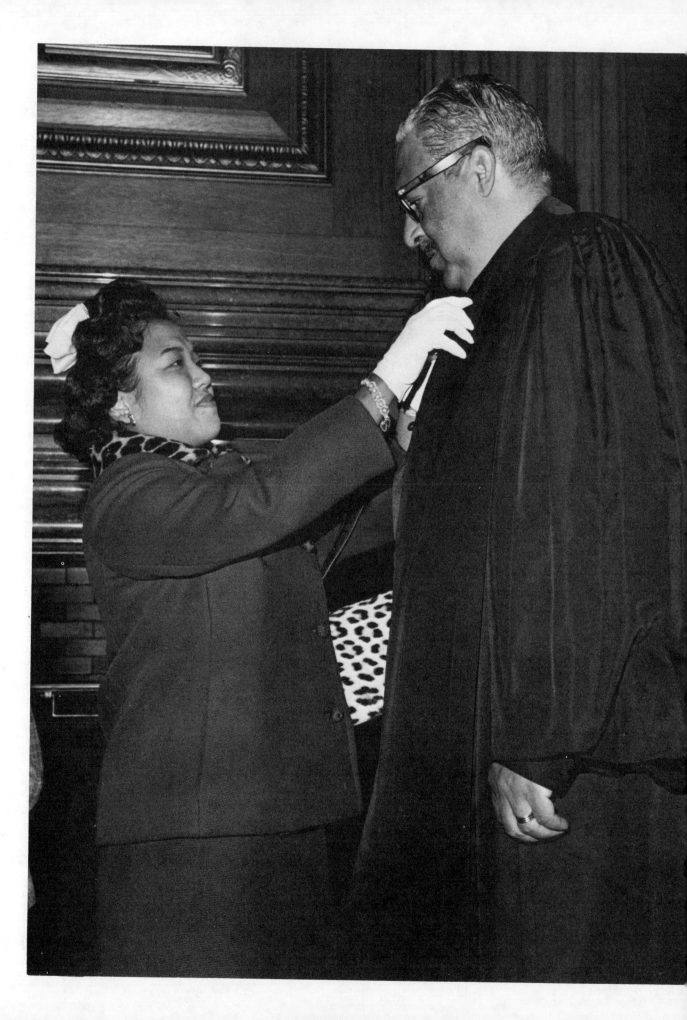

8

SUPREME COURT JUSTICE

❧

O N THE SUNNY morning of June 13, 1967, Lyndon Johnson and Thurgood Marshall faced a battery of television cameras in the White House Rose Garden. The president had just named the solicitor general as his choice for the vacancy on the Supreme Court. "He deserves the appointment," said Johnson. "He is the best qualified by training and by very valuable service to the country." The president paused, then said forcefully, "I believe it is the right thing to do, the right time to do it, the right man and the right place. I believe he has already earned his place in history, but I think it will be greatly enhanced by his service on the Court."

Millions of people rejoiced at Johnson's words. Echoing the sentiments of many of his fellow citizens, Floyd B. McKissick, chairman of the Congress of Racial Equality (CORE), a prominent civil rights organization, said, "This has stirred pride in the breast of every black American."

Thurgood Marshall would be the first native of Maryland to serve on the Supreme Court since Roger Taney, chief justice from 1836 until 1864. Taney had presided over the celebrated case of Dred Scott, a Missouri slave who claimed the right to freedom after living in the free Wisconsin Territory for several years. His case reached the Supreme Court in 1856. Delivering the Court's ruling in 1857, Taney said that because Scott was a Negro, he was "property," not a citizen. Therefore, said Taney, Scott had no rights under the Constitution and no right to institute a

Cissy Marshall makes a last-minute adjustment to her husband's robe before his 1967 U.S. Supreme Court swearing-in ceremony. The 96th man to take the oath, Marshall became the first black justice in the Court's 178-year history.

Marshall listens to a question posed by a member of the Senate Judiciary Committee in July 1967, during the hearings to confirm his nomination to the U.S. Supreme Court. He was sworn in as an associate justice three months later.

lawsuit. (The sympathetic son of Scott's former master later arranged to purchase the black man, whom he immediately emancipated.)

Now, little more than a century after that fateful decision, the great-grandson of a slave stood at the side of the president of the United States. A free American citizen, a distinguished attorney, and a powerful reformer, Thurgood Marshall was about to take his place on the Court where Roger Taney had ruled that blacks were property, not people. Slowly, painfully, but steadily, the nation was moving forward.

Johnson later talked to an interviewer about Marshall. "I figured he'd be a great example to younger kids," said the president. "All over America that day, Negro parents looked at their children a little differently, thousands of mothers looked across the breakfast table and said, 'Now, maybe this will happen to my child someday.' I bet from one coast to the other, there was a rash of new mothers naming their newborn sons Thurgood."

Johnson's announcement sparked an avalanche of comments, most of them positive, in the nation's press. New York City's leading black newspaper, the *Amsterdam News*, called the nomination "a milestone in American history." *Newsweek*, which said Marshall had "probably done as much to transform the life of his people as any Negro alive today, including Nobel laureate Martin Luther King," called him "the legal champion of the Negro revolution." Marshall's nomination, said the magazine, offered "fresh evidence that America may romanticize its radicals, but it more often rewards its reformers. And Marshall is a reformer in the best tradition of the rule of law."

In a letter to the president, Supreme Court Chief Justice Earl Warren said, "All of us know Thurgood, and will welcome him to the Court in the belief that he will make a real contribution." Not everyone, however, agreed: In some quarters, the spirit of Roger Taney lived on. This time, Marshall's confirmation hearings were even more hostile than those he had endured for the Second Circuit court.

Die-hard southern senators did their best to humiliate the nominee during the hearings. South Carolina's Strom Thurmond was the roughest. He confronted Marshall with a list of 60 complex questions about the post–Civil War Congress and its dealings with constitutional issues. Marshall, who had told friends he was determined to "keep a cool head" during the hearings, calmly admitted that he was unable to answer most of Thurmond's questions. Later, when North Carolina's Sam Ervin questioned Marshall's ability to exercise judicial restraint, Senator Joseph D. Tydings of Maryland sprang to the nominee's defense. Marshall's "performance in the last two days," said Tydings pointedly, "is a great testimony to his judicial restraint."

When the Judiciary Committee reported its findings to the full Senate, Thurmond announced that Marshall had failed to pass the simple test of history he had been given. It was "surprising," said Thurmond, that Marshall could not even name the congressional research committee members who had worked on the Fourteenth Amendment in 1868. At this point, Senator Edward Kennedy of Massachusetts interrupted Thurmond. Did the senator from South Carolina, he asked politely, "have that information at hand?" If so, said Kennedy, he would appreciate Thurmond's reading it into the record. Obviously unable to produce the names himself, the flustered Thurmond hastily concluded his remarks and sat down.

Despite the southerners' harassment, Marshall won full Senate approval by a vote of 69 to 11. He took the oath of office one month later, on October 2, 1967. Seated next to President Johnson, the proud

Marshall family—Cissy, Thurgood, Jr., and John William—watched Thurgood Marshall as he placed his hand on a Bible and swore to "administer justice without respect to persons, and do equal right to the poor and to the rich." After taking the oath, a beaming Associate Justice Marshall shook hands with his fellow justices and went to work, joining his colleagues as they admitted a group of lawyers to practice before the Court.

During Marshall's first term, the Supreme Court heard 110 cases. As a former solicitor general, he disqualified himself from participating in 57 of these cases because the government had an interest in them. Of the remaining cases, Marshall wrote 14 opinions, the most significant of which dealt with First Amendment rights and the rights of defendants.

One of these cases, *Interstate Circuit, Inc. v. City of Dallas*, centered on movie censorship and the right to freedom of expression. The city of Dallas had established a review board to decide what films were "likely to incite or encourage delinquency or sexual promiscuity on the part of young persons." Movies so identified were declared off limits to anyone under the age of 16. Challenged by a local film distributor, the legality of the Dallas film board came under Supreme Court review in early 1968. Marshall, speaking for the majority, ruled against Dallas. Because such terms as "sexual promiscuity" were too "vague" to apply with justice, he said, the Dallas film board's actions violated the First Amendment. In this opinion, Marshall emphasized the far-reaching effect of a Supreme Court ruling: "What Dallas may constitutionally do," he pointed out, "so may other cities and states."

Another free-speech case involved an Illinois schoolteacher who had criticized his board of education in a letter to the local newspaper. Fired for writing the letter, the teacher sued the school board; when an Illinois court upheld the board's decision,

The U.S. Supreme Court in 1967, with its newest member, Associate Justice Thurgood Marshall. Seated (left to right) are John M. Harlan, Hugo Black, Chief Justice Earl Warren, William O. Douglas, and William J. Brennan, Jr. In the back row (left to right) are Abe Fortas, Potter Stewart, Byron R. White and Marshall.

the teacher took his case to the Supreme Court. Marshall, again speaking for the majority, said the ruling of the Illinois court implied that the teacher—or anyone else—could be forced to give up his First Amendment right of free speech in order to keep his job. Pointing out that such a premise had been rejected by the Court in numerous earlier decisions, Marshall decided for the teacher, reversing the lower court's decision.

When questioned about his political position, Marshall refused to identify himself with any philosophical or political camp. He did, however, offer clues. "I am not attached to any legal school of thought," he told one reporter. "But I am also not a conservative." As term followed term, his decisions proved that he was, as many court observers phrased it, "his own man." He remained skeptical, wary of change but willing to reconsider any traditions that appeared to be out of touch with the times. But his decisions made it clear that he would never retreat from his lifelong commitment to civil liberty.

"We're over the beginning on civil rights," Marshall had told a *New York Times* reporter in 1965. "There are, of course, plenty of important questions still hanging, involving such things as school picketing and street demonstrations. Now fundamentally, I believe I have the right to picket anybody's house with a sign that says, 'You're a bum.' But that doesn't give me the right to chain myself to the man's door. You just can't chain a doorway, whether it be to courts, homes, or stores."

Picketing was the subject of a 1968 case in which Marshall wrote the majority opinion. When a striking food employees' union picketed a store in a Pennsylvania shopping mall, the mall's owner sued, claiming that the strikers were trespassing on private property. Marshall disagreed. Although it was privately owned, he said, the mall was "clearly the functional equivalent" of a city business block and could not be sealed off from citizens exercising their constitutional rights of free expression and communication. "Peaceful picketing carried on in a location open generally to the public," Marshall concluded, "is protected by the First Amendment."

Some of Marshall's opinions—his ruling on a 1969 obscenity case, for example—created ripples of surprise among Court watchers. The 1969 case *Stanley v. Georgia* began with a police visit to the home of a Georgia man suspected of illegal bookmaking. The police, who had obtained a warrant permitting them to search for evidence of gambling, found something else instead: three reels of film they judged pornographic. Arrested and found guilty of possessing obscene material, the Georgia man appealed to the Supreme Court. The Court overturned the conviction, with Marshall asserting that "mere private possession" of the allegedly obscene films broke no law. His written opinion in the case left no doubt about his sentiments on the matter:

Whatever may be the justifications for other statutes regulating obscenity, we do not think they reach into the privacy of one's own home. If the First Amendment means anything, it means that a state has no business telling a man, sitting alone in his own house, what books he may read or what films he may watch. Our whole constitutional heritage rebels at the thought of giving government the power to control men's minds.

Such opinions strengthened Marshall's reputation for plain speaking. A blunt, direct questioner in court and a skillful debater at the justices' conferences, he seemed as likely to use intuitive common sense as to employ complex, legalistic reasoning. Behind the scenes, too, Marshall's straightforward style set him apart from the stereotype of a mannered and formal judge. Colleagues and clerks alike reported his attitude toward them as relaxed and amiable. Occasionally, however, fellow justices found his informality somewhat jarring.

Warren Burger, who became chief justice after Earl Warren's retirement in 1969, apparently needed a little time to get used to Associate Justice Marshall. In *The Brethren*, their 1979 book about the Supreme Court, authors Bob Woodward and Scott Armstrong quote Marshall's customary greeting to Burger in the Court halls: "What's shakin', Chiefy baby?" At first, the conservative Burger would simply look puzzled, mumble a few words in response, and walk rapidly on. As time passed, however, Burger grew to respect Marshall, and the two men established a cordial and respectful relationship.

Marshall also treated Court visitors to his own brand of humor. One day, he had just entered the justices' private elevator when a group of tourists boarded it by mistake. Assuming that the black man at the controls was the elevator operator, the visitors said, "First floor, please." Marshall responded with his best Uncle Tom imitation. "Yassah, yassah," he said, putting the elevator in motion and delivering the visitors to their destination. According to Woodward and Armstrong, "Marshall regularly recounted

Marshall joins Dr. George Allen (left), President Granville Sawyer, and law school dean Otis King (right) after a 1976 ceremony renaming the Texas Southern University School of Law. Of the approximately 100 men and women graduated each year by the Thurgood Marshall School of Law, about half are black, one-quarter Mexican American, and the remainder white.

Cecilia Marshall, *daughter of the Marshalls' son John and a namesake of her grandmother, enjoys television with her grandfather in the early 1980s.*

the story, noting the tourists' puzzlement and then confusion as they watched him walk off, and later realized who he was."

But Marshall's easygoing personal style was deceptive. Beneath the relaxed appearance and surface humor, he was as shrewd and tough-minded as ever. In the decades that followed his elevation to the high court, he remained unshakably committed to the defense of constitutional rights and the establishment of educational and legal equality for all races. In case after case, Marshall supported the positions of civil libertarians and equal rights advocates. In the beginning of his service as a justice, he often found himself voting with the Court's liberal majority.

But with the election of President Richard Nixon in 1968, the balance of the court began to change, becoming more conservative as the Republican president replaced retiring justices with members of his own choosing. Marshall now became one of the Court's most outspoken and emphatic dissenters. In the *Milliken v. Bradley* case, for example, he wrote a memorable dissent from the majority opinion.

Milliken, a Detroit case, reached the Supreme Court 20 years after the *Brown* decision. By the early 1970s, the South had desegregated many of its schools. The states of the North and the West, however, lagged behind in following the Court's 1954 ruling that separate but equal schools violated the Constitution. Like many other northern cities, Detroit had become a "bull's-eye"—an inner city populated largely by blacks, surrounded by rings of almost entirely white suburbs. As a result, the Michigan city's schools had reverted to a pattern of segregation. Instead of trying to integrate the schools, the Detroit board of education had made segregation even more pronounced by busing black students to black schools, even when white schools were closer, and by encouraging white students to transfer to white schools far from their own neighborhood.

When a group of black parents sued the state, the district court—later backed by the court of appeals—decided in their favor. Detroit, said the courts, must expand its school district to include many of the city's wealthy white suburbs. Students from all over this larger area, continued the courts, must be racially mixed, even if the move required massive busing. The United States Supreme Court, however, reversed the lower courts. Speaking for the now-conservative majority, Chief Justice Burger ruled that the integration plan placed an unfair burden on Detroit's suburban white population. Marshall, one of the four dissenting justices, expressed his opinion in passionate terms.

In Detroit, said Marshall, black children had been "intentionally confined to an expanding core of all-Negro schools immediately surrounded by a . . . band of all-white schools." He asserted that the issue concerned "the right of all of our children, whatever their race, to an equal start in life." America, he countinued, "will be ill-served by the Court's refusal to remedy separate and unequal education, for unless our children begin to learn together, there is little hope that our people will ever learn to live together." After "20 years of small, often difficult steps," Marshall concluded sadly, "the Court today takes a giant step backward."

Regents of the University of California v. Bakke inspired another strong Marshall dissent. The case began when the California institution's medical school rejected Alan Bakke, a highly qualified white applicant. The University of California practiced affirmative action, a program designed to correct the long-term imbalance of black and white students in the nation's colleges and corporations. Because the quota of minority students had filled all the medical school's openings, no slot remained for Bakke, despite his high scores on admissions tests. Claiming reverse discrimination, Bakke sued the university.

Cissy Marshall with her husband in 1988.

Bakke, which reached the Supreme Court in 1978, resulted in a mixed decision: Although race could be considered as one factor in admitting students, ruled the Court, rigid quotas for minorities were not permissible. Marshall thunderously disagreed. The Court, he said, had firmly obligated itself to eliminate racism in public life; now it was once again making a full-scale retreat from its own commitment.

As an associate justice of the Supreme Court, Marshall never hesitated to make his feelings known; outside the courtroom, however, he said little. Before he took his place on the high court, he had been a popular public speaker and the frequent subject of newspaper interviews and magazine profiles. After he ascended to the bench, he strictly limited his public statements, made personal appearances only on social occasions, and gave speeches only to legal gatherings. But in the fall of 1979, when Howard University installed a new law school dean, Marshall made an exception to his policy and addressed the students of his alma mater. His speech contained a mixture of wry humor, advice, and recollections about his mentor, Howard Law School dean Charles H. Houston.

"You know," Marshall said, "I used to be amazed by people who would say that 'the poorest Negro kid in the South is better off than a black kid in South Africa.' So what? We are not *in* South Africa. We are *here*." Warming to his subject, Marshall added, "I am also amazed by people who say, 'You ought to go around the country and show yourself to Negroes and give them inspiration.' For what? These Negro kids are not fools. They know when you tell them there is a possibility that someday they'll have a chance to be the O-N-L-Y Negro on the Supreme Court, that those odds aren't too good. . . . Well, all I am trying to tell you is there's a lot more to be done. . . . There are people who tell us today . . .

Thoroughly at home in the U.S. Supreme Court by 1979, Marshall heads for the Court Robing Room with colleague William Brennan. The Court's tilt to the political right in the 1970s distressed Marshall, but he remained firmly committed to his ideals: Other members of the Court might try to reverse civil rights progress, he thundered in 1989, "but I'm not going to do it."

'Take it easy, man. You made it. No more to worry about. Everything is easy.' Again I remind you of Charlie Houston's words: 'You have got to be better, boy. You better move better.' "

Concluding his speech in a ringing voice, Marshall recalled the day in 1963 when the African nation of Kenya celebrated its independence. "Hundreds of thousands of people," he said, "yelled in unison the watchword of that day and of this day—*Harambee!*—meaning 'Pull together!'" The entire student body rose to its feet, cheering and applauding the former Howard law student.

Anguished by what he saw as more than a decade of backsliding on civil liberties, Marshall spoke out again in a 1987 interview. Although Supreme Court justices almost never comment on political issues, Marshall could not resist answering a reporter who asked him to evaluate President Ronald Reagan's contributions to black America. Reagan, snapped the justice, "has done zero for civil rights."

In September 1989, after 22 years at the Supreme Court, Marshall made a few more political comments, this time before an audience of federal judges. Supreme Court decisions of recent years, he said, had displayed an increasingly restrictive approach to civil liberties. And such decisions, he insisted, "put at risk not only the civil rights of minorities but the civil rights of all citizens." The Court, he asserted, was now deliberately reversing 35 years of progress on civil rights. "We could sweep it under the rug and hide it," said the angry justice, "but I'm not going to do it." No one familiar with Thurgood Marshall's career could doubt his words.

At 81, Marshall's legendary energy may have diminished somewhat, but his convictions had lost none of their fiery intensity. Marshall had never taken foolish risks; neither had he ever run from a battle or compromised his principles. It was Marshall who once told an interviewer how he felt about social justice: "On the racial issue, you can't be a little bit wrong any more than you can be a little bit pregnant or a little bit dead."

History will record Marshall as the first black American to sit on the Supreme Court. But perhaps an even more important achievement was his orchestration of the *Brown* case, which demolished the legal basis for segregation in America. When Marshall took over the NAACP Legal Defense Fund in

1938, racial discrimination was a fact of American life. Black children attended separate, inferior schools. They bathed at separate beaches, drank from separate water fountains, entered theaters from separate doors. When they grew up, society restricted them to jobs at the lowest end of the economic scale. In many parts of the nation, they were denied the right to vote, the right to a fair trial, the right to live where they wanted to live. Not even their lives were safe: In the first half of the 20th century, lynch mobs murdered thousands of black men and women.

In persuading the Supreme Court to rule school segregation unconstitutional, Marshall scored a tremendous victory. The decision by no means eradicated racial prejudice or even immediately eliminated school segregation. In some areas of American life, progress was slow and painful. But *Brown* changed the social climate of the nation, paving the way for laws that prohibited discrimination in housing, employment, public facilities, and the armed services. The decision marked the place in history when the government of the United States stopped sanctioning and supporting racial inequality.

One of the most successful constitutional lawyers of the 20th century, Marshall has also served as a symbol of hope and courage to citizens of all races. Historians agree that, in the long run, no government can succeed or endure without extending justice to all its citizens. By employing legal and peaceful means to advance blacks both politically and socially, Marshall has not only made an immense contribution to all Americans but to the foundation of American justice itself. ◄◊►

CHRONOLOGY

1908   Born Thoroughgood Marshall on July 2 in Baltimore, Maryland

1929   Marries Vivian Burey

1930   Graduates with honors from Lincoln University

1933   Receives law degree from Howard University; begins private practice in Baltimore

1934   Begins to work for Baltimore branch of the National Association for the Advancement of Colored People (NAACP)

1935   With Charles Houston, wins first major civil rights case, *Murray v. Pearson*

1936   Becomes assistant special counsel for NAACP in New York

1940   Appointed director-counsel for NAACP Legal Defense and Educational Fund; with *Chambers v. Florida*, wins first of 27 Supreme Court victories

1944   Successfully argues *Smith v. Allwright*, overthrowing the South's "white primary"; suffers the first of four Supreme Court defeats with *Lyons v. Oklahoma*

1946   Receives Spingarn Medal from NAACP

1948   Wins *Shelley v. Kraemer*, in which Supreme Court strikes down legality of racially restrictive covenants

1950   Wins Supreme Court victories in two graduate-school integration cases, *Sweatt v. Painter* and *McLaurin v. Oklahoma State Regents*

1951   Visits South Korea to investigate charges of racism in U.S. armed forces

1954   Wins *Brown v. Board of Education of Topeka*, landmark case that demolishes legal basis for segregation in America

1955   Following death of first wife, marries Cecilia Suyat

1961   Defends civil rights demonstrators, winning Supreme Court victory in *Garner v. Louisiana*; nominated to Second Circuit Court of Appeals by President John F. Kennedy

1961–65   As circuit judge, makes 98 rulings, all of them later upheld by Supreme Court

1965   Appointed U.S. solicitor general by President Lyndon Johnson; wins 14 of the 19 cases he argues for the government between 1965 and 1967

1967   Becomes first black American elevated to U.S. Supreme Court; as associate justice, continues to support constitutional rights and educational and legal equality for all races

FURTHER READING

Abraham, Henry J. *Justices and Presidents: A Political History of Appointments to the Supreme Court.* New York: Oxford University Press, 1974.

Berman, Daniel M. *It Is So Ordered: The Supreme Court Rules on School Segregation.* New York: Norton, 1966.

Bland, Randall W. *Private Pressure on Public Law: The Legal Career of Justice Thurgood Marshall.* New York: Associated Faculty Press, 1973.

Clayton, James E. *The Making of Justice: The Supreme Court in Action.* New York: Dutton, 1964.

Fenderson, Lewis H. *Thurgood Marshall: Fighter for Justice.* New York: McGraw-Hill/Rutledge, 1969.

Friedman, Leon, and Fred L. Israel. *The Justices of the United States Supreme Court, 1789–1969: Their Lives and Major Opinions.* 5 vols. New York: Chelsea House, 1980.

Kluger, Richard. *Simple Justice.* New York: Knopf, 1976.

Manchester, William. *The Glory and the Dream: A Narrative History of America, 1932–1972.* Boston: Little, Brown, 1974.

Miller, Loren. *The Petitioners: The Story of the Supreme Court of the United States and the Negro.* Cleveland: World Publishing, 1966.

Schwartz, Bernard, ed. *Statutory History of the United States: Civil Rights, Part I.* New York: Chelsea House, 1970.

Schwartz, Bernard, with Stephan Lesher. *Inside the Warren Court.* Garden City, NY: Doubleday, 1983.

William, Juan. *Eyes on the Prize: America's Civil Rights Years, 1954–1965.* New York: Viking-Penguin, 1987.

Woodward, Bob, and Scott Armstrong. *The Brethren.* New York: Avon Books, 1981.

JESSE
OWENS

JESSE OWENS

Tony Gentry

Senior Consulting Editor
Nathan Irvin Huggins
Director
W.E.B. Du Bois Institute for Afro-American Research
Harvard University

1

THE
NAZI
CHALLENGE

ADOLF HITLER AWOKE on the rainy morning of August 1, 1936, looking forward to his grandest day yet as Germany's chancellor. He was to attend the opening ceremonies of the summer Olympics later that afternoon. The eleventh Games in modern history, the Olympic festival was slated to take place in his country's capital, Berlin, with 52 nations participating.

Three years earlier, shortly after he had come to power, Hitler said of the Games, "If Germany is to stand host to the entire world, her preparations must be complete and magnificent." To assure this, he had personally supervised a large part of the planning. With the help of 2,600 men, a stadium that could seat 100,000 spectators was erected out of stone on the western outskirts of the city. A swimming stadium, hockey arena, and dormitories for the athletes were also built. Century-old trees that bordered the city's avenues were dug up and moved to the athletic complex to make a park for the visitors.

A runner bearing the Olympic flame passes through the Lustgarten in Berlin, Germany, to mark the opening of the 1936 Summer Olympics. By staging the Games on a grander scale than the world had ever seen, German chancellor Adolf Hitler hoped to camouflage the evil intentions of his Third Reich from the festival's many visitors.

Adolf Hitler (standing in the car at left) leads a motorcade through the heart of Berlin on August 1, 1936, as he makes his way to the opening ceremonies of the Olympic Games. He expected his German athletes to dominate the action and was unfazed by the question repeatedly asked of him by the press: "Who have you got to beat Jesse Owens?"

Throughout the preparations, the Games were heavily promoted, often with colorful touches. The zeppelin *Hindenburg*, the world's largest airship, towed an Olympic flag across the Berlin sky. Thousands of people, from schoolchildren to soldiers, rehearsed for months, with marching bands and parading regiments slated to take part in the opening ceremonies. More than 3,000 runners were asked to carry the Olympic torch a kilometer each from Athens, Greece—the site of the first Olympic Games—to Berlin, so that the flame would arrive at the huge stadium just as the festivities were about to begin.

At precisely 3:00 P.M., a motorcade of sleek and powerful convertible limousines left Hitler's quarters, with the man dubbed the führer (German for the leader) in the head car. The procession traveled down streets lined with flags bearing the Nazi swastika emblem before turning onto the rain-slick boulevard leading to the Olympic stadium. A fanatical shout went up from the thousands of people lining the route.

Dressed in his military uniform, Hitler stood in the front seat, his eyes set straight ahead. "The Leader came by slowly in a shining car," wrote American novelist Thomas Wolfe, "a little dark man with a comic-opera moustache, erect and standing, moveless and unsmiling, with his hand upraised, palm outward, not in Nazi-wise salute, but straight up, in a gesture of blessing such as the Buddha or Messiahs use." Following the limousines and motorcycles came a runner carrying the Olympic torch on the last kilometer of its 10-day journey.

The ovation that greeted Hitler's arrival in the main stadium was nearly matched by the cheers for the approach of the Olympic torch. As soon as the runner lit the huge fire bowl in the stadium, the procession of the athletes began. Hitler and the 100,000 people surrounding him stood to salute the representatives of all the nations that had come

Twenty-eight thousand members of the Hitler Youth, Germany's national athletic organization for boys, and the Bund Deutscher Mädchen, a similar association for girls, take part in the opening ceremonies of the 1936 Games on May Field, outside the main Olympic stadium in Berlin. Regulated by the Nazi party, both organizations combined sports with politics.

to compete. With martial music blaring over loud-speakers, the athletes marched smartly around the track. Among them were blacks, Jews, Hispanics, Orientals, and Arabs, none of whom fit the Nazi model of a proper human being.

The German coaches had all but purged their Olympic team of any competitors who were not Aryan—native born, white, and non-Jewish. Hitler would have preferred that the other nations do the same. Yet if they saw fit to enter what he considered subhumans alongside his Aryan athletes, then his team would simply have to defeat them, proving to the world the strength of his nation of racially pure supermen.

Radio broadcasts and leaflets had blanketed Germany for months, promoting the brilliance of the nation's athletes, even as Jewish stars, born and raised in Germany, were hounded from the team. So the Games began, with Hitler's Aryans, cheered on by 100,000 spectators, facing off against everybody else. The cards, it seemed, were stacked. With the Germans on their home turf, the world was about to be taught a moral lesson.

Competition began the next day, on Sunday, August 2. The first event was the preliminary eliminations of the men's 100-meter dash, generally considered the most glamorous of the track-and-field events because the winner has the right to call himself "the world's fastest human." German fans held high hopes for their best runner, Erich Borchmeyer, who Americans thought looked more like a football player than a runner. But the Germans also had an eye out for the black American college student Jesse Owens, who held the world record in the 100-yard dash. As he stepped onto the rain-muddied track for his warm-ups, all eyes turned his way, wondering how the unassuming young man would do at this slightly longer distance.

Owens (far right) tries to keep warm on the first day of competition of the 1936 Olympics as he waits his turn in the 12th—and last—heat of the men's 100-meter run. Seated next to him are American sprinters Frank Wykoff (far left) and Ralph Metcalfe (second from right) and Swiss runner Paul Hänni.

Borchmeyer won his preliminary heat in a time of 10.7 seconds. An American sprinter, Frank Wykoff, bettered Borchmeyer's time by a hair in another heat.

Finally, just before noon, Owens got his chance. The hosts had furnished each sprinter with a silver hand shovel to help dig toe holes at the starting line (the aluminum-and-rubber starting blocks used by runners today were unheard-of then). Owens looked over the damp cinder track, which was already pocked and scarred by the feet of other runners, and got down on his knees to dig a foothold.

When the starter fired his gun, Owens shot off his mark, arms and legs pumping, even before the sound of the gun reached the upper seats of the stadium. In just a few steps he attained full speed. He ran with a fluid, easy stride; his eyes looked straight ahead, as if his only opponent were the tape stretched across the track fewer than 100 meters away. His feet hardly seemed to touch the ground.

Owens finished yards ahead of his closest competitor, coasting effortlessly across the finish line in a time that equaled the world record of 10.3 seconds. The crowd went wild. Even fervent Nazis could not ignore the speed of this young man.

Owens in a second-round heat of the men's 100-meter run, crossing the finish line for an unofficial world record of 10.2 seconds. His outstanding performance in the event marked the start of his dominance in the 1936 Olympic Games.

That afternoon, Owens ran in the second round of heats. Again, he made it look easy. No other runner even came close during the race. And this time Owens shaved a tenth of a second off his earlier standard, breaking the world mark. The judges decided that his time had been aided by the wind, however, so they could not award him the record.

That did not matter to Owens or to the crowd. He would run again the next day, and the next. Who could say how fast he might run in the 100-meter semifinals and finals? It was even possible that the 100-meter dash was not his best event. Didn't he also hold world records in the 220-yard dash and the long jump? Moreover, he was clearly at the top of his form, prepared to trounce all comers beneath the gray skies of Berlin.

German youngsters seeking autographs eagerly surrounded Owens on the way back to his room. On the very first day of the Olympic Games, he had proved a sensation. This must have come as a rude surprise to Hitler. These Games were to have been the führer's showpiece. Blond, blue-eyed white men and women from Germany were supposed to capture the spotlight.

But one man changed all that. One American upstaged Adolf Hitler at what was meant to be his greatest glory. One American athlete performed as no one has since, captivating a worldwide audience. One black American athlete made a laughingstock of the Nazis' racist notions, throwing Hitler's challenge right back into his mustachioed face. That man was Jesse Owens.

Within the span of a week, Owens would become an international hero, prompting people everywhere to ask the questions that must have been on the führer's lips as he sat in his special box and watched the races being run: Who is this incredible athlete? Where did he come from? What is he like? How can anyone be so good?

2

"FIGHTING
THE
WIND"

JAMES CLEVELAND OWENS was born on September 12, 1913, in Oakville, Alabama—unimaginably far from the lights and fanfare of Berlin. Nicknamed J. C., he was the tenth (and last) child of Henry and Mary Emma Owens. He had six brothers—Prentice, Johnson, Henry, Ernest, Quincy, and Sylvester—and three sisters, Ida, Josephine, and Lillie.

Like thousands of families, black and white, throughout the South, the Owenses were sharecroppers. This meant that a local landowner, Albert Owens, allowed them to live in a beat-up house on his property and use his farm equipment in exchange for their hard work and half the season's crop from the land they farmed. The Owenses sold the other half of the crop, and with the little bit of money they earned they bought clothing and a few basic supplies.

A predominantly white community of 1,000 residents, Oakville was situated along a red dirt road amid the rolling hills and tall pines of northern Alabama. Most of the Owenses' neighbors were sharecroppers, too. They plowed, behind a mule, the fields

Owens spent his early years in north-central Alabama, on a sharecropper's plantation much like the one shown here. "It was more dozens and dozens of farms," he later said of Oakville, the community in which he was raised, "than a real town."

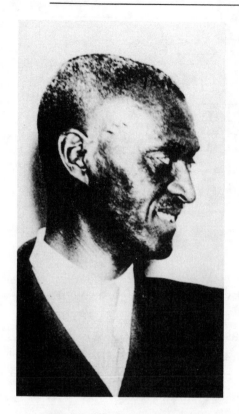

The son of former slaves, Owens's father, Henry, barely managed to scratch out a living in Oakville as a sharecropper. According to Jesse, the senior Owens "had no more earthly possessions than [a] mule and the shredded clothes he wore to shield him from the sun."

in the spring, hoed the long rows of corn and cotton throughout the scorching summer, then picked cotton from sunup to sundown during the backbreaking two-week-long harvest in the fall. Struggling to make their harvest money stretch through the winter, they fretted and prayed.

With so much work to be done, all the Owens children were expected to pitch in. But the youngest son, J. C., gave his parents fits. He was small and sickly, and it was a trial to nurse him through one cold winter after another, especially because his father could not afford to buy any medicine or pay for a doctor. As the drafty old house rattled with every icy blast, little J. C., wrapped in soft cotton feed sacks in front of the stove, coughed and sweated and cried with pneumonia for weeks at a time.

As if that were not enough, terrifying boils appeared on J. C.'s chest and legs. His father had to hold the crying child while his mother practiced surgery in her own home, carving the boils out of his flesh with a red-hot kitchen knife. Years later, in his autobiography, *Jesse*, Owens recounted one of those doctoring sessions in all its harrowing detail: "Real pain is when you don't have any choice any more whether to cry or not, and then maybe you don't even cry because it wouldn't help. I always hated to go to sleep at night, but now for the first time in my life I wanted to pass out. Something inside wouldn't let me. All I felt was the knife going deeper, around and around, trying to cut that thing loose, all I saw were the tears running down my father's face, all I heard was my own voice—but like it was somebody else's from far-off—moaning, 'Aww, Momma, no . . .' "

Through sheer will and the determination of his long-suffering parents, little J. C. somehow survived these brushes with death. And by the age of six, he was well enough to walk the nine miles to school with his brothers and sisters.

School amounted to a one-room shack that doubled on Sunday as the Baptist church for the blacks of the area. The teacher was anybody who had the time and the inclination. During spring planting and at harvesttime, students worked the fields instead of arithmetic problems. In spite of all the drawbacks and interruptions, J. C. learned to read and write.

Meanwhile, his parents struggled to make a better life. First, they moved their family to a larger farm in Oakville, where they worked 50 acres of land. Nevertheless, sharecroppers rarely expected to earn much money, and the Owenses were no exception. The children endured the hard times by concentrating on happier moments: fishing, raccoon hunts, swimming, berry picking, games of hide-and-seek, and schoolboy pranks. "We used to have a lot of fun," Owens recalled. "We never had any problems. We always ate. The fact that we didn't have steak? Who had steak?" His family, like most sharecroppers, did not think of themselves as poor because all their neighbors were poor, too.

With hard work and good weather, a family could pick enough berries for jams and collect enough wind-fallen apples, pears, and peaches to last through the winter. They canned tomatoes and beans from their garden and slaughtered a hog after harvesttime. So even though the Owenses did not have much money, there was usually enough to eat.

And with all that, there was time for play. It was in the low hills of Alabama that J. C. first began to run. He recalled in his autobiography that even as thin and sickly as he was, "I always loved running. I wasn't very good at it, but I loved it because it was something you could do all by yourself, and under your own power. You could go in any direction, fast

Mary Emma Owens proved to be the chief source of inspiration in Jesse's life. Unlike her husband, who had become resigned to a life of poverty, she urged her children to dream of greater things and to work hard to attain them.

or slow as you wanted, fighting the wind if you felt like it, seeking out new sights just on the strength of your feet and the courage of your lungs."

As the Owens family continued to eke out an existence from the red dirt of Oakville, prospects of better opportunities beckoned at last. One of J. C.'s sisters, Lillie, had moved to Cleveland, Ohio, and she soon wrote home that she had found work there earning more money than she had ever seen before. She begged her parents to pull up roots and join her in this worker's paradise.

Around 1920, the Owenses, like many other southern blacks searching for a better way of life, gave up sharecropping and moved to the industrial North. They settled in Cleveland's East Side ghetto (below), which Owens said was "a better world . . . most always" than the one his family had known in Alabama.

Henry and Mary Emma Owens, however, did not jump at the chance to leave their tattered farmhouse amid the cotton fields. The Owens family had roots in northern Alabama that ran back for a century, into slavery days. They had never known anything but farm life. As fellow members of the Baptist church, their friends and family spread for miles around in the northern Alabama hills.

J. C.'s father understood particularly well how ill equipped he was to face urban life. He had never learned to read or write or even to calculate the value of the cotton he harvested. He was a good farmer and a well-respected deacon of the church, but none of that would matter in the big city.

Even so, his wife approached him with their daughter's letter in her hand and a determined sparkle in her eye. She pointed out that the family was not faring too well in the rural South. A move to Cleveland was not such a gamble.

J. C.'s father never stood a chance against his wife's arguments. When he reminded her how un-schooled he was, she asked him if he wanted his 10 children to grow up just as ignorant. When he told her how he would miss the farm life, she waved her hand through their dark, unpainted rooms, showed him the all-but-empty kitchen shelves, ran a finger through the holes in her apron, and laughed.

For Mary Emma Owens, the family had nothing to lose and everything to gain from catching the first train north. And when J. C. turned nine years old, they sent him down the road to sell their mule to a neighbor. With that money, they all bought train tickets, and as their youngest child later recalled, he stood with his folks on the platform at the Oakville station and asked, "Where's the train gonna take us, Momma?" She answered only, "It's gonna take us to a better life."

That better life, however, lay a little more than a train ride away. The Owens family moved into the only apartment they could afford, in a ghetto neighborhood on Cleveland's East Side. Back in the country, the view beyond the windows of their house had expanded for miles across open fields beneath the limitless blue sky of Alabama. In the city, their windows opened onto bedraggled alleys and the walls of the building next door. Emma Owens more often than not kept her curtains closed.

But now that she had convinced the family to move north, J. C.'s mother was not about to forget her dream. She took jobs all over town, cleaning houses and washing laundry, and put her daughters to work doing the same. The older sons took jobs in a steel mill, where the foremen appreciated the strength and endurance the Owens boys had developed in the fields. J. C., too young for such grueling labor, found a part-time job polishing shoes and sweeping up in a cobbler's shop.

But for Henry Owens, who was in his forties, the move north had perhaps come too late. Worn down by a lifetime on the farm, he could not keep up with his sons in the mill and had to settle for whatever part-time work he could find. Still, for the first time in his life, his labor earned him a paycheck. At the end of the week, the family pooled its money to buy luxuries they had only imagined in the South: new shoes, new clothes, and good, sturdy furniture.

The bustling city swirled about them. Mill work proved exhausting, closed in, run by time clocks and strict supervisors. Shysters waited on every corner to cheat a man out of his wages. Around the dinner table in their ghetto home, the Owens family acted out a story repeated in millions of urban households all over the country during the first half of the 20th century—that of rural people in crowded apartments, bewildered and harried by their new environment, weighing in their minds the advantages and disadvantages of the move they had made to the city.

And if the working life seemed worlds apart from the farm, 10-year-old J. C. discovered that Bolton Elementary School was just as far from the one-room schoolhouse back home in Oakville. Everything at Bolton ran in a businesslike fashion. For example, when the busy teacher asked for J. C.'s name, she misunderstood his slow southern drawl and wrote it down as "Jesse." Afraid to interrupt her on his first day of school, the youngster took his seat without comment, and for the rest of his life he was called Jesse instead of J. C.

Unsure of how much schooling her new student had previously received, the teacher assigned Jesse to

While a student at Fairmount Junior High School in Cleveland, Owens formally began his career as a track athlete. He encountered little success in school meets, however, because he had not yet overcome, as he later put it, "the instinct to slack off, give in to the pain and give less than your best, and wish to win through things falling right, or your opponents not doing their best, instead of going to the limit, past your limit, where victory is always found. Because it's victory over yourself."

first grade, where he towered over his younger class-mates. But the little school in Oakville had taught him enough, so he quickly moved up to another class. Even so, he was a couple of years older and a few inches taller than the other children in his classroom.

Bolton, like the community it served, was a ra-cially mixed school. Jesse soon made friends with children from all over the world—Poles, Hungarians, Greeks, Italians, and Chinese. He ran himself ragged exploring his new neighborhood, which seemed so much larger, more exciting, and more dangerous than

At the age of 15, Owens began dating Minnie Ruth Solomon, who later became his wife. "I fell in love with her some the first time we ever talked," he said, "and a little bit more every time after that."

the fields of Alabama. His imagination ran wild. In Cleveland, it seemed, all that limited anyone was how well their legs could keep up with their dreams. For children like Jesse—more energetic, more inquisitive, less set in their ways than their parents were—even a large city's ghetto could seem like a wonderland.

Jesse Owens spent the next three years of his life that way. In addition to working at the cobbler's shop, he held jobs in a greenhouse watering plants and as a grocery store delivery boy. The northern winters, however, kept him in bed fighting it out with pneumonia for weeks. When the time came for him to enter junior high school, Owens probably felt that he knew all about city life. No longer the awkward southern hick, he stayed out of trouble, went to church on Sunday with his parents, and played a mean game of stickball.

Then, at Fairmount Junior High School, Owens's life gradually began to diverge from that of his playground friends. All in one week he met the two people who would change his life. Each in his or her own way would show him a glimpse of a larger world than the one he knew on Cleveland's windy streets and then dare him to chase it.

The first person was a pretty young girl named Minnie Ruth Solomon. Owens must have grinned when she told him her parents had been sharecroppers in Georgia and had just recently moved north to try their hand in the city. It is easy to imagine 14-year-old Jesse, a playful glint in his eye, offering to show her the town.

As Owens recalled in adulthood, for him it was love at first sight: "She was unusual because even though I knew her family was as poor as ours, nothing she said or did seemed touched by that. Or by prejudice. Or by anything the world said or did. It was as if she had something inside her that somehow made

Owens with his first and foremost track coach, Charles Riley. "I'd noticed him watching me for a year or so," Owens said of his junior high school physical education teacher, "especially when we'd play games where there was running or jumping."

all that not count. I fell in love with her some the first time we ever talked, and a little bit more every time after that until I thought I couldn't love her more than I did. And when I felt that way, I asked her to marry me . . . and she said she would." Jesse and Ruth were still too young for marriage, but their puppy love would grow.

The second important person Owens met at junior high was a short, skinny man with a whistle around his neck: Charles Riley, who coached the school's track team. Who knows what the wiry Irishman saw in the happy-go-lucky kid from Alabama? He certainly was not the strongest, the fastest, or even the healthiest student in school. But Riley may have guessed at his potential, or maybe he just wanted to help Owens build up his lungs to fend off his frequent attacks of pneumonia. Whatever the reason, Riley called Owens into his office one day and asked if he would be interested in running a little after school.

Thus began a career that would rewrite the records of track and field, shake up a dictator, and make the name *Jesse Owens* a household word worldwide. ✥

3

"FOUR YEARS FROM NEXT FRIDAY"

T HE TEACHERS AT Fairmount Junior High School knew that most of their students would never go on to high school. In the East Cleveland ghetto, bright youngsters had to grow up fast, helping their families earn a living any way they could. So classes skimmed over English, history, and mathematics, concentrating instead on the kinds of lessons that might help students find and hold jobs as laborers. Boys learned to use tools; girls were taught how to type and cook. Arriving on time, dressing cleanly, and following instructions meant more than test scores did.

Jesse Owens thrived under these conditions. Friendly, compliant, a fastidious dresser, he had never been a whiz at textbooks. Fairmount rewarded his strengths and did not hammer too hard at his weaknesses.

Meanwhile, a passion began to occupy Owens's imagination "so completely," he said, "that whole days would pass when I didn't think of anything else." He began to think of himself as a runner. Coach Charles Riley set up a training schedule for Owens, even though he was too young to compete on the school's track team. Because the youngster held part-time jobs after school, he asked the coach if it would be all right to train in the morning. Riley must have reasoned that if this skinny but eager student was willing to push himself so hard, then he could not

A teenage Owens during his days at East Technical High School in Cleveland. He enrolled at the school in 1930 and quickly became one of its most popular students.

say no. So, most days at dawn the two met, one sipping coffee and watching while the other stretched and jumped and ran.

It was not long before Owens began to look up to Riley almost as a second father. He even called the Irishman "Pop." The coach made sure Owens ate well, bringing him breakfast from his own table or inviting him to dinner with his family. He used their training sessions not only to build up the runner's legs and lungs but to build character as well. Riley told all of his teenage charges not to expect immediate results but always to train for "four years from next Friday." Steady, gradual improvement was the goal.

Riley may have been the first man Owens had ever met who challenged him to test his limitations. Having inherited from his mother the drive to achieve, Owens found in Riley a teacher who woke up early every day to hammer the point home that the biggest obstacle anyone has to overcome is within one's own head. Riley said that a man has to push himself every day, winning out over the tricks his mind plays on itself, in order to reach his potential. Yet he was not one to preach. He taught by quiet example and encouragement.

In the 1920s, most world-class sprinters tried to power down the track, furiously pumping their arms and legs. Riley thought this was unnatural. One day he took Owens to a racetrack to see the relaxed grace of the thoroughbreds as they ran, their hooves seeming to barely touch the turf, their eyes always looking forward, a study in speed. He told Owens and his other students to mimic the horses, to run as if the track were on fire, keeping each foot on the ground for as little time as possible. These characteristics became the hallmark of Owens's running style throughout his career and, through his example, revolutionized the way sprinters everywhere learned to run.

For a year, Coach Riley put Owens through his paces. Then one day he decided to time Owens at the distance of 100 yards. When Owens flew past the coach 11 seconds later, all Riley could do was stand there in openmouthed astonishment. He asked Owens to run the distance again, and again the runner clocked in at 11 seconds—unbelievably fast for a 15 year old. It was time to suit this youngster up for the team.

Riley knew that with such speed Owens would make a good jumper. He signed Owens up to compete not only in the 100-yard and 220-yard dashes but also

"Every morning, just like in Alabama," Owens said of his high school days, "I got up with the sun, ate my breakfast even before my mother and sisters and brothers, and went to school, winter, spring, and fall alike to run and jump and bend my body this way and that for Mr. Charles Riley."

Owens (second from left) in the spring of 1932, when he was coming into his own as a runner. By winning this 100-meter race at the Northern Ohio Amateur Athletic Union Track-and-Field Championships, he automatically qualified for the quarterfinals of that year's Olympic Trials.

in the long jump and high jump. Sometimes, Riley entered him in the hurdles or the 440-yard run, guessing that these races would make the sprints seem easier. Owens quickly repaid his coach's confidence. In his first year on the track team, he broke the world record for junior high school students in the high jump and long jump. When Charlie Paddock, an Olympic gold medalist in the 100-meter dash, came to the school to deliver a speech, Riley introduced him to Owens. From the moment the two shook hands, Owens's only dream was to reach the Olympics.

But as Owens trained ever harder, life at home threatened to dash his dream. His father broke a leg when he was hit by a taxicab, and because of the injury he lost his job. Jesse's brothers, one after the other, were laid off from the steel mill, and when they could not pay their rent they moved their wives and children into their parents' already crowded house. These were the years of the Great Depression, when the nation's economy all but collapsed. Poor people, holding down the most tenuous of jobs, took the brunt of the hard times. Millions of workers all over the United States found themselves penniless and hungry, standing on food lines.

The pressure must have been great for 17-year-old Jesse to drop out of school and do what he could to help the family make ends meet. Credit must go to his mother, who, despite her tough days washing laundry for pennies, convinced her son to continue his education. In 1930, Owens enrolled at East Technical High School, a few blocks from his house. He tried out for the football and basketball teams but soon gave them up when they cut into his running time.

The track coach at East Tech, Edgar Weil, was not the inspiring innovator that Coach Riley had been. But, luckily for Owens, Weil soon asked Riley to be his assistant, and under Riley's continued tutelage Owens came into his own. In the spring of 1932, during his junior year, he proved so dominant a competitor that one newspaper called him a "one-man team." That estimation was not far off the mark. Owens often scored more than half the points for his whole team at track meets.

But again private life intruded on Owens's ambitions. His girlfriend, Ruth, reported one day that she had become pregnant. The two hastily eloped to Pennsylvania in a car driven by a friend, David Albritten. The young couple claimed that they were married in Erie by a justice of the peace. It is more likely, however, that Owens and Solomon did not go through with the wedding, for no marriage license exists from that time. In any event, when the two lovers returned to Cleveland, they faced the wrath of their parents. Ruth's father swore never to let Owens see his daughter again.

Owens could do nothing but concentrate on his running. That summer, he took a big step toward realizing his dream, traveling to Northwestern University to try out for the U.S. Olympic team. But 1932 was not to be the year of Jesse Owens; he did not make the team. In both the 100-yard and 220-yard dashes, he lost to Marquette University sprinter Ralph Metcalfe, who went on to win silver and bronze medals at the 1932 Olympic Games in Los Angeles. Metcalfe was a powerhouse runner of the old school. He and Owens would become firm friends—and archrivals—in the years ahead.

In the trials for the 1932 U.S. Olympic team, Owens got as far as the midwestern preliminaries, where he lost in the 100- and 200-meter races to Ralph Metcalfe (left), then the top American sprinter. Metcalfe later won a bronze medal in the 200 meters and a silver medal in the 100 meters at the 1932 Games in Los Angeles, finishing second in the shorter race to teammate Eddie Tolan (second from left).

When the Olympics were over, some of the runners toured the United States, holding demonstration track meets. It must have come as some consolation to Owens that he won the 100-yard and 220-yard dashes and even finished second behind the 1932 Olympic gold medalist in the long jump, Edward Gordon, when the squad came through Cleveland. But no matter how Owens felt about his performances, he gained valuable experience in competing on an international level.

Owens could not keep his mind entirely on his running, however. On August 8, 16-year-old Ruth gave birth to their baby. A healthy little girl, she was given the name Gloria Shirley. With this, Ruth's high school days were over. She dropped out of school and took a job in a beauty parlor. But she continued to live with her parents, who still would not let Jesse in the house.

By refusing him the responsibilities of fatherhood, the Solomons, perhaps unwittingly, did Owens a

One of the few flaws in Owens's running technique during the early portion of his track career was his start, which was not as explosive as he would have liked. He remedied the problem by making a few adjustments in his takeoff stance and improving his concentration as the starter was about to fire the gun.

favor. Now he could enter his senior year of high school and continue his track-and-field career. As a testament to his popularity, his East Tech classmates (95 percent of whom were white) voted him student body president. As the high scorer and natural leader of the track team, he became squad captain as well.

Owens repaid his admirers with electrifying performances, not losing a race all year. Though he never deliberately drew attention to himself, he was so clearly head and shoulders above the other competitors that all eyes stayed on him, whether he was running a race or landing in the long-jump pit. On May 20, 1933, he concluded his high school career in typically splendid fashion. At the state interscholastic finals that day, he broke the world record for high school students in the long jump, sailing 24 feet, 3⅛ inches.

Then, in June, at the National Interscholastic Meet in Chicago, Owens eclipsed even his own standards. In the 100-yard dash, he tied the world record of 9.4 seconds. In the long jump, he improved his best leap by a remarkable six inches. And then, in the 220-yard dash, he ran a blazing 20.7 seconds, breaking the world record.

The town fathers back home in Cleveland were quick to honor the city's new favorite son. They organized a victory parade as soon as Owens got home. One can only imagine the pride of Henry and Mary Emma Owens as they were helped into the backseat of a convertible, flanking their son, for the slow-moving procession along the broad streets downtown. In the car directly behind theirs rode Charles Riley. Perhaps he guessed that this would be only the first of many victory parades for his favorite student. And somewhere in the crowd one can picture Ruth, holding a daughter who was not quite one year old, helping the baby wave at her father's car going by.

Owens at the age of 19, showing his mother the four medals he won at his final high school meet, the National Interscholastic Championship in Chicago. Among his achievements at this June 1933 tournament were setting a new world record in the 220-yard dash and equaling the world mark in the 100-yard dash.

When the procession stopped at City Hall, the mayor of Cleveland joined several council members in praising the young athlete, happy to discover a hero during such difficult times. They predicted a grand future at whatever college he chose to attend.

Owens let none of the fanfare go to his head. He drove a hard bargain in negotiating with the big midwestern schools that were clamoring for his talents. During the summer, Coach Riley drove Owens all

Cleveland mayor Ray Miller congratulates Owens in June 1933 on his accomplishments at the National Interscholastic Championship. Owens's father (third from left) and mother (far right) were on hand at City Hall for the festivities.

the way to the University of Michigan to tour the campus. But in the end, Owens elected to stay close to home. Ohio State University, in the state capital of Columbus, won the budding star.

In those days, colleges did not give athletic scholarships. Instead, they offered easy jobs at good wages to help students pay their way. After school each day, Owens would have to run a freight elevator at the State House. Having held much more strenuous jobs most of his life, he quickly agreed. Owens even secured a custodial job on campus for his father, but Henry Owens did not have it in him to pull up roots again. He chose to stay home in Cleveland and appreciate his son's exploits long distance.

There was one major hitch in all these arrangements. Owens had just slipped by with a D average in high school, and his report card failed to impress the administrators at Ohio State. The coaches got around this difficulty by having Owens take special tests over the summer. When he passed these, the last door opened.

With the next few years decided upon, Owens could tie up loose ends at home. For spending money, he pumped gas at a filling station. At long last, the Solomons gave in to their daughter's pleas and allowed Owens to visit after work each day. And on weekends, Riley drove him in his Model T to track meets. Once, they even drove as far as Toronto, Canada, for an international competition.

With autumn approaching, the old coach prepared to say farewell to his surrogate son. Pop Riley had started Owens out on the road to glory, instilling in him a will to win and a humility toward the tasks that would face him in the years ahead. Owens was 19 years old, already arguably the world's fastest human. The rest would be up to him.

4

COUNTDOWN
TO THE
OLYMPICS

·(··)·

JESSE OWENS WAS among the handful of blacks that enrolled in an American university in 1933, when the Great Depression caused an unusually low percentage of high school graduates to enter college. Nevertheless, at Ohio State, a school where athletes—particularly football players—are treated like conquering heroes, he fit right in. The coaches made sure he signed up for easy courses, knowing that his secondary schooling had not been the best. And the job running a freight elevator was even easier. Because freight was rarely delivered during his shift at night, he had hours of free time to study on the job. Finally, Owens learned that he could make extra cash traveling about the state on weekends, giving speeches to help promote the school. At that rate, he later recalled, he not only paid for his education but saved enough to send regular checks home to his mother and to help Ruth raise their baby.

Meanwhile, every day, Owens trained for the track season. In January 1934, without ever having run a race in college, he was named to the Amateur Athletic Union (AAU) All-American Track Team. Everything seemed to go well during the first semester but his grades. East Technical High School in Cleveland had done little to prepare Owens for a college curriculum, and having never learned how to study, he quickly fell behind his classmates. At the begin-

Owens at a training session with his track coach at Ohio State University, Larry Snyder. "He was constantly on me," Owens said, "about the job that I was to do and the responsibility that I had upon the campus. And how I must be able to carry myself because people were looking."

507

Not permitted to join Ohio State's varsity squad in 1933–34 because he was still a freshman, Owens (far right) participated instead in freshman meets and regional tournaments, including this February 1934 contest in New York City that was won by Ralph Metcalfe (second from right).

ning of the spring semester, he was put on academic probation and ordered to bring up his grades.

Ohio State's track coach was a young man named Larry Snyder. A character builder as well as a coach, he must have seemed to Owens like a younger, peppier, more ambitious version of Pop Riley. Snyder liked the natural running style Owens had developed in high school, but he believed there was still room for improvement. In the sprints, he concentrated on getting Owens to relax even more—he tended to tense his upper body and arms—and he taught the freshman a more compact crouch at the starting line, which would help him uncoil quickly into a full-speed run. In the long jump, Snyder showed the freshman how to "run through" the air, pumping his arms and legs for more distance as he flew. A dedicated student when it came to track and field, Owens practiced these new techniques with a diligence he rarely applied to his schoolbooks. (Such an attitude toward his classwork would ultimately hurt him in later years.)

According to collegiate rules, Owens, like all incoming students, was not eligible to compete on a varsity team until his sophomore year. After another summer spent pumping gas back home in Cleveland, he traded in his job running the elevator for a more prestigious position as a page for state legislators in the capitol. When he joined the varsity track squad later in the year, the refinements Coach Snyder had taught him began immediately to pay dividends. On February 9, 1935, in his first Big Ten Conference meet, Owens won 3 out of 4 events, placing second in the 70-yard low hurdles. It was plain to all concerned that he would be able to compete successfully on the college level.

Owens must have guessed that he was reaching the top of his form. For seven intense years, he had trained to run and jump with the best. But at the

Big Ten Championships in Ann Arbor, Michigan, on May 25, 1935, he shocked even himself. In the space of 45 minutes, Jesse Owens broke 5 world records and tied another. This feat has never been equaled; it is still considered the greatest single performance in the history of track and field.

Owens's teammates could not believe their eyes. They had seen him wearing hot packs on his back all week after falling down a flight of steps at school. When Coach Snyder, wary of aggravating the injury, wanted to bench him for the meet, they had overheard Owens pleading for the chance to run. Owens later said that he knew he would be all right when he first crouched down for the 100-yard dash. Miraculously, the pain seemed to disappear. And after the starter's pistol sounded, Owens did the same, blazing effortlessly into the lead and tying the world record of 9.4 seconds.

In the 220-yard dash, Owens shaved four-tenths of a second off his previous best time, reclaiming the

By his sophomore year, Owens (far left) had become one of the best-known sprinters in the nation. He is shown here in February 1935, winning the 60-yard dash at the Millrose Games in New York City's Madison Square Garden.

world record. He was also awarded the international record for the slightly shorter distance of 200 meters without having to run that race. Then, in his worst event, the 220-yard low hurdles, he breezed to a new standard of 22.6 seconds. In this race, he finished 10 yards ahead of his nearest competitor. Again, he was allowed the low-hurdles record for the shorter international distance of 200 meters.

It took just one leap for Owens to break the world record in the long jump. At his request, a friend placed a handkerchief beside the pit at the 26-foot mark. Owens soared past the handkerchief, landing 8¼ inches beyond it. This astounding leap was not equaled for 25 years. After such a performance, Owens then took his coach's advice and chose not to try for a longer distance.

Owens at work in 1935: pumping gas at a service station in Cleveland (right) and as a page in Ohio's State House (opposite).

Immediately, autograph seekers and reporters mobbed the new champion. Owens posed for photographers, shook hands, and signed his name all the way back to the dressing room. So many well-wishers crowded the door there that he had to escape through a back window. In the parking lot, patiently waiting in that old Model T, sat Coach Charles Riley, who had cheered with everyone else as Owens rewrote the record books.

As they took the long drive back to Riley's house for a celebratory dinner, the old coach quietly prepared his protégé for the fame that was to come. He

In addition to the sprints, Owens frequently competed in the long jump (right) and the 220-yard low hurdles (opposite). He considered the hurdles to be his weakest event.

explained that life would be different from now on. Owens had been a contender; but in one day he had become a star. Now the top runners in the world would be gunning for him. Fans would surround him. Every move he made would be scrutinized by the press.

No doubt the young runner listened respectfully to Riley's thoughtful advice. But neither man could have guessed that the success they had cultivated for so long would soon be challenged from four different directions. Although none of these challenges came on the track, any one of them might have ended Owens's drive toward the Olympics.

The first challenge arrived in the beautiful person of Quincella Nickerson, a wealthy socialite who took the runner's arm one night in June 1935 after a meet in Los Angeles. Imagine the response back in Cleveland, Ohio, at the Solomon household when the grinning faces of this glamorous couple appeared in the local papers, captioned with hints of a wedding engagement.

Ruth Solomon caught up with Owens by telephone when the track team reached Lincoln, Ne-

Owens (left) at the Big Ten Championships in May 1935, setting a new world record in the 220-yard low hurdles. He usually compensated for his less-than-perfect hurdling technique by soaring rather than skimming over the barriers.

braska. Whatever she told him, he promptly went out and lost all his races at the AAU Championships the next day, July 4. Then he caught the first train back to Cleveland. In the Solomons' living room, which had been off limits to him for so long, he and Ruth were married that afternoon. The event was covered in newspapers nationwide. And the next morning, a chastened young husband, still burning from his first brush with celebrity, left for the East Coast and the relative peace and quiet of track meets there.

Shaken by it all, Owens lost his races to a fine runner named Eulace Peacock. Then he returned home to his new family and his summer job at the filling station, reading in the papers that Peacock now seemed to be the front-runner in the race for the Olympics.

There was no rest for the weary. AAU officials called Owens back to Columbus in August, threatening to bar him from competition. He had received checks totaling $159 during the summer from his page's job at the State House. Part of the sum was for travel expenses, and Owens had used the money to pay for his trip to California. To the AAU, the job seemed suspiciously like a cover-up for an outright athletic scholarship. Owens gave back the money, but it took all the persuasiveness of Ohio State University administrators and Ohio lawmakers to convince the AAU to drop its charges.

When his junior year got underway, Owens received yet another slap in the face. Those same university officials who had argued his case so convincingly just weeks before now suspended him from the track team for the winter season. The reason? Poor grades. They threatened to cut the world-record holder in six events from the team unless he hit the books hard.

If that was not enough, world politics impinged on the young runner, too. The Olympic Games were scheduled to begin in less than a year, in Berlin, Germany. But stories had begun to circulate about German mistreatment of Jews, blacks, Catholics, and political dissidents. Many of the nation's leading newspapers were calling for an American boycott of the Olympics in protest of Adolf Hitler's discriminatory policies, and the AAU made a tentative decision to keep American athletes out of the games.

All that winter, as Owens, unable to compete with his teammates, trained on his own, he could not be sure if he would be granted the opportunity to achieve his grand dream of reaching the Olympics. And worst of all, there was nothing he could do about it. The decision would be made by men in business suits, far from the playing fields.

It must have been a terrible time for the 20-year-old Owens, who faced pressure from all sides. But he remembered the teachings of Coach Riley—to challenge himself, to do his best—and he concentrated on those tasks that were within his control. Gradually, his grades came up, and by the time Owens rejoined the track team for the spring season he had run himself into the best shape of his life.

Against the University of Wisconsin on May 16, just 10 weeks prior to the Olympic Games, Owens ran the 100-yard dash in 9.3 seconds, breaking the world record. While his archrival Eulace Peacock struggled with a hamstring injury, Owens piled up victory after victory, all leading to the Olympic Trials in New York City on June 11 and 12. After an agreeable visit with German chancellor Adolf Hitler, AAU officials had decided that it would be all right for American athletes to compete in Berlin after all. The last barrier to Owens's dream had fallen. Now, after what must have seemed the darkest time since

Owens in July 1935 with his friend Eulace Peacock, who went on to defeat Owens five times in the next nine months. A hamstring injury prevented Peacock from making the 1936 U.S. Olympic team.

Owens performing at the Midwest regional tryouts for the 1936 U.S. Olympic team in the 100-meter run (above, far left) and the long jump (opposite). He wound up qualifying for the squad in those two events as well as in the 200-meter sprint.

his boyhood illnesses in Alabama, the door stood open for him.

At the Olympic Trials, Owens breezed to victory in the 100-meter and 200-meter dashes and in the long jump. His schoolboy pal David Albritten, also a teammate at Ohio State, made the team as a high jumper. Ralph Metcalfe, the 1932 medalist who had

beaten Owens in the trials that same year, also gained
a berth. These were 3 of the 19 black athletes who
would compete for the United States in the 1936
Olympics, 4 times the number who had made the
team 4 years earlier. The big disappointment: Eulace
Peacock. Hampered by his hamstring injury, he finished out of the running at the trials.

Owens married his childhood sweetheart, Minnie Ruth Solomon, on July 5, 1935, in her parents' home.

The night following the trials, Owens joined the other Olympians at a celebratory feast in Manhattan. There he was surprised and honored to find himself seated beside the legendary baseball slugger Babe Ruth. As Owens later recalled, Ruth wasted no time in asking, "You gonna win at the Olympics, Jesse?"

Owens replied, "Gonna try."

"Everybody tries," Ruth said. "I succeed. Wanna know why?"

Owens nodded.

"Because I know I'm going to hit a home run just about every time I swing that friggin' bat. I'm surprised when I *don't!* And that isn't all there is to it. Because I know it, the pitchers, *they* know it too."

Owens grinned at the supreme confidence of the baseball hero. And he did not fail to recognize the good advice hidden in the blustering anecdote. Sometimes, it is not enough to *want* to win. Sometimes, you have to *know* that you will. Owens took the Babe's advice with him on board the S.S. *Manhattan* when it departed for Berlin three days later.

Every kind of distraction awaited Owens during the week-long voyage, from heavy gourmet meals to Hollywood starlets who vied for his arm on the dance floor. To at least one of the Olympians, the distractions proved too much. The beautiful backstroke champion Eleanor Holm Jarrett partied her way to Berlin—and lost her chance to compete when a chaperon discovered her drunk on champagne one morning. Owens was careful to avoid all the premature celebrating. He kept his mind on his destination, performing calisthenics and watching what he ate, while getting to know his fellow Olympians.

There was a lot of time, too, for thinking over all he had been through, for thrilling to the fact that his wildest dream was about to come true. As Pop Riley had said, "Run to beat yourself." As Babe Ruth had suggested, "Know you will win." He would test both of these axioms, to their limit, in the Olympic Games.

All set to make a big noise: Owens in his New York hotel room in mid-July 1936, just before sailing with the U.S. Olympic team to Europe for the start of the Games.

5

THE DREAM COME TRUE

WHEN THE OLYMPIC Games began on August 1, 1936, German chancellor Adolf Hitler had been running his nation for a little more than three years. In that brief amount of time, he had raised the nation from a poor and broken-spirited country, beaten and divided by the Great War of 1914–18 (what is now called World War I), to a position of power in the world. He had put his unemployed countrymen to work building the first superhighways anyone had ever seen. These were broad and straight concrete roads he called autobahns, on which the powerful cars of the 1930s could run flat out, with no speed limit at all.

The skies of Nazi Germany were ruled by enormous hydrogen-filled zeppelins. The most spectacular of these airships, the *Hindenburg*, stretched the length of three football fields and regularly traveled across the Atlantic Ocean carrying passengers in style. And the show of size and strength did not end there. All over Germany, people gladly adopted Hitler's strict programs aimed at making the nation's young people well schooled, physically fit, and proud of their country.

"It all goes so fast," Owens said of the sprint races, "and character makes the difference when it's close."

521

Yet this glittering nation of fast highways and fit youngsters was being built at the expense of the livelihood and freedom of millions of its own people. Hitler's dream nation excluded anyone he did not consider a patriotic native of pure Aryan stock. And with fanatical and relentless energy he set about promoting a form of national pride that thrived on the oppression of anyone who did not fit that description.

When he had been in office just 1 month, Hitler ordered the creation of 50 concentration camps to imprison "enemies of the state." Four months later, 27,000 people—mostly Jews and Communists—were being held under brutal conditions in those camps. Soon, Catholics and members of other religious denominations were forced to join these prisoners in their misery, and thousands of others fled the country in fear.

Astute observers of the strange goings-on in Germany guessed what Hitler was up to. Those autobahns could be used to transport troops quickly and efficiently all over the country. Those zeppelins and the planes being turned out on German assembly lines could be fitted out for wartime purposes almost instantly. And all those schoolboys learning to toss balls accurately into hoops positioned on the ground might just as easily have been throwing grenades. Finally, if the Nazis saw fit to drive out or imprison a large part of their own population, who could say what they might do to other nations in a time of war?

But somehow, few people got the point. Maybe Hitler's clampdown on the German press was the reason. Maybe he charmed the world's leaders into trusting him. Maybe it was simply impossible to believe that a nation beaten into the ground in the ugliest war ever fought, scarcely 17 years earlier, could be thirsting for battle again so soon. Whatever the cause, Hitler began to carry out his plans for genocide

An awe-inspiring symbol of Germany's advanced technology, the zeppelin Hindenberg, *the world's largest airship, navigates the skies of Nazi Germany in 1936.*

and world domination with scarcely a whimper from other governments.

And in sponsoring the 1936 Olympic Games, he expected to pull off yet another coup, because here was his opportunity to hoodwink the people of the world, to perform a magnificent magician's trick directly under their noses. He invited the world's greatest athletes, the reporters with their radio hookups, the statesmen and socialites, right into his nation's capital and dared them to see anything but good.

But for Adolf Hitler, never one to pull his punches, merely sponsoring the Olympic Games was not enough. These sporting events supplied an ex-

Chancellor Adolf Hitler (above) and Owens (opposite) besieged by their respective fans in Germany. "I wanted no part of politics," Owens later said of the 1936 Games. "And I wasn't in Berlin to compete against any one athlete. The purpose of the Olympics, anyway, was to do your best. As I'd learned long ago from Charles Riley, the only victory that counts is the one over yourself."

cellent forum where his notions of Aryan supremacy might be tested. Germany had done well at the 1932 Games in Los Angeles, before Hitler's rise to power. The new chancellor had spared no expense to make sure the Germans would come out victorious this time.

Red-white-and-black Nazi swastika flags were flying from every shop window on June 24, when the U.S. Olympic team came down the S.S. *Manhattan*'s gangway in Bremerhaven, Germany, touching solid ground for the first time in a week. Catching an express train to Berlin, the team marveled at the beauty of the countryside. Berlin itself had been so carefully renovated for the Games that it seemed to sparkle.

The Germans had built a magnificent Olympic Village to house the athletes a few miles west of the city. This idea worked so well that similar villages have been built for every Olympics since then. The Berlin version included comfortable dormitories, a spacious park, a library, a swimming pool, and theaters. Owens roomed with his high school buddy and Ohio State teammate, high jumper David Albritten.

For two weeks, as other competitors arrived from around the world, the American track team worked off its "sea legs" at the practice track in the Olympic Village. Ohio State track coach Larry Snyder was not an official member of the U.S. delegation, but he had traveled to Berlin at his own expense to keep an eye on Owens and Albritten.

It was lucky for Owens that he did. One day, Snyder arrived at the track to find the Olympic coaches trying to change the running style that he, Coach Charles Riley, and Owens had all but perfected over the past several years. Those coaches were trying to alter Owens's effortless gliding run into the powerhouse style they favored, but Snyder stepped in to convince them to leave well enough alone.

Also, Owens had lost his track shoes at the Olympic Trials in New York, so Snyder spent days combing the shops of Berlin for a perfect replacement pair.

But there was nothing Snyder could do about all the autograph seekers and photographers who constantly surrounded his star. Adolf Hitler may have had a grudge against people from what he considered to be inferior races, but German youngsters were fascinated by the American who held all those world records. And Owens, always smiling and happy to oblige, won their hearts with the few German words he had picked up during his stay. He woke up every morning to the sight of curious faces pressed against his dormitory window, yet he handled the fishbowl of celebrity with a down-to-earth sense of humor that belied all the pressure of the upcoming Games.

By the time August 1 arrived, however, he and his teammates were eager to get on with the competition. They marched into the gigantic crater of a stadium to the roar of 100,000 fans and caught their first glimpse of the German chancellor. Hitler stood in uniform and at attention in his flag-draped viewing box, surrounded by his right-hand men: Hermann Goring, Albert Speer, and Joseph Goebbels—all names that would become notorious in the war years ahead.

Owens was largely unconcerned with all the pomp and politics. He had come to Berlin to run and jump. And the next day he got his chance. If he had any doubts about his physical condition after the voyage overseas, he quickly wiped them away in the 100-meter eliminations. Cold, drizzly rain fell most of the day, making the track slow and muddy. But without a word of complaint, Owens astounded the crowd by equaling his own world record of 10.3 seconds. In his afternoon heat, he lowered that time by a tenth of a second, but because of a following wind the new record was disallowed.

Reassured that he was still at the top of his form, Owens slipped on his sweat suit and spent the rest of the afternoon watching Albritten compete in the high jump. Before the day was over, both Albritten and his American teammate Cornelius Johnson had broken the world record in their event. Johnson squeezed out a victory with a remarkable leap of 2.3 meters (7 feet, 6¼ inches). Albritten, having hurt his ankle during the competition, admitted that he was pleased to have won the silver medal. He took it back to his dormitory room that night, where it did not remain alone for long.

The semifinals and finals of the 100-meter race were held the next day. As Owens warmed up for his semifinal heat, a cloudburst sent the spectators scurrying for cover and muddied the track even more. But this was the day Owens had lived for. The dream of a lifetime lay within his grasp.

Later, he would philosophize about the oddity of training so many years for an occasion that would be over in mere seconds. To the runner, he said, the race was both shorter and longer than a spectator could imagine: "To a sprinter, the hundred-yard dash is over in *three* seconds, not nine or ten. The first 'second' is when you come out of the blocks. The next is when you look up and take your first few strides to attain gain position. By that time the race is actually about half over. The final 'second'—the longest slice of time in the world for an athlete—is that last half of the race, when you really bear down and see what you're made of. It seems to take an eternity, yet is all over before you can think what's happening."

According to Owens, people assumed that running 100 meters was just a question of speed. Certainly, that was a lot of it. But against world-class

Owens (right) beating fellow American Ralph Metcalfe in the 100 meters to win the first of his Olympic gold medals. Owens's time of 10.3 seconds equaled the world mark.

One of Germany's most popular athletes, Luz Long (left), with his new friend Jesse Owens. To most people, their spirited competition in the long jump was the high point of the 1936 Olympic Games.

competition, the big challenge appeared in the last half of the race, when every instinct, all those years of training, and sheer courage were called upon to squeeze out every last drop of speed. This was what Coach Riley had been talking about in all his high school lectures when he said to "race against yourself." To go to the limit in this way was a supreme sporting achievement, and Jesse Owens carried it out so brilliantly that he made it look like child's play.

Owens won his semifinal heat easily, in 10.4 seconds. Then, in the 100-meter finals, he burst into the lead at the starting gun and was never challenged. He broke the tape in 10.3 seconds, tying his own Olympic record. Ralph Metcalfe, the Marquette University sprinter who had won two Olympic medals in Los Angeles, finished second, a yard back. But all eyes were on Owens. One British observer marveled, "No sprinter I have ever seen has run in such effortless style. He was in a class above all other competitors;

his arms and legs worked in perfect rhythm, and he carried his running right through the tape."

The results of the race were broadcast on loudspeakers all over Berlin, so, as Owens took his victory lap, shouts in and out of the stadium circled with him. The German crowd had found a hero in the college boy from the United States, and for the rest of the Games, wherever he went, the shout went up: "Yesseh Oh-vens! Yesseh Oh-vens!"

On the victory stand that afternoon, Owens's eyes misted over as he bent forward to receive his gold medal and watched the American flag being raised. He had achieved his dream at last. He would remember this as the happiest moment of his whole career.

It was no such happy moment for Adolf Hitler. Owens bowed to him from the victory stand, and the German chancellor returned a stiff salute, then turned away. The Nazi leader had been working for years to build racial hatred in Germany, and here in just 10 seconds a black American had won the hearts of his countrymen. When an aide suggested that he invite Owens to his viewing box, Hitler savagely replied, "Do you really think that I will allow myself to be photographed shaking hands with a Negro?"

Whether Owens knew that he had been snubbed or not, he did not have time to be bothered by a racist politician. The next day, the preliminaries of the 200-meter race began. For the fourth day in a row, rain fell—this time as a bus drove the American track team to the stadium. Owens had to wear his sweatshirt to stay warm during his elimination heats, which he won handily. Then, while the other sprinters caught a bus back to the Olympic Village, he tried to stay loose for the afternoon's long-jump competition, swallowing a damp sandwich for lunch.

The 100-meter victory had seemed so easy, but the long jump proved anything but. In fact, Owens barely made it into the finals. Each athlete was given three chances to qualify, which should have been two more than Owens needed. But when he ran, still wearing his sweat suit, through the long-jump pit to gauge the steps for his first leap, he was shocked to discover that the judges counted the run-through as his first attempt. Then, when he *did* jump, they said he had committed a foul by stepping over the takeoff board and disqualified the leap.

Now the pressure was on, and suddenly the power of concentration that had helped make Owens such a formidable competitor deserted him. In his autobiography, Owens recalled that this was the most frightening moment of his career: "I fought, fought hard, harder . . . but one cell at a time, panic crept into my body, taking me over."

He credited a German long jumper, Luz Long, with pulling him back together for his last leap. The German, who had already qualified for the finals, walked over and asked in his best English, "What has taken your goat, Jazze Owenz?" Owens had to smile at that.

The tension broken, Long suggested to Owens that in his third attempt he take his very last step several inches before the end of the takeoff board, thus making sure that he did not overstep the board and become disqualified. Owens thanked him for the advice, and with the old confidence returning, raced down the runway for his jump. Even though he leaped before the end of the takeoff board, where the officials begin their measurements, he landed more than 26 feet away, a new Olympic record. Again, Owens ran over to thank the German.

All afternoon, Owens and Long were locked in head-to-head competition for the long-jump gold medal. The Olympic record broke with each leap. Yet through it all they cheered each other on. The crowd had never seen anything like it. Long stood a few inches taller than Owens. He was the perfect picture of the Aryan superman—blond, blue eyed, with a perfectly proportioned physique. But he was not caught up in Hitler's mania for white supremacy. Like Owens, he understood that one competes primarily against oneself, and he seemed genuinely grateful to have at last met a man who could drive him on to a better performance.

Luz Long jumped with a simple, fluid style, his arms thrown high above his head. Owens "ran through" the jump, hitch kicking in midair as Coach Snyder had taught him, to capitalize on his superior speed. With each jump, the crowd erupted in applause. No doubt the Germans wanted their countryman to win, but Owens had already become a crowd favorite, and for once it was easy to join in the friendly spirit of competition that the two long jumpers shared.

In the final round, Long matched Owens's record. The two smiled and shook hands. Then Owens went to the board and jumped even further. More applause. Eventually, Long faltered, overrunning the board. A groan went up around the stadium. And with the gold medal awaiting him, Owens gathered himself for one more jump. With the regal confidence and concentration of a Babe Ruth, he sailed to a new Olympic record of 26 feet, 5⁵⁄₁₆ inches. Luz Long was the first to congratulate Owens, giving him a hearty bear hug in full view of Adolf Hitler.

That evening at the Olympic Village, Owens and Long were inseparable. Though Owens could not speak German and Long knew only a little English, they talked for hours. It turned out that Long had come from a poor family, too. Like Owens, he had a wife and child at home. They spoke about their love for their sport, which offered challenges nothing else could match, and fretted together over racial prejudice in Germany and the United States. By the

Luz Long makes his final leap in the 1936 Olympics long-jump competition. He was, according to Owens, "a supreme example of Aryan perfection . . . one of those rare athletic happenings you come to recognize after years in competition—a perfectly proportioned body, every lithe but powerful cord a celebration of pulsing natural muscle, stunningly compressed and honed by tens of thousands of obvious hours of sweat and determination. He may have been my archenemy, but I had to stand there in awe and just stare at Luz Long for several seconds."

"I decided I wasn't going to come down," Owens said of his final leap in the long-jump competition. "I was going to fly. I was going to stay up in the air forever." He won the Olympic event with a record leap of 26 feet, 5⁵⁄₁₆ inches.

time the Olympic Games ended, the two had become firm friends. And as their relationship was portrayed in newspapers worldwide, they came to represent the way supposed archenemies can overcome their differences. Beyond all of Hitler's flag-waving and speeches, the image of Jesse Owens and Luz Long shaking hands became the overriding symbol of the 1936 Olympics.

Owens awoke the next day to more rain. He breezed through his semifinal heat in the 200 meters, then spent the afternoon watching Americans Ken Carpenter and Earle Meadows win gold medals in the discus and pole vault, respectively. Then, just before sunset, in the 200-meter finals, Owens again proved himself the world's fastest human. On top of all his tutoring by Coaches Riley and Snyder, he had developed a trick or two of his own over the years. One of these accounted in part for his quick takeoffs at the starting gun. Out of the corner of his eye he watched the starter, knowing that there was usually some telltale sign just as the trigger was pulled, and that sign gave Owens a slight jump on his competitors. This technique worked well in Berlin, where the starter habitually bobbed his knees just before pulling the trigger.

Owens knew he would need all his skill to win the 200-meter race. After he had set a new Olympic record of 21.1 seconds in his preliminary heat, teammate Mack Robinson equaled that mark later in the morning. Yet Robinson could not keep up with Owens in the final. Owens held a slight lead coming out of the turn, and when he reached the tape Robinson trailed him by nearly five yards. Owens's time of 20.7 seconds set a new world record for a 200-meter race around a curve. But the crowd had barely finished shouting its approval when the skies opened again. Owens received his third gold medal during a downpour.

At last, the competition had ended for him. He could spend the remaining days in Berlin rooting for his American teammates, enjoying performances by circus animals, dance troupes, and even the Berlin Philharmonic at the Olympic Village, or trying to make out the shadowy images of other athletes on a prototype television set.

Then the U.S. coaches called him to a meeting. They believed the Germans were saving their best runners for the 400-meter relay race, and for that reason they wanted Owens to run the first leg for the American team. Ralph Metcalfe would run the second leg, virtually assuring an American victory in the event. It is not difficult to imagine the anger of

Owens (right) in a 200-meter heat, setting an Olympic record for the distance with a time of 21.1 seconds. In the finals, he bettered the mark by an extraordinary amount, four-tenths of a second, to win his third gold medal. Mack Robinson, an older brother of baseball great Jackie Robinson, captured the silver medal.

sprinters Marty Glickman and Sam Stoller, who had been slated to run the relay, when they were told that they were being bumped from the race. Owens also seemed surprised. He told the coaches he had enough gold medals and to let the others run.

But the coaches would not budge. Glickman and Stoller, the only Jewish members of the U.S. Olympic team, thus became the only two team members who did not compete at the Games. And by making the change, U.S. officials seemed suspiciously close to the racist notions that fueled the Nazi government. Their decision made it plain to all that anti-Semitism was not simply a German problem.

When race day came, Owens, of course, did his best. He handed the baton to Metcalfe with a five-yard lead. Foy Draper started his leg ahead by 7 yards, and Frank Wykoff, who took the baton 10 yards in the lead, lengthened it to 12 by the end of the race. The Americans set a new world record of 39.8 seconds. The Italians won the silver medal, and the Germans came in third. The rumor of a German superteam had amounted to nothing.

Jesse Owens had won his fourth gold medal, an unprecedented feat by a track athlete. He had broken Olympic records in all four events. This achievement overreached his wildest dreams and made him a hero to sports fans worldwide.

One of those fans proved to be Hitler's hand-picked cinematographer, Leni Riefenstahl. She filmed the entire 1936 Olympic Games in a sweeping, lyrical style that highlighted the beauty of each event

Owens competing in the 400-meter relay, on his way to his fourth Olympic gold medal, a record number for a track-and-field athlete.

Wearing the victor's laurels, Owens salutes the American flag during an Olympic medal ceremony. "It dawned on me with blinding brightness," he later said of his Olympic achievements. "I realized: I had jumped into another rare kind of stratosphere— one that only a handful of people in every generation are lucky enough to know."

while downplaying all the hoopla over winners and losers. Jesse Owens was her athletic ideal. In her filming of the 100-meter competition, her cameraman zoomed in on Owens's thigh, neglecting all the other runners to show his perfectly toned muscles in action.

Similarly, her portrayal of the Owens-Long duel in the long jump centers on the soaring grace of their leaps, not on their battle for the gold. Riefenstahl's film, *Olympiad*, is sometimes shown on television, especially during Olympic years, and it is easy for a viewer to be drawn into her awe at the magnificence of athletic achievement and particularly at the seemingly effortless beauty of Jesse Owens in full flight.

As the Americans packed their bags at the Olympic Village, they already looked forward to the next Games. These were to be held in Tokyo, Japan, in 1940, when Owens would be just 26 years old. Certainly, he would be back to compete again.

But the Germans and the Japanese had goals other than sports in mind. A wooden peg in the closet of each dormitory room had been placed there to hold a helmet. Already in the fields near the Olympic Village machine-gun practice could be heard. The village would become an infantry training center as soon as the athletes departed.

World War II would put an end to any talk of a 1940 or a 1944 Olympics. The German swastika flag would become a hated emblem to people all over the world. As Owens carefully packed his four gold medals for the trip home, he could not have known that he would never compete at another Olympics. And he would never again see his new friend Luz Long either. Like Owens's relay-race teammate Foy Draper, Long would die in a foxhole during the war. ❧

6

AFTER
THE
GOLD RUSH

❧

WHAT DOES A 22 year old do when he has achieved his wildest dream? As the possibilities piled up following his Olympic victories, Jesse Owens could not have guessed that this question would torment him for the rest of his life. It had been one thing to aim his formidable talents at the single goal represented by those five interlocked Olympic hoops. Testing himself against the constantly shifting demands of the workaday world would prove a far more difficult challenge.

Coach Larry Snyder wasted no time in coming to Owens's aid. He arrived in the athlete's room the evening following the 400-meter relay race for a private, man-to-man talk. He had not come to discuss race strategy or running form—none of that mattered anymore—but to consider how Owens might best capitalize on his Olympian achievements. At that moment, it seemed there were two options: return to Ohio State to complete his degree or drop out of school to make some money from his newfound celebrity.

Even though Owens was the unparalleled star of the school's track team, Coach Snyder was a practical man, and he knew that offers would soon come pouring in proposing huge amounts for Owens's services. As the Olympic star told a reporter the next morning, "I'm anxious to finish my college career, but I can't

The conquering hero: Owens displays the three gold medals that he won for his individual prowess in the 1936 Olympics.

A hero's welcome: Owens is greeted by his mother and wife (above) in New York City and is cheered by his hometown fans in Cleveland (opposite, at back of lead car) shortly after returning from the 1936 Olympics in Berlin. "You worked—possibly slaved is the word—Jesse, for many years for this," his wife told him. "And you deserve everything they're saying about you and doing for you."

afford to miss this chance if it really means big money. I can always go back and get a degree."

Even before Owens had his bags packed, the offers began to arrive. A California orchestra wired him that it would pay him $25,000 just for introducing songs onstage for 2 weeks. Entertainer Eddie Cantor wanted to share a vaudeville stage with Owens, proposing a $40,000 fee for 10 weeks of work. And Paramount Pictures talked of a movie deal.

All those zeros made the runner's head spin. To a depression-era American, the sums seemed astronomical. All Owens wanted to do was get home, show those medals to his family, and rest a while before sorting out the opportunities.

But the AAU and the U.S. Olympic Committee had other plans. In order to pay team expenses, they had set up post-Olympic track meets all over Europe, and Owens was to be their star gate attraction. Exhausted from a week of record-breaking performances, he had to join his teammates on a trip to Dresden, then on to Cologne and Prague, and back to Bochum, Germany, staging track-and-field exhibitions at each stop. Not surprisingly, the team performed unevenly. If Owens equaled his world record in the 100-meter dash in one city, he lost out to an unknown athlete in the long jump elsewhere.

By the time the team boarded a plane for London, they were homesick, dog tired, and flat broke. Coach Snyder, angry at the shoddy treatment the AAU was showing some of the world's best athletes, called a stop to it right there. After a meeting with university officials, he announced that Owens was simply too tired to go on. He would run one last time in London and then board a ship for New York.

At the London meet, the American team trounced all comers. Owens, however, competed only on the 400-meter relay team. The 90,000 spectators who had come to see the Olympic stars perform could

not have known that they were witnessing the last amateur race Owens would ever run.

But thanks to the arrogance of AAU officials, that is what happened. Avery Brundage and the other businessmen who ran the U.S. Olympic team were not about to lose their star athlete in the midst of such a lucrative tour—at least not without a fight. They told Snyder to make sure Owens caught the plane to the next meet in Stockholm, or else. When Owens failed to board that plane, the outraged officials suspended him indefinitely from amateur competition. Never mind that the entire world knew about his exploits a week earlier on the track in Berlin. Never mind that he was a hero to people everywhere. Once again, the AAU proved its stubborn

"Don't do anything till you see me!" Bill "Bojangles" Robinson (right), one of America's best-known black entertainers, told Owens by ship-to-shore telephone as the Olympic champion made his way back to the United States in August 1936 aboard the Queen Mary. *Robinson arranged for his manager to handle the business offers that came Owens's way.*

narrow-mindedness, punishing its greatest athlete simply for wanting to go home.

At least the suspension freed Owens to do what he wanted: He caught the next ship back to the States. Aboard the *Queen Mary* he relaxed, danced, and regained the 10 pounds he had lost during the stress of the Olympics. By the time he arrived in New York four days later, he felt rejuvenated and ready to face the hero's welcome awaiting him.

And what a hero's welcome it was. Owens's family was brought out on a launch to meet the ship even before it docked in New York harbor. The women smothered him with kisses. Then, at the dock, Owens answered the questions of clamoring reporters until

the great entertainer Bill "Bojangles" Robinson rescued him and his family for a fast-moving motorcade
to Harlem. At Robinson's home, Owens found himself the guest of honor of the city's black luminaries,
who seemed as eager to shake his hand as the German
schoolchildren had been.

Finally, when the party died down, Robinson
took Owens aside and introduced the athlete to his
show-business agent, Marty Forkins. The agent and
the performer had taken sprinter Eddie Tolan under
their wing following his victory at the Los Angeles
Olympics, and they said they would now be happy
to guide Owens through the strange waters of celebrity. His mind spinning with their talk of a Hollywood
fortune, Owens gathered his family to catch a train
back to Cleveland and the well-deserved rest he had
dreamed of ever since he left Berlin.

*Owens with his wife at the Cot-
ton Club in Harlem. Following
the 1936 Olympics, a number of
deals and endorsements for
Owens were arranged at the
nightclub.*

But Owens's hometown fans could not let him
rest without first getting a glimpse of their hero. A
motorcade wound its way through Cleveland's East
Side ghetto and through the fanciest streets in town
on its way to welcoming speeches at City Hall. Then
it was on to Columbus for another victory procession
and more speeches. Finally, three weeks after leaving
the Olympics, Owens got a chance to sleep in his
own bed.

But he was up the next day to haggle with Coach
Snyder and Ohio State administrators over what he
would do next. Everyone agreed that his best bet at
cashing in on his fame was to sign an agency agreement with Forkins. He could always get his college
degree later.

So Owens climbed back on the train for New
York. While in Manhattan, he met his Olympic
teammates as they arrived from Europe, and he rode
in the first car of the ticker-tape parade up Broadway
that honored their return. Once again, Bill "Bojangles" Robinson was waiting for him. At the final

ceremony, held on nearby Randall's Island that afternoon, Owens showed his gratitude to his new friend by giving him one of the gold medals he had won in Berlin.

With all the victory parades out of the way, Owens sat back and waited to pick his way through the many job offers he had received. Then, one by one, before his eyes, they all disappeared. Eddie Cantor backed out of his promise to take Owens on tour, as did the California orchestra that had sounded so eager in Berlin. All the talk of movie deals faded away, too. As Owens remembered years later, "After I came home from the 1936 Olympics with my four medals, it became increasingly apparent that everyone was going to slap me on the back, want to shake my hand or have me up to their suite. But no one was going to offer me a job."

Owens (right) stumping for Republican presidential candidate Alf Landon (opposite, center) in the fall of 1936. An exceptional public speaker, Owens "doesn't so much take [a room] over as envelop it," said one reporter. "He is friendly to all, outgoing and gracious."

To make matters worse, the Olympic champion could not compete in track meets anymore. Signing an agency contract had been the last straw for the AAU. Already angry over Owens's dropping out of the European tour, the organization said that he was now a professional and was therefore ineligible to compete as an amateur ever again.

What was Owens to do now? He did the one thing he knew how to do best: He ran. But this time he was running from a banquet to a radio broadcast to a clothing or food endorsement and back to another banquet, earning $1,000 or so at each stop. Any offer Forkins dug up, Owens took. In the months following his return from Berlin, Owens traveled all over the United States, trading his fame for whatever money he could make. No single job amounted to much, but all together they added up to a small fortune.

Before the year was out, Owens had bought his parents a big house, his wife an expensive wardrobe and jewelry, and himself a spanking new Buick sedan. He even took Charles Riley to an auto showroom, trading in that old Model T for a new Chevy.

When the Republican party asked Owens to campaign for its presidential candidate, Alf Landon, Owens balked at first, saying he did not care much about politics. But when they reminded him that President Franklin D. Roosevelt, the Democratic candidate in the 1936 presidential race, had not even sent a telegram of congratulations following his Olympic victories, Owens changed his mind. Now he was running the political race, too. At whistle-stops all over America, Owens used the speech-making skills he had learned at Ohio State, telling charming anecdotes about his experiences in Berlin and ending each talk with a few words in support of Landon. For this, he earned somewhere between $10,000 and $15,000. All of Owens's public-speaking

In late 1936, Owens's business manager, Marty Forkins (left), arranged for his client to race in Cuba against the country's fastest athlete, Conrado Rodriques. The staging of the race was sabotaged by the Amateur Athletic Union, however, which regarded Owens as a professional and threatened Rodriques with the loss of his amateur status if he took part in the contest.

skills could not help Landon, however. He lost to Roosevelt in a landslide, carrying only two states, Vermont and Maine.

Owens was determined to make a living no matter how he had to do it, and he poured all of his athletic intensity into the project. If no one wanted to hire a black Olympic champion, then he would get along as well as he could. When Forkins offered him the opportunity to race in Cuba on the day after Christmas, 1936, Owens reluctantly agreed to pass up the holiday at home. The race was supposed to be against Cuba's fastest sprinter, Conrado Rodriques. But the AAU, watching every move Owens made, warned Rodriques that by racing against a professional he risked his own amateur standing.

Owens arrived in Havana on Christmas Day only to learn that the race would not go off as scheduled. The fast-talking promoter, however, said he had something else in mind that might work. He asked if Owens would be willing to run against a horse. At first, Owens must have thought this was a joke. Did the promoter know that he had learned to run from watching horses race? What was he to do? He was in Cuba at Christmas, the money was on the table: Why not?

The race took place at halftime of a soccer game. To make matters worse, when Owens jogged onto the field rain came pouring down. Only 3,000 fans remained in the stands. And there at the starting line was his competition, jockey J. M. Contino, astride the thoroughbred Julio McCaw. Owens later said that he felt sick at that moment, realizing what he was about to do. But he went through with it. He lined up with a 40-yard head start and raced 100 yards further down the field, beating the horse by several steps. Then he took the $2,000 payment and went home.

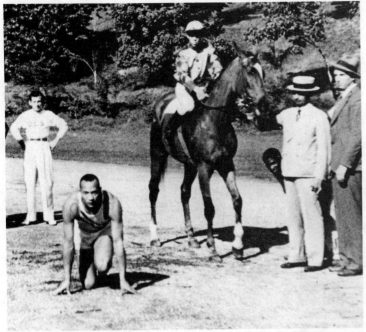

When Owens's match race with Cuban sprinter Conrado Rodriques was canceled, business agent Marty Forkins (far right) arranged for Owens to run against the thoroughbred Julio McCaw. "It was bad enough to have toppled from the Olympic heights to make my living competing with animals," Jesse said. "But the competition wasn't even fair. No man could beat a race horse, not even for 100 yards."

It did not escape Owens's notice how far he had fallen in just four months since the Olympic Games. He was at that moment one of the most famous people in the world, and newspapers everywhere carried photographs of his race against the horse. Some even quoted Owens, saying how good it felt to be out running again. But if fans were dismayed at their hero's misfortune, Owens had never been one to complain. And if racing against horses or campaigning for a politician would help support his family, he would do it again.

This is how, in the weeks following his Olympic triumph, Jesse Owens set the stage for the rest of his life. ✧

7

BARNSTORMIN'

❦

T HE ONLY PERSON who came through on his promise to help Jesse Owens after the 1936 Olympics was Bill "Bojangles" Robinson. The veteran showman fitted the runner out in a white suit and tails, briefed him on holding the attention of a nightclub audience, and helped him win a whopping $100,000 contract to lead a 12-piece black touring band. Ruth Owens was now expecting her second child. She had just picked out a new house in Cleveland and was busy decorating. But she would have to make that house a home by herself, because in January 1937 her famous husband hit the road.

Years later, Owens would laugh while describing to William O. Johnson, Jr., author of *All That Glitters Is Not Gold: The Olympic Games*, his months as a bandleader: "Well, I couldn't play an instrument. I'd just stand up front and announce the numbers. They had me sing a little, but that was a horrible mistake. I can't carry a tune in a bucket. We played black theaters and nightclubs all over hell. One-nighters. Apollo Theater in Harlem and the Earle Theater in Philly—that was big time for blacks."

In January 1937, Consolidated Radio Artists sought to capitalize on Owens's fame by offering him the position of bandleader of a 12-piece orchestra. The music company reportedly paid him $100,000, making it one of the most lucrative deals Owens ever made.

549

Sometimes, Owens would scout out the town he awoke in, and if a baseball game was scheduled there, he would cut a deal for a running exhibition between innings. It was a grueling life, fights often broke out on the dance floors, and Owens missed his family. Finally, he came down with strep throat in Richmond, Virginia, and called it quits, giving up that huge contract for a chance at some home cooking and more than a glimpse of his baby daughter, Marlene.

At that time, freewheeling basketball teams toured the country, dazzling the locals with their prowess. Today, the Harlem Globetrotters are the last of these teams to survive, but in the fall of 1937, when Owens formed a team of Cleveland hotshots he named the Olympians, there were similar groups all over. Owens went out on the road with this crew, which played in large and small towns across America. Before spring came, the Olympians had played 142 games, winning all but 6. As an added attraction, Owens often ran exhibition races at halftime. But when the season ended, the team had barely broken even, and Owens returned home looking for new money-making ventures.

He hired some of the same players for a barnstorming softball team called the Olympics and traveled with them on weekends in the summer. But by now he was finding it difficult to pay his debts, especially the notes on his and his parents' new homes. Coach Riley discovered to his dismay that Owens had covered only the down payment on his Chevy, and Riley had to struggle on his teacher's salary to make the monthly payments.

So Owens decided to get a job. At just over $1,000 for the summer, his position as a bathhouse attendant for Cleveland's recreation department was a far cry from his stipend as a bandleader, but at least it helped pay the bills. Before the summer ended, he

had parlayed that job into a better-paying position as a playground director.

But those legs that had run so far were not ready to quit yet. For the grand opening of nighttime baseball at Ebbetts Field in Brooklyn, New York, Owens showed up to race against the fastest athletes baseball had to offer. At another game in Chicago later that summer, he challenged heavyweight boxing champion Joe Louis to a 60-yard sprint.

And Owens raced against horses, too, learning after a while a few circus tricks to make it easier. As he told William O. Johnson, Jr., "The secret is, first, get a thoroughbred horse because they are the most nervous animals on earth. Then get the biggest gun you can find and make sure the starter fires that big

The Olympians, a basketball team founded by Owens (front row) in the fall of 1937, competed against amateur squads, semiprofessional clubs, and college teams. At halftime of each game, Owens spoke to the crowd and demonstrated his running techniques. On occasion, he also took part in an exhibition race.

Owens races against two of major-league baseball's fastest players, Ernie Koy (left) and Lee Gamble (center), before the start of the first night game ever played at Ebbetts Field in Brooklyn, New York. Owens was narrowly defeated in the 100-yard dash after giving the ballplayers a 10-yard head start.

gun right by that nervous thoroughbred's ear." By the time the jockey got his mount settled down, Owens would be halfway down the track. Still, the races were close.

For Owens, it would never be enough just to hold a job, run a baseball team, and tour as a runner-for-hire. Before long, he had started a dry-cleaning business as well. The first of these establishments opened on Cleveland's East Side, where Owens had grown up. The sign out front read, Speedy 7-Hour Service by the World's Fastest Human. Constantly on the road, Owens left the dry cleaning to business partners and signed on to tour for a while with a team of baseball-playing comedians aptly named the Indianapolis Clowns.

Owens had never been much of a ballplayer, however. He later said that his role came at the end of the game, as the grand finale: "We'd get into these little towns and tell 'em to get out the fastest guy in town and Jesse Owens'd spot him ten yards and beat him." This is why there are old men all over America still telling yarns about racing against Jesse Owens. Many of them actually did.

But maintaining all of these ventures at the same time eventually proved too much for Owens. All at once, the whole world seemed to come crashing down. It started when the Internal Revenue Service demanded payment for back taxes. Owens lost the dry-cleaning business trying to pay that debt. Then, in March 1940, his beloved mother, Mary Emma, his first and greatest inspiration, died at the age of 64. In a car crash that summer, Owens's Buick was totally destroyed. He escaped with a few bruises, but the brush with death was terrifying. As a final blow, his world record in the 220-yard low hurdles fell, another sign of his mortality. When his third daughter, Beverly, was born, Owens realized it was time to take stock of where he was headed.

Owens made the courageous choice to start from scratch. In the fall of 1940, he returned to Ohio State to get his degree. Even though the AAU still refused to allow him to compete as an amateur, Coach Larry Snyder gladly hired him to help with the track team. Owens's entire family moved to Columbus, and he settled into the life of a student.

Yet as hard as he tried, the 27-year-old college junior could not make it work. In September, his father died of a heart attack. Owens mourned while sweating over the tough required courses he had postponed during his glory years. Finally, he had to face the fact that he would never get a diploma. In December 1941, halfway through his second year back in school, he called it quits. His average on a 4.0 scale was just 1.07.

That same month, the Japanese bombed the Pearl Harbor naval base in Hawaii, and the United States entered World War II. Because he was the head of a household, Owens was not drafted into military service, but the government nevertheless found a role for him at home. The Civilian Defense Office put Owens in charge of a national physical fitness orga-

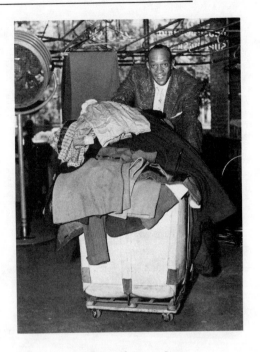

The Cleveland-based Jesse Owens Dry Cleaning Company, established in the summer of 1938, was a business opportunity that Owens said he "grabbed . . . like you grab the baton in a relay race from a man who's almost out of the legal passing zone—just in time." The venture struggled from the start, however, and collapsed less than a year later.

In the fall of 1940, Owens (left) returned to Ohio State with the hope of earning his college degree. He helped pay for his tuition by assisting Larry Snyder as coach of the track team.

nization. For a year, he toured the country setting up exercise programs at black schools and community halls.

Then Owens was offered the best job he would ever hold. Ford Motor Company, which was turning its assembly lines into military factories for the war effort, hired him as a personnel officer for its thousands of black workers in Detroit. This was the perfect job for a man with limitless energy, prestige, and a way of getting along with almost anybody.

Owens started out by mediating difficulties that came up between the company and the United Auto Workers of America union. But by the time the war ended, Owens had expanded his position so that he was helping black workers find better housing, establishing recreation facilities in their neighborhoods, and welcoming new immigrants to the Motor City. At last, he had found work that allowed him to use his talents in a way that not only paid his rent but helped others as well. Not since he had thrilled the crowds at the Olympics had he felt this good.

But when the Germans, and then the Japanese, surrendered in 1945, Owens had to surrender his job as well. With Ford restructuring itself to make cars again, many of the wartime managers, including Owens, were dismissed.

He went back to his old barnstorming ways, touring for a while with the Harlem Globetrotters. At an exhibition in Milwaukee in 1950, at the age of 37, he ran a 100-yard dash in the astounding time of 9.7 seconds, less than half a second off his own world record. One wonders what feats he might have accomplished had the Olympic Games been held during the interim. But he could not go on like that forever. And besides, he had caught a glimpse of another way of life during his years at Ford. Jesse Owens would never be one to stay put for long, but in his remaining

During World War II, the Civilian Defense Office made Owens coordinator of a nationwide physical fitness program. Federal government officials also asked him to supervise the hiring of black workers at Detroit's Ford Motor Company plant, which was serving as a military factory during the war.

Owens, at the age of 34, outruns a 7-year-old pacer, The Ocean, in a 100-yard dash. Pointing out that he "worked as few men ever have," Owens continued to appear in racing exhibitions well into the 1950s.

years he would find a way to combine his need to constantly keep moving with the opportunity to make more money than he had ever imagined earning.

The key was public relations. As American companies grew larger and more powerful in the years after World War II, they spent more money on advertising and on making themselves look good to their customers. Olympic hero Jesse Owens, the first American to put Hitler in his place, seemed the perfect choice to promote their goods.

Today, of course, when athletes and rock stars advertise all sorts of products at every opportunity, public relations of this sort is commonplace. But at that time, during the infancy of television, companies were just beginning to recognize the advantages of having a celebrity sell their wares.

Owens became the self-admitted prototype of the "famous flack." In Chicago, where he moved his family in 1949, he held public relations positions for clothing factories, insurance companies, and dry cleaners while plugging a variety of other products on television and radio. He was so swamped with offers that he had to form his own public relations firm to keep track of them all. Fourteen years after his Olympic triumph, some of the reward for his toil in Berlin had begun to come through.

But as he recalled in his autobiography, it all just meant more work: "People who worked with me or knew me still called me the 'world's fastest human' because I almost never stopped. I'd found that I could get more done with no regular job or regular hours at all, but by being on my own, flying to speak here, help with a public relations campaign for some client there, tape my regular jazz radio show one morning at 5:00 A.M. before leaving on a plane for another city or another continent three hours later to preside over a major sporting event."

Owens's barnstorming days were over. Never again would he have to race against a horse or some cocky local yokel to make ends meet. From the pinnacle of success at the Berlin Olympics, he had fallen very far. But each year, until the day he died, his Olympic gold medals would shine brighter.

8

A
PATCHWORK
QUILT

JESSE OWENS'S SECOND wave of fame began in 1950, when the Associated Press named him the greatest track-and-field athlete in history. He was given the award at a huge banquet in Chicago, where he then lived, attended by 600 business leaders and sportsmen. Owens's acceptance speech sounded a lot like the other speeches he had been giving for years. He reminisced about his rough childhood, used his memory of German long jumper Luz Long to demonstrate how even enemies can overcome their differences, and swore by the difficult lesson he had learned over the past several years—that with hard work, even a poor boy can make good in America.

This was exactly what the business leaders wanted to hear. These were the years of the cold war with the Soviet Union, when Communism became a dirty word in the United States and many people were hounded from their jobs for not seeming patriotic enough. Almost overnight, Jesse Owens became a symbol of the "American way of life." It was not that he was saying anything differently than he ever had before; it was just that now those words readily blended in with the mood of the country. A registered

Owens acting as an American goodwill ambassador, on a tour of India, Malaysia, and the Philippines in 1955. The U.S. State Department asked him to visit the Far East to foster international friendship.

559

Republican ever since his ill-fated campaign for Alf Landon in 1936, Owens soon became a favorite of Republican president Dwight D. Eisenhower.

While corporations scrambled to get Owens to endorse their products, the president sent him overseas as a goodwill representative of the government. On one of these tours, when he traveled through Berlin, he met the son of his long-lost friend Luz Long. It was the youngster who broke the news to Owens that Long had been killed in the trenches during the war. Just as he had done with the high jumper years before, Owens talked with the young man late into the night.

Back in Chicago, Owens joined the board of directors of the South Side Boys Club, where he personally organized programs to help out troubled youngsters in the city's black ghetto. Appointed chairman of the Illinois State Athletic Commission, he worked hard to promote sport as a way out of poverty for poor youngsters. Meanwhile, he kept up his usual schedule of publicity appearances and radio shows, somehow finding time to tour the Far East as a goodwill ambassador for the State Department. This was a backbreaking schedule, and it would only accelerate in the years ahead.

But gradually, as Owens raced from airport to airport, he began to tire of it all. He wrote, "I was getting to be just another old jockstrap. . . . Maybe I was fur-lined, but I was still a jockstrap." When his long-standing world records in the 100-yard dash and 400-meter relay fell, that feeling hit him harder. Jesse Owens was 43 years old now. His daughter Marlene had just enrolled at his alma mater, Ohio State University. Yet he had to admit to himself that he still had not found anything to compare with the youthful thrill of those Olympic Games so long ago.

He never would. One by one, his world records fell, the last being his long-jump mark, which Amer-

ican Ralph Boston overtook at the 1960 Olympics in Rome. Interviewed there about his feelings, Owens shrugged and said, "It's like having a pet dog for a long time. You get attached to it, and when it dies you miss it."

That same year, Owens had the haunting experience of appearing on "This Is Your Life," a television show in which celebrity guests won the mixed blessing of being surprised by faces from their past. Coach Charles Riley, old and feeble by now, made the trip from his retirement home in Sarasota, Florida, to Los Angeles for the show. It dawned on Owens that he had not taken the time to see his old mentor in 15 years. And this was the last time the two would meet. Riley died a few months later.

Owens was aware, too, that he hardly knew his family. All three of his daughters were grown and gone. His wife, Ruth, had done what she could to make a good family life for them all, but like the constant world traveler that he had become, Owens realized that his family existed for him primarily as

Owens at a swimming class in Chicago. In the mid-1950s, he received two government appointments to which he was particularly well suited: secretary of the Illinois State Athletic Commission and executive director of the Juvenile Delinquency Prevention Program for the Illinois State Youth Commission. Both jobs required that Owens travel all over the state, organizing and supervising sports activities.

snapshots in his wallet. Yet he could not stop himself. The constant running had begun to seem like a tread-mill that he could not get off.

Owens campaigned for Richard Nixon in 1960 in a losing presidential battle against John F. Kennedy, and in 1965 he joined the hapless New York Mets at their training camp as a running coach. Even a rup-tured disc suffered while with the Mets, and the re-sulting neurosurgery, did not slow him down for long. Meanwhile, the list of products he endorsed grew and grew. His corporate clients included Ford Motor Company, Sears Roebuck, Atlantic-Richfield, and U.S. Rubber. During the 1968 Olympics, he ap-peared in television advertisements for Schlitz beer.

It was at those 1968 Olympic Games, held in Mexico City, that this self-professed "old jockstrap" really began to feel the pinch of age. As usual, he

Still on the run: Owens shows he remains in excellent form 25 years after his world-record-breaking performances at the Big Ten Championships.

arrived at the Games only to be mobbed by throngs of adoring fans. But as a paid consultant to the U.S. Olympic Committee, he had serious work to do. Nineteen sixty-eight was a year of revolt and upheaval around the world. The civil rights movement and opposition to the Vietnam War raged in the United States, and just one week before the Olympics began hundreds of student demonstrators had been shot by police in Mexico City. To a conservative Republican like Jesse Owens, things seemed out of control.

The great American sprinters that year were Tommie Smith and John Carlos, both students at San Jose State University in California. Tall and powerful, Smith had held 11 world records, and he blazed to a new 200-meter mark of 19.8 seconds in the Olympic final. Carlos won the bronze, finishing less than a step behind. They arrived at the podium to receive their medals barefoot. This was intended as a remembrance of black poverty in the United States. As the American flag rose, they raised their right fists encased in black gloves—a black power salute—and bowed their heads.

This gesture was an elegant example of nonviolent protest, but beamed worldwide by satellite television, it set off a wave of indignation in conservative circles. Jesse Owens, the man whose performance in Berlin had itself seemed a protest against Hitler's racism, was called in to help. He sat down with Smith and Carlos afterward, begging them to apologize. He told them, "The black fist is a meaningless symbol. When you open it, you have nothing but fingers—weak, empty fingers. The only time the black fist has significance is when there's money inside. There's where the power lies." Smith and Carlos looked at this man who had been their hero and realized that more than a generation gap lay between them. They refused to apologize and were promptly kicked off the U.S. Olympic team.

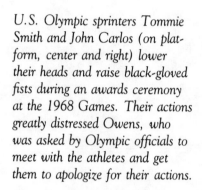

U.S. Olympic sprinters Tommie Smith and John Carlos (on platform, center and right) lower their heads and raise black-gloved fists during an awards ceremony at the 1968 Games. Their actions greatly distressed Owens, who was asked by Olympic officials to meet with the athletes and get them to apologize for their actions.

Owens went home furious. Somehow, he failed to make the connection between their performance in Mexico City and his own in Berlin. With sportswriter Paul Neimarck, he dashed off a book entitled *Blackthink: My Life as Black Man and White Man,* determined to show the world that not all black Americans were militants.

Blackthink, which was published in 1970, is a strange book, filled with a middle-aged man's anger and confusion at a changing world. In it, Owens lashes out at the nation's civil rights leaders, calling them complainers and "pro-Negro bigots." Those civil rights leaders found it hard to forgive Owens for his accusations, particularly this line: "If the Negro doesn't succeed in today's America, it is because he has chosen to fail."

Though the mainstream press supported *Blackthink*, angry letters poured into Owens's Chicago home. His barber refused to cut Owens's hair after reading the book. One reader suggested Owens take another look at the nation he had been racing across for 30 years, including with his letter a copy of the angry autobiography *Soul on Ice* by black militant Eldridge Cleaver. Bewildered by the stir he had caused, Owens sat down and read the book. It opened his eyes to the prejudice and hard times faced by many black Americans, difficulties that, because of his fame, he had been able to skirt most of his life.

So Owens wrote a new book, *I Have Changed*. Published in 1972, it is his apology for the bullheaded arrogance of *Blackthink*. "I realized now," he wrote, "that militancy in the *best* sense of the word was the *only* answer where the black man was concerned, that any black man who wasn't a militant in 1970 was either blind or a coward."

Owens added, however, that for him militancy did not mean violence, unless violence meant survival. He wanted to carve out a middle ground between conservatives and the youthful militants. He called it the "immoderate moderate." Like many Americans of his generation at that time, Owens had been shaken by the events of the 1960s and came out on the other side changed.

Changed, but not slowed down. Writer William O. Johnson, Jr., caught up with him on a speaking tour in 1971 and saw Owens in full stride: "He is a kind of all-around super-combination of nineteenth-century spellbinder and twentieth-century plastic P.R. man, a full-time banquet guest, eternal glad-hander and evangelistic small-talker. Muted, tasteful, inspirational bombast is his stock in trade."

Owens himself might not have argued with Johnson. In *I Have Changed*, he marveled at the half million miles he traveled each year, listing the events of one average week: "In the space of less than seven days, I attended a track meet in Boston, flew from there to Bowling Green for the National Jaycees, then to Rochester for the blind, Buffalo for another track meet, New York to shoot a film called, 'The Black Athlete,' Miami for Ford Motor Company, back up to New York for 45 minutes to deliver a speech, then into L.A. for another the same night."

For years, Ruth had pleaded with her prosperous husband to slow down and enjoy the wealth he had earned. At last, he agreed to move from the hustle and bustle of Chicago to quieter Scottsdale, Arizona. He was 65 years old now, the age when most workers retire. Yet he could not give up the road for the golf links and rarely made it home.

But the great athlete's health gradually began to fail. That winter, he caught pneumonia—the illness that had haunted his childhood. Then, during a speech in St. Louis, Missouri, a few days after Thanksgiving, 1979, Owens had to suddenly leave the stage. He went to see his doctor in Chicago only to hear two terrifying words: lung cancer. Owens had smoked cigarettes for 30 years, and at last the habit had taxed his mighty lungs past their limit.

The doctors treated Owens all winter, only to see him grow weaker. Still, they often caught him on the telephone, lobbying President Jimmy Carter and American athletic officials in an effort to keep them from boycotting the 1980 Olympic Games, which were to be held in Moscow. He lost out in that effort. American athletes did not compete in the 1980 Olympics. But he did not live to hear that news. On March 31, 1980, Jesse Owens died at a hospital in Tucson, Arizona, at the age of 66.

Immediately, plans were made to memorialize the great champion. Two thousand people attended his funeral at Oak Woods Cemetery in Chicago; Ohio

Owens finally received a college degree in 1972, when he was awarded an honorary doctor of athletic arts degree from Ohio State. He received many other accolades in the following years, including the Theodore Roosevelt Award (the National Collegiate Athletic Association's highest honor), the presidential Medal of Freedom, and induction into the Track and Field Hall of Fame.

State University announced that a new track complex would bear his name; athletic awards, scholarships, and annual track meets were created in his honor; and monuments were built to him in his childhood hometowns of Oakville, Alabama, and Cleveland, Ohio. Perhaps the greatest of these memorials was the one in Berlin, Germany. Jesse Owens Strasse became the new name of the street leading to the Olympic Stadium there.

In an effort to make sense of his life, Owens had written in *I Have Changed*: "The lives of most men are patchwork quilts. Or at best one matching outfit with a closet and laundry bag full of incongruous

Owens's granddaughter Gina Hemphill carries the Olympic torch around the Los Angeles Coliseum during the opening ceremonies of the 1984 Olympic Games.

accumulations." Astonishing athlete, advertising man, government emissary—Owens had worn these and many other hats, often at the same time, during his career. Perhaps it was his loss that he never found work that could compare with the athletic challenges of his amateur days, but in the patchwork quilt that he made of his life he touched millions of people in a way that he never could have by following a single line of work.

Owens always knew, however, that his greatest moment had been at the Berlin Olympics in 1936. That was when he proved himself more than a record-breaking athlete; the world discovered that he was a great sportsman as well. His showdown with Nazi chancellor Adolf Hitler has grown into a sports legend, but another aspect of the Games is even more significant. Owens's friendly competition with the German long jumper Luz Long will forever symbolize the way so-called enemies can work together to discover the best within themselves.

Thanks to the adoring attention of filmmaker Leni Riefenstahl's film *Olympiad*, it will always be possible to share the remarkable electric charge that went through the crowd in Berlin's Olympic Stadium in 1936. On the screen, an athlete like no other bursts from the starting line, instantly unfolding into an effortless, fluid stride. His feet seem to barely touch the ground. Before our eyes, he sails past all competitors and into the record books. The race, as Jesse Owens himself said, seems to be over in no time at all and to last an eternity. ❧

Owens's Olympic victories being immortalized in stone at the end of the 1936 Games.

CHRONOLOGY

- - - ❧ - - -

1913	Born James Cleveland Owens on September 12 in Oakville, Alabama
ca. 1922	Moves to Cleveland, Ohio
1927	Enrolls at Fairmount Junior High School; meets Coach Charles Riley
1930	Enrolls at East Technical High School
1933	Equals the world record in the 100-yard dash and breaks the world record in the 220-yard dash at the National Interscholastic Meet; enrolls at Ohio State University
1935	Breaks five world records and equals a sixth at the Big Ten Championships; marries Minnie Ruth Solomon
1936	Breaks the world record in the 100-yard dash; earns a berth on the U.S. Olympic team; wins Olympic gold medals in the 100 meters, 200 meters, long jump, and 400-meter relay; signs agency contract; loses amateur status
1937	Becomes a bandleader and the owner of a basketball team, softball team, and dry-cleaning company
1940	Resumes studies at Ohio State University
1941	Placed in charge of the Civilian Defense Office's national physical fitness program; takes a personnel job with Ford Motor Company
1945	Launches a public relations company
1950	Named the greatest track-and-field athlete in history by the Associated Press; appointed head of Illinois's Athletic Commission and Youth Commission; begins to travel widely as goodwill ambassador for the State Department
1965	Serves as running coach for the New York Mets
1970	Publishes *Blackthink: My Life as Black Man and White Man* and *The Jesse Owens Story*; awarded an honorary doctor of athletic arts degree from Ohio State University
1972	Publishes *I Have Changed*
1980	Dies of lung cancer on March 31 in Tucson, Arizona

FURTHER READING

———————— ❦ ————————

Ashe, Arthur. *A Hard Road to Glory*. New York: Amistad-Warner, 1988.

Baker, William J. *Jesse Owens: An American Life*. New York: Free Press, 1986.

Cromwell, Dean B. *Championship Technique in Track and Field: A Book for Athletes, Coaches, and Spectators*. New York: McGraw-Hill, 1941.

Edwards, Harry. *The Revolt of the Black Athlete*. New York: Free Press, 1969.

Hart-Davis, Duff. *Hitler's Games*. New York: Harper & Row, 1986.

Johnson, William O., Jr. *All That Glitters Is Not Gold: The Olympic Games*. New York: Putnam, 1972.

Kusmer, Kenneth L. *A Ghetto Takes Shape: Black Cleveland*. Urbana: University of Illinois Press, 1976.

Mandell, Richard D. *The Nazi Olympics*. New York: Macmillan, 1971.

Owens, Jesse. *Blackthink: My Life as Black Man and White Man*. New York: William Morrow, 1970.

————. *I Have Changed*. New York: Morrow, 1972.

————. *Jesse: A Spiritual Autobiography*. Plainfield, NJ: Logos International, 1978.

————. *The Jesse Owens Story*. New York: Putnam, 1970.

Robertson, Lawson. *Modern Athletics*. New York: Scribners, 1932.

Wallechinsky, David. *The Complete Book of the Olympics*. New York: Viking Press, 1984.

MADAM
C. J. WALKER

MADAM
C. J. WALKER

A'Lelia Perry Bundles

Senior Consulting Editor
Nathan Irvin Huggins
Director
W.E.B. Du Bois Institute for Afro-American Research
Harvard University

1

"MY OWN FACTORY ON MY OWN GROUND"

Born to former slaves on a Louisiana cotton plantation, Sarah Breedlove Walker spent 20 years as a laundress. At the age of 37, however, she invented a hair-care product that made her the wealthiest black woman in the United States.

STATELY AND HANDSOME, 44-year-old Madam C. J. Walker was brimming with self-confidence as she arrived in Chicago for the 1912 convention of the National Negro Business League (NNBL). She was sure that she could persuade Booker T. Washington, the nation's most influential black spokesman and the NNBL president, to let her address the more than 200 black American entrepreneurs who had journeyed to this Illinois city. Washington had treated her cordially earlier in the year, when she visited Tuskegee Institute, the black vocational school he founded. Moreover, he was aware of Walker's fund-raising efforts for black education.

Poor for most of her life, Walker had invented a new hair-care product when she was 37. By the time she attended the Chicago convention seven years later, she owned and operated her own thriving business, the Madam C. J. Walker Manufacturing Company of Indianapolis, Indiana. Knowing it would encourage them, Walker wanted to tell other black women about her work. Meanwhile, she paid careful attention to the men who addressed the daily sessions.

At the convention's opening meeting, Walker listened closely to one success story after another. Massachusetts real estate broker Watt Terry, for example, told the audience how he had started his career by purchasing a single house; after selling it at a profit, he invested his money and eventually acquired 50 houses and 2 apartment buildings altogether worth half a million dollars.

The accounts of Terry and his fellow businessmen would have been striking under any circumstances. What made them truly remarkable, however, was the race of the speakers. Half a century earlier, almost all the blacks in America had been slaves. In 1860, one of every seven Americans was the property of another.

A handful of owners taught their slaves to read and write and encouraged them to learn skilled trades, but most slaveholders preferred to keep blacks illiterate. Teaching a slave to read, in fact, was a crime in many southern states, and several states passed laws prohibiting blacks from holding jobs that required literacy.

Thus, when the Civil War—and slavery—ended in 1865, blacks were ill equipped to enter the economic mainstream. Those who tried to start their own businesses found it almost impossible to borrow money from white bankers, and blacks who did manage to offer products or services found few white customers. Nevertheless, a number of enterprising blacks established such small but profitable operations as barbershops, catering firms, sail-making shops, funeral homes, pharmacies, and dry-goods stores.

By 1900, when Booker T. Washington, himself a former slave, founded the National Negro Business League to help promote black commerce, the United States boasted some 20,000 black-owned businesses. By the time of the 1912 convention, that number had doubled. But despite these impressive figures, most black Americans still lived in poverty. A black businessman was rare, a black business*woman* even rarer.

Walker found herself especially intrigued by the words of Anthony Overton, who described his Overton-Hygienic Manufacturing Company of Chicago as "the largest Negro manufacturing enterprise in the United States." From the sale of its products, which included cosmetics and baking powder, the Illinois firm had earned more than $117,000 during the previous year. This was just the kind of success Walker hoped to achieve with her own company.

When Overton finished speaking, Washington asked for questions from the audience. George Knox, publisher of the black Indianapolis newspaper *The Freeman*, stood up. "I arise to ask this convention for a few minutes of its time to hear a remarkable woman," he said. "She is Madam Walker, the manufacturer of hair goods and preparations."

Acting as though Knox had not spoken, Washington recognized another audience member. The frustrated Walker suspected that he looked down on her line of work: the manufacture and sale of hair treatments for blacks. Nevertheless, she resolved that the convention would hear from her, even if she had to commandeer the podium. At the next morning's session, she sat patiently through a long lecture by an Indianapolis banker, then another by a Texas banker. As each man returned to his seat, she tried to catch Washington's eye, but with no success.

Finally, while the audience was applauding Washington's remarks about the Texas banker, Walker sprang to her feet. "Surely you are not going to shut the door in my face," she said firmly. "I feel that I am in a business that is a credit to the womanhood of our race. I started in business seven years ago with only $1.50."

The audience looked at her with curiosity. Who was this determined woman with the satiny, cocoa-colored skin and the beautifully groomed hair?

Educator Booker T. Washington, the foremost black spokesman of the early 20th century, founded the National Negro Business League (NNBL) in 1900. Skeptical at first about female entrepreneurs, he ignored Walker at the 1912 NNBL convention, but he later hailed her as "one of the most progressive and successful businesswomen of our race."

"I am a woman who came from the cotton fields of the South," said Walker. "I was promoted from there to the washtub." This line drew a laugh: The position of washerwomen was hardly enviable. "Then I was promoted to the cook kitchen, and from there *I promoted myself* into the business of manufacturing hair goods and preparations," continued Walker in a strong voice. "I have built my own factory on my own ground." Now, serious attention replaced the audience's laughter.

"My object in life is not simply to make money for myself or to spend it on myself," Walker said. "I love to use a part of what I make in trying to help others."

Walker finished her speech and returned to her seat in a wave of applause. When it finally subsided, Knox took the floor. "I arise to attest all that this good woman has said concerning her business," he declared.

That evening, Walker's unscheduled speech was the talk of the convention. Delegates clustered around her after dinner, eager to learn more about this newcomer with the expensive clothes, dignified manner, and firm convictions.

Responding to her colleagues' questions, Walker said she believed that more black women should strike out on their own. "The girls and women of our race," she asserted, "must not be afraid to take hold of business endeavor and . . . wring success out of a number of business opportunities that lie at their very doors."

A few of the men disagreed; their wives, they said, should stay at home and take care of their families. But whether a woman should work or not was not the issue: Most black American women had no choice. Those who were unmarried, widowed, or single parents had to support themselves, and many of the married women had to augment the small incomes their husbands were able to earn.

Black women earned less than any other working group in America. Although a small number had managed to become schoolteachers or nurses, and a few had opened beauty parlors or seamstress shops, most rural black women worked on farms, and most of those in the cities took jobs—when they could find them—as maids, cooks, or laundresses. In the first decade of the 20th century, very few black women earned more than $1.50 per week. (At this point, the average unskilled white worker earned about $11 weekly.)

Walker told the conference delegates about the way her program helped black women. After learning the Walker System of hair care, either at one of her schools or through a correspondence course, a Walker agent could set up shop in her own home, receiving customers and selling Walker products. Her agents, said Walker, enjoyed both newfound independence and an increased income, allowing them to buy homes and send their children to school.

By 1912, Walker had trained more than 1,000 women. They were, she told her listeners, making $5, $10, and even $15 per day. "I have made it possible," she said proudly, "for many colored women

A trio of grocers proudly survey their immaculate shop. Only a generation away from slavery, some 40,000 enterprising black Americans had started their own businesses by 1912.

Friends of Indianapolis's new black YMCA assemble on its steps in 1913. In the front row are (from left) Freeman *publisher George Knox, Madam C. J. Walker, Booker T. Washington,* Indianapolis World *publisher Alex Manning, and YMCA executives R. W. Bullock and Thomas Taylor. Standing at the rear are Walker's longtime business associate, F. B. Ransom (left), and her physician, Colonel Joseph Ward.*

to abandon the washtub for more pleasant and profitable occupation."

As the Chicago convention ended, delegates continued to talk about Madam Walker and her unusual business practices. Even Washington, who had taken no official notice of her, would soon prove he had been impressed by this dynamic, highly motivated woman.

Several months later, Washington and other nationally known black leaders attended the dedication of the new black YMCA in Indianapolis. Sharing the stage with keynote speaker Washington were a number of prominent local blacks—including Madam C. J. Walker. The cosmetics manufacturer had stunned YMCA building-fund officials by contributing $1,000, the largest sum donated by any black benefactor.

Washington told the dedication ceremony's 1,200 guests that the new YMCA would improve the lives of the city's young men. "This building," he said, "should mean less crime, less drink, less gambling, less association with bad characters," and should make its users "more industrious, more ambitious, more economical." Walker must have been warmed when, at the end of his speech, Washington paid tribute to her generosity and her work, which he called "a business we should all be proud of."

At the next NNBL convention, held in Philadelphia a few weeks later, Washington invited Walker to serve as principal speaker. As she walked regally to the podium, he said, "I now take pleasure in introducing to the convention one of the most progressive and successful businesswomen of our race—Madam C. J. Walker."

When Walker concluded her speech, Washington thanked her for "all she has done for our race." Then he added a note Walker must have relished. "You talk about what the men are doing in a business way," he said. "Why, if we don't watch out, the women will excel us!"

That was exactly what Madam Walker intended to do. ❧

2

A HARDWORKING
CHILDHOOD

MADAM C. J. WALKER was born Sarah Breedlove on a Delta, Louisiana, cotton plantation on December 23, 1867. She was the first member of her family to be born free. Perhaps her parents, former slaves Owen and Minerva Breedlove, hoped that her Christmas-season birth was a message of good fortune, a sign that her life would be better than theirs. Optimism, however, could not have come easily to the Breedloves.

The 1867 cotton crop, attacked by bollworms just before harvest time, had been a disaster. When Christmas arrived, the Breedloves had no money to buy presents for Sarah's brother and sister, Alex and Louvenia. Sarah was the family's special and only gift.

Owen and Minerva Breedlove, who were probably born during the 1830s, worked as field hands on Robert W. Burney's Madison Parish (county) cotton plantation. Crops, especially cotton, flourished in the dark, rich soil deposited by the Mississippi River; by 1861, when the Civil War began, Madison Parish had become one of the South's most prosperous farming areas. Because raising and harvesting cotton

Walker was born Sarah Breedlove in this one-room cabin in Delta, Louisiana, in 1867. She was the first member of her family to start life as a free American citizen.

585

required many hands, local planters had acquired slaves in great numbers; blacks in the parish outnumbered whites by almost 10 to 1.

Burney's thousand-acre plantation, one of many that lined this stretch of the Mississippi, included a sprawling manor house nestled among giant oaks and fragrant magnolias. Known as Grand View, the estate offered a sweeping panorama of the bustling city of Vicksburg, across the river in Mississippi.

Steamboats from New Orleans, Memphis, St. Louis, and Louisville plied Vicksburg's harbor, delivering passengers and merchandise on the city's teeming docks and picking up cotton for cloth factories in New England and Europe. Adding to Vicksburg's clatter were the clanking, puffing trains that carried passengers and products east and the ferry boats, their steam whistles hooting, that shuttled goods and people between Vicksburg and Delta.

Vicksburg's location made it a strategic prize during the Civil War. In 1862, Union general Ulysses S. Grant laid siege to the city, hoping to cut communication and supply routes between the Confederacy's eastern and western regions. Grant anchored his gunboats just off Grand View, and used the plantation itself as a battle-staging area.

In an attempt to divert the Mississippi from Vicksburg's strategic bluffs, Union engineers even began to dig a canal through Grand View. The canal project failed, but after almost a year of Union bombardment, the entrenched Confederate forces yielded Vicksburg on July 4, 1863, marking one of the greatest Union victories of the war.

Less than two years later, on April 9, 1865, the South surrendered. The war was over. Like much of the South, Delta lay in ruins, its homes, crops, and livestock destroyed by Union soldiers. Although some newly freed slaves left the plantations, Owen and Minerva Breedlove stayed because they had no other way to support themselves.

Plantation owners, who controlled local governments and state legislatures, often prevented former slaves from buying farmland. After the crop failure of 1867, the federal government ordered black farmers to accept any work they were offered or face arrest for vagrancy. To protect themselves, the Breedloves continued to work for the family that had once owned them, receiving acreage, seed, and tools in return for a share of the crops they raised.

The sharecropping system almost always worked out to the tenants' great disadvantage. Tenants were forced to buy their supplies from the landlord and to process their crops with the landlord's equipment, all at prices he established. At the end of each season of backbreaking labor, "croppers" usually owed their employers more than they had earned. For most, the system amounted to a second bondage.

Unable to afford even one day without working, Minerva Breedlove chopped cotton right up to the day of Sarah's birth. She bore her third child in the drafty, one-room cabin she shared with her family. Although the fireplace at one end provided heat and light, the cabin's roof leaked, and wind whistled through the wooden shutters on its glassless windows. The Breedloves wanted their children to have more than this. They craved education for their offspring because literacy was a symbol of freedom; themselves illiterate, they dreamed of sending Sarah and her siblings to school.

Educating them, however, proved a daunting challenge. Schools for former slaves and their families were scarce, and even these encountered fierce opposition from racists. Refusing to accept blacks' legal right to education, the Ku Klux Klan, the Knights of the White Camellia, the White Brotherhood, and other southern white-supremist groups often burned down black schoolhouses and harassed and even murdered their teachers and pupils.

Another barrier to education for black plantation

Like the child pictured here, Walker went to work in the cotton fields at an early age. Sharecroppers' daughters enjoyed little free time: Along with their mothers, they cooked in the morning, planted and harvested all day, tended the family livestock in the evening, and on Saturday, washed mountains of laundry for white customers.

families was time. Children worked alongside their parents in the cotton fields, leaving only the short periods before planting and after harvesting for school. Sarah probably started working in the fields, carrying water for the older laborers, when she was about five years old. She soon graduated to planting, dropping seeds in the long furrows made by the men and women who pushed the plows.

Every morning, Sarah, Louvenia, and their mother got up at sunrise to cook a breakfast of corn bread, molasses, and fried salt pork. At the same time, they started that night's dinner, preparing the vegetables that would simmer all day in an iron pot. Watching her mother and older sister carefully, Sarah learned quickly. In the evenings, she dug potatoes from the garden, swept the yard, and fed the chickens—whose eggs the family sold for extra pennies.

Saturdays were for laundry, washed in large wooden tubs on the riverbank. From dawn until dark, Sarah, Louvenia, and Minerva Breedlove used wooden sticks and washboards to beat the soil out of their own clothes and those of the white customers who paid them about one dollar per week.

In its own way, laundering was as hard as picking cotton. The huge linen sheets and tablecloths of the Breedloves' customers were heavy and difficult to handle, especially after being soaked in boiling water and strong lye soap. Still, Sarah would recall later, she loved to listen to her mother and the other women sing while they washed; their harmony and rhythm seemed to make some of the job's drudgery evaporate.

Sarah probably heard the older women talk about slavery and their dreams of a better life. Sometimes, when the women's voices blended with the steamboat whistles from the river, Sarah would imagine herself traveling. But most of the time, she and the others simply worked hard.

The combination of endless labor, poor diet, and almost nonexistent medical care left most of the sharecroppers with little resistance to illness. Malaria and yellow fever stalked the hot, humid communities on the Mississippi's banks, regularly taking their toll of women, men, and children. In 1874, when Sarah was seven years old, a particularly severe outbreak of yellow fever claimed many lives in Delta; two of those fatally stricken were Owen and Minerva Breedlove.

Sarah missed her parents terribly, but in the general suffering of the community, her sorrows were overlooked. No one seemed to have time to worry about one lonesome, frightened little girl. The Breedlove children tried to work the land they lived on, but without their parents, they found it impossible. Finally, Sarah's brother, Alex, decided to move to Vicksburg and look for work.

Alone on the farm, Sarah and Louvenia found life harder than ever. Sarah longed to go to school, but she and her sister spent almost all their waking moments at their washtubs, trying to make enough money to stay alive. Only at the end of her long working day did Sarah have even a few moments to call her own; whenever she could, she spent this precious time sitting on the riverbank near the cabin, inhaling the sweet smells of sassafras and flowering plum trees.

On these evenings, she looked across the water at Vicksburg, watching the copper sunlight dance on the windows of the city's elegant homes and long warehouses. She loved to meet the ferry and gaze at the women travelers in their beautiful hats and expensive clothes, so different from her own patched and faded dress.

In 1878, yellow fever struck again. Between July and November, more than 3,000 people around Vicksburg died in the region's worst epidemic yet. To make matters worse, the cotton crop failed that year.

With no work and no money, thousands of blacks, including the Breedlove girls, lost their homes.

They had no choice but to move across the river, where Louvenia hoped she could find work as a washerwoman or servant. Many other Louisiana blacks made the same decision, streaming into Vicksburg in a steady tide. At about this time, the black population—poor, out of work, and in constant dread of the Ku Klux Klan and other racist bands—began to look with interest at a movement known as Afro-American nationalism, or separatism.

Some separatists believed that America's blacks should form all-black colonies outside the United States, particularly in Africa. Others urged their followers to set up new black communities in the

An 1870s photograph shows Vicksburg, Mississippi, which became home for the 11-year-old Walker and her older sister, Louvenia, in 1878. Orphaned and friendless, the two girls made a meager living by washing clothes for wealthy whites.

American West, which promised economic opportunity to people of all races.

Soon after Sarah and Louvenia arrived in Vicksburg, they heard people talking about Dr. Collins, a traveling preacher. Visiting towns along the Mississippi, Collins assured blacks that a ship would soon come to carry them to Africa and deliver them from their "second bondage" of poverty and fear. Collins's talk of deliverance made many people think about the Bible's Moses, who led his people out of bondage and into the Promised Land.

As news of Collins's plan spread, more and more blacks gathered in the towns along the river. But no ship arrived. Stranded, the would-be emigrants further congested the area's already crowded communi-

Benjamin ("Pap") Singleton and his colleague S. A. McClure (right) prepare to board a frontier-bound riverboat in 1879. Singleton, who flooded the South with handbills (opposite page) urging blacks to move to "Sunny Kansas," led hundreds of Exodusters (black settlers) west in the late 1870s.

ties. By early 1879, however, another separatist leader appeared, this one offering a more accessible dream.

Describing Kansas as a land of cheap farmland and freedom from white oppression, black Tennessean Benjamin "Pap" Singleton urged other blacks to join him in a great exodus to the West. Hundreds did, boarding steamboats bound for St. Louis, where they took trains to the frontier. Known as Exodusters, these settlers were to establish several all-black western towns, including Bookertee, Nicodemus, and North Fork Colored.

Standing alone on a Vicksburg dock one day in 1879, 11-year-old Sarah waved as the last boat steamed upriver. She wished she were aboard, sailing away to a new life instead of sharing a drafty shack with her sister and new brother-in-law, Willie Powell, a man she would recall as cruel and contemptuous.

Three years later, Sarah escaped from the domineering Powell. At 14, "to get a home of my own," as she later put it, she married Moses McWilliams, a Vicksburg laborer. She decided his name had a good ring to it: Perhaps, like his biblical namesake, Moses would be a conductor to greener pastures. But jobs were still scarce in the Vicksburg of the 1880s. McWilliams took work where he found it, probably hauling crops to market, repairing streets and railroads, and picking cotton during the harvest season. Sarah continued to work as a washerwoman, as she had since she was a little girl in Delta.

On June 6, 1885, when she was 17, Sarah gave birth to a daughter; she and her husband named their little girl Lelia. Now Sarah was busier than ever, but she was content. If she worked hard enough, she thought, she could someday make Lelia's life easier than her own. Soon after Lelia's second birthday, however, Moses McWilliams was killed in an accident.

At 20, Sarah was suddenly a widow and a single mother. She had no intention of rejoining her sister and brother-in-law, but how could she manage on her own? Discussing her problem with neighbors, Sarah learned that there were jobs for laundresses in St. Louis, where wages were higher than those in Vicksburg. Several acquaintances told Sarah that they had relatives in St. Louis who took in boarders.

All her life, Sarah Breedlove McWilliams had listened to train whistles echoing through the night. With hungry eyes, she had watched steamboats disappear around the river bend to new and exciting places. It was time, she decided, to move on. With a baby on her hip and a boat ticket in her hand, she boarded a northbound riverboat. No matter what the future brought, she told herself, it had to be better than the past.

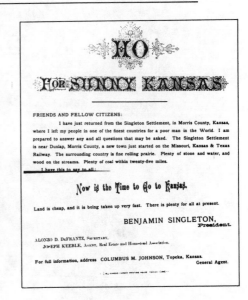

HO For SUNNY KANSAS

FRIENDS AND FELLOW CITIZENS:

I have just returned from the Singleton Settlement, in Morris County, Kansas, where I left my people in one of the finest countries for a poor man in the World. I am prepared to answer any and all questions that may be asked. The Singleton Settlement is near Dunlap, Morris County, a new town just started on the Missouri, Kansas & Texas Railway. The surrounding country is fine rolling prairie. Plenty of stone and water, and wood on the streams. Plenty of coal within twenty-five miles.

I have this to say to all:

Now is the Time to Go to Kansas.

Land is cheap, and it is being taken up very fast. There is plenty for all at present.

BENJAMIN SINGLETON, President.

ALONZO D. DeFRANTZ, Secretary.
JOSEPH KEEBLE, Agent, Real Estate and Homestead Association.

For full information, address COLUMBUS M. JOHNSON, Topeka, Kansas.
General Agent.

3

"I GOT MYSELF A START BY GIVING MYSELF A START"

When Walker arrived in St. Louis, Missouri, in 1888, she joined one of the nation's largest black communities. She also became a member of the St. Paul African Methodist Episcopal Church, a congregation whose members specialized in helping the city's poor.

SARAH McWILLIAMS WATCHED her daughter skip off to school and smiled. Giving Lelia what she lacked herself—an education—made all her sacrifices seem worthwhile.

When the little girl disappeared from view, McWilliams walked through her St. Louis rooming-house hallway to the backyard. There, clustered around the rickety porch, stood her wooden wash-tubs. Years later, she remembered the moment: "As I bent over the washboard and looked at my arms buried in the soapsuds, I said to myself, 'What are you going to do when you grow old and your back gets stiff?' This set me to thinking, but with all my thinking, I couldn't see how I, a poor washerwoman, was going to better my condition."

McWilliams looked at the baskets heaped with dirty clothes, then sighed and wiped her hands on her long, checkered apron. She raised an arm to her forehead, wiped the sweat with her sleeve, and pushed back her calico bandanna. She knew her life was better than it had been when she left Vicksburg six years ago. Still, sometimes she could not help feeling discouraged.

When she and her daughter arrived in St. Louis in 1888, McWilliams had headed for the city's black community. She found it filled with recently arrived people, many of them widowed mothers like herself. In this Mississippi River city of almost half a million residents lived one of the country's largest black populations, some 35,000 people. Swelled by migrants from the Deep South, the black community supported 3 weekly newspapers and more than 100 businesses.

St. Louis's pace was far swifter than Vicksburg's. Hurrying along its clamorous, electric- and gas-lighted streets were white and black Missouri natives, transplanted easterners, and European immigrants. Dress styles ranged from ragged to elegant; vehicles included everything from expensive horse-drawn carriages to shabby peddlers' wagons. By the 1890s, the city would claim the nation's largest brewery, its most important drug manufacturer, and its biggest tobacco factory.

Along the St. Louis riverfront, noisy, brightly lighted saloons and cafés attracted nightly crowds of gamblers, hustlers, and prostitutes. Ragtime, the infectious, syncopated piano music that seemed to come from the heart of black St. Louis, poured from dance halls and bars. People tapped their feet to the rhythms of such popular tunes as "Ragtime Millionaire," with lyrics that captured the hopes and ironic humor of the community: "I'm afraid I may die of money disease / Don't bother a minute about what those white folks care / I'm a ragtime millionaire!"

McWilliams could not imagine herself a millionaire, but she had no trouble in finding work as a washerwoman. It was hard labor and carried no status, but it was better than working as a live-in servant, her only other option. Washing clothes at home meant she could keep an eye on Lelia.

Taking pride in her work, McWilliams carefully scrubbed out spots, added just the right amount of

A laundress scrubs clothes in her backyard tubs. Although Walker continued to hope for a bright future, she sometimes gave in to despair: "I couldn't see," she said, "how I, a poor washerwoman, was going to better my condition."

starch, thoroughly cleaned the rust from her irons, and painstakingly pressed the delicate lace and ruffles of her customers' clothes. When she delivered her laundry, she walked with dignity, a basket of neatly folded clothes balanced atop her head.

McWilliams's delivery route often led her across the Eads Bridge, which spanned the Mississippi River and led to East St. Louis, Illinois. As she walked, she later remembered, she often marveled at the skill of the engineers who had built this great brick-and-steel structure. There must be a way, she had thought, to build a bridge to prosperity for herself and Lelia. In her prayers, she asked God to show her the way.

McWilliams believed God would help her; she also knew she would have to help herself. Working long hours over her steaming tubs, scrimping on necessities, doing without luxuries, she managed to put aside a little money each week. By the time Lelia graduated from high school, her proud mother was able to send her to Knoxville College, a small black institution in Knoxville, Tennessee.

At about this time, McWilliams married again. Little is known of her second husband, John Davis; McWilliams rarely spoke of him except to remark that he was a heavy drinker. She apparently divorced him before her daughter went away to college.

Soon after her move to St. Louis, McWilliams had joined the St. Paul African Methodist Episcopal Church. Established in 1840, St. Paul was the first St. Louis church planned, built, and financed by blacks. Defying the pre–Civil War laws that forbade blacks to learn to read and write, St. Paul sponsored a secret school for its members, and it had long extended its aid to newcomers to the city, helping them find houses and jobs, and supplying them with clothing and other necessities.

The women of the church had proved both friendly and generous to McWilliams. Deeply grateful, she vowed to help others in turn, although she had little money to contribute. After she settled into city life, she joined the Mite Missionary Society, the St. Paul organization that assisted needy members of the community.

Years later, a newspaper article described McWilliams's first activity for the society: "She read in the [St. Louis] *Post-Dispatch* . . . of an aged colored man with a blind sister and an invalid wife depending on him for support. Without acquaintance of any kind with the family, she went among friends

The Eads Bridge forms a backdrop for St. Louis's bustling riverfront in the 1890s. The sight was a familiar one to Walker, who often crossed the bridge with a load of laundry on her head.

in the behalf of the distressed people, succeeding in collecting $3.60 which she gave to them. . . . She felt it was her duty to do even more [so] she arranged for a pound party through which means groceries in abundance were given, also a purse of $7.50."

Among the missionary society's members were a number of prominent, well-educated black women. Through them, McWilliams encountered a new world, peopled with prosperous, cultured blacks. She was dazzled by their stylish dress and formal manners and awed by their ability to organize themselves and become community leaders.

McWilliams was even more impressed by the black leaders who came to St. Louis for the 1904 World's Fair. Mingling with dazzled fairgoers were such luminaries as poet Paul Laurence Dunbar, scholar and political activist W. E. B. Du Bois, and newspaper publisher T. Thomas Fortune. Even the great Booker T. Washington was there, delivering two speeches to spellbound black audiences.

Also taking part in the festivities were 200 delegates of the National Association of Colored Women (NACW). After a meeting at St. Paul church, the NACW members proceeded to the fair, where they listened to an address by Margaret Murray Washington (the wife of Booker T.). Local newspapers ran Washington's picture and reported on her speech, marking the first time that the white St. Louis press had featured positive coverage of any black woman.

Gazing at the immaculately groomed Margaret Washington, Sarah McWilliams reflected on her own appearance. Perhaps, she thought, if she improved it, she might gain some of the self-confidence exuded by Washington and other successful black women. McWilliams always wore neat, crisply starched clothing, the better to advertise her skills as a laundress, but she was self-conscious about her hair;

When Margaret Murray Washington, wife of Booker T. Washington, addressed the St. Louis branch of the National Association of Colored Women in 1904, Walker watched in awe. Washington's calm elegance inspired the 37-year-old laundress to improve her own appearance, starting with her sparse and damaged hair.

broken and patchy, it revealed her scalp in several places.

Countless black women shared McWilliams's hair problems. Sometimes inadequate diets, stress, and poor health caused hair loss; sometimes it was the result of lotions and treatments containing harmful chemicals. Advertisements for hair improvement products—Queen Pomade, La Creole Hair Restorer, Kinkilla, and Ford's Original Ozonized Ox Marrow, for example—crowded the pages of black newspapers.

The manufacturer of Thomas's Magic Hair Grower claimed its product would "cleanse the scalp of dandruff, stop it from falling, and make it grow even on bald spots." Because many blacks looked down on hair straightening as imitative of whites, Thomas's ads stressed that its product was "NOT A STRAIGHTENER." Although they disdained copying white females, few black women wore the traditional hairstyles and elaborate ornaments of their African foremothers, and many yearned for long hair.

The "ideal" American woman of the 1890s had a full bosom, a tiny waist, and a great mass of hair, which she swept to the top of her head. Although not many women of any race could meet all these beauty standards, most tried for lengthy tresses. Women whose hair refused to grow long wore wigs and hairpieces.

Sarah McWilliams asked God to keep her hair from falling out. She also tried a number of patented hair mixtures, including the Poro Company's Wonderful Hair Grower, but with little success. The St. Louis–based Poro Company hired local women to sell its products door to door; for a few months Mc-Williams worked as a sales agent when she was not washing clothes. Then she got a better idea: If she could devise her own hair product, one that really worked for her, she could go into business for herself.

Sketched by artist Charles Dana Gibson, this trio represented turn-of-the-century Americans' ideal woman: wasp waisted, full bosomed, and crowned with long, upswept hair. Few women, black or white, could achieve a "Gibson girl" figure, but most either grew their hair long or wore a hairpiece.

In early 1905, McWilliams informed friends that, with divine help, she had learned how to make the mixture she wanted. God, she later told a reporter, "answered my prayer, for one night I had a dream, and in that dream a big black man appeared to me and told me what to mix up for my hair. Some of the remedy was grown in Africa, but I sent for it, mixed it, put it on my scalp, and in a few weeks my hair was coming in faster than it had ever fallen out. I tried it on my friends; it helped them. I made up my mind I would begin to sell it."

Perhaps because she knew she would be in direct competition with the Poro Company, McWilliams decided to leave St. Louis before starting her new business. She had made one especially good friend in the city: Charles Joseph Walker, a sales agent for a local black newspaper. Except for Walker, she had little reason to remain in Missouri; she had divorced John Davis, and Lelia was still at school in Tennessee.

Once again, McWilliams packed her belongings and headed for a new frontier, this one in Denver.

Countermen await customers in E. L. Scholtz's Denver pharmacy. Family records suggest that the Colorado druggist employed Walker as a cook and that he advised the future cosmetics tycoon about ingredients for her first products: Wonderful Hair Grower, Vegetable Shampoo, and Glossine.

Her brother had recently died, leaving his widow and four daughters in the Colorado city. McWilliams believed they could help each other. For the first time in her life, the 37-year-old woman would leave the Mississippi River area of her birth.

On July 21, 1905, McWilliams arrived at Denver's Union Depot with her savings: $1.50, about a week's pay for her work as a laundress. Colorado's mountains and wide blue skies astonished her, and she found Denver's crisp, dry air a welcome change from the steamy heat of St. Louis. Along the city's wide boulevards, cattlemen, silver miners, land speculators, and frontiersmen jockeyed for their share of the riches and adventure promised by the West.

Colorado's entire population was only slightly larger than that of St. Louis alone. When McWilliams arrived, fewer than 10,000 blacks lived in the state. Even here, where slavery had never taken root, they faced discrimination, but Colorado nevertheless offered blacks the chance to work in state and local government; many had started their own businesses.

Settling into the Mile High City, as Denver is known, McWilliams rented an attic room, joined the Shorter Chapel African Methodist Episcopal Church, and found a job as a cook. According to family records, her employer was probably E. L. Scholtz, a Canadian-born druggist who owned the largest, best-equipped pharmacy west of Chicago. His drugstore compounded both doctors' prescriptions and home medical remedies and tonics.

McWilliams probably consulted Scholtz about ingredients for the hair preparations she was concocting. In any case, she spent her evenings working on her formulas and testing them on herself and her nieces. Finally, she came up with three products that met her requirements. She called them Wonderful Hair Grower, Glossine, and Vegetable Shampoo.

McWilliams saved her money carefully; before long, she could afford to leave her cook's job. To pay her rent, she took in laundry two days each week; the rest of the time she spent in mixing her products and selling them door to door. As a saleswoman, she usually wore a long, dark skirt and a white blouse; she carried her goods in a trim black case.

McWilliams soon proved herself a natural marketer, introducing her products with free demonstrations. After thoroughly washing a woman's hair with her Vegetable Shampoo, the saleswoman applied her Wonderful Hair Grower, a product that contained medication to combat dandruff and other conditions that sometimes caused hair loss. To complete the treatment, McWilliams applied a light oil to the customer's hair, then pressed it with a heated metal comb. This procedure softened the tight curls characterizing the hair of many people of African descent.

McWilliams had targeted her market well: Denver's black women began buying her wares with enthusiasm. At first, she used all her profits for raw materials and advertising. Her ads in the *Colorado Statesman*, a black newspaper published in Denver, generated mail orders, and her personal sales trips produced heartening results.

But McWilliams's best advertisement was herself. A customer who looked at a "before" picture, and then at the saleswoman herself, could hardly fail to be impressed. When McWilliams announced that her long, well-groomed hair was the product of her treatments, the customer was almost sure to place an order.

McWilliams, who had stayed in touch with her St. Louis friend, Charles Joseph Walker, wrote to him about her growing business. After providing a steady stream of advice by mail, Walker, known to all as C.J., showed up in Denver in person. Already fond of each other, the two soon decided to marry; their wedding ceremony took place on January 4, 1906.

Familiar with newspaper promotion campaigns, Walker helped his wife expand her mail-order business. Together, they manufactured and sold such products as C. J. Walker's Blood and Rheumatic Remedy and the newly named Madam C. J. Walker's Wonderful Hair Grower.

Sarah Walker began calling herself Madam not only to identify her marital status but to give her products more appeal. The title also evoked thoughts of the world's fashion and beauty capital, France, where married women were called Madame. In the United States of the 1890s, women had few guaranteed legal rights; they could not vote, and in most states, could not even own property. Worse off, of course, were black women, who were frequently stereotyped as childlike and ignorant. Thus, many black women in the public eye, such as opera singer Madame Lillian Evanti, adopted the title to convey an image of worth and dignity.

By the time the Walkers' business was bringing in $10 per week, C. J. Walker decided it had reached its full potential. Not so his wife: Sarah Walker believed that if they only knew about it, women all over the country would buy her Wonderful Hair Grower. Accordingly, she made plans for an extended sales trip.

Her husband and other advisers predicted she would not even earn enough to pay her expenses. She left anyway, setting out in September 1906 for what would become a year and a half of traveling to nine states, including Oklahoma, Louisiana, Mississippi, and New York. Within a few months, she was making weekly sales of $35, more than twice the salary of the average white American male worker, and 20 times that of the average black woman worker.

By this time, Lelia, now 21 years old, had graduated from college. She moved to Denver to help run the mail-order business while her mother traveled. Elegantly dressed, nearly six feet tall, and regal of bearing, Lelia gave the company added distinction. She also demonstrated a flair for business, but even with the help of her four cousins, Anjetta, Thirsapen, Mattie, and Gladis, she could barely keep up with the orders her mother kept pouring in.

On the road, Sarah Walker was doing more than selling; she was training agents who could demonstrate and take orders for Walker products in return for a share of the profits. By the spring of 1908, she had signed on dozens of representatives and brought her company's monthly income to a breathtaking $400. Running a now vast mail-order operation, she decided to move her company closer to the nation's population centers.

After a visit to Pittsburgh, Walker selected the Pennsylvania city as her new base of operations. A thriving industrial and banking center, Pittsburgh boasted a sophisticated transportation system, a convenient source of steel for Walker's pressing combs, and a rapidly increasing black population.

In Pittsburgh, Walker rented an office on Wylie Avenue, the main street of the city's black community. She shared the bustling neighborhood with 45 churches, 5 lawyers, 22 doctors, and dozens of businesses, including tailor shops, restaurants, funeral

Vegetable Shampoo, one of the Walker company's most popular offerings, promised to ease dandruff and other scalp problems. Most manufacturers of black hair-care products promoted their wares with light-skinned models, but Walker—correctly assuming that customers would respond to a woman who looked more like them—used her own likeness on packages and ads.

parlors, and pharmacies. The area was home to a number of prosperous black families, but most of the city's blacks worked in service jobs or as laborers.

Although the bulk of Pittsburgh's mining and manufacturing jobs went to newly arrived European immigrants, waves of black southerners poured steadily into the city, eager to take whatever work they could find. Businesswoman Walker saw the influx of blacks as a source of new agents and customers.

In the summer of 1908, Sarah Walker's daughter joined her in Pittsburgh. Together, the women opened a beauty parlor and a training school for Walker agents, which they called Lelia College. A graduate from the school would be known, they decided, as a hair culturist.

Word of the new college spread quickly. Applying for entrance were housekeepers, office cleaners, laundresses, and even schoolteachers, women whose needs and dreams Walker understood well. Over the next two years, Lelia College turned out scores of hair culturists, most of whom were delighted with their new careers.

In a letter to Walker, one graduate said, "You have opened up a trade for hundreds of colored women to make an honest and profitable living where they make as much in one week as a month's salary would bring from any other position that a colored woman can secure."

In 1910, the *Pennsylvania Negro Business Directory* ran a feature story about Walker, whom it called "one of the most successful businesswomen of the race in this community." Accompanying the article was a photograph of Walker, showing a woman dramatically changed in the course of only a few years. Posed with her hands clasped behind her back and her long hair pinned atop her head, Walker looked confident and dignified. Her high-necked,

A 1910 photograph of the 43-year-old Walker shows a serene, fashionably attired woman, strikingly different in appearance from the neat but shabbily dressed laundress of earlier days.

lace-bodiced gown more closely resembled her former customers' clothing than the threadbare gingham dresses she had worn during her days as a laundress.

As she rose in her career, Walker found herself sought out by the city's most prominent black citizens, including clergymen and the women who headed community and church organizations. The kind of people she had once admired from afar were now admiring her.

4

GEARING UP

❧

Pittsburgh provided fertile ground for the early growth of Madam C. J. Walker's business. During the two years she spent in the booming Pennsylvania city, Walker trained scores of hair culturists at Lelia College and turned her mail-order and door-to-door operations into a profitable business. Still, she felt restless.

Despite Pittsburgh's commercial potential, Walker yearned for broader horizons; by 1910, she was scouting for a new city in which to establish a permanent national headquarters. When she visited Indianapolis, Indiana, in February, she decided she had found the spot. Sometimes called the Crossroads of America, the midwestern city was situated at the heart of the nation's transportation network, a major asset for a mail-order operation. Also attractive to Walker was Indianapolis's thriving black business community.

Although Indianapolis lacked a major waterway, it had become the country's largest inland manufacturing center because of its access to eight major railway systems. More than 1 million freight cars passed through the city's rail yards annually, and nearly 200 passenger trains arrived and departed daily.

In the first two decades of the 20th century, Indianapolis was the center of America's automobile

Moving from Pittsburgh to Indianapolis in 1910, Walker swung into high gear: She legally incorporated her business, opened a factory, and started assembling the dedicated and talented staff that would help turn her company into one of the nation's top black-owned enterprises.

industry; in 1909, the city built the Indianapolis Speedway. (Originally designed to test-drive cars, the Speedway became a racecourse after the first Indy 500 race in 1911.) The city was also home to scores of large manufacturing and industrial companies.

When he met Walker on her first visit to his city, Indianapolis newspaper executive George L. Knox strongly advised her to settle there. Knox, who published *The Freeman*, one of the nation's most widely read black newspapers, backed his argument for Indianapolis by telling Walker his own story.

Born a slave in 1841, he had arrived in Indianapolis in 1864. After spending some years apprenticed to a black barber, he opened his own 10-chair barbershop in one of the city's large hotels. Knox used his access to his wealthy white customers to advance himself economically and politically; by the late 1890s, he had become the city's leading black businessman and the state's most powerful black Republican.

His own success, Knox assured Walker, was by no means unique in Indianapolis. The black community's main thoroughfares, Indiana Avenue and North West Street, were lined with thriving businesses: cafés, offices, and such assorted enterprises as Belle Davis's catering firm, Oliver Martin's coal company, and Archie Greathouse's saloon and restaurant.

Knox probably also mentioned H. L. Sanders, a former hotel waiter who had become America's most prosperous black uniform manufacturer. At the time of Walker's visit, Sanders, his wife, and their 25 employees were producing uniforms and work clothes for hospital aides, hotel workers, janitors, and domestic employees across the nation.

After noting the natural assets of Indianapolis and observing the civic pride of Knox and other Indianapolis boosters, Walker made up her mind. "I was so impressed with [Indianapolis] and the cordial welcome extended," she said later, "that I decided to make this city my home."

Leaving her 24-year-old daughter—who had married John Robinson, a Pittsburgh hotel worker, in 1909—in charge of the company's Pittsburgh operations, Walker moved to Indianapolis with her husband in the spring of 1910. Shortly after she settled in, Knox introduced her to another recent arrival, a young black attorney named Robert Lee Brokenburr. Born in 1886 in Hampton (then Phoebus), Virginia, Brokenburr had attended Hampton Institute—Booker T. Washington's alma mater—and graduated from the Howard University Law School in 1909.

At Knox's recommendation, Walker hired Brokenburr as a part-time legal adviser. In September 1911, he filed articles of incorporation for the Madam C. J. Walker Manufacturing Company, a corporation that would "manufacture and sell a hairgrowing, beautifying and scalp disease–curing preparation and clean scalps with the same."

Listed as the new company's officers were Walker, her husband, and her daughter. Walker, who hoped Brokenburr would work for her full time, asked the young lawyer to serve as acting president and treasurer of the company's board of directors. More interested in law than business, he declined the offer.

During her travels, Walker had met another young attorney, Freeman Briley Ransom. Born in Grenada, Mississippi, in 1882, Ransom had studied at Columbia University Law School, moved to Indianapolis in 1911, and set up his own law office. In exchange for room and board in Walker's home, he gave her free legal advice.

As her travel schedule became heavier, Walker realized she needed someone with legal expertise to oversee her company's day-to-day operations. After much discussion, she persuaded Ransom to sign on as general manager and attorney; still maintaining his

Robert Lee Brokenburr, a graduate of Howard University, started working for Walker in 1910. Soon afterward, the 24-year-old Virginia-born attorney filed articles of incorporation for the Madam C. J. Walker Manufacturing Company, a business that would make and sell "a hairgrowing, beautifying and scalp disease–curing preparation and clean scalps with the same."

Lelia College graduate Alice Kelly was a Kentucky schoolteacher when she met Walker in 1911. Spotting the self-assured young woman as an ideal employee, Walker hired her, sent her to Indianapolis, and soon named her forewoman of the Walker company's bustling factory.

private law practice, Brokenburr agreed to become the company's assistant manager.

Brokenburr and Ransom frequently disagreed on political and philosophical issues, but they respected each other and worked well as a business team. And, like many young black professionals of the time, they shared a sense of pioneering; Walker knew she could count on them to protect her business interests while she was traveling.

With her daily operations now under firm control, she began focusing her attention on the company's future, seeking skilled people to help her expand it. Everywhere she went, she recruited new Walker agents and employees for her main office. On one southern sales trip, she met Alice Kelly, a teacher at Kentucky's Eckstein Norton Institute. Impressed with the younger woman's decisive, confident manner, Walker offered her a job.

Kelly learned quickly, and Walker soon named her forewoman of the Indianapolis factory. Walker also hired one of Kelly's former students, Violet Davis Reynolds, as her private secretary. So impressed was Walker with the tall, self-assured Kelly, in fact, that she even entrusted her with the company's secret hair-grower formula, until then known only by Walker and her daughter.

Kelly's strong-willed personality—and the fact that she knew the secret formula—created tension between her and Ransom. Aware of the conflict between her two top executives, Walker urged them to settle their differences. "They worked that out," another Walker employee recalled years later, "because they knew they'd have to get along to do what Madam wanted them to do."

The more successful Walker became, the more she wanted to improve her communications skills. Acutely aware of her own lack of formal education, she sought the cultured Kelly's advice on social etiquette, penmanship, public speaking, letter writing, and literature. Acting as both traveling companion and tutor, Kelly often accompanied her boss on sales trips.

Walker continued her lessons at home and in her Indianapolis office. Each morning, as she sat at her desk reading the newspapers, she asked secretary Reynolds or bookkeepers Lucy Flint and Marie Overstreet to look up unfamiliar words in the dictionary. Thus, as she educated herself, she educated her staff; she knew that her company's continued success depended on knowledgeable employees.

Walker's many sales trips, as well as her extensive advertising campaigns in the nation's black newspapers, brought daily product orders from all over the United States. Walker got especially good results from the advertisements she placed in George Knox's widely circulated paper, *The Freeman*.

C. J. Walker, an experienced newspaper sales agent, probably designed his wife's most effective ad, one that described Walker's business success and included testimonials from satisfied customers and company agents. The Walker advertisements stood out from those of other hair-care companies because they included dramatic photographs showing Walker before and after using her most popular product, Wonderful Hair Grower.

Within a year of her arrival in Indianapolis, Walker announced a set of impressive statistics: Her company now had 950 agents nationwide and a monthly income of $1,000. She put her profits back into the business, expanding her factory and hiring new employees. Situated in the heart of the city's black community, the Walker company employed neighborhood women almost exclusively. After an intensive training program in hair and beauty culture, the graduates served a stream of eager customers, giving them scalp treatments, restyling their hair,

As Walker's private secretary, Violet Davis Reynolds did more than type, file, and take dictation; her responsibilities also included helping her boss acquire the education she had missed. Whenever Walker came across an unfamiliar word, she asked Reynolds and other office workers to look it up, thus broadening the knowledge of all concerned.

F. B. Ransom, Walker's general manager, checks out an order in his Indianapolis office. Starting his association with Walker as a part-time lawyer, Ransom would eventually become her second-in-command and most trusted adviser.

and administering manicures and massages.

Always serious about her work, Walker also found time for culture and amusement. She became a patron of the arts, often hosting concerts and poetry readings, and she gradually filled her home with art objects. On her walls hung oil paintings she had commissioned from black artists; in her parlor stood a mahogany baby grand piano, along with a custom-made phonograph and a harp, both covered with gold leaf. Walker often spent her evenings listening to recorded music, reading in her library, or playing Flinch, a popular card game of the day, with friends.

Fascinated by the era's grand theaters and thrilling silent films, Walker had also become an enthusiastic moviegoer; among her favorites were Charlie Chaplin's comedies and the elaborate epics of director Cecil B. De Mille. One afternoon, however, Walker's expectation of a pleasant hour at the cinema turned to disappointment and anger.

Arriving at Indianapolis's Isis Theatre, she gave the ticket seller a dime, standard admission price at the time. The agent pushed the coin back across the counter. The price, she said, was now 25 cents. Responding to Walker's quizzical look, the seller explained that the admission price had gone up—but only for "colored persons."

Furious, Walker went home and instructed attorney Ransom to sue the theater. He duly filed a complaint, accusing the Isis and its agents of practicing "unwarranted discrimination because of the color of this plaintiff" and asking for the imposition of a $100 fine. (No further records of the suit exist; the theater probably settled the complaint out of court.)

Walker, who rarely took half measures, next sent for an architect. For some time, she had been thinking about building a larger factory and office building. Now she decided to begin work at once. Completed some years later, the Walker Building would cover an entire block in downtown Indianapolis—and would include an elegant movie theater specifically operated for the city's black residents.

Few members of Indianapolis's black population—about 10 percent of the city's 233,650 people in 1919—escaped encounters with discrimination. Obviously, Walker was no exception, but her wealth and prominence gave her entrée into some areas closed to most blacks. The city's bankers, for example, treated her cordially—as they would treat any customer who deposited thousands of dollars each year. Recognizing her efficiently run company as a solid investment, Indianapolis banks willingly lent her money for expansion.

Walker also received a warm welcome in the city's department stores and automobile showrooms. One white jeweler, apparently color-blinded by Walker's purchases of silverware and diamonds, made it a point to rush out of his shop and greet her whenever he saw her car arrive.

Although she enjoyed driving herself, Walker employed a chauffeur to take her on pleasure trips.

On summer evenings, she sat in the backseat of her luxurious automobile with Alice Kelly or her nieces, Anjetta and Thirsapen Breedlove, as her driver piloted the car around Indianapolis. Gliding past the expensive homes on the city's north side, then through the industrial districts, the chauffeur maneuvered the vehicle through streets crowded with horses and wagons, automobiles, bicycles, streetcars, and the electric trains known as interurbans.

The Isis Theatre, a popular Indianapolis movie palace, established a new admissions policy in 1912: White patrons would continue to pay a dime, but the price for "colored persons" went up to a quarter. Outraged, movie-lover Walker immediately sued the Isis for "unwarranted discrimination."

In the midst of her success, Walker began to have serious disagreements with her husband about control of the company and plans for its expansion. Business differences spilled over into the couple's personal life, finally resulting in an agreement to end the marriage. Sarah Walker filed for divorce in late 1912, but she would retain her husband's name for the rest of her life. Ironically, C. J. Walker remained a Walker agent for the rest of his life.

5

LADY BOUNTIFUL

A FTER HER DIVORCE, Walker became even more involved in her company, which, by the end of 1912, employed some 1,600 agents and produced weekly—instead of monthly—revenues of nearly $1,000. Meanwhile, Walker's daughter—recently divorced but now known as A'Lelia Walker Robinson—was beginning to extend the company's East Coast operation into New York City.

On one of her frequent visits to Indianapolis, A'Lelia Robinson noticed 13-year-old Mae Bryant, a neighborhood girl who sometimes ran errands for the Walker enterprises. Because Mae had long, thick hair, Robinson thought she would make an excellent model for Walker products.

Etta Bryant, a poor widow who had recently moved to Indianapolis with her children, agreed to let her daughter model. As the Walker women came to know Mae better, they realized she was not only a good-natured but an unusually bright child, one who might benefit from the advantages their wealth could provide.

Mae spent more and more time with the Walkers. Eventually, the childless Robinson asked Etta Bryant to let her adopt Mae. She would, she assured Bryant,

Seated in the back of their elegant touring car, Walker (right) and her daughter, A'Lelia, prepare to take a spin around town. Although she was an excellent driver, Walker usually rode behind her chauffeur, Otho Patton.

619

Long-haired Mae Bryant was 13 years old when A'Lelia Walker Robinson hired her as a model for Walker products. Charmed by the bright, attractive young woman, Robinson eventually adopted her, providing Walker with her only grandchild.

give the girl a good education and be sure she kept in constant touch with her family in Indianapolis. Aware that Robinson could give Mae much more than she herself could, Bryant consented to the adoption.

When Robinson returned to Pittsburgh, Mae went with her. And when Walker came through on her sales trips, she often picked Mae up, taking her along to learn the business. With her new granddaughter, Walker spent much of the summer of 1912 along the East Coast and in the upper southern states, giving lectures and promoting business at conventions held by black religious, fraternal, and civic organizations.

After each lecture, Walker asked her audience to endorse her as the "foremost colored businesswoman in America," a title she hoped would give her an edge over her competitors. Most of the groups obliged willingly.

In July 1912, Walker attended the annual conference of the National Association of Colored Women, held in Hampton, Virginia. There she met Mary McLeod Bethune, the 37-year-old founder of the Daytona Normal and Industrial Institute for Negro Girls. Determined to bring schooling to a Florida area that offered blacks no education at all, Bethune had struggled to open her tiny institute in 1904. By 1912, the school, at that point accepting boys as well as girls and known as the Daytona Educational Industrial Training School, had expanded vastly.

Impressed by Bethune and her work with black youngsters, Walker volunteered to lead a fund-raising effort for the school's benefit. The two women's mutual respect led to a lifelong friendship.

From Virginia, Walker continued her tireless pilgrimage, speaking and demonstrating her products at black churches, Masonic lodges, and public halls. By train and by car, she visited hundreds of communities, sometimes traveling with her nieces, sometimes with her granddaughter. The young women helped with the demonstrations and other chores, peppering each town with Walker leaflets and booklets, then signing up new Walker agents. When a community was too small for a scheduled train stop, Walker and her aides tossed company literature to the crowds waiting along the tracks.

Because telephone service at the time was limited and sometimes unreliable, Walker depended on the mail to communicate with her staff. From the road, she wrote almost daily letters to her daughter and to Ransom, instructing them on company operations, describing her sales efforts, and relating personal tidbits and details. Back in Indianapolis, each day's mail delivery brought hundreds of dollars worth of orders from Walker and her agents. In a May 1913 letter to Walker, Ransom said, "Your business is increasing here every day. I think you are the money making wonder of the age."

Ransom, who looked on himself as Walker's financial watchdog, sometimes gently scolded her for what he regarded as extravagance. In one letter to him, Walker said, "Am writing to let you know I have given a check for $1,381.50 to the Cadillac Motor Co. Won't you see to it that the check is cashed? . . . I guess you think I am crazy, but I had a chance to get just what Lelia wanted in a car. . . ." Ransom's response: "No, I don't think you crazy, but think you very hard on your bank account. I take pleasure in the fact that there can hardly be anything else for you to buy, ha, ha!!"

Convinced that the company needed a base in New York City, A'Lelia Robinson persuaded her mother to buy a house there. For its location, Robinson selected Harlem, the uptown Manhattan area then just starting to attract black residents. By the late spring of 1913, Robinson had acquired a town house on 136th Street, near Lenox Avenue,

A'Lelia Walker Robinson, who posed for this portrait around 1907, moved to New York City in 1913. Intrigued with Harlem, the city's burgeoning black community, she talked her mother into buying a house there and then turned it into a stylish residence and beauty salon. The place delighted Walker. "There is nothing to equal it," she said, "not even on Fifth Avenue."

which she turned into living quarters and a beauty salon.

Arriving in New York with Alice Kelly in the midst of the renovation, Walker was delighted with what she saw. "In regards to this house," she wrote Ransom, "you will agree with Lelia when she said that it would be [a] monument for us both. . . . The Hair Parlor beats anything I have seen anywhere, even in the best Hair Parlors of the whites. There is nothing to equal it, not even on Fifth Avenue." Walker was not alone in her admiration for her daughter's handiwork. The *Defender* called the new establishment "the most completely equipped and beautiful hair parlor that members of our Race ever had access to."

Delighted with the project or not, Walker could not stay in one place for long. She spent the rest of that summer and early fall traveling with her chauffeur, Otho Patton, in her new seven-passenger Cole touring car. This time, the Walker women hit a score of East Coast cities, including Philadelphia, Atlantic City, Baltimore, and Washington, D.C.

In the nation's capital, Walker gave speeches in 10 churches, among them the First Baptist Church in Georgetown and the downtown Metropolitan AME Church. Lecturing on "The Negro Woman in Business," she told audiences how she had achieved success through hard work and careful planning, then urged other women to follow her example and establish their own businesses.

"Now I realize that in the so-called higher walks of life, many were prone to look down upon 'hair dressers,' as they called us," she told her listeners. "They didn't have a very high opinion of our calling, so I had to go down and dignify this work, so much so that many of the best women of our race are now engaged in this line of business," she added proudly.

Walker's host in Washington was R. W. Thompson, national correspondent for *The Freeman*. "Mme

This photograph, one of a series that illustrated Walker's Text Book of Beauty Culture, *shows Alice Kelly receiving a hot-comb treatment. The hands belong to Walker herself.*

Walker," he later wrote, "is essentially a business-woman, and no matter where she goes or on whatever errand, she talks business. She . . . never loses the opportunity to emphasize to her sisters the importance of their getting into the world of business, of acquiring a footing in the soil, making themselves financially independent and setting an example for all people of thrift, industry and the practical application of their mental training."

The more Walker traveled and the more new ideas and new people she encountered, the more possibilities she saw. On her way home from Washington, she began thinking about expanding her business overseas. People of African descent—potential customers—lived all over the world, she reasoned. Central America, the Caribbean, and South America had heavily concentrated black populations. Why not develop an international market?

After some quick research on the area, Walker sailed for the West Indies in November 1913. Five days later, she arrived in Kingston, Jamaica, with her touring car and enough products and clothes to last three months. With Jamaica as her base, she visited Cuba, Haiti, Costa Rica, and the Panama Canal Zone, demonstrating her Walker Hair Care Method just as she had done throughout the United States. And just as they had done in the United States, women flocked to see her, to buy her goods, and to sign on as her agents.

When she returned to Indianapolis in January, Walker found her office and factory employees working furiously to fill the ever-mounting product orders. To celebrate her success, she engaged entertainer Noble Sissle and invited a throng of relatives and friends to a spring dance. At Walker's home, guests admired her fine Oriental rugs and antique furniture, nibbled delicate hors d'oeuvres, and sipped punch served from a huge silver bowl. Sarah Breedlove Walker had come a long way from a sharecroppers' cabin in Louisiana.

The following summer, Walker made a whirlwind tour of the Northeast, tirelessly promoting her products and giving dozens of speeches. As usual, audiences received her with enthusiasm. "My lecture Monday night was a grand success," she wrote business manager Ransom from one New England town. "The house was packed. The people applauded so I hardly had time to talk. . . . I have been entertained two and three times a day ever since I've been here. Haven't had a day or evening to myself."

Walker, who made increasingly frequent trips to New York, liked the city better with each visit. Harlem, buzzing with politics, business, music, and theater, gave her renewed energy. She found herself sought out by the black community's most prominent residents: composer and conductor James Reese Europe, who had performed at Carnegie Hall in 1912; Fred Moore, publisher of *New York Age*; Shakespearean actor Richard B. Harrison, who had toured with

Walker's friend William Monroe Trotter (1872–1934) edited a crusading Boston newspaper, the Guardian, and founded the National Equal Rights League. Considered radical at the time, Trotter's demands for racial integration and social justice foreshadowed the national civil rights movement of the 1960s.

poet Paul Laurence Dunbar; and Philip A. Peyton, a real estate speculator whose Afro-American Realty Company had helped open Harlem to black tenants and homeowners. By 1915, Walker was spending almost as much time in New York as in Indianapolis. She began to think about moving east.

Life in the Midwest, however, continued to provide challenge and excitement. Walker's home attracted people of all political persuasions; she agreed with few entirely, but she relished the debates produced by deeply held, conflicting ideas. Among her guests in the spring of 1915, for example, was the conservative Robert Russa Moton, an associate of Booker T. Washington and president of the National Negro Business League. To ensure an evening of spirited dialogue, Walker also invited a group representing widely divergent political opinions: journalist George Knox, Indianapolis YMCA secretary Thomas Taylor, and attorneys Robert Brokenburr and F. B. Ransom.

On another spring evening, Walker received a visit from journalist and activist William Monroe Trotter. The first black member of Phi Beta Kappa, the national scholarship fraternity, Trotter had graduated from Harvard College in 1896. He became publisher and editor of the *Guardian*, a crusading Boston newspaper, and later founded the National Equal Rights League. Admired by many, Trotter had also become a center of controversy because of his opposition to Booker T. Washington's politically conservative philosophy.

Walker differed with Washington herself, particularly on the issue of women in leadership roles, but she deeply respected him as a ground-breaking educator. And although she disagreed with most of Trotter's criticisms of Washington, she admired his political activism and dedication to racial justice. No matter what their positions on the political spectrum, Walker took a broad view of all blacks who worked for what she called "the betterment of the race."

By late summer Walker was traveling again, this time to previously untapped markets in Colorado, Utah, Montana, Oregon, Washington, and California. By now, she had added an effective new dimension to her lectures: a slide show featuring illustrations of her hair-care system along with photographs of black leaders and schools and businesses founded by blacks.

Shortly after her return to headquarters, Walker made an announcement: She had decided to move to New York City. Her manufacturing operation, she said, would remain in Indianapolis under the management of Ransom, Brokenburr, and Kelly.

Walker's associates greeted her announcement with some alarm, and many tried to persuade her to reconsider. Ransom protested vigorously, insisting that the move would be too expensive, and that it would interfere with Walker's ability to run the business. But Walker had made up her mind. She wanted to live in New York, the center of progressive black thinking and activity.

The night before Walker left Indianapolis, she sat in her bedroom gazing at a faded picture of her father, thinking about how far she had come in her 48 years. As a large group of friends waited for her below, she reminisced about her arrival in Indianapolis six years earlier. Few people had heard of her then; now she was known as "the foremost businesswoman of the race."

Less than a decade earlier, Walker had been struggling to meet her own expenses. Now people called her Lady Bountiful for her contributions to orphanages, schools, and other charities. As she headed downstairs, she heard voices raised in song. The melody was "Auld Lang Syne": "Should auld acquaintance be forgot . . ."

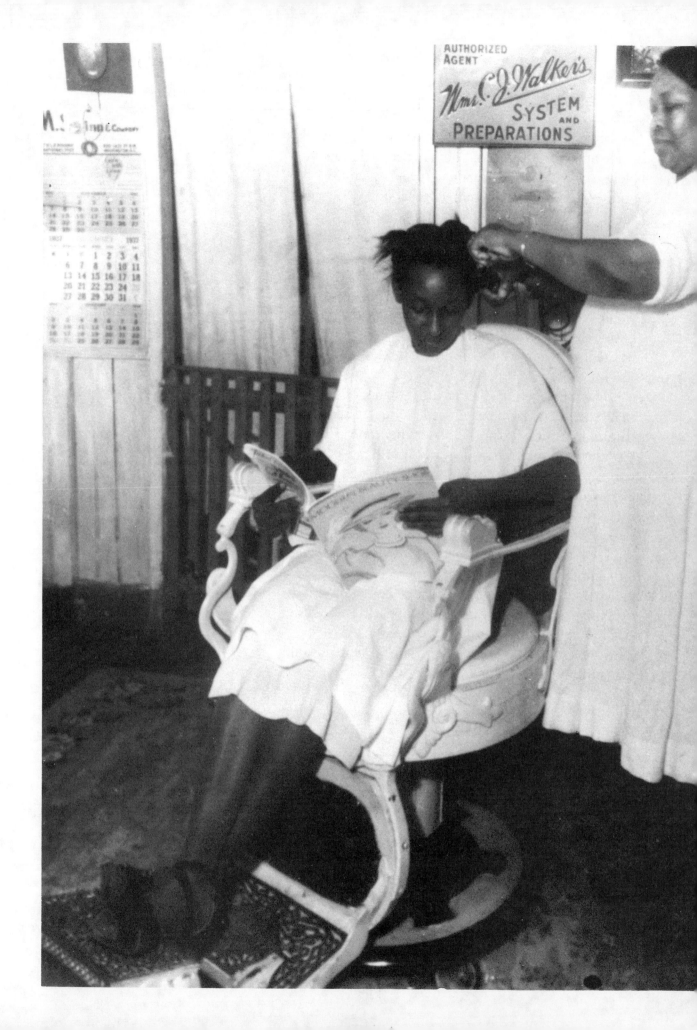

6

"DON'T SIT DOWN AND WAIT"

⟪❧⟫

A T THE ROOT of Madam C. J. Walker's astonishing success lay her self-confidence, boosted by her first sale and increased by those that followed. That sense of assurance, born of economic independence, impressed other women, impelling them to buy her products and to follow her example. She briskly encouraged them to do both.

Addressing the 1914 convention of the National Negro Business League, held in Muskogee, Oklahoma, Walker had said: "I am not merely satisfied in making money for myself, for I am endeavoring to provide employment for hundreds of the women of my race. I had little or no opportunity when I started out in life, having been left an orphan. . . . I had to make my own living and my own opportunity! But I made it! That is why I want to say to every Negro woman present, don't sit down and wait for the opportunities to come. . . . Get up and make them!"

Helping to make those opportunities, Walker hired black women at all levels, from factory worker to national sales agent. By 1916, she employed

Working in her home beauty salon, a Walker agent demonstrates her skills. Walker's program enabled thousands of black women to find independence and self-esteem. "I have all I can do at home," reported one agent happily, "and don't have to go out and work for white people in kitchens and factories."

629

20,000 agents in the United States, Central America, and the Caribbean. These women often wrote letters expressing their feelings about working for Walker: Florida agent Lizzie Bryant, for example, said, "I have all I can do at home and don't have to go out and work for white people in kitchens and factories."

At the time, black women workers in the North earned an average weekly salary of $10; their southern counterparts brought home less than $2 per week. Walker-trained women fared much better. "A diploma from Lelia College of Hair Culture is a Passport to Prosperity," assured one advertisement. In a 1913 letter to the company, Mrs. Williams James of Columbus, Ohio, said, "We have been able to purchase a home and overmeet our obligations. Before I started out as an agent in Madam Walker's employ, I made the regular working woman's wage, but at this writing I average $23 a week."

"Open your own shop. Secure prosperity and freedom. Many women of all ages, confronted with the problem of earning a livlihood have mastered the Walker System," read a typical Walker ad. In an era of wildly exaggerated advertising, the Walker claims were rather modest. They were also truthful. Almost any woman with drive, determination, and creativity could pass the Walker course, whether she took it by mail, at one of the Lelia Colleges in Pittsburgh, New York, or Indianapolis, or from Walker and her traveling instructors.

One of Walker's top representatives, Marjorie Stewart Joyner, credited her husband's mother with her success. Telling her story years later, Joyner said that as a recent graduate of a white beauty school, she had offered to shampoo and style her mother-in-law's hair. But Joyner's technique, learned on naturally straight Caucasian hair, failed to work on her relative's hair.

Instead of being angry, the elder Mrs. Joyner gave her daughter-in-law some advice. "She said she had heard of a black woman who was coming to Chicago to teach a course about our hair," Joyner recalled later. "And she gave me $17 to take the course."

Teaching that course was Madam C. J. Walker, who showed Joyner how to use a hot steel comb to dry and soften the hair. Joyner, who found the process "amazing," repaid Walker by demonstrating the "French marcel wave," a technique she had learned in the white beauty school. Impressed, Walker asked the young woman to join her company.

Joyner opened her own Walker beauty salon in Chicago; several years later, she became a recruiter and trainer of Walker agents and then national supervisor of the Lelia Colleges and all Walker Beauty Schools. With Joyner and others as instructors, the Walker company eventually opened a dozen beauty schools.

In late 1916, Walker began offering her courses to black colleges throughout the South. Many schools accepted her plan, which included the installation, without charge to the colleges, of campus beauty parlors and training centers. Mary McLeod Bethune responded enthusiastically to the proposal. "For the past four years my girls and myself have been using your Wonderful Hair Grower," she wrote Walker in March 1917. "We have proven it to be very beneficial indeed and would be glad to place it in [the Daytona Educational Industrial Training School] as a course of study."

Hairdressing and barbering had a long tradition in the American black community. In the days of slavery, black men and women often tended to their masters' hair. Centuries earlier in Africa, hairstyles, their versions as varied as the hundreds of tribes inhabiting the continent, had denoted marital status, age, and social status. African women spent hours,

Marjorie Stewart Joyner, trained in a white beauty school, botched the job when she tried to style her mother-in-law's hair. After she enrolled in Walker's classes, however, she became a master of her trade and opened her own Walker salon.

even days, creating intricate, beautiful braids into which they wove shells, beads, and other ornaments. Some women wore wigs made of human and animal hair or plant fibers; others dyed their hair with soot or colored it with red clay. Whatever they did with their hair, African women did proudly.

By the 20th century in America, slavery had severely damaged black pride. Although blacks managed to retain some vestiges of their African heritage in language, music, religion, and food, their white masters had forcibly eliminated many other traditions. Blackness had come to signify bondage; Negroid hair and features to suggest inferiority.

Many blacks harbored ambivalent feelings about themselves, an uneasy mixture of racial pride and self-hatred born of their unique experience of oppression. As scholar and activist W. E. B. Du Bois once put it: "One ever feels his two-ness—an American, a Negro; two souls, two thoughts, two unreconciled strivings; two warring ideals in one dark body."

Because of widespread racial mixing, many 20th-century American Negroes had European and Native American as well as African ancestry. Their multi-racial biological heritage reflected itself in the shade of their skin and the texture of their hair. It also left them with the tricky task of defining who they were in American society.

When it came to black women and their hair, the question seemed all the more loaded. A black woman might be proud of her heritage and, at the same time, eager to match the prevailing standards of "white" beauty. Acutely aware of the image debate, Walker sought to create a look that was truly Afro-American and that also addressed women's concerns about their appearance. Her solution: to urge women to concentrate on grooming and on emphasizing their own good points without trying to imitate whites.

"Right here let me correct the erroneous impression held by some that I claim to straighten the hair," she once told a reporter. "I want the great masses of my people to take a greater pride in their personal appearance and to give their hair proper attention. . . . And I dare say that in the next ten years it will be a rare thing to see a kinky head of hair and it will not be straight either."

Walker considered the ritual of her system as important as any resulting hairstyle. She taught her agents to create an atmosphere in which their customers would feel pampered and valued. The personal attention gave women a chance to focus on themselves, boosting their confidence and self-esteem in the process. For black women, who rarely found themselves valued in American society, the psychological lift was enormous.

Walker agents learned a philosophy of inner and outer beauty. "To be beautiful," asserted the Walker Beauty School textbook, "does not refer alone to the arrangement of the hair, the perfection of the complexion or to the beauty of the form. . . . To be beautiful, one must combine these qualities with a beautiful mind and soul; a beautiful character. Physical and mental cleanliness, together with [good health] are essential to attain loveliness."

Most manufacturers of black hair-care and cosmetic products featured glamorous mulatto or idealized white women in their ads. Not Walker. She used her own photograph on her products and in her advertisements, allowing customers to see that she, like many of them, was a black woman with decidedly Negroid facial features. The ads seemed to say: Buy Walker's products and look like Walker; look like Walker, and you too may achieve her success.

Walker promoted that notion among her agents as well as her customers. In one letter about literature for her agents, she told her attorney, "In those circulars I wish you would use the words 'our' and 'we' instead of 'I' and 'my.' "

The Walker agents' handbook stressed the impor-

Walker's advertisements covered all bases. This one, which ran in The Messenger *and other publications, includes the entrepreneur's photograph, pictures of her offices and salons, descriptions of her products, an invitation to become a Walker agent, a plug for the Lelia Colleges, and a block of hard-hitting copy: "All Mme. C. J. Walker's Inventions are reliable," asserts the ad.*

tance of keeping accurate financial records, spotless beauty salons, and an impeccable appearance. "See that your hair always looks well . . . to interest others," the handbook counseled. Walker also encouraged her agents to be socially conscious community leaders, urging them to contribute part of their profits to charity.

Walker customers were encouraged to take treatments, but Walker knew that not all black women could afford them. "Do not be narrow and selfish to the extent that you would not sell goods to anyone because they do not take the treatment from you,"

Walker told her agents. "We are anxious to help all humanity, the poor as well as the rich, especially those of our race."

Genuinely interested in aiding other blacks, Walker also knew that her own well-publicized philanthropy increased sales. Every time she donated money to a black institution, she linked the purchase of Walker products with the well-being of black America.

Whenever she could, Walker spent her money in the black community. Constructing a group of houses for Indianapolis blacks in 1916, for example, she employed 50 black workers. "My business is largely supported by my own people, so why shouldn't I spend my money so that it will go back into colored homes?" she remarked to a reporter. "By giving my work to colored men they are thus able to employ others and if not directly, indirectly I am creating more jobs for our boys and girls."

As her agents increased in number and local influence, Walker decided to create a national organization for them. Modeled on some of the benevolent societies of the time, The Madam C. J. Walker Hair Culturists Union of America was designed to foster cooperation among the agents and to protect them from competitors who were imitating Walker products and selling inferior goods at lower prices.

In August 1917, more than 200 delegates met at Philadelphia's Union Baptist Church for the group's first national convention. The hall hummed with excitement as the women arrived, each probably wondering who would win the prize for most successful sales agent of the year. They were also eager to tell Walker how they were educating their children, purchasing homes, and contributing to the charities in their communities.

As Walker entered the assembly hall, all the well-coiffed heads turned in her direction. In her

Proudly wearing their membership badges (opposite page), delegates to the first annual convention of the Madam C. J. Walker Hair Culturists Union of America assemble in Philadelphia in 1917. Addressing her agents, Walker (front row, center) recommended an active approach to selling: "Hit often and hit hard," she urged. "Strike with all your might."

speech, "Women's Duty to Women," Walker praised her agents, then reminded them of their responsibility to use their own success to advance other women. "I want to show that Walker agents are doing more than making money for themselves," she said. She also gave them advice on selling, which she compared to a battle. "Hit often and hit hard," she said. "Strike with all your might."

Most of all, she urged the women to pursue their dreams as she had pursued her own. "Perseverance is my motto," she told them. "It laid the Atlantic cable. It gave us the telegraph, telephone, and wireless. It gave to the world an Abraham Lincoln, and to a race freedom. It gave to the Negro Booker T. Washington and Tuskegee Institute. It made Frederick Douglass the great orator that he was, and it gave to the race Paul Laurence Dunbar and to poetry a new song."

Pursuing her theme, Walker said, "If I have accomplished anything in life it is because I have been willing to work hard. I never yet started anything doubtingly, and I have always believed in keeping at things with a vim. There is no royal flower strewn road to success, and if there is I have not found it, for what success I have obtained is the result of many sleepless nights and real hard work."

That hard work was clearly paying off. A few months before the Philadelphia convention, F. B. Ransom had given Walker an optimistic annual financial report. "At the rate you are going," he wrote, "we have now but five years before you will be rated as a millionaire."

Reporters, fascinated by Walker's wealth, often asked her about her net worth. Replying to a query from a *New York Times* reporter in late 1916, she said, "Well, until recently it gave me great pleasure to tell . . . the amount of money I made yearly, thinking it would inspire my hearers. But I found that for so doing some looked upon me as a boastful person who wanted to blow my own horn. . . . I will say, however, that my business last year yielded me an annual income which runs into six figures and I'm going to try to eclipse my 1915 record this year."

A year later, Walker responded to another press inquiry by saying, "I am not a millionaire, but I hope to be someday, not for the money, but because I could do so much to help my race." ❧

7

"WE SHOULD PROTEST"

❧

In 1916, WHEN Walker arrived in Harlem, a wave of black southern migrants was reaching its peak in New York and other northern cities. Sparking the migration was the promise of good jobs and a better life.

Coming after two years of boll weevil invasions, the summer floods of 1915 had made intolerable living conditions even worse for poor southerners. Jobless, homeless, and hungry, many blacks were forced to look for work outside the region. World War I, which had begun to ravage Europe in 1914, drastically reduced the supply of European immigrants. To fill positions in northern factories, employment agents swept through the South, ready to hire anyone willing to work, black or white.

The hundreds of thousands of blacks who fled the South between 1915 and 1920 sought not only work but escape from lynchings and segregation. As the *Defender*, a black Chicago newspaper, put it, "To die from the bite of frost is far more glorious than at the hands of a mob."

Of all the northern cities, New York—specifically, Harlem, the cultural and intellectual

---

Walker, who loved cars, pilots a snappy electric coupé, a vehicle especially popular with women in the century's first two decades. At top speed, an electric car moved no faster than 30 miles per hour, but it traveled silently, operated easily, and could run for 35 to 50 miles on one battery charge.

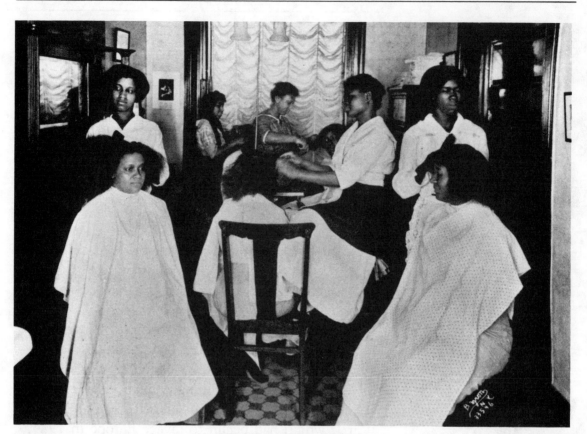

A'Lelia Walker Robinson (seated, front left) patronizes the beauty parlor of her namesake Lelia College in New York City. Among the busy salon's attendants is A'Lelia's daughter, Mae, who stands on the left side of the window at rear.

mecca of black America—exerted the strongest pull, not only on the southerners but on blacks across the nation. It was Harlem's residents who established trends in the black community; their tastes in music, books, art, and fashion influenced styles far beyond their city's borders.

In the realm of cosmetics and skin care, two recent European immigrants, Elizabeth Arden and Helena Rubenstein, dictated white fashion. For black women, the queen of beauty culture was a recent immigrant from Indianapolis, Madam C. J. Walker.

Walker's success mirrored the spirit of possibility many sensed in Harlem. Her elegant four-story, brick-and-limestone town house, which she shared with her daughter and granddaughter, quickly became a focal point for Harlem's elite. Harlemites vied for invitations to Walker's lavish dinner parties and musical evenings, which featured melodies played on her ceiling-high organ and on the gold-leafed harp and phonograph she had brought from Indianapolis.

Walker's 136th Street residence also housed Lelia College, which graduated 20 Walker hair culturists every 6 weeks. Also on the building's ground floor was the expansive Walker Hair Parlor; here, black women from all over Manhattan and Brooklyn experienced the Walker Method of hair care as they sipped tea and coffee in the calm, pearl gray surroundings. Helping Walker train the students and manage the salon were her daughter and granddaughter, Mae.

As Mae's 19th birthday approached, her mother and grandmother decided it was time to broaden her education and prepare her to take on more responsibility in the Walker company. In September 1916, A'Lelia enrolled Mae in Spelman Seminary in Atlanta, Georgia, the nation's first college for black women.

Meanwhile, the family business continued to prosper. In October, Walker factory shipping clerk Raymond Turner wrote his boss from Indianapolis: "We have more mail than anyone at the post office. . . . Miss Kelly sent a big shipping order to Mrs. Robinson of 13,234 Grower, 3,904 Glossine and 1,002 shampoos." In Pittsburgh alone, the Walker operation was bringing in $2,000 a week from sales of such popular products as Wonderful Hair Grower and Vegetable Shampoo.

The company's energetic chief executive had continued to act as its principal sales agent, traveling from state to state, making speeches, organizing demonstrations, and taking product orders. By the fall of 1916, however, the 48-year-old Walker was ready to turn some of this exhausting travel over to others; she knew she could count on Alice Kelly, former schoolteacher Alice Burnette, and her other handpicked, carefully trained executives to do the job. Departing on a swing through the South in September, Walker declared it would be her last.

From each stop, Walker sent a report back to headquarters. After visiting Salisbury, North Carolina, for example, she wrote happily, "I was very much flattered at the splendid turnout to hear my lecture. Both black and white came. They were all loud in their praise." In a note from Savannah, Georgia, she said, "My trip here was a howling success in that I have been able to get before thousands of people and all the big guns have shown me the greatest courtesies and kindness." And from Mississippi, she wrote, "I surely made a hit in Natchez and am sure we'll get some good business from there."

When Walker reached Washington, Georgia, she found the city in the midst of a disappointing cotton-harvesting season and consequent hard economic times. "I'm having quite a deal of success here with the work," she wrote, "but I've found so many poor people who cannot raise $25.00 that I've decided to let them have the trade for $10.00. . . . I put them on their honor to pay whenever they can."

From Georgia, Walker went on to the towns of her childhood. "Delta was honored Sunday," reported the local paper, "by a visit of the richest negro woman in the world, [Madam] C. J. Walker. . . . The visitor was very quiet and unassuming and a fine example to her race." In Delta, Walker received a warm welcome from Anna Burney Long, owner of the plantation where Walker had been born and the great-granddaughter of the man who had owned Walker's parents, Minerva and Owen Breedlove. After chatting with Long, Walker walked down the muddy road to the cabin where she and her family had lived.

She stood outside, remembering her parents, remembering her childhood. No one, she reflected, could have dreamed that little Sarah Breedlove would grow up to be the wealthiest black woman in America. Recalling the moment, Walker said she could not help but enjoy a sense of deep satisfaction and triumph.

Still, something was bothering her. All her life, she had possessed boundless energy, enabling her to help both herself and other people. Lately, however, she had noticed an occasional overwhelming sense of fatigue: Although her spirit was always willing, sometimes her body was not. Walker's doctor had warned her of high blood pressure, chiding her about her high-fat diet and her frantic pace, but she had found it almost impossible to slow down.

Then, traveling through Clarksdale, Mississippi, in mid-November, she was reminded of her own mortality. She wrote to Ransom about the event: "After leaving the church, we had to cross a railroad track. As soon as the car we were in got on the track we heard a man yelling, 'Get out of the way!' We looked around in time to see a freight train backing down on us, not a bell ringing or anything. The chauffeur in the nick of time put on more gas and shot forward. The train all but grazed the back of the car in which we were riding. I haven't been myself since."

The doctor who examined Walker after the near catastrophe advised her to take a long vacation. "I think instead of coming home, I will go to Hot Springs where I can really get rest and quietude," she wrote Ransom. "The doctor advises me to take not less than six weeks rest." At the bottom of Walker's letter, her traveling companion typed a postscript: "Dear Mr. Ransom," it said, "Thank goodness we have finally persuaded Mme. Walker to take that much needed rest. Today the doctor told me she was on the verge of a nervous breakdown. . . . You keep telling her after she gets to Hot Springs to remain there for the six weeks."

Mae Walker Robinson takes a break between classes at Spelman Seminary, the Atlanta, Georgia, college she entered in 1916. Known since 1924 as Spelman College, the school—the first U.S. institution of higher education for black women—was founded in 1881 as the Atlanta Baptist Female Seminary.

Walker obediently settled into a health spa in Hot Springs, Arkansas, but she still found it hard to relax. Within days of her arrival, she wrote to Ransom again: "I promise you I am going to let all business alone and look strictly after my health except little things which I am going to write to you about now. Ha. Ha."

Situated on the edge of central Arkansas's Ouachita National Forest, Hot Springs featured dozens of wells bubbling with steaming, mineral-laden water that was said to cure a variety of ailments. Wealthy visitors from all over the United States "took the waters" at Hot Springs and relaxed in the area's elegant, European-style bathhouses. The tense, over-tired Walker, her associates thought, was in the right place to relax—if she could manage to sit still for a few weeks.

Hoping to keep her at Hot Springs, Walker's daughter and Alice Kelly joined her there for the Christmas holidays. The three women spent much of their time at the luxurious bathhouse owned by the Knights of Pythias, a black fraternal organization. Every morning, Walker soaked herself in hot mineral water as she sipped a soothing herbal tea, then showered in a spray of brisk water jets. Afterward, wrapped in hot towels, she rested in a darkened room. Completing the regimen was a massage with fragrant oil.

Surprising her family and friends, Walker stayed at Hot Springs until February. Then, full of renewed energy, her promise to quit the road forgotten, she set off on a two-month trip through Texas and Louisiana. Along with her returned health came a surge of record-breaking business.

In April 1917, soon after Walker returned to New York, the United States entered World War I. The conflict triggered a debate in Harlem and throughout black America: Should black men enlist to fight? Many said yes, sure that their country would reward their loyalty with respect. Others, however, put civil rights before world war; they believed their country should grant them full rights as citizens before asking them to risk their life.

This group had very real reason for concern. Many whites felt threatened by blacks' increasingly outspoken stance and by their abandonment of the moderate approach of Booker T. Washington and his followers. On the rise since the end of the post–Civil War Reconstruction period, racism had reached terrifying proportions by the beginning of the 20th century's second decade.

The 1912 election of Democratic president Woodrow Wilson reversed much of the progress blacks had made after the Civil War. Campaigning for office, Wilson had promised black leaders that he would treat members of their race with "absolute fairness," that he would encourage their employment in federal agencies, and that he would establish a National Race Commission to study the health, education, and economic status of blacks.

After his election, Wilson—the first southerner to occupy the White House since the Civil War—reintroduced racial segregation in the nation's capital, forced many blacks from their federal jobs, and backed away from the Race Commission project.

By the beginning of Wilson's second term, the antiblack backlash was in full force. Zealously spurring it on was the Ku Klux Klan, the secret organization founded after the Civil War to reestablish white supremacy in the South. Klan "Knights" roamed the countryside, burning fiery crosses, kidnapping, flogging, and murdering minority citizens, especially blacks. Inspired by these hooded night riders, American racists embarked on an orgy of lynchings: Between 1885 and 1916, nearly 3,000 blacks met violent death at the hands of white mobs.

Despite such horrors, despite social and economic inequality, and despite the federal government's lack

A poster advertises The Birth of a Nation, *an immensely popular 1915 movie that portrayed blacks as docile servants, corrupt politicians, or bloodthirsty rapists. Despite its historical inaccuracy and blatant sensationalism, the film reinforced some whites' belief that blacks deserved few political and economic rights.*

of interest in its black constituents, a number of prominent black leaders believed that members of their race should cooperate in the nation's war effort. Such a demonstration of loyalty, they believed, would prove to whites that blacks had an equal stake in the nation's welfare and therefore deserved equal rights as citizens.

Among this group of committed people were two leaders of the National Association for the Advancement of Colored People (NAACP): W. E. B. Du Bois, editor of the NAACP magazine, *The Crisis*, and NAACP field secretary James Weldon Johnson. Both men advised blacks to "close ranks" with white America in support of the war effort.

Strongly approving the Du Bois–Johnson approach, Walker lent her name—by now widely known in both the black and the white communities—to the government's black-recruitment effort. She threw herself into the cause with her usual enthusiasm. Visiting training camps around the country, she offered moral support and encouraged young black enlisted men to become outstanding soldiers.

After Walker's visit to his post, one sergeant wrote her a letter. "We all remember you," he said. "We have often spoken of you and of the words of consolation which you gave us at Camp Sherman, Ohio, on the eve of our departure. Those words have stayed with the boys longer than any spoken by anyone that I have known or heard of."

Then, in the summer of 1917, major race riots swept several American cities. The worst of these bloody uprisings took place in East St. Louis, Illinois, where mobs murdered 39 blacks, seriously injured hundreds of others, and drove thousands of families from their homes. In some cases, whites torched the homes of blacks, then shot them as they tried to escape. As assailants drowned, burned, and beat black children, women, and men, white policemen either watched calmly or helped the mobs.

After the riot, a profound sense of outrage united the nation's blacks. Adding to their anger and grief was the knowledge that thousands of young black men had demonstrated their support for America by joining the armed forces—knowledge particularly galling to those who, like Walker, had endorsed enlistment. In Harlem, Walker joined other leading citizens to design a way to express the community's pain and to demand an end to unchecked mob violence. The result: the Negro Silent Protest Parade, staged in Manhattan on July 28, 1917.

Shortly after noon on that Saturday, some 10,000 black New Yorkers began a somber, purposeful march down Fifth Avenue. Block after block, no sound broke the city's hush but the dirgelike roll of muffled drums and the muted thunder of marching feet. More than 20,000 spectators, silent as the marchers, lined the avenue.

In the parade, dark-suited men carried banners and signs protesting Jim Crow laws, mob violence, and disfranchisement. Treat Us so That We May Love Our Country, read one banner. The female marchers, who included a number of Walker agents, wore white dresses and escorted rows of neatly dressed children.

Heartened by the public show of solidarity, Walker and her colleagues pressed on, hoping they could persuade national officials to make lynching a federal crime. (Like murder—which it was—lynching was a state, rather than a federal crime; because the southern states where it was most often committed almost never prosecuted lynchers, civil libertarians hoped for a special federal law banning the barbaric practice.)

The Harlem group composed a petition, then requested a meeting with President Wilson to discuss

Marchers fill Manhattan's Fifth Avenue during the Negro Silent Protest Parade in 1917. Sparked by a murderous attack on blacks in East St. Louis, Illinois, and organized by Walker and her associates, the parade drew 10,000 participants and twice as many spectators.

the issue. Along with Walker, James Weldon Johnson, and W. E. B. Du Bois, the petition signers included the Reverend Adam Clayton Powell, Sr., of Harlem's Abyssinian Baptist Church; Harlem realtor John E. Nail; and *New York Age* publisher Fred Moore. Although the petition was low-keyed and courteous in tone, it made its point unmistakably clear.

"Mobs have harried and murdered colored citizens time and time again with impunity, culminating in the latest atrocity at East St. Louis," said the text in part. "We believe that this spirit of lawlessness is doing untold injury to our country. . . . We ask, therefore, that lynching and mob violence be made a national crime punishable by the laws of the United States."

In response to the Harlem delegates' request, Wilson's secretary, Joseph Tumulty, promised them an appointment with the president. On August 1, four days after the Silent Parade, Walker and her friends presented themselves at the White House with their petition. As scheduled, Tumulty appeared in the executive waiting room at exactly 12 o'clock. He greeted the group cordially—then said the president was busy signing a bill dealing with farm animal feed. Wilson, Tumulty said, would be unable to see the black petitioners.

Walker and her friends had not come to Washington expecting miracles. They knew Wilson's views on racial matters reflected the Old South; they knew he had abandoned the projected Race Commission; they knew of the remark he had made to a group of black leaders in 1913: "Segregation is not humiliating but a benefit, and ought to be so regarded by you gentlemen." Still, the Harlemites had hoped the president would understand the urgency of their message, and that he would keep his appointment with them. Vastly disappointed, they presented their petition to Tumulty and left the White House.

The group went on to visit several senators and congressmen to ask for their support. Congress eventually appointed a committee to investigate the East St. Louis riot. Its members also introduced two new antilynching bills; like all the others, however, they met defeat at the hands of southern legislators.

Despite the government's failure to move against lynching, Walker believed there might be political leverage in staying involved, and she continued to urge blacks to support the war effort. Addressing a convention of Walker agents in August 1917, she advised her listeners "to remain loyal to our homes, our country and our flag." At the same time, however, she maintained that blacks should keep on fighting for justice and equal rights.

"This is the greatest country under the sun," she said. "But we must not let our love of country, our patriotic loyalty cause us to abate one whit in our

Walker admired newspaperwoman Ida Wells-Barnett, and the fiery antilynching activist returned the feeling. "To see her phenomenal rise," said Wells-Barnett of Walker, "made me take pride anew in Negro womanhood."

protest against wrong and injustice. We should protest until the American sense of justice is so aroused that such affairs as the East St. Louis riot be forever impossible."

Just as Walker had encouraged her agents to become community leaders, she now encouraged them to become political lobbyists (individuals who try to influence lawmakers on behalf of special-interest groups). After listening to Walker's 1917 speech, the agents voted to send a telegram to Wilson:

Honored Sir: . . . Knowing that no people in all the world are more loyal and patriotic than the Colored people of America, we respectfully submit to you this our protest against the continuation of such wrongs and injustices [as the East St. Louis race riot] and we further respectfully urge that you as President of these United States use your great influence that congress enact the necessary laws to prevent a recurrence of such disgraceful affairs.

(A year later, Wilson finally issued a public statement about lynching. The president, reported the *New York Times* on July 27, 1918, denounced "mob spirit and mob action as emulating German lawlessness," and urged the country's governors, law officers, and citizens to "actively and watchfully" bring an end to lynching. His mild words, followed up by no specific proposals for controlling lynching, had no apparent effect on the ongoing violence against blacks.)

Realizing that her wealth and high visibility made people listen to what she said, Walker became increasingly outspoken on political issues. Sometimes, her self-confidence led her to take militant stands avoided by her more cautious associates. She surprised many of them, for example, by advertising in *The Messenger*, a socialist newspaper published by future labor leader A. Philip Randolph.

Randolph made no secret of his distaste for Walker's "frivolous" society parties, but he also publicly praised her political and economic efforts for blacks. He had good reason to respect Walker's achievements as a businesswoman: *The Messenger* was largely funded by income from a beauty salon owned by his wife, Lucille Green, a close friend of Walker's and one of the first graduates of Walker's Lelia College in New York.

Deeply involved in her business and increasingly committed to political activities, Walker still found time to plan and build her dream house. In late 1916, she had bought a large piece of land in Irvington-on-Hudson, a wealthy community just north of New York City. Her purchase of the property, perched on the eastern bank of the broad Hudson River, had originally raised eyebrows among Irvington's white residents.

"On her first visits to inspect her property," reported the *New York Times*, "the villagers, noting her color, were frankly puzzled, but when it became known that she was the owner . . . they could only gasp in astonishment. 'Impossible!' they exclaimed. 'No woman of her race could own such a place.' To say that the village, when the report was verified, was surprised, would be putting the case mildly. 'Does she really intend to live there, or is she building it as a speculation?' the people asked."

The *Defender*, on the other hand, regarded the situation with some amusement. Walker's purchase of the Irvington estate, said the black newspaper, had "created a furore, for one of the Race was invading the sacred domains of New York's most sacred aristocracy."

Happily looking forward to her new home with its panoramic views of the river and the towering New Jersey Palisades, Walker paid no attention to the controversy. And, as things turned out, her neigh-

The New York Times

Wealthiest Negro Woman's Suburban Mansion

Estate at Irvington, Overlooking Hudson and Containing All the Attractions That a Big Fortune Commands

To own a country estate on the banks of the Hudson has been the dream of many a New Yorker. It is a dream come true in the case of Mrs. Sarah J. Walker, the city's wealthiest negro woman, Mrs. Walker, or Mme. Walker, as she is more generally known, has built a $250,000 home at Irvington. Twelve years ago she was a washerwoman, glad of a chance to do any one's family wash for $1.50 a day. Her friends now acclaim her the Hetty Green of her race. They say she has a cool million, or nearly that.

Ground for the Walker dwelling was broken eight months ago, and a large gang of workmen have been kept busy ever since. Although the house is nearly completed, it will not be ready for occupancy for several months. When it is finished it is to be one of the show places on the Hudson. Of late Mme. Walker, in her high-powered motor car, has been a familiar visitor in Irvington. On her first visits to inspect her property the villagers, noting her color, were frankly puzzled. Later, when it became known that she was the owner of the pretentious dwelling, they could only gasp in astonishment.

"Impossible!" they exclaimed. "No

red tile, is in the Italian renaissance style of architecture, and was designed by V. W. Tandy, a negro architect. It is 113 feet long, 60 wide, and stands in the centre of a four-and-a-quarter-acre plot. It is fireproof, of structural tile with an outer covering of cream-colored stucco, and has thirty-four rooms. In the basement are a gymnasium, baths and showers, kitchen and pantry, servants' dining room, power room for an organ, and storage vaults for valuables.

The main entrance is on the north side. The visitor enters a marble room, whence a marble stairway leads to the floor above. On the first floor are the library and conservatory, a living room

21 by 32 feet, furnished in Italian style,

maids of all work. In addition to these she has a social secretary and a nurse. On the third floor are also bathrooms, a billiard room, and a children's nursery. Mme. Walker loves children. They are frequent guests at her home. She provides toys for them, likes to see them at play, and does what she can to make them happy.

Plans for furnishing the house call for a degree of elegance and extravagance that a princess might envy There are to be bronze and marble statuary, sparkling cut glass candelabra, paintings, rich tapestries, and countless other things which will make the place a wonder house.

On the side of the house facing the river is a terraced veranda 72 feet long

the South, and New England. She is content to let her chauffeur drive the big cars. She has, however, a small electric coupé which she drives herself on shopping tours.

Mme. Walker is preparing to entertain her friends on a large scale in the new house. She will have as her companion most of the time her daughter, Mrs. Lelia Walker Robinson, associated with her in business.

"I was born forty-nine years ago," she said in speaking of her life, "was married at 14, and was left a widow at 20 with a little girl to support. If I have accomplished anything in life it is because I have been willing to work hard. I never yet started anything doubtingly, and I have always believed in keeping at things with a vim. When, a little more than twelve years ago, I was a washerwoman, I was considered a good washerwoman and laundress. I am proud of that fact. At times I also did cooking, but, work as I would, I seldom could make more than $1.50 a day. I got my start by giving myself a start. It is often the best way. I believe in push, and we must push ourselves.

"I was at my tubs one morning with a heavy wash before me. As I bent over the washboard and looked at my arms buried in

Irvington Home of Wealthy Negro Woman, Now Nearing Completion.   Brown Bros.

By 1917, Walker was news, even in the white press. Reporting on her mansion, the New York Times *noted that it was "in the most exclusive part of Irvington Village." Of Walker, the paper said, "Twelve years ago she was a washerwoman, glad of a chance to do any one's family wash for $1.50 a day. Her friends now . . . say she has a cool million, or nearly that."*

bors' chilly attitude thawed soon after she moved in. "Mme. Walker's unassuming ways kept down any possible friction that might have arisen due to her presence," one observer noted later. "Instead of dislike, her neighbors have learned to respect her."

The new house was nearing completion in September 1917, when Walker attended the 10th annual convention of the National Equal Rights League in Manhattan. At the meeting, she met an old acquaintance, journalist and antilynching crusader Ida B. Wells-Barnett. The businesswoman and the activist had first met several years earlier, just as Walker was starting her business.

"I was one of the skeptics that paid little heed to her predictions as to what she was going to do," Wells-Barnett recalled years later. "To see her phenomenal rise made me take pride anew in Negro womanhood."

After hosting a banquet for the convention's officers, Walker invited Wells-Barnett to visit with her and to inspect her new house. The visitor appeared properly impressed with the sunken Italian garden, the swimming pool, and the sweeping terraces, but she wondered about the size of the place. "I asked her on one occasion what on earth she would do with a thirty room house," Wells-Barnett noted in her autobiography. "She said, 'I want plenty of room in which to entertain my friends. I have worked so hard all my life that I would like to rest.' "

Rest, of course, was exactly what Walker usually managed to avoid. Several weeks after Wells-Barnett's visit, the entrepreneur's blood pressure shot up, and her physician sent her to a medical clinic in Battle Creek, Michigan. There, doctors made an announcement she did not want to hear: If she had any interest in remaining alive, she "must give little or no attention again to business or heavy social activities."

8

RACE WOMAN

N O MATTER WHAT her doctors said, Walker could not—or would not—slow down her hectic pace. Within a week of her release from the Battle Creek clinic, she traveled to Des Moines, Iowa, to speak at an NAACP fund-raising banquet.

Walker put up a good front, but George Woodson, the local attorney who introduced her to the audience in Des Moines, realized she was not in the best of health. "The eloquent force which she put into that speech in spite of her nervous state, greatly alarmed me," he wrote to F. B. Ransom. "I took her pulse in the reception room after the meeting and tried to get her away from the great mass of common people who crowded about her to admire and compliment her. But it was no use. She loved those common people and just would not leave them."

Walker thrived on the knowledge that her success could inspire and help other black Americans. She also thrilled to the enthusiasm she inspired in her audiences. From Des Moines, she embarked on a string of appearances designed to raise money for the NAACP. "I had a crowded house and applause all through the lecture," she wrote Ransom from Chi-

Walker—uncharacteristically—relaxes at home. Despite frequent warnings from her doctor, the dynamic entrepreneur found it hard to take it easy: "I promise you I am going to let all business alone and look strictly after my health," she once wrote attorney F. B. Ransom. Then she added, "Ha. Ha."

cago. "I would have to wait for them three minutes to get quiet before I could begin again." She went from Chicago to Indianapolis, then to Columbus, Ohio, and Pittsburgh. "I have packed houses everywhere I have gone, notwithstanding the downpour snow," she noted happily.

Meanwhile, Walker's "dream of dreams," her new home in Irvington, was almost ready for occupancy. By the late spring of 1918, she had finished most of the decorating, sparing no expense in her effort to create a breathtaking environment for herself, her daughter, and her granddaughter.

Walker lined the walls of the elegant main hall with handmade tapestries and filled the hall's cabinets with bronze and ivory statuettes collected from her travels. In the dining room, she installed hand-painted ceilings and recessed lighting to create a fairy-tale atmosphere for her dinner guests. She stocked the paneled library with works by great American authors from Paul Laurence Dunbar to Mark Twain, along with rare books from all over the world.

The drawing room contained not only a grand piano trimmed in 24-carat gold leaf but an organ whose music was piped through the entire house. From the first floor, a broad, curved marble staircase led to the lavish bedrooms above. Gazing from the windows of her own chamber, furnished with a four-poster bed canopied in red velvet, Walker could see the New Jersey Palisades across the river. The view was slightly reminiscent of the Vicksburg bluffs of her youth, but light-years from her present circumstances.

Breathlessly reporting on what it called Walker's "wonder house," the *New York Times* credited it with "a degree of elegance and extravagance that a princess might envy." After describing the interior and the gardens, the paper noted that "the garage [has] apartments for the chauffeur and gardener. Mme.

Walker maintains four automobiles. . . . She is content to let her chauffeur drive the big cars. She has, however, a small electric coupé, which she drives herself on shopping tours."

Soon after the Walker women moved into their luxurious residence in June 1918, they entertained Enrico Caruso, the era's most celebrated opera star. Learning that the Walkers had not yet named their new home, Caruso made a suggestion: The place, he said, reminded him of the grand estates of his homeland, Italy; why not use letters from A'Lelia's name—LElia WAlker RObinson—and call it a villa? The idea appealed to his hostesses, who thereupon christened the magnificent house Villa Lewaro.

Walker took immense pleasure in the villa, a place "that only Negro money had bought." She once said she thought of her home as a black institution, a monument that would "convince members of [my] race of the wealth of business possibilities within the race, to point to young Negroes what a lone woman accomplished and to inspire them to do big things."

To help look after her villa, Walker sent for the butler and housekeeper, Mr. and Mrs. Bell, she had employed in Indianapolis. As soon as the couple arrived, Walker went to work in her garden, labor that she found extremely relaxing. Writing to a friend later that summer, she said, "Every morning at six o'clock I am at work in the garden, pulling weeds, gathering berries and vegetables. [You] should see me now . . . all dressed up in overalls. . . . I am a full-fledged 'farmerette.' We are putting up fruit and vegetables by the wholesale."

Calmly planting seedlings and pruning rosebushes, Walker seemed to be following her doctor's orders at last. But in midsummer, she received a tempting invitation from the National Association of Colored Women. Walker had been the main contributor to the NACW drive to pay off the mortgage

Ransom exchanged hundreds of letters with Walker over the years. Even though the two had become close friends, their correspondence retained a formal tone: Walker addressed the attorney as "Mr. Ransom" and signed her mail "Yours respectfully, Mme. C. J. Walker." Ransom, in turn, always wrote to "Dear Madam."

on the home of black abolitionist Frederick Douglass; now the NACW proposed to honor her at its annual convention. The meeting would be held in Denver, the city where Walker had started her business 13 years earlier. Delighted, she promised to attend.

Walker, who had made the largest individual contribution ($500) to the Douglass fund, played a key role in the mortgage-burning ceremony. As the audience sang "Hallelujah, 'Tis Done," NACW president Mary B. Talbert held the mortgage document as Walker touched a burning candle to its edge. Watching the paper crumble to ashes, the crowd rose to its feet with a storm of applause.

A few weeks after the convention, the National Negro Business League honored Walker and Vertner W. Tandy, the architect who had designed both her Manhattan town house and her suburban villa. Tandy, New York State's first certified black architect, had attended Tuskegee Institute, where Booker T. Washington had encouraged him to study architecture. By 1917, when he began designing Walker's home, Tandy had already completed many schools, churches, and private residences. Addressing the NNBL audience, he said, "There is one person who has contributed more to architecture for Negroes than any person or group of persons in this country and that person is . . . Madam C. J. Walker."

As Walker thanked him, she was probably thinking of the house party she had scheduled for late August. Guest of honor at the weekend celebration was to be Emmett J. Scott, former private secretary to Booker T. Washington and a principal founder of the NNBL. Walker had planned her party as a tribute to Scott's recent appointment to an important government post: special assistant to the secretary of war in charge of Negro affairs.

Walker's guest list read like a copy of *Who's Who in Black America*. Invited to the gala were leading black Baptist and Methodist ministers, educators

Dean William Pickens of Morgan College and Charlotte Hawkins Brown, founder of Palmer Memorial Institute; political activists Ida B. Wells-Barnett and A. Philip Randolph; newspaper publishers Fred Moore of the *New York Age* and Robert Sengstacke Abbott of the *Chicago Defender*.

Also asked to the celebration were several white NAACP members, including board chairman Joel Spingarn; president Moorfield Storey; secretary Mary White Ovington; and vice-president and treasurer Oswald Garrison Villard, editor of the *New York Evening Post*.

Others invitees included bibliophile Arthur Schomburg; Jesse Moorland, senior secretary of the YMCA's Colored Men's Department; banker Maggie Lena Walker; AME bishop and NAACP board vice-president John Hurst; NAACP assistant secretary Walter White; NAACP field secretary James Weldon Johnson and his brother, composer J. Rosamond Johnson; physician and former minister to Haiti Henry Watson Furniss; composer and concert singer Harry T. Burleigh; Margaret Murray Washington; poet William Stanley Braithwaite; and Carter G. Woodson, founder of the Association for the Study of Negro Life and History.

The Villa Lewaro weekend proved an immense success. Writing to Walker later, Emmett Scott said, "It will be a very great pleasure during all the years to come that we were the first official guests entertained at Villa Lewaro. The wonderful gathering of friends . . . was beyond compare. No such assemblage has ever gathered at the private home of any representative of our race, I am sure."

The party had included more than good food and lighthearted conversation; guests had also talked of such serious matters as the situation of black soldiers in Europe. Everyone had heard the frontline reports about heroic actions by black troops, particularly those of Harlem's own 369th Regiment. Popularly

Workmen put the finishing touches on Villa Lewaro, Walker's opulent mansion on the east bank of New York's Hudson River. The estate's title, suggested by a visiting Italian opera singer, derived from the name of Walker's daughter, LElia WAlker RObinson.

A'Lelia Robinson pauses in the drawing room at Villa Lewaro. Although she appreciated the comfort and beauty of her mother's mansion, A'Lelia found life in Irvington too staid; she preferred the bright lights and lively parties of Harlem.

known as the Hell Fighters, the 369th had been in ongoing combat for longer than any other American regiment and had been the first Allied unit to reach Germany's Rhine River.

Everyone had also heard reports of widespread racism within the military. Walker and her friends were beginning to wonder how black soldiers would fare when they returned to the United States. Would the nation reward their heroic efforts with new respect? Or would white America continue to treat these men as second-class citizens? The group at Lewaro resolved to fight for the rights of returning black veterans.

As the war dragged on into 1918, the Walker women became increasingly involved in the civilian war effort. Madam Walker promoted the sale of war bonds in the black community and joined the advisory board of the Motor Corps of America, a war-relief support effort. A'Lelia drove an ambulance for the Motor Corps, helping to transport wounded black returnees. She also worked with the Circle for Negroes' War Relief, supervising the making of bandages and other first-aid supplies.

The war finally ended in Allied victory on November 11, 1918. Like the rest of the nation, Walker rejoiced, celebrating with friends in Boston and sending all her employees home for the day. The following month, she accepted an invitation from Mayor John F. Hylan of New York to help the city welcome the troops home from Europe.

As Christmas approached, Walker went into her usual preholiday whirl, ordering festive meals, decorating her house, and choosing gifts for her family, friends, and employees. On December 23, her 51st birthday, mountains of Christmas cards competed for space with an avalanche of birthday greetings from friends and admiring strangers.

Walker's holiday guests began arriving on the afternoon of Christmas Eve. One of her best friends,

Hallie Queen, later wrote a description of the next few days:

Christmas Eve was spent most happily with music and song. Madame retired early as she usually did. At twelve o'clock, however, she awakened everyone who had gone to bed to wish him a "Merry Christmas."

Early Christmas morning, when we returned to the house [after church], we found Madame waiting for us before a glowing fireplace. Christmas greetings and gifts were exchanged and enjoyed until breakfast time.

It was significant that in that beautiful state dining room, with its wonderful furnishings and rich indirect lighting and all the material good that life could expect, Madame insisted upon our kneeling while she returned to God thanks for the gift of the Christ child and for all other gifts that had come to her. The theme of her prayer was humility and awe in the presence of God.

First, there was a distinguished minister, Rev. Brooks of Baltimore, who charmed us with stories of his European travels; then Mrs. [May Howard] Jackson, the brilliant moulder [sculptor] of human faces; her husband, W. T. S. Jackson, the mathematician; Lieut. O. Simmons, the army officer; a wounded overseas soldier wearing a *croix de guerre* [a French medal for heroism] and a sailor from a recently torpedoed vessel; Mr. Williams, the politician; Mr. [Lloyd] Thomas, one of Madame's secretaries; Mrs. [Agnes] Prosser, her sister-in-law; and I who had no claim to greatness other than that I was her friend.

After dinner we went into the wonderful music room and listened to old Christmas carols or read in the library from the magnificent selection of books owned by Mme. Walker.

Christmas night we motored in to New York City to attend a basketball game at the Manhattan Casino. Mme's entrance was the signal for an ovation and she was at once requested to throw the ball from her box.

The following day was to be a great day for she had been invited by the Mayor of the City to go out on his boat and observe the return of the Atlantic Fleet.

So ended . . . Christmas . . . and it was impressed upon my mind a memory of her goodness, devotion, reverence, humility and faith. ❧

9

THE LEGACY

BY JANUARY 1919, the Madam C. J. Walker Manufacturing Company had become black America's most successful business. Sales for 1918 had topped a quarter of a million dollars; with the introduction of five new products in 1919, Walker's accountants expected the company's income to rise still further.

Walker's financial health was booming, but her personal health was not. In early 1919, her doctor, Colonel Joseph Ward, put his foot down: It would be nothing less than suicide, he said, if a woman with her soaring blood pressure maintained a day-to-day involvement with business. Walker must leave her company in the capable hands of her attorney, her agents, and her sales representatives.

Reluctantly, Walker obeyed Ward's orders—up to a point. She continued to stay in regular contact with her main office, and to direct corporate development and long-range sales strategy. She also started spending more time on political activity.

During the recently ended war, Walker had concluded that if black Americans were to attain

Walker (second row, second from the left) reunites with a group of old friends outside the Indianapolis YMCA, the building she had helped endow in 1913. Standing in the first row (second from the left) is George Knox, the newspaper publisher who persuaded Walker to settle in the Indiana city in 1910; fourth from the right in the back row is Robert Lee Brokenburr, the attorney who joined Walker's company during its early days in the Midwest.

663

their full rights as citizens, they would have to assert themselves in all aspects of national and international affairs. After the war, she paid careful attention to the peace negotiations, conducted in Paris between defeated Germany and the victorious Allied nations: the United States, Great Britain, France, Italy, Japan, and 23 other powers.

Walker and many of her colleagues feared that the peace treaty negotiators would ignore the rights of both black Americans and blacks in Europe's African colonies. Hoping to influence the treaty makers, several black leaders—W. E. B. Du Bois and William Monroe Trotter among them—decided to hold their own Paris meetings. Du Bois organized a group called the Pan-African Congress; Trotter, who had already founded the National Equal Rights League (NERL), held a meeting to elect delegates to his own alternative Paris peace conference. Among those selected as representatives were Walker and her friend Ida Wells-Barnett.

Walker's association with NERL alarmed her chief of operations. "You must always bear in mind that you have a large business, whereas the others who are going have nothing," Ransom lectured his boss. "There are many ways in which your business can be circumscribed and hampered," he added, "so as to practically put you out of business." In other words, Ransom, who considered NERL a radical, possibly even subversive organization, feared that Walker's connection with it could turn people against both her and her products.

NERL, which campaigned for integration and social justice, might have served as a model for the civil rights organizations of the 1960s. Although its demands seem moderate today, some cautious blacks did indeed regard it as dangerous. Walker, however, mapped her own path as usual. She valued Ransom's judgment, but she did not always agree with him and sometimes ignored his advice.

Home from the war, a wounded member of the Harlem Hell Fighters greets a Manhattan well-wisher in 1919. Although she was apprehensive about the future of the nation's black veterans, Walker was sure of one thing: "They will come back," she said, "to face like men whatever is in store for them and like men defend themselves, their families, and their homes."

Trotter, denied a passport by the State Department, never managed to field a Paris delegation. Du Bois, who did convene his Pan-African Congress in the French capital, presented his delegates' resolutions to members of the official peace conference, but to no avail. The Treaty of Versailles, signed in June 1919, would contain no guarantees of equality or self-determination for the world's people of color.

Disappointed but not discouraged, Walker continued to speak out for her race. She was particularly emphatic about the debt America owed its black veterans. Her strong stand on the issue brought sharp criticism from Colonel William Jay Schieffelin, the white treasurer of the Welfare League of an all-black infantry unit. Schieffelin, who believed blacks should

Walker, representing the International League of Darker Peoples (ILDP), attends a 1919 New York City conference with S. Kuroiwa (center), Japan's delegate to the Versailles Peace Conference. ILDP members, who also included future labor leader A. Phillip Randolph and Harlem clergyman Adam Clayton Powell, Sr., hoped to ensure the postwar rights of nonwhites through an alliance with the Japanese and other non-European peoples. Their efforts failed; the Treaty of Versailles included no special provisions for people of color.

take a very soft approach to the rights question, told Walker that her strident demands would do more harm than good. Walker, being Walker, refused to back down one inch.

"Their country called them to defend its honor on the battlefield of Europe," she told Schieffelin, "and they have bravely, fearlessly bled and died that that honor might be maintained."

Warming to her theme, she continued, "And now they will soon be returning. To what? Does any reasonable person imagine to the old order of things? To submit to being strung up, riddled with bullets, burned at the stake? No! A thousand times no! . . . They will come back to face like men whatever is in store for them and like men defend themselves, their families, and their homes."

Her fury spent for the moment, Walker closed her remarks in a somewhat milder tone. "Please understand," she told Schieffelin, "that this does not mean that I wish to encourage in any way a conflict between the two races. . . . My message to my people is this: Go live and conduct yourself so that you will be above the reproach of anyone—but should but one prejudiced, irrational boast infringe upon [your] rights as men—resent the insult like men."

During the first few months of 1919, Walker stayed close to home, writing political letters, hosting occasional dinner parties, and enjoying Villa Lewaro. Then, in late April, her friend Jessie Robinson, one of the first Walker agents and the wife of newspaper publisher C. K. Robinson, asked her to come to St. Louis to help launch the new line of Walker products. Although Walker was suffering from a severe cold, she decided to make the trip.

On Easter Day, a few days after she arrived in St. Louis, Walker became seriously ill. Alarmed, the Robinsons arranged for their doctor and his nurse to accompany their friend back to New York. At Walker's request, the St. Louis couple chartered a private railroad car on the era's fastest train, the 20th Century Limited. Other passengers, according to Walker's secretary, Violet Reynolds, expressed great curiosity about their fellow traveler, this mysterious "'colored woman' whose room was filled with flowers."

As the train sped across Ohio and Pennsylvania, Walker talked about all her still-unfinished business: She intended to build a girls' school in Africa, to construct a new office building and factory, and to put up a housing development for the poor in Indianapolis. She also wanted to take a European vacation that summer.

Arriving in Irvington weak but still determined, Walker got down to business at once, ordering her accountants to donate $5,000 to the NAACP's antilynching fund. News of the gift, announced a few days later at the NAACP's Anti-Lynching Conference at Manhattan's Carnegie Hall, brought a standing ovation from the 2,500 delegates. Walker's contribution, the largest the organization had ever received, so moved the convention that one wealthy black farmer from Arkansas pledged another $1,000 on the spot. Supporters, each of them expressing hope for Walker's recovery—"God spare you to the race and humanity," said a typical message—pledged $3,400 more within a week.

But Colonel Ward held out little hope for his patient. The effect of her high blood pressure, he said, had hopelessly damaged her kidneys. After she heard Ward's diagnosis, Walker sat by the fireplace in her bedroom, pulling her heavy, cream-colored silk shawl tighter around her shoulders. Then she summoned Ransom.

When the attorney arrived, Walker gave him a list of groups she wanted to help. "Madam Walker gave $25,000 to colored organizations and institutions," reported the *New York Age*. "Intimate friends believe she fully realizes the seriousness of her condition and wanted to do what she could for deserving race institutions before passing away."

One morning, Walker managed a faint smile as her secretary read her the latest letter from A'Lelia, who was traveling through Central America on a sales trip with Mae. Eliciting the smile was A'Lelia's news: She had decided to marry Ward's protégé, Dr. James Arthur Kennedy, who had just returned from Europe with the croix de guerre.

A few days later, Walker's nurse heard her say, "I want to live to help my race." Then she slipped into a coma. On the following Sunday morning, the *Chicago Defender* would later report, the day "dawned bright and warm. Outside, where the trees and lawn were green and pretty, the flowers blooming and the birds merrily singing, all was gaiety and happiness.

"Inside, where several people gathered around a beautiful four-posted bed and watched a magnificent soul go into eternity, all was grief and sorrow." Breaking the silence, the paper continued, Dr. Ward "turned to those around the bedside and said, 'It is over.' " Sarah Breedlove Walker, 51 years old, died on May 25, 1919.

Notified of her mother's death, A'Lelia rushed home from Panama. Meanwhile, 1,000 mourners attended funeral services at the Villa Lewaro, which concluded with a reading of Walker's favorite Bible passage, the 23rd Psalm. "Farewell, farewell, a long farewell," said the minister. When A'Lelia and Mae arrived, they joined a circle of close friends and accompanied Walker's rose-covered casket to Woodlawn cemetery, where it was buried after a brief graveside ceremony.

Tributes began to pour in at once. Walker's friend Mary McLeod Bethune called Walker's life "an unusual one." It was, said Bethune, "the clearest demonstration, I know, of Negro woman's ability recorded in history. She has gone, but her work still lives and shall live as an inspiration to not only her race but to the world."

Among the countless grieving admirers was journalist and author George Samuel Schuyler. Writing in *The Messenger*, he said, "What a boon it was for one of their own race to stand upon the pinnacle and exhort the womanhood of her race to come forth [and] lift up their heads." Walker, he added, "had given dignified employment to thousands of women who would otherwise have had to make their living in domestic service."

W. E. B. Du Bois, who wrote an obituary for *The Crisis*, said, "It is given to few persons to transform a people in a generation. Yet this was done by the late Madam C. J. Walker. . . . [She] made and deserved a fortune and gave much of it away generously."

Indeed, Walker's concern for those in need became even clearer after her death. Her will named A'Lelia as her principal heir, then listed dozens of organizations and individuals as beneficiaries. She

Wearing one of her trademark jeweled turbans, A'Lelia Walker Robinson strikes a jaunty pose in 1925. After her mother's death, A'Lelia became something of a Harlem legend, famous for her flamboyant style and lavish, celebrity-studded gatherings. Like her mother, she died in middle age, suffering a fatal stroke at the age of 46 in 1931.

Walker's business outlasted its founder by several decades: Here, Walker Beauty School graduates and officials—including Walker's friend and 1919 hostess, Jessie Robinson (seated third from right)—assemble in St. Louis in the 1930s.

established a $100,000 trust fund, its proceeds to go to "worthy charities," and left sums ranging from $2,000 to $5,000 to such institutions as the Colored Orphans' Home in St. Louis, the Home for Aged and Infirm Colored People in Pittsburgh, the Haines Institute in Georgia, the NAACP, and Tuskegee Institute.

America's first black, self-made female millionaire, Walker never forgot her roots. A child of poverty, she eagerly shared her immense wealth with the needy. Deprived of an early education, she made a point of supporting schools. Born to former slaves, she vigorously exercised her rights as an American citizen, using her economic and personal power to strengthen her community and urging others to follow her lead.

Walker's success sprang from her innovative line of beauty products and techniques. But the Walker

Method involved more than cosmetics: It taught black women to develop their natural beauty, thus improving their self-esteem and enhancing their confidence.

The Walker company employed thousands of people, both during its founder's lifetime and for decades afterward. Today, countless black Americans can name a relative—an aunt, a grandmother, perhaps an uncle—who served as a Walker agent. Walker's products enabled these women and men to educate their children, build homes, and start other businesses.

By recounting her own story, Walker encouraged black women and men to pursue their dreams. "I promoted myself," she often told her audiences. "I had to make my own living and my own opportunity! But I made it! Don't sit down and wait for the opportunities to come. Get up and make them!"

A woman of extraordinary courage and vision, Walker paved the way for the generations that followed her. The grit and determination that carried her from a cotton field to a mansion, from penniless obscurity to riches and national recognition, continue to inspire Americans who yearn to realize their own possibilities.

CHRONOLOGY

———— ✺ ————

1867   Born Sarah Breedlove on December 23 in Delta, Louisiana

1874   Orphaned when both parents die in yellow fever epidemic

1878   Moves to Vicksburg, Mississippi, with sister, Louvenia

1882   Marries Moses McWilliams

1885   Gives birth to daughter, Lelia

1887   Widowed when McWilliams dies; moves to St. Louis with daughter

1905   Moves to Denver and develops formula for Wonderful Hair Grower

1906   Marries Charles Joseph Walker and changes name to Madam C. J. Walker

1908   Moves to Pittsburgh and opens Lelia College

1910   Moves to Indianapolis and builds factory

1912   Travels throughout United States selling products and speaking to major black organizations; donates $1,000 to Indianapolis's black YMCA; divorces C. J. Walker; becomes grandmother when daughter adopts Mae Bryant

1913   Travels to Caribbean and Central America on sales trip

1916   Moves to Harlem in New York City

1917   Convenes first annual Madam C. J. Walker Hair Culturists Union of America Convention; visits President Woodrow Wilson, urging him to make lynching a federal crime

1918   Completes and moves into Villa Lewaro, a Hudson River mansion; becomes millionaire as Walker company annual sales exceed $250,000

1919   Contributes large sums to NAACP antilynching fund and other causes; dies on May 25 at Villa Lewaro

FURTHER READING

Barnett, Ida B. Wells. *Crusade for Justice.* Chicago: University Chicago Press, 1970.

Bird, Caroline. *Enterprising Women.* New York: Norton, 1976.

Gatewood, William, Jr. *Slave and Freeman: The Autobiography of George L. Knox.* Lexington: University of Kentucky Press, 1979.

Giddings, Paula. *When and Where I Enter.* New York: Morrow, 1984.

Hine, Darlene Clark. *When the Truth Is Told: I. History of Black Women's Culture and Community in Indiana 1875–1950.* Indianapolis: National Council of Negro Women, 1981.

Huggins, Nathan. *The Harlem Renaissance.* London: Oxford University Press, 1971.

Jones, Jacqueline. *Labor of Love, Labor of Sorrow.* New York: Basic Books, 1985.

Lewis, David Levering. *When Harlem Was in Vogue.* New York: Knopf, 1981.

Logan, Rayford W., and Michael Winston. *Dictionary of American Negro Biography.* New York: Norton, 1982.

Painter, Nell Irvin. *Exodusters.* New York: Knopf, 1977.

Sterling, Dorothy, ed. *We Are Your Sisters: Black Women in the Nineteenth Century.* New York and London: Norton, 1984.

JESSE
JACKSON

JESSE JACKSON

Robert Jakoubek

Senior Consulting Editor
Nathan Irvin Huggins
Director
W.E.B. Du Bois Institute for Afro-American Research
Harvard University

1

RAINBOW EXPRESS

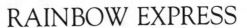

Shortly after lunchtime on July 14, 1988, a blazing summer afternoon, the Reverend Jesse L. Jackson departed Chicago for the Democratic National Convention in Atlanta. He was, so far as anyone could recall, the first person seeking the presidential nomination of a major American political party to go to its national convention by bus.

It was, to be sure, not Greyhound he traveled. His vehicle was a nicely appointed motor coach with a kitchen, television sets, and two spacious seating areas. On the outside, beneath the bus windows, several Jackson for President signs held the smiling likeness of the candidate and advertised the point of the trip. Jackson would be leading a parade of 7 chartered buses—the Rainbow Express—on the 715-mile journey southward.

Climbing aboard, Jackson hoisted a thumbs-up gesture to the small band of admirers on the sidewalk, waved to the considerably larger group of reporters and photographers, then gave his wife a farewell kiss.

Presidential hopeful Jesse Jackson, traveling by Rainbow Express—a seven-bus cavalcade—to the 1988 Democratic National Convention in Atlanta, stops to greet well-wishers in Houston, Texas. Accompanying the Chicagoan on his 715-mile trip to Atlanta were relatives, aides, friends, and 125 journalists.

Jacqueline Jackson, as her husband later noted, possessed the "good sense" to travel to Atlanta by plane.

Inside the bus, Jackson threaded his way through his children, his aides, and his friends toward one of the deeply cushioned seats. Dressed in jeans and a white polo shirt, he looked perhaps 15 years younger than his age of 46 and he moved with the ease of a college quarterback.

His face, with its wide-set eyes and trimmed mustache, and his voice, with its rhythmic cadences learned in the black churches of the Deep South, were among the best known in America. For two decades, Jackson had been a presence on the national scene, first as a lieutenant of Martin Luther King, Jr., during the civil rights movement of the 1960s, then as the founder of a social reform organization called People United to Serve Humanity (PUSH). And always, and seemingly everywhere, Jackson appeared as the outspoken foe of what he perceived to be racism, imperialism, and economic injustice.

In 1984, responding to the plea, "Run, Jesse, Run," Jackson had sought the Democratic presidential nomination, representing what he called a Rainbow Coalition of blacks, of the poor, of women, of homosexuals, of the unemployed. His campaign captured the fevered attention of the media and whipped up powerful storms of controversy; still, he had finished far behind Walter Mondale in the Democratic presidential sweepstakes.

Jackson kept right on running, and in 1988, to no one's surprise, he again became a candidate for president. But this time, to everyone's surprise, he won primaries and swept caucuses. At the Democratic convention in Atlanta, he would have 1,200 delegates committed to his name.

He had outrun and outlasted every Democratic hopeful except one: Governor Michael S. Dukakis of Massachusetts. Then, in a series of spring primaries from New York to California, Dukakis and Jackson had gone head to head, and the diminutive governor had soundly whipped the tall preacher. As Jackson left Chicago for Atlanta, it was all over but the shouting. Controlling the votes of 2,800 delegates, Dukakis had the nomination locked up.

Jackson had nevertheless pressed ahead with his campaign, refusing to concede, passing up every chance to get behind Dukakis. By staying in the race, Jackson hoped to pressure Dukakis into selecting him as his running mate. Jackson believed that by making such a strong showing for the presidency, he had staked a claim to the vice-presidential nomination. He stated his case: If the vice-presidential nominee should be "someone who can mobilize a mass of Democrats, I've done that. If it's someone who is not limited to regional appeal, I've won primaries from Vermont to Puerto Rico, from Mississippi to Michigan, from Texas to Alaska."

But Michael Dukakis had not the slightest intention of picking Jesse Jackson. In the first place, every public opinion poll showed that a Dukakis-Jackson ticket would be doomed; too many white voters would desert it for the Republicans. Furthermore, Dukakis did not want as his vice-president a man who had never held public office, who stood considerably to Dukakis's left on most matters of policy, and whose charisma and eloquence vastly exceeded his own.

Yet Dukakis had to give the *impression* he was seriously considering Jackson. To have done otherwise would have been a slap in the face to Jackson and Jackson's loyal supporters. And if they, the black Democrats who had nearly unanimously backed Jackson in the primaries, did not vote for Dukakis in November, the governor was sure to lose.

On the Fourth of July, Dukakis had attempted to cultivate his rival. The governor and his wife, Kitty, invited Jesse and Jacqueline Jackson to their home

Jackson and his wife, Jackie, attend a Boston Pops concert with Massachusetts governor Michael Dukakis on the Fourth of July, 1988. All smiles on the surface, the Jacksons were inwardly raging about what they considered high-handed treatment from Dukakis, at this point the almost certain Democratic presidential candidate.

just outside Boston for a holiday dinner, followed by the annual Boston Pops concert and fireworks display on the Charles River.

Nothing went right. The Jacksons arrived an hour and a half late, partly because no one met them at Logan Airport. The Dukakises, unaware of Jackson's allergy to milk, served a meal of creamy New England clam chowder and salmon poached in milk. And just when Dukakis and his guest settled down in the living room to discuss the vice-presidency, the governor's daughters entered the room, offering ice cream for dessert. At the concert, a famished Jackson ordered fried chicken from a vendor and Dukakis strained to make small talk. There was, of course, a chance for some serious political talk after the concert, but Dukakis said he felt sleepy.

The evening left Jackson in a foul mood. "He felt he had been treated like a nigger," said a friend.

Compared to what happened next, the dinner was a stunning social success. The governor and his campaign continued the charade that Jackson was under serious consideration for vice-president. Dukakis dispatched his senior adviser, Paul Brountas, to conduct a lengthy interview with Jackson. At its conclusion, Brountas said that whomever Dukakis selected, Jackson would be among the first to know, well before the choice became public. "Reverend Jackson," Brountas pledged, "you're not going to read about it in the newspapers."

To be fair, he did not. He heard the news from a reporter. On the morning of Wednesday, July 13, as he disembarked from a plane at National Airport in Washington, D.C., newspeople closed in, each asking what he thought of Dukakis's choosing Senator Lloyd Bentsen of Texas to be his running mate.

Jackson was dumbstruck. His jaw tightly set, obviously trying to control his temper, he pushed past the reporters and said nothing. Later in the day, he explained that he was really not upset about having been left in the dark. "No, I'm too controlled," he said. "I'm too clear. I'm too mature to be angry. I am focused on what we must do to keep hope alive." For once, his words were entirely unpersuasive. He appeared very angry.

From Dukakis's headquarters in Boston came the lame explanation that it had all been a foul-up. No offense had been intended; staff members just could not locate in time the telephone number of the Cincinnati hotel where Jackson had spent the night. Jackson supporters were not buying it. Many believed it to be a calculated snub. "They weren't simply careless," said Maxine Waters of California.

There matters stood when the Rainbow Express rolled out of Chicago on its way to Atlanta. Jackson,

Meeting reporters in Washington, D.C., on July 13, 1988, Jackson learns that Michael Dukakis has bypassed him in selecting a running mate; only days earlier, the probable Democratic presidential nominee had promised to inform Jackson privately about his choice for vice-president. Although Jackson claimed he was "too mature to be angry" about the selection of Texas senator Lloyd Bentsen, he was visibly steamed by Dukakis's method of handling it.

leader of the Democratic party's left wing, obviously felt shunned, not only by Dukakis's apparent discourtesy but by the selection of Bentsen, a conservative Texan. "Mr. Bentsen represents one wing of the party, I represent the other wing," Jackson proclaimed. "It takes two wings to fly, and so far, our wing is not connected."

The Democratic convention appeared headed for a crash landing. Party leaders desperately wanted a harmonious, united show in Atlanta, and Jackson was promising to give them anything but. In the Jackson camp, there was talk of demonstrations in the streets of Atlanta, of divisive fights over the party platform, even of Jackson himself challenging Bentsen for the vice-presidential nomination from the floor of the convention. "This party was hanging by a thread in Atlanta," Jackson's aide Ron Brown recalled.

As the Rainbow Express roared southward along Interstate 65, the mood in the candidate's motor coach was surprisingly upbeat. Jackson's five children lifted everyone's spirits. "It's fun. It's family time. We laugh a lot," said one daughter.

More than 125 reporters, photographers, and television crew members squeezed onto the buses, and their presence guaranteed Jackson a prominent place on the evening news and in the next morning's newspapers. The bus caravan was meant as a plain reminder of the Freedom Rides of the early 1960s, the time when young blacks, traveling on interstate buses into the Deep South, challenged the racial segregation found in the facilities of public transportation.

Late on Thursday afternoon, July 14, the Rainbow Express rumbled into Indianapolis. Only a few curious pedestrians turned to watch the buses pass by, but that evening at a rally in the Christ Missionary Baptist Church, Jackson found the sort of enthusiasm and acclaim that had long sustained his campaigns. He was, after all, a preacher, and these were his people—the devout black churchgoers who had been the first to raise the cry: "Run, Jesse, Run."

Handmade Jackson for President signs decorated the walls and hung from the church balcony. More than 1,000 people filled the church, which had no air-conditioning, on one of the hottest nights of the hottest summer in a half century. "I was born against the odds," Jackson cried, sweat pouring from his face. "I grew up against the odds. I stand here against the odds. I am an odds breaker and a dream maker. I will never surrender."

The next morning, the Rainbow Express moved southward once more, sweeping past the brown fields of corn and soybeans stunted by the summer's drought. At all times, several black Mercury sedans—the vehicles of the Secret Service agents assigned to protect Jackson—kept pace alongside the candidate's bus. In Louisville and Nashville on Friday and in Chattanooga on Saturday, Jackson stopped for rallies at the way stations of his campaign, the black churches. At each, in words nearly identical to those he had spoken in Indianapolis, he defiantly expressed his aims.

Frequently, the helicopters of local television stations hovered above the Rainbow Express, collecting shots of the caravan for evening news broadcasts. The missed phone call, and Jackson's response to it, kept the spotlight trained on him, and he was doing nothing to lessen the tension between himself and Dukakis. At one point, he suggested that former president Jimmy Carter might mediate his dispute with the governor. Dukakis flatly rejected the idea.

Early Saturday afternoon, July 16, the express pulled up alongside Interstate 75 in Calhoun, Georgia, for two passengers. One was Bert Lance, a beefy, freewheeling Georgian who had briefly directed the federal budget during the Carter administration. Over the last few years, he had emerged as an unlikely but influential Jackson adviser. The other new passenger was Dan Rather, the high-strung, high-powered anchorman of CBS News.

At the side of the highway, oblivious to the horrendous traffic jam the stopped buses were causing, Jackson and Rather embraced and exchanged pleasantries. What could say more about Jackson's place at the center of things? Dan Rather, the most famous newsperson in America, had come to him and was riding his bus to the Democratic convention.

Arriving in Atlanta four hours late, the Rainbow Express proceeded to Piedmont Park, where several thousand Jackson partisans had been patiently waiting all afternoon. Nearly a century before, on the same spot, Booker T. Washington had delivered his famous "Atlanta Compromise" speech, in which he urged his fellow blacks to exchange political and social equality for economic advancement.

Compromise was not on Jesse Jackson's mind. He demanded a significant place for himself and his supporters in the Democratic party. He requested equity, partnership, and shared responsibility. "I don't mind working," he said of his role in the party. "I'll go out and pick the voters. I'll go back and bale up some votes. But when I get to the Big House, I want to help count the cotton."

He had stretched his pique with Dukakis too far. His remarks in Piedmont Park clearly cast him as the field hand and Dukakis, the man in the "Big House," as the slaveholder. And what did he mean when he proposed partnership and shared responsibility? After all, there were two, not three, places on the national ticket.

If Jackson had any desire for a large future in the Democratic party—and he most certainly did—the time had come to fold his hand. If he continued to shun Dukakis, he would be remembered as the man who wrecked the Democratic convention and spoiled the party's chances for victory in November. In a profession that places an extravagant value on party loyalty, such a memory would be hard to overcome.

Hardly a political innocent, Jackson knew this as well as anyone. So, on Sunday evening, July 17, when a telephone call from Dukakis reached him at the Fox Theatre, where he was attending a gospel concert, he readily took it in a backstage holding room. And when the governor proposed a breakfast meeting the next morning at 8:30, he quickly agreed to be there.

On Monday morning, in Dukakis's suite at the Hyatt Regency, over a breakfast of cereal, fruit, and coffee, the two rivals got down to brass tacks. The atmosphere was decidedly uncomfortable. Dukakis griped about Jackson's "Big House" remark, saying he did not appreciate being compared to a slaveholder. Jackson, in no uncertain words, deplored the missed phone call. For several hours, it went back and forth. "They got it out on the table and they cleared the air," said a Jackson associate.

In the late morning, Lloyd Bentsen joined the meeting; soon afterward, the three men, wreathed in smiles, appeared together at a press conference in the hotel basement. Dukakis complimented Jackson. Jackson complimented Dukakis. And then, in a moment everyone had been waiting for, Jackson pledged his support for the Dukakis-Bentsen ticket and promised a harmonious convention. There would be no demonstrations, a minimum of dissent over the party platform, and no opposition to Bentsen's nomination for vice-president.

And what had Jackson received in return for his cooperation? Precious little. Dukakis did not budge an inch when it came to issues of foreign and domestic policy, making no attempt to accommodate Jackson's agenda. Nor did he offer Jackson a job in a Dukakis administration. All Jackson got were some

Delegate Julia Hicks leads a cheer for her candidate on the last day of the 1988 convention. Even at this point, no one was sure what to expect from Jackson: Would he continue to shun Dukakis, or would he urge his backers to support the ticket? Not until his rousing speech at the end of the convention did Jackson make his intentions clear.

changes in party rules concerning the selection of convention delegates for 1992, an assurance that members of his staff would be employed by the Dukakis campaign, and, for himself, the use of a chartered plane during the fall campaign.

Seeing Dukakis and Jackson arm in arm at the press conference, most Democrats breathed a sigh of relief. Their party was whole again. Among Jackson's ardent partisans, however, the feelings were rather different. "A plane for Jesse to campaign for Dukakis. So what?" snorted a Jackson delegate from Mississippi. Hosea Williams, an old ally from the civil rights movement, saw matters in a similar light: "Basically, Dukakis got Jesse in that meeting and told Jesse to go to hell."

For the media, Jackson put up a brave front, denying that he had lost a thing, but his family and his closest advisers knew he was depressed. His campaign was over. He had, for all the world to see, come out second best in his altercation with Dukakis. All that remained for him in Atlanta was his speech to the convention on Tuesday night.

Prior to the speech, Jackson recalled, several party officials asked him which governor or senator he would like to have present him to the convention. "None of them," he replied. "Who do you want then?" they asked. "The Jackson Five," he said. A singing group? "The Jackson Five I'm referring to are my kids."

On Tuesday evening, before a throng bursting the seams of Atlanta's Omni Center, the five Jackson children, Jacqueline, Yusef, Jonathan, Santita, and Jesse, Jr., one after the other, came to the rostrum and spoke of their father. "We, the children of Jesse and Jacqueline Jackson, are proud to be Jacksons," proclaimed Jesse, Jr.

At three minutes before 11 o'clock eastern time, Jesse Jackson, dressed in a dark gray pin-striped suit; a pale blue shirt with a highly starched, long-pointed

*His image projected on the huge
television screens above him,
Jackson (center) rocks listeners
with his powerful convention
address. In the 55-minute speech,
repeatedly interrupted with cheers
and applause, Jackson reached
out to the nation's poor and
pledged to support the Democratic
ticket.*

collar; and a red tie with white polka dots, stepped to
the microphones. He smiled and showed the thumbs-
up sign to the delegates and spectators in the hall.
They cheered him madly and waved red-and-white
Jesse! signs.

At last, when the demonstration showed signs of
subsiding, Jackson started to speak. His voice was
hoarse. "When I look out at this convention, I see
the face of America, red, yellow, brown, black, and
white. We are all precious in God's sight—the real
rainbow coalition."

From his front-row box seat, Jimmy Carter listened intently. Fifty-five minutes later, when Jackson
finished, the former president would say he had just

heard "the best speech ever given at a convention, certainly in my lifetime."

Jackson spoke of his mentor, now 20 years dead: "Dr. Martin Luther King, Jr., lies only a few miles from us tonight. Tonight he must feel good as he looks down upon us. We sit here together, a rainbow, a coalition—the sons and daughters of slave masters and the sons and daughters of slaves sitting together around a common table, to decide the direction of our party and our country. His heart would be full tonight."

In her seat, Coretta Scott King, the great man's widow and someone who had always been wary of Jackson, brushed away a tear.

The hoarseness had vanished from Jackson's voice. So had the petulance that had colored his dispute with Michael Dukakis. He spoke of love and common ground, of unity and working together. To the enormous television audience, mostly white and mostly middle class, he described his people—the poor and the dispossessed.

"Most poor people are not on welfare. . . . I know. I live amongst them. I'm one of them. I know they work. I'm a witness. They catch the early bus. They work every day. They raise other people's children. They work every day. They clean the streets. They work every day. They drive vans with cabs. They work every day. They change the beds you slept in in these hotels last night and can't get a union contract. They work every day."

His voice now exploding into a shout, now retreating to a husky whisper, Jackson had the audience in the palm of his hand.

In a modest two-bedroom apartment in southeast Atlanta, Betty Strozier sat close to her television set, not wanting to miss a word of Jackson's speech. Now and then she clasped her hands and silently nodded. For the past 19 years, she had raised 3 sons by herself. She worked every day as a seamstress, and she made

$9,000 a year. "We don't have a lot, but what we have is ours," she said. "Black people have always learned to make do."

An Atlanta cabdriver said that during the speech "not a driver drove, not a hooker hooked. We all found bars with TVs."

Proudly, Jackson spoke of himself: "I know abandonment and people being mean to you, and saying you're nothing and nobody, and can never be anything. I understand. . . . I'm adopted. When I had no name, my grandmother gave me her name. . . . So I wouldn't have a blank space, she gave me a name to hold me over. I understand when you have no name. . . .

"Born in a three-room house, bathroom in the backyard, slop jar by the bed, no hot and cold running water. I understand. . . .

"My mother, a working woman. So many days she went to work early with runs in her stockings. She knew better, but she wore runs in her stockings so that my brother and I could have matching socks and not be laughed at at school. . . .

"Every one of these funny labels they put on you, those of you who are watching this broadcast tonight in the projects, on the corners, I understand. Call you outcast, low down, you can't make it, you're nothing, you're from nobody, subclass, underclass— when you see Jesse Jackson, when my name goes in nomination, your name goes in nomination."

For at least the 50th time, the Democratic convention applauded his words. He was nearly finished. "You must not surrender," he said. "You may or may not get there, but just know that you're qualified and you hold on and hold out. We must never surrender. America will get better and better. Keep hope alive. Keep hope alive. Keep hope alive. On tomorrow night and beyond, keep hope alive.

"I love you very much. I love you very much."

2

THE DRIVING FORCE

TALL AND GRACEFUL, with a fine figure, Helen Burns was one of the prettiest girls in Greenville, South Carolina. What's more, she had the best singing voice in her class at Sterling High School, a voice so good that eventually five music colleges offered her scholarships. But during the spring of 1941, when she was 16, her hopes for a singing career and her dreams of a brighter life turned to dust. She found out she was pregnant, and because of that, she faced dishonor and shame.

She faced it first at home. Her mother, Matilda Burns, had been through the same thing herself, having as a teenager borne Helen out of wedlock. Ever since, she prayed Helen would avoid her own fate—no husband, hard days working as a maid for a white family, never having enough time or money or anything else. Enraged at her daughter, she offered nothing in the way of sympathy. "It's your responsibility," she said.

Matters were just as bad at church. Word of Helen's pregnancy spread quickly, and when it got to the worshipers at the Springfield Baptist Church, they voted to expel her from the congregation. Only later, when she confessed, "I have sinned against the church," was she restored to membership. And as if

Jesse Burns, pictured here at the age of 13, became Jesse Jackson when his mother's husband, Charles Jackson, legally adopted him in 1957. Fond of Jackson, the boy also developed a warm relationship with his blood father, Noah Robinson, Sr.

693

her mother's anger and the church's hard heart were not sufficient, Helen had to endure the sneers of her classmates and the scorn of family and townspeople. Thirty years later, a relative would still speak of Helen's pregnancy as "this terrible, dishonorable disgrace."

Who could blame her for running away? With the baby's father, she fled to Chicago. But escape proved to be no solution, and before long she returned to Greenville, hearing once more her mother say the coming baby was "your responsibility."

"I gladly accepted," Helen recalled years later. "I said, O.K., that singing career is over. I was committed to being a real mother."

Early on the morning of October 8, 1941, Matilda Burns sent for a midwife, Minnie Mason, and at 9:00 A.M., she delivered Helen's baby, a 7-pound, 4-ounce boy. "It seemed the child was in a hurry to get here," Mason said. "By the time the doctor arrived, I had just wrapped him in a blanket and laid him in bed with his mother." Helen and Matilda named the infant Jesse Louis Burns, his first two names coming from his father's side of the family.

"He was a charmer from the start," said a neighbor. "Always causing everything. He'd give you a little old sexy smile. I couldn't stand it. I'd run up those steps and bite him."

Two years after her son's birth, on October 2, 1943, Helen married Charles Jackson, a 24-year-old postal worker. Like millions of other wartime newlyweds, the Jacksons had only a brief time together. Charles, who had been drafted into the armed services, was dispatched to his unit shortly after the wedding. As everyone in the black neighborhoods of Greenville seemed to know, Charles was not Jesse's father. Yet Helen wanted her son to believe otherwise. Time and again, she showed little Jesse a photograph of Charles in his soldier's uniform and said, "Your father's coming home soon."

When Jackson did come home from the war, he followed his wife's lead. "I never told him I was not his father because I didn't want him to grow up thinking he was different," Jackson recalled. "At four and five years old he was calling me Daddy, following me around, tugging at my knee."

The neighborhood children were less accommodating. By the time Jesse was about six, they had begun a cruel taunting on the playground at Happy Hearts Park. "Your daddy ain't none of your daddy," they chanted at Jesse. "You ain't nothing but a no-body, nothing but a no-body."

In tears, Jesse would run home to his mother's embrace. "He cried a lot," she remembered. "He would try to be very brave. He never came home and repeated the things they said—you had to read the expression on his face." Bit by bit, from his mother, from his grandmother, from his playmates, Jesse found out the truth, and he stopped calling Charles Jackson "Daddy."

Jesse did not have to look far to find his blood father. Noah Robinson was one of the best-known black men in Greenville, and at the time of Jesse's birth, he lived right next door to Matilda Burns and her daughter, Helen. "I didn't have any children by my own wife," Robinson said years later. "Helen, she was pretty, she was a baby—we just got to liking each other, and it all started. Then Helen said to me, 'I'll have a child for you.' I said, 'Well, you know I'm married, I can't do that kind of thing.' Well, it happened. Everybody in town knew."

And everyone talked about it. But Robinson was not one to let the gossip of a small town get in his way. He was a man on the move and he was after success. When Jesse came to know him as his blood father, Robinson was a valued employee of the Ryan

Greenville, South Carolina (pictured on a postcard from the early 1940s), was a pleasant, quiet city of 60,000 residents when Jackson was born there in 1941. Like other southern communities of the era, however, Greenville was also a city of strictly enforced racial segregation.

textile mill and had settled his family into Greenville's best black neighborhood. His fieldstone house, the one with a wrought-iron *R* on the chimney, sat on a large, shady corner lot and had a basketball court in back and a brick wall in front and along the sides.

Tall, barrel chested, and brown skinned, Robinson had as a young man fought his way to a Golden Gloves championship. Long after hanging up the boxing gloves, he stayed a slugger, becoming particularly combative if he was on the receiving end of a racial slur. As one of his sons would say years later, "Few whites got funny with Daddy. He'd punch them out." Once, at the Ryan mill, a white executive gave a few pokes to Robinson's posterior. In a flash, Robinson spun around and launched a right hook that knocked his tormentor out cold.

For punching a white, let alone a white boss, virtually every other southern black would have been fired instantly, perhaps even driven out of town. Not Noah Robinson. He had the good fortune to be employed by John J. Ryan. Remarkably, the mill owner fired the white executive, explaining that he liked Robinson's spirit. During the years that followed, Ryan continued to patronize and promote Robinson. When Robinson wished to take his family to Philadelphia for a summer visit, it was Ryan who bought them first-class tickets on the Crescent, the premier train of the Southern Railway.

Thereafter, the Robinsons took the Crescent to Philadelphia every summer, no one among them enjoying the trip more than Noah Robinson, Jr., who was 10 months younger than Jesse Burns. Noah, Jr., seemed to have been born lucky. He inherited his father's golden brown skin and aquiline nose, lived in the fine house with its own basketball court, and when it came to his education, had John J. Ryan pulling strings to gain his entry into an exclusive Catholic school.

When he was seven or eight, young Noah became aware of his half brother, Jesse. "I was playing on the playground with a group of boys and some lady called me over," he recalled. "She whispered to me, 'See that kid over there with the curly hair, well, he's your brother.' " At home that evening, said Noah, Jr., his father "sank down in the telephone chair and explained what had happened."

All along, Robinson had kept track of Jesse, often going to the playground or schoolyard to watch him from a distance. Now and then, he slipped Helen Jackson some money for the boy, and each Thanksgiving and Christmas he sent her an overflowing basket of seasonal delicacies. But Noah's wife drew the line at any closer relationship. Unsurprisingly, she had no desire to be reminded of her husband's affair with Helen. "I'd want to be with him so bad," Robinson said of Jesse.

Jesse felt the same way. There were days when he would sneak up to the fieldstone house with the wrought-iron *R* on the chimney and stare into a window, hoping to catch a glimpse of his father. "Sometimes I wouldn't see him right away and Noah

Junior would tell me he was out there," Robinson recalled. "No telling how long he could have been there. As soon as I would go to the window and wave, he would wave back and run away."

Jesse was never invited in, and when the Robinsons left for their annual summer vacation in Philadelphia, Jesse stayed in Greenville, feeling miserable and deserted. "I didn't know until Jesse was a big boy that he used to cry when the rest of us would take off and leave him behind," Robinson said.

Eventually, the Robinsons and Jacksons patched things up. By the time Jesse was a teenager, he was a regular and welcome visitor to his blood father's home. But those early years of rejection, of being told by his playmates he was a "nobody," of always being on the outside looking in, left their mark.

"If your father says my blood is your blood, but really you're denied, it has to affect you on the inside," Jesse's schoolboy coach said nearly 40 years later. "If you've got a lot of pride, and Jesse has that, this can get painful. I think that was the driving force behind whatever he's done."

Having seen the well-to-do Robinsons, Jesse knew he was missing a great deal. "You sense these distinctions," he told writer Gail Sheehy in 1987. "You long for the privileges other people have." In truth, the Jacksons had more than most. Charles earned a steady $3,000 per year from the post office, and Helen, who had attended beauty college after giving up on a singing career, brought in additional income as a hairdresser.

"We were never poor," Charles Jackson insisted. "We never wanted for anything. We've never been on welfare, because I was never without a job. We never begged anybody for a dime. And my family never went hungry a day in their lives."

Jackson provided his stepson with more than financial support: In 1957, when Jesse was 16, he legally adopted him. By then, Jesse had come to love the man he called Charlie Henry. He later dedicated a collection of his speeches "to Charles Jackson, who adopted me and gave me his name, his love, his encouragement, discipline and a high sense of self-respect."

Until Jesse was in the sixth grade, the Jacksons lived on University Ridge Street, near Furman University, in a three-room cottage with a coal bin beneath the floorboards and a toilet on the back porch. In the early 1950s, they moved to Fieldcrest Village, which the city directory of the time described as "a housing project for the colored located at the end of Greenacre Road." The federally funded complex consisted of square brick buildings divided into two-story row houses. It was a step up in the world for the Jacksons. Their home had a living room and kitchen downstairs and two bedrooms and a bath upstairs. They needed the larger space; it was also home for Helen's mother, Matilda, and for Jesse's half brothers, Charles and George.

The black neighborhoods of Greenville were tightly knit and self-supporting. "There were two or three people in the neighborhood who just kept big

Sterling High School's popular football coach, Joseph D. Mathis, counsels Jackson (center) and his teammates during halftime of a 1957 game. Mathis spotted Jackson as a winner early on: "I told him he was going to be heir apparent to great things," recalled the coach of his star quarterback.

pots of vegetable soup on," Jesse Jackson recalled. "When folks didn't have any food, they couldn't go to the Salvation Army because they were black. They couldn't get Social Security; they couldn't get welfare. But folks had a tradition of being kind to one another, because that was our roots."

Matilda Burns, matriarch of the house and called Aunt Tibby by nearly everyone, took a particular interest in Jesse. She told him he was special, that someday he would be some*body*: "Nothing is impossible for those who love the Lord," she said. "Come hell or high water, if you got the guts, boy, ain't nothing or nobody can turn you around." Above all, she taught him never to forsake hope. "So, every goodbye ain't gone," she would say. "Just hold on; there's joy coming in the morning."

Early on, Jesse showed signs of realizing his grandmother's hopes. Family legend has it that when he was five he announced, "One of these days I'm going to preach." However precocious, it was not an unlikely ambition. Jesse had heard from his mother that the Robinsons had produced a long line of Baptist ministers. Closer to home, his grandmother was the soul of religious devotion. Helen and Charles Jackson both sang in the church choir and had pictures of Jesus Christ on their walls and mantel.

At the age of nine, Jesse won a church election to the National Sunday School Convention, and once a month, at Sunday services, he spoke about the organization's business to the full congregation. To do so, he had to overcome both stage fright and a slight stutter in his speech.

"We developed a life-style built around the Bible," Jesse Jackson once said; for his stepfather, that meant his children were not only devout but hardworking. Jesse started working when he was six, picking up wood scraps in a lumberyard. From then on, before and after school and during the summer,

he worked at whatever jobs were open to a black youngster: hawking concessions at Furman games, shining shoes, ushering at a movie theater, caddying at the Greenville Country Club, and, by the time he was in high school, waiting on tables at the Poinsett Hotel.

Jesse's grandmother was not alone in thinking him special. "He stood head and shoulders above everybody at the age of six and could he talk," J. D. Mathis, his school coach, recalled. "I told him he was going to be heir apparent to great things."

On the white side of town, just about no one believed that Jesse or, for that matter, any black person was in the slightest way special. For the 60,000 residents of Greenville, white supremacy and segregation were facts of life, and as far as the whites were concerned, the sooner a youngster like Jesse learned it, the better. One day, he recalled later, "I went to catch a bus with my mother, and the sign above the bus driver's head said Colored Seat from the Rear. . . . My mother had to pull me to the back. I said I wanted to sit up front. She said, 'Let's go.' She pinched me."

Jackson (back row, third from right) stands next to his best friend, Owen Perkins (wearing dark tie), in a 1958 portrait of Sterling High's Camera Club. An honors student and sports star, Jackson also participated in almost every extracurricular activity his school offered.

Betty Davis, Sterling High's Miss Basketball of 1958, leaves her coronation ceremony on the arm of the school's tall, handsome basketball star, 17-year-old Jesse Jackson.

He risked more than a pinch by defying the customs of segregation. The corner grocery, a hangout for Jesse and his friends, was run by a white man named Jack. "We used to run in there and play with him, so I always thought of him as a friend," Jesse Jackson said.

One day, as shoppers crowded the aisles and Jack sliced bologna for a customer, Jesse rushed in. "Jack, I got to go right away and I got to have some candy," he shouted. Jack ignored him. Jesse repeated his demand. Again, no response. So Jesse whistled at the storekeeper. Jack dropped the bologna, reached under the counter for a .45 caliber revolver, and aimed it at Jesse's face. "Goddamn you," he screamed, "don't you ever whistle at me no more as long as you live." Everyone froze. "That store was full of black folks," Jesse recalled, "but not one of them moved and I didn't either."

Faced with Whites Only signs on theaters, restaurants, drinking fountains, and rest rooms, the blacks of Greenville did what they could to preserve a measure of dignity. "We would say we didn't want to drink water because we weren't thirsty," Jackson remembered, "or we didn't want to eat because we weren't hungry, or we didn't want to go to the movie theater because we didn't want to see the picture. Actually, we were lying because we were afraid."

They addressed the inequity of segregation in small ways—mocking the oppressive whites, for example. A schoolmate remembered how Jesse "used to make up jokes about whites, how foolish and stupid they were. He used to have me in stitches. He used to turn things around. The white and black football teams couldn't play together. And Jesse would always say, that's because they're scared they'd get whupped. Because the black team is better."

He was probably right about the football squads. Sterling High School, with Jesse Jackson playing quarterback, steamrollered nearly every team it played. "Jesse was the kind of kid you wanted as a quarterback," said his coach, "clean and an all-American type. He was big and he could take a punch and then dish out a blow."

Jesse was the picture of confidence when he took over as quarterback his junior year. Even the team's seniors, who were accustomed to pushing underclassmen around, respected him. In the huddle during one game, an older player, a wide receiver, said he doubted that Jesse could get the ball to him on a long fly pattern. "It'll be there—just make sure you are," Jesse snapped. And it was.

Unlike some other athletes, Jesse was as attentive to textbooks as he was to playbooks. "He was the only football player I ever had that asked for his assignment if he was going to miss class because of football practice," said a Sterling teacher. "The others would make excuses." It paid off. Jackson compiled an academic record so strong that, as a senior, he was chosen for the National Honor Society. "Growing up taught me to make A's; when you do people have to hang around you. With D's, they don't," he said.

But it was his athletic gifts that brought stadium crowds to their feet and that had girls, as Coach Mathis said, "falling all over themselves to get to Jesse." He heard the cheers year-round, playing not only football but basketball and baseball, too.

Every school has its all-around athlete. At Sterling it was Jesse Jackson. At Greenville High, the white school across town, Mr. Everything was Dickie Dietz. Sterling and Greenville, of course, never met on the field, but in pickup games, whites and blacks played ball together—until, as Jackson recalled, "the police would catch us and run us off." In these encounters, Jackson apparently got the best of Dietz. But for the local newspaper, it was all Dietz.

Jackson (25) offers a big smile in this 1959 yearbook shot of the Sterling High basketball team. The young athlete's skills attracted attention both on and off the court; according to Coach Mathis, the girls of Greenville "fell all over themselves to get to Jesse."

On the same night during one football season, Dietz kicked the extra point in a 7–6 win, while, at Sterling's Sirrine Stadium, Jackson had switched to halfback and scored all three of his team's touchdowns. The next day's paper headlined Dietz's heroic extra point. "Way down at the bottom of the page," Jesse remembered: "'Jackson makes three touchdowns. Sterling wins.' We lived with that kind of imbalance."

In the spring of 1959, a group of major league baseball scouts arrived in Greenville and invited the local talent to a tryout camp. Jackson and Dietz both showed up. A fireballing pitcher, Jesse had been striking out batters right and left, but it was Dietz, a slugging catcher, whom the scouts really wanted to see. "They asked me to pitch," Jackson said, "and guess who was doing the hitting? Dickie Dietz!"

For the first time in an organized competition, it was Jackson against Dietz, Sterling versus Greenville, black against white. Sitting together in the bleachers, several dozen blacks cheered themselves hoarse. "Yaaay, Jesse!" they screamed.

Dietz foul-tipped one pitch. That was it—the only wood he laid to one of Jackson's pitches. Three times the mighty Dietz struck out.

The blazing exhibition so impressed the scout for the San Francisco Giants that he offered Jackson a contract that carried a $6,000 signing bonus and an opportunity to play B-level ball in the minor leagues. That was quite a lot of money in 1959, twice what Jackson's stepfather earned in a year at the post office. Then Jackson discovered that the Giants had signed Dietz to a contract for A ball and handed him a bonus worth $95,000.

"I don't want this," Jackson informed the Giants.

He was going to college. "Six thousand seems big, but it can go fast," he explained years later. "I knew a college education would be less risk and greater return."

3

"I ONLY WANT MY FREEDOM"

H EY, NIGGER, OVER here!" the red-faced men in the bleachers at Textile Hall would shout. Jesse Jackson would haul over his vendor's tray of soft drinks, and somebody would give him a dollar, then want change for a ten. It was all in a night's work if you were black and sold concessions at the basketball games of Furman University.

Watching the games, Jackson dared to dream of a day when he would wear the purple and white of Furman, play on the court in Textile Hall, and, with his exploits, thrill the same fans who now yelled, "Hey, nigger, over here." He would show them.

It was not to be. Furman had never admitted a black and, in 1959, had no intention of doing so. However, in Bob King, a Furman coach, Jackson had a friend. Knowing of his desire to attend college and impressed by his athletic skills, King helped Jackson obtain a football scholarship to the University of Illinois. While the leading universities in Dixie stayed lily-white, the football powers of the Big Ten recruited talented southern blacks and were glad to have them on their rosters.

Jackson arrived in Champaign, Illinois, in the late summer of 1959. He expected to pick up where

The biggest man on campus: Quarterback Jackson carries the ball for his alma mater, North Carolina Agricultural and Technical State University in Greensboro. Jackson was not only a football star but an honors student and president of the student body.

he had left off in high school, calling the signals and heaving touchdown passes, but a coach of the freshman team set him straight. Blacks were running backs, linemen, and ends. "You people," the coach kept saying. Dutifully, Jackson lined up at left halfback, then at left end. Inwardly he seethed. "It was traumatic for me," he said, "black players being reduced to entertainers."

Jackson was no happier away from the football field. Set on a sprawling campus, with an enrollment of 25,000 and a formidable academic reputation, the university seemed remote, even hostile, to the newcomer from South Carolina. Blacks had long been accepted as students, but seldom as equals. "We were reduced to a subculture at Illinois," Jackson observed. "The annual interfraternity dance was the social event of the fall, only the black fraternities weren't invited. My black friends and I were down at the Veterans of Foreign Wars listening to 45s while the white folks were jumping to Lionel Hampton in the gym. Live."

Unhappy about what he had found in the integrated North, Jackson left Illinois after his freshman year, not to return. In the fall of 1960, he enrolled at North Carolina Agricultural and Technical State University, a predominantly black state college in Greensboro. "North Carolina A&T was my choice because that was where the sit-ins started and it was the students who started them," Jackson explained.

Eight months before Jackson's arrival in Greensboro, four North Carolina A&T freshmen, Ezell Blair, Jr., Franklin McCain, Joe McNeil, and David Richmond, had walked downtown and entered the F. W. Woolworth store. When they reached the lunch counter, they sat down. By so doing, they had broken the law and custom of segregation. The counter was for whites and whites only.

A black waitress had approached the young men. "Fellows like you make our race look bad," she said,

and refused to serve them. The four smiled under-standingly but remained in their seats and stayed there until the store closed. The next morning they were back, once more patiently waiting to be served. Nineteen more students had joined them. On the following day, February 3, a total of 85 students showed up. Organized by then, they began to sit in shifts of several hours each. The sit-in movement had been born.

The sit-ins raced across the upper South like wildfire. Over the following year, 50,000 students, white and black, all of them quietly determined to end segregation in eating places, took the simple, eloquent step of sitting down and waiting. They faced a barrage of hostility from whites, who screamed obscenities, poured condiments over them, and pressed lighted cigarettes into their skin.

But the demonstrations worked. By the end of 1961, rather than see their businesses hopelessly

North Carolina A&T students stage a sit-in at the whites-only lunch counter of a Greensboro variety store in 1960. Such courageous protests prompted Jesse Jackson to enter the largely black state college that fall.

disrupted, store owners in 200 southern cities had desegregated their lunch counters. The peaceful protest, born on a North Carolina campus, had scored a significant victory in the American civil rights movement. Was it any wonder Jesse Jackson decided to enroll at North Carolina A&T?

A&T, which also had a football team, welcomed the refugee from Illinois. The team played on lumpy fields ringed by splintery wooden bleachers, light-years from the splendor of the Big Ten, but it did not matter to Jackson. At A&T he was the quarterback, calling the plays, running the show. An outcast at Illinois, he became the biggest man on campus in Greensboro—Saturday's hero, student body president, honor student, and second vice-grand basileus of Omega Psi Phi, his fraternity.

As in high school, Jackson had an eye for the young women in his vicinity and they for him. At first, though, his interest in Jacqueline Lavinia Davis, a 17-year-old freshman, was not romantic. Struggling with his term paper ("Should Red China Be Admitted to the United Nations?"), Jackson had approached Davis for some advice. After talking a while, she must have wondered why he was asking. Jesse "was a bit too fast, a bit too full of himself" to be interested in what anyone else had to say. "He didn't appeal to me initially," she said. "I was from a puritanical culture and I thought he was a little too quick in formulating opinions."

She would change her mind.

Born in Fort Pierce, Florida, in 1944, Jackie Davis came from a family of migrant farm workers. The oldest of five children, she never knew her father, but she had the protection and unbounded love of her mother, who supported her family by picking beans for 15 cents an hour. For a time, Davis considered becoming a nun, then decided on college and North Carolina A&T. In 1961, she was studying psychology and sociology.

Leaders of North Carolina A&T's sororities and fraternities gather for a campus conference in 1962. Standing third from the right is the second vice-grand basileus of Omega Psi Phi, aka Jesse Jackson.

Davis let no one wonder where she stood politically. Highly intelligent and intensely committed to the civil rights movement, she participated in demonstrations and was known on campus as a fiery champion of left-wing causes. She was also known as a beauty. An inch over five feet tall with a stunning figure, she possessed an air of absolute confidence.

Jackson found himself smitten. As he and Davis began seeing more of one another, what started as discussions of politics and world affairs turned to intimacy and laughter. Jackson was Davis's first boyfriend, and he was determined to be her last. On campus one day, to the delight of his friends, he shouted, "Hey, Jackie, you're going to marry me."

And she did. Sometime in 1962, she discovered she was pregnant. "I think Jesse did it to catch me," she speculated in 1987. "Because he kept asking me, 'Are you feeling sick?' A baby? I hadn't thought about a baby." In late 1962, they had a quiet wedding at Jackson's home in Greenville. "We got married and established family security. We broke the cycle," Jackson said, alluding to his and Davis's backgrounds of illegitimacy and single-parent households. On July 16, 1963, Jackie Jackson gave birth to their first child, a daughter they named Santita.

Although she dropped out of college to make a home and raise a family, Jackie Jackson retained her independence. "I did not marry my husband to imprison him," she once said. "Nor did he marry me to place me in a prison." Over the years, the Jackson marriage has been one of respect and equality. "He loves basketball," she once remarked, attempting to explain their relationship. "It doesn't make me happy to go and watch him play basketball. So, therefore, I love to swim. I think life is as simple as agreeing that you play basketball and I swim."

By 1963, Jesse Jackson had become the leader of student activism at A&T. With the same confidence he showed on the football field, he led columns of marchers from the campus to the local restaurants, theaters, and public buildings that barred or segregated blacks. Part of a southern campaign sponsored by the Congress of Racial Equality (CORE), the Greensboro protests proved, beyond any doubt, that Jesse Jackson was a man people followed.

On June 6, 1963, the demonstrators decided to intensify the protest, to deliberately court arrest, and to fill the jails with students whose only crime was demanding an end to segregation. That afternoon, Jackson, wearing a sharply pressed suit and a snap-brim hat, led several hundred demonstrators into downtown Greensboro. Reaching the intersection in front of the municipal building, they sat down and refused to budge. "I know I am going to jail," Jackson said to them. "I'm going without fear. It's a principle that I have. . . . I'll go to the chain gang if necessary."

With the students encamped on the street and traffic snarled for blocks, a police captain approached Jackson. "Now you've done it," he sputtered. "You're really messing up now." Jackson returned the captain's stare. Then, in a broad gesture, he pointed to the municipal building, headquarters of the city government that condoned and enforced segregation. "No," he said, "It's not me, Captain, they're the ones that are messing up."

The police moved in and arrested 278 of the demonstrators, including their leader, on charges of inciting a riot. Like nonviolent protesters before him, Jackson refused to post bond, preferring jail to any compromise with injustice. "I'm going to jail because I refuse to let another man put a timetable on

Detective William Jackson escorts activist college student Jesse Jackson to jail after arresting him for "inciting a riot"—actually, for organizing a peaceful protest against segregation—in June 1963. The two Jacksons, who crossed paths in numerous arrest situations, often engaged in philosophical discussions and eventually became good friends.

North Carolina A&T's president, Samuel Proctor, gives Jackson a hearty handshake and a medal for scholastic excellence in 1963. Proctor, who saw a fine potential clergyman in the 21-year-old South Carolinian, helped him get a scholarship at the Chicago Theological Seminary.

my freedom," he explained. "We aren't asking for integration. We're asking for desegregation and there's a difference. I only want my freedom."

When he left jail a few weeks later—the police dropped the charges—Jackson was a bigger man on campus than he had ever been before. Greensboro had caved in. Wanting peace and quiet rather than daily demonstrations, the city desegregated its downtown. Moreover, the national civil rights movement had taken notice of the tall young man from A&T. He became a field director for CORE, marked by the organization's director, James Farmer, as a rising star.

That summer, 21-year-old Jesse Jackson graduated from A&T with a degree in sociology. Before the commencement exercises, he had decided on his next step: a career in the ministry. He passed up a scholarship to Duke University Law School, and with the counsel and assistance of A&T president Samuel Proctor, secured a Rockefeller fellowship to the Chicago Theological Seminary.

Jackson's decision had followed a period of considerable soul-searching. "One night he woke up and said he had an odd dream," said his former A&T roommate Charles Carter. "He said he thought he had been called to preach. He was shaking. I never saw him look so serious before."

The choice of the ministry was not altogether a matter of midnight visions. As a boy, Jackson had taken pride in the preachers who had cropped up in every generation of the Robinson family. Later, his enthusiasm for the ministry had cooled as he began to look down on the fundamentalist, fire-and-brimstone theology of the black church. "For a long time I reacted negatively to the whole preaching thing," he said, "because of my hang-up on traditional preaching and traditional preachers."

The civil rights movement restored his ambition. It had been born in the black churches of the South and its leaders were ministers. Jesse Jackson meant to join them.

With his wife and daughter, Jackson moved to Chicago and began his seminary studies in early 1964. "I really thought by going to seminary school it would be quiet and peaceful and I could reflect," he said. He described his days there as "precious," but in the spring of 1965, six months before his graduation, he dropped out of school and headed for Selma, Alabama. There, in the heart of the old Confederacy, Martin Luther King, Jr., was leading a crusade to secure for southern blacks the most elemental right of citizenship: the right to vote. ❧

4

A PATCH OF BLUE SKY

MARTIN LUTHER KING, JR., was the commanding moral force of his generation—the visionary leader of the civil rights movement. Beginning with the Montgomery bus boycott of 1955, King and the organization he founded, the Southern Christian Leadership Conference (SCLC), spearheaded a non-violent revolution against segregation in the American South. The defenders of the old order, that of white supremacy, fought them every step of the way, answering the peaceful protests of the SCLC with jailings, clubbings, lynchings, and midnight bombings.

It was what King expected, even desired. The nation, he believed, had to see and understand the true nature of racial persecution. So, in 1963, on their television screens and in their newspapers, middle-class Americans witnessed the horror of Birmingham, Alabama, where King was thrown into solitary confinement at the city jail and where his disciples, many of them children, were mangled by police attack dogs and knocked senseless by high-pressure water hoses.

By 1965, as a result of the previous year's federal civil rights act, the Whites Only signs had come down in the restaurants, theaters, and hotels of Dixie. But they remained in place on the ballot boxes. King's last great effort in the South was directed against the fear and discrimination that kept southern blacks off the voting rolls. For their campaign, he and the SCLC selected Selma, Alabama, the seat of a county where 15,000 blacks were eligible to vote but only 325 did. "We are demanding the ballot," he cried.

On Sunday, March 7, 1965, 600 marchers, nearly all of them black, massed at Brown Chapel in Selma to begin a protest march to Montgomery, the state capital, 54 miles away. The protesters got as far as the Edmund Pettus Bridge on the edge of Selma. There, a phalanx of local and state policemen awaited them. In a few minutes, tear gas was clogging the air, and defenseless marchers were being clubbed by police in riot gear and trampled by a mounted posse brandishing cattle prods. It was a bloodbath.

That evening, along with film of the gruesome spectacle, network television ran an appeal from King to his fellow clergy. Come to Selma, he pleaded, we will march again.

In Chicago, Jesse Jackson watched the events of Bloody Sunday and knew he had no choice but to answer King's appeal. He went straight to Selma. When he got there, Jackson did not melt into the throng of marchers but broke for the front ranks. "I remembered getting a little annoyed," said Andrew Young, one of King's principal aides, "because Jesse was giving orders from the steps of Brown Chapel and nobody knew who he was. All the other marchers came up getting in line, but Jesse, assuming a staff role, automatically started directing the marchers."

Jackson, wearing a porkpie hat and denim work clothes, spoke in a voice that carried across the street. "I thought it strange that he would be making a speech," recalled Betty Washington, a correspondent for the Chicago *Daily Defender*, "when he was not on the SCLC staff and had not been included in any

of the strategy meetings. He just seemed to have come from nowhere. Like, who *was* he? But he spoke so well, I recorded his statement anyway. I had the feeling that one day he might be important."

Jackson's audacious behavior caught the notice of the Reverend Ralph Abernathy, King's right-hand man and closest friend. "There was something about him that impressed me," Abernathy said of Jackson. "I could see the leadership potential in him." When Jackson asked if there were any openings on the SCLC staff, Abernathy took it up with King.

King was skeptical. He "did not agree with me that we ought to employ this young man on the basis of my experience with him during that short time," Abernathy recalled. "Reluctantly he went along, though."

Martin Luther King, Jr. (front row, at right of flag), leads 10,000 civil rights marchers on the last leg of their monumental 54-mile trek from Selma, Alabama, to Montgomery in March 1965. Holding hands with King is his wife, Coretta; next to her is SCLC aide Hosea Williams. Other notable marchers are labor leader A. Philip Randolph (second from left), Ralph Abernathy (fourth from left), and diplomat Ralph Bunche (sixth from left).

It was Jackson's good luck that the SCLC was just then shifting its attention from South to North. Selma, for the time being, would be King's last effort in the South. The campaign there and the successful completion of the march to Montgomery helped ensure congressional approval of the Voting Rights Act of 1965. With the federal government stepping in to register and protect previously disfranchised southern blacks, the last pillar of legal segregation had fallen.

What now most troubled King was the plight of northern blacks. They had long had equality before the law, but all too often, they endured lives of crime, illness, and poverty in dilapidated inner-city slums. King meant to do something about it by bringing the SCLC north. He chose to begin in Chicago, Jackson's new hometown.

Placed on the SCLC payroll at $3,000 a year, Jackson was assigned to work under James Bevel in Chicago. Bevel liked the new recruit and carefully instructed him in the ways of nonviolent protest. Jackson was amazed at how much Bevel knew. "Bevel was the real creative genius of that period," he said later, "one of the most creative thinkers I've ever been exposed to." And, he might have added, one of the most colorful.

King tolerated, even appreciated, Bevel's lively nature. His skill as an organizer and eloquence as a speaker were too great to do otherwise. A newcomer such as Jackson soon found that free spirits such as Bevel fit right in at the SCLC. A staff member recalled that the "SCLC was a very rowdy place," and, he could have said, one chronically short of money and often in organizational disarray. But never, ever, was it lacking in purpose.

Its purpose in 1965 and 1966 was open housing in the nation's second city. Blacks constituted the largest ethnic group in Chicago, and nearly all of them lived in slums on the south and west sides of town. The rest of the city was white, and that was the way the white working-class residents wanted it to stay. "Most Chicago whites hated blacks," wrote local newspaperman Mike Royko. "The only genuine difference between a southern white and a Chicago white was in their accent."

Running Chicago was its red-faced, pudgy—and incomparably shrewd—mayor and political boss, Richard J. Daley. "Under Daley," wrote historian Theodore H. White, "ethnic municipal politics were to reach their classic triumph as an art form, as distinctively American as baseball." As long as they were loyal Democrats, Chicagoans could find a place in Daley's machine or on the city payroll. This was true not only for the Irish, Jews, Poles, and Czechs, but for blacks as well. However, as everyone knew, the upper rungs on the political ladder were painted white.

Jackson had been active in Democratic politics while he was at A&T, campaigning for North Carolina's Democratic governor, Terry Sanford. To show his appreciation, Sanford gave his young supporter a letter of introduction to Daley. Shortly after he returned to Chicago, Jackson called on Daley and presented the letter. The mayor looked it up and down. "See your ward committeeman," he said. Daley was suggesting that if Jackson pounded the pavement of his precinct for a few elections and proved he could turn out the vote, then, perhaps, some job for him might be found. Something like— the mayor thought for a moment—coin collector on one of the city toll roads.

Jackson had called on Daley to establish a working relationship with city hall, not because he wanted a job. He was committed to the battle for civil rights and had no intention of leaving the SCLC. Thousands of Chicago blacks, however, would have

SCLC official James Bevel speaks at a black Chicago church in the mid-1960s. Once a successful rock and roll performer, Bevel had experienced a religious conversion and become a Baptist clergyman. By the time Jackson went to work for him in 1965, he was a veteran civil rights activist.

In 1965, when Chicago mayor Richard J. Daley (opposite page) met Jackson (above) for the first time, the old political boss regarded the young black activist as nothing more than an eager job seeker. In the years to come, Daley would learn he had made a serious misjudgment.

jumped at Daley's suggestion. It was through such patronage and favors that the Daley machine controlled the black vote and, for a long while, black behavior in Chicago. Black community leaders, particularly in the older, established South Side, were Daley's people. "Negro ministers may think they're servants of God, but they're servants of Daley—or maybe that's the same thing," joked one black politician.

"We entered a different world when we came to this northern city in 1966, a world we didn't fully understand," wrote Ralph Abernathy of the SCLC in Chicago. Driving a borrowed Cadillac, Jackson showed King and Abernathy around. The two ministers expressed amazement at the size of the city's sprawling South Side. "That's nothing," said Jackson. "Wait till you see the West Side." He took them there. Abernathy remembered "looking over at Martin and both of us shaking our heads. The number of people living in the squalid devastation was beyond our comprehension."

The public phase of the SCLC's Chicago campaign got under way on July 10, 1966—Freedom Sunday—with a lakefront rally at Soldier Field followed by a King-led march to City Hall. On Monday morning, King and 11 colleagues, including Jackson, met with Daley. The mayor pledged cooperation (although nothing too specific) and said that he too hated slums and was going to clean them up.

Keep stalling and maybe King will go away, seemed to be Daley's strategy, and so far, it seemed to be working. But at the Monday morning meeting, Al Raby, a local activist who had begun the Chicago open-housing movement and who had invited King to town in the first place, looked Daley straight in the eye. "I want you to know we are going to begin direct action, immediately," Raby said bluntly. Daley, who had a short fuse, lost his temper, and the meeting wound up as a shouting match.

Daley was angry because he was worried. By direct action, Raby meant that blacks from the inner city planned to march into the white blue-collar neighborhoods that excluded them. Such a move would pit two groups of Daley's staunchest supporters—blacks and white ethnics—against one another, a confrontation that could mean nothing but bad news to the mayor.

On the evening of July 29, a group of 50 protesters arrived in the all-white Gage Park neighborhood and settled down in front of the offices of the Halvorsen Realty Company. The demonstration's leaders—Jackson, Bevel, and Raby—announced that they would stay there all night to protest the firm's policies of discriminating against blacks. By 9 o'clock, more than 1,000 enraged whites had descended on the demonstrators. Although several dozen policemen strained to keep them back, the whites got close enough to shower the visitors with debris and racial epithets. The demonstrators retreated.

The next day, their number swollen to 500, the demonstrators returned to the Halvorsen office in Gage Park. This time, bottles and bricks hit both Jackson and Raby. On Sunday, Raby led a car caravan into Marquette Park, another all-white community. Before the day was over, 15 of the demonstrators' cars, all of them unoccupied, had been overturned and set afire.

On August 5, King himself led a procession into Marquette Park. Its residents greeted the 1964 winner of the Nobel Peace Prize with a hail of stones and broken glass. A rock struck King on the side of his head and he sank to one knee. "I would never forget the look in the eyes of this man who had survived Birmingham and Montgomery and Selma," wrote *Time* correspondent Robert Sam Anson. "It was of sheer terror." Although he was not badly hurt, King was appalled by the ferocity of northern whites. "I think the people from Mississippi ought to come to Chicago to learn how to hate," he said.

The marches continued. On Sunday, August 7, Jackson directed 2,000 protesters into the Belmont-Cregin neighborhood. When they stopped marching to kneel in prayer, they heard the neighborhood whites singing a familiar tune, an advertising jingle for a brand of frankfurters. Its lyrics, though, had been changed:

> I wish I were an Alabama trooper,
> That is what I would truly like to be:
> I wish I were an Alabama trooper
> 'Cause then I could kill the niggers legally.

The following day, with King out of town, Jackson announced the next target of the protest: Cicero, the tightly packed suburb just across Chicago's western city limit. The plan sent a shudder through nearly everyone who heard about it. Cicero promised to be not only the protest's next stop but its last.

A community of 70,000 people, every one of them white, Cicero held 2 claims to fame: During the 1920s, it had cheerfully welcomed the gangster Al Capone; and in 1951, when a black family purchased a house there, 4,000 whites had started a riot that ended only with the dispatch of the National Guard. "We expect violence," Jackson admitted. No one disagreed. "Jesus, they won't make it," said a Cicero politician. "If they get in, they won't get out."

Jackson's announcement caught the SCLC and the Chicago organizers off balance. The protest leaders had discussed going to Cicero but had reached no decision. King, away on SCLC business in Mississippi, was "a little angry," Abernathy recalled. "He had not wanted to tip off our future plans and . . . our demoralized army did not want to hear about even more difficult battlegrounds at a time when they were encountering enough trouble in Gage Park and Marquette Park."

To some of his colleagues in Chicago, Jackson had become a show horse, one no longer willing to pull with the team. "Jesse would often make major policy statements without clearing them with anyone," said Don Rose, a Chicago organizer. "The march announcement came one night when the cameras were on him. He couldn't resist saying something sensational."

King, too, had begun to speculate about Jackson's motives: Was he interested in the movement or in himself? Bevel often stood up for his friend when King questioned his devotion. "He's crude 'cause he's young," Bevel would say.

"No, he's ambitious," King would reply.

But no matter what the SCLC inner circle thought of Jackson, the organization stood behind his pledge of a march to Cicero and tentatively scheduled it for late August. Meanwhile, protests in other all-white neighborhoods kept on. It was too much for Mayor Daley. Marches day after day, combined with the specter of a racial holocaust in Cicero, brought him if not to his knees at least to the conference table.

After a series of meetings, Daley and the SCLC leaders reached an agreement on August 26: The city of Chicago would enforce the open-housing laws, and from then on, realtors would be compelled to stop discriminating against blacks.

King was ecstatic. Canceling plans for future Chicago-area marches, he announced that "the total eradication of housing discrimination has been made possible." Others, however, were not so sure. "I don't know," said Bevel when asked about the pact. "I'll have to think about it."

Bevel's doubts were well founded. As things turned out, Daley and his administration gave the agreement lip service but little else. The mayor had succeeded in stopping the marches and in getting King out of town. With that, his interest in open

Martin Luther King, Jr. (left), kneels in prayer with other SCLC members before beginning a civil rights demonstration. Although they were often beaten, jailed, and vilified by racist whites, King and his followers maintained a firm policy of nonviolence throughout their campaign.

housing quickly evaporated. A generation later, Chicago still possessed the most racially segregated housing patterns of any large American city.

Realizing he had been outmaneuvered, King attempted to turn Chicago blacks against their mayor; in late 1966, the SCLC launched a voter-registration drive. King might as well have decided to go 15 rounds with Muhammad Ali. When it came to registering voters and counting their ballots, Daley was the undisputed heavyweight champion. The SCLC got nowhere. In April 1967, Daley cruised to reelection for a fourth term, in the process capturing 73 percent of the total vote and a staggering 83 percent of the black vote.

In the midst of the storms over open housing and voter registration, there appeared a patch of blue sky for the SCLC, and it was largely Jackson's doing.

When Bevel had arrived in Chicago to set up an SCLC office, he brought along plans to implement Operation Breadbasket, the organization's economic arm. Founded in Philadelphia by the Reverend Leon Sullivan, transplanted to Atlanta and the SCLC in 1962, Breadbasket aimed to expand black employment at companies whose products blacks bought. If a company refused to hire more blacks, or if it discriminated against its existing black employees, then black consumers, organized by their ministers, would boycott the firm. Breadbasket also sought to encourage white-controlled businesses to invest in black-owned banks and companies.

Breadbasket appealed to Jackson, who found it particularly valuable in Chicago. With so many black preachers in the grip of the Daley machine, church endorsements of the open-housing campaign were few and far between. "It was clear that the ministers preferred a separate, but related program to the movement," Jackson recalled. Placed in charge of the Chicago operation by King in November 1965,

Jackson recruited more than 200 ministers to its banner within a few months.

The Breadbasket strategy was straightforward. First, identify firms that did business in black neighborhoods but that employed few blacks. Second, approach the company's executives and request they mend their ways. If that failed, begin picketing the company's retail outlets and encourage black consumers to take their trade elsewhere. A consumer boycott was a powerful weapon. "We are the margin of profit of every major item produced in America from General Motors cars on down to Kellogg's Corn Flakes," Jackson said.

Breadbasket first targeted Country's Delight Dairy, a company with no black drivers or sales representatives. At their first meeting, the dairy's executives told the Breadbasket ministers, in so many

Jackson and Ralph Abernathy exchange a hug before going into action at a Washington, D.C., protest march in the late 1960s. One of the first members of the civil rights movement to spot Jackson as a natural leader, Abernathy called him "a genius at motivating people."

words, to get lost. Within days, picket lines appeared in front of stores carrying Country's Delight products, and black consumers were buying other brands. After a week of seeing their milk sour in the groceries, dairy executives had a sudden change of heart. Within 30 days, a company spokesman announced, the dairy would hire 44 new black workers.

Strengthened by success, Operation Breadbasket swept through the rest of the dairy business in Chicago. By the end of the summer of 1966, 3 more dairies had agreed to provide blacks with 119 new jobs. "You can't beat them," groused a dairy boss. "They got that weapon and you have to respect it. If you don't you can go broke."

In August, Breadbasket began a boycott of Pepsi. Caving in quickly, Pepsico, Inc., came up with 32 new jobs. The bottlers of Coca-Cola, 7-Up, and Canfield surrendered without a fight, together promising 100 openings for blacks.

King was impressed with Breadbasket's achievements, particularly when he contrasted them with the dismal open-housing and voter-registration drives in Chicago. Jackson's stock rose. King doubled his SCLC salary, to $6,000 a year, and in early 1967 gave him control of the entire Operation Breadbasket program. Jackson responded by drafting strategies for expanding Breadbasket into other cities and into other fields, particularly those involved with helping black-owned businesses.

Jackson's relationship with King had its ups and downs. During 1967, it headed downward as King found it increasingly difficult to control his subordinate's activities. Jackson stayed in Chicago, preferring to run Operation Breadbasket from there rather than moving to SCLC headquarters in Atlanta, where he might have been monitored more closely. William Rutherford, the SCLC executive director, remembered King saying to him, "Jesse Jackson's so independent, I either want him in SCLC or out— you go whichever way you want to, but one way or the other, he's a part of SCLC or he's not a part of SCLC."

Sometimes it seemed Jackson just rubbed King the wrong way. "Martin had problems with Jesse because Jesse would ask questions," one associate said. He also tended to argue and press his case long past the point of accomplishing anything other than irritating King. King's interests in 1967 and early 1968 focused on opposing American involvement in Vietnam and organizing the Poor People's March on Washington. The more he concentrated on these projects, the less he wanted to hear about Operation Breadbasket.

And the less patience he had for arguing with Jackson. On a Saturday in late March 1968, during an exhausting, contentious SCLC meeting in Atlanta, Jackson made no attempt to hide his scorn for some of King's plans. Others did the same. King could take no more of it and abruptly got up to leave. Jackson rose and followed him to the door. King stopped in his tracks, spun around, and snapped, "If you are so interested in doing your own thing that you can't do what the organization is structured to do, go ahead. If you want to carve out your own niche in society, go ahead, but for God's sake don't bother me!"

Four days later, King left Atlanta to offer his help to some striking sanitation workers in Memphis, Tennessee. ❦

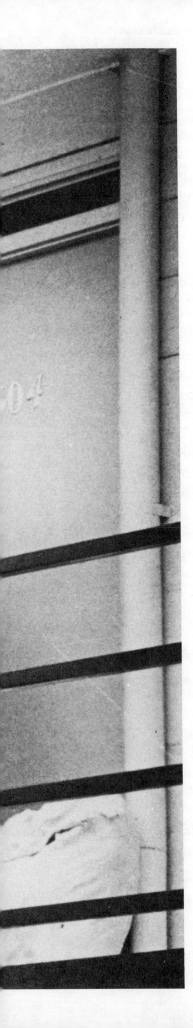

5

THE HEIR APPARENT

THERE WAS A chill in the early evening air in Memphis, and the driver of the white Cadillac limousine called up to Martin Luther King, Jr., waiting on the second-floor balcony of the Lorraine Motel, and said he had best bring a topcoat. "O.K.," came the reply.

Down in the motel courtyard, gathered around the Cadillac, killing time until they all got into the big car and went to dinner, were five of King's lieutenants: Andrew Young, James Bevel, Chauncey Eskridge, Hosea Williams, and, in a brown turtleneck shirt, brown trousers, and brown shoes, Jesse Jackson.

Jackson's mood also might well have been brown. He had come to Memphis with the others to organize a march on behalf of the striking garbage collectors, but his relations with King were chillier than the evening air. Far from regretting the tongue-lashing he had given Jackson the previous week in Atlanta, King had repeated it the night before. "Jesse, just leave me alone," he had said. "Go any place you want to, do anything you want to do, but leave me alone."

Martin Luther King, Jr. (center), and his aides Jackson and Ralph Abernathy gather on the balcony of the Lorraine Motel shortly after their arrival in Memphis, Tennessee, on April 3, 1968. Standing at the same spot the next day, King fell to the bullets of assassin James Earl Ray, an escaped white convict who later confessed to the murder and received a 99-year prison sentence.

There was no place Jackson wanted to go. "Don't send me away," he had begged King.

But on the balcony that evening, seeing Jackson downstairs by the white car, King had said to him, loud enough for everyone to hear: "I want you to come to dinner with me." Could it be the sign he was back in King's good graces?

Jackson smiled and took the moment to introduce Ben Branch, a musician who played for Operation Breadbasket in Chicago and who would be performing at a rally for the Memphis strikers that evening. "Ben, make sure you play 'Precious Lord, Take My Hand' at the meeting tonight," King said, leaning forward as he talked, placing both hands on the balcony railing. "Sing it real pretty."

It was one minute past six on April 4, 1968. King had not yet moved to fetch his topcoat. Ralph Abernathy was inside the room, number 306, that he shared with King, splashing on some of his roommate's Aramis aftershave lotion.

There came a muffled explosion, the kind that sounds like a car backfiring or a firecracker going off. The men around the Cadillac instinctively ducked for cover. Abernathy turned and through the open door of room 306 saw King's body sprawled on the balcony. He rushed out and found his friend lying in a spreading pool of blood. The right side of his jaw had been blown away.

"Martin, Martin, this is Ralph. Do you hear me? This is Ralph." King's lips moved, but no words came. An hour later, at five minutes past seven, he was pronounced dead. He was 39 years old.

The assassination of Martin Luther King, Jr., was a national tragedy. As soon as the bulletins of the shooting flashed onto radio and television, agonized and enraged blacks stormed into the streets. Over the next several days, rioting scarred and, in some cases, demolished the black neighborhoods of 126 cities.

Thirty-nine people died in the arson, looting, and gunfire. The carnage seemed a horrible negation of King's philosophy and legacy of nonviolence.

For Jackson, the assassination was a personal tragedy. King was his idol and inspiration, his mentor and moral conscience. Nevertheless, what his SCLC colleagues saw in the hours following the murder was not the picture of a grief-stricken disciple.

By every account of the shooting, Ralph Abernathy was the first to reach King. Then came Andrew Young, who raced upstairs from the courtyard. Following Young was James Laue, an observer from the Department of Justice occupying a nearby room, who placed a folded towel under King's bleeding head. Abernathy held his dying friend in his arms and on his lap. At six minutes past six, an ambulance arrived.

A mule-drawn caisson carries King's coffin through the streets of Atlanta. Among those accompanying the fallen leader are Jackson (last row, second from the left) and, at left rear of coffin, SCLC executive vice-president Andrew Young.

Hosea Williams recalled that after Jackson went up the staircase, "He just stood there. Then, I think he ran for a phone to call Coretta." In Atlanta, Coretta Scott King had just returned home from shopping. Jackson informed her of the shooting, advised her to come to Memphis, and to soften the news, said her husband had been wounded in the shoulder.

At 6:25, camera crews from the television networks started arriving. "Don't talk to them," Jackson ordered the other SCLC staffers. Minutes later, said Williams, "I was in my room. I looked out and saw Jesse talking to these TV people. . . . I heard Jesse say, 'Yes, I was the last man in the world King spoke to.' "

Jackson flew to Chicago later that evening. Early the next morning, after what had been a virtually sleepless night, several SCLC staff members mustered in a room at the Lorraine. The television, its volume low, was tuned to NBC's "Today Show." "Somebody called me," Williams said, "'Come quick, look who's on TV.' " It was Jackson, wearing the brown turtleneck from the night before. It was smeared with blood. To the amazement of his comrades in Memphis, Jackson was saying it was the blood of Martin Luther King, Jr., and that it had gotten there when he cradled the fallen leader in his arms.

The media picked up and held on to Jackson's version of the assassination: "Jesse ran to the balcony, held King's head, but it was too late," reported *Time*. The press also accepted Jackson's claim to the top: In 1969, *Playboy* called him "King's heir apparent."

There was, however, a question of precisely how much King's legacy was worth. During the last few years of his life, King had lost considerable standing in black America. His principles of nonviolence and integration had come under assault from all directions. The Black Muslims preached black separatism. Stokely Carmichael and H. Rap Brown promoted

Black Power. The Black Panthers embraced Marxist ideology and armed themselves for what they said was an inevitable war with whites. These black militants drew their greatest strength in the ghettos of northern cities, the very places where, as his failures in Chicago had shown, King was his weakest.

Jackson meant to succeed where King had failed. "Jesse was probably the only one . . . who could attract the urban young and still work on the program of nonviolence," said a Chicago associate. "It was an effort to update the spirit of Dr. King in the northern urban context, an effort to get kids who seemed to be going off in another direction."

Ralph Abernathy took over the leadership of the SCLC. Jackson's vehicle would be Operation Breadbasket; his message, black economic power.

Jackson's manner was in direct contrast to King's. A product of Atlanta's black aristocracy, King had projected an image of probity, carefully dressed in a somber suit, white shirt, and a skinny tie held motionless by a pearl tiepin. If he changed clothes for a protest, he put on the raiment of the rural poor: bib overalls, a denim shirt, and rough work boots.

The young blacks in the ghettos of Chicago and New York and Cleveland plainly did not emulate men who dressed like that, like accountants or sharecroppers. They dressed as Jackson did, in striped vests and bell-bottom trousers, in dashikis, leather coats, gold medallions, and, in what became a symbol, sneakers. "I'm a man of the streets, not of the office," Jackson said. When the Chicago Theological Seminary awarded him an honorary degree in 1968, he accepted it wearing the traditional cap and gown. Then, for all to see, he removed the robe to reveal Levi's and a turtleneck.

Operation Breadbasket survived on Jackson's speeches. Without Jackson to whip up support, there would have been no picket lines, no boycotts, no educated consumers. Every Saturday morning in

Newly named an honorary doctor of divinity by Chicago Theological Seminary, Jackson reveals his standard outfit of turtleneck shirt and jeans beneath his academic robe. Moments after the June 1969 award ceremony ended, Jackson went back to leading a hunger-protest march from Chicago to Springfield, the Illinois capital.

Reporters, photographers, policemen, and protesters listen as Jackson, speaking outside the governor's mansion in Indianapolis, Indiana, in July 1969, demands the hiring of more black state workers. Jackson's fiery, energetic leadership of Operation Breadbasket, which attempted to expand black employment at companies whose products blacks bought, made the SCLC organization a smashing success.

Chicago's Capitol Theater, Jackson presided over a Breadbasket rally, an affair that was equal parts church service, political rally, lecture, and concert. Before he rose to deliver his message of pride and economic self-help, the Breadbasket choir and a 13-piece jazz band would bring the audience to a state of hand-clapping, body-swaying excitement with up-tempo versions of old standard hymns. Then Jackson, tall and handsome, would step to the pulpit and say, "Good morning, brothers and sisters. Repeat after me":

> I am—Somebody!
> I may be poor, but I am—Somebody!
> I may be on welfare but I am—Somebody!
> I may be uneducated, but I am—Somebody!
> I may be in jail, but I am—Somebody!
> I am—Somebody!
> I must be, I'm God's child.
> I must be respected and protected.
> I am black and I am beautiful!
> I am—Somebody!
> SOUL POWER!!!

After each line, he paused and the devoted audience repeated his words.

Jackson stressed the necessity of blacks patronizing black businesses: "Rather than looking through the Yellow Pages we have to start looking through the black pages. The trouble is that Negroes have been programmed by white folks to believe their products are inferior. We've developed a generation of Oreos—black on the outside, white on the inside."

It was a riveting performance, one he repeated countless times in countless places. "Nobody could do more with a crowd of potential supporters waiting to be told what to do," wrote Abernathy. "He instinctively knew their hearts, and he was a master of the right phrase to bring out their passion. When he spoke to such crowds he always quickened their blood."

Jackson carried his appeal across the country, traveling constantly, inspiring the young urban blacks who heard him. They listened to Jackson with something approaching awe as he explained the tactics of protest: "Turn on the pressure and don't ever turn it off. Don't forget one thing: When you turn on the gas you gotta cook or burn 'em up."

The country preacher, as he had taken to calling himself, enraptured the national media as well. Jackson, in Abernathy's words, "could promote a press conference on the smallest pretext and end up the lead story on the evening news." Within the space of five months in late 1969 and early 1970, Jackson received two of the garlands of American celebrity: an interview in *Playboy* and a front-cover story in *Time*.

He had less success in transforming Operation Breadbasket from a local to a national organization. During 1967 and 1968, he had led a highly effective boycott against A&P supermarkets in Chicago. Attempting the same thing in other cities, however, proved tough going. Jackson staged several protests at A&P's headquarters in New York City (getting arrested for one in 1971), but the firm resisted all his pressure. Other efforts at a nationwide campaign also fizzled. "The main problem with Breadbasket," wrote Abernathy, "was that it never existed outside of Chicago, except on paper; and even the paper organization was sketchy and full of holes."

Jackson's growing fame was coupled with a growing family. On March 11, 1965, soon after he arrived in Selma to join the voting rights protest, he got the news of the birth of his second child, Jesse Louis Jackson, Jr. In early 1966, Jackie Jackson gave birth to another boy, whom the couple named Jonathan Luther. He was followed by a third son, Yusef Dubois, in 1970, and in September 1975, by a daughter, Jacqueline Lavinia. Growing up, the children sometimes saw their peripatetic father only a few days a month; it fell to Jackie Jackson to run the house and raise the children.

In 1970, the Jacksons moved into a 15-room Tudor-style stucco house on tree-lined Constance Avenue, a few blocks from Lake Michigan in a pleasant, integrated neighborhood on Chicago's South Side. With Jesse home, the house was the scene of constant movement. To the front door trooped the official visitors—the press, out-of-town politicians, and business leaders. They were greeted and entertained in the front parlor, a room furnished with leather couches and velvet curtains. Friends and close associates used the back door and gathered in the dining room, a cheerful space that also housed some of Jackie's half-refinished antiques and Jesse's seldom-used golf clubs.

Among the callers was Jackson's half brother, Noah Robinson, Jr. Needing someone to run the business end of Breadbasket, Jackson had selected his half brother, now a graduate of Philadelphia's prestigious Wharton School of Finance and Commerce. Things had changed dramatically since Greenville. Once the outsider, it was Jesse whose picture was on the cover of *Time*, Jesse who could dazzle Noah by taking him to dinner with Diana Ross.

"I wanted to help him and please my father as well," Jackson said of his reasons for hiring his half brother. He placed Robinson at the head of the Breadbasket Commercial Association (BCA), a new agency charged with helping black businesses secure contracts from white-owned firms. With Robinson calling the shots, the BCA got off to a fast start; in the first half of 1970, it secured $16 million worth of contracts for black companies.

Unfortunately, Robinson seemed to view Breadbasket not only as a social service organization but as a means to personal profit. The half brothers' partnership lasted less than a year. In late 1970, Jackson fired Robinson, but when Robinson left, he took the BCA with him. Using its name, he went right on brokering contracts and soon became a construction subcontractor himself. Because the law required a certain amount of the work on federally funded projects to be set aside for minority contractors, Robinson had a very good thing going. "I wasn't ashamed of making millions," he said. As for his relations with Jackson after their blowup in 1970: "We didn't speak to each other for five years," said Robinson.

Jackson's relationship with Ralph Abernathy was deteriorating, too. Abernathy's tenure as SCLC chief was not a happy one. "Martin Luther King *was* the SCLC," said one associate, suggesting that no successor would have had an easy time. Abernathy, though, did a particularly bad job of it. Under his ineffective leadership, members left and contributions dried up. Jackson, theoretically a subordinate, won the lion's share of media attention, consolidated more and more power in Chicago, and displayed open contempt for Abernathy.

At the end of each year, the SCLC required Breadbasket to present a complete, orderly accounting of its finances. "What we got from Chicago was little more than a paper bag full of canceled checks

Recently suspended from a Boston high school for wearing his dashiki (a loose-fitting, African-style shirt) to class, Glen Grayson (second from left) discusses the clothing issue with friends. Black teenagers all over the country found they could relate to Jackson, whose sharp dress style reflected their own tastes.

and receipts—and more of the former than the latter," Abernathy recalled.

The relationship between the two men worsened steadily until, in late 1971, it exploded. The immediate cause was Jackson's handling of Black Expo, a yearly celebration and trade fair sponsored by Operation Breadbasket. Begun in 1969, Black Expo offered an opportunity for black companies to display their wares; for black leaders to state their cases; for writers, entertainers, athletes, and scholars to encourage black pride. A smashing success, it attracted huge crowds; tens of thousands descended on Chicago's International Amphitheater and paid their admission to see Expo's attractions.

It was Jackson's show. At the 1970 Expo, all mention of Abernathy was dropped from the exhibits even though the SCLC, as Breadbasket's parent, was the official sponsor. In 1971, Jackson went a step further, secretly incorporating Expo under its own charter and thereby severing its tie with the SCLC.

Fighting back, Abernathy ordered an audit of Black Expo's books. At about the same time, the *Chicago Tribune* began digging into the same field. Both the accountants and the reporters discovered a serious discrepancy: The gate receipts for Expo did not match the number of people attending. Unaccounted for was a sum somewhere between $100,000 and $400,000.

Jackson had generally steered clear of Expo's financial affairs, but as the fair's organizer, he was responsible for any financial discrepancies. On December 3, 1971, a typically snowy Chicago day, Abernathy and the SCLC board came to town and convened at a hotel near Chicago-O'Hare International Airport to decide Jackson's fate.

Marching outside in the snow, several picketers carried signs with a message for Abernathy: "Don't Get Messy with Jesse." Inside, the SCLC chief and his board met in a conference room and went over

Jackson leaves the Chicago conference room where, on December 3, 1971, he received a 60-day suspension from the SCLC for an accounting discrepancy involving Operation Breadbasket. Fuming at the reprimand, Jackson waited only nine days before announcing his resignation from the SCLC and his establishment of a new organization, PUSH, which now stands for People United to Serve Humanity.

the books. Several times Jackson tried to join them. "We are not ready to see you now," Abernathy scolded. "Wait until you're called." After three hours, he at last summoned Jackson. The board had decided to suspend him, with pay, from all SCLC activities for 60 days. After that, Jackson could resume his place as the head of Operation Breadbasket.

It amounted to a mere slap on the wrist, but Jackson was having none of it. On December 12, 1971, he announced his resignation from the SCLC. To his followers in Chicago he said, "I love the organization that I grew up with. . . . But I need air. I got to grow." ✺

6

OPERATION PUSH

With George Wiley (right) of the National Welfare Rights Organization, Jackson directs participants in the Children's March for Survival, a 1972 demonstration held in Washington, D.C.

ON DECEMBER 12, 1971, the very day Jackson sent a telegram of resignation to Abernathy, an imposing group of black Americans assembled in a suite of the old Commodore Hotel, next door to New York City's Grand Central Terminal. Some—singers Roberta Flack and Aretha Franklin, for example— were instantly recognized celebrities. Others—such as Carl Stokes, former mayor of Cleveland, Ohio, and Richard Hatcher, mayor of Gary, Indiana—were political wheelhorses. Al Johnson, a Chicago Cadillac dealer, was anonymous but rich. Ed Lewis and Clarence Jones, of *Essence* magazine and the *Amsterdam News* respectively, represented the black press. Junius Griffin of Motown Records represented himself and a large bank account.

These people, who had assembled at Jackson's invitation, laid the groundwork for a new organization, one crafted to supplant Operation Breadbasket. They would help finance it, and Jackson would run it. "We don't care what you call the movement as long as you stay the same," an admiring businessman told Jackson.

Less than two weeks later, on Christmas Day 1971, Jackson was in Chicago to unveil the new movement, Operation PUSH (People United to Save Humanity). "A new child has been born," he proclaimed.

The nation's first black congresswoman, Shirley Chisholm of New York, announces her support of Democratic presidential candidate George McGovern in July 1972. Chisholm had sought the nomination herself but gave up when she realized she had little backing from the black male politicians of her party.

To some extent, PUSH was old wine in a new bottle. Most of Operation Breadbasket's staff owed their jobs and loyalty to Jackson and came to PUSH with him. The same was true for the allegiances of the Chicago ministers who had backed Breadbasket's various campaigns. In the way of objectives, PUSH borrowed Breadbasket's goal of black economic growth: new jobs, companies, and products.

Yet PUSH, which eventually changed its name to People United to *Serve* Humanity, was different from Breadbasket. In the first place, Jackson was altogether on his own. There was no SCLC, no Ralph Abernathy looking over his shoulder. PUSH also had a clear political purpose. King and Abernathy had kept the SCLC out of electoral politics, but as stated in its initial prospectus, PUSH aimed "to elect to local, state, and federal office persons committed to human, economic, and social programs."

Richard J. Daley did not strictly fit that description. For some time, Jackson had been gunning for him, and in early 1971, as Daley launched his bid for a fifth term, Jackson had proposed himself as a candidate for mayor. When Jackson supporters failed to come up with enough petition signatures to place his name on the ballot, he announced he would run as a write-in candidate. Giving up on that tactic at the last minute, he finally endorsed Richard Friedman, a liberal Democrat who had the solid support of Chicago's reformers. On election day, Daley rolled to another 4 years in City Hall with 71 percent of the vote. For his part in the struggle against the mayor, Jackson collected 35 write-in votes.

Thirty-five votes! In the dining rooms and corridors of the LaSalle Hotel, stamping grounds for Chicago's regular Democrats, the Daley men had themselves a long, loud laugh. For six years, Jackson had been a thorn in their sides. His activism and appeal had threatened to undercut the machine in the city's black wards. But now, they roared, when it really counted, on election day, the "country preacher" drew a miserable 35 votes.

A year later, the hilarity had long since died, because by then Jackson had beaten the old pros at their own game.

"See Dick Daley." For years, every Democrat thinking of running for president had heard and taken that advice. As boss of Chicago, Daley also bossed the big Illinois delegation to the Democratic National Convention, and at the four conventions from 1956 to 1968 he had delivered the delegation's bloc of votes to the winning candidate. The 1972 convention promised to be no different.

Meanwhile, Jackson had been doing his level best to make it a very different sort of election year. During the fall of 1971, he tried to get off the ground a black political party. He suggested Representative John Conyers of Michigan as its presidential candidate. The plan never flew. The Congressional Black Caucus, a recently formed organization of blacks in Congress, adamantly opposed the idea.

There already was a black candidate in the race: Representative Shirley Chisholm of New York was seeking the Democratic nomination. But she received little support from most black leaders. Jackson, for one, never seriously considered backing Chisholm. Instead, he endorsed Senator George S. McGovern of South Dakota, the most liberal candidate in the field. A passionate opponent of the Vietnam War, McGovern was in charge of a full-scale revolt within the Democratic party. In his ranks were the young antiwar protesters, feminists, environmentalists, welfare rights activists, and, after April 1972, Jesse Jackson.

McGovern presented Jackson with an opportunity to even some scores with Daley. A clause in the

Democratic party's newly adopted charter (written a few years earlier by a commission cochaired by McGovern himself) required each delegation to the convention to include blacks, women, and young people in a number precisely proportionate to their numbers in the general population. The 59 delegates, handpicked by Daley and elected in March, were, unsurprisingly, mostly white, male, and old. "I don't give a damn about the McGovern rules," snorted the mayor.

Joining with Chicago alderman William Singer, Jackson demanded that the party unseat the 59 delegates loyal to Daley because the delegation clearly violated the new rules. Jackson and Singer orchestrated a hurried selection of an alternative 59 delegates, most of them young, more than half of them women, a third of them black, one of them Jesse Jackson. Daley responded with characteristic directness: He tried—unsuccessfully, as it turned out—to have Singer arrested.

Which delegation would it be, Daley's or the Jackson-Singer slate? The decision would be made by a credentials committee and then voted on by the full convention. At the last minute, Jackson proposed a compromise: Seat both delegations, and give half-votes to each side. Daley was in no mood for a deal. For the mayor, who had been attending Democratic conventions since before Jackson was born, it was to be all or nothing.

It was nothing. Meeting in Miami Beach, the convention, firmly controlled by the McGovern forces, voted 1,486 to 1,372 to unseat the delegates of Richard J. Daley. The people loyal to the man who routinely produced the largest Democratic majorities of any American big city were replaced by 59 reformers led by Jesse Jackson. For Chicago, it was a political earthquake. The party regulars had been booted from their own convention.

For the long-suffering foes of the Daley machine, though, it was a moment of the highest jubilation. On the convention floor that hot July evening, the new delegates rejoiced. Theodore H. White observed with wonder "the sight of black people jumping and hugging each other with glee as Dick Daley was humiliated."

Over the next four nights, through the platform debates, through the nomination and acceptance speech of George McGovern, the television cameras kept returning to the Illinois standard where, in the words of Gary Hart, McGovern's manager, there "loomed the imperious, almost regal countenance of the dashiki-clad Jesse Jackson. The saucer-shaped Martin Luther King medallion around his neck stood out like a beacon."

After the convention, McGovern's prospects sank like a stone. Running on a platform far to the left of the political mainstream, he managed to make the not particularly popular incumbent, Richard M. Nixon, unbeatable. In November, McGovern swept Massachusetts and the District of Columbia; Nixon carried the 49 remaining states.

Even so, 1972 was a political watershed for Chicago blacks. After the Democratic convention, Jackson had returned to the Illinois city and begun a campaign to defeat two Daley Democrats. One was Roman Pucinski, running for the U.S. Senate against Republican Charles Percy. The other, and for Jackson the far more important target, was Edward Hanrahan, the Cook County state's attorney (prosecutor).

In December 1969, Hanrahan had directed police officers to make an early-morning raid on a headquarters of the militant Black Panther party. The police, investigators later discovered, fired more than 100 shots, in the process killing 2 Panther leaders. Hanrahan and Daley declared the raid a triumph for

Jackson chats with George McGovern at a 1972 PUSH banquet in Chicago. The event, which drew 10,000 high-paying diners, raised much-needed funds for Jackson's new movement and also provided much-needed political exposure for candidate McGovern, Jackson's choice for president.

law and order. Jackson called it murder and said Hanrahan must be voted out of office even if it meant casting a ballot for his Republican opponent, Bernard Carey.

"We're going to see to it that every black person in Chicago gets instructions on how to vote a split ticket," Jackson announced. Getting Chicagoans to vote Republican was only slightly less difficult than getting the crowd at Wrigley Field to pull for the Mets against the Cubs, but Jackson was as good as his word. With Ralph Metcalfe, an anti-Daley congressman, working the back rooms, Jackson hit the street. "Don't worry, I repeat, about Democrat and Republican," he told the crowds. "You ain't neither one, you're black, and you're trapped. White folks been saying black folks ain't sophisticated enough to split tickets, well, they just ain't been speaking our language."

On election night, it was Jackson's language that was spoken. Normally, the black wards of Chicago voted 90 percent Democratic. About this precentage voted for McGovern and Metcalfe, running for reelection. Yet Pucinski, on the same ticket, lost the South Side to Percy. And in the race for state's attorney, Chicago blacks vented their fury by giving Bernard Carey, the Republican, an amazing 62 percent of their votes.

Hanrahan's defeat was a crowbar thrown into the gears of the Daley machine. Using his powers of investigation as the new state's attorney, Carey probed Chicago's government, uncovered corruption nearly everywhere he looked, and ultimately secured the indictments and convictions of several close Daley associates. If Jackson had not got blacks to vote a split ticket on election day 1972, none of it would have happened.

The Democratic machine wheezed along—Daley won reelection easily in 1975—but the desertion of

Frozen by astonishment, two aides to Chicago mayor Daley, John Touhy (left) and Clyde Choate, serve as launching pads for a joyful Jackson at the 1972 Democratic National Convention. Prompting both the agony and the ecstasy was the news that Jackson's delegate slate had just defeated Daley's by a vote of 1,486 to 1,372.

black voters cost it a good deal of horsepower. When, just before Christmas 1976, the 74-year-old mayor dropped dead of a massive heart attack, the fabled Chicago organization virtually died with him.

As for Jackson's part in the emergence of black political independence, Ralph Metcalfe acknowledged that he "played a major role." However, in the congressman's view, Jackson did not "have the people who are willing to go from door-to-door and do the precinct work. They may pack his Saturday meetings, but the people don't go out and ring doorbells." Jackson answered such critics by saying simply, "I'm a tree shaker, not a jelly maker."

And at times during the 1970s, it seemed as though he and PUSH were shaking every tree in the

Visiting a high school in Soweto, an all-black district of Johannesburg, South Africa, Jackson joins students in the black power salute. The PUSH leader, who was cheered at every stop he made, told South Africa's blacks that their stuggle for freedom had much in common with the struggle of American blacks.

forest. PUSH organized protest marches, trade fairs, and forums on everything from tax reform to voter registration. It sent Jackson to Africa for talks with the continent's leaders and to Washington for meetings with the president and testimony before congressional committees. It sponsored all-star basketball games, a Christian revival, and, in 1974, Hank Aaron Day in honor of the Atlanta Braves outfielder who smashed the all-time home run record set by Babe Ruth.

Until the mid-1970s, the most significant work of PUSH was similar to the work previously done by Operation Breadbasket: securing agreements, or, as they came to be called, covenants, with large corporations. "If [blacks] account for 20 percent of a firm's sales," Jackson explained, "then that firm must give us 20 percent of its advertising dollar, 20 percent of its banking business, and 20 percent of its jobs."

Companies often gave up without a fight. Fearful of lost trade and disruptions in business, executives accepted covenants before the first picketers appeared. By early 1975, PUSH had secured covenants with Schlitz and Miller beers, Avon Products, Quaker Oats, and General Foods.

On January 15, 1975, Jackson was in Washington, D.C., planning to lead a demonstration at the White House in favor of jobs for young, unemployed blacks. Striding to his place at the head of the march, he passed through the columns of young demonstrators recruited by PUSH. As he did so, his expression grew as cold as the blustery winter day. Many, if not most, of the demonstrators were in no condition to protest anything. They were drunk. They were high on drugs.

Appalled, Jackson abruptly canceled the march. Even if there were jobs, who would hire these individuals? "The door of opportunity is open for our people," he said angrily, "but they are too drunk, too unconscious to walk through the door." He vowed to do something about it.

Over the next year, Jackson turned the focus of PUSH away from economics and toward education by launching PUSH-Excel, a campaign designed to encourage young blacks to stay in school and study, to abandon drugs and alcohol, and to develop a sense of self-esteem. By promoting self-help and old-fashioned morality, PUSH-Excel proposed to combat the problems of illiteracy, drug abuse, and teenage pregnancy that afflicted the nation's inner cities.

Develop your willpower, Jackson told young blacks: "For if you get willpower, you'll get voting power and you'll get political power and you'll get economic power and you'll get social prestige. If you get willpower, you'll have a power that the boss can't fire. You'll have a power that jail cells can't lock up."

Introduced first in a number of Chicago high schools, PUSH-Excel spread rapidly. By 1979, 22 school districts had implemented variations of the program, which required the active participation of not only students but of teachers, parents, and administrators. The programs that got off to the fastest, most enthusiastic start were those kicked off by Jackson himself. Students responded to him and his chant of "I am Somebody!"

For many youngsters, Jackson's campaign marked the first time anyone had asked them to excel at anything other than shooting jump shots or applying makeup. To the girls in his audiences, he said, "You cannot spend more time in school on the cultivation of your bosom than your books. If you are to be the right kind of woman, you cannot have a fully developed bottom and a half developed brain." The boys heard equally blunt talk: "You're not a man because you can make a baby. They can make babies through artificial insemination. Imbeciles can make babies. You're only a man if you can raise a baby, protect a baby, and provide for a baby."

The message was black self-reliance. "Nobody will stop us from killing ourselves," he would insist. "Nobody will make us catch up. We will have to rely on ourselves to overcome history."

In December 1977, Dan Rather of CBS News interviewed Jackson for the popular Sunday evening television program "60 Minutes." Millions of viewers heard Jackson describe PUSH-Excel's efforts to save the country's black youth by mobilizing schools and communities.

One of the show's viewers was a man propped up with pillows in the bed of a hospital room in Minneapolis. He was Hubert H. Humphrey, U.S. senator from Minnesota, once vice-president, once the Democratic nominee for president, the most respected liberal politician of his generation. He was dying of cancer. The next day, Humphrey placed a call to Joseph Califano, the secretary of Health, Education, and Welfare in the new Democratic administration of President Jimmy Carter.

In a weak, rasping voice, Humphrey asked Califano if he had watched "60 Minutes" the night before. The secretary said yes. "Well, then you saw what I saw," said Humphrey. "I want you to talk to Jesse Jackson and help him. He's doing something for

Inspired by Jackson's pitch for PUSH-Excel, Chicago high school students hand him written assurances that they will study harder, refuse drugs, and avoid casual sex. Jackson pulled few punches when he talked to teenagers: To the boys, for example, he said, "You're not a man because you can make a baby. Imbeciles can make babies. You're only a man if you can raise a baby."

those kids. I've talked to him this morning and told him I'd talk to you. Now you get down to your office and help him. Will you do that for me?"

Califano immediately summoned Jackson to Washington. The secretary was perhaps taken aback to hear his visitor say that the PUSH-Excel program was not yet fully developed and that, right at the moment, it did not need federal funding. But Califano would not take no for an answer. He said that a developed program was not really necessary and that the government would assist in putting together a surefire proposal to get some money.

A month later, PUSH-Excel received a federal grant for $45,000. Five months later, $400,000 rolled in. It was just the beginning. Between 1976 and 1982, 3 federal agencies granted PUSH-Excel $5 million.

Unfortunately, PUSH-Excel never got fully developed. "The problem with Jackson's program," Califano admitted, "was his inability to sustain its momentum when he was not present, its dependence on his charisma." A one-time PUSH enthusiast described what happened at Washington High

School in Los Angeles: "As long as Jackson was on hand, the program worked. At Washington the success rate in signing up students to commit to the program was excellent. The school administrators got behind it and clamped down on troublemakers or kids involved in drugs and illegal activities. But without Jackson's charisma, the kids gradually lost enthusiasm."

In school after school, the story was the same: PUSH-Excel offered no day-to-day provision to monitor student performance or to keep parents and teachers involved. "PUSH didn't push, except Jesse," concluded a New York youth director.

Worse, no one seemed to know how all the money was spent. "While Jesse was flying around the country, things in Chicago were in absolute chaos," said a PUSH official. When the federal government got around to auditing PUSH-Excel's books, it uncovered an accountant's nightmare. "Our problem is that the man keeping the records died, and the records don't seem to exist," said a government spokesman. Eventually, federal officials demanded repayment of an unaccounted-for $1.4 million. In 1988, PUSH-Excel agreed to repay $550,000 and the case was closed.

The days of cabinet secretaries anxious to fund such programs as PUSH-Excel ended with Ronald Reagan's election to the presidency in 1980. Convinced that the conservative Reagan administration was out to "discredit and destroy PUSH," Jackson returned to his earlier theme of black economic empowerment. In 1981, PUSH initiated a new campaign of boycotts against such companies as Coca-Cola, Burger King, and the Heublein Corporation, owner of Kentucky Fried Chicken.

The first boycott targets gave up in a hurry. In 1981, Coca-Cola agreed to increase its black-owned franchises and to place a black director on its board.

A year later, Heublein greatly expanded the number of Kentucky Fried Chicken franchises available to blacks, even agreeing to help finance some of the new owners. As for locating those blacks wishing to become owners and franchisees, the covenants included a special clause: "Operation PUSH has volunteered to help . . . identify qualified applicants." Jackson explained, "All we ever did was recommend a list."

The name Noah Robinson, Jr., appeared on more than one of the lists. In 1975, after nearly five years of not speaking to one another, Jackson telephoned Robinson and suggested they let the wound heal. "I'm preaching brotherhood, but I'm not practicing it," Jackson said. They made their peace. Each knew the other so well, and they knew, too, why they had such trouble getting along. "I'm not interested in making money. . . . It's hard for Noah to relate to my value system and its hard for me to relate to his," Jackson said. Robinson quickly took full advantage of the famous Jackson name. One month after Jackson signed the covenant with Coca-Cola, Robinson received a Coke distributorship. Just as Jackson began negotiating with Heublein, Robinson won a supplier contract with Kentucky Fried Chicken. When Jackson took on the fast-food chains, Robinson wound up with a string of Wendy's, Bojangles, and Church's Fried Chicken outlets in Chicago and New York.

"I'm not in business with him, never have been," Jackson insisted, and Robinson would forever wonder why not. He told friends he simply could not understand his half brother's lack of interest in getting rich. He understood ambition though, and, in late 1983, he had no trouble getting the point when Jackson revealed his newest idea: "I think I'm going to run for president of the United States."

7

"OUR TIME HAS COME"

·◊·

Jackson surveys the crowd at Operation PUSH's annual voter-registration rally in Cleveland, Ohio. Year after year, Jackson had waged a nonstop campaign to persuade young blacks to register and vote. By 1983, thousands were willing and eager to cast their ballots—for Jackson himself.

ON AUGUST 27, 1983, at the Lincoln Memorial in Washington, D.C., Jesse Jackson stood exactly where, precisely 20 years earlier, Martin Luther King, Jr., had delivered his most famous speech. "I have a dream," King had said to the tens of thousands who came to the nation's capital to march for civil rights, "that my four little children will one day live in a nation where they will not be judged by the color of their skin, but by the content of their character."

"We must continue to dream, but the dream of 1963 must be expanded to meet the realities of these times," said Jackson to the crowd observing the 20th anniversary of the March on Washington. It was time for blacks to assert their political power, for them to register and vote: "Hands that picked cotton in 1864 will pick a president in 1984," said Jackson.

President Ronald Reagan had to go, Jackson thundered, and African Americans, like David facing Goliath, could lay low "the repressive Reagan regime" with their votes. It was also time for blacks to run for office: "Run! Run from disgrace to amazing grace. Run! Run from the outhouse to the statehouse to the courthouse to the White House. Run! But hold on to your dreams."

Harold Washington, surprise successor to the mighty Dick Daley, confers with staunch supporter Jackson. Washington's capture of the Chicago mayoralty delighted the nation's blacks—especially, perhaps, the celebrated figure to whom Daley had once offered a job as a minor city functionary.

The crowd's cadence started during Jackson's speech and reached a crescendo as he finished. "Run, Jesse, run!" the audience at the Lincoln Memorial chanted over and over, louder and louder. "Run, Jesse, run!"

It was a cry Jackson had heard all through the spring and summer as he waged a voter-registration drive in the churches and schools of black America. Signing up at each Jackson stop, new voters made it plain for whom they wished to vote: "Run, Jesse, run." With broad hints that, yes, indeed, he might just run for president, Jackson did nothing to discourage their hopes.

A black president? Ever since the 1983 race for mayor of Chicago, anything seemed possible. In February, Harold Washington, a relatively obscure black congressman from Chicago's South Side, had won the Democratic mayoral nomination by beating two white candidates: Jane Byrne, the incumbent, and Richard M. Daley, son of the late boss. Two months later, in a bitter, racially polarized general election, Washington edged his Republican opponent, Bernard Epton, a white man whose theme song was "Bye, Bye Blackbird."

However narrow, Washington's victory sent an emotional charge through black communities everywhere. A number of big cities had elected black mayors, but Chicago, where Richard J. Daley once ruled and where Martin Luther King, Jr., had so visibly failed, was a city with very special symbolism. Jackson was as exhilarated as anyone over Washington's election.

Jackson was still infuriated, however, by the behavior of the party's leading liberals during the mayoral primary. Senator Edward M. Kennedy of Massachusetts had endorsed Byrne, and former vice-president Walter Mondale, the odds-on favorite for the 1984 presidential nomination, had backed Daley.

The siding of Kennedy and Mondale with the white candidates "forced us to consider new options," Jackson said. "One option, of course, was to take it. Another option was to withdraw. Another option came to me: Why don't we run somebody in the [presidential] primary?" That somebody, naturally, was Jesse Jackson.

The idea of a black running for president, however, was rooted in more than the ambition of one man. With remarkable uniformity, blacks believed Ronald Reagan hostile to their interests, and for three years, their anger at his administration had been rising steadily. Reagan's apparent indifference to civil rights, along with his policies of tax cuts for the wealthy, accelerated defense spending, and reduced social programs, seemed to them dangerously wrongheaded. Their dismay with the president placed them against the prevailing political wind; as the 1984 election approached, Reagan's popularity among whites was soaring, but blacks felt an increasing sense of political isolation.

Although the nation's black political leadership was opposed to Reagan, it was divided on the question of a Jackson candidacy, or, for that matter, of any black candidacy. An impressive number of black mayors and congressmen had already committed to Walter Mondale. The former vice-president, a protégé of Hubert Humphrey's, possessed a flawless record in support of civil rights and promised, if elected, to reverse the Reagan policies. Furthermore, Mondale had a chance to win; Jackson did not.

Joe Reed, a leading black Democrat from Alabama, summed up the feelings of many: "We elected to tell the truth, and that was, we didn't think Jesse could get nominated, and if he got the nomination, he couldn't win." Mayor Coleman Young of Detroit was more blunt: "Jesse has no experience and he has no platform and he has no chance." Virtually every black big-city mayor seemed to agree. Only Richard Hatcher of Gary, Indiana; Marion Barry of Washington, D.C.; and Kenneth Gibson of Newark, New Jersey, wound up in the Jackson camp.

By the fall of 1983, having heard the cry "Run, Jesse, run" from every audience he addressed, Jackson decided the "black leadership family" was very much out of touch with the black rank and file. On October 30, 1983, in an interview with Mike Wallace on CBS's "60 Minutes," he declared his candidacy. Four days later, he kicked off his campaign for the nomination with a 3½ hour rally at the Washington, D.C., Convention Center. "Our time has come," he announced.

Few presidential campaigns run with clocklike precision, and Jackson's, in its early days, was no exception. It was chaos, and Jackson admitted it: "No fund-raising machinery, no budget, no knowledge of how to rent a plane or how to deal with the Secret Service and the traveling press corps. We learned all that on the job."

The other candidates for the nomination—Mondale, Senators John Glenn of Ohio, Gary Hart of Colorado, Ernest Hollings of South Carolina, and Alan Cranston of California, former Florida governor Reubin Askew, and, in a last hurrah, George McGovern—all had far more impressive operations, bigger campaign bank accounts, and seasoned professionals running things. However, to no one's knowledge had a Glenn speech ever been interrupted by shouts of "Run, John, run," nor was Mike Wallace in the habit of offering Hart or Hollings 20 minutes of air time on the country's top-rated news program.

Mondale, always freshly barbered and wearing a dark suit, white shirt, and red tie, was miles in front. But although he had grabbed every endorsement in sight, when he started to speak in his nasal monotone, his listeners had to be forgiven for recalling the last time they had consulted an undertaker.

Jackson, by comparison, was a live wire. Gone were the leather jackets and dashikis—he now favored suits as conservative as Mondale's—but the electricity that had energized the old Saturday morning Breadbasket and PUSH convocations was still running at full current. Enormously proud that one of their own was in the race for the top prize, blacks responded to his oratory with a fervor the other candidates could only dream about. The white media, endlessly curious about black America's favorite son, lavished on him the interviews, magazine covers, and evening news soundbites that placed him in the stratosphere of celebrity.

At Christmastime, 1983, Jackson completely stole the political show by halting his campaign and flying to the Middle East, where he negotiated the release of Lieutenant Robert Goodman, a U.S. naval aviator being held prisoner by Syria. On December 4, 1983, while attacking a Syrian position in Lebanon, Goodman, a 27-year-old black bombardier-navigator, had been shot down and captured. (In one of its periodic military adventures in the Middle East, the United States had intervened to support the beleaguered government of Lebanon.) The Reagan administration seemed neither particularly concerned about Goodman's plight nor on good enough terms with Syria to negotiate his release.

Jackson, on the other hand, got on well with Syrian president Hafez al-Assad and with most other Arab heads of state. This amiability stretched back to 1979, when Jackson had toured the Middle East with a delegation of prominent American blacks. What prompted their visit was President Jimmy Carter's firing of Andrew Young, Jackson's old SCLC colleague, from his post as U.S. ambassador to the United Nations. Carter had dumped Young after learning of the ambassador's secret meeting with a representative from the Palestinian Liberation Organization (PLO), the militant group demanding the

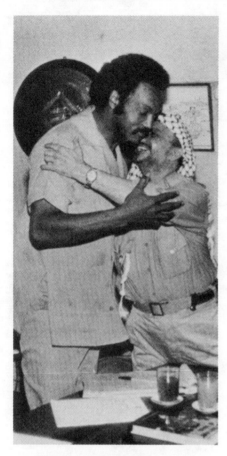

Visiting Beirut, Lebanon, during his 1979 tour of the Mideast, Jackson gets a hug from Yasir Arafat, leader of the Palestine Liberation Organization. Jackson's cordial relationship with Arafat infuriated many supporters of Israel, but it paved the way for the American politician's future negotiations with the Arab world.

establishment of an independent Palestinian state on territory occupied by Israel.

Black leaders hit the ceiling at Young's dismissal. Some accused American Jews of pressuring Carter; others denounced the traditional American policy of unswerving support for Israel. On tour in the Middle East, Jackson was photographed embracing PLO leader Yasir Arafat and leading a number of largely puzzled Palestinians in the "I am Somebody" chant. His conduct appalled Israelis and American Jews, just as surely as it delighted the Arab world.

So it was that when Jackson appealed to Syria for the release of Lieutenant Goodman, President Assad replied with an invitation to come and talk things over. Trailed by a retinue of clergymen, aides, Secret Service agents, and reporters, Jackson headed for Damascus. It was risky business. He had received no official encouragement at all—Reagan refused his telephone call—and a skeptical press was calling the trip shameless grandstanding. Even the airman's father, fearful that intervention might worsen his son's plight, asked Jackson not to go.

In Damascus, Jackson argued with Syrian officials that freeing Goodman would break the "circle of pain" in American-Syrian relations. After one lengthy conference, he suggested concluding with a prayer and turned to a fellow American, Nation of Islam leader Louis Farrakhan, who delivered an Islamic prayer in faultless Arabic. This display both touched and impressed the Syrians. Three days later, on January 3, 1984, Syrian officials summoned Jackson and handed him good news: Goodman was a free man.

JESSE DID IT! screamed the headline of the *New York Daily News*. Even Jackson's political rivals had to hand it to him. "It is impressive, yes," said Walter Mondale. As soon as their plane touched down in Washington, Jackson and Goodman sped to the

White House for a ceremonial welcome home by President Reagan.

In the Rose Garden, with Vice-president George Bush and cabinet members forming a solemn tableau, Jackson was the radiant star. "Reverend Jackson's mission was a personal mission of mercy and he has earned our gratitude and admiration," the president said. His tone was gracious, but he was far from pleased by Assad's turning Goodman over to a political foe.

In one bold stroke, Jackson had dramatically answered the noisy critics who said he was all talk. New life surged through his campaign for president. A poll of Democrats in New Hampshire, site of the first primary and a state with a tiny black population, put him in third place with 16 percent of the vote.

Then, with one stroke more, he threw away nearly all he had won.

On the morning of January 25, 1984, Jackson arrived at Washington's National Airport and, before his plane took off, dropped into the cafeteria for breakfast. When he saw Milton Coleman, a black *Washington Post* reporter covering his campaign, he waved him over to his table. "Let's talk black," Jackson said. It was something he frequently said to black correspondents—his way of declaring that the conversation that followed would be off the record. Coleman understood that in any story he wrote, nothing Jackson said could be directly attributed to him.

The talk turned to an upcoming meeting at which Jackson and several *Washington Post* editors would discuss the candidate's views on foreign policy. Questions about Israel, Coleman said, were certain to be asked. Fine, said Jackson, but he would not be intimidated. He continued: "All hymie wants to talk about is Israel. Everytime you go to hymietown, that's all they want to talk about."

Lieutenant Robert Goodman, an American naval flier shot down and captured by Syria in late 1983, matches the broad smile flashed by his rescuer. Ignoring skepticism from the Ronald Reagan administration and the American public, Jackson had flown to Damascus and persuaded the Syrians to release Goodman.

"Hymie" was new to Coleman, but he assumed, correctly, that Jackson was referring to Jews and that "hymietown" meant New York, the city with the nation's largest Jewish population. For the time being, Coleman did nothing. "I filed it away in my head," he recalled.

But when he learned that other black reporters had heard Jackson say much the same thing, Coleman decided to pass the information along to Rick Atkinson, a *Post* reporter who was writing a story about Jackson's chilly relations with Jews. On Monday, February 13, Atkinson's story appeared in the *Post*. Near the end were two brief paragraphs:

> In private conversations with reporters, Jackson has referred to Jews as "hymie" and to New York as "hymietown."
>
> "I'm not familiar with that," Jackson said Thursday. "That's not accurate."

The revelation soon became front-page news. On February 18, the *Post* editorialized that Jackson's hymie remarks were "ugly," "degrading," and "disgusting." Jackson, said the paper, should present "an explanation and an apology." Five days later, the *New York Times* finally offered its first coverage of the incident. By then, leaders of Jewish organizations were expressing outrage at Jackson's slur.

For the best part of two weeks, Jackson stuck to his denial. On "Face the Nation," he said, "It simply isn't true, and I think the accuser ought to come forth." That satisfied no one in the press, and the controversy gathered fury.

On February 25, the storm nearly became a hurricane. It was Savior's Day, a holy event on the calendar of the Nation of Islam, the Black Muslim sect led by Louis Farrakhan. A mesmerizing speaker, Farrakhan was a regular at Jackson rallies, warming up the crowd, then introducing the candidate, which was what he did on Savior's Day in Chicago.

With Jackson a few feet away, Farrakhan declared: "I say to the Jewish people who may not like our brother, when you attack him you attack the millions who are lining up with him. You are attacking all of us. If you harm this brother, I warn you in the name of Allah, this will be the last one you do harm." Jackson listened and, in his own speech, said nothing to contradict Farrakhan's open threat to the nation's Jews.

Jackson's advisers were horrified: Matters were bad enough without this apparent tolerance for Farrakhan. Now, said several Jackson staffers, unless something was done right away, the entire campaign might explode. The day after his appearance with Farrakhan, Jackson went before a candidates' forum at a crowded synagogue in Manchester, New Hampshire. "In private talks we sometimes let our guard down and we become thoughtless," he said. "It was not in a spirit of meanness, an off-color remark having no bearing on politics. . . . However innocent or unintended, it was wrong."

But damage had been done. On February 28, Jackson captured only five percent of the primary vote in New Hampshire, finishing a poor fourth behind Hart, Mondale, and Glenn. What was worse,

Forced to honor Jackson because of his rescue of Goodman, Ronald Reagan acts the genial host in the White House Oval Office. The president said Jackson had earned the nation's "gratitude and admiration," but insiders knew he was seething about the Democratic contender's coup.

Farrakhan continued to breathe fire into the controversy. In a March 11 radio broadcast, the minister announced that Milton Coleman, the black reporter who had revealed Jackson's hymie remark, was a "traitor," a "Judas," and an "Uncle Tom." Farrakhan issued a warning to Coleman: "One day we will punish you with death." The Nation of Islam leader also found something nice to say about the German dictator Adolf Hitler: "The Jews don't like Farrakhan, so they call me Hitler. Well, that's a good name. Hitler was a very great man."

Editorialists outdid one another in expressing outrage at Farrakhan's threatening message to Coleman and his praise of Hitler. Even Jackson's rivals for the Democratic nomination, who up until then had kept quiet, roused themselves. Mondale called Farrakhan's remarks "an outrage," and Hart said that if he were Jackson, he "would repudiate the support of Mr. Farrakhan."

Jackson did not particularly care what Gary Hart thought he should do. In February, Jackson had publicly apologized at the New Hampshire synagogue, and he was not about to make it a monthly habit. He severed whatever remaining ties Farrakhan had to the campaign, said his threat to Coleman was "wrong," and condemned the minister's "message." But he refused to condemn the messenger. "Jesus repudiated the politics of assassination," said Jackson, "but he did not repudiate Judas." His mind was set. Despite badgering from the press and pleas from prominent Democrats, Jackson would not repudiate Farrakhan.

"I felt very black at this point," Jackie Jackson recalled. "White people were saying now, little children, you're not grown up. . . . I thought it was very arrogant of white people to ask us to explain Farrakhan, to ask us to disassociate ourselves from him. . . . We were treated very colored."

Nation of Islam leader and longtime Jackson supporter Louis Farrakhan addresses a Boston audience in the mid-1980s. His unconcealed anti-Semitism made him a huge political liability for presidential hopeful Jackson, who denounced only Farrakhan's message, not the man himself.

A great many blacks agreed. Beginning in February with the hymie story and on into the spring with the Farrakhan storm, Jackson's support among blacks grew both broader and deeper. His hopes of winning anything beyond a token vote from whites evaporated with the controversy, but black ballots would sustain him through the primaries.

"We are the poorest campaign, with the richest message," said Jackson at nearly every stop as he flew from state to state in a slow, creaking Lockheed Electra, a relic from the prejet age. After New Hampshire, the scene shifted to the South, where, on March 13, Super Tuesday, Alabama, Georgia, and Florida voted. Jackson still lacked money and organization, but he was back home, and that was sufficient for many black voters in the Deep South. His campaign tapped the wellspring of black pride. "He makes me feel sooo good," exulted a young black student. A black schoolteacher said it did not matter whether Jackson won or not. Pointing to her class, she said, "Just so they have somebody to look up to. Just so we have somebody to idolize." "He's us, that's all," said a black nurse.

With its large black population, the South could have been friendly territory for Jackson on Super Tuesday. But Mondale, with the support of the region's black leadership, cut into his strength. In Alabama, Birmingham mayor Richard Arrington put his political organization to work for the former vice-president. In Georgia, Coretta Scott King and Andrew Young, now mayor of Atlanta, also did what they could for Mondale. On primary day, Jackson captured roughly 20 percent of the vote in Alabama and Georgia and 12 percent in Florida.

After Super Tuesday, the race for the Democratic nomination came down to three men: Mondale, Hart, and Jackson. Mondale, weighted down by all his endorsements, had stumbled badly coming out of the blocks, losing New Hampshire to the youthful-looking Hart. But by winning Alabama, Georgia, and, a week later, Illinois, he reestablished himself as the front-runner. In April, he flattened Hart in the New York and Pennsylvania primaries, virtually assuring himself of the nomination.

Jackson placed third in each of the northern primaries, sweeping the big-city black vote. Black politicians stood by Mondale, but it was getting very lonely for them. In Pennsylvania, Mayor Wilson Goode of Philadelphia boosted Mondale; 78 percent of the city's black voters supported Jackson. Representative Charles Rangel of New York also recommended Mondale; 87 percent of black New Yorkers cast ballots for Jackson.

"I want to be respected and heard," Jackson said, and he attained those goals, thanks largely to a series of televised debates. "Jackson had the greatest natural ease and assurance of any Democratic candidate," wrote William A. Henry III of the candidates' encounter at Columbia University during the New York campaign. "He had an almost intuitive gift for making exactly the right adjustments of manner and intonation to fit any circumstance."

Jackson realized that a lot was riding on each appearance. "Suppose I had made big classical errors in the debates," he later said to columnists Jules Witcover and Jack Germond. "It would have embarrassed my people. They would have said, 'You know, I told you we were not ready.' "

They said anything but. "I see Jesse on TV with all those big people, and I just puff up. I know he's not going to be president, but he could be," said a black Philadelphian.

While Jackson more than held his own in the televised debates, he steadily lost ground in the process of selecting delegates to the Democratic convention. The system favored a candidate such as Mondale, one who had the backing of party bigwigs and showed strength among all groups of Democrats. It worked against Jackson, whose great strength was among blacks. (In Pennsylvania, for example, he got only three percent of the white vote.) After all the primaries had been run and all the delegates had been named, Jackson had 21 percent of the popular vote, but only 11 percent of the delegates.

In June, following the final primaries, Jackson took off on a swing through Central America and Cuba. Presidential candidates traditionally campaigned within the borders of the United States, but Jackson was hardly a traditional candidate. His journey to Panama, El Salvador, Cuba, and Nicaragua dramatized his strong opposition to the U.S. government's policies in the region. Since it had seized power in 1959, Fidel Castro's Communist regime in Cuba had endured the near total enmity of every American president, Democrat and Republican alike. The Reagan administration, which had worked up a similar hatred of Nicaragua's Sandinista government, openly sponsored an anti-Sandinista military insurgency, the Contras.

Jackson, in common with the American left, believed "we must completely reverse Ronald Rea-

Taking time out after a grueling season of primaries in 1984, the 42-year-old Jackson prepares to shoot a few baskets in the backyard of his Chicago home.

Cuban leader Fidel Castro greets Jackson at Havana's Presidential Palace in June 1984. Repeating his Syrian success of early in the year, Jackson persuaded Castro to let him take almost 50 prisoners—22 of them Americans—back to the United States. This time, Americans had mixed reactions: Some applauded; others accused Jackson of overstepping his role as a private citizen.

gan's policies in Central America." He favored assisting the Sandinistas "in their attempt to build a more just society" and advocated normal diplomatic relations with Cuba. "We have much to learn from the Cubans," he insisted. "They have much to learn from us."

Castro gave the "Moral Offensive"—Jackson's name for his journey—its warmest reception. Meeting the American's plane at the Havana airport, the Cuban leader said, "He honors us with his visit."

Jackson reciprocated. The next afternoon, speaking at the University of Havana, he proclaimed: "Long live Cuba! Long live the United States! Long live Castro! Long live Martin Luther King! Long live Che Guevara! Long live our cry of freedom! Our time has come." It was not every day a candidate for the Democratic presidential nomination linked the name of America's great apostle of nonviolence with those of Castro and his aide Guevara.

Later the same day, Jackson led Castro into the First Methodist Church of Havana and offered a prayer for peace. "I'll fear no evil, for Thou art with me," he prayed. "Thy rod and Thy staff comfort me." Then he added, "Hold on, Cuba! Hold on, Castro! Hold on, Nicaragua!"

Jackson did not leave Cuba empty-handed. Castro agreed to release into Jackson's custody 22 Americans and 26 Cubans being held in Cuba's prisons. Most of the Americans had been convicted of drug dealing and smuggling. The Cubans had been imprisoned for what the Castro government labeled "behavior injurious to the nation"—in short, political dissent.

Jackson brought nearly 50 newly released prisoners home with him, but this rescue, unlike that of Lieutenant Goodman, produced only muted acclaim. While some Americans applauded Jackson's Cuban mission, others wondered about the propriety of a private citizen dealing with the head of a Communist state. Speaking for many of Jackson's critics, James Reston of the *New York Times* said flatly, "He is interfering with the constitutional rights of the president and Congress to conduct foreign policy."

The controversy whipped up by Jackson's Central American excursion did not last very long. Within two weeks of his return, the Democratic National Convention opened in San Francisco. ❧

8

"WE'RE WINNING"

ONE EVENING IN late 1983, after a long campaign day, Walter Mondale was having a drink with reporters in the bar of a New Hampshire motel. "How are you going to handle Jesse?" he was asked.

Mondale puffed his cigar, then replied with a laugh, "Veerry carefully."

Throughout the campaign, Mondale did exactly that. While he slugged away at Gary Hart and the others, with Jackson he pulled his punches or did not even swing. "What I decided to do," Mondale later explained to Jack Germond and Jules Witcover, "was to disagree in a dignified way with Jesse Jackson . . . and try to give him the dignity and respect he deserved as a candidate for president, to recognize the profound nature of this new effort by a black in America and what it meant to millions of black Americans." The former vice-president feared that anything beyond the gentlest criticism of Jackson would alienate millions of blacks whose votes Mondale required if he was to stand a chance of defeating Ronald Reagan. In other words, he had to have Jackson's goodwill and endorsement.

About to deliver his eagerly awaited 1984 convention speech in San Francisco, Jackson offers his admirers a buoyant salute. He went on to stun them with the campaign's most electrifying oratory: "Leave the racial battleground" for the "moral high ground," he urged. "America, our time has come!"

He was not to win them easily. Jackson knew that as long as he withheld an endorsement, he would remain at the center of things, the subject of speculation and attention—a major player in the Democratic party. He tried to make the most of his position, pressing demands on Mondale and hinting he might sit out the fall campaign. As they gathered in San Francisco for their convention in July, nearly every Democrat seemed to be asking, What does Jesse want?

For one thing, he wanted changes in the platform, calling on the party to endorse stronger measures for affirmative action, a reduction in defense spending, a policy of no first use of nuclear weapons, and an end to the system of runoff primaries when no candidate got a majority—a system, Jackson argued, that discriminated against blacks. Already under attack for being too liberal, Mondale had no wish to let the platform drift further to the left and rejected each Jackson proposal.

The sole concession Mondale made to Jackson was handing him a prime-time spot for his speech to the convention—eight o'clock eastern time, Tuesday evening. Neither Mondale nor anyone else knew what Jackson planned to say. Robert Beckel, who had negotiated with Jackson on Mondale's behalf and who had given him the 8:00 P.M. slot, tried to get a preview of Jackson's text. "You've really got to give a great speech," he said as he and Jackson stood on a balcony of the Fairmont Hotel and gazed at the San Francisco skyline. "I've got a lot invested in you."

"Well, I'll tell you this, Beckel," replied Jackson, delighting in the nervousness of the Mondale camp. "You're either going to be a chimp, a chump, or a champ."

As the time for Jackson's speech approached, Dan Rather on CBS was promising great things. This speech was going to be something; get the whole family together, the anchorman advised, even "get grandma in." By now, much of the country wanted to know, What does Jesse want? His speech drew the largest television audience of the convention.

He began with what amounted to an apology for the hymietown remark and the Farrakhan mess. "If in my low moments, in word, deed, or attitude, through some error of temper, taste, or tone, I have caused any discomfort, created pain, or revived someone's fears, that was not my truest self," he said. "As I develop and serve, be patient. God is not finished with me yet."

Jackson was in top form. He spoke of his constituency as "the damned, the disinherited, the disrespected, and the despised," and of America as "a rainbow—red, yellow, brown, black, and white—we're all precious in God's sight." He laced into the policies of the Reagan administration and issued a call for Democratic unity: "We are much too intelligent, much too bound by our Judeo-Christian heritage, much too victimized by racism, sexism, militarism, and anti-Semitism, much too threatened as historical scapegoats to go on divided from one another." He concluded: "Our time has come! No lie can live forever. Our time has come. We must leave the racial battleground and come to the economic common ground and the moral high ground. America, our time has come!"

Jackson's address was the high point of the convention, perhaps of the 1984 Democratic campaign. When Mondale delivered his acceptance speech two nights later, he seized the moment to tell the nation he planned, if elected, to raise everybody's taxes. Mondale wound up in November carrying only the District of Columbia and his home state of Minnesota. Reagan, who had proclaimed that it was "morning again in America," won all the rest.

There was never the slightest doubt that Jackson meant to run for the 1988 nomination. With the ashes of the Mondale disaster still glowing, he announced the formation of the National Rainbow Coalition, a political action committee designed to publicize and finance his activities until the 1988 campaign officially began. He traveled the country incessantly, building grass-roots support, appealing to those who were having a hard time.

This time, Jackson planned a broader-based and more professional organization. "In 1984 we went through the experience of an exhilarating campaign, but we were all spirit and not much body," he explained to a supporter in early 1986. "We need both ministers, who were our original base, and politicians, but now we need politicians more so we're not labeled some kind of fringe. We've got to expand the Rainbow Coalition."

No one would label Gerald Austin "some kind of fringe." A well-regarded professional who had run several successful campaigns in Ohio, Austin signed on as Jackson's campaign manager. He was committed to the Jackson cause. "Before I took this job I traveled a few days . . . with Jackson to see how we got on," he told Elizabeth Colton, the campaign press secretary. "After I saw him in action a few times, I began to think: This guy can go all the way. Jesse Jackson can be elected president. And that's the way I'm now running this campaign."

On October 24, 1987, in Raleigh, North Carolina, Jackson formally announced his candidacy. "I want to be president of the United States of America," he said. His competition for the Democratic nomination was, if anything, less imposing than it had been in 1984. Back for a second go at it, Gary Hart had the look of a front-runner, but he careened into the starting post. In the spring of 1987, less than a week after announcing his candidacy, he was found to be keeping steady nighttime company with a woman decidedly not his wife. A few days later, after facing such questions from reporters as "Have you

After officially announcing his candidacy for the 1988 Democratic presidential nomination before a crowd in Raleigh, North Carolina, Jackson kisses his wife and gets set to battle for the prize. Pitted against five white candidates, he started fast, shooting to the front of the pack in the early stages of the race.

ever committed adultery?" Hart gave up and withdrew from the race.

The vacuum created by Hart's pullout was not easily filled. Although Democratic prospects looked brighter than they had four years earlier, the party stars—Governor Mario Cuomo of New York and Senator Sam Nunn of Georgia—left the stage to their understudies. In Cuomo's case, it was another northeastern governor, Michael Dukakis of Massachusetts, and in Nunn's, it was Senator Albert Gore, Jr., of Tennessee. Rounding out the field, hoping for lightning to strike, were Representative Richard Gephardt of Missouri, Senator Paul Simon of Illinois, and former governor Bruce Babbitt of Arizona.

The good news for Jackson was that few voters knew anything about these candidates. Everybody, of course, had heard of Jackson; on the basis of name recognition, he shot to the front of the public-opinion polls. Furthermore, none of the white candidates had anything resembling Mondale's ties to the black community. This time around, Jackson could count on rock-solid black support.

He was dealt another ace with the revised schedule of the nominating process. Eager to nominate a moderate white southerner, conservative Democrats had prevailed on party officials to group together 14 southern primaries on a single election day, Super Tuesday, March 8, 1988. They hoped a moderate, by sweeping the South, would pick up enough momentum to be unstoppable. They miscalculated badly. It was Jackson, the exact opposite of a white moderate, whose interests were served by the Super Tuesday strategy. His best states, by virtue of their large black populations, were in the South.

In the two weeks prior to Super Tuesday, Jackson crisscrossed the South, rallying his loyal constituency and reaching across the past to old foes. After a speech in Beaumont, Texas, for example, he met Bruce Hill, a local union leader. "Back in 1965 I was with you in Selma," Hill said. Clearly delighted, Jackson at once started talking about the great battle against white supremacy. Hill interrupted: "No, no. I was there, but I was on the other side." He had been a member of the Ku Klux Klan. Jackson stared at him. "But Jesse, today I'm on your side!" Hill exclaimed.

The men embraced. "It summed up the beauty and the promise of the Jackson campaign: He was the candidate willing to reach out to anyone," journalist

Walter Fauntroy, Washington, D.C.'s nonvoting congressional representative, links arms with Jackson and Coretta Scott King during a demonstration in the nation's capital. King's belated but welcome 1988 acceptance of Jackson as her husband's heir supplied the Jackson campaign with a powerful shot in the arm.

Roger Simon wrote of the incident. "Even to those who had once despised him or had shouted racial epithets at him or had tried to lynch him."

There were other such moments. In Selma itself, Jackson was greeted by Joe T. Smitherman, then as in 1965 the town's mayor. Twenty-three years earlier, he too had been on the other side. Now, he gave Jackson the key to the city and then joined him for a walk across the infamous Edmund Pettus Bridge, site of Bloody Sunday. Smitherman admitted he had been wrong all those years before, and Jackson, deeply touched, said it was time "to forgive each other, redeem each other, and move on."

On Sunday afternoon, March 6, two days before the voting, Jackson attended worship services at the Ebenezer Baptist Church in Atlanta, the church of Martin Luther King, Jr. Visiting the historic church four years earlier, on the eve of 1984's Super Tuesday, Jackson had been pointedly snubbed by the King family, few of whom turned out to hear him preach.

On this Sunday, however, Coretta Scott King accompanied Jackson to her husband's tomb. Together they laid a wreath on the grave and together they prayed. These actions held great significance. However reluctantly, with whatever misgivings, Coretta King had symbolically passed the torch of leadership to Jesse Jackson.

On Super Tuesday, Jackson did well—very well. He won the primaries of 5 states (Georgia, Alabama, Louisiana, Mississippi, and Virginia), placed second in the remaining southern states, and captured 353 delegates to the national convention. Dukakis won in Texas and Florida, and in the five northern and western states voting that day. Gore of Tennessee salvaged a little of the original plan behind Super Tuesday by carrying five states in the upper South.

The race was left with three candidates: Jackson, Dukakis, and Gore. Dukakis offered himself as the cool, experienced master of public policy, the creator and guardian of the Massachusetts Miracle, his state's supposedly booming economy. Uncertain about which face to present to the electorate, Gore settled on promoting a hawkish foreign policy and deriding his opponents as advocates of "retreat, complacency, and despair."

Jackson plainly stood to the left of his two adversaries. While Gore and Dukakis accepted certain aspects of the Reagan years, such as lower tax rates and big defense budgets, Jackson demanded radical change. On the campaign trail, he directed his sharpest remarks at huge multinational corporations—"barracudas," he called them—that did "economic violence" by opening plants abroad.

"Your jobs went to South Korea and Taiwan and South Africa and Chile," Jackson told the unemployed. The government, he said, had to control private enterprise to the extent that "its investment decisions are made in the best interests of the community." Jackson envisioned a vastly expanded welfare state, offering comprehensive health care, new housing projects, bigger welfare checks, and larger food stamp benefits. To pay for it, he would cut defense spending, raise taxes, and borrow against public-employee pension funds.

After Super Tuesday, the primary trail led north, first to Illinois, where Jackson ran second to Simon—whose candidacy had been diminished to "favorite-son" status—and then to Michigan. Jackson did not go into Michigan with very high hopes. Dukakis had the backing of the Michigan party apparatus and an ally in Mayor Coleman Young of Detroit, one of the handful of black elected officials in the country not supporting Jackson.

Well before the Michigan voting, Dukakis stopped campaigning and returned to Boston to look after some state business. His private polls showed him 10 points ahead of Jackson (Gore was not contesting the state), and he figured he had it wrapped up. Coleman Young, however, was not so sure. On election eve, he attended a Greek-American fund-raiser with a Dukakis aide. Fifteen hundred people wildly cheered every mention of Dukakis, a fellow Greek American. "You see how excited these people are about Michael?" Young asked the aide. "I got a whole city like that for Jesse."

On Saturday evening, the Dukakis high command gathered at its Boston headquarters, ready to watch the vote from Michigan and celebrate the inevitable triumph. But early on, things started going very wrong. As the votes poured in, Dukakis's shocked media adviser asked, "Jesus, where are all these black people coming from?"

They came from the old factory towns of Flint and Lansing and from the housing projects and neighborhoods of Detroit. In overwhelming numbers, they gave up their Saturday for Jesse Jackson. In the 2 congressional districts of Detroit, 50,000 people voted. One district went 25–1 for Jackson, the other

Jackson and influential Democrat Clark Clifford emerge from a spring 1988 conference to talk to reporters about the new "bonding of the Democratic party." During the meeting, representatives of several candidates who had dropped from the race—and who had once savagely criticized Jackson—offered him their assistance.

17–1. By casting approximately 45 percent of the total vote, Michigan blacks handed Jackson a stunning victory. The final statewide count: Jackson, 55 percent; Dukakis, 29 percent.

On Monday evening, March 28, Dan Rather led off the "CBS Evening News" by announcing, "Jesse Jackson has become the front-runner." *Newsweek* devoted its lead to the "Michigan Miracle." *Time* splashed his photograph on its cover with the caption, "Jackson!?" In the accompanying story, the news magazine reported that "for the first time in the nation's history, a major political party was grappling with one of the biggest what-ifs of all: What if Democratic voters actually nominate a black man for president?"

The white elders of the party, who four years earlier had not given Jackson the time of day, started wondering the same thing, and a few tried to accommodate themselves to the changed political landscape. In early April, Jackson met a group of Democratic leaders over breakfast in a private dining room of the Jefferson Hotel in Washington. Clark Clifford, a courtly, white-haired, impeccably tailored Washington lawyer whose days of influence stretched back to the Truman administration of the late 1940s, assured the candidate that there was no "Stop Jackson" movement. If Jackson happened to be nominated, said Clifford, he would have the benefit of "the best brains the party and the country have to offer."

Despite Clifford's encouraging words, not a single senator, governor, or state chairman endorsed Jackson. In the Wisconsin primary of April 5, he captured only 28 percent of the vote; Dukakis won with 48 percent and was quickly reestablished as the likely nominee. Michigan, the pundits now said, had been a fluke.

Jackson had a chance to prove them wrong. On April 19, New York voted, and on the face of it, his prospects looked good. More than a quarter of the votes in New York were cast by blacks, and this time, Gore was making a stand. In a 3-man race, with 40 or 45 percent of the vote, Jackson might win.

In New York, however, Jews also accounted for a quarter of the electorate; for them, Jackson's hymie-town remark and his association with Farrakhan were vivid memories. And if by chance people had forgotten, Edward I. Koch, mayor of New York, was around to help them remember.

"I'm the Paul Revere," said the mayor as he galloped off to warn voters about Jackson. In fact, he was the head of a city whose racial relations were as poisonous as any in the country. Energetic and colorful, Koch had enjoyed wide popularity during his first two terms, but his abrasive style—"slime," "dummy," "poverty pimp," and "wacko" were favored descriptions of his political rivals—had also fueled the fire between black and white.

After endorsing Gore, Koch dragged the Tennessee senator around the city to the usual campaign stops but paid him scant attention. It was Jackson he was after. "And he thinks maybe Jews and other supporters of Israel should vote for him?" Koch said of Jackson. "They have got to be crazy!" Then came

In August 1988, four months after New York's bitter and divisive primary, Jackson offers a handshake of truce to New York City mayor Ed Koch. Standing between the two is Manhattan Borough President David Dinkins, who was to become, in 1989, the city's first black mayor.

the Koch litany: Jackson was against Israel; he would, if elected president, "bankrupt the country in three weeks and leave it defenseless in six weeks."

"Ed Koch is an idiot, even by New York standards," replied Gerald Austin. Jackson was unhappy with the remark. "You keep forgetting," he informed Austin, "you're the campaign manager, I'm the spokesman." Jackson preferred not to get into the gutter with Koch.

He also preferred not to try to improve relations with New York's Jews, avoiding Jewish groups and refusing to march in the big Salute to Israel Parade on Fifth Avenue just before election day. Jews, he was certain, had their mind made up about him: "Children in this city have been taught to fear. That's not right. Jewish children have been taught to fear me. That's not right."

"Jesse showed contempt and arrogance!" Koch bellowed after Jackson failed to show up for the parade. "He is treating Jews with contempt and arrogance."

There were times when Jackson wanted to let the mayor have it, but he continued his discreet, turn-the-other-cheek approach. "In some sense I came out of New York victorious, because my mettle under heat was shown," he reflected later. "I had the capacity to take a punch without my knees buckling. And enough strength not to react, to keep my composure."

He did not come out of New York victorious in any conventional sense. Dukakis won the primary with 51 percent of the vote. Jackson polled 37 percent, and Gore, smothered by the mayor's embrace, trailed with 10 percent.

The bright optimism that had followed the Michigan Miracle was gone for good. For three wonderful weeks, it had been castles in the air for Jackson and his entourage as they considered vice-presidential

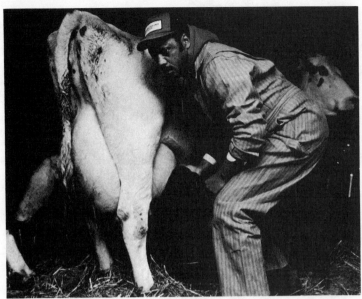

Jackson demonstrates his campaign skills at an Iowa farm. Like any sensible politician, he knew that winning voters' hearts involves more than defining issues and taking positions: Equally crucial are cow milking, baby kissing, and hand shaking.

candidates, cabinet appointments, and new directions in foreign policy. Now, with New York's vote counted, Jackson stood before his cheering supporters in the Sheraton Centre. His eyes glistened with tears. Beside him, Jackie was weeping.

"Dr. Martin Luther King's heart is rejoicing tonight," he said. "We're winning. We've climbed the tough side of the mountain and we can keep on climbing, step by step by step."

In 1988, there were not many more steps for him to take. After New York, Gore sensibly withdrew, reducing the field to Dukakis and Jackson. It was one on one, black against white, a race Jackson could not win. Over the next six weeks, Dukakis pounded Jackson in primaries from Pennsylvania to California. And, as Mondale had done four years before, the governor handled Jackson with kid gloves, ignoring his program and campaign but refusing to criticize him.

After Dukakis won the party's nomination that July, Jackson dutifully campaigned for him, traveling the country in a chartered jet and urging his audiences to register and to vote Democratic. Dukakis

left most blacks cold, but on election day, 9 out of 10 voted for him—a showing for which Jackson could rightfully claim much of the credit. But in spite of Jackson's effective electioneering, Dukakis fell flat on his face. After running a dull, confused campaign, he saw George Bush cruise to an easy victory in November.

In early 1989, as Bush was settling into the White House, Jackson announced that he was moving from Chicago to Washington, D.C. The change of address sparked instant rumors that Jackson intended to run for mayor of the District of Columbia, a city whose vast, poor, overwhelmingly black sections were wracked by crime and virtually ruled by drug dealers. If he decided to run for mayor, he would, given his great popularity in the District, almost certainly win.

And if Jackson became mayor of Washington, as Hendrick Hertzberg of the *New Republic* put it, "No longer could it be said that Jesse Jackson had never been elected anything, had never held public office." Jackson, however, had no interest in the job. "I want to serve," he said in March 1990, "but not as mayor." Instead, he announced himself as a candidate for statehood, or "shadow," senator from the District of Columbia, a new post created by the city government to lobby Congress for statehood. "Statehood for the District of Columbia," said Jackson, "is the most important civil rights and social justice issue in America today."

Facing minimal opposition and solidly supported by most Washingtonians, Jackson was confident about the election. At this point, however, his support among members of the black political establishment was far from solid. Black politicians knew they had to win the votes and confidence of whites to get elected. A number of these political figures—including Virginia's Douglas Wilder, the nation's first black governor; and David Dinkins, New York City's first black mayor—indicated that they considered

Jackson too controversial, too black. "The move is mainstream now," said a Dinkins associate.

Jackson's convention manager in Atlanta, Ron Brown, who in 1989 had become the first black to head the Democratic National Committee, echoed the sentiments of the Dinkins camp. Talking to a reporter about Jackson, Brown said, "Here is a guy who is brilliant, got great political instincts, been right on most of the issues . . . but as happens so often, not only in politics but in life, he just might not be the right message carrier."

The "right carrier" or not, Jackson swept to victory in the 1990 race for District of Columbia shadow senator. His new office paid no salary, had no budget, carried no clear responsibilities, and entitled its holder to no vote in Congress. Nevertheless, Jackson expected the Democrats in the Senate to admit him to their caucus and include him in their decision-making processes. "After traveling this country in two presidential campaigns and getting seven million votes," he declared, "I have *earned* the right to be part of the national governing body."

Three months before the election, in August 1990, Jackson heard the news that Iraq had invaded its neighbor, the oil-rich nation of Kuwait. Bush quickly responded by dispatching American troops to the Arabian desert, organizing international sanctions, and threatening Iraq's dictator, Saddam Hussein, with attack unless he withdrew from Kuwait. Like most other American politicans, Jackson immediately announced his support of the president's actions in the Mideast.

By mid-August, it was clear that Hussein was not going to retreat. Moreover, he announced that several thousand Americans and other foreign nationals were not free to return home. They were, in no uncertain terms, hostages.

Jackson decided that what he had done for Robert Goodman in 1984 he could do for the

Like hundreds of others at the 1988 Democratic National Convention, Los Angeles delegates Lillian Mobley (left) and Marva Smith find themselves in tears as they listen to Jackson (opposite page) deliver his spellbinding address. Former president Jimmy Carter described the Jackson effort as "the best speech ever given at a convention."

As singer Roberta Flack, an old friend and political supporter of Jackson's, looks on with amusement, Jackson clowns backstage with Flavor Flav of the rap group Public Enemy. Jackson featured a broad variety of guests, ranging from entertainers to attorneys, from civil rights leaders to former members of the Ku Klux Klan, on "Jesse Jackson," the syndicated television talk show that he began in the fall of 1990.

hostages held by Iraq. In late August, he proposed a trip to Baghdad, where he would appeal to Hussein for release of at least some of the hostages. After receiving a positive response from Iraq, Jackson departed New York City with his son Jonathan and 13 others.

Within a week, Jackson was conducting a two-hour interview with Hussein. At its conclusion, Hussein grabbed his visitor's hand and said, "You will take the women and children who are allowed to leave, along with four of the men who appear to be sick." Even after getting Hussein's approval, however, Jackson had to spend many hours negotiating with uncooperative Iraqi officials.

Watching Jackson in action, journalist Milton Viorst found him to be "at his best." When Jackson dealt with the Iraqis, Viorst wrote later, "as nearly as I could grasp it, his technique consisted of measured drafts of pleading, rational argument, cajolery, flattery, and moral importuning."

A few days after his conversation with Hussein, Jackson left Baghdad in an Iraqi Air 747 loaded with nearly 300 American, British, and French hostages. It was a considerable accomplishment. Back home in the United States at long last, one hostage—perhaps speaking for all—cried, "Thank God and Jesse Jackson!"

Two months after returning from Baghdad, Jackson entered a new profession: television journalism. "Jesse Jackson," a talk show syndicated by the Time-Warner communications corporation and produced by Quincy Jones, debuted in October 1990. Aired on Sunday evenings, the program featured roundtable discussions of political issues high on its host's agenda.

An early "Jesse Jackson" show, for example, centered on civil rights and included such diverse voices as those of Louisiana State Representative and former Ku Klux Klan leader David Duke, feminist lawyer Gloria Allred, conservative columnist Richard Viguerie, and Kweisi Mfume, a Baltimore congressman and vice-chairman of the Congressional Black Caucus. "So many of the disfranchised have given me their support over the years," said Jackson. "If they look for the weekend TV show to discuss civil rights 1990, this is the only place they'll see it discussed in depth."

Indeed, Jackson's is the strongest and most eloquent voice reminding America that equality is still a goal, not a reality. Whatever his future holds, he is sure to remain a presence, a force, in American life. Poverty and racism will not soon disappear, and the people from whom Jackson comes, and for whom he speaks, will continue to need a champion.

Back in the spring of 1988, Jackson shared a platform in San Francisco with Andrew Young. Ever since the March day in 1965 when he had watched the tall young stranger from Chicago invite himself to address the crowd in Selma, Young had wondered about Jackson. Over the years, his doubts had persisted.

As Jackson talked, Young listened intently. When Jackson spoke of going to a place the other candidates had not—to the side of those dying from AIDS—Andrew Young, a man who had heard thousands and thousands of speeches, found himself moved to tears. When Jackson finished, the two men embraced.

That evening at his hotel, still feeling the emotion from Jackson's words, Young wrote a private note to his old comrade and had it delivered by hand. It read: "You make me feel proud and humble when I hear you speak. Martin would be proud, too. You have my full endorsement as the moral voice of our time."

CHRONOLOGY

— ✿ —

1941   Born Jesse Louis Burns on October 8 in Greenville, South Carolina

1957   Takes surname of adoptive father, Charles Jackson

1962   Marries Jacqueline Davis

1963   Graduates from North Carolina Agricultural and Technical State University; enrolls in Chicago Theological Seminary

1965   Leaves seminary in senior year to work with the Reverend Martin Luther King, Jr., and his Southern Christian Leadership Conference (SCLC); takes charge of Operation Breadbasket, the SCLC's economic arm

1971   Leaves SCLC to form Operation PUSH (People United to Serve Humanity)

1984   Runs for nomination as Democratic presidential candidate; secures release from Syria of captured U.S. pilot; loses nomination to Walter Mondale

1988   Runs for Democratic nomination; makes strong showing but loses to Michael Dukakis

1990   Arranges release of 300 hostages from Iraq; starts television talk show, "Jesse Jackson"; elected nonvoting Senate representative from Washington, D.C.

FURTHER READING
———— •◊• ————

Abernathy, Ralph David. *And the Walls Came Tumbling Down.* New York: HarperCollins, 1990.

Colton, Elizabeth. *The Jackson Phenomenon.* New York: Doubleday, 1989.

Garrow, David. *Bearing the Cross: Martin Luther King, Jr., and the Southern Christian Leadership Conference.* New York: Morrow, 1966.

Germond, Jack, and Jules Witcover. *Wake Us When It's Over: Presidential Politics of 1984.* New York: Macmillan, 1985.

————. *Whose Broad Stripes and Bright Stars? The Trivial Pursuit of the Presidency 1988.* New York: Warner Books, 1989.

Goldman, Peter, and Tom Mathews, et al. *The Quest for the Presidency: The 1988 Campaign.* New York: Simon & Schuster, 1989.

Henry, William A., III. *Visions of America: How We Saw the 1984 Election.* Boston: Atlantic Monthly Press, 1985.

House, Ernest L. *Jesse Jackson and the Politics of Charisma: The Rise and Fall of the PUSH/Excel Program.* Boulder, CO: Westview Press, 1988.

Landess, Thomas H. *Jesse Jackson and the Politics of Race.* Ottawa, IL: Jameson Books, 1985.

McKissack, Patricia C. *Jesse Jackson: A Biography.* New York: Scholastic, 1991.

Reed, Adolph L., Jr. *The Jesse Jackson Phenomenon: The Crisis of Purpose in Afro-American Politics.* New Haven: Yale University Press, 1986.

Reynolds, Barbara. *Jesse Jackson: The Man, the Moment, the Myth.* Chicago: Nelson-Hall, 1975.

Sheehy, Gail. "Jesse Jackson: The Power or the Glory?" *Vanity Fair* 51 (January 1988).

Simon, Roger. *Road Show.* New York: Farrar, Straus & Giroux, 1990.

Stone, Eddie. *Jesse Jackson.* Los Angeles: Holloway House, 1988.

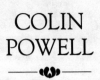

COLIN
POWELL

COLIN POWELL

Warren Brown

Senior Consulting Editor
Nathan Irvin Huggins
Director
W.E.B. Du Bois Institute for Afro-American Research
Harvard University

1

"A COMPLETE SOLDIER"

The first black to serve as chairman of the Joint Chiefs of Staff (JCS), Colin Powell is all smiles as he poses with JCS members (from left to right) U.S. Navy admiral Carlisle A. H. Trost, U.S. Air Force general Larry D. Welch, and U.S. Air Force general Robert T. Herres on November 7, 1989. Powell was asked to head the JCS three months earlier, shortly after being promoted to four-star general.

SHORTLY AFTER THREE o'clock on the afternoon of October 3, 1989, in Arlington, Virginia, the doors of the Pentagon, nerve center of the U.S. Department of Defense, swung open to release a steady stream of people into an immense, carefully manicured courtyard. The 20,000 men and women who oversee the global operations of the world's most powerful military force had been ordered by the Pentagon's head, Secretary of Defense Richard B. Cheney, to stop working so they could formally welcome a new person into the Defense Department's chain of command. At 3:30 on this bright fall afternoon, U.S. Army general Colin Luther Powell would officially assume his duties as the 12th chairman of the Joint Chiefs of Staff (JCS) of the U.S. armed forces.

The selection of General Powell to replace Admiral William J. Crowe, Jr., as the nation's highest-ranking military officer represented a landmark event not only for the Pentagon but for the entire American military. Powell had not earned his commission at one of the regular service branch academies, such as the U.S. Military Academy at West Point, New York, or the U.S. Naval Academy at Annapolis, Maryland. He had instead graduated from the Reserve Officers' Training Corps (ROTC) at the City College of New York. At age 52, he would be the youngest person ever to head the JCS.

Departing JCS chairman Admiral William J. Crowe, Jr., is congratulated on September 29, 1989, by his successor during a retirement ceremony at the U.S. Naval Academy in Annapolis, Maryland. Powell became the highest-ranking military officer in the U.S. Department of Defense when he replaced Crowe as JCS chairman.

Far more important, however, Powell had risen from a childhood of poverty to a position of power and influence that no black American had achieved before. He was about to become the first black to head the U.S. military.

At precisely 3:30 P.M., Powell, tall and imposing in a dark green dress uniform, stepped into the courtyard and strode confidently to a podium bearing the Department of Defense seal. The crowd grew quiet as the general, his face framed by a pair of dark-rimmed reading glasses, his chest covered with service decorations, began his acceptance speech. His wife of 27 years, Alma, along with their 3 grown children—Michael, Linda, and Annemarie—stood among the listeners, as did former secretary of defense Frank C. Carlucci, who had taken notice of Powell in the early 1970s and had helped nurture his career.

Powell recognized the importance of his appointment, and his emotionally charged speech showed it. The responsibilities of his new post left him feeling "humbled and proud," he said. "I'm also very mindful today," he continued, "that the period we are entering may be the most historic period in the postwar era. It will be a time of hope, a time of opportunity, a time of anxiety, of instability, of uncertainty, and, yes, a time of risk and danger. But we are not afraid of the future."

Determined to be a firm leader, Powell proceeded to pierce the fog of doubt that had dogged the American military ever since the humiliation of the Vietnam War. "The constant must be to ensure that our armed forces always remain good," he said, "that they always have what is needed to accomplish their mission, that they are never asked to respond to the call of an uncertain trumpet. We owe them, and the nation, and the world no less."

As chairman of the Joint Chiefs of Staff, Powell would be able to make good on this pledge. The JCS chairman is the principal military adviser to the president, the secretary of defense, and the National Security Council (NSC). He is also the leader of the roughly 2 million active-duty and 1.5 million reserve members of the U.S. armed forces. According to the Historical Division of the JCS, the chairman's responsibilities include:

assisting the President and the Secretary of Defense in the strategic direction of the armed forces; preparing strategic and logistics plans and net assessments; providing for the preparation and review of contingency plans; advising the Secretary of Defense on requirements, programs, and budgets; developing doctrine for joint employment of the armed forces; formulating and coordinating policies for the training and education of the armed forces; providing U.S. representation on the United Nations Military Staff Committee; and performing such other duties prescribed by law or by the President and the Secretary of Defense.

The chairman also presides over the JCS meetings and serves as spokesman. All the while, he must be a shrewd politician because it is his duty to maintain a balance of funding and power among the various military branches and to lobby for the military's interests in Congress.

President Franklin D. Roosevelt established the JCS in 1942, one month after the United States entered World War II. Initially, the JCS was the American half of the Combined Chiefs of Staff (CCS), the supreme military body for the joint British-American war effort. The four officers who represented the U.S. military at CCS strategy sessions were formally known as the Joint U.S. Chiefs of Staff. In addition to conferring with their British counterparts, they served as a military advisory committee to the president on the use of armed forces.

The National Security Act of 1947 reorganized the JCS to meet the needs of postwar America. Made up of the heads of the U.S. Army, Navy, and Air Force, the JCS was authorized to provide for the strategic direction of the military forces and to serve as the principal military advisory body to the president and the secretary of defense. The position of chairman, its holder to be nominated by the president and confirmed by the Senate, was created in 1949.

When Powell became chairman, he not only reached an unheard-of position for a black in the

Secretary of Defense Richard B. Cheney swears the 12th JCS chairman into office on October 3, 1989, at the Pentagon in Arlington, Virginia. Powell's wife, Alma, holds the Bible for her husband as he recites the oath.

armed forces but had attained it in record time. His list of qualifications was impressive indeed. During his previous 31 years in the army, he had received 2 decorations for valor in the Vietnam War, had held commands in Korea and West Germany, and had served as both the senior military assistant to the secretary of defense and as the National Security Council adviser under President Ronald Reagan. In addition, Powell had been promoted to the army's highest rank, four-star general, four months prior to being nominated to head the JCS. None of the

The newly sworn-in JCS chairman reviews an honor guard at the October 3, 1989, induction ceremony hosted by Defense Secretary Dick Cheney (left) at the Pentagon. Powell agreed to serve a second term as chairman when his two-year appointment neared its conclusion in 1991.

generals who preceded him as chairman had earned a fourth star faster than Powell had.

On Defense Secretary Cheney's recommendation, President George Bush had selected Powell for the post over 36 more senior officers. "The president wasn't exactly a tough sell," *Newsweek* magazine quoted a White House source as saying. "He thinks the world of Colin." Bush confirmed this sentiment in a speech on August 10, 1989. "Colin Powell has had a truly distinguished military career and he's a complete soldier," the president said. "He will be a key member of my national security team."

Democrat Sam Nunn of Georgia, the chairman of the Senate Armed Services Committee (which must approve any presidential military appointment), agreed with Bush. Nunn remarked upon hearing of Powell's appointment that the general would bring "tremendous . . . talent, insight, and experience" to the position. John Warner of Virginia, the committee's ranking member of the Republican party, echoed the strong feelings of approval for Powell's nomination. "It would have been easy to pick the next most senior officer," Warner commented. "But here, a deep selection was made, which conveys to me [that] some thought went into the decision." The full Senate confirmed Powell's appointment without a single dissenting vote two days after the Armed Services Committee approved his nomination.

Neither the Senate nor the Armed Services Committee made any mention of Powell's race. Yet the choice of a black to fill the nation's highest military position, especially when a conservative Republican administration controlled the White House, could not help but cause some surprise. A friend of Powell's remarked in an interview with *Jet* magazine, "Before this, the only blacks constantly around a U.S. President were valets and the first family servants."

Powell understood as well as anyone that his appointment was of great significance to black America. During much of the nation's history, the U.S. military had excluded blacks from its ranks or had limited them to segregated units under the command of white officers. It had taken many battles on numerous fronts before the military had become an institution that based opportunity on merit rather than race.

Powell was quick to acknowledge that he owed a tremendous debt to the many blacks who had fought to be treated by the U.S. military on equal terms with whites. His new post, he declared to a convention of black journalists shortly after he was nominated as chairman of the JCS, "would not have been possible without the sacrifices of those of our soldiers who served this great nation in war for 300 years previously. . . . All is on the backs and the contributions of those who went before me."

For the most part, though, Powell preferred to look ahead, for he was taking over as chairman of the JCS at a pivotal time in American history. The United States faced unprecedented global changes as its principal adversary in the postwar era, the Soviet Union, released its grip on Eastern Europe and seemed willing to end the cold war. As the warming of relations between the Soviet Union and the United States shifted the focus of global tensions from superpower rivalry to regional threats in the Americas and the Middle East, Congress became more interested in arms control and in reducing the federal budget than in funding a military for tensions that seemed all but over.

As the new chairman of the JCS, it was Powell's responsibility to allocate the money in the military's $290 billion budget and make decisions about the size and role of the U.S. armed forces—decisions that would strongly affect their future. His acceptance speech at the Pentagon indicated that he was prepared for the task. Powell's stirring words left no doubt that he intended to lead the armed services into this new era aggressively. He also clearly intended to help restore public faith in the military's ability to carry out the missions assigned to it.

Powell concluded his Pentagon introduction ceremony by reviewing an assembly of troops in parade formation. The long lines of blue-clad soldiers stood at attention, their rifles resting on the ground and their ceremonial flags waving in the breeze. Their new leader strode firmly in front of this racially mixed group, his posture and expression radiating self-assurance and natural ease with command. That Colin Powell now stood at the pinnacle of American military power spoke volumes about his own abilities—and about how much the armed forces had changed since the time of his birth. ✦

2

"MAKE SOMETHING OF YOUR LIFE"

᪣

The future army general at age 15 is flanked by his mother, Maud; sister, Marilyn; and father, Luther. Colin's parents preached to both their children the importance of a good education and personal achievement.

COLIN LUTHER POWELL was born on April 5, 1937, in New York City's Harlem district. Formerly an area of open farmland and country estates, Harlem became a residential neighborhood in the late 19th century, when a mixture of wealthy and working-class whites moved there to escape Manhattan's congested downtown area. To keep pace with the growing demand for housing, real estate developers constructed magnificent town houses and apartment buildings in this uptown section. By 1900, Harlem had emerged as one of the most desirable places to live in the city.

These developers overestimated the demand for housing, however, and by the early 1900s many apartments in Harlem were empty because not enough people could afford to live in such a high-rent district. Desperate to fill the vacant apartments, Harlem landlords drastically lowered their rents. The sudden availability of quality housing attracted large numbers of blacks seeking to escape the racial violence and poor living conditions in the city's congested West Side ghetto, and they moved to Harlem in droves. By the beginning of World War I, 50,000 blacks resided in Harlem and formed a vibrant community with a middle-class standard of living.

Colin's parents, Luther Theopolis Powell and the former Maud Ariel McKoy, arrived in Harlem during the early 1920s, when the community was at its most prosperous. Both parents were from the island of Jamaica and had left their Caribbean homeland in the hope of finding their fortune in the United States. Like so many other immigrants drawn by the booming American economy during the 1920s, they settled in New York City, the thriving metropolis at the mouth of the Hudson River; with its bustling port and enormous wealth, the city seemed to offer limitless opportunity to anyone who sought a better life.

Neither Luther Powell nor Maud McKoy had finished high school, and so they had little choice but to join the large pool of working-class immigrants that served as the backbone of the city's labor force. Luther, a husky young man with a pleasant, round face, found work as a shipping clerk in a garment factory. At a picnic one day in the Bronx, New York City's only mainland borough, he met Maud McKoy. Shortly afterward, the pair married and made their home in Harlem.

Meanwhile, Harlem had begun to take on a special allure. As it became one of the few areas in the country where blacks could enjoy an unusually high quality of life, its writers, musicians, and actors celebrated their racial heritage and promoted their own culture. This awakening of black artistic and intellectual achievement came to be known as the Harlem Renaissance.

Yet underneath the surface of this growing, closely knit community lay the symptoms of decline. By 1930, 200,000 of New York City's 327,000 blacks lived in Harlem, and they were all crowded together in an area that had housed only a quarter of that number 15 years earlier. When the Great Depression began to ravage the nation in the 1930s, Harlem was especially hard hit. Long lines of unemployed people

"MAKE SOMETHING OF YOUR LIFE" 809

in search of food and clothing stretched in front of the local churches and charity organizations. Families evicted from their apartments because they could not pay the rent crowded into the homes of relatives or lived on the street. What had previously been one of New York City's most beautiful areas began to deteriorate rapidly.

It was into this black community, in desperate decline but still treasuring proud memories, that Colin Powell was born. He lived in Harlem until he was three years old; then his parents decided it was time to relocate. In 1940, Luther and Maud Powell packed their belongings; and with Colin and his sister, Marylin, who was five and a half years older than him, in tow, they followed the city's ever

Young Colin with a few of his friends from the Hunts Point, New York, neighborhood in which he grew up. So many minorities lived there, Powell said later, that he "didn't know what a 'majority' was."

expanding elevated railway line northeast, across the Harlem River to the Bronx.

The Powells settled in Hunts Point, a working-class neighborhood in the southeastern section of the borough. The family made its home in a walk-up apartment building on Kelly Street. In time, the area would reach the extreme levels of urban decay and devastation that have come to characterize Harlem. But in the 1940s, residents called the borough "the beautiful Bronx," and Harlemites who moved into Hunts Point's blue-collar neighborhood felt that they had moved up in the world.

Although the local population was mainly Jewish, Hunts Point contained a mixture of New York City's various immigrant groups. Jews mixed freely with blacks, Irish, Italians, Poles, and Puerto Ricans, and their children mingled unselfconsciously in play. As a result, young Colin never paid much attention to the color of his skin. "I grew up in a neighborhood where everybody was a minority," he recalled. "I never thought there was something wrong with me because I was black."

The fact that his parents came from Jamaica also contributed to Colin's lack of self-consciousness about his race. Even though blacks in Jamaica were British subjects, they rarely experienced the sort of racial oppression that many black Americans, particularly those in the southern states, endured. When Powell's parents arrived in the United States, they did not view themselves as second-class citizens, and they never allowed their children to think that way either.

Instead, Luther and Maud Powell instilled in their son and daughter a strong faith in the Anglican church and a healthy respect for formal education. They wanted Colin and Marylin to do well in life and insisted that getting ahead in America depended on learning as much as possible. As a result, the Powell children often received lectures from their parents to "strive for a good education. Make something of your life."

Luther and Maud Powell also told their children that only hard work and perseverance could lead to success. Colin recalled later, "There was something of a tradition of hard work being the way to succeed, and there was simply an expectation that existed in the family—you were supposed to do better. And it was a bloody disappointment to the family if you didn't."

Colin's parents certainly led by example. Each morning, Luther Powell left home at an early hour to catch the elevated train to his job in New York City's Garment District, and he remained there all day, never returning home from work until at least 7:00 or 8:00 in the evening. Maud Powell found a job as a seamstress, and she too spent many long hours doing her work. "It wasn't a matter of spending a great deal of time with my parents discussing things," Colin remembered. "We didn't sit down at night . . . and review the work of the day. It was just the way they lived their lives."

Even though both his parents worked, young Colin never went unsupervised during the day. Maud's mother, who was known to everyone as Miss Alice, and other relatives stayed with him and his sister to enforce discipline. In addition, nearby families made a habit of watching one another's children. Marylin recalled years later that "when you walked down the street, you had all these eyes watching you."

In spite of this upbringing, Colin showed few signs during his childhood of responding to his parents' desire that he apply himself in school. Early on in elementary school, when he was about eight years old, he attempted to play hooky. The young truant estimated the time wrong, however, and arrived

At Morris High School in the South Bronx, Powell lettered in track and was elected class representative. He also served as treasurer of the Service League (above), a group that performed helpful deeds at the school.

home too early. A family friend caught him, and a family discussion ensued. In the days that followed, an adult was always present to take Colin by the hand and lead him to the classroom door.

Colin, however, did not change his ways. As a fifth grader at Public School 39, he was such a lackluster student that he landed in the slow class. At both Intermediate School 52 and Morris High School, he continued to apply himself indifferently. In his own words, he "horsed around a lot" and managed to keep his grades only barely above passing. His unspectacular marks kept him from realizing an ambition to attend the Bronx High School of Science, one of the nation's finest schools.

By this time, Colin had developed into a tall, strong teenager with a natural flair for leadership. At Morris High School, he was elected class representative, served as treasurer of the Service League, whose members helped out around the school, and lettered in track. Neighborhood youths learned not to push him around. He moved freely among Hunts Point's various racial groups and even managed to learn some Yiddish while working after school at Sickser's, a store that sold baby furniture. In his free time, Colin and his best friend, Gene Norman, raced bicycles along the sweeping curve of Kelly Street or played games of stickball.

When Colin graduated from Morris High School in early 1954, he said that he wanted to become an engineer; but in reality, he had very little idea of what he wanted to do with his life. His parents, insisting that he lift himself out of Hunts Point's "$40-a-week, lower blue-collar environment," made it clear that they expected him to go to college. Colin had no particular urge to get a higher education, but he had a deeply ingrained sense of obedience to his mother and father. If they expected him to attend college, he would go.

Colin applied to New York University and to the City College of New York. Despite his low grades, both institutions accepted him. Tuition costs helped Colin narrow down his choice. New York University charged students $750 per year to attend. The City College of New York, situated on 138th Street in upper Manhattan, enrolled any graduate from a New York City high school for only a token $10 fee. Accordingly, on a cold winter day in February 1954, Colin took a bus to Manhattan and began his life as a City College student.

Colin enrolled in City College's engineering program, and he did moderately well at first, ending his initial semester with a B average. But during the summer of 1954, he took a mechanical drawing course, and it proved to be the most miserable summer of his life. When, on a boiling hot afternoon,

Powell showed little interest in pursuing a military career around the time that this photograph for the 1954 Morris High School yearbook was taken. His stated ambition was to become an engineer.

his instructor asked him to imagine a cone intersecting a plane in space, Colin decided that he had had enough of engineering and dropped out of the program.

Colin decided to change his major to geology, not because of any strong interest in the subject but because he thought it would be easy. He did not push himself very hard and saw his average creep down to a C.

Nevertheless, Colin was about to display his first real enthusiasm for a school-related activity. During his first spring at City College, he had noticed uniformed members of the Army Reserve Officers'

Training Corps walking around the campus. The ROTC offered students military training that could lead to a commission as an officer in the U.S. Army. Colin decided that he liked the serious look of the members of the Pershing Rifles, the ROTC drill team, who wore small whipped cords on their uniform shoulders.

Colin already possessed a mild interest in the military. In high school, he had closely followed the unfolding of the Korean War. His interest aroused, Colin signed up for the ROTC for the fall semester of 1954 and pledged himself to the Pershing Rifles.

At that point, Colin had no intention of making the army a career. He wanted only to find a way to escape from New York City for a while and, in his own words, "have some excitement." Besides, joining the ROTC would help him find work. He expected to serve no more than two years in the army after graduating from college "and then come home and get a real job." But as it turned out, he had stumbled onto his life's calling.

3

BUFFALO SOLDIERS

❧

WHEN COLIN POWELL entered City College's ROTC program in the fall of 1954, he was taking advantage of an opportunity that was relatively new to black Americans. The U.S. Army and its officer training programs had not always welcomed blacks with open arms. Even though black soldiers had displayed their skill and heroism countless times during the nation's wars, the United States refused to desegregate its armed forces until 1948.

The U.S. military's long history of discriminating against blacks began with the first settlers. As these colonists established their homes along North America's eastern coast during the late 17th and early 18th centuries, they formed local militias to protect themselves from hostile Native Americans. Every able-bodied man who could shoulder a musket—a description that included many freed blacks and slaves—served the community during an emergency.

As the slave trade grew and America's colonial leaders began to fear that slaves would turn their weapons on their white masters, laws were formed to bar blacks from serving in the militia. Virginia

Troop E of the Ninth U.S. Cavalry assembles for a group portrait en route to the Philippines in 1900. One of the first all-black combat regiments, the Ninth Cavalry was originally stationed in the Old West, where its members became known as the Buffalo Soldiers.

One of the 185,000 blacks who served with distinction in the Civil War, drummer boy Jackson (above, right) stands proudly in full uniform, a vast improvement over the rags he wore (above, left) before enlisting in the Union army. Shortly after the war, the federal government established the regular army's first all-black regiments, thereby opening a door of opportunity for blacks who wanted a career in the military.

enacted the first such law in 1639; Massachusetts instituted similar legislation in 1656. Hartford, Connecticut, followed suit in 1661 after blacks and Native Americans in the area attempted a revolt.

By the middle of the 18th century, blacks throughout the colonies were allowed to serve in militias only as laborers, cooks, musicians, and in other noncombat roles. Still, from time to time there arose emergencies in which it became necessary for whites to allow blacks to join them on the firing line. In 1715, for example, North Carolina whites armed their slaves to help turn aside an attack by the Yamasee and Creek Indians. Most whites did not feel very comfortable with this solution. "There must be great caution used," one of them said on the subject of distributing weapons to blacks, "lest our slaves when arm'd become our masters."

Among those who agreed with this view was George Washington, who commanded the patriots' forces, the Continental army, during the American Revolution. In October 1775, half a year after British troops clashed with the patriot militia for the first time, he banned all blacks from enlisting in the Continental army. It was not until the following year, after the British formally invited free blacks and slaves to join their side, that Washington, facing a critical shortage of manpower, permitted blacks to fight alongside whites.

By the time the American Revolution ended in 1783, about 5,000 blacks had served in the revolutionary forces. They had proven extremely capable and dedicated, yet the mistrust that whites felt toward armed blacks quickly reasserted itself. In 1792, Congress passed a law limiting the recruitment of state militias to white men between the ages of 18 and 45. Most states interpreted the new law as a total ban on black enrollment.

Nevertheless, in the 19th century—as in colonial times—necessity prompted white military leaders to bend the law by drawing on the black population for manpower. Hastily formed black militia units helped fight British forces in the War of 1812. Half a century later, a shortage of white volunteers during the Civil War forced Northern generals to form black regiments without official permission. President Abraham Lincoln had expressly prohibited blacks from serving in the Union army because he feared it would anger most of the white soldiers and cause tension in the ranks. He also felt that allowing blacks to fight the Confederacy might jeopardize the allegiance of the few slaveholding states that had remained loyal to the Union.

In 1879, Henry Flipper became the first black to graduate from the U.S. Military Academy at West Point, New York. It took another 69 years, however, for the armed forces to become fully integrated.

As the Civil War dragged on, Massachusetts governor John Andrews declared that Northerners no longer cared whether their soldiers traced their roots "from the banks of the Thames or the banks of the Senegal." The Union simply needed more troops. Lincoln agreed that more soldiers were needed, and in 1862 he authorized the arming and training of blacks. By the end of the war, the U.S. Bureau of Colored Troops had recruited and trained more than 185,000 black soldiers.

Despite this large number, blacks constantly faced discrimination in the Union army. They were assigned to segregated units under the command of whites and were given menial tasks to perform. On those occasions when they were allowed to fight alongside whites, they displayed the same degree of courage that their ancestors had shown in earlier wars. The most celebrated black Civil War unit was one of the first: the 54th Massachusetts Regiment, which spearheaded an unsuccessful assault on a Confederate fort in South Carolina. Led by a young white colonel named Robert Gould Shaw, the 54th lost more than half its men during an attempt to capture Fort Wagner. All told, more than 38,000 black soldiers died in the Civil War.

After the war ended, Congress awarded blacks a permanent place in the army. Four all-black regiments were formed: the 24th and 25th Infantry regiments and the Ninth and 10th Cavalry regiments. As with the black regiments established during the Civil War, white officers led these units. Federal officials instituted one other significant measure: They stationed all four regiments out west to remove them from public view. The Native Americans in the western territories likened the short, curly hair and the stamina of these men to the plains buffalo's and christened them the Buffalo Soldiers.

The Buffalo Soldiers soon showed that they were excellent fighters, yet the army still treated them like outcasts. During the Spanish-American War in 1898, the Ninth and 10th Cavalry regiments were sent to Cuba but had to fight on foot because they were not supplied with horses. Both regiments helped ensure an American victory in the pivotal battle at San Juan Hill, although neither one received much credit for its effort. Soon-to-be-president Theodore Roosevelt and his white Rough Riders, who also participated in the battle, downplayed the Buffalo Soldiers' contribution and claimed the lion's share of the victory for themselves.

Discrimination toward black soldiers showed itself once again in 1906, when a riot broke out in

Brownsville, Texas, and the men of the 25th Infantry, stationed on the edge of town, were accused of starting the violence. Even though there was no clear-cut evidence against the black troops, President Theodore Roosevelt called for three entire companies to be dishonorably discharged from the army. As a result, 167 soldiers, some with up to 27 years of military service and several having already been awarded the Congressional Medal of Honor, were booted out of the army. None of them received any pension, benefits, or back pay, let alone any official recognition of their past service.

Despite these incidents, a few blacks began to make headway in the army's hierarchy. In 1879, Henry Flipper became the first black to graduate from the U.S. Military Academy at West Point. Ten years later, Charles Young, the third black to graduate from the academy, took his military career a few steps further. By the end of World War I, he had become a high-ranking officer.

After he left West Point, Young taught military science at Wilberforce University, commanded the Ninth Cavalry during the Spanish-American War, and served as military attaché to both Haiti and Liberia. In 1916, he headed a squadron of the 10th Cavalry and helped General John ("Black Jack") Pershing pursue the Mexican revolutionary Pancho Villa. Young's heroics during this campaign earned him the rank of lieutenant colonel.

But even Young was a victim of discrimination. By the start of World War I, he seemed poised to become the nation's first black general. In 1917, however, army physicians blocked his promotion by declaring the 53-year-old officer physically unfit for active duty. Outraged, Young proved his fitness by riding the 500 miles from his Ohio home to Washington, D.C., on horseback. Still, army doctors refused to reinstate him. He was kept out of the

service until shortly before the end of World War I. By that time, all chance of his being promoted to general had passed.

The army's treatment of Young during World War I exemplified its handling of black soldiers, most of whom ended up serving as laborers. Those who were sent into combat had to contend with inadequate training, poor equipment, and unenthusiastic white commanders. They were also barred from using the same facilities as whites.

Prior to the war, blacks had hoped their participation in the conflict would earn them greater respect from white America. Instead, they continued to face discriminatory treatment. Of the 370,000 blacks who served in the military during World War I, only 5

Black officers were a rarity in World War I, as the armed forces averaged 1 black officer per every 2,600 black soldiers. None of the black officers, including these members of the 367th Infantry, 77th Division, held a rank higher than colonel.

held officers' commissions in the army; none held a commission in the air corps.

By the time Colin Powell was born, the situation had hardly improved; indeed, the army showed little desire to end segregation in its ranks. It was not until 1940, when the United States was preparing to enter World War II, that a few of the barriers finally began to crumble. The military established several black combat units and officer candidate schools for the training of blacks as combat pilots. Moreover, Benjamin O. Davis, Sr., broke new ground when he was named the nation's first black general. The army, however, refused to renounce its policy of segregation or to stop relegating black recruits to service units.

When given the opportunity, black troops served with distinction. The 92nd Infantry Division, nicknamed the Buffalo Division after the black troops who had fought in the American West, won 65 Silver Stars, 162 Bronze Stars, and 1,300 Purple Hearts. The all-black 332nd Fighter Group, commanded by Col-

Benjamin O. Davis, Sr. (below, right), and his son, Benjamin O. Davis, Jr. (below, left), were among the first blacks to rise to the top of the military. In 1940, the army promoted the senior Davis to brigadier general—the first black American to attain such a high rank. Fourteen years later, the junior Davis became the first black general in the air force.

onel Benjamin O. Davis, Jr., son of the first black general, destroyed 260 enemy planes and damaged 148 others in 1,579 missions. Its pilots were awarded more than 800 medals.

In light of such gallant efforts, criticism of the army's segregation policy grew stronger during the mid-1940s. A. Philip Randolph, Walter White, and other black leaders stepped up their campaign to desegregate the armed forces. Finally, in July 1948, President Harry S. Truman gave in to the demands and issued two landmark executive orders: He desegregated the armed forces and called for government agencies to institute fair employment practices. The door for equal opportunity had begun to open for Colin Powell and other black Americans. ⬩

U.S. armed forces remained racially segregated until 1948, when President Harry S. Truman ordered an end to discrimination in the military "as rapidly as possible." By the time the Korean War began two years later, most combat troops, including the Second Infantry Division (above), had become integrated.

4

"HEY, THIS IS FUN!"

❧

While attending City College of New York, Powell became commander of the Pershing Rifles, the Reserve Officers' Training Corps (ROTC) precision drill team; he also served as president of the Cadet Officers' Club and graduated at the top of his ROTC class. "There was no specific point," he later said of his decision to make the army his career. "I just never found or saw anything I liked better."

THE SAME YEAR that Colin Powell enrolled in City College's ROTC program, the Pentagon announced that the army had become totally desegregated. Blacks who entered the military in 1954 would find their chances for advancement limited only by their ability. And no recruit would make more of this newly won opportunity than Powell.

It dawned on the teenager right away that military life suited him. He liked the physical activity and the discipline that the ROTC program demanded of him. He also enjoyed the camaraderie he felt among the members of the Pershing Rifles as they went through their drills in New York City's 369th Armory. As a result, he did not bring the same carefree attitude to the ROTC program that he did to other courses. For the first time ever, he received A's for his work. "Hey, this is fun!" Powell said of the ROTC in his sophomore year. He had at last found a pursuit that appealed to him.

One of the things the ROTC did for Powell was to give him his first look at black life in other parts of the United States. A few months after he turned 19 years old, he enrolled in a training program at Fort Bragg, North Carolina, for the summer. His father saw him off from New York City, unsure how Colin would survive his first encounter with southern racism. In the South, Jim Crow laws (a term that originated in the popular blackface minstrel shows of the late 19th and early 20th centuries) gave racial prejudice full legal backing by restricting black access in public accommodations.

Jim Crow laws assigned blacks to inferior schools and hospitals and demanded that they use separate restaurants, drinking fountains, toilets, and waiting rooms. These laws also required separate seating sections for blacks in the rear of buses, trains, and movie theaters and banned them from using city parks and beaches. All told, Jim Crow laws touched on practically every aspect of black southern life.

Powell's upbringing in Hunts Point's racial melting pot had not prepared him for the antiblack attitudes he encountered in North Carolina. "It was only [when I arrived]," he said later, "that I had brought home to me in stunning clarity the way things were in other parts of the United States." By the time the summer was over, he had become much more determined to make something of himself.

This new outlook revealed itself after Powell returned to City College. He encouraged his ROTC classmates to work harder and was appointed head of the Pershing Rifles. During his senior year, he attained the ROTC's highest rank, cadet colonel. And by the time he graduated from City College in 1958, he stood at the top of his ROTC class.

After graduation, Powell was commissioned as a second lieutenant in the army and received a weekly salary of $60. Despite his strong showing in the ROTC program, he did not have very great expectations for his future. No black American had ever risen higher than the rank of brigadier, or one-star, general. "If you do everything well and keep your nose clean for 20 years," his superiors told him, "we'll make you a lieutenant colonel." Powell set his sights on meeting that goal. A career officer with 20 years of service was eligible to retire from the military with a full pension, which meant solid financial security to a son of immigrant parents.

Second Lieutenant Powell embarked on the typical nomadic life of a young army officer. He went first to Fort Benning, Georgia, the home of the army's Infantry School. There he took courses in airborne infantry and attended classes for the small commando units, known as Rangers, that specialized in surprise raids.

After completing his training in Georgia, Powell shipped out for West Germany, where he joined other U.S. soldiers in maintaining a watch on the troops of the Warsaw Pact nations. He served first as a platoon leader, then became the commander of a rifle company. By the time Powell returned to the United States in 1960, he was a first lieutenant. His climb up the military's ladder of success had begun.

Indeed, the 24-year-old first lieutenant had already managed to make a favorable impression on his superiors. The army assigned him to take over as battalion adjutant in an infantry battalion stationed at Fort Devens, Massachusetts. Normally, this post was assigned to a higher-ranking officer than a first lieutenant—usually, to a captain—and brought with it responsibility for all decisions regarding the battalion's personnel.

(The smallest unit in the U.S. Army is a *squad*, which comprises 5 to 10 soldiers and is commanded by a noncommissioned officer, usually a sergeant. A group of several squads, amounting to 30 to 50 soldiers, is called a *platoon*; it is most often headed by a lieutenant. Three to four platoons form a *company*, which is usually led by a captain. Three to five companies make up a *battalion*, which is generally overseen by a lieutenant colonel.)

From December 1962 to November 1963, First Lieutenant Powell was stationed in Vietnam (above and opposite page), where he served as military adviser to a South Vietnamese infantry battalion. He returned to Southeast Asia in June 1968 for a second tour of duty, this time as an infantry battalion executive officer and assistant chief of staff, and he continued to see action in the Vietnam War until July 1969.

Powell's natural ease with people made him well suited for his new job as battalion adjutant. His commanding officer, Colonel William Abernathy, taught him the ropes. Powell later declared that he "learned a lot from Bill Abernathy about how to treat soldiers." In turn, Powell struck the colonel as "wise beyond his years" in dealing with problems of discipline and morale, perhaps because Powell himself had not always been especially motivated. In any event, the first lieutenant "performed magnificently," Abernathy said later. "He was always thinking and planning ahead."

Powell was still stationed in Massachusetts in 1962 when he went on a blind date while on leave in Boston. His companion for the evening was Alma

Johnson, an attractive young speech pathologist from Birmingham, Alabama. "He was absolutely the nicest person I had ever met," she recalled. He also seemed different from most other servicemen. When Alma asked him when he would be getting out of the army, he replied that he intended making it a career. "Everyone else I knew in the army," Alma said later, "had the days and minutes of their remaining service counted."

Favorably impressed, Alma Johnson agreed to see Powell again and again over the next few months. During the summer, the couple decided to wed, even though Powell had received word he would be leaving the States by year's end for reassignment in Southeast Asia. They were married on August 25, 1962.

At the end of 1962, Powell took leave of his wife to join the rapidly growing American military force in Vietnam. Since the mid-1950s, the United States had been helping to bolster the South Vietnamese government against attacks by the Communist rebels of North Vietnam. But by the early 1960s, the South

Vietnamese government had become so endangered that President John F. Kennedy sent thousands of American military personnel, under the guise of advisers, to fight alongside the South Vietnamese troops. Powell's assignment was to serve as an adviser to a South Vietnamese infantry battalion patrolling the jungles along the Laos border.

By the spring of 1963, Powell was leading a combat unit near the North Vietnamese border. There he received word that Alma, who had moved to Birmingham to live with her parents while her husband was stationed overseas, had given birth to a boy, Michael. More than half a year would pass before Powell's tour of duty ended and he could return to the States to see his first child.

One day that summer, Powell and his men were wading through a Vietnamese rice-paddy field when he stepped on an enemy trap, a sharpened stake (known as a punji stick) that had been concealed just below the surface of the water. Powell impaled his left foot on the stake with such force that it came out the top of his boot. The army shipped him to the nearby coastal city of Hue to treat his wound. He returned to the jungle a few weeks later with his first combat decoration, the Purple Heart, to show for his injury.

While Powell was braving the dangers of Vietnam, his wife was in the middle of a different kind of battle. Her hometown of Birmingham had a well-deserved reputation as being the most segregated city in the South. With that in mind, Martin Luther King, Jr., and other black leaders decided to make Birmingham a focal point of the civil rights movement. "We knew that as Birmingham went, so would go the South," said a King aide, Wyatt T. Walker. "And we felt that if we could crack that city, then we could crack any city."

Powell takes a break outside his barracks during his second tour of duty in Vietnam. The lessons he learned from the Vietnam War led him to conclude that an army should not enter into combat unless it had a clear objective. "If you finally decide you have to commit military force," he said, "you've got to be as massive and decisive as possible. Decide your target, decide your objective, and try to overwhelm it."

The showdown in Birmingham came to a head in early May 1963, when more than a thousand youngsters took part in a massive civil rights demonstration organized by King. The Birmingham city government responded with a brutal show of force. Birmingham's public safety commissioner, T. Eugene ("Bull") Connor, ordered his men not only to arrest the protesters but to repulse them. Scores of firemen employed high-pressure water hoses to repel the demonstators, slamming them to the ground and knocking them senseless. Mobs of policemen unleashed German shepherd attack dogs and looked the other way as angry whites brutally beat some of the marchers.

Alma's father, J. C. Johnson, who had been a principal in one of the city's all-black high schools, brought home stories of the racial violence. As the tumult reached its peak, he watched over his wife, his daughter, and her infant son, Michael, with a shotgun.

Powell arrived in Birmingham that Christmas, having recently won a Bronze Star for heroism in addition to his Purple Heart. The realization that he had risked his life for his country while his family's safety had been threatened by city officials left him enraged. "I was hit full force with what had happened in my absence," he recalled. "I was stunned, disheartened, and angry." Thereafter, he became a solid supporter of the civil rights movement.

Powell felt the sting of southern racism firsthand after he received orders to leave Birmingham and report once again to Fort Benning. One day, when he was trying to find a house in the area so his wife and son could join him in Georgia, he stopped at a restaurant for a hamburger. The waitress asked Powell if he was a student from Africa. When Powell told her no, the woman asked him, "A Puerto Rican?"

"No," Powell answered.

Powell freed himself from this wreckage after a helicopter in which he was riding crashed in a Vietnamese jungle. He then pulled a GI from the burning craft—an act of bravery that subsequently earned him the Soldier's Medal.

"You're Negro?"

"That's right."

"Well," the waitress responded, "I can't bring out a hamburger. You'll have to go to the back door."

Powell made a point of returning to the restaurant after President Lyndon B. Johnson signed the Civil Rights Act of 1964 into law on July 2. Among other measures, this law prohibited segregation in public facilities and forbade employers from practicing racial discrimination. "Then I went back to the restaurant," Powell recalled, "and got my hamburger."

That same year, Powell requested and received permission to attend the army's Command and General Staff College at Fort Leavenworth, Kansas—he had not forgotten his parents' lectures about the value of a good education. Meanwhile, Powell himself was becoming a parent once again. In 1965, while he was still stationed in Kansas, his wife gave birth to their second child, Linda. Another daughter, Annemarie, was born to the Powells in 1971.

Halfway through his Leavenworth course work, Powell asked the army to let him attend a civilian graduate school and add a master's degree to his City College degree in geology. "Your college record isn't good enough," the officer in charge responded. Angrily, Powell buckled down and graduated from Leavenworth second in a class of 1,244. Despite his efforts to prove he was "good enough," Powell did not receive permission to enter a program of graduate study. Instead, the army sent him back to Vietnam.

American involvement in Vietnam had gradually been escalating, and by 1968 it had turned into overt military action. Furthermore, in an increasingly desperate attempt to protect the South Vietnamese regime, the U.S government had progressively raised the number of troops it sent to Vietnam. By June 1968, when Powell joined the American forces in Vietnam as an infantry battalion executive officer and assistant chief of staff with the 23rd Infantry Division, he was one of more than 500,000 servicemen stationed there. He watched with increasing skepticism as the American troops failed to bring the war to a successful close despite their advanced technological weapons and high-powered aircraft.

Shortly after Powell arrived in Vietnam, a stroke of luck pulled him out of constant combat duty in the jungle and placed him on the road to high command. The *Army Times* had just published a story about the year's top five Leavenworth graduates, and the article had caught the eye of the commander of the 23rd Infantry. "I've got the number two Leavenworth graduate in my division, and he's stuck in the boonies?" he shouted at his subordinates. "I want him on my staff!" Powell thus became the division's assistant chief of staff.

From time to time, Powell still went out on combat missions. On one occasion, he accompanied a helicopter unit into the jungle. The pilot tried to set down the craft in a small clearing, but a rotor blade struck a tree and the helicopter crashed. Before the fuel tanks could explode, Powell pulled the pilot from the burning wreckage, a feat that earned him the Soldier's Medal, awarded for voluntarily risking one's life in a noncombat situation.

Powell's second Vietnam tour ended in July 1969. Upon returning to the States, he received permission to continue his education. That fall, he began work on a Master of Business Administration (MBA) degree at George Washington University in Washington, D.C. His reason for pursuing an MBA was quite simple. "Good business managers," he explained years later, "are needed in the Department of Defense."

5

THE CORRIDORS OF POWER

O N JULY 9, 1970, 12 years after he first received a commission in the U.S. Army, Colin Powell was promoted to lieutenant colonel, the rank he had been told it would take him 20 years to attain. The 33-year-old officer now had a guaranteed retirement pension, which gave him and his family a growing sense of security. The following year, he graduated from George Washington University with an MBA. His future seemed secure, whether or not he chose to remain in the army.

In 1972, a stroke of fate similar to the one that had placed him on the 23rd Infantry Division staff landed Powell his first political appointment. He was working as a research analyst in the office of the vice-chief of staff at the Pentagon when he received a phone call from the army's personnel department. "Colin," the caller said, "the Infantry Branch wants one of its people to become a White House Fellow. We want you to apply."

The White House Fellowship program sponsors promising military officers to serve for one year as an assistant in various departments of the executive

In September 1973, Lieutenant Colonel Powell arrived in South Korea to command the First Battalion of the Second Infantry Division's 32nd Infantry Regiment. He resumed his climb up the federal government ladder the following year, when the army rotated him back to the United States and he took a staff job at the Pentagon.

branch. This internship is highly coveted because it grooms talented officers for a role in government policy-making. Powell agreed to apply for a fellowship.

His interview was conducted by Frank Carlucci, a small, wiry deputy secretary from the Office of Management and Budget (OMB). A former foreign service official who had won a State Department medal for rescuing a group of Americans from an angry mob in what is now Zaire, Carlucci took an immediate liking to the lieutenant colonel. Powell received word shortly after the interview that of the more than 1,500 applicants for the fellowship, he was 1 of the 7 people chosen to become a White House Fellow.

Powell's good fortune did not end there. Carlucci invited him to serve as his assistant at the all-important OMB. In effect, the OMB oversees the operations of the executive branch. The OMB helps the president put together the nation's budget for each fiscal year, controls the administration of the budget after Congress has approved it, and provides the president with information on the performance of each government program. Thus, Powell's new assignment not only involved him in the fiscal planning of the executive branch but also gave him a broad view of how it worked. He felt that he had landed what he termed a "dream job."

Along with assisting Carlucci, Powell worked with Carlucci's boss, OMB director Caspar W. Weinberger, who had recently been appointed to the post by President Richard M. Nixon. A tough-minded politician, Cap Weinberger displayed such a willingness to streamline federal finances that he was given the nickname Cap the Knife.

Powell's stint at the OMB proved a turning point in his life. His ability to carry out tasks with extreme competence and little fuss made a lasting impression

on both Carlucci and Weinberger, each of whom was a rising star in Washington politics. Because of their support, Powell would always find the corridors of power open to him in the years that followed.

After Powell's term as a White House Fellow expired in 1973, the army sent him to South Korea in September to take command of the First Battalion of the Second Infantry Division's 32nd Infantry Regiment. Racial tension and a growing drug problem within the regiment had expanded into a major problem. The army was looking for Powell to smooth out the problems and restore a sense of discipline.

Powell quickly displayed the forceful command style that would become his hallmark. He discharged the malcontents—"bums," he later called them—and ordered the drug users put in jail. He ran everyone else four miles each morning and spent the rest of the day working them equally hard; by nightfall, no one

Battalion Commander Powell meets with his junior officers in Korea. He has since attributed his rise in the military to his belief that "there are no secrets to success; don't waste time looking for them. Success is the result of perfection, hard work, learning from failure, loyalty to those for whom you work, and persistence."

Located at Fort Lesley J. McNair in Washington, D.C., the National War College offers a course of study that emphasizes the planning and implementing of national security policy. Powell enrolled there in 1975 and graduated from the college with distinction in late 1976.

had enough energy left to cause trouble. All the while, he emphasized a spirit of cooperation. Within a few months, Powell's approach had yielded clear-cut results. Blacks and whites worked together peacefully and socialized with one another as well.

In 1974, Powell returned to the Pentagon, this time as an operations research analyst in the office of the assistant defense secretary. The army, however, apparently had greater things in store for him. The next year, Powell received word that he had been accepted into the National War College at Fort Lesley J. McNair in the nation's capital.

Founded by the Joint Chiefs of Staff in 1946 to promote understanding among the various branches of the armed forces and to bridge any communications gap between the Defense and State departments, the National War College has since evolved into an institution that provides education in national security policy to selected military officers and career civil service employees of federal departments and agencies concerned with national security. The 10-month academic program emphasizes the study of major issues likely to affect the national security of the United States.

In 1975, Powell, along with nearly 100 officers of comparable rank from the various armed forces and about 40 civilians, began his studies at the National War College. The curriculum would round out his knowledge of the armed forces and their role in national security policy. His course work would also help him learn how to plan and implement national strategy.

In February 1976, while he was still enrolled at the National War College, Powell received a promotion to full colonel. Two months later, partway through his second semester at the college, his superiors pulled him out of school and gave him another field command. He was made brigade commander of the 101st Airborne Division, based at Fort Campbell, Kentucky.

Powell's appointment to the division's Second Brigade brought with it a large measure of prestige. The 101st had fought with distinction during World War II and, along with the 82nd Airborne Division, now made up the army's entire mobile attack force. If the army needed to respond quickly to a military crisis, Powell could almost certainly expect to find himself in the thick of the action.

During his tenure as commander of the Second Brigade, Powell once again showed himself to be a hard-driving, energetic leader. But when the opportunity arose, he revealed another side of his character. A battalion commander in Powell's unit, Lieutenant Colonel Vic Michael, hurt his back after he slipped and fell while getting out of a helicopter. Michael tried to shrug off the injury, but Powell sent him to a doctor. The physician found that spinal surgery was needed to repair the injury.

Powell refused to follow normal army procedures, which would have resulted in another officer assuming command of Michael's battalion. Instead, he helped Michael's junior officers run the battalion and kept the position open until Michael underwent surgery and was healthy enough to resume his duties. "Powell could have ended my career, but he had faith in me," Michael said later. "He acted like he owed me something. I will never forget his understanding for me as a soldier and a human being."

Powell graduated with distinction from the National War College in late 1976. The following summer, after serving as brigade commander for a little more than a year, he returned to the Pentagon as a military assistant in the office of the deputy defense secretary. During his previous postings in Washington, he had served under Republican administrations, first Nixon's and then Gerald Ford's.

Now, a Democrat, Jimmy Carter, sat in the White House, which meant that Powell was working for another Democrat, Deputy Secretary of Defense Charles W. Duncan, Jr.

The change in the political climate made no difference in the way the Pentagon's top brass perceived Powell. He had not been labeled a Republican or a Democrat (in actuality, he considered himself an independent) because he had never shown any leanings toward either of the nation's two main political parties. First and foremost, he was a military officer, and as such he preferred to leave politics to others and perform his duties regardless of which party the national elections had placed in control of the Pentagon.

Powell remained at the Pentagon until 1979, when he briefly went to work at the newly established Department of Energy. His immediate boss at the Defense Department had just been named the new secretary of energy and had invited Powell to come along. "I went to the Department of Energy with him for two to three months," Powell later said of Duncan, "to help him get set up."

Duncan, in turn, took the colonel under his wing and taught him how to achieve his goals in the maze of federal bureaucracy without ruffling any feathers. One of Duncan's rules of thumb, Powell now jokes, stuck with him for life. "When I told [Duncan] something awful had happened," Powell recalled, "he said, 'Well, Colin, if all else fails and we have no choice, tell the truth.'"

In the summer of 1979, at age 42, Powell reached yet another milestone in his military career. On June 1, the army promoted him to brigadier general. When he pinned the general's star on his uniform, he joined the small but growing number of blacks who had risen through their own hard work and merit to such a high rank. He had now achieved much more than he ever thought possible when he had decided to pursue a career in the army.

Powell's fortunes would soon change once again. In the 1980 presidential election, the Republican party regained control of the White House, with former California governor Ronald Reagan soundly defeating Carter's bid for a second term in office. Reagan wasted little time in calling on an old friend, Caspar Weinberger, to head the Pentagon as defense secretary. Weinberger promptly tapped his deputy from the OMB, Frank Carlucci, for the post of deputy defense secretary. As they began to staff their department, both Carlucci and Weinberger remembered the promising young White House Fellow from their days at the OMB. Carlucci called Powell to the Pentagon, and when he invited the brigadier general to serve as his assistant once again, Powell accepted.

His first love, however, remained his role as soldier. Powell vastly preferred being a field commander to holding a bureaucratic position in the Pentagon. Yet the higher he rose on the military's ladder of success, the more removed he became from his desire to command troops. Since his last tour in Vietnam, he had spent only two years as a field commander: one in Korea and one with the 101st Airborne.

In the spring of 1981, Powell's wish to return to the field was granted; Weinberger appointed him assistant commander of the Fourth Infantry Division at Fort Carson, Colorado. Happy to be back with the troops, he spent the next two years at the post. In the spring of 1983 came a similiar assignment; this time, he was made the deputy commanding general of the Army Combined Arms Combat Development unit at Fort Leavenworth.

But Powell was not destined to remain in the field for very long. Events soon conspired to pull him away from his command and bring him back to the Pentagon.

Powell "is extraordinarily bright, articulate, and with excellent judgment," said Frank C. Carlucci, who became Powell's immediate boss at the State Department in 1972 and at the Pentagon in 1980. "Nobody could provide you with better guidance in this building or in the United States government."

6

WEATHERING
THE STORM

A general discussion: General Powell confers with General Mikhail A. Moiseyev, the Soviet Union's first minister of defense and chief of the general staff, aboard the USS Intrepid. Meeting with foreign military officials was one of the many duties Powell performed during his first decade with the Defense Department.

In THE SPRING of 1983, Defense Secretary Caspar Weinberger began to search for a new senior military assistant. The name he placed at the top of the list of leading candidates was that of his former colleague Colin Powell. Happily situated at Fort Leavenworth, Powell had little desire to give up his command. But when Weinberger contacted him, the general knew enough to interview for the position. His career might lose its momentum if he refused the job outright.

Instead of declining the post, Powell told the defense secretary that he preferred "being close to the troops." His comment did little good. Weinberger wanted Powell on his Pentagon staff, and so in June 1983 the general and his family reluctantly moved back to Washington, D.C.

Powell may have displayed an initial lack of enthusiasm for the position, but he certainly labored hard at it. Emulating his father's work habits, he arrived at the Pentagon every morning by 6:30 and returned home after seven o'clock each evening. As easygoing as he was tactful, he became indispensable to Weinberger. Powell screened staff members before they met with the defense secretary and reviewed memos and documents before they reached Weinberger to prevent unnecessary details from wasting the secretary's valuable time.

It did not take long for Powell to earn high marks for fairness from the department's employees. Not one to play favorites, he gave anyone who wished to speak with Weinberger a chance to do so. He clashed only with those who attempted to establish a private channel to the defense secretary.

Powell rarely expressed his own thoughts to Weinberger. He regarded his job as that of department coordinator; it was his duty to convey the staff members' views and ideas to the defense secretary. As a result, his Pentagon colleagues began to think of him, in the words of one associate, as "more of an expediter than a global thinker."

In effect, Powell functioned as Weinberger's chief of staff. According to Pentagon assistant secretary Michael Pillsbury, Powell "was the real secretary of defense. All paper, in or out, went through Colin. All meetings of substance Colin had to attend, or there was no meeting." An admiring Weinberger leaned heavily on his aide. He later remarked that Powell "knows what he's talking about and he always knows all of the buttons to push."

It did not take long for the Weinberger-Powell team to become the talk of the Pentagon. Wherever Weinberger went, Powell accompanied him. During Powell's tenure as senior military assistant, he traveled with Weinberger to more than 35 countries. Before long, Powell was awarded a second general's star and was elevated to the rank of major general.

Powell's performance as senior military assistant gained him not only Weinberger's confidence but also that of the Joint Chiefs of Staff. As a result, he was asked to play a major role in helping the Reagan administraion carry out a more aggressive approach to foreign policy.

The first time Powell took part in a major military action as a Pentagon official was when the United States invaded Grenada on October 25, 1983. Earlier in the month, revolutionaries on the tiny Caribbean island had put Maurice Bishop, the prime minister, under house arrest. This political coup threatened to strengthen the ties between Grenada's new Marxist government and both Cuba and the Soviet Union.

According to the Reagan administration, Grenada's association with the two Communist nations jeopardized American interests in the region. Moreover, its internal turmoil threatened American students who lived there. When the Organization of Eastern Caribbean States appealed to the United States to help restore order and democracy on Grenada, the president acted swiftly, sending 1,900 marines along with several hundred Caribbean troops to the island to overthrow the newly installed government.

Weinberger assigned Powell the task of convincing White House officials to allow the armed forces to carry out the invasion, code-named Urgent Fury, as the Defense Department saw fit. It also became Powell's responsibility to brief the White House about the course of the invasion. All told, the entire operation took less than a week to complete and was, according to government officials, an unqualified success.

Less successful was a scheme devised by Robert McFarlane, Reagan's national security adviser, to sell antitank and antiaircraft missiles to Iran. As head of the National Security Council staff, McFarlane was responsible for overseeing the operation of the staff

Powell served as senior military adviser to Secretary of Defense Caspar W. Weinberger from 1983 to 1986. Powell, Weinberger said, "is one of the very best persons I have ever worked with in any of the positions I've had. He has excelled in everything he has touched, and he always will. I don't think you can find anyone who has anything bad to say about Colin Powell, which is an extraordinary thing when you've been around Washington as long as he has— in highly sensitive and vital assignments."

as well as the workings of the NSC system. But he was hoping to accomplish far more than that.

The NSC had been formed in 1947 to serve as a forum for advising the president on matters relating to the nation's security. Attending the NSC meetings in addition to the president are the vice-president, the state and defense secretaries, the chairman of the JCS, the director of the Central Intelligence Agency (CIA), and the so-called NSC adviser, whose actual title is assistant to the president for national security affairs. The civilian and military officials who make up the NSC advisory staff contribute to the proceedings by monitoring the world situation, coordinating research involving various government agencies, and providing information and recommendations to the council.

The NSC staff was established in part to act as a watchdog, curbing the competition between the State and Defense departments as they shaped foreign policy. Over the years, however, NSC advisers managed to broaden their influence in American affairs by turning their agency into an independent policy-making body. Henry Kissinger, for one, virtually controlled the nation's foreign policy when he served as NSC adviser during the Nixon administration.

McFarlane, too, attempted to exercise his power, but he did it in a way that threatened to bring down the entire Reagan administration. The first hint that he had exceeded his authority came in the summer of 1985, as Powell was entering his third year as senior military assistant. Powell received an apparently routine request from the NSC. It wanted information on the price and availability of sophisticated TOW wire-guided antitank missiles for sale abroad.

Powell delivered the information, considering his action, as he later explained to the *Washington Post*, "a routine service that I would provide to any department." He did not know that McFarlane was planning to sell the TOW missiles to win the release of American hostages held in Lebanon by Iranian-backed Islamic extremists.

McFarlane's scheme violated both the president's policy of not aiding Iran during its ongoing war with neighboring Iraq and his publicly stated promise not to make bargains with terrorist groups. Despite these strong words, Reagan's loose management style allowed the NSC staff to sell war matériel to Iran without his approval or any other form of official supervision. On August 20, 1985, the NSC staff put the plan into operation, making a small arms delivery to Israel, America's chief ally in the Middle East. Acting as go-between, the Israelis bought the missiles from the United States and then shipped them to Iran. Approaching the deal in this circuitous way allowed McFarlane to maintain he was not doing anything illegal.

After the NSC staff inquired about the TOW missiles, it approached Powell for information about HAWK antiaircraft missiles. Meanwhile, McFarlane arranged to ship more TOW missiles to Iran. A second delivery was made on September 14.

Both Powell and Weinberger, along with Secretary of State George Shultz, opposed the arms deal as soon as they uncovered what the NSC staff was up to. But they were unable to stop it. In January 1986, one month after McFarlane resigned as national security adviser, the new head of the NSC staff, Rear Admiral John Poindexter, persuaded Reagan to authorize direct arms shipments to Iran in the hope of winning the hostages' release. Now that the deal had the president's approval, Weinberger chose Powell to carry out the transfer of weapons from Pentagon stockpiles to the CIA, which arranged to ship them to Iran.

Despite the presidential order to go ahead with the sale, the attempt to exchange arms for hostages still troubled Powell. He wrote a memo to Poindexter, reminding him of the legal requirement to notify Congress of any arms transfers, such as those that were now taking place. Poindexter, well aware of the outcry that would result if Congress found out about the arms sales and of the potential political damage to the president if the scheme was uncovered, ignored Powell's memo.

Powell chafed to get away from Washington, D.C., and return to a field command. In June 1986, Weinberger let him go. Powell was appointed to command the U.S. Army V Corps stationed in

Lieutenant Colonel Oliver L. North is sworn in at a 1987 investigation into the Iran-contra affair. Powell was among the few people implicated in the wide-ranging scandal to be found innocent of any wrongdoing.

Frankfurt, West Germany. This assignment put him directly in charge of 72,000 active-duty combat troops. At the same time, Reagan authorized Powell's promotion to lieutenant general, the army's third-highest rank, superseded only by full general and general of the army. With a prestigious field command and three stars sewn on his shoulder, Powell said that he was "probably the happiest general in the world."

A few months later, the storm broke. On November 13, the president appeared on television to confirm reports that the United States had secretly sold arms to Iran, and a national uproar ensued. The situation grew worse when Attorney General Edwin Meese revealed that the NSC staff had diverted part of the $48 million Iran had paid for the arms, using the funds to supply military aid to the contra rebels fighting Nicaragua's Sandinista government.

This second scheme, run by NSC staff member U.S. Marine Corps lieutenant colonel Oliver L. North, directly violated a 1984 law passed by Congress that prohibited all military aid, direct or indirect, to the contras. Poindexter had supported North's illegal operation and had deliberately concealed it from the president. Reagan appointed a review board headed by former senator John Tower to investigate the scandal.

The Tower Commission found among the documents concerning NSC operations a note handwritten by North. The memo listed the people in the government who knew about the secret arms deals with Iran. Third on the list of 16 people, after Shultz and Weinberger, stood the name of Colin Powell.

The general testified privately in front of congressional committees about his role in the scandal, which became popularly known as the Iran-contra affair. He testified alone, in private sessions, because

Congress felt it inappropriate to question him publicly alongside Pentagon officials of lower rank.

The investigators found no evidence of any
wrongdoing on Powell's part. He had acted as a staff
member rather than as a policymaker and had properly followed orders from his superiors in coordinating
arms transfers to the CIA. The discovery of his memo
to Poindexter, reminding the national security adviser of his responsibility to notify Congress of the
arms sales, won Powell respect and approval on
Capitol Hill. He emerged from the Iran-contra scandal as one of the few participants to survive with an
unblemished reputation.

7

"MR. PRESIDENT, I'M A SOLDIER"

❦

Powell gives President Ronald Reagan his daily 30-minute briefing on national security. "I'm principally a broker," Powell said of being deputy national security adviser and national security adviser, posts he held from January 1987 to January 1989. "I have strong views on things, but my job is to make sure the president gets the best information available to make an informed decision."

WHEN COLIN POWELL was told he was being appointed commander of the Army V Corps, he anticipated a long tour of duty in West Germany. He had seen enough of Washington, D.C.'s political jungle to realize all over again that he preferred being stationed with the troops. He also hoped his new assignment would lead to a promotion as the U.S. Army's chief of staff. Therefore, when Frank Carlucci called him six months into his command with an offer of a new White House position, Powell instantly responded, "No way."

Carlucci had recently accepted a new job, too. The Iran-contra affair had forced John Poindexter to resign as national security adviser, and in a bid to restore the National Security Council's tarnished image, President Ronald Reagan had appointed the universally respected Carlucci as Poindexter's replacement. Carlucci saw at once that the scandal had left the credibility of the 190-member NSC staff on the brink of collapse, and he desperately needed someone with Powell's diplomatic and leadership skills to help rebuild the shattered organization. That was why he had telephoned Powell in Frankfurt: to ask his former assistant to become deputy national security adviser.

857

An aerial view of the Pentagon, the massive limestone building in Arlington, Virginia, that houses the Defense Department. Powell's many duties as a high Pentagon official have included the administering of the department's multibillion-dollar budget.

Powell's refusal did not discourage Carlucci. He called twice more in an effort to get Powell to change his mind. On the third try, Carlucci sounded so desperate that a wavering Powell phoned him back and pleaded his involvement in the Iran-contra affair as a reason for rejecting the post. "Frank," he said, "you should know I've been questioned about Iran-contra because of those TOW missiles and may be asked to testify. That could be a problem."

"Colin, I've talked to everybody," Carlucci responded. "You're clean. I wouldn't ask you to give up this command if I didn't need you. The commander in chief needs you."

"If he really wants me," Powell said reluctantly, "then I have to do it."

The next evening, Powell's phone rang again. When he picked up the receiver, he heard the president's voice on the line. Reagan attempted to add his own influence to Carlucci's pleas. "I know you've been looking forward to this command," the president told Powell, "but we need you here." It was unthinkable to Powell to turn down a request from one's commander in chief. "Mr. President, I'm a soldier," he replied, "and if I can help, I'll come."

Powell rejoined Carlucci in Washington, D.C., at the beginning of 1987. Together the two men began the task of restoring life to the NSC. Powell took over the job of reorganizing the staff to comply with recommendations made by the Tower Commission. Poindexter had kept all NSC departments separate from each other, which had allowed Oliver North to run his illegal contra operation without control or comment from any other part of the NSC. Powell introduced a clear chain of command while at the same time encouraging discussion among the NSC staff and related government agencies on most policy items.

"Like Frank," Powell said, "I am a great believer that the interagency process works best when everybody has a chance to say his piece and get his positions out on the table. . . . When we forward the final decision package to the president or present it to him orally, everybody who played knows he has been properly represented and had his day in court." Under Carlucci and Powell's leadership, the NSC staff revived quickly and began to assume its proper place in the government.

Carlucci occasionally broke with NSC tradition by letting his deputy give the president his daily 30-minute briefing on national security. Carlucci hoped to give Powell a chance to develop a personal relationship with the chief executive, and he was not disappointed; Reagan instantly took a liking to the general. The president appreciated that Powell treated him courteously but without the overzealousness that many senior military officers displayed in his presence. The two men also shared a common bond: Each had been a youthful underachiever who had nonetheless managed to become a success.

For his part, Powell failed to show any resentment toward Reagan over the president's opposition to several pieces of civil rights legislation aimed at advancing blacks' rights. The general contented himself with working slowly to improve the president's sensitivity to the problems of black America.

Shortly after Powell took over as Carlucci's deputy, a tragic accident almost robbed him and Alma of their only son. Michael had followed his father into the army and at the age of 24 had become a first lieutenant. He was stationed in West Germany when his jeep overturned, breaking the young officer's pelvis in six places. Four days after the accident, Michael arrived at Walter Reed Army Hospital in Washington, D.C., for surgery.

A stunned Powell sat by his son's bed, fearful that Michael might not survive and that if he did, he might have to spend the rest of his life in a wheelchair. "You'll make it!" the general repeatedly said to his son, practically willing him to live. "You want to make it, so you will make it!"

Michael survived the surgery but remained in the hospital for a year. Then he returned to his parents' home in Fort Meyer, Virginia, to convalesce. Continual therapy eventually enabled him to walk again. When he was finally fit enough to go back to work, he left the army and joined the Defense Department.

On November 5, 1987, while Michael was still in the hospital, a changing of the guard in the Reagan administration placed Colin Powell in a leading role on the national stage for the first time. This newly won position came Powell's way when Caspar Weinberger approached Howard Baker, Reagan's chief of

National Security Adviser Powell discusses a proposal for a United States–Soviet Union medium-range missile treaty with (from left to right) White House Chief of Staff Howard Baker, Senator Robert Dole, and Senator Alan Simpson. This meeting was held as part of the preparations for a May 1988 summit conference between President Ronald Reagan and Soviet Union leader Mikhail S. Gorbachev.

staff, and said he wanted to resign as defense secretary. Baker promptly escorted Weinberger to the Oval Office to talk over the situation with the president.

Reagan accepted Weinberger's resignation after the latter assured him the main reason why he wished to leave the government was his wife's poor health. The president then began to discuss with Weinberger and Baker who should become the next defense secretary. All three men agreed on Carlucci. There was one last matter to settle: Who should succeed Carlucci as national security adviser? Powell's name was suggested. "I think that's a great idea," Reagan responded. "Nobody else was considered," Baker later said of the meeting.

Indeed, Powell's reputation for integrity and his hand in rebuilding the NSC staff made him a doubly good choice. Moreover, his lack of a personal political agenda recommended him as an administrator who could continue to restore the NSC to its proper role as a watchdog over the State and Defense departments.

Only one issue stood a chance of preventing Powell's appointment. After uncovering Rear Admiral John Poindexter's role in the Iran-contra affair, the Tower Commission had strongly recommended that no military officer ever again be appointed national security adviser. Powell himself agreed with the commission's recommendation. In October 1987, just one month prior to Weinberger's resignation, Powell had told the *New York Times* that in his opinion only civilians should fill this sensitive post.

Yet Powell was by now so popular in government circles that his nomination to the post of national security adviser met with few objections. He continued to state that he supported the idea of a civilian serving as national security adviser. But Powell also said publicly that "the transcendent principle is that a President should have who he wants."

In late December 1987, Powell became Reagan's sixth national security adviser. The 10 months he had spent as Carlucci's deputy enabled the 50-year-old general to adapt smoothly to the national security adviser's daily routine. At 6:30 each morning, he arrived at his corner office on the first floor of the White House's west wing. For 30 minutes, he studied intelligence reports on military and political activities around the world. At 7:00 A.M., Carlucci and Secretary of State George Shultz joined him for a conference. After two more hours of private conversations and phone calls, Powell seated himself on a sofa across from Reagan and gave the chief executive his daily national security briefing.

"It was a heck of a homework quiz," Powell later said of these presidential briefings. "I would give him warning of what was coming our way, or sometimes just philosophize: for example, what was happening

General Powell and First Captain Cadet Kristin Baker, the U.S. Military Academy's first female brigade commander, meet the press at West Point. In recent years, Powell has made himself accessible to the public so as to encourage others to rise as high as they can. "If you check my stats around here," he told Ebony magazine, "you'll find I've been to elementary schools, junior high schools, high schools trying to get the message out every way I can."

in the Soviet Union or how Congress was reacting to a particular issue. It was a challenge, but it becomes a natural one because you're doing it every day."

The president and the soldier maintained the cordial relationship they had established during Powell's tenure as Carlucci's deputy. As was his style, Powell did not press his views on Reagan but tried to influence him with carefully reasoned arguments. The general's tact and persuasiveness, for example, played a large part in convincing the president to back away from his cherished policy of sending the contras military aid in their fight against the Sandinista government of Nicaragua. Although Powell personally supported the rebels' goals, his political instincts told him an attempt to send more military aid to the contras would not survive the public's outrage over the Iran-contra affair. Instead he helped persuade Reagan to push for a face-saving compromise that would allow shipments of food and medicine to the rebels but ban all transfers of arms.

In fulfilling his role as national security adviser, Powell tried to avoid appearing overly sympathetic to the military point of view. He also worked long and hard at locating a middle ground in disputes between the State and Defense departments over foreign policy. Cabinet politics in the waning days of the Reagan administration often made this task difficult. No longer opposed by the strong and crusty Caspar Weinberger, George Shultz tried to assume control of the administration's foreign policy. As a result, Powell was often forced to back Carlucci to keep the balance of power between the State and Defense departments intact.

Powell usually handled these disputes with the utmost diplomacy. When Shultz suggested various ways to remove Panamanian dictator Manuel Antonio Noriega from power, such as kidnapping him or setting up a rival government in exile, Powell did not immediately tell the secretary of state that he opposed the plan. Instead he checked with other NSC members to see how they felt about Shultz's proposal. Discovering that they opposed it as well, Powell convened a fully staffed NSC meeting. Arranging for the matter to be discussed in an open forum let Shultz see for himself that it was not the general alone who disapproved of the plan.

There was only one aspect of his job that Powell did not appear to relish: the constant media exposure. Now that he was the administration's national security spokesman, every word he uttered in public seemed to take on special significance. His newfound visibility prompted Powell to remark to an interviewer, "You'd better have a hell of a lot of information [as a White House official]. You cannot be wrong. If you're wrong, you're a headline."

Powell also complained about the weekly ritual of talking to reporters. "Why do I have to talk to these people every week?" he asked White House press spokesman Marlin Fitzwater shortly after taking over as national security adviser. "All they ever want to know is who did what to whom. They never ask about substance."

Powell may have viewed the media as a necessary evil, but reporters liked the general. He had got off on the right foot, winning their respect during his first month as national security adviser. While accompanying the president to a lavish New Year's Eve celebration in Palm Springs, California, he had dropped in on a party for the Reagan press corps. A television producer, having heard that the general might show up, had arranged a surprise or two to test Powell's mettle.

The producer had ordered a pair of cakes to be baked for the party, both of which were meant to recall the sins of past national security advisers. One of the desserts was molded to look like a key, to serve

Side boys salute General Powell as he arrives for a change-of-command ceremony on the USS John F. Kennedy. Powell was promoted to the rank of four-star general in 1989.

as a reminder of the time Robert McFarlane had brought a key-shaped cake (to symbolize the unlocking of doors) to a secret meeting in Iran during the arms-for-hostages deal. The other cake, in the shape of a Bible, was baked in honor of a trip to Iran that John Poindexter's associate Oliver North had made in support of the deal; the lieutenant colonel had brought his Iranian contacts a Bible signed by the president.

Powell did not lose his composure for an instant when he spotted the cakes. Instead he shared in the joke—to the point of posing with them for photographs. "That's Colin Powell," said one of the reporters on hand. "He's a General but a damn nice guy."

Regardless of how much Powell disliked dealing with the media, he became very good at it. His role in coordinating the efforts of policymakers and technical advisers during the December 1987 summit conference between Reagan and Soviet Union leader Mikhail S. Gorbachev resulted in his making frequent appearances on television news broadcasts. Powell developed a calm, cool, and self-possessed persona for the screen. The only time he lost his composure in front of the cameras occurred when a reporter for the "Nightwatch" news program asked him a personal question about his parents. Powell could not speak for a moment. Finally, he said in a voice full of emotion, "Well, Mom, Pop, you brought us up right. All of us. I hope you're happy. I hope you're proud of what we do."

The media naturally focused on Powell's race, but he felt strongly that it should not influence people's judgment of him. "What my color is is someone else's problem, not mine," he told a television interviewer. "People will say, 'You're a terrific Black general.' I'm trying to be the best general I can be." Nonetheless, he recognized that by working hard and earning respect for his abilities, he was helping to open doors to other blacks.

Powell tried to be more than just a role model. He made himself accessible to interviewers representing black publications, spoke out against racism at public appearances, and lent his support to the civil rights movement as best he could from the Reagan White House. "I am . . . mindful that the struggle [against racism] is not over," he said at a January 1988 meeting of a black political studies organization, ". . . until every American is able to find his or her own place in our society, limited by his or her own ability and his or her own dream."

An incident that occurred shortly after Powell took over as national security adviser demonstrated the importance he attached to supporting black rights. A blizzard broke out on the day he was scheduled to speak at a luncheon given by one of Washington, D.C.'s oldest black patriotic organizations, the James Reese Europe American Legion Post. When his secretary offered to cancel the appointment because of the foul weather, Powell simply responded, "No, I have to go." He then spent 2 hours driving through the snow to give a half-hour speech to 12 people on the contributions of blacks to the American military.

Although Powell supported the civil rights movement, many black leaders felt he was betraying his race by serving a president whom they viewed as hostile to their cause. During a speech Powell gave in January 1988 at the Joint Center for Political Studies, several black officials walked out of the room after he began to speak in favor of the administration's policy to continue business ties with South Africa, a nation that endorsed racial segregation. Powell "will not attain hero status from the masses of black people," said civil rights leader and politician Jesse L. Jackson, "because Reagan has been so indifferent . . . to blacks."

Powell disagreed with Jackson. "Surprisingly, most black American groups I talk to are proud of the fact that I have this job," he told the press. "The fact that I have this job is a credit to the President. . . . He knew me and he gave it to me." Despite their differences, Jackson and Powell have developed a warm friendship, each admiring what the other has accomplished.

Indeed, Powell has succeeded in leaving almost no political enemies in his wake. Even his occasional opponent George Shultz has honored him. In September 1988, the secretary of state bestowed on Powell the Secretary's Award, given out annually for "distinguished contributions to the development, management, or implementation" of U.S. foreign policy. Shultz cited Powell for his role in coordinating Reagan's two summit meetings with Gorbachev.

Powell's widespread popularity prompted many political observers to call on George Bush, who was on course to succeed Reagan in the White House, to make Powell his running mate during the 1988 presidential election. Other people had their own ideas about where Powell's career was headed. NSC insiders regarded him as a strong candidate for U.S. Army chief of staff, a position that was to open up in early 1990. Frank Carlucci, who said that Powell had done a better job running the NSC staff than he had, speculated that the general might even become chairman of the Joint Chiefs of Staff.

As the end of Reagan's second term in office drew near, not even Powell could predict what his own future might hold. Rumors began to spread that he would be asked to stay on as national security adviser if Bush won the 1988 presidential election, but Powell brushed them aside and waited until all the votes were in. Bush won the election handily; a short time later, he called in Powell and delivered the news. "I think I ought to have my own national security adviser," said the president-elect.

When word began to spread that Powell would be leaving his White House post, U.S. Army chief of staff General Carl Vuono phoned him with an offer. "If you want to come home to the army, we have a job for you," Vuono said. A New York City booking agent approached Powell as well, telling him he could make far more money on the lecture circuit than he could in the army. The speech agent offered Powell a contract worth more than $100,000.

The general was so overwhelmed by his choices that he sat down with a pen and a sheet of paper and made two columns. He labeled one of them "Reasons to stay in the army" and the other "Reasons to leave the army." He easily found a dozen items to put in the first column; he wrote only one word under the second heading: *Money*. Powell decided to follow his heart and return to active duty in the army.

Before Reagan left office, the president followed through on Vuono's offer and promoted Powell to the rank of four-star general. He also named Powell commander in chief of the U.S. Forces Command at Fort McPherson in Atlanta, Georgia. With this appointment, the former ROTC graduate found himself in charge of all the army's troops in the continental United States. The men and women under his authority included 250,000 active-duty troops and 300,000 reserves. If, as happens in a time of crisis, the National Guard was to be activated, Powell would control more than 1 million soldiers, or almost two-thirds of the army's worldwide combat strength. ❧

8

THE BEST MAN FOR
THE JOB

IN EARLY 1989, as Colin Powell assumed his post as commander in chief of the U.S. Forces Command, George Bush took over the reins of the federal government. Powell felt distant from the incoming regime, separated by more than the miles between Washington, D.C., and Atlanta. Personal alliances were very important to the new president, and Powell could not claim any close bonds of friendship to Bush's inner circle—certainly not in the way that his association with Frank Carlucci and Caspar Weinberger had tied him to Ronald Reagan.

What's more, the 1988 presidential campaign had left the general feeling uneasy about Bush. His campaign had tried to stir up racial fears by running a television commercial about Willie Horton, a convicted black rapist who had been furloughed from prison under a Massachusetts law supported by Governor Michael S. Dukakis, the Democratic candidate in the race. While on leave, Horton had raped a white woman—a crime that the commercial blamed on Dukakis, implying that rampaging blacks would threaten the nation if the governor were elected president. This smear tactic deeply disturbed Powell and added to his misgivings about the new administration. Consequently, when the president offered to make him director of the CIA, Powell turned Bush down.

There appeared to be only one government position that would entice the general into returning to Washington, D.C. In August 1989, it came his way. The new secretary of defense, Dick Cheney, a member of the House Intelligence Committee during Powell's term as national security adviser, phoned him with an offer to become chairman of the JCS. "I have recommended that the president appoint you," said Cheney, who held Powell in very high regard. "He has accepted my recommendation."

After his conversation with Cheney, Powell called his wife. "Alma," he said, "we're moving again. The president's making me chairman of the Joint Chiefs."

The choice of Powell to replace the retiring JCS chairman, William Crowe, Jr., met with widespread praise. But approval of Powell's appointment was not unanimous. A number of high-ranking military officers resented the fact that the president had bypassed dozens of candidates with more seniority in favor of a general who had received his fourth star just a few months earlier and had spent more time holding government jobs than commanding combat troops.

Powell, these officers grumbled, had climbed to the chairmanship on his political connections rather than on his military expertise. "In his last 20 years in the service, he served 5 years with the operational units and the other 15 years in Washington," retired rear admiral Eugene Carroll told the *Congressional Quarterly*. As a result, many younger officers would interpret Powell's success as a cue to "come to Washington; serve your political mentors; make

friends where it counts . . . and avoid those trips to the troops."

Powell's lack of long-term command experience had also caused Bush and Cheney some concern. Cheney had originally favored appointing Crowe's deputy as chairman, which would have permitted Powell to spend the next two years getting more seasoning as a commander before moving into the JCS chairmanship when the position reopened in 1989. After considering their options more closely, both Bush and Cheney decided that Powell was already the best man for the job.

Powell officially became the JCS chairman on October 3, 1989. According to a government observer writing about the general at one of his first JCS meetings, "If a stranger had come into the room and been told that one person there was new to his job, he would never guess it was Powell. The new

Defense Secretary Dick Cheney (left) confers with Powell at a Senate Armed Services Committee hearing. The top two officials in the Defense Department, Cheney and Powell have worked closely together since the latter became JCS chairman on October 3, 1989.

Chairman was utterly confident. He absolutely filled the room. There was a quality about him that announced, 'Hi, get the hell out of the way, I'm Chairman.'"

World events quickly put Powell to the test. Within his first few months in office, the American military had to deal with small crises in Panama, the Philippines, and El Salvador. The quick succession of these events prompted Powell to comment afterward, "I've had several cold showers. From time to time, when you least expect it, when everyone thinks the world is quiet, someone pulls on Superman's cape."

In the first emergency, revolutionaries eager to overthrow Panamanian dictator Manuel Noriega sought American assistance; certain that an attempted coup was destined to fail, Powell recommended against aiding the rebels. The second international crisis involved another military coup, this one in the Philippines, where the United States had an important air base and naval station; the JCS chairman advocated the use of American warplanes to put down the rebellion. Powell's third "cold shower" occurred when a civil war in El Salvador placed some Green Berets, part of the U.S. Army's special-operations force, in grave danger; Powell called for additional troops to go into San Salvador to rescue the soldiers.

In late 1989, Powell met with Bush to discuss an even more sensitive assignment. The president, outraged by the international drug-smuggling activities encouraged by Noriega, wanted the Panamanian dictator physically removed from power. Powell preferred to negotiate a deal with Noriega: The United States would drop all drug-smuggling charges against him if he would relinquish control of the government.

Powell changed his mind, however, when Noriega's soldiers killed a U.S. marine in Panama. The JCS chairman spent the better part of the next two months with General Maxwell R. Thurman of the Southern Command, devising a plan for 26,000 U.S. troops to invade Panama and hunt down Noriega. Their plan became known as Operation Just Cause.

The American invasion commenced on December 20. "We will chase him," Powell said of Noriega as Operation Just Cause unfolded, "and we will find him." As promised, the operation proved swift and successful. Unprepared for such a massive, lightning-like strike, Noriega was cornered by U.S. military forces and brought to Florida to face drug-trafficking charges.

Throughout Operation Just Cause, Powell held frequent press briefings to let the American public know that its troops were in total command of the operation. Ever since the Vietnam War, the nation's military leaders had shied away from sending soldiers into combat for fear of a public outcry over the resulting casualties. Powell's experiences in Vietnam had convinced him that a halfhearted commitment of troops, no matter how sophisticated their weaponry, achieved little against a determined enemy. Such an approach led only to a prolonged conflict, with plenty of casualties and little public support.

In situations that called for military force, Powell preferred to make the initial blow strong enough to guarantee a quick, clean success. "Strike suddenly, decisively, and in sufficient force to resolve the matter" was his opinion. "Do it quickly; and . . . do it with a minimum loss of life."

Despite this philosophy, Powell was never especially eager to use force. He had, in fact, taped to his Pentagon desk a quotation from the ancient Greek historian Thucydides: "Of all manifestations of power, restraint impresses men most." Powell had seen the horrors of battle in Vietnam and understood there was no such thing as a risk-free operation or a clean bombing attack. What's more, he knew that another inconclusive war, like the one in Vietnam, would

Powell addresses crew members aboard the battleship USS Wisconsin, stationed in the Persian Gulf as part of Operation Desert Shield, in September 1990, one month after Iraqi troops invaded Kuwait. To prepare for the deployment of American forces in the Middle East, Powell intensively studied the history of the region. "I always like to have a context for what I do," he said, "so I know I'm in the right stadium and I'm playing the right game. Then I can go on the field and play it. History helps put me in that context."

seriously jeopardize the standing of the American military both at home and abroad.

Yet by early 1991, Powell would find himself in charge of the largest U.S. military action since Vietnam.

On August 2, 1990, the Bush administration was stunned by reports that 80,000 Iraqi troops commanded by President Saddam Hussein had just invaded neighboring Kuwait. Iraq's military action gave Hussein control of Kuwait's vast oil fields and put his army in position to strike further southward, into oil-rich Saudi Arabia. The fear that Iraq, which boasted the Middle East's largest and best-equipped army, would soon gain control of most of the world's oil supply forced oil prices to rise sharply and sent shock waves through almost every nation's economy.

Bush responded to the invasion with a firm warning. Hussein's action "will not stand," he promised the American public. "This will not stand."

Privately, Powell was dismayed to hear Bush promising to liberate Kuwait without first consulting his military leadership. Moreover, the general favored a strategy of containing Hussein's ambitions with economic sanctions, not with the use of force. In public, however, Powell backed his president and advised him that a token show of strength would not intimidate Hussein into withdrawing from Kuwait. "You can't put a ship in the [Persian] Gulf and lob shells and do anything," Powell said. If the president really wanted to turn back the Iraqi army and at the same time reaffirm America's role as a preeminent world power, he should act quickly and send as many troops to the Persian Gulf as possible.

At Bush's behest, Powell drew up the plans for what became known as Operation Desert Shield, the largest deployment of American forces since the Vietnam War. Within days after Bush approved of the plan, U.S. troops began to arrive in the Saudi Arabian desert, where they were joined by a coalition of United Nations (UN) forces. By November, 180,000 U.S. soldiers were stationed near the Saudi border, keeping a watch on Hussein's army across the desert in Iraq and Kuwait.

The Bush administration's rapid deployment of troops did not go uncriticized in the States. Many people said they did not want to see American lives lost in what they regarded as a purely foreign dispute. Undeterred, Powell defended the use of U.S. troops to help settle an international affair. "I certainly agree that we should not go around saying that we are the world's policeman," he said, "but guess who gets called when suddenly someone needs a cop."

Donning the mantle of international peacekeeper did not seem to go far enough, according to the president and his defense secretary. Neither the defensive position of the coalition-led forces nor the economic sanctions that the UN had imposed on Iraq were convincing Hussein to withdraw. As a result, Bush and Cheney told Powell on November 8 to double the American presence in the Persian Gulf. The added troop strength would not only improve

Powell greets U.S. airmen while visiting military facilities in the Saudi Arabian desert during the Persian Gulf war. Said one of his associates, "If there was ever anybody who could communicate with the private fixing a broken tank tread and in the next second talk with the president, it's Colin Powell."

Saudi Arabia's defenses but also give the allied forces enough offensive capabilities to confront Iraq.

Powell did not support the idea of launching a desert offensive in the Middle East. Fearing that, as in the Vietnam War, thousands of American soldiers would die needlessly and that such an outcome would erode public support for the military, he preferred to continue pressuring Iraq with economic sanctions. But when Powell told his opinion to the president, Bush responded, "I don't think there's time politically for that strategy."

Accordingly, Powell set about turning the president's wishes into reality. He began to orchestrate a massive build up of troops and tanks, ships and aircraft, in the Middle East. As he told the Senate Armed Services Committee, "My job is to make sure that if it is necessary to go to war, we go to war to win." If diplomacy could not resolve the crisis, Iraq would receive the full weight of allied military might in swift and crushing blows.

At a press conference, Powell outlined in simple terms the strategy for defeating the Iraqi army. "First we're going to cut it off," he said, "and then we're going to kill it." All the while, he hoped that the two months it would take to transform Operation Desert Shield into Operation Desert Storm, an attack force large enough to defeat Iraq's 1 million-man army, was enough time for the crisis to be resolved peacefully.

In early December, another alarm for war sounded: The UN Security Council authorized "all necessary means" to expel Hussein from Kuwait if he did not withdraw his troops by January 15, 1991. "Should military action be required," Bush told the American public, "this will not be another Vietnam. This will not be a protracted, drawn-out war."

To make sure the allied victory would be rapid, Powell met separately with White House officials and the nation's military leaders, acting as a liaison

A longtime acquaintance of Powell's, General H. Norman Schwarzkopf was the chief architect of Operation Desert Storm, the 1991 campaign to liberate Kuwait from occupying Iraqi troops. Powell served as Schwarzkopf's link to the president and Congress during the Persian Gulf war and was responsible for convincing the government to support what proved to be a very successful military plan.

between the two. He let the strategists under his command—particularly the head of U.S. Central Command in Saudi Arabia, General H. Norman Schwarzkopf—work out the details of the military operation; Powell took it upon himself to convince the president and Congress of the resulting plan's merit. He also coordinated the United States' war strategies with those of its allies. Making stops throughout Europe and the Middle East, he established a unified command-and-control system for the 18 nations preparing to engage in battle with Iraq.

On January 15, the UN deadline passed without Hussein withdrawing his forces from Kuwait. Less than 24 hours later, multinational forces unleashed a massive air assault on the Iraqis. It was the largest air strike in history. Allied forces flew more than 1,000 missions in the first 14 hours of combat, more than

President George Bush (fourth from right) holds a national security briefing in the White House's Oval Office on February 25, 1991, the day after allied forces launched a ground offensive in the Persian Gulf war. Attending the meeting are (from left to right) Powell, Chief of Staff John Sununu, Defense Secretary Dick Cheney, Vice-president Dan Quayle, Secretary of State James A. Baker III, and National Security Adviser Brent Scowcroft and his deputy Robert Gates.

double the number of sorties flown by U.S. pilots during the heaviest period of fighting in Vietnam.

By February 23, continued allied air strikes had paralyzed Iraq's military command-and-communications systems and had saddled the Iraqi army with tremendous losses. At that point, allied ground troops went on the offensive. One hundred hours later, the Iraqi president, with his army in shambles and virtually cut off from all means of retreat, agreed to withdraw from Kuwait and meet every other UN demand.

The speedy, complete, and relatively bloodless victory for the allies—less than 200 Americans were killed in the Persian Gulf war—turned Powell, Schwarzkopf, and the rest of the U.S. military into national heroes. Congressmen proposed to promote the two men to the rank of General of the Army, which would make them the first generals to wear five stars since Omar N. Bradley was accorded that honor in 1950. In addition, both officers reminded people of an equally popular military leader, general-turned-statesman Dwight D. Eisenhower, and they began to hear their names mentioned as potential political candidates.

Powell did not like the sudden barrage of attention that surrounded him in the months following the end of the Persian Gulf war. He commented despairingly to a colleague about the growing political speculation, "I can't tell you how much I hate this. I don't control my life anymore."

For a while, Powell tried to avoid publicity as much as possible, to the point of asking *U.S. News and World Report* to substitute a planned cover story on him with one on Schwarzkopf. (The magazine refused his request.) In the relatively few free moments he had left to himself, Powell pursued a favorite hobby—repairing broken-down Volvos—and spent time with his wife and three children: Michael, 28, a student at Georgetown University's law school; Linda, 26, a television actress and employed in New York at a major corporation; and Annemarie, 20, a junior at the College of William and Mary.

To questions about his political future, Powell gave a standard response: "I have no interest in politics at the moment." Yet the constant rumors that he would replace Vice-president Dan Quayle on Bush's 1992 reelection ticket deeply bothered Powell. In mid-March 1991, the JCS chairman finally felt compelled to telephone the vice-president and state outright that he had no desire to become the president's running mate in the next election. Powell's actions subsequently bore him out. That May, he accepted Bush's invitation to serve two more years as JCS chairman, which precludes him from seeking any other employment until his second term as chairman ends in 1993.

Powell and his wife, Alma, along with Defense Secretary Dick Cheney (fourth from left), greet returning prisoners of war, including U.S. Navy lieutenant Jeffrey Zaun (third from left), at Maryland's Andrews Air Force Base on March 10, 1991. Powell's resolute, commanding image appeared often in the media during the Persian Gulf war and helped boost his standing with the American public.

In the meantime, formidable challenges await Chairman Powell. The Bush administration, facing continual pressure to lower the massive federal debt, has been urged to cut the national defense budget. Powell has agreed that military spending should be decreased, especially in light of the end of the cold war and the Soviet Union's greatly reduced global ambitions. But he has also made it clear that the armed forces have to remain well funded if they are to respond effectively to regional crises such as the one in the Persian Gulf. "Peace through strength vanishes as a possibility," he told journalist Carl Rowan, "if there is no strength."

In the months following the Persian Gulf war, Powell went to work restructuring the U.S. military in response to a declining Pentagon budget. He teamed up with Cheney and other Defense Department officials in determining which domestic bases could be closed down or consolidated without causing serious disruptions to military operations. In addition, he contended with being a role model, which he regarded as one of the most important—and most gratifying—offshoots of his job. Reaching the top of the military, he said, has helped raise "the expectation level a little higher" for other blacks.

But not all blacks were supportive of Powell's high position. Shortly before the start of the Persian Gulf war, he withdrew as marshal of a parade honoring Martin Luther King, Jr., because associates of the slain civil rights leader felt that being a JCS chairman was not in keeping with King's commitment to nonviolence. Several months later, the audience at a Congressional Black Caucus meeting told Powell they were upset that a disproportionately large number of blacks had been asked to risk their life in the Persian Gulf war. (According to the Defense Department, blacks made up only 12 percent of American society but accounted for 25 percent of the forces in the Persian Gulf.)

In defense of the military, Powell echoed Bush's words: "To those who question the proportion of blacks in the armed services," the president said on February 25, "my answer is simple. The military of the United States is the greatest equal opportunity employer around."

Powell could have answered the critics just as easily by telling them about his trip to Fort Leavenworth less than a year earlier. In July 1990, he returned to the Kansas military base to break ground for a memorial to the Ninth and 10th Cavalry regiments, a project he had launched during his tenure as deputy commanding general. The monument was being built on the site of the former Buffalo Soldiers' barracks, and by digging into the soil, Powell had taken part in a ceremony to honor the black soldiers who had struggled long and hard for fair treatment in the military.

Back home in the Bronx on April 15, 1991, Powell throws out the first ball of the new baseball season during opening day ceremonies at Yankee Stadium. "The real story," he has said of his rise from the streets of the South Bronx to the top of the military, "is that yes, I climbed, and I climbed well, and I climbed hard, and I climbed over the cliff, but always on the backs and the contributions of those who went before me. And your challenge, and my challenge is to tell our young people throughout the land, black, white, whatever coloration, that they've got to prepare themselves, they've got to be ready."

But rather than dwell on America's history of racism, Powell has elected to focus in his numerous public statements on the many opportunities the nation offers. "As much as I have been disappointed in my lifetime that we didn't move as fast as we might have, or that we still have forms of institutional racism, we have an abiding faith in this country," he said to the *Washington Times*. "Hurt? Yes. Disappointed? Yes. Losing faith or confidence in the nation? No."

As a result, Powell devotes as much of his packed schedule as possible to visiting schools and preaching his gospel of hard work. He tells black youths, "Don't let your blackness . . . be a problem to you. Let it be a problem to somebody else. . . . Don't use it as an excuse for your own shortcomings. If you work hard . . . success will come your way."

On April 15, 1991, the JCS chairman returned home to the Bronx, riding along the sweeping curve of his old block, Kelly Street, before arriving at Morris High School to speak to its current crop of students. Powell had not been back to the school since his 1954 graduation. "I remember the front door," he said to the assembly in a sentimental voice. "I remember the auditorium. I remember the feeling that you can't make it. But you can."

His tone rising, Powell encouraged the youngsters to avoid using drugs and to remain in school until they received their diplomas. Then, like a commander giving his troops their final instructions, he told the students: "Stick with it. I'm giving you an order. Stick with it." ❧

APPENDIX: AWARDS AND HONORS

The military awards and decorations and other honors bestowed on Colin Powell include the following:

Air Medal

Army Commendation Medal with two Oak Leaf Clusters

Bronze Star Medal

Congressional Gold Medal

Defense Distinguished Service Medal with two Oak Leaf Clusters

Defense Superior Service Medal

Distinguished Service Medal, U.S. Army

Joint Service Commendation Medal

Legion of Merit with Oak Leaf Cluster

Presidential Medal of Freedom

President's Citizens Medal

Purple Heart

Secretary of Energy Distinguished Service Medal

Secretary of State Distinguished Service Medal

Soldier's Medal

CHRONOLOGY

1937   Born Colin Luther Powell on April 5 in the Harlem district of New York City

1940   Moves with his family to Hunts Point in the Bronx

1954   Graduates from Morris High School; enrolls in the City College of New York (CCNY); joins the U.S. Army Reserve Officers' Training Corps (ROTC) at CCNY

1958   Graduates from CCNY at the top of his ROTC class; commissioned as second lieutenant in the U.S. Army; attends Infantry Officers' Basic Training and Airborne and Ranger schools

1959   Serves as platoon leader and rifle company commander in West Germany

1960   Becomes battalion adjutant at Fort Devens, Massachusetts

1962   Marries Alma Johnson; arrives in Vietnam to serve as adviser to an infantry battalion

1963   Son, Michael, is born; Powell is wounded in action in Vietnam and receives the Purple Heart

1964   Enrolls in the Command and General Staff College

1965   First daughter, Linda, is born

1968   Powell arrives in Vietnam to serve as infantry battalion executive officer and assistant chief of staff, G-3, 23rd Infantry Division

1969   Enrolls in George Washington University (GWU)

1970   Promoted to lieutenant colonel

1971   Earns a Master of Business Administration degree from GWU; second daughter, Annemarie, is born

1972   Powell is selected as White House Fellow; serves as special assistant to the deputy director of the Office of Management and Budget (OMB); promoted to major

1973   Assumes command of the First Battalion, 32nd Infantry in South Korea

1974   Becomes operations research analyst in the office of the assistant defense secretary

1975   Enrolls in the National War College

1976   Assumes command of the Second Brigade, 101st Airborne Division at Fort Campbell, Kentucky; graduates with distinction from the National War College

1977   Serves in the Intermediate Office of the secretary of defense and as senior military assistant to the deputy secretary of defense

1979   Serves as executive assistant to the secretary of energy; promoted to brigadier general

1981   Becomes assistant commander for Operations and Training, Fourth Infantry Division at Fort Carson, Colorado

1983   Serves as deputy commander at Fort Leavenworth, Kansas; becomes senior military assistant to the secretary of defense

1986   Assumes command of the U.S. Army V Corps in Frankfurt, West Germany; testifies before the Tower Commission about role in the Iran-contra affair

1987   Becomes deputy national security adviser and national security adviser

1989   Promoted to four-star general; named commander in chief of the U.S. Forces Command at Fort McPherson in Atlanta, Georgia; becomes chairman of the Joint Chiefs of Staff (JCS); directs an invasion of Panama to apprehend General Manuel Noriega

1990   Directs the Operation Desert Shield campaign in the Middle East

1991   Oversees successful U.S. effort in the Persian Gulf war; accepts a second term as JCS chairman

FURTHER READING

Adler, Bill. *The Generals: The New American Heroes*. New York: Avon Books, 1991.

Binkin, Martin, and Mark J. Eitelberg. *Blacks in the Military*. Washington, DC: Brookings Institution, 1982.

Dalfiume, Richard M. *Desegregation of the United States Armed Forces: Fighting on Two Fronts, 1939–1953*. Columbia: University of Missouri Press, 1969.

Davis, Benjamin O., Jr. *Benjamin O. Davis, Jr., American: An Autobiography*. Washington, DC: Smithsonian Institution, 1991.

Fletcher, Marvin E. *America's First Black General*. Lawrence: University Press of Kansas, 1989.

Fowler, Arlen. *The Black Infantry in the West, 1869–1891*. Westport, CT: Greenwood Press, 1971.

Leckie, William H. *The Buffalo Soldiers: A Narrative of the Negro Cavalry in the West*. Norman: University of Oklahoma Press, 1985.

Morris, M. E. H. *Norman Schwarzkopf: Road to Triumph*. New York: St. Martin's Press, 1991.

Motley, Mary. *The Invisible Soldiers: The Experience of the Black Soldier, World War II*. Detroit: Wayne State University Press, 1987.

Nalty, Bernard C. *Strength for the Fight*. New York: Free Press, 1986.

Prados, John. *Keepers of the Keys: A History of the National Security Council from Truman to Bush*. New York: Morrow, 1991.

Smith, Graham. *When Jim Crow Met John Bull: Black American Soldiers in World War II in Britain*. New York: St. Martin's Press, 1988.

Woodward, Bob. *The Commanders*. New York: Simon & Schuster, 1991.

INDEX
·❧·

Daley, Richard M., 758
Dallas, Texas, 399–400
Dance Theatre of Harlem, 9
Daniel, Price, 415
Davids, Tice, 276
Davis, Benjamin O., Jr., 825
Davis, Benjamin O., Sr., 824
Davis, Edward, 171
Davis, John, 597–98, 601
Davis, John W., 362, 425, 426
Davis, Nelson, 341–42, 344
Defender, The, 84
Degler, Carl, 53
DeKalb County, Georgia, 177–78
Delany, Martin R., 39
Delaware River, 300
Delta, Louisiana, 585, 586, 589, 593, 641–42
Denver, Colorado, 601–2, 604, 605
Detroit, Michigan, 109–10, 123, 409, 410, 554
Dexter Avenue Baptist Church, 149, 152–53, 155–56, 158, 168, 171, 174, 226
Dietz, Dickie, 703–5
Dinkins, David, 786
Dixon, Jeremiah, 277
Doby, Larry, 93
Dodson, Media, 372
Dorchester County, 265, 287, 288, 296
Douglas, Stephen A., 43–44
Douglass, Frederick, 6, 39, 263, 275, 291, 305, 319, 320, 322, 323, 324, 343, 349, 658
Douglas, William O., 448
Draper, Foy, 534, 537
Drew, Benjamin, 310
Dresden, Germany, 540

Du Bois, W. E. B., 72–73, 74, 83, 322, 380, 599, 631, 645, 647, 663, 664, 668
Dukakis, Kitty, 681
Dukakis, Michael S., 9, 680–83, 685–88, 690, 777, 780–82, 784–86, 873
Dunbar, Paul Lawrence, 599, 624
Duncan, Charles W., Jr., 844
Durant, Henry, 337

Earle Theater, Philadelphia, 549
Eastern Shore, 263, 277, 281, 285, 287, 289, 291, 293, 296, 297, 300, 309, 311, 313, 315
Eastland, James O., 438
East St. Louis riot, 645, 647, 648–49
East Technical High School, 499, 502, 507
Ebbets Field, Brooklyn, 551
Ebenezer Baptist Church, 133–35, 142, 144, 148–49, 176, 239, 247
Ebony, 370
Edmund Pettus Bridge, 221, 223–25
Eisenhower, Dwight D., 95, 96, 169, 174, 179, 432, 560, 885
Elijah Muhammad, 106–7
Elliott, Roderick, 421
Ellison, Ralph, 88
El Salvador, 876
Emancipation Proclamation, 181, 327, 359, 428
Ennets, Maria, 325
Ennets, Stephen, 325
Epton, Bernard, 758

Ervin, Sam, 457
Eskridge, Chauncey, 731
"Ethiopia, Thou Land of Our Fathers," 83
Evans v. Newton, 446–48
Evanti, Madame Lillian, 604
Evers, Medgar, 205
Exodusters, 592

Fair Employment Practices Commission, 142, 412
Fairmount Junior High School, 491, 495
Farmer, James, 99, 182–83, 713
Farrakhan, Louis, 762, 764–67, 775
Faubus, Orval, 95, 431–32
Fauntroy, Walter, 189
Federal Bureau of Investigation (FBI), 211–16
Federal Housing Administration, 409
Federation of Colored Women's Clubs, New York, 346
Feinberg Law, 440
Fernandina, Florida, 329–30
Fieldcrest Village, 699
Fifteenth Amendment, 403, 405
Fifth Amendment, 440
Figg, Robert, 424
Fire Next Time, The (Baldwin), 88
First Amendment, 439, 460
First International Convention of the Negro Peoples of the World, 82–83
First Baptist Church, 153–63, 184
Fitzwater, Marlin, 866

Flack, Roberta, 743
Flipper, Henry, 822
Ford Motor Company, 554,
  555, 562
Forkins, Marty, 523, 545, 546
Fort Benning, Georgia, 829,
  834
Fort Bragg, North Carolina,
  827
Fort Campbell, Kentucky,
  843
Fort Carson, Colorado, 845
Fort Devens, Massachusetts,
  829
Fort Leavenworth, Kansas,
  835, 845, 887
Fort Lesley J. McNair,
  Washington, D.C., 842
Fort McPherson, Georgia,
  854
Fort Sumter, 326
Fort Wagner, 333–34
Fourteenth Amendment, 359,
  361, 364, 374, 426,
  440, 448, 450, 452
Fourth Amendment, 450
Frankfurt, West Germany,
  854
Franklin, Aretha, 743
Franklin, John Hope, 33, 80
Frederick Douglass's Paper, 275
Freeman, The, 579, 609, 621
Freedmen's Bureau, 50, 67
Freedom Rides, 98–99, 129,
  182–87, 191, 684
Fugitive Slave Act, 255, 284,
  290, 291, 305, 326
Furman University, 699, 707
Furnas, J. C., 307

Gaines, Lloyd, 397–98
Gandhi, Mohandas
  (Mahatma), 97,
  145–46, 161, 174

Garner v. Louisiana, 436
Garrett, Thomas, 289–90,
  301, 314, 315, 325,
  342
Garrison, William Lloyd, 38,
  275
Garvey, Marcus, 81–84
Geneva, New York, 337
Georgetown Day School, 452
George Washington
  University, 837
Gephardt, Richard, 778
Germany, 475, 521–22, 524,
  529
Germond, Jack, 769, 773
Ghana, 167–68
GI Bill, 413
Gibson, Kenneth, 760
Gibson Island Club, 371
Glenn, John, 760, 766
Glickman, Marty, 534
Goebbels, Joseph, 526
Goode, Wilson, 768
Goodman, Andrew, 445
Goodman, Robert, 761–63,
  771, 787
Gorbachev, Mikhail S., 868
Gordon, Edward, 501
Gore, Albert, 777, 780–81,
  784–85
Göring, Hermann, 526
Grant, Ulysses S., 47, 338
Gray, William, 9
Great Depression, 389, 499,
  507, 808
Green, Harriet, 264, 266,
  268, 278, 297–99, 312,
  313–14, 342
Green, Lucille, 651
Green Berets, 876
Greenville, South Carolina,
  693–705, 712
Greenville High School, 703,
  705

Grenada, 849
Griffin, Junius, 743
Guardian, The, 74

Haiti, 32–33, 275, 822
Halvorsen Realty Company,
  723
Hamilton, Charles Clarence,
  434
Hanrahan, Edward, 747–48
Harlan, John Marshall, 69
Harlem, New York, 7, 77–78,
  82, 84, 172–73, 399,
  542, 620, 623, 624,
  638, 639, 643, 646,
  807–9
Harlem Globetrotters, 550, 555
Harlem Property Owners
  Association, 78
Harlem Renaissance, 7,
  84–88, 380, 808
Harpers Ferry, Virginia, 45,
  305, 319, 321–24
*Harper v. Virginia Board of
  Elections*, 450
*Harriet Tubman: Conductor on
  the Underground Railway*
  (Petry), 285
Hart, Albert Bushnell, 334
Hart, Gary, 747, 760, 766,
  768, 773, 776–77
Hart, Phillip A., 439
Hartford, Connecticut, 818
Hartsfield, William, 177
Harvard University, 387
Hastie, William Henry 385,
  386, 471
Hatcher, Richard, 743, 760
Hawkins, Coleman, 85
Henry, William A., III, 768
Hertzberg, Hendrick, 786
Higginson, Thomas
  Wentworth, 316–17,
  320, 330, 339, 343

Malcolm X, 8, 106–7, 108
March on Washington, 205–7
Marquette University, 500,
  528, 534
Marshall, Annie, 369–70
Marshall, Burke, 200
Marshall, Cecilia, 431, 444,
  452, 458
Marshall, Elizabeth, 372
Marshall, John William, 444,
  452, 458
Marshall, Norma, 370–72,
  374–75, 379, 384, 427
Marshall, Thoroughgood,
  368–69, 377
Marshall, Thurgood, 93–94
  awarded Spingarn Medal,
    407
  childhood, 367, 371, 372
  death of first wife, 427
  early education, 375, 379
  family background,
    367–72
  family life, 444, 452
  judgeship on Court of
    Appeals, 437–41
  law practice, 389–91
  law school, 382–87
  leisure activities, 452–53
  marries Cecilia Suyat,
    431
  marries Vivian Burey,
    382
  and NAACP, 385,
    391–92
  personal encounters with
    prejudice, 375–76,
    381, 397, 406
  personality, 376, 377,
    385, 399, 431,
    445, 461
  physical description, 419
  public speaking, 464–65
  as solicitor general, 445–52

Supreme Court
    appointment,
    457–58
Supreme Court
    nominations,
    455–57
Supreme Court tenure,
    457–67
Marshall, Thurgood, Jr., 444,
  452, 458
Marshall, Vivian, 382, 396,
  426, 427
Marshall, William Aubrey,
  371, 375, 379
Marshall, William Canfield,
  371, 374, 375, 383
Mason, Charles, 277
Mason, Minnie, 694
Mason-Dixon line, 277, 285,
  289
Mason Temple, 124, 127–29,
  243
Mathis, J. D., 701–3
Matthews, Army, 376
Mays, Benjamin, 143
Meadows, Earle, 532
Meese, Edwin, 854
Memphis, Tennessee, 121,
  123–29, 243–44,
  246–47, 731–34
Memphis garbage strike,
  124–29, 243–44,
  246–47
Meredith, James, 233
Messenger, The, 649, 650, 668
Metcalfe, Ralph, 500, 516,
  528, 533, 748–49
Mezzrow, Milton "Mezz," 85
Mexico City, Mexico, 562,
  564
Michael, Vic, 843
Miller, Elizabeth, 345
Miller, Loren, 411
Milliken v. Bradley, 462–63

Mississippi Freedom Summer,
  102
Mississippi River, 585, 586,
  589, 591, 596, 597,
  602
Missouri Compromise, 41–43,
  44
Mite Missionary Society,
  598–99
Mohawk Valley, 310
Mondale, Walter, 680,
  758–62, 766, 768–69,
  773–75, 785
Monroe, James, 34
Montgomery, Alabama,
  96–97, 149, 151–65,
  167–68, 170–74,
  183–85, 188, 190,
  220–27, 720, 723
Montgomery bus boycott,
  155–65, 167–68, 170,
  188
Montgomery, James, 330,
  332, 342
Montgomery Improvement
    Association (MIA),
    157–62, 164–65,
    170–71, 185, 435
Moore, Fred, 623, 647, 658
Morehouse College, 34,
  142–44
Morgan v. Virginia, 406
Morris High School, 812–13,
  889
Morrison, Toni, 88
Motor Corps of America, 659
Murphy, Carl, 391, 426, 429
Murray, Donald Gaines, 394,
  396
Murray v. Pearson, 394–96
Muslim Mosque, Inc., 107

Nabrit, James, 415
Nalle, Charles, 255–61, 324

PICTURE CREDITS
❧

THE AFRICAN AMERICANS

AP/Wide World Photos: pp. 94, 101, 111; The Bettmann Archive: pp. 16, 21, 32, 44, 49, 83, 84; Brown Brothers: pp. 78, 79; Solomon D. Butcher Collection/Nebraska State Historical Society: pp. 40–41; Culver Pictures: p. 86; Ralph Fitzgerald/LGI: p. 60 (bottom); Forbes/LGI: p. 62; Ernest Haas/Magnum Photos: p. 63 (top); Patrick Harsron/LGI: p. 64; Courtesy Harvard University Archives: p. 74; Historical Pictures Service: pp. 68, 72, 76–77, 88, 89; Library of Congress: pp. 4–5, 13, 15, 17, 18, 20, 22, 25, 35, 39, 42, 46, 47, 51, 52, 54–55, 56, 66, 71; Louisiana State Museum: p. 27; Missouri Historical Society: p. 45; National Museum of African Art, Eliot Elisofon, Smithsonian Institution: p. 14; National Portrait Gallery, Smithsonian Institution: p. 7; New-York Historical Society: p. 28; The New York Public Library, Astor, Lenox and Tilden Foundations: p. 93; The Saint Louis Art Museum: pp. 10–11; Schomburg Center for Research in Black Culture, New York Public Library, Astor, Lenox and Tilden Foundations: pp. 73, 75; Donna Sinisgalli: p. 12; Sophia Smith Collection, Smith College: p. 38; UPI/Bettmann: pp. 9, 70, 80, 87, 90, 96, 98, 99, 103, 104–5, 106, 107, 108, 109, 112, 114; Valentine Museum, Richmond, VA: p. 67; Jack Vertoogian: pp. 57, 58, 59 (bottom), 60 (top), 61, 63 (bottom); Alex Webb/Magnum Photos: p. 59 (top).

MARTIN LUTHER KING, JR.

Bob Adelman/Magnum Photos: pp. 192–93; AP/Wide World Photos: pp. 120–21, 123, 125, 129, 133, 140–41, 157, 160, 172, 175, 189, 196, 209, 231, 233; James H. Karales/Peter Arnold, Inc.: pp. 226–27; Boyd Lewis/Atlanta Historical Society: p. 136; Library of Congress: pp. 185, 207, 213; Joseph Louw, *Life* Magazine © 1968, Time Inc.: p. 245; Danny Lyon/Magnum Photos: p. 194; Charles Moore/Black Star: p. 203; Courtesy Morehouse College: p. 143; NAACP, New York, NY: p. 152; *New York Daily News* Photo: p. 173; Schomburg Center for Research in Black Culture, New York Public Library, Astor, Lenox and Tilden Foundations: pp. 130–31, 142; Scott Photo Services, Montgomery, AL: p. 149; Stoughton/Lyndon Baines Johnson Library: pp. 210–11; John Tweedle/The Hartman Group: pp. 180–81; UPI/Bettmann: pp. 118–19, 135, 145, 147, 154, 163, 165, 166, 170, 179, 183, 186, 191, 195, 199, 201, 202, 204, 208, 212, 215, 216, 219, 221, 223, 228–29, 235, 237, 238, 242–43, 246, 247; Washington, D.C., Public Library System © Clover International: p. 119; *Washington Star* Collection, *Washington Post*: p. 240; Dan Weiner/Magnum Photos: p. 150.

HARRIET TUBMAN

The Bettmann Archive: pp. 256, 264, 267, 271, 274, 275, 280, 282, 288, 289, 291, 297, 302, 307, 315, 320, 323, 324, 327, 331, 332, 334, 338, 340, 345; Cayuga County Historian: pp. 343, 346, 348; Library of Congress: pp. 254, 311; Louisiana Collection, Tulane University Library, New Orleans, LA: p. 298; Maryland Historical Society: p. 286; National Archives: pp. 287, 323, 329, 333; National Portrait Gallery, Smithsonian Institution: p. 326; Schomburg Center for Research in Black Culture, New York Public Library, Astor, Lenox and Tilden Foundations: pp. 252–53, 258–59, 260, 261, 262, 268, 269, 276, 277, 278, 279, 284, 290, 292, 294, 301, 304, 306, 309, 313, 316, 321, 330, 336, 347; Frederic Jean Thalinger, Library of Congress: pp: 253, 350; UPI/Bettmann: pp. 272, 318.

THURGOOD MARSHALL

AP/Wide World Photos: pp. 355, 363, 365, 433, 439, 449; The Bettmann Archive: pp. 404, 423; Courtesy of Justice and Mrs. Thurgood Marshall: pp. 366, 373, 374, 375, 378, 383, 388, 451, 461, 462, 463, 465, 468; Culver Pictures: pp. 369, 412, 422; Library of Congress: pp. 354–55, 356, 359, 370, 380, 381, 386, 387, 395, 396, 401; Schomburg Center for Research in Black Culture, New York Public Library, Astor, Lenox and Tilden Foundations: pp. 360, 364, 391, 392, 406, 408, 414, 417, 425, 428; UPI/Bettmann: pp. 384, 420, 430, 432, 435, 436, 438, 440, 442–43, 445, 447, 454, 456, 459.

JESSE OWENS

Cleveland Picture Collection/Cleveland Public Library: p. 489; Cleveland Public Library Photo Collection: 545, 551; Stanley L. McMichael Collection/Cleveland Public Library: p. 486; Museum of Modern Art/Film Stills Archive: p. 477; Ohio State University Archives: pp. 506, 511, 513, 528, 535, 554, 567, 570; Owens Collection, courtesy of Ohio State University: pp. 492, 510, 518, 556; Private collection of Fred Rennert: pp. 474–75, 476, 479,

480, 531; Schomburg Center for Research in Black Culture, New York Public Library, Astor, Lenox and Tilden Foundations: pp. 509, 536, 548–49, 564; UPI/Bettmann: pp. 472–73, 482–83, 485, 490, 494, 497, 498, 503, 504, 508, 512, 514, 515, 516, 517, 519, 520–21, 524, 525, 527, 532, 534, 538, 540, 541, 542, 543, 544, 546, 547, 552, 553, 558–59, 561, 562, 568; UPI/Bettmann, courtesy of Cleveland Public Library: pp. 484, 501, 523, 555; Wide World Photos, Los Angeles Bureau: pp. 500.

MADAM C. J. WALKER

The Bettmann Archive: pp. 601, 665; Brown Brothers: pp. 597, 659; The Byron Collection, Museum of the City of New York: p. 640; Denver Public Library, Western History Department: p. 602; Indiana Historical Society, Bass Photo Collection 74523: pp. 616–17; Kansas State Historical Society, Topeka, KS: pp. 592, 593; Library of Congress: pp. 575, 590–91, 599, 607; Madam Walker Collection, Indiana Historical Society Library: pp. 614 (neg.# A77), 662–63 (neg.# C2042); From *The Messenger*, Schomburg Center for Research in Black Culture, New York Public Library, Astor, Lenox and Tilden Foundations: p. 634; Missouri Historical Society, Robert Benecke photo, Riverfront #193: p. 598; Museum of Modern Art/Film Stills Archive: p. 646; Courtesy of the NAACP Public Relations Department: p. 648; Schomburg Center for Research in Black Culture, New York Public Library, Astor, Lenox and Tilden Foundations: pp. 579, 581, 587, 625, 650, 660; The Walker Collection of A'Lelia Bundles: pp. 574–75, 576, 582, 584–85, 594, 605, 608, 611, 612, 613, 618–19, 620, 621, 623, 628–29, 631, 636, 637, 638–39, 643, 654–55, 657, 666, 669, 670, 672.

JESSE JACKSON

AP/Wide World Photos: pp. 676–77, 678–79, 727, 730–31, 735, 736, 741, 749, 750, 753, 756, 758, 769, 772–73, 782, 785, 787, 788; *Greensboro Daily News*: p. 713; Greenville Cultural Exchange: pp. 692, 699, 701, 702, 704; Otis Hairston: pp. 706, 711, 714, 716; Bettye Lane: pp. 723, 742; Reuter/Bettmann: p. 682; Richard D. Sawyer: p. 696; UPI/Bettmann: pp. 684, 687, 689, 709, 719, 721, 722, 725, 733, 739, 744, 747, 762, 764, 765, 767, 770, 777, 779, 783, 786, 790.

COLIN POWELL

ABOUT THE AUTHORS

———— ❦ ————

THE AFRICAN AMERICANS

HOWARD SMEAD is a lecturer in history and Afro-American studies at the University of Maryland and the director of night research at the *Washington Post.* He is the author of *Blood Justice: The Lynching of Mack Charles Parker* and *The Redneck Waltz.*

MARTIN LUTHER KING, JR.

ROBERT JAKOUBEK holds degrees in history from Indiana University and Columbia University. He is co-author of *These United States,* an American history text-book. For Chelsea House's BLACK AMERICANS OF ACHIEVEMENT series he has written *Joe Louis, Jesse Jackson,* and *Martin Luther King, Jr.,* the latter of which was selected by the National Council for the Social Studies and the Children's Book Council as one of the notable 1989 children's trade books in the field of social studies.

HARRIET TUBMAN

M. W. TAYLOR is the former editor of the *New York Times* and *Los Angeles Times* syndicates and also served as an editor at *Life* magazine. Currently a New York City–based book editor and writer, she is coauthor of *Facts on File Dictionary of New Words.*

THURGOOD MARSHALL

LISA ALDRED first became interested in Thurgood Marshall while taking a course in civil rights history at Duke University. She graduated magna cum laude from Duke in 1981 and earned a law degree from the University of North Carolina in 1985. She then joined a law firm in Chapel Hill, North Carolina, before moving to Arizona to work on a constitutional law project involving the Navajo Indians. She is currently an adjunct professor at the University of North Carolina School of Law, where she teaches legal writing.

JESSE OWENS

TONY GENTRY holds an honors degree in history and literature from Harvard College. Formerly an award-winning news and feature editor at WWL Newsradio in New Orleans, he now works in New York City, where he is an avid runner and hopeful marathoner. His poetry and short stories have been published in *Turnstile* and *Downtown*. He is also the author of *Paul Laurence Dunbar* in the Chelsea House BLACK AMERICANS OF ACHIEVEMENT series.

MADAM C. J. WALKER

A'LELIA PERRY BUNDLES is the great-great-granddaughter of Madam C. J. Walker. Currently a producer with ABC News's "World News Tonight" in Washington, D.C., she was educated at Harvard and Radcliffe Colleges and Columbia University Graduate School of Journalism. Bundles, who lives in Alexandria, Virginia, frequently gives speeches about Madam Walker.

JESSE JACKSON

ROBERT JAKOUBEK holds degrees in history from Indiana University and Columbia University. He is co-author of *These United States*, an American history textbook. For Chelsea House's BLACK AMERICANS OF ACHIEVEMENT series he has written *Joe Louis*, *Jesse Jackson*, and *Martin Luther King, Jr.*, the latter of which was selected by the National Council for the Social Studies and the Children's Book Council as one of the notable 1989 children's trade books in the field of social studies.

COLIN POWELL

WARREN BROWN, a native of Texas, is a freelance writer currently living in Cincinnati, Ohio. He has written several books for young adults, including biographies of Roald Amundsen and Robert E. Lee.

ABOUT THE
CONTRIBUTING EDITORS
——————— ❦ ———————

DANIEL PATRICK MOYNIHAN is the senior United States senator from New York. He is also the only person in American history to serve in the cabinets or subcabinets of four successive presidents—Kennedy, Johnson, Nixon, and Ford. Formerly a professor of government at Harvard University, he has written and edited many books, including *Beyond the Melting Pot, Ethnicity: Theory and Experience* (both with Nathan Glazer), *Loyalties,* and *Family and Nation.*

NATHAN IRVIN HUGGINS, one of America's leading scholars in the field of black studies, helped select the titles for the BLACK AMERICANS OF ACHIEVEMENT series, for which he also served as senior consulting editor. He was the W.E.B. Du Bois Professor of History and of Afro-American Studies at Harvard University and the director of the W.E.B. Du Bois Institute for Afro-American Research at Harvard. He received his doctorate from Harvard in 1962 and returned there as a professor in 1980 after teaching at Columbia University, the University of Massachusetts, Lake Forest College, and the California State University, Long Beach. He was the author of four books and dozens of articles, including *Black Odyssey: The Afro-American Ordeal in Slavery, The Harlem Renaissance,* and *Slave and Citizen: The Life of Frederick Douglass,* and was associated with the Children's Television Workshop, National Public Radio, the Boston Athenaeum, the Museum of Afro-American History, the Howard Thurman Educational Trust, and Upward Bound. Professor Huggins died in 1989, at the age of 62, in Cambridge, Massachusetts.